Computerized Adaptive Testing

From Inquiry to Operation

Edited by

William A. Sands
Brian K. Waters
James R. McBride

AMERICAN PSYCHOLOGICAL ASSOCIATION

Washington, DC

Published by
American Psychological Association
750 First Street, NE
Washington, DC 20002

Copies may be ordered from
APA Order Department
P.O. Box 92984
Washington, DC 20090-2984

In the United Kingdom and Europe, copies may be ordered from
American Psychological Association
3 Henrietta Street
Covent Gardens, London
WC2E 8LU England

Typeset in Century Schoolbook by G&S Typesetters, Inc., Austin, TX

Printer: Braceland, Philadelphia, PA
Cover design: Minker Design, Bethesda, MD
Technical/production editor: Edward B. Meidenbauer

Library of Congress Cataloging-in-Publication Data
Computerized adaptive testing : from inquiry to operation / edited by
  William A. Sands, Brian K. Waters, and James R. McBride.
     p.   cm.
  Includes bibliographical references and index.
  ISBN 1-55798-442-5 (acid-free paper)
  1. Psychological tests—Data processing.   2. Computer adaptive
testing.   I. Sands, William A.   II. Waters, Brian K.   III. McBride,
James R.
BF176.2.C65   1997
153.9'3'0285—dc21   97-25695
                                                         CIP

British Cataloguing-in-Publication Data
A CIP record is available from the British Library

Printed in the United States of America
First edition

Contents

To Brad, Friends Forever, Kathy Moreno

Brad, Best Wishes, Vince

Brad — I miss the meetings of the CAT Psychometric Committee. Thank you for all of your contributions to them! — Bruce

Brad, I miss our Psychometric discussions. Best wishes! — Dan

To Brad, the best co-author ever! I miss working together! Becky

About the Editors and Contributors

The Editors

W. A. (Drew) Sands has spent most of his career in military personnel research. He earned a B.S. in Social Sciences and an M.A. in Counseling and Testing Psychology from The American University in Washington, DC. In 1967, he joined the Naval Personnel Research and Development Laboratory in Washington as a personnel research psychologist. In 1973, Mr. Sands transferred to the Navy Personnel Research and Development Center (NPRDC) in San Diego, CA. In 1980, he became the Head of NPRDC's Computerized Personnel Accessioning Systems Branch of the Personnel Systems Department. He managed the R&D team that developed the Navy Personnel Accessioning System (NPAS) and the Computerized Adaptive Screening Test (CAST). In 1983, he became Head of the Computerized Testing and Accessioning Division in the Personnel Systems Department, which was focused on the CAT version of the Armed Services Vocational Aptitude Battery (CAT-ASVAB). In March 1986, he became Director of the Personnel Systems Department at NPRDC, where he planned, directed, and evaluated the overall scientific research program in personnel screening, selection, classification, and performance assessment. As the Officer-in-Charge, he had the lead laboratory (NPRDC) responsibility for the Joint-Service CAT-ASVAB Program. Mr. Sands retired from civil service in March 1994, returned to the Washington, DC area, and is conducting research for various organizations as a consultant with Chesapeake Research Applications. He has authored over 110 book chapters, journal articles, technical reports, and professional presentations in psychological testing (paper-and-pencil and computerized adaptive tests); personnel screening, selection, and classi-

fication; survey design and analyses; computer-based vocational guidance; artificial neural networks; and, expert and decision support systems.

Brian K. Waters is Program Manager of the Manpower Analysis Program of the Human Resources Research Organization (HumRRO). He joined HumRRO in 1980, after retiring from the Air Force, where he taught and was Director of Evaluation at the Air War College, was an R&D manager and researcher with the Air Force Human Resources Laboratory and a navigator. He holds a Ph.D. and M.S. in Educational Measurement and Testing from Florida State University, and an M.B.A. from Southern Illinois University. His doctoral dissertation in 1974 was one of the earliest empirical studies of CAT, and he has over 20 years' experience with CAT R&D. He is a fellow of the American Psychological Association (APA) and a former President of the APA Division of Military Psychology. He has authored over 100 journal articles, books, and professional papers, primarily dealing with the selection, classification, and testing of military and civilian personnel.

James R. McBride is a Principal Scientist with HumRRO. A research psychologist, he has been involved in research and development related to CAT since 1972. During his doctoral studies in psychometric methods at the University of Minnesota, he was a research assistant to David J. Weiss, and participated in Weiss' pioneering CAT research for the Office of Naval Research. Since completing doctoral training in 1976, he has done test development and personnel research for the Army Research Institute for the Behavioral and Social Sciences (ARI), NPRDC, The Psychological Corporation, and HumRRO. At NPRDC, he was Principal Investigator on a variety of CAT-related projects ranging from the exploratory development work that provided the first empirical demonstration of CAT's efficiency for military personnel testing, to the design and development of prototype systems intended for nationwide administration of computerized adaptive versions of the ASVAB. At NPRDC, he designed and directed the development of the first complete computerized systems for adaptive ASVAB administration. At the time of his departure from NPRDC, he was Director of the Personnel Systems Department, with responsibility for the entire spectrum of scientific research related to Navy personnel selection, classification, and testing. He joined The Psychological Corporation in 1984, as Director of its Computer-Based Testing Group; later, his responsibilities there extended to all development and research related to tests designed for personnel assessment in business, government, and career development. Between 1984 and 1990, he designed and directed development of a number of computer-based testing systems, including the first commercial application of CAT: The Computerized Adaptive Edition of the Differential Aptitude Tests. Since joining HumRRO in 1990, he has continued his involvement in R&D on computer-based testing in general, and CAT in particular. He directed the development of one of the first CAT systems used for personnel selection in industry for a Fortune 100 HumRRO client. He has provided consulting services in computer-based testing to several other private sector firms, and has been a member of an expert panel advising the U.S. Department of Labor on the development and evaluation of a CAT version of the General Aptitude Test Battery (GATB). He is currently directing the HumRRO project team responsible for modifying the Army's Computerized Adaptive Screening Test for use by all of the Armed Services.

The Contributors

David L. Alderton is the author or co-author of numerous journal articles on individual differences in spatial ability, problem solving, and intelligence. After receiving his Ph.D. in Educational Psychology from the University of Santa Barbara in 1986, Dr. Alderton joined the NPRDC staff, where he played a major role in several projects to develop and validate new tests. He now works at the Centers for Disease Control and Prevention, where he is conducting behavioral surveillance research for the prevention of HIV infection.

Jane M. Arabian is Assistant Director for Enlistment Standards in the Directorate for Accession Policy, Office of the Secretary of Defense. She plans and formulates policy on military enlistment standards (i.e., aptitude, education, moral character, age, citizenship) as well as the DoD Student Testing Program. Dr. Arabian also serves as the Executive Secretary for the Defense Advisory Committee on Military Personnel Testing. She is an author of over 30 journal articles, professional papers, and technical reports in the areas of experimental psychology, health psychology, and military selection and classification testing and has presented formal research papers and invited addresses at over 50 professional conferences. Dr. Arabian earned her Ph.D. in Experimental Psychology at the University of Toronto.

Bruce M. Bloxom obtained a Ph.D. in Psychometrics from the University of Washington in 1966. He is presently a research psychologist at the Defense Manpower Data Center (DMDC), Monterey, California, where he has served as Chief of the Quality Control and Analysis Branch as well as Acting Chief of the Personnel Testing Division. Prior to his time at DMDC, he was Professor of Psychology at Vanderbilt University.

Linda T. Curran was a psychologist with the Personnel Testing Division of the DoD Manpower Data Center in Arlington, Virginia from 1991 until she died in June 1997. She was responsible for coordination between DoD staff in the Washington area and the Testing Division staff in Monterey, California. She received her doctorate from the University of Texas in Educational Psychology (specializing in psychometrics) and a Bachelor's degree from Baylor University. She chaired two groups: One reviews technical and policy matters related to the research and development of the ASVAB and the other is involved in the nationwide implementation of CAT-ASVAB. She also was the manager of the program to norm the CAT-ASVAB and an interest measure called the Interest-Finder. Her experience included conducting testing and training research for five years at the Air Force Human Resources Laboratory, consulting with Jeanneret and Associates to develop selection tests for various oil companies for three years, and developing and validating tests for the University of Texas for seven years.

Paul A. Gade is Chief of the Organization and Personnel Resources Research Unit at the U.S. Army Research Institute for the Behavioral and

Social Sciences. He is a Fellow of the American Psychological Association (APA) and the Inter-University Seminar on Armed Forces and Society, and is past President of the Military Psychology Division of APA. Dr. Gade was the research manager in charge of the Computerized Adaptive Screening Test (CAST) development for the Army's JOIN system.

Rebecca D. Hetter worked in CAT-ASVAB research at the NPRDC from 1984 to 1996. Before joining the CAT-ASVAB project and also at NPRDC, she worked in U.S. Naval Academy research and developed a biographical questionnaire currently used in applicant selection. Prior to joining NPRDC in 1978, she was an instructor in the Psychology Department at Southwestern College in San Diego, a systems programmer at the University of California, San Diego, and a systems programmer in the Division of Biometrics at the Western Reserve University Medical School in Cleveland. Currently, she is an operations research analyst at the Defense Manpower Data Center, Monterey Bay, California.

C. Richard (Dick) Hoshaw, a retired Navy Reserve Captain and senior-level civil servant, was Program Manager for CAT-ASVAB at the Bureau of Naval Personnel from 1982 to 1987. Beginning in 1979, he was Navy policy representative to the CAT Inter-Service Coordinating Committee and later served many years as Chairman of the Policy Committee of the CAT-ASVAB Working Group. He was the first United States representative to NATO's Research Study Group on Computer-Based Assessment of Military Personnel (RSG-15). He is presently retired and living in Alexandria, Virginia.

Irwin Hom is a computer specialist providing hardware, software, and networking solutions. With a degree in computer science, he was one of the principal software designers for the CAT-ASVAB program that operated on the HP-Integral PC. In addition, he has developed and contributed to numerous projects for the federal government and private agencies. Currently he is the software systems developer for the Human Resources Research Organization (HumRRO) where he is rewriting the CAT-ASVAB software to run on the personal computer platform.

William F. Kieckhaefer. Mr. Kieckhaefer's 24-year career includes 17 years of management and supervisory experience. For the past 12 years as head of RGI's Personnel Systems Division, he has led and managed projects directly related to ASVAB ranging from CAT-ASVAB to the Dynamic Spatial Test Battery. During this period, he has directed data collection from over 300,000 study participants at locations nationwide. He has extensive experience interfacing with USMEPCOM, the MEPS, and such related organizations as DMDC, NPRDC, and ARI. Mr. Kieckhaefer has led recruitment and training of TAs, remote test site set-up and operation, development of data, and material security measures for a nationwide network of test sites. He has full responsibility for all operations of RGI's Division including resource control, staffing, planning and administration. Mr. Kieckhaefer has an M.S. in Industrial and Organizational Psychology.

Deirdre J. Knapp earned her Ph.D. in industrial and organizational psychology from Bowling Green State University in 1984. While at the ARI (1985–1987), Dr. Knapp was responsible for the Computerized Adaptive Screening Test (CAST) research program. Since moving to HumRRO, Dr. Knapp has worked primarily on the design and administration of performance assessments. This testing experience has covered many different contexts (e.g., performance assessment for promotion systems, criterion measurement for selection and classification test validation research, occupational certification programs) and many different types of jobs and organizations (e.g., Army enlisted and civilian occupations, federal agencies, and private organizations). Most notably, Dr. Knapp spent seven years as task co-leader of the performance measurement portion of the Project A/Building the Career Force research program sponsored by the U.S. Army.

Gerald E. Larson received an M.S. degree in experimental psychology from San Diego State University in 1983. Since then, while serving as a research psychologist at NPRDC, he has worked on numerous projects concerning individual differences in cognitive abilities and personality.

Clessen J. Martin served as CAT-ASVAB Program Manager from 1987 until the program was transferred to DMDC in 1994. Prior to joining the Department of the Navy, he was a research psychologist for the Army Research Institute for the Behavioral and Social Sciences and the Air Force Human Resources Laboratory. Before joining DoD in 1979, he was Professor and Head of the Psychology Department at Texas A&M University and Professor at Michigan State University. Currently, he is a personnel research psychologist at the Defense Manpower Data Center, DoD Center—Monterey Bay, California.

Kathleen E. Moreno is the Chief of the Data Quality Control and Analysis Branch, Personnel Testing Division, at the Defense Manpower Data Center (DMDC)—Monterey Bay. Ms. Moreno has worked on the CAT-ASVAB project for the past 16 years. She was hired as a graduate student at the Navy Personnel Research and Development Center (NPRDC) in 1981. In 1983, she became a government employee, working as a personnel research psychologist on the CAT-ASVAB program. In 1990, Ms. Moreno became director of the Operations and Testing Division at NPRDC, responsible for all CAT-ASVAB empirical research and development, including the Operational Test and Evaluation (OT&E). From 1994 to 1996, before leaving NPRDC to join the staff at DMDC, Ms. Moreno was the Director of the Personnel and Organizational Assessment Department, managing a wide variety of research projects in these areas, including CAT-ASVAB. Over the years, Ms. Moreno has been involved in all aspects of the CAT-ASVAB program, from early psychometric development to development and evaluation of an operational system for full-scale implementation. She has worked on the program in the roles of both research psychologist and project director, managing the CAT-ASVAB program. She is currently a key player in the nationwide implementation of CAT-ASVAB.

Bernard A. Rafacz attended St. Francis College and Pennsylvania State University where he received advanced degrees in Mathematics and Statistics. After teaching high school mathematics and physics for two years, he served in the U.S. Army for two years developing computerized weapons testing systems. For most of his career, Mr. Rafacz has worked with NPRDC, San Diego, as a computer scientist. During this time, he has developed personnel selection/assignment and job skill matching procedures, with special emphasis on the design, development, and testing of computer hardware/software systems for personnel testing systems for DoD and other Government agencies.

Daniel O. Segall has been the chief technical advisor and psychometric architect for the CAT-ASVAB program for over a decade. He has authored over 50 journal articles, book chapters, conference papers, and manuscripts on adaptive testing. In addition to his work for the DoD, Dr. Segall has acted in an advisory capacity to other adaptive testing efforts for the Departments of Labor and Justice.

His association with the CAT-ASVAB program began in 1983, working on one of the first large-scale validity studies of CAT. In 1985, he went to work for NPRDC, and shortly thereafter was appointed to represent the lead laboratory on the Joint-Service CAT-ASVAB Technical Committee. In 1993, he was appointed Chair of the Manpower Accession Policy Working Group Technical Committee which reviews and advises on technical aspects of ASVAB R&D. Recently, Dr. Segall moved to the DMDC, where he plays a central role in the design, execution, and analysis of R&D studies for CAT-ASVAB and related efforts.

W. S. (Steve) Sellman is Director for Accession Policy, Office of the Secretary of Defense. His office develops policies and procedures that annually drive the enlistment of more than 400,000 men and women into the active and reserve components and the commissioning of more than 20,000 new officers. He has been conducting research in military manpower, psychological testing, literacy training, and selection and classification for 30 years, and has authored more than 75 journal articles, professional papers, and technical reports. Past president of the American Psychological Association's Division of Military Psychology, Dr. Sellman earned his Ph.D. in Industrial/Organizational Psychology at Purdue University.

J. Bradford (Brad) Sympson studied psychology and psychometrics at the University of Minnesota. From 1979 to 1981, he worked at Educational Testing Service with Dr. Frederick M. Lord, one of the original developers of the theory behind CAT. In 1981, Brad moved to NPRDC in San Diego, where he worked on development of the experimental and operational CAT-ASVAB systems. He is now affiliated with Analytic Systems, a private consulting firm.

Vincent D. Unpingco is a computer specialist at the Defense Manpower Data Center (DMDC). He has been a government employee for the past 27 years, working in computer system development. Mr. Unpingco has a long history of working on innovative, state-of-the art systems. Some of these include the Space Transportation System (Space Shuttle and Missile Launch), the Planning, Programming, and Budgeting System (PPBS), various criminal investigative and intelligence systems, world-wide logistical systems, financial management systems, personnel management systems, and communication systems. In 1987, Mr. Unpingco transferred to NPRDC, working on the CAT-

ASVAB program. Since that time, he has served as the government's lead computer expert in the design, development, evaluation, and implementation of the operational CAT-ASVAB system.

Frank L. Vicino received his B.A. in Psychology from Hunter College, New York City; M.S. from the University of Maryland in Experimental Psychology; and Doctorate from Western Colorado University in Psychological Measurement. As Head of the Personnel Assessment Research Division at NPRDC, Dr. Vicino and his staff are engaged in cutting-edge research in computerized testing technology and models, Joint-Service testing, new test development, new selection and classification technology, and theories of evaluation and assessment. He has directed, supervised, and evaluated professional training programs in behavioral science, statistics, and computer sciences. Dr. Vicino is a member of the American Educational Research Association, American Psychological Association, American Association for the Advancement of Science, Western Psychological Association, International Military Testing Association, and the National Academy of School Executives.

C. Douglas Wetzel has conducted research at NPRDC that broadly spanned testing, and training technologies. Dr. Wetzel conducted psychometric simulation studies on item selection strategies used for CAT-ASVAB. He oversaw the development of a large computer-based educational software system and developed Navy courseware. He conducted research to extend the use of video-teletraining beyond lecture courses to training involving hands-on laboratories. He is the principal author of a book entitled "Instructional Effectiveness of Video Media."

Lauress L. Wise directed the Personnel Testing Division at DMDC from 1990 through 1994. In that capacity, he supervised ASVAB research and development activities, including research on options for the operational implementation of CAT-ASVAB. Prior to his position at DMDC, Dr. Wise earned a Ph.D. in psychometrics from the University of California, Berkeley and worked for 16 years as a research scientist with the American Institutes for Research, concentrating on test development, validation, and use. Dr. Wise is currently President of HumRRO, in Alexandria, Virginia and maintains an active involvement in testing and test use issues.

Martin F. Wiskoff is currently a Director/Senior Scientist for BDM Federal Inc. in Monterey, CA. He was previously a Senior Scientist for the Defense Personnel Security Research Center in Monterey, CA and Director of the Manpower and Personnel Laboratory at NPRDC, San Diego, CA. Dr. Wiskoff is a fellow and past president of the Division of Military Psychology of the American Psychological Association. He is also founder and editor of *Military Psychology*, a journal published by the Division of Military Psychology.

John H. Wolfe received his B.S. degree in mathematics from the California Institute of Technology in 1955 and M.A. in psychology from U.C. Berkeley in 1963. After working as a Mathematical Statistician for the Bureau of Census and a Senior Programmer at UNIVAC, he joined NPRDC as an Operations Research Analyst. There, for the next 30 years, he worked on network flow models for personnel assignment, artificial intelligence applications to computer-assisted instruction, and CAT. From 1986 to 1994, he organized and led a group for the Navy's research on new computerized aptitude tests. Since his retirement from NPRDC in 1994, he has continued to do writing, independent research, and consulting on personnel research problems. He is best known for his statistical clustering program NORMIX.

Preface

This book incorporates the ideas and work of many dedicated people, from a variety of professional disciplines, who have made significant contributions to the Computerized Adaptive Testing—Armed Services Vocational Aptitude Battery (CAT-ASVAB) Program from inception in 1979 to the present. A review of the Table of Contents illustrates the large number of authors involved in writing chapters for this book. Numerous other individuals, both inside and outside of the Navy Personnel Research and Development Center (NPRDC), made important contributions over the years. However, four individuals should be singled out for special recognition, based upon the critical roles they played in the success of the CAT-ASVAB Program.

Dr. W. S. Sellman, Director for Accession Policy, Office of the Assistant Secretary of Defense (Force Management Policy) provided vision, on-going guidance, and support for the program from the beginnning until the present. The CAT-ASVAB Program developed as a Joint-Service program, with each Service playing a role, and having its own perspective. Dr. Sellman's central, Department of Defense (DoD) perspective has kept the CAT-ASVAB Program focused on the eventual goal of full-scale, nationwide, DoD implementation of a scientifically sound and practical testing innovation.

Dr. M. F. Wiskoff created the CAT research capability at NPRDC, where the vast majority of the research and development for CAT-ASVAB has been accomplished. He convinced NPRDC management of the merits of the CAT concept, created the organizational structure for the program within his Manpower and Personnel Laboratory, hired new professionals from outside the Center and reassigned key personnel assets from other areas within his laboratory. As the first Officer-in-Charge of the Joint-Service CAT-ASVAB Program, he chaired the CAT-ASVAB Working Group, and

headed the CAT-ASVAB Program Office, which included a uniformed officer from each of the Services. His contributions to CAT-ASVAB were crucial to the Program's birth and growth.

Mr. C. R. Hoshaw, and subsequently, Dr. C. J. Martin, were key players in the Department of Navy. In the role as policy representative for the lead Service (Navy), they provided a strong headquarters advocacy. As career civilians, they provided a Bureau of Naval Personnel "corporate memory" for the CAT-ASVAB Program. This was essential in working with a succession of rotating senior Naval officers, who were responsible for the program over the years. In addition, they coordinated funding support essential for sustaining the program over many budget years and cutbacks.

This book would never have come to life without the efforts of Mrs. Margie Sands, Ms. Lola Zook, and Ms. Emma James. Mrs. Sands was the Administrative Assistant to Marty Wiskoff at NPRDC during most of the CAT-ASVAB Program. She edited the book chapters from the perspective of someone who had first-hand knowledge of the program over the years. Mrs. Zook served as the HumRRO technical/copy editor. Ms. James (HumRRO) typed many iterations of the entire book. The editors appreciate their important contributions.

The book was produced, in part, through an Army Research Institute for the Behavioral and Social Sciences (ARI) delivery order contract: Contract for Manpower and Personnel Research and Studies (COMPRS). Dr. Ron Tiggle (ARI) was the delivery order Contracting Officer's Representative. Dr. Jane M. Arabian, Assistant Director for Enlistment Standards in the Directorate for Accession Policy, Office of the Assistant Secretary of Defense (Force Management Policy), was the delivery order monitor.

The editors wish to thank Julia Frank-McNeil,

Director of APA Books, and Ed Meidenbauer, the book's technical/production editor, for their help in the publishing of the CATBOOK. The views, opinions, and findings contained in this book are those of the authors and editors. They should not be construed as representing an official Department of Defense position, policy, or decision, unless so designated by other official documentation.

Foreword

This book documents the U.S. Department of Defense's (DoD) research, development, and implementation of computerized adaptive testing (CAT) from its early research and development in the 1960s and 70s through its operational implementation into DoD enlistment testing in the 1990s. Much can be learned from the tale of this trailblazing evolution of CAT into the DoD enlistment test battery, the Armed Services Vocational Aptitude Battery (ASVAB). Its story is both rich and informative.

Each year DoD administers the ASVAB to nearly two million young men and women. In addition to operating the world's largest testing program, DoD strives to operate the best testing program. During the 1960s, a new testing method, CAT, was receiving research support from the Office of Naval Research (ONR). CAT showed promise for significantly improving the way aptitudes of new recruits were measured.

At ONR, Drs. Marshall Farr and Charles Davis guided and funded early CAT research. Some of the ONR-supported work focused on the statistical techniques of item response theory (IRT) that allow examinees' scores to be expressed on the same score scale, even though they respond to a different set of test questions. That theoretical development of IRT was crucial to achieving CAT advances. Later research, during the 1970s, developed and evaluated a wide variety of CAT issues and alternative methods for CAT test administration, including procedures for tailoring the choice of test questions to individual ability. By the early 1980s, DoD and the Military Services had begun extensive studies of CAT and to plan a CAT system for administering the ASVAB in operational enlistment testing.

In 1984, the DoD CAT-ASVAB program received an unexpected push forward by Lieutenant General E. A. Chavarrie, then Deputy Assistant Secretary of Defense (Military Manpower and Personnel Policy). The General was scheduled to present the keynote address at the Military Testing Association (MTA) conference in Munich, Germany. Part of his speech covered the status of CAT research in the American military. However, the day before the conference opened, the General visited several German recruiting offices, where he saw applicants taking the German enlistment test via computer. It apparently made quite an impression on him, especially since the very next day he planned to go before over 250 MTA conferees from 10 countries to say that the U.S. would not be operationally implementing its computerized testing program for another five years. He then changed his prepared speech and announced to the MTA audience that CAT-ASVAB development in DoD would be completed within two years. As a result, developmental work on CAT-ASVAB assumed a renewed urgency. Despite the sense of urgency created by the speech, major psychometric, economic, and political issues remained to be resolved before CAT-ASVAB could become the operational enlistment testing battery in DoD.

Although the most noticeable change in the new method of testing was that the test was administered by computer, a more important difference between this method and paper and pencil (P&P) tests is that each examinee answers a potentially unique set of test questions "tailored" to his or her ability. CAT allows examinees to answer only questions that are suited to their own individual abilities, by selecting (tailoring) after each item response the next item to be presented to an ex-

Much of this foreword is based on W. S. Sellman, "Computer Adaptive Testing: Psychometrics, Economics, and Politics," presented to the Workshop on Computer-Based Assessment of Military Personnel. Brussels, Belgium: NATO Defense Research Group, November 26, 1991.

aminee based upon his or her performance on previous items. This contrasts with conventional P&P group testing, which requires all examinees to take the same set of items, thus forcing many people to spend time on questions that may be either too easy or difficult for them.

It is imperative that ASVAB scores be accurate reflections of the ability levels of new military recruits. DoD annually reports the aptitude levels of new recruits to Congress and the American public using a percentile scale that enables comparisons across Services and time. Thus, each version of the ASVAB must be "calibrated" correctly against the normative population. Otherwise, scores lose their psychometric meaning and cannot be interpreted properly. Unfortunately, the forms of the ASVAB in use from 1976 through 1980 were miscalibrated due to technical errors in their norming, inflating the reported scores of low aptitude examinees. This ultimately resulted in the enlistment of over 300,000 young people who would not have qualified for military entry if they had received accurate test scores. Numerous studies have shown that brighter recruits return the investments in their recruiting, because, when compared with their lower scoring peers, they are more trainable, perform better on the job, have lower rates of discipline actions, and are more likely to complete their obligated tours of duty. Thus, the psychometric strength of the CAT-ASVAB is a major issue for DoD.

Another major psychometric hurdle faced by CAT researchers was equating the P&P-ASVAB with an ASVAB administered adaptively by computer. The ability to equate P&P and computerized adaptive tests would enable DoD to transition to CAT-ASVAB knowing that it could still track recruit aptitude across Services and time. When DoD began CAT research, the researchers had no experience base describing how to equate the two types of tests. Fortunately, with the early help of some of the most eminent psychometricians in the nation, including Drs. Darrell Bock, Bert Green, Jr., Frederick Lord, Mark Reckase, Fumiko Samejima, and David Weiss, progress was made toward equating the two types of tests.

In the mid-1980s, DoD began studies to examine the relationship between CAT-ASVAB scores and recruit performance in technical training. The validity coefficients for CAT-ASVAB turned out to be similar to those of P&P-ASVAB. This was not surprising, since CAT-ASVAB used the same types of questions (e.g., verbal, mathematics, and technical information) found on the operational P&P-ASVAB.

For the past several years, DoD has conducted studies equating P&P-ASVABs with CAT versions of ASVAB with large samples of military applicants. Today, DoD is confident that a person taking a CAT-ASVAB test would receive the same ability estimates if he or she took the P&P version. Equating the two types of the ASVAB (P&P and CAT) was essential for the scores to be interpreted against the normative base or against previous distributions of recruit aptitude. A large portion of the credit for this technical advance is attributed to Drs. Bruce Bloxom and Daniel Segall of the Defense Manpower Data Center.

Before CAT-ASVAB could become operational, DoD had to demonstrate its relative economic costs and benefits for military selection and classification. During the late 1980s, DoD sponsored a cost-benefit analysis of the CAT-ASVAB. It would be prohibitively expensive to buy computers for all 1,000 locations where the ASVAB was to be administered. Consequently, a variety of siting strategies were explored that either took the test to the applicant or the applicant to the test. In particular, DoD considered (a) transporting all applicants to a small number of centralized sites; (b) additional testing at high volume sites; and (c) testing of applicants at portable locations. Costs for each of these strategies were computed, along with costs of P&P-ASVAB testing under existing procedures. The results showed that CAT-ASVAB would increase costs over the P&P-ASVAB by $17 million for centralized testing and by $132 million for portable testing over the economic life of the system.

At the same time, the benefits of CAT-ASVAB were evaluated. It was shown that using a more valid test during selection and classification would reduce personnel costs through enhanced performance in training and on the job, and result in lower first term attrition. It costs approximately $20,000 each to recruit and train replacements for recruits who do not complete their obligated tour of duty. Unfortunately, the validity of CAT-ASVAB was not appreciably higher than that for the P&P-ASVAB at the time of that first cost–benefit study. As a result, DoD was not able to demonstrate improved enlistment processing through the use of CAT-ASVAB, nor could it justify the costs of purchasing computers for enlistment testing.

Computerized testing expands the types of tests which can be administered. Among the new types made possible by computerizing tests are psychomotor tracking, cognitive processing, and short- and long-term memory, which are difficult to present in a P&P mode of testing. If such tests proved more valid than conventional tests, then testing effectiveness could be improved. The results of the cost–benefit analyses prompted DoD to initiate a new phase in the CAT-ASVAB program—development and validation of tests that could only be administered via computer.

A second cost–benefit analysis of six alternative CAT-ASVAB concepts of operation was completed in 1993 (Hogan, McBride, & Curran, 1995). The second study focused on operational costs (e.g., recruiting costs) and took into account the significant decreases in computer costs since the earlier cost–benefit study. Each of the alternative concepts of operation was found to generate savings over the baseline P&P-ASVAB concept.

DoD has made substantial progress in the development of computerized tests. Today, much is known that previously was only speculation. For example, CAT reduces testing times by almost one half. CAT-ASVAB also enhances the image of the military with applicants for enlistment who view the technology as an indicator that the military is technically sophisticated. Applicants tend to prefer taking a computerized test over a P&P test. It provides more precise measurement for those at the extremes of ability (i.e. high and low aptitude people), although the P&P measure still works better psychometrically for those of average ability. Equivalent scores can be obtained whether P&P or CAT versions of the ASVAB are administered. Finally, new measures which can only be administered by computer have shown improvements in the prediction of training and on-the-job success.

The operational military supports CAT-ASVAB because of its potential to reduce testing time, thereby saving valuable recruiting resources. But CAT-ASVAB could prove even more beneficial once fully implemented. It will not only be easier to incorporate new tests such as psychomotor tests and develop new items via on-line item calibration, but it also will be possible to tailor an enlistment testing session to include Service-specific tests for applicants. Technical issues aside, CAT-ASVAB provides a superior testing situation for all applicants to military service, regardless of their aptitude. Individuals who would struggle through typical P&P tests find CAT to be challenging, but not overwhelming. They do not encounter large numbers of items far beyond their capabilities. Higher aptitude individuals, on the other hand, are challenged by CAT-ASVAB and, hopefully, positively influenced by the military's high technology image. It provides a winning situation for everyone.

DoD had to deal with psychometric, economic, and political issues before implementing an operational CAT-ASVAB system. Most of these problems have been solved. Others are being tackled currently with a sense of urgency. But there are still lessons to be learned and hard decisions to be made as recruits are tested by computer. Obviously, the science and politics of CAT-ASVAB involve complex problems that offer significant challenges.

The well-justified pride of DoD and Service policy makers and researchers, including civilian scientists working under contract, is conveyed in the following pages. This book captures the story of CAT-ASVAB implementation in DoD. It documents technical information that will be helpful to other scientists and the test development community in general as computerized testing becomes the standard test delivery method for large-scale testing programs. Hopefully, the knowledge, experience, and lessons learned contained in the "CATBOOK" will guide, instruct, and even inspire those who see today's technology as the stepping stone to the future of psychological measurement.

W. S. Sellman, Ph.D.
Director for Accession Policy
Office of the Assistant Secretary of Defense
(Force Management Policy)
U.S. Department of Defense

Jane M. Arabian, Ph.D.
Assistant Director for Enlistment Standards
Office of the Assistant Secretary of Defense
(Force Management Policy)
U.S. Department of Defense

PART
I

Background

For the most part, the major parts of this book are organized chronologically, and their chapters document a sequence of milestones in the research and development that led to the introduction of CAT into operational use in the administration of U.S. military personnel selection and classification tests. This first part is an exception to that chronological order: Its four chapters present the context in which the CAT-ASVAB program was conducted and provide perspectives on the program from the points of view of several individuals who were intimately involved in it, either at its outset or through some of its critical periods.

At the core of the CAT-ASVAB program is the Armed Services Vocational Aptitude Battery, which since 1976 has been used for enlisted personnel selection and classification by all four of the U.S. Armed Services, as well as the Coast Guard. An appreciation of ASVAB's content, its purposes, and the size and complexity of the system in which it is administered should be helpful to the reader because these matters simultaneously provided the motivation to pursue the development of CAT-ASVAB and a set of constraints on its features. The first chapter, by Sands and Waters, is an aid to that appreciation. It describes the ASVAB itself, the two different testing programs in which it is used, and some key details of the administration of one of them: The ASVAB Enlistment Testing Program, which administers the tests in hundreds of locations to applicants for military enlistment. Chapter 1 also introduces the concept of CAT, and describes some of the features which made it attractive as an alternative to paper-and-pencil administration of the ASVAB.

In a sense, **Chapter 1** provides historical and practical perspectives on the program. Chapters 2, 3, and 4 provide three additional perspectives: Those of key personnel responsible for setting policy for the program, managing the re-

search and development effort in the lead laboratory, and planning and directing the development of the adaptive tests themselves and the computer system needed to administer them.

Chapter 2 represents the perspective of policy and program management. Its authors, Hoshaw and Martin, had responsibility for advocating the program in the headquarters offices of the lead Service, the U.S. Navy. It fell to them to ensure continuing support for CAT-ASVAB research and development within an organization with a large number of competing priorities.

Chapter 3 reflects the perspective of laboratory R&D management, which was especially challenging in this case because CAT-ASVAB was a Joint-Services, coordinated program. Wiskoff provides a historical overview of the major stages of the program, including the development of an R&D capability, the performance of early research, and the transition of responsibility for the program from one agency (the Marine Corps) to another (the Navy). His chapter goes on to address a number of management-related topics, including the special problems of obtaining support from upper management, from policy makers in Navy headquarters, and from the organizations that set priorities for funding R&D programs. All of these issues were intertwined with the research and development itself. Wiskoff addresses those interrelationships as they affected the program's technical thrusts, including psychometric research, delivery system development, economic analysis, and other topics. At the chapter's conclusion, Wiskoff offers recommendations for others engaged in the management of R&D programs with multiple constituencies similar to the Joint-Services arena in the Department of Defense.

In **Chapter 4**, McBride provides a perspective on the program from a technical point of view, addressing the two principal thrusts of CAT-ASVAB

R&D: Design and development of computer systems to deliver adaptive tests, and the research needed to develop and evaluate computerized adaptive versions of the tests that make up the ASVAB. His chapter provides a summary of the state of the art in adaptive testing at the outset of the program, and enumerates specific areas of psychometric research in which the CAT-ASVAB program broke new ground. McBride points out a number of research topics in which the CAT-ASVAB program did pioneering work. The topics addressed in Chapter 4 represent a research and development agenda that is as applicable today as it was in 1979 to any organization contemplating the conversion of an existing test battery to a computerized adaptive format.

Introduction to ASVAB and CAT

W. A. Sands and Brian K. Waters

The Armed Services Vocational Aptitude Battery (ASVAB) and computerized adaptive testing (CAT) are the topics of central importance throughout this book. The purpose of this introductory chapter is twofold: (1) to provide the reader with a brief introduction to ASVAB and CAT, and (2) to consolidate basic information on these two topics, providing a framework for the more detailed presentations in the following chapters.

Military Personnel Screening

Aptitude testing plays a central role in the military personnel screening process. Indeed, the military places far more emphasis on aptitude testing as a selection tool than does the civilian sector. This difference is the result of a number of factors:

• The majority of individuals in the primary age group of applicants targeted by the military (17–21 years old) has no significant employment history to aid in selection decisions.

• The military selects people for a wide variety of training and jobs.

• The overall military screening process is quite expensive, in part because of the large numbers of people involved. Group-administered tests offer efficiencies in time, cost, and psychometric precision that are quite appealing.

• The large number of people tested enables the military to conduct large-scale, empirical studies to obtain evidence for the validity, reliability, fairness, and differential impact of tests on various subgroups. This information is useful in meeting current professional standards for the use of employment tests (American Educational Research Association, American Psychological Association, & National Council on Measurement in Education, 1985; American Psychological Association, 1980).

Historical Antecedents

The early history of military testing is briefly characterized by Eitelberg, Laurence, and Waters, with Perelman (1984).[1]

The American military was a pioneer in the field of aptitude testing during World War I. In 1917 and 1918, the Army Alpha and Army Beta tests were developed so that (1) military commanders could have some measure of the ability of their men, and (2) personnel managers could have some objective means of assigning the new recruits. The Army Alpha test was a verbal, group-administered test used primarily by the Army for selection and placement. The test consisted of eight subtests—including verbal ability, numerical ability, ability to follow directions, and information—and served as a prototype for several subsequent group-administered intelligence tests. The Army Beta test was a nonverbal, group-administered

---

[1] Additional information on the history of the U.S military's use of aptitude screening tests may be found in a number of Department of Defense publications, (for example: Eitelberg et al., 1984; ASVAB Working Group, 1980; and Department of the Army, 1965).

counterpart to the Army Alpha test. It was used to evaluate the aptitude of illiterate, unschooled, or non-English-speaking draftees. . . .

The Army General Classification Test (AGCT) of World War II largely replaced the tests of World War I. The AGCT was described as a test of "general learning ability" and was intended to be used in basically the same manner as the Army Alpha (i.e., an aid in assigning new recruits to military jobs) (Eitelberg et al., 1984, pp. 14–15).

Between World War II and 1976, each of the Services employed its own set of tests to determine initial eligibility for enlistment and for subsequent classification decisions. These tests included measures of general trainability and specific aptitudes considered important to the Services.

The Selective Service Act (1948) mandated the development and use of a common basis for determining U.S. military enlistment eligibility. At that time, the Army General Classification Test (AGCT) was the most widely used personnel screening instrument in the military. This test became the model for the Armed Forces Qualification Test (AFQT), the Joint-Service selection test designed to address the congressional mandate. The AFQT became operational in 1950.

The original AFQT contained three types of items: Verbal, arithmetic reasoning, and spatial relations. Since that first version, various content changes have been introduced. During the period 1972–75, the Services were not required to use the AFQT. Rather, each Service was permitted to use its own test battery and conversion tables to estimate the AFQT score for each person (ASVAB Working Group, 1980).

Armed Services Vocational Aptitude Battery (ASVAB)

In 1966, the Department of Defense (DoD) directed the individual Military Services to explore the development of a single, multiple-purpose aptitude test battery that could be used in high schools. This direction was designed to prevent costly duplication by the military and schools, and to encourage equitable selection standards across Services (DoD, 1992).

Since 1976, the ASVAB has been the common selection and classification battery for the four (DoD) Services and the Coast Guard (Department of Transportation). New forms of the battery have been produced approximately every three to four years. At the time of this writing, P&P-ASVAB Forms 20 through 22 and CAT-ASVAB Forms 01 and

02 are currently used in the Enlistment Testing Program, while P&P-ASVAB Forms 18 and 19 are used in the DoD Student Testing Program.

ASVAB Testing Programs

DoD student testing program (DoD-STP). The ASVAB was introduced into the high school setting during the 1968–69 school year. DoD provides the ASVAB, an interest inventory, and a host of supporting materials to participating schools free of charge. The benefit to the schools is a well-researched, multiple-aptitude test battery to provide career guidance and counseling services to students. This benefit is especially important to schools in an era of budget reductions, as the ASVAB program sometimes is the only vocational guidance information available to counselors and their students.

According to Wall (1995), the purposes of the AS-VAB Career Exploration Program (CEP) are to:

• Provide information to students about their abilities, interests, and personal preferences

• Provide information to students on civilian and military occupations

• Help students identify civilian and military occupations that have characteristics of interest to them

• Identify for the Services aptitude-qualified individuals who may be interested in joining the military

ASVAB as a counseling tool. The ASVAB CEP provides a comprehensive set of educational and career counseling tools for the student and school counselor for their use as the student learns career decision skills. The program includes ASVAB scores, a DoD-published interest inventory, and exercises designed to help students identify their personal preferences (DoD, 1992).

Interest-Finder. DoD's license to use the Self-Directed Search (SDS), a commercially published interest inventory, expired in July 1995. Therefore, DoD developed an interest inventory, the Interest-Finder, which was implemented in the DOD-STP during the 1995–96 school year. Like the SDS, the Interest-Finder uses Holland's classification codes (Holland, 1973) to cluster interests into related occupational areas. The instrument has extensive research and development underlying its use in the schools.

ASVAB career exploration program counseling materials. A number of ASVAB CEP printed materials are currently provided to participating schools and students. These materials can be obtained from local military recruiters or from ASVAB Education Services Specialists at Military Entrance Processing Stations (DoD, 1992). Current ASVAB CEP printed materials include:

- ASVAB 18/19 Educator and Counselor Guide

- ASVAB 18/19 Counselor Manual

- ASVAB 18/19 Technical Manual

- ASVAB 18/19 Student and Parent Guide

- Exploring Careers: The ASVAB Workbook

- Military Careers

ASVAB as a high school recruiting tool for the military. A major benefit of the DOD-STP to the military is the recruiting leads provided by the results. ASVAB score information enables Service recruiters to focus on students who will be likely to qualify for enlistment. Hence, the DOD-STP serves as a mechanism to pre-qualify student recruiting prospects. The ASVAB is administered in about 14,000 schools. The number of students tested in the schools has been decreasing, with 931,000 tested during the 1990–91 school year, 882,000 in 1991–92, and 880,294 in 1992–93 (Branch, personal communications, 1995).

Enlistment testing program. The Military Services began using the ASVAB in 1976. In FY 1993, about one half million prospects took the ASVAB for active duty (358,755), Reserve (73,244), and National/Air National Guard (67,383) recruiting programs (Branch, personal communication, 1995). As with the DOD-STP, the Defense drawdown has led to decreasing numbers of military applicants taking the ASVAB since 1988.

Active, Reserve, and much National Guard ASVAB testing, is conducted in 65 Military Entrance Processing Stations (MEPSs) and their nearly 700 associated, satellite Mobile Examining Team Sites (METSs). The MEPSs and METSs are part of the U.S. Military Entrance Processing Command (USMEPCOM), a Joint-Service agency headquartered in North Chicago, Illinois, which is responsible for administering the ASVAB, physical examination and medical qualification, and other enlistment processing activities for the Armed Forces. USMEPCOM essentially handles all enlistment processing activities from the time that a

prospect begins the testing program until he or she ships to a Service recruit training center.

Military entrance processing stations (MEPSs). The approximately 65 MEPSs (the number is shrinking during the Defense drawdown) are geographically dispersed applicant processing centers which have ASVAB testing rooms, answer sheet scanners and computer equipment, medical and physical examining facilities, and offices for Service career counselors (classifiers) to interact with prospects about options for military jobs, training class seats, and shipping dates. The ASVAB is administered by military personnel in the MEPSs, in a carefully controlled testing environment.

Mobile examining team sites (METSs). Each MEPS has several relatively small, satellite testing sites which operate under its control. In a given METS, testing frequency may range from less than once per week to several times a week. METSs are located in various types of facilities, ranging from post offices and other public buildings to leased space. The METSs administer the ASVAB and some specialized Service tests; qualifying applicants who wish to continue the screening process proceed to the MEPS for medical and physical examinations and other processing. The ASVAB is administered at the METSs by part-time Office of Personnel Management (OPM) test administrators (TAs). The answer sheets are optically scanned at the MEPS, generally a day or two following METS testing, although recruiters are given an unofficial hand-scored AFQT score for their applicants immediately after ASVAB testing.

ASVAB tests. At present, the paper-and-pencil (P&P) version of the ASVAB contains 10 tests. The name, description, and testing time for each are presented in Table 1-1 on the following page. They include eight power (relatively unspeeded) tests (Arithmetic Reasoning [AR], Word Knowledge [WK], Paragraph Comprehension [PC], Mathematics Knowledge [MK], General Science [GS], Mechanical Comprehension [MC], Electronics Information [EI], and Auto and Shop Information [AS]); and two speeded tests (Coding Speed [CS] and Numerical Operations [NO]). The first four are measures of general trainability, while the following four tap learned abilities predictive of success in specific jobs and clusters of military jobs. The two speeded tests predict performance on certain military tasks that require highly speeded activities or rapid information processing. Factor analytic studies of the ASVAB have consistently yielded four factors—Verbal (WK, PC, and

Table 1-1 Armed Services Vocational Aptitude Battery (ASVAB) Tests: Description, Number of Questions, and Testing Time[a]

ASVAB Test Title and Abbreviation	Description	Number of Questions	Testing Time (Minutes)
Arithmetic Reasoning (AR)	Measures ability to solve arithmetic word problems	30	36
Word Knowledge (WK)	Measures ability to select the correct meaning of words presented in context and to identify best synonym for a given word	35	11
Mathematics Knowledge (MK)	Measures knowledge of high school mathematics principles	25	24
Paragraph Comprehension (PC)	Measures ability to obtain information from written passages	15	13
General Science (GS)	Measures knowledge of physical and biological sciences	25	11
Mechanical Comprehension (MC)	Measures knowledge of mechanical and physical principles and ability to visualize how illustrated objects work	25	19
Electronics Information (EI)	Measures knowledge of electricity and electronics	20	9
Auto and Shop Information (AS)	Measures knowledge of automobiles, tools and shop terminology and practices	25	11
Coding Speed (CS)	Measures ability to use a key in assigning code numbers to words in a speeded context	84	7
Numerical Operations (NO)	Measures ability to perform arithmetic computations in a speeded context	50	3
	Totals	**334**	**144**[b]

[a] Source: Eitelberg, M. J. (1988). *Manpower for Military Occupations*. Washington, DC: Office of the Assistant Secretary of Defense (Force Management and Personnel), p. 68.

[b] Administrative time is 36 minutes, for a total testing and administrative time of 3 hours.

GS), Quantitative (AR and MK), Technical (EI, MC, and AS), and Speed (CS and NO) factors (cf: Waters, Barnes, Foley, Steinhaus, & Brown, 1988).

ASVAB operational use. The ASVAB is used for two main purposes in military enlisted accessioning: selection of new recruits from applicants, and subsequent classification of recruits into one of the many jobs available. Scores from AR, WK, PC, and MK are combined into the Armed Forces Qualification Test (AFQT) composite score for each applicant. The AFQT measures trainability and predicts job performance in the military. AFQT has been shown to be valid for these uses in the four Military Services and the Coast Guard. AFQT scores are calculated on a percentile scale ranging from 1 to 99. They are reported to Congress by "AFQT Categories," shown in Table 1-2.

ASVAB norms development. Prior to 1980, ASVAB scores were statistically referenced to the population of all male military personnel on active duty on December 31, 1944. This 1944 reference population served as the normative base for U.S. military selection tests until the mid-1970s. Since 1984, ASVAB scales have been based upon ASVAB

testing of a nationally representative sample of over 12,000 youth 18 to 23 years old (DoD, 1982). The study was part of the National Longitudinal Survey of Youth Labor Force Behavior (NLSY79), sponsored jointly by DoD and the Department of Labor (DoL). The NLSY79 has provided the current normative base for all ASVAB test and composite scores (Waters, Laurence, & Camara, 1987). DoL

Table 1-2 Armed Forces Qualification Test (AFQT) Categories by Corresponding Percentile Scores and Level of "Trainability"

AFQT Category	AFQT Percentile Score Range	Level of Trainability
I	93–99	Well Above Average
II	65–92	Above Average
IIIA	50–64	Average
IIIB	31–49	Average
IV	10–30	Below Average
V	1–9	Well Below Average/ Ineligible for Enlistment

Note: From the Department of Defense, *Defense Manpower Quality: Volume 1* (Washington, DC: Office of the Assistant Secretary of Defense (Manpower, Installations, and Logistics), 1985, p. 9.

and DoD are presently planning for a computer-based renorming of the ASVAB, scheduled for 1997.

ASVAB Summary

The ASVAB and its predecessor military tests are exemplars in large-scale, multiple-aptitude selection and classification testing programs. Extensive research and development programs have produced an efficient, accurate, and useful testing program for selecting and assigning hundreds of thousands of young persons annually. With its extensive use in experimental, and now operational, test and evaluation in CAT, the ASVAB provides a solid basis for the future of military personnel selection and classification.

Computerized Adaptive Testing (CAT)

Traditionally, large-scale aptitude testing has used conventionally-administered, paper-and-pencil, multiple-choice tests. Psychometric developments in item response theory (IRT) (Lord, 1980a), in conjunction with advances in computer technology, have made an alternative approach, CAT, feasible (McBride, 1979).

Description

As the name indicates, a CAT instrument is computer administered. Less obvious is the way in which the test dynamically adapts itself to an examinee's ability during the course of test administration. In a conventionally administered, paper-and-pencil aptitude test, every examinee takes the same items, typically in the same order, regardless of the item's appropriateness for a given examinee's ability level. Administering easy items to a high ability applicant is wasteful, as correct responses provide relatively little information about that examinee's ability. In addition, the person may become bored with test items that offer no challenge and may respond carelessly, introducing additional measurement error. Similarly, administration of hard items to a low-ability examinee is wasteful as incorrect answers do not provide much information on that person. Moreover, low-ability examinees are likely to find most items too difficult, and may become frustrated and respond randomly, also introducing additional error into the testing process. In contrast, a CAT instrument

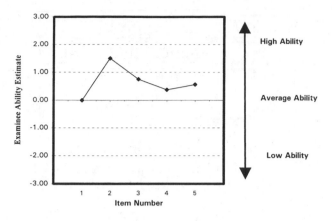

Figure 1-1
Hypothetical 5-Item Computerized Adaptive Test Results.

"tailors" the test to each examinee, as information is collected and evaluated *during* test administration.

The adaptation process can be illustrated with a hypothetical, 5-item test, shown in Figure 1-1 (Wiskoff, 1981). At the beginning of the test, we have no information about the ability level of the examinee, so we assume that person is average in ability (theta = 0.00). Therefore, an item of average difficulty is chosen for administration. Let us suppose that the examinee correctly answered the first item. Our initial ability estimate (average ability) is updated (in this case, raised to theta = 1.5), and a second (more difficult) item is chosen for administration. Now, suppose that the examinee selected an incorrect answer to the second item, suggesting that it was "too hard." Again, the computer updates the ability estimate (this time in a downward direction to theta = 0.75). Then, the next item is selected for administration at that difficulty level. This third item would be less difficult than the second item, reflecting the latest estimate of the person's ability. Suppose that the examinee also answered this third item incorrectly. Again, the ability estimate is updated (lowered to theta = 0.38) and the next item is chosen. Item 4 would be easier than the third item. If the examinee correctly answered this item, the ability (theta) estimate would be raised, and a more difficult item (theta = 0.56) would be presented as the last item in this hypothetical, 5-item adaptive test.

This process of selecting and administering a test item, scoring an examinee's response, updating his or her ability estimate, and choosing the next item for administration continues until a specified stopping rule is satisfied. The stopping criterion might be administration of a predeter-

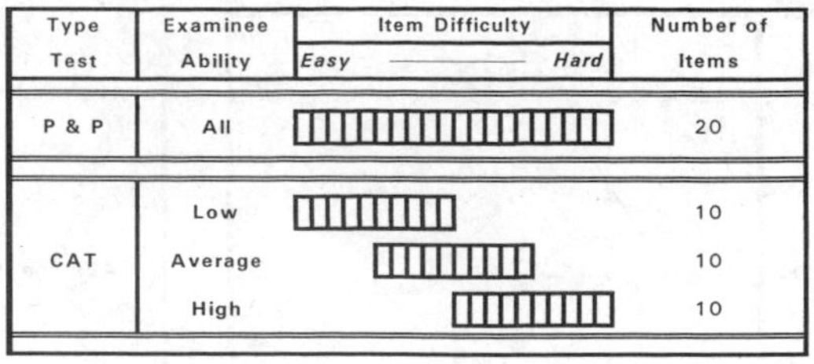

Type Test	Examinee Ability	Item Difficulty (Easy — Hard)	Number of Items
P & P	All		20
CAT	Low		10
	Average		10
	High		10

Figure 1-2
Test Item Utilization for Paper-and-Pencil
Tests and Computerized Adaptive Tests.

mined number of items (fixed-length testing), reduction of the standard error of measurement to a pre-specified level (variable-length testing), or a hybrid combination of the two stopping criteria (see Chapter 5 for discussion).

In comparison to a paper-and-pencil test, the adaptive nature of the CAT instrument produces a very efficient testing session, as illustrated in an example in Figure 1-2. In the example, all paper-and-pencil (P&P) examinees take all 20 test items, regardless of their ability. However, in the CAT test, a low-ability examinee takes a subset of 10 relatively easy items, a person of average ability takes 10 items in the mid-range of difficulty, and a high-ability person takes a subset of 10 relatively difficult items. In the hypothetical situation portrayed in Figure 1-2, the CAT instrument entails only half the number of items (10) required of the P&P test (20) for comparable test precision, producing a substantial savings in test administration time.

Advantages of CAT

Administrative. A CAT version of a test offers four adminstrative advantages over a P&P version of the same test. Reduced test session length is the first advantage. Since each item presented to a particular examinee is appropriate for the current estimate of that person's ability level, no items are wasted. The number of test items administered in an adaptive test is substantially lower than in a traditional test. This reduction is made possible by obtaining more information about the examinee's actual ability per item administered. This, in turn, reduces the test length required to yield a fixed level of measurement precision.

A second administrative advantage of CAT is test session flexibility. The P&P-ASVAB is a group-administered test battery with all examinees starting and ending the test battery together. All examinees are given instructions by the test administrator (TA), and all examinees take each test in the battery simultaneously. Persons finishing a test early must wait for the entire scheduled time for that test to end. Then, all examinees move ahead in lock-step fashion to the next test. In contrast, examinees can begin CAT-ASVAB, individually, at any time. Test battery administrative instructions are provided by the microcomputer. When an examinee finishes a test, that person can proceed directly to the next test. This flexibility increases examinee flow, making the overall testing process more efficient.

A third administrative advantage of CAT is greater standardization. Although P&P-ASVAB is administered with a standard set of instructions and specified time limits for each test, the actual practice may be less standardized than is desirable. The testing procedures are more standardized for a CAT instrument, as the computer precisely controls the test administration.

Fourth, CAT administration simplifies test revision. Revision of a P&P-ASVAB is a time-consuming, logistically cumbersome, and expensive process. After a large supply of experimental items is developed, they are organized into sets of over-length forms and administered to groups of recruits in basic training. Since the schedule in recruit basic training is typically quite full, scheduling test administration sessions can often be problematic. The collected data are scored, then analyzed to cull out items that exhibit poor psychometric characteristics. Those items that survive the process are organized into operational-length test forms. The test forms must then be printed and distributed nationwide.

In CAT-ASVAB, a few embedded experimental items can be administered routinely as each person takes the operational battery. Performance on the experimental items has no impact on a person's scores. Administration of experimental items is transparent to both the examinee and the TA. Thus, the computer provides an opportunity to collect a wealth of item data for future item calibration, without the disruption and lengthy development process necessary in P&P-ASVAB form revision.

Scoring. A computer-based delivery system reduces errors that occur due to reliability problems with optical scanning equipment used to score the P&P-ASVAB. In addition, the possibility for clerical error is greater when hand-scoring takes place. Finally, CAT-ASVAB results are available virtually immediately. If policy permits, scores can be given to the applicant and to the recruiter immediately after the test battery is completed.

Measurement precision. The measurement precision of the typical P&P test is peaked around the average ability level of the target population. This means that most of the items cluster around medium difficulty, while there are relatively few easy or difficult items. Although this strategy of test development usually produces high measurement precision for "average" people, the measurement precision for examinees at both ends of the ability distribution is typically considerably less. Since each CAT-ASVAB test is designed to be appropriate for each examinee's ability level, measurement precision is improved for both low- and high-ability examinees, while matching the precision of P&P-ASVAB for average-ability examinees.

Test security. Use of CAT-ASVAB significantly improves test security. There are no test booklets to be stolen or marked. The actual test items are stored in volatile random access memory (RAM) in the microcomputer system. This means that even if an examinee stole the computer, the items would not be compromised, as the information in volatile RAM disappears immediately when the computer is disconnected from its power source.

Motivation/image. CAT-ASVAB offers advantages in the areas of examinee motivation and military image. Studies have shown that examinees clearly prefer taking a test on a computer to taking a P&P test. Further, the use of microcomputers in the military personnel accessioning process conveys a "high tech" image of the Services to the applicants. This image should assist military recruiters in meeting their goals.

Future tests. A final area in which CAT-ASVAB offers significant advantages is that it provides a microcomputer-based delivery platform which can be used to administer tests that would be impossible via paper-and-pencil. An example would be a target acquisition and tracking test, which would involve dynamic test items, presented on a computer screen.

Use of the computer to administer tests also makes it possible to measure and record an examinee's response latency for each item. The speed with which an examinee responds to a test question can augment the information provided by the correct/incorrect dichotomous scoring of the item. This may enhance the predictive effectiveness of the ASVAB for some criteria.

CAT Summary

Currently, CAT-ASVAB is being operationally evaluated in five MEPSs and one METS. DoD has decided to implement CAT-ASVAB in MEPSs, and nationwide implementation in METSs is being considered. Conversion of the DOD-STP ASVAB testing to computerized delivery is in the future, if at all, because of logistical, technical, and practical problems in conducting a standardized, computer-based testing program in nearly 15,000 schools. Whatever the outcome of METS and STP implementation decisions, the CAT-ASVAB promises to be one of the largest, if not the largest, operational implementation of CAT in history.

Summary

This chapter was designed to familiarize readers new to the ASVAB program and/or CAT with the concepts, jargon, and applications of the two major focuses of this book, making it unnecessary to redescribe the ASVAB and CAT in each of the following chapters. The 15-year research and development program that has led to CAT-ASVAB operational adoption provides a valuable history of the design, development, implementation, and evaluation of a major CAT effort. The lessons learned are documented in the forthcoming chapters, written by many of the professionals who did the work throughout the years.

Policy and Program Management Perspective

Clessen J. Martin and C. Richard Hoshaw

The purpose of this chapter is to address CAT-ASVAB development issues from a Navy headquarters management perspective. The Department of the Navy (DoN) served as the Executive Agent for the Department of Defense (DoD) CAT-ASVAB program from 1979 to 1994 and was responsible for the research and development (R&D) required for the development and evaluation of the feasibility of implementing CAT in DoD. Politics, policy, and psychometrics all had their players on the CAT-ASVAB stage. This chapter is about choreography in the Joint-Service arena. There was never any shortage of personnel who wanted to direct, stage, and choreograph the performance.

Joint-Service Perspective

All persons involved in CAT-ASVAB development, whether it was policy, technical, or financial, had an organizational affiliation and allegiance. This was not the case with the position of Program Manager for CAT-ASVAB. Although the Program Manager was a Department of Navy employee, the fundamental direction came from the Directorate for Accession Policy in the Office of the Assistant Secretary of Defense (OASD) for Force Management and Personnel. It is the Directorate for Accession Policy that has the responsibility for the military testing program and it was this office that provided the impetus for funding the CAT-ASVAB program. Many Navy admirals did not understand this fact and often had the mistaken idea that CAT-ASVAB funds were coming out of Navy personnel budgets that would otherwise be available for other Navy

personnel projects. The fact was that CAT-ASVAB funds would never have been available had it not been for the OASD designation of DoN as Executive Agent.

The management of CAT-ASVAB from a Navy headquarters perspective was foremost a public relations and funding effort. It was a Joint-Service venture and impacted many levels of the military bureaucracy and many different organizations within DoD. Ultimate success of the program meant that all the concerned parties would agree to implement CAT-ASVAB at some future date. The initiation date was 5 January 1979 and the implementation decision date was 13 May 1993. Over the course of those 14 years and 5 months, it was necessary to secure approval of literally hundreds of requests ranging from designation of Executive Agency to the timing and scoring of the ASVAB tests. The concerned parties in 1979 ranged from the Office of the Assistant Secretary of Defense for Manpower, Reserve Affairs and Logistics (MRA&L), the admirals and generals from each of the Services who were in charge of military manpower policy, and the recruiters who scheduled military applicants for testing. In addition, there were three Service personnel laboratories representing the Army, Air Force, and Navy in addition to one contractor organization supporting the Marine Corps. For most of the decisions, both policy and technical, there had to be Joint-Service consensus beginning with the Joint-Service Technical Committee, Joint-Service Policy Committee, Manpower Accession Policy Steering Committee (MAP), and the Defense Advisory Committee (DAC) on Military Personnel Testing. It is not an exaggeration to state that for every decision, most everyone had to be onboard. Maybe with misgivings at times, but they had to be onboard. This meant that there had to be open and frank discussion of both policy and technical issues. There had to be a give-and-take attitude and all parties had to have their say. Because your Service was designated Executive Agent did not mean that you could carry a big stick. In fact, the opposite was often the case. The Executive Agent had to be responsive to the input from all of the Services. This was not always easy for some to accept.

An illustration of the psychometric approval process in the Joint-Service CAT-ASVAB program concerned setting time limits for the ASVAB tests. The process described below is not unique to CAT and is the same for most all psychometric issues today related to ASVAB. Most of the CAT-ASVAB tests present 15 items. Early in CAT development the Navy Personnel Research and Development Center (NPRDC) psychometric personnel decided that the maximum time allowed for each test would be based on the 95th percentile of completion times from an earlier experimental CAT-ASVAB system. The total time for the test approached that of the paper-and-pencil test. This proposal was first presented to the CAT-ASVAB Working Group Technical Committee. This committee was composed of individual Service psychometric representatives plus a technical representative from Headquarters, U.S. Military Entrance Processing Command (USMEPCOM). USMEPCOM is responsible for the daily processing of potential recruits and administers the ASVAB. This proposal was discussed and a vote taken to implement the resulting decision. Next, the proposal went to the CAT-ASVAB full working group which is composed of both policy and technical representatives from the four Services and USMEPCOM. At this meeting, the proposal was discussed and after consultation with their respective technical representatives, the policy representatives voted. When this proposal was approved by the CAT-ASVAB Working Group, it was then presented to the Defense Advisory Committee on Military Personnel Testing (DAC). The DAC is a specially appointed civilian oversight committee mostly composed of eminent psychometricians from universities or major test publishing firms. After DAC approval, the MAP, composed of admirals and generals (one or two star level) was briefed on the overall approach and its approval solicited. Often, depending on the proposal, a great deal of orchestration within the Joint-Service arena was necessary to ensure success along this perilous journey. It was not at all un-

Table 2-1 CAT-ASVAB Service Responsibilities—1979

DEPARTMENT OF THE NAVY
Serve as Executive Agent for Management and R&D
Plan, Program and Budget for R&D
Chair the CAT Inter-Service Coordinating Committee (CATICC)
Develop Psychometric Methodology
Conduct Operational Test & Evaluation for CAT-ASVAB Systems

DEPARTMENT OF THE ARMY
Procure and/or Lease CAT-ASVAB Delivery System
Introduce CAT-ASVAB throughout USMEPCOM
Assure Army and USMEPCOM Participation in CATICC

DEPARTMENT OF THE AIR FORCE
Develop CAT-ASVAB Item Pools
Participate as a Member of CATICC

common for members of the Services' recruiting commands to be observers at some or all of these meetings and they inquired about the "so-called" time savings touted for CAT-ASVAB and why the recommended time limits were being imposed. One could never be certain about the fate of any issue or decision until it had come before both the DAC and the MAP. It must be pointed out that the Chairman of the MAP was the OASD Director for Accession Policy and the Executive Secretary for the DAC was the OASD Assistant Director for Accession Policy. Without this arrangement, it is doubtful that CAT-ASVAB would ever have been implemented.

Table 2-1 presents the Services' responsibilities and illustrates the Joint-Service aspect of the early CAT-ASVAB program. Navy was also charged with determining the cost advantages of CAT-ASVAB, developing the necessary psychometric methodology, and providing a "test bed" for developing items and procedures during the development phase. The Army was to participate as a member of CATICC, to procure the operational testing equipment, and to implement CAT-ASVAB throughout the USMEPCOM system. The Air Force was to participate in CATICC and had the prime responsibility for the development of item banks for CAT-ASVAB.

Marine Corps Perspective

An initiating 5 January 1979 memorandum from the Under Secretary of Defense for Research and Engineering and the Principal Deputy Assistant Secretary of Defense for Manpower, Reserve Affairs and Logistics named the DoN as Executive

Agent for CAT-ASVAB Management and R&D. Management responsibility was assigned to the Marine Corps and R&D activities were assigned to NPRDC as the lead laboratory for development and further evaluation of the feasibility of implementing CAT in DoD. Also important was the fact that the DoN was to chair the CAT Inter-Service Coordinating Committee (CATICC) and since the Marine Corps was given lead Service management responsibility, the Chairman of CATICC was a Marine Corps officer, Major Frank Yohannon. It was logical to designate the DoN as Executive Agent because NPRDC had developed the capability of doing CAT-ASVAB research and the Marine Corps had been supporting some CAT research with NPRDC since 1977. However, it must be emphasized that there was some CAT-ASVAB expertise in both the Army and Air Force personnel labs. The Air Force Human Resources Laboratory (AFHRL) was conducting research related to the development of CAT item pools and Dr. Raymond Christal was in the process of establishing the Learning Abilities Measurement Program, a basic research program having as its central objective the use of computers to administer cognitive tests.

The first author was working with Dr. Christal at the time and a name was needed for the project. Since both had a rather fundamental religious background, the acronym LAMP was chosen. It came from the Biblical phrase, "A LAMP unto my feet." Suffice it to say, computerized testing was a serious matter if not somewhat divine. The Army Research Institute for the Behavioral and Social Sciences (ARI) was also in the process of developing an adaptive testing research program; however, this research program was not operating until the CAT lab was established at the Army Engineer School at Fort Belvoir, Virginia. Thus, there was a fair amount of support for computerized testing among R&D personnel and all the Service laboratories were involved.

In 1980–81, the Marine Corps Program Manager formed a procurement team to prepare a Request For Proposals (RFP) for competitive bidding on a CAT-ASVAB delivery system. To his credit, he approached the program just as one would approach the development and acquisition of any defense system. He was well schooled in the procedures outlined in the *Federal Acquisition Regulations 5000*. These regulations provide very specific guidelines regarding contracting requirements, competitive bidding, contracting methods, and contract management. He was also successful in securing Marine Corps financial support as well as Navy funding.

Table 2-2 Marine Corps Procurement Strategy

Stage	Development Activity
1A	Formulation of a cost-effective design and implementation plan
1B	Demonstration of a Prototype System
2	Development of a Production System plus Test & Evaluation
3	Full Scale Production and Implementation

The early CAT-ASVAB procurement strategy in Table 2-2 included three stages. Stage 1 involved the awarding of three separate contracts for parallel and independent development of a CAT-ASVAB prototype system. Stage 1A was devoted to the formulation of a cost-effective design concept and a system implementation proposal. Stage 1B involved development and demonstration of a prototype system. Stage 2 involved the development of a production system and the test and evaluation of the system in a USMEPCOM environment. Stage 3 envisioned the production and nationwide implementation of the CAT-ASVAB system. Stage 1 contracts were awarded in December 1981 to three competing firms: Bolt, Beranek, and Newman; McDonnell Douglas Astronautics Company; and WICAT Systems, Inc. This approach had one rather important advantage in that it produced a competitive environment for all aspects of the developing system. If the contractors did not have adaptive testing experts already employed, they hired consultants who brought differing views to many of the psychometric issues. This aspect was important during the system's formative development.

At this point in history, there was guarded optimism. Individuals at all levels (military and civilian) realized that this was an unproven technology and that there were a host of hardware, software, and psychometric issues which had to be addressed. Technical personnel were generally optimistic; however, recruiters and USMEPCOM personnel were more hesistant in their endorsement, but everyone was willing to assume their fair share of the duties. There was from the very beginning and at every level the issue of the cost-benefit aspects of the CAT-ASVAB system. It was common to hear the remark that "computers cost more than paper and pencils and there is no way for CAT-ASVAB to be cost-effective." But at this point, CAT-ASVAB was an R&D activity and many took a wait-and-see attitude.

Joe Young, a commander at Headquarters, USMEPCOM, was a tireless supporter of the system and conducted two major studies analyzing possible reconfiguration of the testing sites. His study analyzed travel distances and times for present and potential reconfigured sites for literally hundreds of Mobile Examining Team Sites (METSs). METSs are scattered throughout the United States and provide testing convenience for recruiters and applicants. This information will be of value in the future should this issue reappear. One of the greatest handicaps that the CAT-ASVAB program faced was that CAT had to operate within an existing testing configuration. This configuration constraint is present in many different aspects of CAT-ASVAB, including siting strategies, number right score, and item pool "forms."

The ASVAB Steering Committee (later renamed the Manpower Accession Policy Steering Committee [MAP]) at its 17 November 1982 meeting approved a list of broad criteria for the evaluation of the systems under development by the three contractors. At this time, the first author was the Army's representative to CATICC. Because he had worked at the AFHRL on the initial phase of the LAMP and was involved with Army's Project A, he realized the need for future CAT systems to have the flexibility to add new computerized tests. The Air Force and Army submitted letters from their respective laboratories endorsing a ninth major evaluation criterion related to design flexibility/ expandability. The resulting proposed evaluation criteria for the CAT-ASVAB prototype systems were: *Performance* (response time, screen display, memory); *Suitability* for MEPSs and METSs (portable, little facility modification, operate in normal office environment); *Reliability* (restart at point of failure, malfunctions less than 1 per 1,000 tests, no loss of test data upon failure); *Maintainability* (no skilled technician required in MEPSs or METSs and integrated logistic support); *Ease of Use* (no computer experience required either for test administrators (TAs) or examinees); *Security* (no printed copies, password-only access); *Affordability* (cost-competitive with ASVAB); *Psychometric acceptability* (Interchangeable with paper-and-pencil ASVAB); and *Expansion/Flexibility* (capability of adding new computerized tests). The ASVAB Steering Committee met on 17 November 1982 and approved the CAT-ASVAB criteria to be used in the evaluation of the three prototype systems.

Critical design reviews of the systems occurred during January through March, 1983 amid fierce weather during these three months. The critical design reviews were held in Boston, Denver, and Orem, Utah. At all three sites there was a lot of snow and freezing temperatures. At these critical design reviews, a dozen or so CAT-ASVAB policy and technical personnel would attend. On several occasions, either the contractor wasn't ready, the planes couldn't fly, or the weather forecasts were ominous. On one such visit to Boston, the group stayed at a motel in Cambridge. There was four feet of snow on the ground and in sub-zero temperatures the motel fire alarm sounded twice between 2 and 4 am. Fortunately, evaluation of the prototype systems occurred during the beautiful months of July and August 1983.

Early Financial Perspective

The major concern at DoN Headquarters during CAT-ASVAB development was funding. In 1983, an unexpected Navy comptroller action cancelled, without opportunity to reclama, DoN's CAT-ASVAB budget commitment of $1.2 million. This created a management crisis within Navy's budget hierarchy. Through prompt Program Manager action, it was possible to effect internal reprogramming actions that saved $500,000 for CAT R&D activity. This was the first of several budget battles during the 1980s decade. In most instances, detailed budget defense by the Program Manager prevailed. During this period, the second author served as Special Assistant to DoN's Director of Military Plans and Policy, while guiding five successive admirals as they presented DoN's positions at the DoD Executive Service meetings. Later on, recognizing the critical need for budget support, the DoD Deputy Assistant Secretary for Military Personnel & Force Management, with Congressional support, issued a Defense Guidance Directive which required full funding of the CAT-ASVAB program by the Services for 1987–91.

The CAT-ASVAB program was funded from both research and development (R&D) dollars as well as operation and maintenance (O&M) funds. During the 1980s, there was approximately $600,000 available each year from R&D funds and about $2 million from O&M monies. However, these amounts fluctuated from year to year and sometimes within a year. If the Navy comptroller was required to provide funding for some unexpected requirement, then there usually was a fixed percentage taken from all personnel projects. In 1994, the first author computed the amount of money taken from CAT-ASVAB as a result of these unexpected Navy requirements. Since the program's inception in 1979, the total amount was slightly in excess of $1 million. The bottom line budget point of all this is that the Navy profited by being lead Service for CAT-ASVAB when it came to O&M funds.

R&D funding was a different issue. These funds were difficult to obtain, but there was more latitude in spending research money than in O&M money.

The progress of CAT-ASVAB did not go unnoticed in Congress during this period. The Honorable Les Aspin, Chairman of the Military Personnel and Compensation Subcommittee of the House Committee on Armed Services, in September 1983 correspondence to the Secretary of Defense, Honorable Casper W. Weinberger, expressed his support for the CAT-ASVAB system. This correspondence was the result of Congressional action which eliminated funding for the program in fiscal year (FY) 1984. Congressman Aspin requested that the Department of Defense ensure that adequate funding be included and fenced in the FY 1985 budget. He stated that he would vigorously support these funds during next year's authorization activities. Aspin's correspondence would become important documentation for later budget reclama efforts and, of course, he later became Secretary of Defense.

While the above budget battles were taking place, the Stage II RFP was finalized in January 1984. Stage II involved full-scale development of the CAT-ASVAB hardware and software systems. Stage II was scheduled to begin in April 1984 and end in June 1985. At this time, there was growing concern about the management of the program. The Marine Corps Program Manager appeared to be operating independently of the Joint-Service participants and the timelines for implementation by the contractors were a concern to everyone. Furthermore, the Marine Corps was losing interest in the program. As early as August 1983, the Assistant Secretary of the Navy (Manpower and Reserve Affairs), in a memorandum to the Under Secretary of Defense for Research and Engineering and the Assistant Secretary of Defense (Manpower, Reserve Affairs and Logistics), stated that completion of Stage II would satisfy the tasking as outlined in the original ASD 5 January 1979 memo. Also in this memo was the statement that the Marine Corps had recommended that lead Service responsibility be transferred from the Marine Corps to the Navy.

The Stage II RFP was finalized and proposals had been received from the three contractors early in 1984. There was general agreement that one of the contractors was considerably ahead of the other two. This had also been evident in the evaluation of the prototype systems at the end of Stage I. It appeared that the lead contractor could complete Stage II in two years and that full-scale

implementation could begin in 1986 or 1987. The first author, at this time the Army's representative to CATICC, consulted with the Army's policy representative, Mr. Lou Ruberton, and they were of the opinion that all funds should be awarded to the lead contractor for Stage II development. However, this was not to happen. The Stage II proposals were evaluated, but were never awarded. It appeared to most of the CATICC members that the Marine Corps was on its way out of the CAT business, and Navy was going to take over the CAT-ASVAB Program. Finally, in November 1984, Lieutenant General E. A. Chavarrie, USAF, the Deputy Assistant Secretary for Military Personnel and Force Management, attended the Military Testing Association's (MTA) annual conference in Munich, Germany. He learned a great deal about how other countries were planning to use computerized testing. Although adaptive testing was not operational at this point, computerized linear testing was operational. Also at the time of the MTA Conference in Munich, plans were being finalized in DoN to transfer the lead Service responsibility from the Marine Corps to the Navy. On 18 December 1984, Dr. Richard S. Elster, the Deputy Assistant Secretary of the Navy for Manpower, sent a memorandum to the Director for Manpower Plans and Policy at Headquarters, Marine Corps recommending that Navy assume lead Service responsibility for the program. Lead Service responsibility transferred to the Navy on 18 January 1985.

Change in Approach and DoD Perception

At the November 1984 MTA meeting in Munich, General Chavarrie met with the directors of the Service personnel research laboratories. During this meeting, there were detailed discussions regarding the scientific requirements that had limited the implementation of the CAT-ASVAB system. In his address to the MTA meeting, General Chavarrie challenged the Service personnel to accelerate the CAT efforts. On 2 April 1985, he issued a memorandum to the MAP in which he requested discontinuance of the original multi-stage procurement strategy for CAT-ASVAB and endorsed an Accelerated CAT-ASVAB Project (ACAP) implementation to be conducted by NPRDC.

At this time, the first author consulted with Mr. Ruberton from Army Headquarters and then called NPRDC to express misgivings about this turn of events. It was clear that NPRDC had made a bid

Table 2-3 CAT-ASVAB Service Responsibilities—1985

DEPARTMENT OF THE NAVY
Serve as Executive Agent for CAT-ASVAB Management
Conduct R&D by Navy Personnel Research and
    Development Center
Plan, Program, and Budget for R&D
Chair CAT-ASVAB Working Group

DEPARTMENT OF THE ARMY
Procure and/or Lease CAT-ASVAB System
Implement CAT-ASVAB Throughout MEPSs and METSs
Participate as a Member of the CAT-ASVAB Working
    Group

DEPARTMENT OF THE AIR FORCE
Continue Development of CAT-ASVAB Items
Participate as a Member of CAT-ASVAB Working Group

for the CAT-ASVAB program and the contractor approach was history. One day later, the Honorable Lawrence Korb, Assistant Secretary of Defense, (Manpower, Installations and Logistics) issued another memorandum to the MAP outlining Service responsibilities for implementation of an operational CAT-ASVAB by FY 1987. Service responsibilities are presented in Table 2-3.

The only change was that now NPRDC was in charge of CAT-ASVAB development. The DoN was to serve as Executive Agent for overall management of research, development, implementation and scientific support of the system and NPRDC was to serve as lead laboratory. Further, the Navy was to plan, program and budget for R&D throughout the life-cycle of the system. The Department of the Army (DA) was to serve as Executive Agent for O&M of the CAT-ASVAB system. Army was given the prime responsibility for procurement and/or leasing of the delivery system hardware. It was also responsible for introducing the system throughout USMEPCOM and its network of MEPSs and METSs. These responsibilities assigned to DoN and DA were incorporated in the DoD Defense Guidance for FYs 1987–1991.

Many of the Joint-Service personnel who had been members of CATICC were less than overjoyed about the discontinuance of the contractor multistage approach. To a certain extent, the CAT-ASVAB program lost some of the Joint-Service loyalty because the perception among many persons was that it was an NPRDC R&D program. And there was no question that NPRDC had developed and expanded CAT expertise to the point that it was regarded by many as the center of excellence in CAT technology. None of the other Service laboratories

had the critical mass of expertise of NPRDC. In early 1985, CATICC was replaced by the CAT-ASVAB Working Group: The first meeting was held 26–27 February 1985. The MAP was briefed on NPRDC's plan to develop ACAP on 12 April 1985.

ACAP faced its share of challenges. In the early phase of ACAP, the Marine Corps CAT-ASVAB policy representative sent an eight page, single-spaced letter to his MAP member, a one-star general, critical of the ACAP project. The substance of the letter was that it was an experimental R&D project and involved an unproven and untested technology; it was expensive and never could be cost-effective; and because of the weight of the equipment could never be implemented in the METSs. The weight issue was a serious one. In fact, the original Stage II proposal specified a weight no greater than 45 pounds for each examinee station. Another issue which has always been raised in relation to the CAT-ASVAB program is, "If it ain't broke, don't fix it." This attitude began to be expressed more frequently and, in fact, nothing was broken. The paper-and-pencil (P&P) ASVAB system was working very well.

There were serious CAT-ASVAB perception problems at DoN Headquarters all during ACAP development and implementation. Part of the problem related to how NPRDC obtained research funds. Each researcher or group of researchers had to obtain sponsorship at headquarters. They were all in competition for the same funds. In addition, during this time the Bureau of Naval Personnel (BUPERS) had established a position of Scientific Advisor to the Chief of Naval Personnel. However, the CAT program at NPRDC never had to seek a sponsor because DoN was assigned as Executive Agent. Navy had lead Service responsibility, and NPRDC was designated lead laboratory. Over time, there developed some considerable jealousy and animosity among some researchers toward the CAT program and these negative views were often expressed to the DoN hierarchy. During ACAP development, the CAT-ASVAB Program Manager not only had a Joint-Service "public" relations responsibility, but also a "project" relations responsibility within BUPERS.

There were ACAP psychometric challenges. One challenge was to equate CAT-ASVAB to the P&P-ASVAB and to have CAT-ASVAB provide scores of record in FY 1987. It was assumed that if the system were approved for nationwide implementation, there would be a time period requiring CAT-ASVAB to be on the same metric as the P&P-ASVAB and the scores would have to be interchangeable. Table 2-4 presents the milestone schedule for ACAP

Table 2-4 Accelerated CAT-ASVAB Project (ACAP) Schedule

Development Activities	Timelines
Score Equating Development (SED)	February 1988–December 1988
MAP Approval of Equating Tables	June 1990
Score Equating Verification (SEV)	September 1990–April 1992
Operational Test & Evaluation (OT&E)	June 1992–Fall 1996

implementation. As is obvious from Table 2-4, the goal of having CAT-ASVAB scores of record in FY 1987 was not achieved.

An ACAP Psychometric Decision List which was formalized in July 1987 contained approximately 100 psychometric issues related to the operational use of the ACAP system. Most of these items required discussion and final approval by the CAT-ASVAB Technical Committee, as well as presentation to, and endorsement by, the DAC. Most of these issues involved new psychometric territory for the Joint-Service technical personnel, especially equating, and the future of the program was dependent upon doing it correctly. ACAP equating consisted of two separate phases. The first phase, Score Equating Development (SED), began in February 1988 and involved six MEPSs. SED data collection was completed in December 1988. The MAP finally approved the provisional equating tables in June 1990. This interim period was necessary to conduct the data analysis, prepare the SED report, and to obtain MAPWG and DAC approval. The second phase, Score Equating Verification (SEV), began in September 1990 at the San Diego MEPS, and represented a major milestone in CAT-ASVAB history. For the first time, military applicants' scores of record were based on CAT-ASVAB. The formal completion of SEV was in April 1992.

Cost–Benefit Issues and Program Redirection

In October 1987, the first author replaced the second author as Program Manager of CAT-ASVAB at DoN Headquarters and as the United States Representative to NATO's Research Study Group on Computer-Based Assessment of Military Personnel (RSG-15). His first duty was to brief the NATO RSG-15 group, the DAC, and the MAP on the cost-benefit aspects of the CAT-ASVAB system. Because economic factors were of major importance in CAT-

ASVAB implementation deliberations, various economic analysis efforts were conducted beginning as early as the contractor 3-stage procurement strategy.

The first large-scale economic analysis involving all MEPSs within the contiguous 48 states was conducted in 1987 by a team of two contractors, Automated Sciences Group and CACI, Inc. Federal. The approach used involved determination of costs associated with four different concepts of operation. Major cost categories were development, equipment procurement, implementation, and recurring or operations and support costs. MEPS input was obtained both with respect to life-cycle costs and feasibility issues. Benefit results were based upon the dollar value of improved job performance due to a better person-job match resulting from increased validity of the CAT-ASVAB testing program. Life-cycle costs and benefits were then calculated by the use of a traditional utility formula. Computation of the utility of alternative testing strategies was based on the difference in life-cycle costs between P&P-ASVAB and CAT-ASVAB. Dollar benefits were directly related to the number of persons recruited, their tenure, the standard deviation of performance in dollars, the difference in validity between two testing systems, and the selection ratio. Suffice it to say, that recipients of these briefings were not impressed with the utility dollar formulation. Military personnel wanted to see actual dollar savings in their personnel budgets, but the results showed that all CAT-ASVAB concepts of operation would increase testing costs under existing policies and constraints (see Chapter 23).

The CAT-ASVAB program was in jeopardy at this point in its history. The popularity of the program was at its lowest during the last half of 1988, especially among military and civilian personnel in the Joint-Service arena. Inspection of Table 2-4 shows that Score Equating Development was nearing completion, but there were no equating tables and none were in sight. In August 1988, Admiral Jeremy M. Boorda became Chief of Naval Personnel and after assuming this position, he requested a briefing on the CAT-ASVAB program. When he was informed of the funds that had been spent, he indicated that the following year would be the last year for the expenditure of R&D money. However, O&M money would still be available. Admiral Boorda was supportive of the CAT program, but he felt that the program had taken more than its share of R&D money and there were other personnel research programs he wanted to support.

The one committee which has consistently supported CAT-ASVAB has been the DAC. During this period, the DAC was receiving briefings related to the psychometric issues involved in ACAP and was becoming very familiar with the Psychometric Decision List. In turn, the DAC was providing invaluable guidance on behalf of this program and always recommended support for CAT-ASVAB. The DAC had no criticism of the cost-benefit analyses and the use of the utility dollar formulation. Of course, it helped that Dr. Frank Schmidt, who had distinguished himself in the validity generalization and test utility analysis arena, was chairman of the DAC when the utility formulation was being briefed. The membership of the DAC always included at least one member, and usually two, who were experts in CAT and supportive of CAT-ASVAB.

It was clear that to save the program a new direction had to be taken. Since all the Service laboratories were involved in research on new computerized tests, the Director for Accession Policy, Dr. Wayne S. Sellman, decided that Joint-Service support for computerized testing could be strengthened by emphasizing the potential for the use of new types of computerized cognitive tests in the accessioning system. The plan was that when the cost-benefit analysis was briefed to the MAP in December 1988, the conclusion would be that major dollar benefits could possibly be realized through new computerized tests. At this meeting, the CAT-ASVAB program was redirected to determine the validity of an Enhanced Computer Administered Test (ECAT) battery.

The central aspect of the program redirection was the design and conduct of a Joint-Service validation study of new computerized tests which had been under development in the Service laboratories. A Technical Advisory Selection Panel (TASP) was formed early in 1989 to select new tests to be included in the ECAT battery. ECAT validation data collection began at the Navy's Great Lakes Recruit Training Center in February 1990 and was completed at the Army's Ft. Knox in April 1992. Even though ECAT validation results were not encouraging with respect to incremental validity, some of the tests appeared to be promising with respect to the issue of adverse impact. More importantly, ECAT revived to some extent Joint-Service support for computerized testing and DoD personnel researchers saw CAT-ASVAB as providing a "platform" for new types of computerized tests which would eventually aid in the assignment of new recruits to appropriate military jobs.

The redirection of CAT-ASVAB was accomplished without any additional funds being programmed for this effort. Although the priority was clearly the ECAT Validation Study, the ACAP milestone schedule was still in place and expectations were that this project would also be completed. A great deal of credit is due to Mr. Drew Sands, successor to Dr. Wiskoff as OIC in 1987, and to the dedicated group of CAT-ASVAB researchers at NPRDC for their continued pursuit of the ACAP milestones in spite of the additional demands made on them by the redirection effort.

ACAP Success and Implementation

Two aspects of the CAT-ASVAB program are specially noteworthy. First, from a policy perspective, the CAT program was rescued in December 1988 when the MAP endorsed the program redirection and approved the ECAT Joint-Service validation study. There was always a basic acceptance of computer testing technology and its promise for the future among high ranking military personnel. Demonstrations of the ECAT battery were always greeted with great interest and perceived relevance to future military selection and classification testing systems. However, when the results from ECAT became available, it was clear that none of the new computerized tests showed marked increases in validity over ASVAB alone. To show a .02 or .03 validity increase for ECAT did not impress military or civilian personnel. But by this time, results had been obtained from the SEV phase of ACAP, and it was demonstrated that CAT-ASVAB could be equated to the P&P-ASVAB and that the scores were interchangeable.

During the later phase of SEV, Captain James Kinney became Director of the Recruiting and Retention Programs Division within the BUPERS. It was in this division where the CAT Program Manager resided. Although this division had experienced many reorganizations since CAT's inception in 1979, it had always been responsible for the overall administration of the CAT-ASVAB program and had reported to the Navy's MAP representative. Captain Kinney was very knowledgeable about recruiting. He became immediately aware of the advantages of CAT-ASVAB, especially in relation to the shortened testing time, the time savings this would afford recruiters and the variable starting times, thus making one-day processing possible at the MEPSs. His reasoned enthusiasm for CAT-ASVAB and his rather straightforward approach within the Joint-Service arena resulted in MAP approval of an Operational Test & Evaluation (OT&E) of the system in selected USMEPCOM sites. Captain Kinney also made several suggestions regarding the cost-effectiveness of the CAT system, namely savings in recruiter time as a result of shortened testing time, one-day processing at USMEPCOM and variable start times for CAT-ASVAB examinees. In the history of CAT-ASVAB, no one single military officer gave more support than Captain Kinney. Although he was a program supporter, in his attempt to assist the Program Manager in obtaining funding for the OT&E, he repeatedly made the claim that CAT-ASVAB would become operational after the OT&E; hence, DoN would no longer have the same funding responsibility. This viewpoint ignored the fact that a feasibility study, and then an OT&E for METS testing, were still a part of the R&D milestone schedule. But DoN's support for this program was waning and Kinney's successor took the position that it was time for DoN to be relieved of its Executive Agent responsibility. Therefore, DoN ceased its funding for CAT-ASVAB beginning in October 1994.

The CAT-ASVAB program's most historic milestone was the 13 May 1993 meeting of the MAP. At this meeting, the Committee approved in concept the implementation of CAT-ASVAB in all MEPSs during 1995. This decision was based on a 1992 cost-effectiveness analysis which indicated an annual savings of $3.3 million from CAT-ASVAB at all MEPSs (Chapter 23). In October 1994, the Executive Agency responsibility for CAT-ASVAB was transferred to the Defense Manpower Data Center (DMDC) in Monterey, California. The Personnel Testing Division of DMDC is responsible for the operational ASVAB testing program and will be responsible for future implementation activities associated with CAT-ASVAB.

Special mention and tribute needs to be paid to two individuals. First, the Army's policy representative, the late Mr. Lou Ruberton, was an unfailing supporter of CAT-ASVAB and took the first author under his tutelage in 1982. Many lessons were learned working with and for Lou during the program's formative years. The most important lesson came from his example of cooperation within the Joint-Service arena, while at the same time representing the DA's policy concerns. Lou was a tough bargainer, but at the end of the day he always came down in support of those issues and programs which strengthened the United States military. From CAT-ASVAB's inception in 1979, he ensured Army's participation. As early as 1985, he had arranged for the Army to program funds for the implementation of CAT-ASVAB. To assist in the development and implementation of the ACAP system, some of Army funds were transferred to NPRDC for the purchase of computers. This was a legitimate use of the Army money because from the beginning of the program, the DA was responsible for the procurement of the CAT-ASVAB delivery system.

Second, and especially noteworthy, was the support given the ECAT program by Admiral Boorda when he was Chief of Naval Personnel (CNP). Admiral Boorda was CNP during ECAT validation and requested that he be administered the battery of new tests. Upon completion of the battery, he was very impressed and remarked to the first author that "if the results were promising he wanted the Navy to implement the tests in the recruit training centers if they did not become part of the ASVAB." His idea was that the new computerized tests could assist the Navy in making job assignments for those recruits who had not been assigned school seats at the end of basic training. This classification strategy continues to be a viable option and offers important research opportunities for the future.

At the time of this writing, CAT-ASVAB (ACAP) is operating successfully in San Diego; Los Angeles; Jackson, Mississippi; Baltimore and Washington, DC. However, most important is that on 9 October 1996, the new CAT-ASVAB system was successfully implemented in the Denver MEPS. During the remainder of 1996 and 1997, the new CAT-ASVAB system will be implemented in the other MEPSs.

Summary

The Marine Corps began its development of CAT-ASVAB following the procedures outlined in the *Federal Acquisition Regulations* in 1979. These procedures are the guidelines for the development and procurement of weapon systems within the DoD. In the development of such systems, it usually takes 14 to 17 years from concept development to implementation. Furthermore, the probability of completing Joint-Service acquisition projects is considerably less than single service acquisitions. If January 1979 is accepted as the beginning of the concept development phase and September 1990 is considered the beginning of CAT implementation, given this was the first time CAT scores became scores of record; the CAT-ASVAB system required a 12-year development cycle. The length of the CAT-ASVAB development cycle was comparable to the development of other major systems.

Success of the CAT-ASVAB program from a policy management perspective depended upon Joint-Service cooperation. This meant that both scientific and policy matters had to be considered in a straightforward and democratic manner. For most all issues, the ultimate decision was based on a vote at the working group and steering committee level. Once DAC and MAP support had been obtained, then the Services and USMEPCOM accepted their marching orders and moved toward the next milestone. CAT-ASVAB progress and acceptance was always incremental and at times the increments were rather small, but the ever continuing advance in computer technology and the associated Zeitgeist helped in keeping the CAT-ASVAB vision alive.

In addition to Joint-Service cooperation, another important factor was the recognized psychometric competence of the Manpower Accession Policy Technical Committee. The sophistication represented in the Psychometric Decision List and the many briefings given to the DAC based on issues from this list served to convince DAC members of the psychometric competence of DoD testing personnel. There was no doubt that DoD was advancing the frontiers of computerized testing in a scientific and rigorous fashion.

Finally, a policy and management perspective chapter would not be complete without mentioning the important role played by the Director for Accession Policy, Dr. Wayne S. Sellman, from the Office of the Assistant Secretary of Defense (Force Management Policy). Although Joint-Service cooperation and psychometric competence were important to CAT's success, the real catalyst was clout. Of the many reclamas prepared by the CAT-ASVAB Program Managers to restore Navy funding, mention was always made of Dr. Sellman's Office as the agency designating DoN as Executive Agency for the CAT-ASVAB Program. His reputation within the Joint-Service arena as an honest and highly respected member of the Senior Executive Service was always the single most important factor in the restoration of program funding. Senior Navy officers would always inquire, whether the project was sponsored by Dr. Sellman's office. The answer was yes, and he controls Navy's recruiting budget too. Dr. Sellman was always willing to assist in any way he could, and often helped to keep the Joint-Service personnel focused. He was even present at the critical design review in Cambridge, Mass. during that very cold January winter in 1983 when the fire alarms were sounded, twice. It is important to emphasize Dr. Sellman's role in the development of CAT-ASVAB. When obtaining support from senior military personnel, it was always necessary to refer to DoD sponsorship of the program. His official position and personal reputation were the most important factors in the eventual success of this Joint-Service program. Future implementations of computerized testing programs should note the importance in having high-level support for their program for the fiscal and policy battles that inevitably face all large-scale R&D implementation efforts.

3

R&D Laboratory Management Perspective

Martin F. Wiskoff

This chapter describes the development and conduct of the computerized adaptive testing version of the Armed Services Vocational Aptitude Battery (CAT-ASVAB) program from the perspective of the performing organization. More specifically, the chapter will focus on the research group within the Navy Personnel Research and Development Center (NPRDC) that initiated, executed, and coordinated the effort. The view presented is that of a research organization looking inward at itself and its parent center (NPRDC), and outward to all the other personnel research laboratories, contractor and headquarters organizations, and advisory committees.

The program required consideration of the following four issues that many laboratory research programs have to address: (1) maintaining support from headquarters policy-makers and laboratory management, (2) planning and performing the research, (3) adjusting to changing requirements over time, and (4) addressing implementation of the system. An additional, significant element in this case was the need to conduct a Joint-Service program and accommodate the requirements of the individual Services.

The first section of this chapter provides a framework for understanding the perspective of the NPRDC research group during the three major phases of its increasing responsibility: (1) initiating a CAT research capability and conducting a small, mostly in-house program; (2) performing the major portion of the research under Marine Corps Headquarters direction; and (3) serving as Officer-in-Charge of the Joint-Service program. In the second section, the focus is on management is-

sues such as obtaining and maintaining higher level support, staffing the program, obtaining funding, interfacing with other research organizations and review committees, dealing with changing requirements, and exchanging CAT technology with other countries. The third section covers topics relevant to the technical program, such as planning the in-house and contract research and coordinating with other organizations performing research under the auspices of the program. The final section is a brief postscript on the lessons learned by the NPRDC research group, and some recommendations concerning the development and implementation of a large-scale CAT system.

Major Stages of the Laboratory Program

The potential of the computer to support military personnel functions such as screening, selection, and classification was the subject of growing interest and research in the 1960s. For example, the first computer-based systems to assign recruits into military jobs were introduced in the mid-1960s. The research antecedents of applied adaptive testing are described in Chapter 5.

Initiating a CAT-ASVAB Research Capability

The primary stimulus to the initiation of a CAT-ASVAB research program at NPRDC was the potential for CAT that was surfacing from three sources: (1) the extensive Office of Naval Research (ONR)-sponsored psychometric research on item response theory (IRT) and basic research issues of CAT; (2) the experimentation by the Service research laboratories into computer administration of tests to military recruits; and (3) the landmark U.S. Civil Service Commission (now the Office of Personnel Management) program to develop a CAT version of its Professional and Administrative Career Examination (PACE).

Two major events in 1976 provided a rationale and need for the NPRDC decision to develop a program of CAT research. In January, the Joint-Service Armed Services Vocational Aptitude Battery (ASVAB) replaced separate Service selection and classification multiple-aptitude test batteries. This dictated that future changes to Service selection and classification procedures, including possible administration of tests by computer, would have to be decided within a Joint-Service framework. In addition, immediately after introduction of the paper-and-pencil version of the battery (P&P-ASVAB), many problems surfaced with the accuracy of the test scores and with the security of the test battery. The second event was that the Civil Service Commission CAT research program was being terminated because of the decision to discontinue use of the PACE.

By 1976, NPRDC had developed expertise in applying computer technology to personnel issues such as automated assistance to the selection and classification of enlisted personnel. In addition, a major effort was underway to assist Navy Recruiting Command by introducing automation into the personnel accessioning process. This research program was called the Navy Personnel Accessioning System (NPAS). One major component of NPAS was the aptitude testing function, employing a CAT approach. This system is described in Chapter 7.

In 1977, the Marine Corps provided funding to NPRDC for research into CAT to investigate the potential to reduce test compromise, a problem that had surfaced with the introduction of P&P-ASVAB. Reports of recruiting personnel coaching applicants, asking applicants to remember test questions and choices for use by later applicants, or outright stealing of test booklets were being heard. The Marine Corps was concerned that the P&P-ASVAB had insufficient backup capability if test compromise became widespread. Because CAT-ASVAB would not administer the same questions in the same order to all applicants, and would be less subject to physical loss than test booklets, it held promise for reducing test compromise.

Chapter 6 describes the project conducted in response to this Marine Corps requirement. A key aspect of the work was the experimental CAT capability that was established at the Marine Corps Recruit Depot (MCRD) in San Diego. This facility enabled testing of the system, provided visibility to the program, and demonstrated that recruits could be successfully tested by computer. Comparisons of paper-and-pencil with computerized testing were conducted, including studies which found that recruits preferred being tested by computer. The fact that MCRD was located close to NPRDC facilitated demonstrations of CAT to Service and Office of the Secretary of Defense (OSD) policy makers. The importance of this early experimental site in obtaining and maintaining support for CAT-ASVAB cannot be overstated.

Results of the Marine Corps-sponsored project were encouraging, leading to a request by the Deputy Assistant Secretary of the Navy for Manpower to consider the potential for operational use of CAT. This request generated an OSD study in 1978 to evaluate the possible use of CAT-ASVAB as a replacement for P&P-ASVAB. NPRDC provided significant input into this study, which led to a recommendation that a CAT-ASVAB program should be initiated as a Joint-Service program.

Performing the Research Under Marine Corps Lead

The Marine Corps was designated lead Service within the Department of the Navy (DoN) and given management responsibility for CAT-ASVAB. A program management office was established at Marine Corps Headquarters in Washington, DC. NPRDC was designated lead laboratory for research and development to include providing technical and scientific expertise for CAT-ASVAB system development and for CAT psychometric methodology and procedural development. In actuality, NPRDC served as the technical expert on all phases of the CAT project, including the development of a delivery system for the adaptive test battery.

Coordination between Marine Corps Headquarters and NPRDC was initially effective and productive. As the program evolved however, it was difficult at times to separate technical from managerial responsibilities and this caused friction between NPRDC, the other Service laboratories, and the Marine Corps. For example, the Services were uncomfortable that technical reviews of potential CAT-ASVAB hardware and software were being coordinated by Marine Corps Headquarters, rather than by NPRDC or another R&D laboratory.

Serving as Officer-in-Charge of the CAT-ASVAB Program

In June 1983, the Marine Corps recommended that the Navy assume lead Service responsibility for CAT at the completion of Stage II of the CAT system design. Stage I (concept development and demonstration) was scheduled to be completed in August 1983. Full scale development (Stage II) was scheduled to commence on 1 April 1984 and be completed during June 1985. In fact, Lieutenant General Chavarrie (Deputy Assistant Secretary of Defense for Military Personnel and Force Management) provided encouragement (see Chapter 4) in November 1984 to the Services to accelerate the CAT program. This led to the cancellation of Stage II and its replacement with the Accelerated CAT-ASVAB Project (ACAP). In conjunction with this policy decision, the lead Service role was transferred to the Navy in January 1985.

As a result of this decision, NPRDC became responsible for chairing the Computerized Adaptive Testing Inter-Service Coordinating Committee (CATICC), later renamed the CAT-ASVAB Working Group (CATWG). A concurrent decision conferred responsibility upon the NPRDC Director of the Manpower and Personnel Laboratory as the Officer-in-Charge of the CAT-ASVAB Program. Navy Headquarters in the Bureau of Naval Personnel (BUPERS) retained the important management functions of obtaining funding for the program and liaison with management representatives of the other Services and OSD. The Marine Corps retained responsibility for funding a portion of the research program.

The reassignment of responsibilities greatly enhanced management of the program during the mid-1980s, when critical decisions concerning program direction needed to be made. The working relationship between NPRDC personnel and the Navy Headquarters program manager was constructive and harmonious. This significantly contributed to the effective planning and conduct of the program.

Support and Organizational Issues

Different types of support were solicited from NPRDC management at different stages of the CAT-ASVAB program evolution. First it was necessary to convince management that the area of CAT research was a viable one and that funding should be allocated to assess its merits.

Management and Policy Maker Support

Marine Corps requirements necessitated a modest increase in personnel resources. However, the major decision point occurred in 1978, just prior to the OSD memorandum creating the CAT-ASVAB program. Because the program was Joint-Service, and therefore different from other programs at NPRDC, Navy management needed to be persuaded to accept lead laboratory responsibility.

The Navy and OSD policy makers had to be convinced that CAT was a promising research area and that it could improve the capability to assess applicants for military service. In addition, the credibility of NPRDC to pursue research in this area had to be established. During the 1977–78 timeframe, briefings, demonstrations, and meetings turned skepticism into endorsement, as policy makers became more aware of the promise of CAT, and the responsible manner in which the Services were approaching the research. It should be noted that once the decision was made to initiate the CAT research, OSD support was strong and unswerving throughout the entire life of the program. This support was absolutely critical for the success of the CAT-ASVAB undertaking.

Funding Support

The Department of Navy (DoN) was designated as the Executive Agency for the Joint-Service CAT-ASVAB program with responsibility for overall program management. DoN had the assignment to provide the research personnel and funding needed to support the research, development, test, and evaluation required to assess and implement CAT-ASVAB. While the Marine Corps was designated lead Service, the Navy and the Marine Corps were assigned joint responsibility for funding. It became the NPRDC responsibility, in conjunction with Navy and the Marine Corps Headquarters personnel, to determine the type and amount of funding needed to pursue the research.

A mix of research and operational funding would be necessary to address all aspects of the program. Within the R&D designation, it was important to have funding provided across the range of exploratory development through engineering development. It was also necessary to adjust the balance of funds across these categories as the research program evolved.

It is very difficult for a laboratory, by itself, to obtain and protect funding, especially if it is geographically distant from research sponsors.

Strong headquarters advocacy from both the Marine Corps and the Navy was absolutely essential for obtaining resources for the CAT-ASVAB program. Once the Navy became lead Service, the support provided by the Navy policy representative in the BUPERS (a civilian) was a critical element in maintaining stability and sustaining the program through changes in direction and turnover of military management personnel.

Staffing and Organization

Considerable effort was devoted to staffing and organizational elements such as obtaining personnel positions, finding suitable people, and creating the organizational structures to optimize program and personnel operations. Initially the CAT-ASVAB staff consisted of one mid-level research psychologist. At its peak, the in-house program employed about 30 full-time personnel and seven student assistants.

Government research laboratories generally have personnel ceilings that they cannot exceed. Within NPRDC there were severe limitations on positions and intense competition among the various research departments, which were seeking to expand their programs. Considerable lobbying of NPRDC management for positions was necessary, especially because the CAT program supported a Joint-Service, rather than an exclusively Navy requirement. OSD provided some assistance by assigning four positions to NPRDC exclusively for the CAT-ASVAB program.

Another way to expand a program is to transfer personnel from other programs, thus obtaining positions and individuals at the same time. However, when the CAT-ASVAB program began, few NPRDC researchers had the requisite skills. Over time, the staff grew by a mix of selective transfers, retraining of personnel within the department, and outside hiring.

In the mid-1980s, the NPRDC organizational structure itself changed and three laboratories were formed to strengthen the internal coordination of programs and the representation of NPRDC to the outside world. There were initially two departments within the Manpower and Personnel Laboratory, with one containing the CAT-ASVAB program. As this program expanded, in both funding and personnel, NPRDC management was persuaded to establish a separate department. Thus, CAT-ASVAB evolved from a very small research project in 1977, to a research program, and then into a multimillion-dollar-a-year research department.

Subsequent budgetary reductions and organizational decisions by NPRDC management resulted in recombination of the two departments. Over time, the success of the CAT-ASVAB program (as described elsewhere in this book) had personnel and organizational implications. Eventually, the primary requirement within CAT-ASVAB shifted from research to implementation, and this was reflected in the transfer of resources and responsibilities from NPRDC to the Defense Manpower Data Center (DMDC) in 1994. By the end of 1994, only a small CAT-ASVAB research capability still existed at NPRDC and a CAT-ASVAB support capability was being developed within DMDC.

Oversight and Coordination

Interaction was extensive with all of the government organizations and oversight committees concerned with CAT-ASVAB. Two factors drove this requirement. The first was the creation of the program as a Joint-Service effort involving both CAT-ASVAB research and possible implementation of the research product. Since each of the Service laboratories had been assigned their own research and support responsibilities by the January 1979 memorandum, they were partners within the CAT-ASVAB program. CAT-ASVAB as a possible replacement for P&P-ASVAB was of considerable operational concern to each Service. The second factor giving rise to intense coordination was the advisory and policy committees that had oversight of the CAT-ASVAB program.

Oversight. Three committees played a significant role in CAT-ASVAB development:

• The **Computerized Adaptive Testing Inter-Service Coordinating Committee** (CATICC) was the principal forum for providing review and direction to the program. It was chaired by the Marine Corps from 1979–84. The CATICC was replaced by the CAT-ASVAB Working Group (CATWG) in 1985, with the chair shifting to the Officer-in-Charge of the program, located at NPRDC (the lead R&D laboratory). This committee was made up of both research and policy representatives of the Services, U.S. Military Entrance Processing Command (USMEPCOM), and the Office of Assistant Secretary of Defense Directorate for Accession Policy. NPRDC was responsible for briefing the CATWG on the status of the CAT-ASVAB program, indicating changes that needed to be undertaken, and modifying the program in response to CATWG's decisions. All the Services played very active roles and provided significant input to this Joint-Service working group.

· The **Defense Advisory Committee on Military Personnel Testing** (DAC) is composed of recognized experts in the fields of psychometrics, testing, and personnel measurement from universities and private research organizations. The DAC was created in the aftermath of the P&P-ASVAB misnorming and other problems in the late 1970s. The DAC continues to this day as an external oversight committee to maintain high standards within the DoD personnel accession testing program. NPRDC briefed the DAC at its quarterly meetings and, as lead laboratory, was held ultimately responsible for all R&D aspects of CAT-ASVAB.

· The **Manpower Accession Policy Steering Committee** (MAP) is composed of flag-level representatives of the Services' manpower and policy headquarters organizations and the Commander of USMEPCOM. The MAP is primarily responsible for policy on operational ASVAB matters, but also functions to approve the direction of ASVAB and related research programs. Since MAP representatives base their decisions (at least in part) on recommendations from their respective Service policy representatives, all projects within the CAT-ASVAB program had to be coordinated with the individual Services. Often extensive lobbying was needed to coordinate Service positions.

Program coordination. Although the program had been established as a joint effort of the Services, the impetus and momentum were provided by the Navy and OSD. The other Services, including the Marine Corps in the later stages, were concerned primarily with maintaining their own research programs and the stability of the operational P&P-ASVAB. It was essential, therefore, in the planning for CAT-ASVAB to meet the Services' future requirements for personnel testing.

Chapter 7 documents the early cooperative effort between NPRDC and the Army Research Institute for the Behavioral and Social Sciences (ARI) to design and implement the Computerized Adaptive Screening Test (CAST). This important program provided evidence of the viability of CAT for military personnel testing and established a precedent for cooperative research among Service laboratories. During the critical years of CAT-ASVAB development, ARI was itself heavily involved in a major personnel research program (Project A), with the goal of revising and expanding future selection and classification test instruments. Army interest in CAT-ASVAB was mostly driven by the desire to obtain a computerized platform for the administration of new tests developed under Project A.

During the 1970s and 1980s, the Air Force was Executive Agent for the operational P&P-ASVAB. The Air Force did not see implementation of CAT-ASVAB as a strong requirement, both because its selection and classification process was functioning well and because the Air Force would stand to lose Executive Agent responsibility with the implementation of CAT-ASVAB. Similar to the Army, the Air Force Human Resources Laboratory (AFHRL) expressed interest in using the CAT-ASVAB computer platform for implementing new tests being developed within their Learning Abilities Measurement Program.

USMEPCOM, as the Joint-Service command responsible for the operational administration of P&P-ASVAB, had constant concerns about its replacement by CAT-ASVAB. The policy position taken by USMEPCOM at any one time toward CAT-ASVAB issues depended to some extent upon the Service uniform worn by the flag officer at its helm. It was essential that NPRDC provide evidence to USMEPCOM that CAT-ASVAB could be implemented with minimum disruption of its operating procedures. The need was a recurring one, due to the personnel turnover in the USMEPCOM Commander position.

Program equilibrium was maintained over the years by the combined efforts of the NPRDC research group, Headquarters Navy, and OSD policy representatives. While the strong Headquarters Marine Corps support waned once lead Service responsibility shifted to the Navy, the Marine Corps Operations and Analysis Group within the Center for Naval Analyses continued to play a significant role in CAT-ASVAB psychometric development.

Changes in Research Requirements

Research requirements changed frequently over the life of the program, primarily as a result of the extensive scientific and policy oversight mentioned earlier. Guidance and recommendations from the advisory groups resulted in significant modifications to the NPRDC research program. For example, at a number of working group meetings one of the Service laboratories presented data or a proposal that required NPRDC to conduct subsequent research. In addition, the DAC often requested further studies or analyses that necessitated reprogramming of NPRDC resources. Some of these requirements caused considerable modifications of the CAT-ASVAB research milestones.

The two changes with the greatest impact resulted from OSD-directed studies. The CAT-ASVAB schedule under the original timeline for Stage III called for implementation in 1990–91. Lieutenant General Chavarrie considered this timeline unacceptably long and, in Fall 1984, directed faster implementation. The Accelerated CAT-ASVAB Project (ACAP), designed in response to this requirement, included a philosophical as well as a programmatic reorientation. During early CAT-ASVAB development, the philosophy had been that only a custom-developed computer-based delivery system could meet the CAT-ASVAB system criteria established by the Services. However, by 1984–85, advances in microcomputer technology showed promise for being able to address CAT-ASVAB requirements in the Military Entrance Processing Stations (MEPSs) and Mobile Examining Test Sites (METSs). The CAT-ASVAB program changed direction in 1985, with the decisions to de-emphasize reliance on contractor support and to employ off-the-shelf computer hardware in the CAT-ASVAB delivery system.

In 1989, OSD directed that a large-scale study of the Enhanced Computer Administered Tests (ECAT), be conducted to evaluate whether the validity of the ASVAB could be improved by adding new tests. The rationale for the study was to determine whether new types of tests administered via computer could result in cost savings for the military, thus justifying the introduction of a CAT-ASVAB system. This requirement introduced a whole new set of studies and caused major milestone changes. NPRDC was able to reduce the resulting timeline somewhat by formulating and obtaining approval for a revised research strategy.

The reorientation of research emphases in response to changing requirements was the single most difficult issue that the CAT-ASVAB program faced. Despite this, the program was able to meet approved time schedules and actually achieved operational status in September 1990, a full year ahead of the projected date. Even though great progress was being made, NPRDC research personnel were frustrated because other research organizations that had started research on computer testing programs after the initiation of CAT-ASVAB were reaching full operational implementation more quickly. Recognition that CAT-ASVAB was being subjected to the most stringent set of guidelines ever imposed on a Defense personnel research program only somewhat tempered the frustration.

Technology Exchanges of Computerized Testing Research With Other Countries

A source of significant pride to NPRDC researchers was the direct and indirect assistance provided to other computerized testing research programs, both in this country and overseas. In 1979, the United States was the only country investigating CAT programs for military personnel accessioning. In 1981, a visit by the author to military research facilities in Belgium and the Federal Republic of Germany assisted them in starting CAT research programs. Over the years, considerable technology transfer took place via document exchanges, site visits, conferences, and exchange programs (e.g., NATO and The Technical Cooperation Program) with personnel from Australia, Belgium, Canada, Germany, Great Britain, Holland, Israel, and New Zealand.

Research Management Issues

This section focuses on aspects of managing the CAT-ASVAB research program; details of the specific projects are contained in later chapters of this book. While NPRDC had the lead laboratory responsibility, research in support of the CAT-ASVAB program was also being performed by the other Service laboratories, their contractors, and ONR contractors. In addition, Joint-Service coordination and decision-making concerning many technical aspects of the program was extensive.

The many research activities that were planned and undertaken over the life of CAT-ASVAB can be categorized into three areas: (1) psychometric research, (2) delivery system development, and (3) implementation issues. Some of the work, such as that reported in this book, included landmark studies that are notable contributions to the research literature and were essential to CAT-ASVAB development. Other studies that seemed valuable at the time they were conceived were later overtaken by the changing orientation of the program and had no long-term value. This situation is probably typical of major multi-faceted research endeavors.

Psychometric Research

One of the first studies commissioned was the development of a master plan, by a panel of five leading experts in the field, for the psychometric research needed to evaluate the acceptability of CAT-ASVAB as a replacement for the P&P-ASVAB (Green, Bock, Humphreys, Linn, & Reckase, 1984a). This very detailed and demanding plan served as early guidance for formulating and conducting psychometric studies. Over time, however, the psychometric plan was significantly modified and expanded because of CATICC and CATWG input, and DAC recommendations. The specific psychometric studies conducted in response to the requirements are documented elsewhere in this book, but what needs to be noted here is the significant amount of redirection that occurred over time. Difficult as it was for research personnel to cope with the restructuring and redirection, it benefited the psychometric credibility of the CAT-ASVAB program and achieved the critical goal of maintaining DAC support.

Delivery System

NPRDC faced a formidable task of conceiving and conducting a program of research to design a CAT-ASVAB delivery system. In-house studies in the 1970s and early 1980s had demonstrated that CAT could be administered by off-the-shelf hardware systems, although the systems were not very portable. However, the requirements formulated by the Services for an operational CAT-ASVAB system were clearly beyond the capability of computer systems available at the time the program was undertaken.

Therefore, in conjunction with Marine Corps Headquarters, a major contractual project (the CAT-ASVAB delivery system research competitive procurement described earlier) was launched in 1980 to design a customized hardware system that would meet all the CAT-ASVAB system requirements. During this time, NPRDC researchers continued to monitor the state-of-the-art in computer hardware and were encouraged by the advances being made. When the ACAP was started in 1985, attention once more shifted to off-the-shelf systems. Under ACAP, NPRDC was responsible for systems design as well as the psychometrics, making it easier to integrate the two components. ACAP is described in greater detail in Chapters 14, 19, and 20.

In retrospect, probably little could have been done to avoid the perturbations in the system design phase of the program. In 1979, computer technology was simply not ready to address CAT-ASVAB requirements. Much of the early effort by NPRDC and Service researchers served as a learning experience, while they waited for computer hardware technology to catch up with the functional requirements of the CAT-ASVAB system.

Implementation Issues

The issues surrounding psychometrics and computer delivery systems were far easier to deal with than developing a plan to implement the CAT-ASVAB system, primarily because it was difficult to aim at a moving target. While it was certain that CAT-ASVAB would be administered in the MEPSs, the question of where and in what form CAT-ASVAB would replace the P&P-ASVAB at the METSs had still not been decided. To some extent, the decision was hampered by both the costs of, and concerns about, the security of a "portable" CAT system at the METSs.

By 1983, a preliminary economic analysis of CAT-ASVAB compared P&P-ASVAB and CAT-ASVAB system costs and benefits for a 10-year life cycle. Subsequent studies also attempted to provide documentation on the cost feasibility of a CAT-ASVAB system. However, each of the Services and USMEP-COM had its own view of the final configuration of a CAT-ASVAB system. To complicate matters further, some of the Service researchers and policy makers changed over the course of the program. To NPRDC personnel, it felt a little like being on a slippery slope with a continual taking and giving of ground. There was always confidence that the top of the hill would be reached, but no assurance of what would be found, or when. Chapter 23 provides greater detail on the studies that were conducted to develop concepts for the operational administration of CAT-ASVAB.

Monitoring and Coordination of CAT-ASVAB Research

As indicated earlier, individual Service laboratories and their contractors were performing research in direct support of the CAT-ASVAB program, and ONR was supporting a vigorous program of contractor-conducted basic research. NPRDC provided a portion of the funding for Service R&D projects. Throughout its history, the CAT-ASVAB program was governed by a critical timeline philosophy, which involved establishing a series of milestones and critical paths for reaching the milestones. Monitoring of research progress, both within and external to NPRDC, was essential for maintaining control over program direction, progress, and accomplishments. NPRDC in-house and contractor research was monitored on an on-going basis. Information on external research progress was obtained informally through interactions among Service laboratory research personnel and more formally through CATWG meetings.

In 1985, a CAT-ASVAB program office was created at NPRDC, under the direction of the Officer-in-Charge, and staffed by representatives of the Services. The Air Force, Marine Corps, Navy, and

Army each provided a uniformed representative for this office to assist in monitoring and coordinating research, and to provide feedback to their parent agencies.

Postscript

The CAT-ASVAB program was a unique endeavor within the personnel R&D world because of the combination of three factors: (1) the presence of an emerging theoretical approach (IRT) coupled with an applied technology (CAT); (2) conduct of the program by Service R&D laboratories within the Joint-Service arena; and (3) extensive, high-level management and technical oversight from outside the laboratories. While this combination of factors is probably unlikely for some time to come, especially because of Defense cutbacks, it might still be instructive to reflect on lessons learned by the performing laboratory.

There is a great deal of pride in having successfully shepherded a program of such significance. From a laboratory perspective, there are three major accomplishments: (1) CAT-ASVAB is being implemented and will result in considerable improvements in DoD selection and classification procedures; (2) major contributions were made to the body of psychometric knowledge; and (3) assistance was provided to other computerized testing personnel research programs, both within the United States and in other countries.

Some major frustrations occurred along the path to success. The program seemed to stretch out for too many years, although perhaps 15 years is not unreasonable for a system with such national implications. The Joint-Service nature of the effort and the heavy external oversight created difficulties in planning and programming resources. Coping with the political infighting and territorial issues among all the CAT-ASVAB stakeholders was a learning experience, and painful at times.

Recommendations for Future CAT R&D

A final few thoughts about how a personnel R&D laboratory should approach similar programs in the future are:

• *Responsibility Acceptance and Allocation*—Carefully consider whether to undertake a Joint-Service program. While such a program can be effectively managed by a Service laboratory, housing the program in a central DoD facility is probably preferable. This would provide better control for the DoD manager and reduce conflict among the Services. Create a clear division of responsibilities between headquarters and the research laboratory. Headquarters personnel should not direct research projects.

• *Time Requirements and Milestones*—Don't underestimate the time to conduct the program, but also recognize that there will probably be extreme pressures to complete it more quickly than may be feasible and that additional requirements may be placed on the program which will extend the timeline.

• *Management and Technical Staff*—Develop a research staff that can adapt to the changing requirements which will inevitably occur during the life of the program. The more specialized personnel technical capabilities, if needed, can always be obtained by contracting with outside sources.

• *Future Technology Projection*—Obtain the best projections on state-of-the-art technology at the time the program will be completed and structure the technical program to be in consonance with the projected *future* technology status.

• *External Reviews and Requirements*—Recognize the value of outside technical reviews in enhancing the quality and credibility of the program. However, attempt to establish some controls over being driven by unnecessary requests to conduct additional research that extend the program's timeline.

• *Public Relations and Marketing*—Establish a capability to brief and demonstrate the program to research sponsors and policy makers as early as possible. The program, once initiated, needs to be constantly marketed.

• *Program Transition*—Plan for research program termination as carefully as you plan for program startup and growth. This should include the transition of the program from research to operational status, and plans for the organization that will assume the operational responsibility.

CHAPTER

4

Technical Perspective

James R. McBride

The remaining chapters of this book represent over 15 years of applied psychometric research and development that culminated in a decision by the Department of Defense to implement computerized adaptive administration of the ASVAB in Military Entrance Processing Stations (MEPSs) nationwide, and to use that same technology to collect data for national norms in the 1997 Profile of American Youth. This chapter provides an overview of the CAT-ASVAB program from a technical perspective.

The CAT-ASVAB was the first high-stakes testing program to produce operational scores using a CAT system. The CAT-ASVAB research and development (R&D) program was also the locus of a number of other significant "firsts." For example, the CAT-ASVAB R&D team was the first to:

• Develop a complete multiple-aptitude battery of adaptive tests

• Develop a micro-computer based adaptive testing system capable of displaying graphical test items

• Deliver adaptive tests on a network of personal computers

• Demonstrate the construct equivalence of conventional and adaptive multitest batteries

• Establish the predictive validity of a battery of adaptive tests

• Develop technical standards for evaluating adaptive tests

• Develop and apply technology for equating conventional and adaptive tests

At the outset of the CAT-ASVAB program, none of these things had ever been accomplished, or even attempted. From a technical perspective, then, CAT-ASVAB represents a breakthrough on a number of technical fronts. This chapter outlines the R&D program that led to these breakthroughs, by presenting an assessment of the state of the art as it existed in early 1979 in each of several dimensions affecting the development of CAT, and discussing how the CAT-ASVAB developers advanced the state of the art in each one.

One important element in this story is time. Prior to January 1979, the CAT-ASVAB program had been a small-scale, exploratory development effort, proceeding at a deliberate pace with moderate resources. With the January 1979 decision, all that changed. Overnight, the project became a Joint-Service effort to "develop and evaluate CAT for use in administering the Armed Services Vocational Aptitude Battery." What's more, the original schedule proposed by some officials in the Department of the Navy—the Executive Agent for CAT-ASVAB development—called for CAT-ASVAB research and development to be completed in just three years, an unrealistically short time given the psychometric research and development needed. Although that timeline was later changed to five years, even that schedule was most ambitious. To come as close as possible to carrying out CAT-ASVAB development on that schedule, plans were made to conduct simultaneously some major project components that would normally be done in sequence.

The most significant instance of this compression was that development of a delivery system suitable for nationwide use was begun before evidence had been developed that CAT was suitable for administering the ASVAB. In effect, the CAT project became two projects conducted parallel to each other. One of these parallel projects entailed designing and developing a computerized delivery system—hardware and software to administer the ASVAB—intended for nationwide use in the Military Entrance Processing System. The other parallel project entailed developing and evaluating all the psychometric aspects of a computer-administered, adaptive version of ASVAB. Each of these two parallel projects is addressed separately below.

Delivery System Design and Development

A "delivery system" is a matched set of computer hardware and software capable of presenting test questions to the examinee, performing the computations necessary between adaptive test items, selecting the best question to present next, determining when to stop testing, and recording and reporting the results in the medium and format necessary to satisfy the requirements of the application. Although a number of experimental computer systems for adaptive testing had been developed over the preceding decade, no systems capable of operational use in a testing program as large and complex as ASVAB existed in 1979.

Developing a computer system to administer an adaptive version of ASVAB was a very different technical undertaking in 1979 than a similar project would be today, because the microcomputer industry was in its infancy. Prior to January 1979, virtually all computerized adaptive testing research and development had involved the use of mainframe computer systems or minicomputers. Microcomputers represented a new and highly promising technology, but one with an unknown future. A number of microcomputer systems were available commercially, but few had been used for test administration, and virtually none had been used as vehicles for adaptive testing. The contrast between the microcomputers of that era and those of the present day is almost astonishing, and the differences had important implications for the feasibility of CAT-ASVAB.

In the 1980s, work progressed to develop a computer-based system to administer the operational ASVAB, and to implement adaptive testing for its power tests. The completed system was intended to replace the printed ASVAB throughout the Military Entrance Processing Stations (MEPSs)

and their associated Mobile Examining Team Sites (METSs).

Delivery System Requirements

At first glance, it might seem almost trivial to develop a computer system to administer the ASVAB, given the availability of powerful computers, and many years of development and application of computer-based instructional systems. Several considerations made this aspect of the project more demanding than is immediately apparent, however. One is the need for the system to be highly portable. This requirement reflects the nature of the METSs, many of which are rooms used only occasionally for ASVAB examining.

Another consideration is the nature of adaptive testing (which is well described by Lord, 1980a; Urry, 1983; and Weiss, 1974a). Unlike traditional tests, adaptive tests are dynamic; test items are chosen one at a time, to match the difficulty of the test to the apparent ability of the examinee. In the case of the adaptive ASVAB, the item selection rationale is based on item response theory (Lord, 1952, 1980a) and requires some computation after every test item is administered. The computer system must perform all the computations very rapidly, so that there is no noticeable delay between the examinee's response to the current test item and the computer's response to the examinee. The need for a consistent, rapid system response had implications for the design of the delivery system. For example, time-shared computer systems with large numbers of interactive terminals may not be able to achieve the necessary response time. In fact, all the candidate CAT-ASVAB system designs were based on local area networks of dedicated microcomputers.

Another peculiarity of adaptive testing with implications for system design, is the need for large banks of test items. Each adaptive ASVAB test draws its items from a large bank, preferably 100 to 500, calibrated test items. Since there would be eight or nine adaptive tests in CAT-ASVAB, permanent mass storage of 900 to 4,500 test items was expected to be required, in addition to mass storage of computer software and test results.

A further consideration was the size and dispersal of the existing paper-and-pencil test delivery system: In the Enlistment Testing Program alone, ASVAB is administered to applicants for enlistment in hundreds of sites throughout the U.S. and its possessions. (Another version of ASVAB is administered in over 14,000 secondary schools, but the

CAT-ASVAB system is not presently intended to automate that testing program.) The CAT-ASVAB system must be large enough to support historically experienced volumes of test administration, portable enough to serve mobile sites as well as the MEPSs, and cost-effective as an alternative to the printed ASVAB.

Functional reliability is one of the most important attributes of a system to replace the printed ASVAB. The design of the CAT-ASVAB system must include provisions to ensure that the system can conduct testing when scheduled, can resume functioning after being interrupted by a delivery system failure, and can retain the data needed to reconstruct and resume interrupted tests. These provisions include design features such as interchangeable equipment modules, hardware redundancy, and redundant storage of data after each transaction between the examinee and the system.

Two other considerations are communications and security. Test results at each mobile site must be communicated daily to the host MEPS, and summary data must be transferred daily from each MEPS to data banks at USMEPCOM headquarters. In addition, the system must have adequate communications capability to support the propagation of software updates—including computer programs and operational as well as experimental test item banks. Security of item banks is an important requirement of the system; this refers to security from interception during data communications as well as to security of mass storage files from unauthorized access.

Finally, an overriding consideration is the human factors issue. The users of the CAT-ASVAB system will include applicants for enlistment—predominantly men and women aged 17 to 23—and military and civilian test administrators. None of these users is expected to be an experienced computer user. Computer experience at any level should not provide an advantage in test performance, and should not be a prerequisite for use of the system by examinees or test administrators.

A more complete statement of requisite characteristics of the delivery system is contained in McBride (1982). The requirements of adaptive administration of the ASVAB, combined with considerations specific to its use in the MEPSs and METSs, were deemed to necessitate development of a custom-designed delivery system. The controlling criteria seemed to be three: (1) The computer had to be capable of displaying ASVAB graphical items, as well as text, with fidelity close to that of ASVAB's printed test items. (2) The computer system had to react to examinee input without distracting response time delays; for practical purposes, an upper limit of a 2 second response time was desirable. (3) The delivery system as a whole had to be capable of being deployed everywhere USMEPCOM administered ASVAB tests to enlistment applicants. At the program's outset, those tests were administered in 68 MEPSs, and in over 900 METS facilities.

Time-shared computer systems, often used to deliver computer-based training, in principle seemed capable of this. In practice, however, time-shared systems proved to be inadequate because their response times to examinee input were too slow or too variable to be satisfactory for administering standardized tests. For example, NPRDC's first computer used for adaptive testing research was a time-sharing Burroughs 1717 minicomputer capable of serving 10 or more terminals simultaneously. However, when it was used for a particularly computation-intensive adaptive testing strategy, the computational load was such that, for all practical purposes, test administration was limited to a single terminal; any more than that and the system response times were distractingly long—often a minute or more.

Software systems for adaptive testing research had been developed for use on real-time computer systems capable of simultaneously controlling multiple test administration terminals. However, these fell short, either because of practical limitations on the number of terminals they could control or because they could not support the graphical display requirements of ASVAB tests such as Mechanical Comprehension—or both.

In short, by 1979 highly promising adaptive research had been conducted in several quarters, using a variety of specially developed experimental CAT-ASVAB delivery systems, but none of those systems was capable of administering the full range of ASVAB test content, or of nationwide deployment in the MEPSs and their associated METSs. All CAT delivery systems up to that time had employed large computers—mainframe or minicomputers—that controlled multiple terminals. The test administration terminals either were on site with the computer, or were in remote locations connected to the host computer by telephone lines and modems. Because voice-grade telephone lines often proved to be unsatisfactory, expensive, specially conditioned lines suitable for data transmission often had to be used. Microcomputers of the kind so ubiquitous today simply did not exist; their predecessors—computers based on 8-bit microprocessors and possessing limited memory and mass storage capacity—had only recently become available commercially. Although the potential was recognized, no microcomputer system had as yet been used for adaptive test administration.

Analysis of System Needs

Thus, a major technical challenge at the outset of the CAT-ASVAB program was to identify or develop a computer system capable of meeting the functional requirements of an adaptive version of all the ASVAB tests, and the widely distributed test administration requirements of the nationwide system of MEPSs and METSs. Although detailed functional specifications had to await the results of some of the psychometric research and development described elsewhere in this volume, it was possible to specify broad functional requirements.

To this end, the Navy entered into an arrangement with the U.S. Office of Personnel Management (OPM) to draft a set of functional specifications. Earlier, researchers within OPM had planned a computer system to administer an adaptive version of the OPM's Professional and Administrative Career Examination (PACE). Unfortunately, those plans were abandoned when OPM discontinued using the paper-and-pencil PACE tests as part of a consent decree. However, the government's investment in CAT technology was not in vain; OPM's Paul Croll prepared a functional specifications document that became the foundation of the Navy's CAT-ASVAB system development plans (Croll, 1982).

In another technology-sharing agreement between government agencies, the Air Force's Federal Computer Performance Measurement and Simulation Center (FEDSIM) agreed to act as a consultant to the Navy in planning how best to go about developing the CAT system. Some of the key decisions reached in consultation with FEDSIM advice can be summarized in four points: (1) The computation-intensive nature of the most promising adaptive testing strategies, combined with the need for consistently short system response to examinee input, made it unlikely that remote terminals served by a central computer system would provide satisfactory performance in administering the ASVAB. (2) The least costly means of satisfying CAT-ASVAB's computing requirements would probably be to use microcomputers at each site to control the adaptive test administration. (3) Because the microcomputers then available commercially were not deemed adequate, a microcomputer system capable of meeting CAT-ASVAB's functional requirements would have to be developed for the

purpose. (4) Developing such a system within the CAT development timeframe was clearly beyond NPRDC's capabilities, and would entail substantial technical risk. A competitive contract development program could minimize the risk, while providing a substantial incentive for contractors to meet the ambitious project schedule.

With those four points as premises, FEDSIM recommended that the Navy undertake a competitive "flyoff" as a means of CAT-ASVAB system development: In the first stage of the competition, contracts would be awarded to two or more firms to independently prepare competing system designs and to develop working prototypes. In later stages, the contractors with the best designs would compete against each other for the right to develop the operational version of the nationwide CAT-ASVAB system. Croll's (1982) functional specifications, along with descriptions of ASVAB and the MEPS/METS system, were incorporated into a formal Request for Proposal (RFP) that was issued to dozens of interested firms. Ultimately, three firms were awarded contracts for the first stage of the flyoff, and the development of a nationwide CAT delivery system for ASVAB was begun.

The Flyoff

As mentioned above, independent, parallel contracts were awarded to three different firms. Each of the three was to become familiar with adaptive testing and with the functional requirements of a nationwide system to administer ASVAB by computer, to conduct design studies, and to build working prototypes of their designs. Competition for future stages of the system development project was to be limited to the three firms performing the first stage.

There were dramatic differences in the technical approaches taken by the three design contractors. Bolt, Beranek, and Newman (BBN), a Massachusetts-based high-technology firm, designed a multiterminal system driven by custom-built circuit boards, each with its own microprocessor. A local system could contain up to 12 test administration terminals. Each terminal consisted of a high-resolution graphics display, and a light pen used to answer multiple-choice test questions. Each terminal was controlled by its own circuit board, which included an 8-bit microprocessor, 64-kilobyte memory, and graphics display circuitry. All of these circuit boards were mounted in a single S-100 bus enclosure, enabling them to share a single hard disk drive that stored all of the test administration software, the test item banks, and test result files. The S-100 bus was an industry standard interface bus for 8-bit Zilog Z-80 and Intel 8080 microcomputers. The BBN design, in effect, consisted of parallel computers sharing mass storage and a common communications bus. Although the BBN design used 8-bit processors with limited memory, it was optimized for the purpose of administering CAT-ASVAB.

A second competitor was McDonnell-Douglas Aeronautics Company (MDAC), based in Aurora, Colorado. MDAC chose off-the-shelf computers and designed some customized components. MDAC also developed customized software to link the computers in a resource-sharing local network, giving each computer access to CAT-ASVAB computer programs and item banks stored on a hard disk drive on the network server. The computers used in the MDAC design were early IBM-PC compatible computers manufactured by Hewlett-Packard. Although each examinee station was a computer closely resembling today's PCs, the processors were early 1980s Intel 8-bit technology, and memory capacity was limited. MDAC designed a customized keypad as the examinee's test response input device.

The third competitor was WICAT Systems, of Orem, Utah. Originally a software firm in the computer-based instruction industry, WICAT had developed its own line of microcomputers because of a lack of suitable equipment from other manufacturers. WICAT's system was superficially similar to BBN's: Each examinee station consisted only of a display monitor and input device, and multiple examinee stations were controlled by a single piece of equipment. However, in WICAT's design, a single, powerful microprocessor controlled multiple examinee stations, rather than having a dedicated microprocessor for each one. WICAT's choice of microprocessors was the Motorola 68000 series, a processor that was much more powerful than the processors used in the other two designs.

All three prototype CAT systems satisfied the CAT-ASVAB functional specifications, and performed satisfactorily in operational demonstrations to a Joint-Service evaluation panel. The next stage in the planned development of the delivery system was competitive advanced development—updating one or more competitors' designs to include refinements on the prototypes and to incorporate the latest technology. By this time—late 1984—the microcomputer industry had matured to the point where off-the-shelf equipment was much more suitable for CAT-ASVAB functional requirements. Consequently, following a policy deci-

sion to accelerate the development of CAT-ASVAB, contractor development of the delivery system was abandoned in favor of in-house development using commercially available computer systems. NPRDC took upon itself the task of developing a system suitable for nationwide use, and selected the Hewlett-Packard Integral Personal Computers (HPIPCs)—a portable computer based on the Motorola 68000 microprocessor—as the vehicle for the CAT-ASVAB delivery system.

That system, which came to be known as ACAP because it was the vehicle for the accelerated CAT-ASVAB project, was developed successfully. It represented a "second generation" in the design and development of a delivery system for operational implementation of CAT-ASVAB. From 1986 through 1996, it was used as the delivery system for continuing CAT-ASVAB research and development. Beginning in 1990, it was in limited operational use in five MEPSs and one METS as part of the operational test and evaluation phase of the CAT-ASVAB system.

Partly because of the success of the operational test and evaluation of CAT-ASVAB, a policy decision was made to implement CAT-ASVAB nationwide in all 65 MEPSs. However, the HP-IPCs used in the IOT&E were no longer being manufactured, so it was necessary to convert the CAT-ASVAB system to another computer platform. In recognition that IBM-PC-compatible computers had become a de facto standard, the PC-compatible platform was selected as the third generation in the evolution of the CAT-ASVAB delivery system. The CAT-ASVAB software system originally developed for use on the HP Integral computers was converted for use on PC-compatibles, and additional psychometric research was carried out to ensure that ASVAB scores from the third-generation CAT-ASVAB system were equivalent to scores for the paper-and-pencil version of ASVAB.

Providing an Interim Delivery System

Initiating development of a CAT-ASVAB delivery system addressed the need for a computer system to administer ASVAB tests upon successful completion of CAT-ASVAB research, but it did nothing to address the need to evaluate the psychometric merits of CAT as a replacement for the printed version of the ASVAB. The delivery system would not be ready for operational use for several years. This presented a dilemma: On the one hand, empirical research data were needed to evaluate CAT and to justify any subsequent decision in favor of operational use of a CAT-ASVAB delivery system in the ASVAB program; on the other hand, no such data could be assembled without a delivery system for CAT-ASVAB tests. To resolve the dilemma, the Navy decided to develop an interim system to deliver experimental CAT tests. The interim system would not have to be suitable for nationwide use in the MEPSs and METSs of USMEPCOM, but would need to be fully capable of administering CAT versions of all the ASVAB tests in a research setting.

That interim delivery system, the experimental CAT-ASVAB system, was developed at NPRDC under the direction of John H. Wolfe. Its functional features are described in detail in an NPRDC special report (Quan, Park, Sandahl, & Wolfe, 1984) that includes the computer program's source code in an appendix. Its development coincided with the beginning of the explosion of the personal computer movement; the Apple II computer was on the way to commercial success, and the IBM-PC computer had just been introduced. Wolfe considered the capabilities of all commercially available microcomputers, and ultimately selected the Apple III for use in the experimental CAT-ASVAB system. That choice may seem odd today, but at the time the Apple III was superior to other computers in memory, graphics, programming language (PASCAL), and networking potential. Like other microcomputers of the time, the Apple III had just an 8-bit microprocessor; however, while its competitors were limited to 64 kilobytes of random access memory (RAM), the Apple III's base configuration included 128 kilobytes, and an expansion to 256 kilobytes was soon available. Its graphics capability was likewise superior to that of its competitors; a capability to display "high-resolution" graphics[1] was essential in a computerized ASVAB delivery system, because graphical figures are inherent in ASVAB's Mechanical Comprehension test items, as well as in some items of other ASVAB tests. A sophisticated higher level programming language interpreter, Apple III PASCAL, was delivered with Apple III computers. An extension of PASCAL, which was a standard language taught to computer science students at the time, Apple III PAS-

CAL was vastly superior to the BASIC language interpreters that were common on most other 8-bit computers; this greatly facilitated software development for the experimental CAT-ASVAB system. Finally, a third-party product available at the time of the Apple III's introduction made it possible to join up to eight Apple IIIs in a network sharing a single mass storage device—a 10-megabyte Corvus brand Winchester (hard) disk drive. Shared mass storage was crucial to the experimental system, because the system software and item banks required greater storage capacity than the built-in floppy disk drives provided, and the least expensive Winchester disk drive at the time cost more than a computer.[2]

Software development for the Apple III-based experimental CAT-ASVAB system was completed in 1981. Over the next several years, that system was used to administer prototype computerized and adaptive versions of ASVAB tests to thousands of research subjects—mostly military recruits—on military bases throughout the country. The research data obtained from those experimental, prototype CAT tests provided the first direct empirical evidence of the success of CAT as an alternative means of administering the ASVAB. The following section will address that subject in more detail.

CAT-ASVAB Psychometric Research and Development

One of the first actions taken at the outset of the project to develop CAT-ASVAB was an assessment of where we stood in terms of what was needed to develop a computerized adaptive version of the battery suitable to replace the conventional, paper-and-pencil version. Chapter 5 summarizes the state of the art in some detail; the following overview, however, should be helpful in presenting this technical perspective.

The delivery system, discussed at length above, is the most visible component of a CAT system. It is, however, only one of the essential components of such a system. Four additional components must be present in an adaptive testing program: One is a psychometric foundation—a valid, defen-

---

[1] When first introduced, the Apple III's graphics resolution was 560 pixels horizontal by 192 vertical; the vertical resolution could be effectively doubled, resulting in 560 x 384 resolution, by means of a technique known as interlaced video. In comparison, the IBM-PC then required the addition of a graphics adapter to make it capable of 300 x 200 resolution; years later, the Enhanced Graphics Adapter (EGA) standard improved this to 400 x 300. Although far higher graphics resolution is attainable on today's PC computers, most programs use no more than the "VGA" standard of 640 x 480.

[2] Today, microcomputers are typically equipped with both floppy disk drives that can store more than 1 megabyte, and "hard" disk drives with more than 200 megabytes. In 1980, however, personal computer floppy disk drives seldom exceeded 200 kilobytes storage capacity, and hard drives were exotic, very expensive, and had less than a tenth of current capacities.

sible theoretical basis for administering different questions to different people, yet expressing all the results on a single scale. A second component of an adaptive test is an item bank—a large set of test questions which measures the domain of interest and which has psychometric characteristics that will make them useful for adaptive testing. A third component is a "strategy" for adaptive testing—a set of procedures for sequentially choosing which test questions to administer at each stage of the test. Yet a fourth component is an experience base—a body of research, development, and empirical evidence—which justifies confidence in the usefulness and validity of adaptive testing as an alternative to the conventional version. The paragraphs that follow discuss each of these essential components in turn, and summarize the status of each of the projects at the outset in early 1979.

Psychometric Foundation

Item response theory (IRT), as advanced by Birnbaum (1968), Lord (e.g., 1970, 1980a) and Rasch (1960; Wright & Douglas, 1977), provided the psychometric foundation for CAT-ASVAB. The signal contribution of IRT to CAT is that IRT provides a basis for locating test questions and examinees on the same scale, for tailoring the difficulty of the test to the ability level of the examinee, and for expressing all scores on the same scale even though examinees have taken tests consisting of very different sets of test questions. IRT was already well developed at the outset of the program, although practical applications were few. Computer simulation studies conducted by McBride (1976b), by Vale (1975), and by Wetzel and McBride (1983) showed that adaptive tests based on IRT were more efficient than adaptive tests based on traditional test theory.

To make IRT useful as a basis for adaptive testing, what was needed were practical means of (1) "calibrating" banks of test items (fitting IRT models to item response data), (2) selecting test items adaptively, and (3) scoring the adaptive tests—all using IRT procedures. The most formidable of these was the requirement for item calibration. Fortunately, several analytical methods for fitting IRT models to large sets of test items had been proposed, and computer programs to implement them had been developed. Most notable were computer programs for fitting normal ogive and logistic ogive IRT models to data. Practical programs for normal ogive models included ANCILLES (Schmidt & Gugel, 1975) and NORMOG

(Bock, 1972). Programs for logistic ogive models included BICAL (Wright & Mead, 1977) and LOGIST (Wood, Wingersky, & Lord, 1976).

In the course of the development of IRT, several alternative families of mathematical functions were proposed for use in modeling response propensity as a function of ability; in general, these were ogive functions which express the probability of a correct item response as an increasing but nonlinear function of the examinee's location on the ability scale. By 1979, practitioners wishing to use IRT for test design and scoring had to choose (1) whether to use normal or logistic ogive response functions, and (2) if they chose logistic functions, whether to use a simple 1-parameter model developed by Rasch (1960) or more powerful, but also more complex 2- and 3-parameter models first developed by Birnbaum (1968). The normal ogive models were developed first—as explicated in Lord's 1952 monograph—and had the advantage of familiarity: Statisticians and psychometricians were generally familiar with the normal distribution function on which they are based. The logistic ogive functions, however, were more mathematically tractable. In time, IRT practitioners for all practical purposes abandoned normal ogive models in favor of the logistic models, so the first of the two choices was made almost by default.

The second choice—among 1-, 2-, and 3-parameter logistic models—was more difficult. The 1-parameter logistic (1PL) model had the advantage of simplicity: In cases where the data conformed to the 1PL model, Rasch had shown that the number-correct score was a sufficient statistic for estimating an examinee's location on the underlying ability scale. Wright and others showed that 1PL item parameters could be estimated from a minimum of item response data. These advantages of the 1PL model were offset by the fact that the model made no provision for differences in item discriminating power, nor for the possibility of answering an item correctly by chance. Proponents of the more complex logistic IRT models pointed out that the appealing mathematical properties of the 1PL model may not be obtainable in cases where the data do not conform to the model. In particular, the number correct score is not a sufficient statistic for estimating ability if items differ in discriminating power, or if they can be answered correctly by chance—as in the case of multiple-choice items.

The 3-parameter logistic (3PL) model includes provisions for chance responding as well as for variations in item discriminating power, by virtue of its lower asymptote and slope parameters.

Although 2-parameter logistic models were not completely abandoned, the 3PL model was more widely adopted, and debate ensued between proponents of the 1PL model (such as Wright, 1977) and those of the 3PL model (such as Lord, 1980a). At times the 1PL versus 3PL debate seemed to take on theological dimensions, with proponents of each one dogmatically advancing the cause of their favorite models, and proclaiming dire consequences to users of the competing model.

In point of fact, both the 1PL and the 3PL models are practically useful for test design, test analysis, and test score interpretation. Lord, long an advocate of the 3PL model for use with multiple-choice items, himself suggested that the 1PL model might be preferable in cases where item parameters had to be estimated from small sample data (Lord, 1980a). On the other hand, when enough item response data are available to estimate its parameters accurately, the use of the 3PL model is preferable for scoring tests (estimating ability) that consist of multiple-choice items. Lord (1970) showed analytically that the 3PL model has appreciable efficiency advantages over the 1PL model: Using the 1PL model to score multiple choice tests sacrifices some measurement precision, and is tantamount to shortening the test (and therefore making it less reliable).

Urry (1970) used computer simulation to compare the reliability of adaptive tests based on the 1PL model and the 3PL model; his results showed convincing evidence that the 3PL model was advantageous for adaptive tests with multiple-choice items, provided that all items in the adaptive item bank had high slope parameters—slope values of .80 and higher (e.g., Urry, 1974b). Lord likewise observed that highly discriminating items were required for adaptive tests to yield efficiency advantages over conventional tests.

In summary: From the outset of the CAT project, IRT was chosen as the basis for adaptive test design and administration. From among the different item response models available at the time, the 3PL model was selected for use. That decision was based on both practical and empirical grounds. Practically speaking, logistic models were much more tractable mathematically than models based on the normal ogive, and computer programs to estimate item parameters were better developed for logistic models. The 3PL model was chosen over the 1PL (Rasch) model because all ASVAB test items were multiple choice, and in principle cannot be fitted well by a model that does not allow for chance success. This decision was bolstered by the results of Urry's research showing the 3PL's greater psychometric efficiency in multiple-choice adaptive tests.

Item Banks

Adaptive testing makes heavy demands on test items. To measure a trait, an adaptive test dynamically selects a different set of test items for each examinee. The choice of test items is response-contingent; each examinee is administered a subset of the items in a fairly large bank of test items. Furthermore, each trait to be measured requires its own item bank. Since the 10-test ASVAB battery includes eight power tests, at least that many adaptive test item banks would be needed.[3] (Two of the ASVAB tests are highly speeded tests not amenable to adaptive testing.)

It was considered desirable for the number of items in the bank to exceed substantially—say, by a ratio of 5 or 10 to 1—the number of questions an individual examinee will encounter (Ree, 1977). In the context of ASVAB testing, this would suggest a need for banks of 50 to 150 calibrated items in each of the non-speeded ASVAB test content areas. "Calibrated" becomes the operative word here; calibrating items entails fitting IRT models to item response data. From the beginning, the 3PL IRT model was the model of choice for CAT-ASVAB. At the time, the LOGIST program (Wood, Wingersky, & Lord, 1976) was considered to be the best available program for fitting the 3PL model. Conventional wisdom at the time was that LOGIST required response data from 1,500 to 2,500 examinees per item.[4] The data requirements implied by that figure constituted a significant practical obstacle because, unlike some major testing programs such as the Scholastic Assessment Test (SAT), the ASVAB testing program did not include routine administration of tryout or experimental items or test sections. To collect the volume of item response data needed to develop an adaptive ver-

---

[3] CAT-ASVAB includes not eight, but nine tests. P&P-ASVAB's Auto and Shop Information test is represented by two separate adaptive tests, Auto Information and Shop Information, in CAT-ASVAB. Ability estimates for the two tests are combined to form a single Auto and Shop Information test score.

[4] Subsequently, alternative programs for estimating IRT model parameters have been introduced that use more efficient estimation methods and require far smaller examinee samples. The BILOG program (Mislevy & Bock, 1981) for example, uses marginal maximum likelihood, and requires 1,000 or fewer examinee responses per item.

sion of ASVAB, special arrangements would have to be made to administer hundreds of new test items to thousands of examinees for research purposes alone.

In addition to the substantial volume of item response data needed to prepare item banks for adaptive testing, research by Lord (1970) and Urry (1970) had shown that adaptive testing demanded higher quality (more discriminating) test items than conventional testing, as well as more variability in item difficulty. The practical effect of these distribution/discriminating power requirements was that only about one item in three would be acceptable for use in adaptive testing. Thus, developing eight ASVAB adaptive test banks of 50 to 150 items each could be expected to entail preparing 150 to 450 items in each area, administering them to tryout samples of examinees, and ultimately discarding about two-thirds of them because of inadequate discriminating power. The sheer number of test items needed, coupled with the substantial item response data requirements for item calibration, made CAT-ASVAB item bank development a formidable undertaking.

At the beginning of the program, available item bank assets fell far short of what would be required for CAT-ASVAB. Previous adaptive testing research within the DoD had involved, at most, two or three test content areas, not all of which had been closely aligned with ASVAB test content specifications. For example, McBride and Martin (1983) had conducted adaptive testing research using tests of verbal and quantitative abilities. Their experimental adaptive test of verbal ability used a calibrated item bank containing over 150 items, but the item format specifications were somewhat different from those of ASVAB's Word Knowledge test. Their adaptive test of quantitative ability used word problems very similar in format to ASVAB's Arithmetic Reasoning test; however, the item bank contained only about 75 calibrated items. An item bank had also been developed and calibrated for an adaptive test of reading comprehension similar to ASVAB's Paragraph Comprehension test; that item bank contained fewer than 40 items, and because item response data from fewer than 500 examinees were available, item calibration had been based on a 1PL model rather than the preferred 3PL model.

In short, as the program to develop CAT-ASVAB began, there was a daunting shortfall in item bank resources. It was quite apparent that developing the item banks needed for adaptive versions of ASVAB tests would be a significant undertaking.

Two more considerations had implications for the magnitude of the effort that would ultimately be involved. One was the medium of test administration used to collect response data for items intended for use in computer-administered tests. Although it would be far more efficient to collect large quantities of item response data by means of paper-and-pencil administration of the experimental test items, there was no assurance that item response propensities would be the same for computer-administration as they were for printed test administration. If they were very different, the IRT model parameter estimates used to control the computer-administered adaptive tests, but derived from printed administration, might be seriously in error.

A second consideration was the distribution of the trait in the examinee samples used to gather item calibration data. Because calibrating IRT models is tantamount to fitting a non-linear model of the regression of response propensity on ability, it was considered important to have the full range of the ability distribution represented in the examinee samples. This seemed to preclude using military recruits as the source of item response data, because military personnel selection standards eliminated most individuals in the lowest third of the distribution of general cognitive ability. While the full range of abilities might be represented in applicants for enlistment in the Armed Services, the lower tail of the ability distribution would not be represented among military recruits.

The response to the two considerations just described was tempered by practical considerations. Because of the large volume of item response data that would be needed to develop large banks of calibrated items for use in an adaptive ASVAB battery, it was practically infeasible to collect the data by means of computer administration—it had to be done by means of printed administration, or not at all.[5] The ability range consideration was more compelling. Examinee samples used for item calibration had to include the low end of the ability range.

---

[5] Concerns about differences in item response propensities between computerized and printed test administration were allayed to some extent by the success of previous CAT research, in DoD and elsewhere, using test items that were calibrated from paper-and-pencil test data (e.g., Weiss, 1974a; Urry, 1974b; McBride & Martin, 1983). Later research at NPRDC compared item response data collected in print and on computers, and found differences in the parameter estimates to be small and of little practical consequence in computerized adaptive tests of ASVAB abilities. Chapter 16 presents the results of that research, as does Segall (1989).

Consequently, a standard for CAT-ASVAB item response data collection was established that is followed to this day: IRT model calibration data were collected by administering experimental tests to applicants in the MEPS system.

The practical implications of this decision were enormous. Test item response data needed to calibrate the first experimental CAT-ASVAB item banks were collected by adding about one hour of experimental testing to the usual applicant examination procedures; over 250,000 applicants for enlistment took these experimental tests.[6] Similar large-scale experimental item response data collection would take place several times in the course of CAT-ASVAB research and development, as additional CAT-ASVAB item banks were developed—for research versions of CAT-ASVAB at first, and later for alternate "forms" of item banks intended for use in operational versions of CAT-ASVAB.

Two generations of CAT item banks were developed initially. The first, referred to as the "prototype item bank," was needed to provide item banks for use in a validity demonstration study that began in 1982. The second, the "operational item bank" development, was intended to provide the item banks for use when the CAT system became operational.

For the "prototype item bank," the Air Force Human Resources Laboratory (AFHRL) developed nine large sets of experimental ASVAB-type test items —one set for each of nine adaptive ASVAB tests.[7] These were first administered to samples of military recruits; based on data from those recruit samples, items were screened out if they did not appear to be sufficiently discriminating for adaptive testing. The items that passed this screening process were later administered for model calibration purposes to large samples of applicants—over 100,000—by USMEPCOM. The item response data were analyzed by Sympson and Hartmann (1985) using a modified version of the LOGIST (Wood, Wingersky, & Lord, 1976) computer program for fitting the 3PL response model. This effort yielded

nine sets of calibrated test items, one set corresponding to each of the power test content areas of ASVAB.

For the "operational item bank," nine more large sets of test items were written and screened under the direction of the AFHRL. About 200 test items in each of the nine content areas were selected for calibration. As with the prototype item bank, these items were administered to large groups of applicants for military enlistment. This data collection took place in 1983, and was followed by item analyses to calibrate the items for use when the CAT-ASVAB system became operational. Details of the operational item bank development and calibration have been described by Prestwood, Vale, Massey, & Welsh (1985). Later, test security considerations led to a decision to have at least two alternate "forms" of CAT-ASVAB. Each CAT-ASVAB "form" required a separate item bank. Additional test items were produced and calibrated to provide sufficient numbers of test items for two separate item banks.[8]

Adaptive Testing Strategy

A difficult decision was the choice of psychometric strategy to employ for adaptive testing in the CAT system. An adaptive testing "strategy" is a specific combination of procedures used to administer the adaptive test. Any number of combinations are possible. One defining characteristic of any adaptive testing strategy is the criterion used to select the test items administered to an individual examinee. The criterion may imply a specific psychometric foundation; for example, selecting test items to match item difficulty to examinee ability implies that item difficulty and person ability are expressed on the same scale, as is the case in IRT. The item selection criterion may also require updating the test score periodically during the test; for example, matching difficulty to ability one item at a time requires updating the ability estimate (a form of test scoring) after each item response. In the context of the CAT system, an "adaptive testing strategy" consists of three methodological components: methods for (1) estimating the examinee's ability level, (2) selecting items sequentially, and (3) deciding when to stop testing.

Within the framework of adaptive tests based on IRT, two ability estimation methods had been used

---

[6] Prospective CAT-ASVAB test items were screened prior to this step, by administering them to much smaller samples of military recruits, and discarding those not meeting statistical quality criteria. Thus, only the most promising test items were included in the experimental test booklets administered to applicants. Large numbers of applicants were required because time limitations precluded administering more than a few dozen items to any one applicant.

[7] Although there are just eight power tests in the ASVAB battery, a decision was made early in the project to include nine adaptive tests. This was done in recognition that ASVAB's Auto and Shop Information test includes items from two very different content areas: Automotive Information and Shop Information.

[8] Additional CAT-ASVAB item banks are under development at this writing. When they are complete, there will be at least four "alternate forms" of CAT-ASVAB—each "form" defined by a separate item bank.

extensively. The first is maximum likelihood estimation, as described by Lord (1980a) for the 3PL response model; the second is Bayesian sequential estimation, as proposed by Owen (1969, 1975) and explicated by Urry (1983) for the 3-parameter normal ogive response model. Promising newer methods, such as those developed by Bock and Mislevy (1981) and by Tsutakawa (1984), had not been tried systematically in conjunction with adaptive testing, and thus were not initially considered for use in the CAT-ASVAB system.

Among methods for sequentially choosing test items in adaptive testing, there are two major categories: methods based on optimization of some mathematical function, and methods that employ simpler, non-optimal branching rules (McBride, 1976a). Examples of optimization-based item selection methods include the Bayesian-motivated procedure suggested by Owen (1969), and the "maximum information" approach implied in Lord (1980a, chapter 10). Owen's procedure selects the one item in the bank that will minimize the expected value of the variance of the Bayes posterior distribution of ability; as implemented by Urry (1977, 1983). That procedure requires intensive computation after each item to select the next one. Lord's maximum information procedure selects the item with the largest value of the "information function" in the vicinity of the current ability estimate. Unlike the Urry/Owen procedure, Lord's method can be implemented by referring to tables of item information function values computed in advance, and thus has far smaller real time computation requirements. The most promising of the branching-rule based item selection procedures was the stratified adaptive ("stradaptive") method advanced by Weiss (1974b).

The simplest criterion for stopping an adaptive test is test length—stopping when a pre-specified number of items has been administered. However, computer-controlled test administration, combined with the sophisticated ability estimation methods of IRT, offers an appealing alternative: Stopping when a specific degree of measurement precision has been attained. In principle, this would result in constant measurement precision throughout the range of ability (subject to the limitations of the item bank). A constant-precision stopping criterion can be implemented in conjunction with any of the IRT-based ability estimation procedures, provided that the ability estimate is updated after each test item. In general, the constant-precision stopping rules will result in variable-length adaptive tests.

Strategies of adaptive testing had been the subject of research and development for some time prior to 1979 (e.g., Lord, 1970; Weiss, 1974a). Although there was room for still more research in this area, enough was known about some strategies to justify confidence in their effectiveness, and to be able to compare them in terms of psychometric characteristics. Most of what was known in this area was the result of either analytic or computer simulation studies. Such studies were carried out either to assess psychometric characteristics of a specific adaptive testing strategy, or to compare two or more strategies. By 1979, for example, computer simulation studies of adaptive testing strategies had shown that strategies which employ IRT for item selection and for updating ability estimates tended to be more efficient than strategies based solely on traditional test theory (e.g., McBride, 1976b; Wetzel & McBride, 1983). This efficiency advantage, however, was achieved at some cost: In some cases, the IRT-based strategies require a substantial amount of computation between test items; the strategies based on traditional test theory require none.

The computational requirements of an adaptive test strategy were a significant consideration in 1979, for two reasons: (1) Most adaptive testing programs had to pay for computation time on mainframe computers or minicomputers; the more computation involved, the more costly the adaptive testing strategy. (2) Computation-intensive strategies could tax the capacities of the host computer systems, resulting in unacceptably slow response by the computer system to an examinee's answer to a test question. Research by McBride (1976b) had shown that one of the most promising IRT-based adaptive testing strategies, Owen's (1969) Bayesian sequential procedure favored by Urry (1977), involved 100 times more computer processing than the least computation-intensive strategies, such as the stratified adaptive strategy proposed by Weiss (1974b). Computational requirements were especially a concern in the case of microcomputers, which had only recently been introduced, because computations were much slower than those performed by the more powerful large computers. Conceivably, microcomputers might be too slow for satisfactory implementation of some IRT-based adaptive test strategies. A separate section of this chapter deals specifically with computer system issues in adaptive testing.

To guide the choice of an adaptive testing strategy, one would like to know certain psychometric properties of tests which employ specified strategies. Research in adaptive testing strategies prior to the CAT-ASVAB program was usually designed to evaluate the psychometric characteristics of a particular strategy. Few data were available in 1979 for comparing alternative strategies in terms of their psychometric characteristics, and even where data existed (e.g., Vale & Weiss, 1975; Crichton, 1981), they were not generalizable. Consequently, a series of computer simulation studies was undertaken at NPRDC to compare alternatives.

The first simulation study (reported by Wetzel & McBride, 1983) compared four adaptive testing strategies; the evaluation focused on the measurement precision of the resulting adaptive tests. Owen's Bayesian sequential tailored testing strategy (Owen, 1969) was compared to three others: A maximum likelihood-based approach, a hybrid procedure which combined Owen's ability estimation procedure with the maximum information item selection procedure suggested by Lord (1980a, Chapter 10), and the stradaptive procedure proposed by Weiss. Little difference was found in the measurement precision of the first three strategies, but all three optimization-based strategies yielded appreciably greater measurement precision than the simpler stradaptive procedure.

While the Wetzel and McBride (1983) simulation results clearly favored item selection procedures which employed optimization, a pragmatic consideration makes them less appealing: Selecting the mathematically "optimal" item at each step in an adaptive test produces predictable sequences of test items. This would make the tests highly vulnerable to compromise. Hulin, Drasgow, and Parsons (1983) recommended random selection from a set of 30 or more "optimal" items to combat this problem. Wetzel and McBride (1986) found that this defense against compromise involved a tradeoff between security and measurement precision. Like Hulin et al., they simulated adaptive tests in which items were randomly chosen from an optimal subset of the full item pool; however, the Wetzel and McBride (1986) study systematically varied the size of the set. They found that measurement precision deteriorated rapidly as the set size increased beyond 10 items. However, they also found that the advantages of choosing the optimal item could be approximated by a randomization strategy in which the number of candidate items in the set was made smaller as the test progressed.

As a result of their computer simulation studies comparing various adaptive testing strategies, Wetzel and McBride developed evidence supporting the choice of a hybrid strategy that used Owen's Bayesian procedure (to update the ability

estimate after each item), Lord's maximum information look-up table (to select items with minimal computation between items), and random choice of items from a progressively smaller set of nearly optimal items (to improve security with minimal loss of measurement precision). The Wetzel-McBride hybrid strategy is essentially the same one used in the CAT-ASVAB system today, except for the security feature. CAT-ASVAB now uses an item security procedure that controls the exposure rate of each item with a requirement that AFQT items be less exposed than non-AFQT items (see Chapter 13).

Research Evidence Base

Up to this point, this chapter has focused on four components that are prerequisites to the *administration* of computerized adaptive tests: A psychometric foundation, a technical strategy for adaptive testing, suitable banks of test items, and a computerized delivery system. Once these four components have been developed, it is possible to administer CAT tests, but it is not yet appropriate to use them. For that, there is a fifth prerequisite: A body of research evidence to support the validity of the CAT tests for their intended uses. This section provides the technical perspective on the development of validity evidence for CAT-ASVAB.

The body of research evidence supporting CAT was small in 1979 but growing rapidly. Theoretical and analytical research dating from the 1960s had provided encouraging evidence that adaptive testing could be a highly efficient approach to measurement,[9] but there had been relatively few instances in which computerized adaptive tests had actually been developed, and none in which such tests had been fully evaluated for potential use. In research at the U.S. Civil Service Commission, Urry (1977) and his colleagues had successfully demonstrated the psychometric efficiency advantage of CAT over conventional test design in a test of a single trait, verbal ability. Research by McBride (1979) likewise showed CAT tests of verbal ability to be more efficient than conventional tests in terms of reliability.

Other research, such as work reported by Johnson and Weiss (1980) and by Hornke and Sauter (1980), was not so successful in this regard, possibly due to shortcomings in the quality of the adaptive test items. Lord (1980a) made the important

---

[9] The research antecedents of DoD's CAT-ASVAB program are presented in more detail in Chapter 5.

observation that an adaptive test based on test items with low to moderate discrimination parameters would be less efficient than a conventional test, not more so; the crucial variable was the discriminating power of the test items. Furthermore, all of the empirical CAT research that had been attempted at the time had involved adaptive tests of a single ability; no one had, as yet, developed a CAT version of a complete multiple-aptitude test battery such as the ASVAB.[10]

In short, the promise of adaptive testing's efficiency, shown in theoretical analyses and computer simulation studies, had been achieved in real applications of adaptive testing, but not consistently. Moving from theoretical results to practical applications of CAT would require not only achieving the promised efficiency advantages consistently, but also establishing convincing evidence of the validity of CAT-ASVAB tests—construct validity as well as criterion-related validity. In addition, because the CAT-ASVAB program was specifically intended to develop an alternative to the conventionally administered ASVAB, it was essential for the CAT-ASVAB battery to be capable of being used interchangeably with the paper-and-pencil version.

This background provides the frame of reference for understanding the technical perspective on the CAT-ASVAB program. Its mission was to develop and evaluate CAT-ASVAB as a possible replacement for the P&P-ASVAB, a battery used by each of the Armed Services for personnel selection and assignment decisions. Each Service establishes its own enlistment standards; so the use of ASVAB test scores varies from one Service to another. However, all of the Services use composites of two or more ASVAB test scores as a basis for personnel classification decisions, such as assignment to entry-level job specialty training. Whatever the technical merits of CAT in general, the CAT version of ASVAB had to be similar to the printed version in terms of test content, and equivalent to it in terms of what the constituent tests measured (construct validity) and how the tests predicted practical outcomes such as training performance (criterion-related validity). Additionally, test scores from the CAT version had to be interchangeable with scores of the printed version, to allow military personnel managers to make personnel decisions on a common basis, regardless of which version of the battery an individual applicant had taken.

These requirements translated into the technical agenda of the program: (1) to develop a full battery of computer-administered, adaptive ASVAB tests, and a computer system to deliver them; (2) to establish their equivalence to the conventional ASVAB in terms of validity for the battery's traditional uses; (3) to equate the CAT and printed versions of the battery, so that they could be used interchangeably; and (4) to accomplish all three of the preceding items in a manner consistent with professional standards.

This agenda was accomplished in waves. In the first wave, we developed a partial battery of adaptive tests, along with the experimental computerized delivery system developed by Quan et al. (1984). The equivalence of CAT-ASVAB tests to their conventional counterparts was evaluated for the first time in this wave. In the second wave, we expanded the adaptive test battery to include equivalent versions of every test in the ASVAB, including the two speeded tests (the speeded tests of the CAT-ASVAB are computer-administered, but not adaptive). During the second wave, the construct equivalence of CAT and conventional ASVAB was first demonstrated, along with the predictive validity of the CAT battery, in samples of Navy personnel. The third wave of the CAT-ASVAB program expanded the scope of the validity comparison to include all four Armed Services, along with a broader range of occupational specialties. The fourth wave marked the beginning of the transition of CAT-ASVAB from experimental to operational use, as two parallel CAT-ASVAB item banks were developed, along with a delivery system intended for full-scale operational use by USMEPCOM. The fifth wave accomplished the final essential step in readying CAT-ASVAB for operational use: Equating the adaptive and printed versions of the battery. Each wave is described in more detail below.

The First Wave

The partial battery was administered to Navy recruits, and its tests were compared to the same tests in the printed battery in terms of reliability, internal structure, and predictive validity. This first wave of CAT-ASVAB research provided an opportunity for the project to fail, but not to succeed: If the partial battery of CAT-ASVAB tests fell short of the printed tests in reliability or validity, the

---

[10] Malcolm Ree (1977), however, reported the development of a prototype CAT version of the Armed Forces Qualification Test (AFQT) component of the ASVAB for evaluation in feasibility and validity studies in the San Antonio Armed Forces Entrance and Examining Station. It included three tests—Word Knowledge, Arithmetic Reasoning, and Space Perception.

project would probably be terminated, but it could not be deemed a success until the reliability and validity of a full battery of computerized ASVAB tests was satisfactorily demonstrated.

This first wave represented the first time a battery of computerized adaptive tests was developed and validated. The project gave rise to a number of new psychometric issues. For example: How should the equivalence of tests of the same trait, administered in different media, be judged? How should the equivalence of adaptive and conventional tests be evaluated? How could adaptive tests based on IRT be equated to conventional tests based on classical test theory? While the first wave was still in progress, it became apparent that existing professional standards[11] did not provide an adequate basis for evaluating the equivalence of conventional and computerized adaptive versions of the same test battery. Thus, another agenda item was added to the CAT-ASVAB program: Developing a set of standards for evaluating whether the yet-to-be-developed CAT-ASVAB battery was a satisfactory alternative to the conventional, printed version. Charles Davis, of ONR, provided the means to do this by commissioning an independent panel of experts, chaired by Bert F. Green, Jr.,[12] to develop a framework for evaluating CAT-ASVAB. The Green committee's report (Green et al., 1982) laid out an evaluation plan that incorporated most of the Navy's plans for CAT-ASVAB development and evaluation, and added to those plans a substantial and rigorous research agenda. That report later became the basis for a seminal article on standards for evaluating adaptive tests (Green et al., 1984); additionally, the *Guidelines for Computer-based Tests and Interpretations* (APA, 1986) are based in part on some recommendations of the Green committee. The point to be noted here is that the first set of standards for evaluating adaptive tests was developed as an integral part of the CAT-ASVAB program.

Also as part of the first wave of CAT-ASVAB development, the first comparisons of the validity of a printed test battery and counterpart computerized adaptive tests, and the first assessments of the construct equivalence of a battery of adaptive and conventional tests took place. The data to support these developments were obtained by administering a partial battery of CAT-ASVAB tests to Navy re-

cruits during basic training. The battery included experimental adaptive versions of five ASVAB tests: Word Knowledge, Arithmetic Reasoning, Paragraph Comprehension, General Science, and Math Knowledge. Since all Navy recruits take the ASVAB prior to enlistment, their ASVAB scores could be obtained from their personnel records. The recruits who participated in the CAT-ASVAB tests also were given an ASVAB retest, using a different form of the printed battery. Thus, when data collection was completed, we had records of the recruits' pre-enlistment ASVAB scores, post-enlistment scores on an alternate form, and post-enlistment scores on the five CAT-ASVAB research tests. The validity of the post-enlistment adaptive and conventional ASVAB tests was assessed by computing the correlations of their test scores with pre-enlistment ASVAB scores. These correlations were compared, test by test, for counterpart adaptive and conventional tests. The researchers' hope was that the adaptive tests' correlations with pre-enlistment scores would be approximately equal to those of the conventional retest scores; this hope was realized (see Chapter 6).

Construct equivalence of the adaptive and conventional tests was evaluated by means of factor analysis. The NPRDC researchers (see Chapter 11) performed exploratory factor analysis of the correlation matrix of all the available test scores: Pre-enlistment ASVAB scores, post-enlistment alternate form ASVAB scores, and scores on the five experimental CAT tests. The results were easily interpretable: The experimental CAT tests had patterns of factor loadings that were nearly identical to those of the counterpart ASVAB tests—both pre-enlistment and post-enlistment. Cudeck (1985) later performed more sophisticated covariance structure analyses based on the same data. His analyses confirmed that the internal structure of the partial battery of adaptive tests was virtually identical to that of the counterpart conventional ASVAB tests. These analyses of the partial battery of CAT-ASVAB tests represented the first time that adaptive versions of a test battery were shown to be equivalent to a conventional test battery in validity and internal structure.

The Second Wave

In the second wave, the experimental CAT-ASVAB was extended to include computerized versions of all of the tests in the ASVAB, and for the first evaluation of the equivalence of the full CAT battery to the printed version of ASVAB. Developing the

---

[11] The 1979 Joint Standards of the American Psychological Association, the American Educational Research Association, and the National Council on Measurement in Education.

[12] The other panel members included R. Darrell Bock, Robert L. Linn, Mark D. Reckase, and Lloyd Humphreys.

full battery entailed expanding the experimental Apple III delivery system to include the capability to administer graphics-based test items, along with development and IRT calibration of adaptive test item banks in the content areas missing from the partial battery: Auto and Shop Information, Electronics Information, and Mechanical Comprehension. In addition, the full experimental battery of computerized ASVAB tests included computer-administered versions of the two speeded tests of the ASVAB: Numerical Operations and Coding Speed.[13]

Once the full experimental CAT battery was ready, a CAT validity demonstration effort was begun, using Navy recruits as subjects. The Navy designated six occupational specialties (called "ratings" in Navy terminology) for the study. Recruits scheduled for entry-level training courses in the six ratings took the experimental CAT battery and the P&P-ASVAB retests. Later, when these recruits had completed technical specialty training, the correlations of their P&P-ASVAB and CAT scores with their training performance were evaluated.

The Third Wave

By the end of the second wave of the project, a full battery of experimental CAT tests had been developed, tried out, and shown to be equivalent to the printed battery in terms of predictive validity and factor structure, in samples of Navy recruits. The third wave of the CAT-ASVAB program expanded the scope of the validity comparison to include all four Armed Services, along with a broader range of occupational specialties. Each of the four Services designated a small number of training courses to participate in the demonstration. About 250 recruits scheduled for attendance at each of the courses took the experimental CAT battery, and were also retested with alternate forms of selected ASVAB tests. Each of the examinees was followed through subsequent technical training, and training performance data were collected. When data collection was complete, there were several blocks of psychometric information for each examinee in

the sample: Pre-enlistment ASVAB test and composite scores, counterpart experimental CAT test scores, experimental ASVAB alternate form test scores, and training performance data. The predictive relations between CAT test and composites were assessed, and found to be closely comparable to those of the printed ASVAB. Although no new ground was broken in the third wave, the results corroborated the earlier findings that CAT-ASVAB was equivalent to the printed battery in terms of predictive validity. This gave the other Services more confidence that the new technology would not work to the detriment of their ASVAB-based personnel selection and classification systems (see Chapter 11).

The Fourth Wave

The fourth wave of the project marked the beginning of the transition of CAT-ASVAB from experimental to operational use. In this wave, NPRDC developed two parallel CAT-ASVAB item banks, which would serve as "alternate forms" of the battery, and a delivery system intended for full-scale operational use by USMEPCOM. The new item banks were improvements over the experimental item bank, with broader distributions of highly discriminating items; Segall, Moreno, and Hetter describe their development in Chapter 11. In Chapter 14, Rafacz, Hetter, Wilbur, and James describe development of the delivery system. It consisted of a completely new suite of software for administering and monitoring operational CAT-ASVAB tests. Designed specifically for use in MEPSs and METSs, the system featured portable computers, and was capable of operating on a single computer or in a local network in which multiple test administration computers were monitored continuously from another computer in the network.

This new CAT-ASVAB system included a number of features missing from the experimental Apple III system (Rafacz, 1995). As mentioned above, the system was highly portable, so that the same computer models could be used in METSs as well as the MEPSs. Additionally, for the first time the system included two new provisions for test security: Alternate forms, and a procedure developed by Sympson and Hetter (1985) for limiting item usage to the same frequencies as the printed tests; Chapter 13 describes their procedure. The new system also included provisions for "seeding" experimental test items in each CAT-ASVAB test; it thus provided a means of gathering response data needed to calibrate new items by embedding them

---

[13] The speeded tests presented technical challenges of their own. How to format them for computerized presentation represented one challenge. Another was how to adjust time limits to account for the substantially faster pace at which examinees can respond to computer-presented items, compared to typical response rates on counterpart printed tests. Later, Greaud and Green (1986) suggested what is now standard practice in CAT-ASVAB: Using rate scores, rather than number correct scores, on the computerized versions of the speeded tests.

unobtrusively in the middle of each operational test. In principle, this feature could lead to the eventual elimination of the need for large-scale administration of experimental tests for the purpose of item calibration (see Chapters 11, 12, and 26).

The Fifth Wave

Before CAT-ASVAB would be acceptable for operational use, CAT-ASVAB scores had to be equated to those of the printed ASVAB, so that military personnel selection and classification criteria based on ASVAB composites and cutting scores could be used with confidence with CAT-ASVAB scores. While equating old and new forms of a test is done routinely in major testing programs, no testing program had as yet attempted to equate adaptive and conventional tests. CAT-ASVAB would be the first testing program to break this new ground.

Equating CAT and paper-and-pencil versions of ASVAB tests would not be a routine task. Although ample evidence had been accumulated to support the equivalence of printed and computerized adaptive ASVAB tests, equating them presented a special challenge, because of the characteristic differences in psychometric precision. Specifically, printed ASVAB tests tend to achieve maximal precision at a single point on the score scale; at scores above and below that point, measurement precision drops off substantially. In contrast, adaptive tests are less variable in measurement precision; they could be expected to be about as precise as their conventional counterparts at the maximum, and far more precise elsewhere on the score scale. This fact presents an interesting paradox: Despite the ample evidence that CAT-ASVAB is equivalent to the printed version in terms of both criterion-related validity and construct validity, CAT-ASVAB tests are not strictly parallel to their printed counterparts because of these precision differences. In fact, because the CAT-ASVAB tests use a different score metric than the printed tests—the real number line rather than the number of items answered correctly—equating them was even more challenging.

To address the difficult technical problems of equating CAT-ASVAB to the paper-and-pencil version, the Office of Naval Research convened a panel of outside experts. Their report (Green, Bock, Linn, Lord, & Reckase, 1984) proposed a solution to this problem. Later, Segall independently solved this technical problem by adapting the common practice of equipercentile equating to the special problem of equating score scales that differed in terms of both measurement precision and the metric itself. Segall's approach, and his results, are described in Chapter 19.

Summary

This chapter has endeavored to provide a technical perspective on the challenges and technical accomplishments of the CAT-ASVAB program. Perhaps the most important aspect of that perspective is the recognition that in the course of the project, the DoD researchers who developed CAT-ASVAB were the first to attempt, and the first to accomplish, a significant number of milestones in applied psychometrics. These milestones are summarized above; many are described in more detail in the chapters that follow.

II

Evaluating the Concept of CAT

In the last 20 years, CAT has evolved from a promising concept to a practical reality. Along the way, the feasibility, validity, and usefulness of the concept had to be demonstrated before making a commitment to invest resources in the development of a CAT version of the entire ASVAB. Early CAT research focused on proof of concept as opposed to full-scale development. The three chapters of this part document the evolution of CAT from basic research to its first modest application by a DoD agency.

Chapter 5 sets the stage for the entire CAT-ASVAB development program by describing the state of the art immediately preceding its inception. By the mid-1970s, a great deal of research had been conducted that provided the technical underpinnings needed to develop adaptive tests, but little research had been done to corroborate empirically the promising results of theoretical analyses and computer simulation studies. In this chapter, McBride summarizes much of the important theoretical and simulation research prior to 1977. In doing so, he describes a variety of approaches to adaptive testing, and shows that while many methods for adaptive testing had been proposed, few practical attempts had been made to implement it. Furthermore, the few instances of adaptive testing were based primarily on traditional test theory, and were developed in laboratory settings for purposes of basic research. The most promising approaches, those based on item response theory and evaluated analytically or by means of computer simulations, remained to be proven in the crucible of live testing.

In the introduction to Chapter 5, McBride characterizes adaptive testing circa 1977 as "a promising but unproven application of psychometric technology." In **Chapter 6**, he describes the design and results of the first proof-of-concept research done within DoD to evaluate CAT from a psychometric point of view. This research was conducted as part of an exploratory development project sponsored by the U.S. Marine Corps. This chapter describes the computer software system developed as a testbed for this research, and summarizes two ground-breaking research studies that demonstrated, for the first time, that the theoretical efficiency of IRT-based CAT could be achieved in practice. A third study, based on the data collected in the first two, provided the first practical demonstration of the structural equivalence of adaptive tests to their paper-and-pencil counterparts. The positive outcomes of those three studies provided the impetus for the inception of the Joint-Services program to develop and evaluate a CAT version of the entire ASVAB battery.

In **Chapter 7**, Sands, Gade, and Knapp describe the first application of CAT to personnel assessment in DoD: The U.S. Army's Computerized Adaptive Screening Test, known as CAST. CAST was introduced in 1984 as a more efficient alternative to a paper-and-pencil test, the Enlistment Screening Test. The purpose of both tests was to give military recruiters a means to forecast a candidate's aptitude qualification for military service by predicting his or her score on the Armed Forces Qualification Test composite of the ASVAB. Knowing who is likely to qualify for enlistment results in more efficient use of recruiters' time and other resources. The chapter summarizes the motivation for developing CAST, as well as its design, development, functional features and validation. Finally, the authors cite CAST as an example of cooperation among the Services, and provide a glimpse of related future developments.

Research Antecedents of Applied Adaptive Testing

James R. McBride

What is now known as the CAT-ASVAB program officially started in January 1979; it had its real beginnings, however, in a Marine Corps exploratory development effort that began in 1977. This chapter summarizes the state of the art in computerized adaptive testing (CAT) at the outset of the exploratory development of CAT-ASVAB, in the form of a review of relevant research conducted prior to 1977.

At that time, adaptive testing was a promising but unproven application of psychometric technology that, for the most part, had been the subject of theoretical analysis and, more recently, computer simulation. Today, CAT is being used in a number of operational testing programs; in almost every instance, the adaptive tests are based on item response theory (IRT), and are administered on personal computers. In 1977, IRT was barely out of its infancy; most approaches to adaptive testing were based on traditional test theory. In the few instances in which CAT had actually been tried, the computers used were costly mainframes and minicomputers. The explosive growth of the microcomputer industry would not occur until several years later. Indeed, microprocessors were just beginning to be used in small computers; "personal computer" was an unfamiliar term.

Adaptive Testing Research Prior to 1977

CAT was conceived as an alternative to conventional testing, and pursued because of its supposed advantages. As a result, the psychometric research that preceded the CAT-ASVAB program involved comparing one or more adaptive testing strategies with conventional test designs. The research can be classified along two dimensions: The source of the data, and the approach used to make the comparisons.

Four different kinds of data sources were represented in the adaptive testing research literature. They are referred to here as live testing, real data simulation, theoretical analysis, and computer simulation. Live testing data, of course, are obtained by administering adaptive and conventional tests to samples of examinees; comparisons can then be based on both test scores and item response level data. Real data simulation involves collecting item response data conventionally, but simulating adaptive testing by choosing subsets of the item responses in a sequence based on one or more adaptive testing methods. Both live testing and real data simulation require expensive and time consuming test administration to collect data; the amount of data needed to design and evaluate adaptive testing often made this prohibitive.

The remaining two data sources made actual test administration unnecessary. Theoretical analyses are usually based on IRT. By specifying an item response model, a set of item parameters, and specific levels of ability, properties of a test design strategy—such as conditional means, measurement error, or test information—can be deduced analytically. In cases where theoretical analysis is not practical, computer simulation studies can produce similar results by sampling item responses using random number generators to produce data based on specific item parameters, ability levels, and item response models.

Two different approaches to comparing test designs were widely used. Before IRT was well understood, the approach used most often was to compare two test design methods in terms of their correlations with a criterion—for example, correlations of adaptive and conventional test scores with scores on a reference test. The alternative, and more sensitive, approach was to compare properties of the two design methods as a function of ability level; this approach was typically used in research applications of IRT. F. M. Lord seems to have instituted this approach, by comparing tests in terms of their measurement precision (test information), which varies with ability level.

The remaining sections of this chapter present thumbnail summaries of the research literature, organized according to the four data sources named above.

Early Live Testing Research

Before the beginning of the CAT program, virtually all live-testing studies of adaptive tests involved branching strategies. These strategies select items sequentially from a predetermined logical branching structure. Examples include the "flexilevel" strategy (Lord, 1971a), two-stage testing (Lord, 1971b), pyramidal (Larkin & Weiss, 1974) and "stradaptive" strategies (Weiss, 1974b). All of the examples cited used classical item parameters (proportion correct and item-total correlation coefficients) to place items at specific points in the branching structure, and thus to specify item selection contingencies. A short summary of live testing research involving each of these strategies is presented in the following paragraphs.

Flexilevel Testing

Lord (1971a) proposed the flexilevel test design: Test items were arranged in order from easiest to hardest, and the middle item in the order was administered first. After each correct answer, the examinee was to take the next more difficult item not already administered; after each wrong answer, he or she was to take the next easier item. Testing stopped when the examinee had answered half of the items plus one; the total number of items in a flexilevel test was always an odd number. The flexilevel procedure was designed for printed administration, with item scoring and branching done by the examinee, following simple instruc-

tions. Correctly following the branching instructions resulted in every examinee answering a contiguous sequence of items. The test score was determined by the examinee's score on the last item in this sequence.

Although Lord (1971a) proposed the procedure, and presented analytical data on its psychometric properties, Olivier (1974) seems to have been the first researcher actually to administer flexilevel tests. He compared a 20-item paper-and-pencil (P&P) flexilevel test of verbal ability with three 20-item conventional tests, in terms of reliability and validity for predicting scores on an independent criterion test. He found the flexilevel tests to have lower reliability and validity than the conventional tests; in addition, about 15 percent of the flexilevel test examinees were excluded from his analyses because errors they made in following the branching instructions prevented their tests from being scored. Betz and Weiss (1975) compared conventional and flexilevel tests administered by computer. They found the same degree of test-retest reliability for both kinds of tests; their research design did not permit other comparisons, such as validity.

Two-Stage Adaptive Testing

In a two-stage test, scores on a short initial (first stage) test are used to select one of several different tests to be administered at the second stage. Betz and Weiss (1973) used computers to administer 40-item conventional and two-stage tests to independent groups of college students. They found comparable levels of test-retest reliability for both kinds of test. Although their research design permitted no other comparisons with conventional tests, they did find that their first stage tests were too easy for the examinees as a group, which may have somewhat degraded the adaptive tests' psychometric properties. Later, Larkin and Weiss (1975) improved the design of the first stage test, but, because their research design included no external criteria, no comparison of the merits of two-stage testing with conventional testing was possible.

Pyramidal Adaptive Testing

In this strategy, also called the "staircase" method (Lord, 1974), items are arranged into a lattice-like structure based on difficulty. Every test starts with the same item; every examinee answers the same number of items. Each item after the first is selected by branching through adjacent nodes in the lattice so as to converge on items that closely match their difficulty with the examinee's ability.

Larkin and Weiss (1974) administered 15-item pyramidal tests by computer, and later (1975) administered two-stage and pyramidal tests to independent examinee groups in the same experiment. They found that scores on both adaptive tests had respectable test-retest correlations, but they concluded that the two-stage test (improved after the 1973 Betz and Weiss experiment) showed superior tailoring properties, as gauged by proportion correct scores. The mean on the pyramidal test was 53 percent correct, compared to 57 to 66 percent correct on the two-stage tests. The latter figure was close to the optimal difficulty, given that five-alternative multiple choice items were used. None of the Larkin and Weiss data made it possible to compare the two stage tests with other strategies in terms of other psychometric figures of merit.

The Stradaptive (Stratified Adaptive) Strategy

Weiss (1974a) proposed this adaptive testing method, in which a pool of items is sorted into mutually exclusive sets—strata—based on item difficulty. Adaptive testing proceeds by branching from one stratum to another, contingent on right or wrong answers to the immediately preceding item. At each level, the first unused item in the stratum is administered. Weiss proposed this as a variable-entry, variable length adaptive strategy, which differentiates it from the otherwise similar pyramidal strategy. Different examinees could start at different levels of difficulty, depending on a priori information about their expected ability levels—for example, based on grade in school. Testing could continue until a stopping criterion had been attained—for example, responding at chance level.

Waters (1974; 1975) administered alternate forms of a stradaptive verbal ability test by computer to 55 entering college students in an investigation of its reliability, validity (correlation with an external criterion measure), and practical utility. He administered a 50-item conventional test, constructed from the same items, to an independent group for comparison. His analysis examined three variants of the stradaptive strategy. For each one, the reliability and the external validity were higher than those of the conventional test. Although these reliability and validity differences were not statistically significant, the three variants of the stradaptive test were from 36 to 60 percent shorter, on average, than the 50 item length of the conventional comparison test. Waters' was the first live testing study to demonstrate superior efficiency in an adaptive test, but the results were not definitive because his conventional tests were too easy (the mean was 75 percent correct) for optimal measurement in his sample.

Vale and Weiss (1975) conducted a similar study with college students as the subjects, and compared stradaptive and conventional tests in terms of internal consistency reliability, test-retest correlations, and correlations with an external criterion measure. They found that the stradaptive test had higher internal consistency (.94 vs. .91) than the conventional test, and comparable re-test reliability, despite being an average of 34 percent shorter. These results were ambiguous, however, because of differences in item discriminating power that favored the adaptive strategy.

Summary

The live testing studies summarized here fall into two categories. Some were designed to compare adaptive strategies with conventional test designs on psychometric criteria. The Olivier (1974) and Waters (1974) studies fall into this category. The results of those studies were mixed, in part due to methodological problems that may have caused one test design or another to be at a disadvantage.

The other category included research designs that did not provide an adequate frame of reference for comparing test designs. The studies by Betz and Weiss (1974) and Larkin and Weiss (1974) certainly fall into this category. The Vale and Weiss (1975) study reported many comparison statistics, but involved such extensive adjustments for nuisance variables that the comparisons were somewhat dubious.

This critique points up a fundamental problem in comparing different test strategies by means of live testing. The problem is one of controlling the influence of such variables as test length, test difficulty, test item discriminating power, and test reliability. Vale and Weiss (1975) recognized these problems and called for more research with better designs.

Real Data Simulations

Adaptive tests could be simulated from paper-and-pencil test item response data by selecting item responses one at a time, using the item selection criterion of almost any adaptive testing strategy.

This was an economical approach to evaluating adaptive testing, since: (1) it did not require the development of computer software to administer the adaptive tests, and (2) it did not require collecting any new data, if the researcher had access to item response data from already developed tests.

Real data test simulation research usually used correlational methods to evaluate the adaptive tests, and to compare them to conventional test designs. Unfortunately, research based on this approach was often methodologically flawed. A frequent practice was to compute the correlations of scores on the simulated adaptive test with total scores on the parent conventional tests, or to compare the adaptive and parent test scores' correlations with an external criterion measure. These correlations were always high, and the adaptive tests were, by design, shorter than the parent tests. Some researchers interpreted such results as evidence of adaptive testing efficiency, forgetting that the correlations were part-whole and therefore overstating the shorter tests' reliability and precision.

A summary evaluation of real data simulation might be stated this way: Real data simulation is an inexpensive, efficient approach to understanding how an adaptive test might work. However, it is not very useful for comparing adaptive and conventional testing unless there is some kind of control over spuriously high part-whole correlations. Such controls were rarely used; consequently, the favorable assessment of adaptive testing based on real data simulation studies largely had to be discounted.

Theoretical Analyses of Adaptive Testing

Theoretical analyses based on IRT provided one alternative to the use of costly, methodologically messy live testing experiments with adaptive testing. Birnbaum (1968) was one of the first to apply what is now known as IRT to the analysis of tests' measurement precision as a function of ability level. IRT specifies the functional relationship between ability and the probability of a correct response to any given item. Items vary according to the parameters of their response functions; if those parameters are known, IRT allows each item's mean and variance to be calculated at any ability level.

A local independence assumption allows those statistics to be combined across all the items on a test, so that the expected value of the test scores and their variance can be calculated directly, at any ability level. Straightforward derivations allow measurement error, as well, to be calculated as a function of ability level. Birnbaum introduced the use of the "test information function"—inversely related to the square of conditional measurement error—as an analytic tool for designing, evaluating, and comparing tests. If a test's IRT item parameters were known, test information functions could be used to evaluate the psychometric characteristics of that test, and to compare them with those of any other test.

Lord (e.g., 1970) applied this theoretical tool to the analysis of various "mechanical" adaptive test design strategies, and to comparisons of each adaptive strategy against conventional test designs. He focused on peaked conventional tests as a frame of reference—tests designed to discriminate at a single point on the ability scale—and compared each adaptive design against a comparable peaked test design. The use of theoretical analyses allowed Lord to control all of the nuisance variables—such as test-to-test differences in test length, item difficulty distributions, item discriminating power—that had contaminated so many of the live testing comparisons of adaptive and linear tests. It also allowed him to manipulate those variables systematically, and thus to study the effects of such things as item discrimination power and test length on each test's measurement properties.

One thrust of Lord's results was that at least some adaptive test designs showed dramatic superiority over peaked conventional tests, in terms of measurement precision, at ability levels that were distant from the peaked test's center. Furthermore, the higher the discriminating power of the test items, the greater the advantage of the adaptive tests, and the narrower the range in which peaked conventional tests were superior. Lord cautioned, however, that it might not be possible in practice to assemble large adaptive test item banks with item discrimination parameters large enough to achieve the theoretical advantage. Subsequent experience proved this concern to be unfounded.

Computer Simulation Studies of Adaptive Test Strategies

The theoretical studies of adaptive testing, exemplified by the work of Lord, focused on various mechanical branching strategies and idealized conditions such as free response test items with identical discrimination parameters. These idealized conditions made the theoretical analyses feasible, and demonstrated the potential for adaptive testing. The results of these studies did not, however, readily generalize to realistic test development situations involving multiple-choice items with random distributions of difficulty, item discriminating power, and susceptibility to guessing. Theoretical analysis would be difficult, if not impossible, for adaptive tests using multiple-choice items with realistic distributions of item parameters. Computer simulation studies were feasible in such circumstances; in short order, simulation studies of adaptive tests' "behavior" supplanted pure theoretical analysis almost completely.

Simulation studies of adaptive testing strategies contained the best elements of live testing and theoretical analyses. They resembled live testing studies in their use of realistic distributions of item psychometric characteristics, and in their reliance on item response data from samples of "examinees." They resembled theoretical analyses in their computation of conditional test data—that is, data for a number of specific levels of ability. The principal difference between simulation studies and the other two was in the source of the data. Simulation study data were obtained by using Monte Carlo techniques to generate simulated item response data based on the IRT model parameters of the "items" specified for an adaptive or conventional test.

Early simulation studies of adaptive testing followed three different paths. One approach was to use simulation techniques to generate global summary statistics for a given testing procedure. Urry and his colleagues (e.g., Urry, 1970, 1971, 1974b) typically used this approach to compute "fidelity" coefficients—correlations of simulated test scores with the ability being measured. A second approach was to use simulation studies to corroborate results obtained in live testing studies. Betz and Weiss (1974, 1975) and Vale and Weiss (1975) conducted simulation studies that were closely parallel to their empirical studies of two-stage, pyramidal, and stradaptive testing strategies, respectively.

The third approach has been to use simulation studies to investigate the conditional psychometric properties of tests—that is, their properties at various levels of ability. This approach is parallel to Lord's theoretical analyses, in which he reported psychometric characteristics as a function of ability level. Numerous researchers used this approach in the 1970s, and reported conditional values of such psychometric characteristics as test information (Betz & Weiss, 1975; Lord, 1975; Samejima, 1976; Vale & Weiss, 1975), mean test scores (McBride & Weiss, 1976), and mean proportion correct (McBride, 1975).

Regardless of the approach taken, the motivation behind most adaptive test simulation studies of the 1970s was to compare the measurement properties of an adaptive test strategy with those of a conventional test design. Below is a summary of the results of some of those computer simulation strategies; Weiss and Betz (1973) reviewed earlier work along these lines.

Computer Simulation Strategies

Flexilevel testing. Betz and Weiss (1975) conducted simulation studies that paralleled their live-test comparisons of 40-item flexilevel and conventional verbal ability tests. Unlike the live tests, the simulation studies had large samples (n = 10,000) of simulated "examinees," and a variety of criteria for comparing the tests, including fidelity coefficients, parallel forms reliability coefficients, and test information function values. Their results showed the flexilevel tests to be slightly superior to the conventional tests in all respects. However, the flexilevel test items used in the simulation studies had somewhat higher item discrimination parameters than the conventional test items. Consequently, the favorable results obtained for the flexilevel tests were somewhat ambiguous.

Two-stage testing. Using a design similar to the one they used to evaluate the flexilevel strategy, Betz and Weiss (1974) simulated administering parallel forms of a 40-item conventional test and two different two-stage tests to large examinee samples. One two-stage test (TS1) had item parameters identical to the test those authors had administered previously to live examinees (Weiss & Betz, 1973). The other two-stage test (TS2) was designed to improve on certain shortcomings of TS1. The simulation study results showed TS1 to be inferior to the conventional test in terms of fidelity coefficient values, parallel forms reliability, and test information. TS2 was found to be superior to both other test designs in all respects. However, TS2 had higher item discrimination parameters than either TS1 or the conventional tests, so its general superiority could not necessarily be ascribed to its adaptive nature.

Stradaptive tests. Vale and Weiss (1975) conducted a series of simulation studies with samples of 15,000 simulated examinees to compare conventional tests against two variants of a stradaptive test design. They replicated each study, systematically varying item discriminating power, test length, and the availability and quality of prior information about examinee ability (which they used to vary the initial difficulty levels of the stradaptive tests). Their criterion variables included fidelity coefficients, estimated test score information functions, and an index of how equivalent the measurement precision was across ability levels. They conducted separate evaluations of fixed and variable length adaptive tests. The results of their fixed-length test simulations will be summarized first, followed by the simulations of variable-length tests.

For the fixed-length stradaptive tests, test score fidelity coefficients increased directly with both item discriminating power and test length. The peaked conventional test's fidelity coefficient was superior to that of the stradaptive test for the lowest level of item discriminating power ($a = .50$). The stradaptive tests had greater fidelity than the conventional peaked tests at higher levels of item discrimination ($a = 1.0$ and 2.0). In terms of test information, the stradaptive tests had higher values of average information and of the equiprecision index, and their superiority over the conventional tests grew larger as test length and item discrimination parameter values increased. Vale and Weiss (1975, p. 41) concluded that "the Stradaptive strategy can produce better measurement than comparable conventional tests in terms of amount of information provided, equality of information provided at different ability levels, and in some conditions, in terms of correlations of scores with ability."

The studies of variable-length stradaptive tests departed from the paradigm of the fixed-length test studies. Like the fixed-length test studies, their simulation studies of variable-length stradaptive tests included investigations of the influence of item discriminating power. However, Vale and Weiss introduced some new wrinkles into this part of their simulation studies. For one, they also evaluated the use of variable entry level—initial stradaptive test difficulty levels based on prior fallible information about each examinee's ability level. For another, they simulated stradaptive tests with randomly varying item discriminating power (mimicking real testing conditions) in addition to their simulations of three levels of constant item discrimination (a = .50, 1.00 or 2.00). The criterion for terminating each variable-length stradaptive test was based on recent patterns of right and wrong answers. The comparison conventional tests were all the same length: 40 items.

The results were somewhat different from the fixed-length stradaptive test results. For one thing, fidelity coefficients of the stradaptive tests were lower than those of the conventional tests in the case of item discrimination parameters of $a = .50$ and 1.00; this was despite the fact that these stradaptive tests averaged 40 or more items in length. In contrast, for the case in which all $a = 2.00$, the stradaptive tests' fidelity coefficients were markedly higher than the conventional tests, despite being considerably shorter on average (28 items) than the conventional tests' 40-item length.

Also of interest, the stradaptive tests, using a random distribution of a-parameter values, demonstrated greater efficiency than the conventional tests, as follows: (1) For the stradaptive tests with the constant test entry-level condition, the fidelity coefficient was comparable to the 40-item conventional test with all $a = .50$, even though the average stradaptive test was shorter than 40 items; (2) For the variable entry level condition, the stradaptive tests were not only shorter than the conventional tests, but also superior in terms of the fidelity coefficient.

Bayesian sequential testing. Owen (1969, 1975) proposed an adaptive testing strategy based on Bayesian statistical procedures for design and analysis of sequential experiments. Owen's approach was adopted by Urry for use in an adaptive personnel testing system then under development by the U.S. Office of Personnel Management (OPM). A modified version of it is used in the CAT-ASVAB system. Simulation studies of Owen's Bayesian sequential strategy were conducted by a number of investigators in the 1970s, including Urry (1971), Jensema (1974a), Vale (1975), and McBride (1975), and McBride and Weiss (1976). Some of the most noteworthy results from these simulation studies are summarized here.

Urry favored variable-length testing using Owen's Bayesian sequential strategy. In this variant of the Bayesian sequential strategy, an individual's test is stopped as soon as the Bayes posterior variance, which typically decreases after each successive test item is scored, drops below a pre-specified target. This results in test scores with approximately equivalent measurement error. Urry and his colleagues typically evaluated tests in terms of fidelity coefficients; in fact, they used a specific value of the fidelity coefficient to specify the posterior variance target. Urry's earliest simulation studies of Owen's Bayesian strategy explored the effect on fidelity of adaptive tests' item pool characteristics including item discriminating power, item difficulty distributions, and items' susceptibility to guessing.

In one of his earliest simulation studies, Urry (1971) evaluated three different item pool designs, along with two different termination criteria—one lenient and the other more stringent. Two of the simulated item banks used idealized distributions of item difficulty—evenly spaced values of the IRT b-parameter—with all a-parameters fixed at 1.60, and all "guessing" c-parameters fixed at .20. The third item bank in this simulation study had 80 items; the item parameters were set equal to the item parameters of a real 80-item published test. In all three simulations, testing stopped as soon as either (1) the target posterior variance had been reached, or (2) 30 items had been administered.

The adaptive tests simulated using the ideal item banks yielded fidelity coefficients of .92 for the lenient criterion and .94 for the stringent criterion; average test lengths were 12 and 18 items, respectively. The adaptive test using the published test's 80-item bank had an average length of 27.5 items (with a 30-item ceiling), and achieved a .951 fidelity coefficient. (For comparison, Urry simulated administering the entire 80-item test conventionally, and found it to have a fidelity coefficient of .949 when so administered—even though it was 52.5 items longer.) Thus, the idealized item banks resulted in more efficient adaptive tests than the published test's item bank. Based on these results and those of other simulation studies that he conducted, Urry suggested a prescription for assembling an item bank for adaptive testing: Select items with a wide and uniform distribution of difficulty parameters, with high discrimination parameters (no a less than .80), and low guessing parameters (no c greater than .33).

A colleague of Urry, Jensema (1974a, 1974b) conducted simulation and analytic studies of Owen's Bayesian strategy in which he systematically varied test length, item discriminating power, and the magnitude of the guessing parameter. Jensema also tried fixed-length as well as variable-length adaptive tests. Like Urry, Jensema's studies focused on the fidelity coefficient as the figure of merit for evaluating the tests. Jensema's results demonstrated clearly that the fidelity coefficient varies directly with the magnitude of the item discrimination parameter, a, inversely with the size of the guessing coefficient, c, and directly with test length. Jensema (1974a) presented curves showing the relationship of the fidelity coefficient to test length, for each of several combinations of a- and c-parameter values.

Vale (1975) conducted a series of simulation studies comparing several adaptive strategies as well as two conventional test designs. Under conditions of no guessing, he found a fixed-length Bayesian strategy to be superior to all other strategies evaluated, in terms of test information throughout the normal range of ability.

McBride also conducted simulation studies of fixed-length Bayesian adaptive tests. His study was concerned with the properties of the Bayesian test score as an estimator of underlying ability. His study varied item discriminating powers, but kept test length constant at 30 items, and used a constant guessing parameter of .20. Results showed that the Bayesian test scores were accurate estimators of ability; the estimates had essentially no bias, except at the lowest value of simulated item discriminating power. As item discrimination increased, fidelity coefficients increased and mean errors of estimate decreased.

Jensema (1972, 1974b) conducted simulations, using both real and artificial data, of variable-length Bayesian adaptive tests based on a 58-item bank with parameters based on those of a state pre-college test. The simulations included both fixed- and variable-entry level; the latter used prior information to determine the initial ability estimate and difficulty level. Based on the results, Jensema concluded that (1) even with a small, relatively poor item pool, the Bayesian adaptive tests were substantially shorter than conventional tests, but no less valid; (2) with a suitable item pool, it is possible to estimate ability very accurately with as few as 10 to 15 items when item discrimination parameters are high; and (3) variable entry level tests using valid prior information were no more valid than fixed entry level tests, and were not appreciably shorter except when pretest information correlated .90 with the ability being measured—at which level there was little need to administer tests.

In another simulation study, Jensema (1974a) compared fixed- and variable-length Bayesian adaptive testing, using fidelity coefficients as the criterion for comparison. The results led him to conclude that the magnitude of the fidelity coefficient is a function of item discriminating power in the case of the fixed-length tests. In contrast, with variable-length tests, the fidelity coefficient is determined by the target posterior variance, provided that adequately discriminating items are available. Since the items in real item pools vary in discriminating power, he concluded that fidelity cannot be predicted accurately as a function of test length, while it is implicitly specified by the posterior variance criterion for variable-length tests.

Urry (1974a) conducted simulation studies of variable-length Bayesian adaptive tests using a bank of 200 simulated items with parameters selected from those of 700 verbal test items he had calibrated from real data. His criterion for evaluating tests was a reliability estimate—the squared fidelity coefficient. He compared the "reliability" coefficients from the simulation data against the observed reliability coefficients of 15 alternate forms of a 60-item actual test of verbal ability. The real-data reliability coefficients ranged from .86 to .90; the simulated Bayesian adaptive tests achieved this range of reliability in 10 to 15 items. Urry concluded that these simulation data demonstrated that the Bayesian adaptive test strategy was capable of achieving the same reliability as conventional tests four to six times as long.

All of the adaptive test simulation data reported thus far ignored the effects of errors in item parameter estimation. That is, they used the same item response model parameters both to generate artificial item response data and to implement the adaptive test scoring and item selection procedures. Had they used fallible item parameter estimates for item selection and ability estimation, results might have been somewhat less favorable to the adaptive tests.

Recognizing this, Schmidt and Gugel (1975) performed simulation studies to evaluate the effect of fallible item parameter estimates on the results of the variable-length Bayesian adaptive test strategy. Two parallel simulation studies, one using the known item parameters throughout, and the other using fallibly estimated item parameters as the basis for item selection and scoring were conducted. In each of the studies, data from eight different test termination criteria were reported; these criteria ranged from .30 (for a target fidelity coefficient of .84) to .05 (fidelity target .97).

Using known item parameters to control the adaptive tests, Schmidt and Gugel found the mean test length ranged from 2.6 items for the least stringent termination criterion (.30) to 13.9 for the most stringent one (.05). When the simulations were conducted using the fallibly estimated item parameters, mean test lengths were even shorter, ranging from as few as 2.0 items for the less stringent criterion to 11.9 items for the most stringent

one. The fidelity coefficients of the tests using fallible item parameters were slightly lower than the target fidelity values.

Schmidt and Gugel attributed their results—adaptive tests that were shorter and somewhat less reliable than expected, when fallible item parameter estimates were used—to a tendency of the Bayesian adaptive item selection procedure to capitalize on item parameter estimation errors, in effect selecting items with overestimated discrimination parameters. However, although the use of fallible item parameters resulted in a slight degradation in measurement precision, the adaptive tests remained highly efficient compared to conventional tests.

McBride (1975) and McBride and Weiss (1976) also conducted simulation studies of Owen's Bayesian procedure, in both its fixed- and variable-length configurations. To eliminate the influence of item bank size and difficulty parameter distribution, their simulated adaptive tests used an "infinite" item pool, by providing an artificial item with difficulty parameter equal to the current ability estimate at every stage of each individual test. Having observed that real item pools often had substantial correlations between item difficulty and discrimination parameters, McBride and Weiss included such phenomena in the design of the simulation studies; thus, some of the simulated item pools had substantial correlations (positive or negative) between the a- and b-parameters, while others had zero correlation. They also conducted separate studies, with and without guessing, by varying the c-parameters across studies.

In the case of variable-length Bayesian adaptive tests with guessing possible, McBride and Weiss found that average test length was strongly related to ability level and to any systematic correlation between the difficulty and discrimination parameters. That is, when the a- and b-parameters were positively correlated, mean test length decreased as ability level increased. When a- and b-parameters were negatively correlated or uncorrelated, they found that mean test length varied directly with ability: Low ability examinees' tests were much shorter than those of high ability examinees on average. Irrespective of the item parameter intercorrelations, they observed a curvilinear relationship between the Bayesian ability estimates and underlying ability: Low ability examinees were systematically overestimated, while high ability levels were systematically underestimated. This regression effect is characteristic of Bayesian estimators, but had not been noted by previous investigators, such as Urry and his colleagues, whose research focused on the value of fidelity coefficients.

Maximum likelihood strategies. Several adaptive testing researchers suggested strategies that employed maximum likelihood ability estimation and used item information function values as criteria for adaptive item selection. Included among them were strategies proposed by Lord (1977), Reckase (1974), and Samejima (1976). Lord's strategy, the most comprehensive, will be described here.

Lord (1977) proposed the "Broad Range Tailored Test" (BRTT), a specific application of the maximum likelihood approach. As a preparatory step, item parameters are estimated from conventional test data, and every item's information function value is computed at each of a number of discrete ability levels spanning a broad range of the ability scale. At each ability level, the items are then sorted in descending order of the information function values; resulting in rank ordering all items by their information function values at every ability level. During the adaptive test, a maximum likelihood estimate of examinee ability is computed after every item; the closest of the discrete ability levels is located, and the first unused item in the sorted list is administered next. This process continues until the test termination criterion has been achieved. Lord proposed a fixed test length of 25 items; however, the procedure could also be used with variable-length tests, using test information functions—which can be computed along with the ability estimate—to specify measurement precision.

Lord proposed, and used computer simulation to evaluate, a specific implementation of this procedure. It had a bank of 182 items taken from four major standardized verbal ability tests. IRT parameters for these items were available and were used in the simulations. In his simulations, Lord compared the results to three forms of the Preliminary Scholastic Assessment Test (PSAT), adjusted to the same 25-item length as the BRTT. His criterion for comparison was the conditional standard error of measurement—in effect, the inverse square root of the test information function. He concluded that "the tailored test is better than the 25-item PSAT at all levels of ability."

Lord's proposal for the BRTT was significant in several respects. For one, it was among the first applications of maximum likelihood ability estimation to adaptive testing. Perhaps most important was that it was a concrete proposal, based on a real bank of test items, for an adaptive test that could be applied in a specific testing program.

Summary of the Simulation Literature

Like the live-testing studies summarized earlier, prior to 1977 most simulation studies of CAT involved comparisons of the psychometric properties of adaptive and conventional test designs. Only Vale (1975) used computer simulation studies to compare different adaptive testing strategies—Owen's Bayesian sequential procedure and Weiss' stradaptive one—against one another. Because those simulation studies were limited to 24-item adaptive tests using free-response items, it was not clear that the results (which favored Owen's procedure) would generalize to different test lengths or to adaptive tests using multiple-choice test items.

Although few data were available in the mid-1970s for comparing different strategies for adaptive testing, the analytic studies conducted by Lord (1970, 1971c) and his computer simulation studies (Lord, 1977), Urry (1970, 1971, 1974a), Vale and Weiss (1975) and others effectively settled the question of the relative merits of adaptive and conventional test designs. Individually and in the aggregate, those studies demonstrated that well-designed adaptive tests were superior to conventional tests in terms of measurement precision. Compared to conventional tests, adaptive tests could achieve higher test reliability (or "fidelity"), attain higher levels of measurement precision in the upper and lower extremes of the ability scale, and reach a given level of precision in substantially fewer items.

In short, by the middle of the 1970s, a great deal of analytical and simulation research had demonstrated the theoretical potential of adaptive testing to surpass conventional testing. Absent, however, were any large-scale practical demonstrations of adaptive tests' superiority, as well as any substantial body of data comparing the psychometric merits of different adaptive testing strategies.

There were other unresolved technical issues as well. One of them had to do with broad classes of item selection strategies. Another issue had to do with adaptive test stopping rules; a third was whether to use information available prior to test administration to influence the course of the adaptive test. Each of these topics is discussed below.

Classes of item selection strategies. Even though adaptive testing was not in practical use at the time, an evolution in item selection strategies took place in the 1970s. Before that time, all adaptive testing strategies employed rigidly structured branching rules for item selection. Examples of such strategies include the pyramidal, flexilevel, and stradaptive strategies; each of those strategies required items to be positioned in a prespecified branching structure in advance of test administration. In effect, the selection of the next item to administer was governed by a mechanical branching rule (McBride, 1976a).

In contrast to those strategies were new strategies that had recently evolved. What distinguished the new strategies was their use of mathematical optimization for item selection. In these new strategies, a statistical estimate of the examinee's location on the ability scale was updated after each test item was answered, and the item that maximized some objective mathematical function was selected to be administered next. These new item selection strategies can be termed "mathematical" strategies. Examples of mathematical strategies include Owen's Bayesian sequential strategy and Lord's BRTT.

In theory, the mathematical strategies' measurement properties should be superior to those of the mechanical strategies, since the objective function used to select test items is the same function used to assess measurement precision. In the case of Owen's Bayesian procedure, the measure of precision is the variance of the posterior distribution of ability; the optimal next item is the one with the smallest expected value of the posterior variance. In the case of Lord's BRTT, the measure of precision is the test information function; the optimal next item is the one with the highest information value at the currently estimated ability level.

In practice, optimal item selection is probably not fully achieved, because of errors in the estimated item parameters. It was possible that one or more of the mechanical strategies would be as good as the optimal strategies for all practical purposes. This was important to know at the time, because the computation-intensive nature of the mathematical strategies made item selection rather slow on the computers then available—particularly on microcomputers such as Apple II and the original IBM-PC, which had 8-bit processors, often without mathematical coprocessors.

Adaptive test stopping rules. Conventional tests end when the examinee has completed every item, or when the test time limit expires. Adaptive tests may also end when all items have been answered, in the case of a "fixed-length" test. An alternative stopping rule leads to "variable-length" adaptive tests, in which examinees continue to be presented with test items until they attain a specified degree of measurement precision. This is possible in the case of the mathematical adaptive testing strategies, because they have a measure of measurement precision available after each test item. Test designers can take advantage of this by stopping the test as soon as a target level of measurement precision has been attained. This would result in different test lengths for different examinees—variable test length—in contrast to the ordinary practice of administering the same number of test items to all. Weiss (1974a), Urry (1974a), and Samejima (1976) all favored variable test length to achieve equal measurement precision for all examinees. Lord (1977), on the other hand, seemed to prefer fixed test length, judging by his proposal for the 25-item BRTT.

The choice of fixed- versus variable-length in the mathematical adaptive test strategies was a matter that had received little research attention in the 1970s; choice of one alternative or the other seemed to be made on the basis of personal preference. Advocates of variable-length adaptive tests argued that it was highly desirable from a statistical point of view to measure ability with equal precision for all examinees. Advocates of fixed-length adaptive tests pointed out that this may entail enormous variability in the test length required to achieve it, giving rise to very long tests in some cases. In computer simulations of Owen's Bayesian strategy, McBride (1975) demonstrated that the test length required to attain a specified degree of precision (gauged by the Bayes posterior variance) was strongly correlated with ability: On average, low ability examinees took much shorter tests than high ability examinees. This could lead to questions of equity. Additionally, if the adaptive test ability estimates were later transformed or combined into composite test scores for score reporting purposes, equal precision might not be preserved at all score levels.

Use of differential prior information. Adaptive tests usually start with a test item appropriate to examinees of average ability. In some cases, prior information about examinees' ability is available; for example, 12th graders are known to perform better on average than 9th graders on most aptitude tests. This prior information can be used to select items of different difficulty levels for different examinees; an adaptive test that includes this feature is called a "variable entry level" adaptive test. Intuitively, it would seem advantageous to employ variable entry levels in an adaptive test whenever there is reliable prior information about examinees' ability levels. Simulation studies conducted in the 1970s by Jensema (1972) and by Vale and Weiss (1975), however, did not bear this out.

Jensema's simulation study compared tests with constant and variable entry levels, using Owen's Bayesian strategy with a variable-length stopping rule. Jensema systematically varied the correlation between the prior information and actual ability. His primary criteria for evaluating the procedures were two: (1) the value of the resulting fidelity coefficient (the correlation between actual ability and the estimated value from the adaptive test), and (2) the mean number of items needed to attain the variable-length stopping criterion. Jensema concluded that differential prior information had little effect on these criteria except in the unrealistic case in which it correlated .90 with actual ability.

Vale and Weiss (1975) simulated stradaptive tests in which prior ability information was available that correlated .50 with actual ability. Their criteria for evaluation included fidelity coefficients and mean test information function values. Their data did not show that the use of prior ability information had any clear advantage in terms of these criteria.

Summary

As the review above indicates, by 1977 theoretical analyses and computer simulation studies clearly showed the potential measurement superiority of adaptive test strategies over conventional tests under certain conditions (e.g., Lord, 1970, 1971a, 1971b, 1971c; Urry, 1970; Vale, 1975). On the other hand, live-testing comparisons of adaptive and conventional tests had produced mixed results, some favoring the conventional tests (e.g., Betz & Weiss, 1973; Olivier, 1974) while others favored the adaptive tests (e.g., Larkin & Weiss, 1974; Waters, 1974, 1975). In many of the live-testing studies results were clouded by (1) failure to control relevant variables such as test length, item discriminating power, and difficulty levels of the conventional tests (e.g., Vale & Weiss, 1975;

Waters, 1974, 1975) or (2) loss of experimental data due to test administration irregularities (e.g., Olivier, 1974).

Further clouding the interpretation of live-testing research comparisons of adaptive and conventional tests was the fact that no major study had employed one of the mathematically-based adaptive strategies such as Owen's Bayesian strategy or the maximum likelihood/maximum information strategy used in Lord's BRTT. Well-designed, well-controlled live-testing studies that employed the most promising adaptive test strategies and avoided the flaws and pitfalls of so many previous studies were needed.

In addition to the lack of a conclusive empirical demonstration of the theoretical advantages of adaptive tests over conventional ones, there was no clear evidence of which adaptive testing strategies were superior to others. This kind of evidence could be obtained by means of computer simulation studies comparing different adaptive test strategies. However, as the research review above has shown, most of the computer simulation studies were intended either to describe the psychometric behavior of a single adaptive strategy or to compare a single adaptive strategy against a conventional test design. Of all the computer simulation research reviewed in this chapter, only the study by Vale (1975) compared two or more adaptive testing strategies. As discussed earlier, the narrow scope of that study limited the generality of its results. Nor was it possible to infer which strategies were superior to others by comparing results across studies. This was prevented by the fact that the research designs and criterion variables differed too much from study to study to support even indirect comparisons.

In conclusion, the adaptive testing research prior to 1977 showed the following: (1) adaptive testing had the potential for substantial efficiency advantages over conventional tests; (2) the potential advantages of adaptive testing had not been convincingly demonstrated in research with real tests and live examinees; (3) there was a proliferation of different strategies for adaptive testing, but little basis on which to compare them against one another, and (4) few data were available to evaluate variations such as the use of different stopping rules and use of differential prior information to set variable entry levels.

6

The Marine Corps Exploratory Development Project: 1977–1982

James R. McBride

This chapter describes the first exploratory empirical studies of the merits of computerized adaptive testing (CAT) for enlisted personnel selection testing. These studies were conducted as part of a program of exploratory development of CAT managed by the U.S. Marine Corps. The research itself was carried out by the Navy Personnel Research and Development Center (NPRDC) between 1977 and 1982.

By 1977, staff members at Marine Corps Headquarters had developed an interest in CAT as a potential solution to some practical problems associated with the administration of the ASVAB. Their interest was spurred by two events in particular: The first was a conference of CAT researchers held in Washington, DC in 1975 (Clark, 1975), at which research papers presented theoretical and empirical data showing significant advantages of CAT over conventionally designed and administered tests. The second event was a program at the U.S. Civil Service Commission to develop a tailored testing version of the Professional and Administrative Career Examination (PACE), then required of applicants for many entry-level civil service positions. Simulation studies conducted by Vern Urry and his associates at the Civil Service Com-

mission indicated that adaptive tests would make it possible to introduce substantial efficiencies in PACE administration. Small-scale pilot studies corroborated the simulation study results (Urry, 1970).

The Marine Corps Manpower Directorate, eager to assess CAT's potential for testing enlisted personnel, tasked NPRDC to develop exploratory CAT-ASVAB tests and to evaluate the feasibility and utility of the new technology. This chapter describes the research that was conducted, and the results.

Background

From the inception of this project, its planners were in close touch with the findings of researchers who were conducting pioneering work in CAT. Among the matters of concern were computer equipment, usability, and the applicability of computer simulation studies of CAT to "live" human populations.

Computer Equipment

CAT was not really even possible until the 1960s, due to hardware limitations. By the 1970s, computers capable of interactive testing and training were widely available, but they bore little resemblance to the personal computers of today. Instead, computers tended to be classed as "mainframes"

LtCol William Osgood, LtCol John Creel, Maj Michael Patrow, and Dr. Stephen Gorman were among the key planners at Headquarters, U.S. Marine Corps. Much of the success of the exploratory CAT project is due to their vision, support, and resourcefulness.

and "minicomputers." Mainframes were large, very expensive, and costly to operate and maintain, and usually served a diverse variety of users. Some mainframe computers were used in interactive systems that served large numbers of users on a time-sharing basis. Weiss (1975) observed that time-shared systems made poor platforms for computer-based testing because of unreliability of system response time, particularly when many terminals were in use simultaneously. He preferred minicomputers operating in real time (rather than time-sharing), and delivering reliable—and immediate—response to test-takers' input. Minicomputers were considerably less expensive than mainframe computers, but in the mid-1970s they typically cost in excess of $50,000, and often more than $100,000. In short, the cost of computer equipment for use in test administration was potentially prohibitive.

Usability

At the time, computer use tended to be the domain of specialists. Relatively few people had any experience with computers, and many professed to be intimidated by them. Computer phobia was part of the *zeitgeist* of the 1970s, and there was genuine concern that ordinary people could not take tests that required use of computer terminals.

Applicability of Academic Research Results

Some of the best research on adaptive testing used computer simulation to evaluate the psychometric characteristics of various approaches to conventional and adaptive test design. The computer simulations used model sampling to generate item responses, rather than using live examinees. IRT parameters and examinee ability are known quantities in such studies, which makes quantitative evaluation quite precise. Model-based computer simulation provided a means of evaluating some important features of adaptive testing rapidly and inexpensively.

However, to the extent that live examinees differ from computer models in their item response propensities, results from simulation studies may not apply to actual tests, conventional or adaptive. Additionally, some constructs—such as item and test information function (TIF) values—can be measured in simulation studies, but have no direct counterpart in live testing studies. These con-

siderations suggest that the results of computer simulation studies of adaptive tests should be regarded as theoretical findings that must be confirmed or disconfirmed empirically.

One of the principal attractions of adaptive testing was its potential to reduce test length without sacrificing reliability or measurement precision. Some research reports overstated the case, however. For example, some research administered a shortened version of a conventional test, and reported the part-whole correlation between the short and long versions as a "reliability" coefficient. In other cases, well-designed research studies failed to replicate the typical psychometric advantages of adaptive tests over conventional ones. This was especially evident for adaptive testing strategies that used classical item difficulty indices and mechanical branching rules for item selection, in contrast to IRT difficulty parameters and mathematically optimal item selection rules (Weiss, 1975).

Purpose

The thrust of this project, which was the immediate predecessor of what is now the CAT-ASVAB program, was proof of concept—that is, to demonstrate empirically the advantages of adaptive testing that had been shown in theoretical analyses and simulations. The project began with a set of objectives that could be expressed as practical questions: (1) could a computer system suitable for adaptive administration of military personnel tests be developed? (2) would computer terminals be a successful and appropriate medium for administering tests to examinees representing a broad range of backgrounds and ability levels? And most important, (3) would CAT administered in a military personnel selection setting show practical evidence of the theoretical advantages claimed on the basis of analytical and simulation studies? If so, would these advantages be sustained in a battery of tests similar to the ASVAB? The purpose of the exploratory development research reported in this chapter was to address these questions.

At that time, a number of different adaptive testing strategies had been described (e.g., by Weiss, 1974a). The strategies differed in their theoretical underpinnings, and in the technical procedures they employed for selecting items, for estimating ability, and for determining when to stop the test. The focus of this exploratory project was on evaluating the psychometric characteristics of CAT-

ASVAB, and comparing CAT to conventional tests in terms of measurement reliability, validity, and efficiency. Although some aspects of the CAT-ASVAB research relied heavily on computer simulation, this evaluation necessarily involved administering adaptive tests to human examinees. At the outset of the project, no computerized testing facilities were available to do this, so the capability had to be developed. The development and use of CAT, and the software to deliver the tests, provided a direct answer to the questions about feasibility and usability. Data collected using those tests and delivery systems provided answers to the psychometric questions.

The exploratory development project proceeded through a series of three research studies. The earliest study involved a single adaptive test, and used a computer system that in the end was deemed unsuitable for continued experimental work. Later studies in the series included adaptive tests of additional abilities, and used more capable computer facilities. In the end, the project yielded both psychometric data and a wealth of practical experience in the design of computer-based testing software and delivery systems. The psychometric data provided encouragement for more advanced research and development of adaptive testing. The practical experience directly influenced the design of an entire battery of adaptive tests parallel to the conventional ASVAB, and the development of computer systems to deliver them successfully.

Study 1: The First Adaptive Tests of Military Recruits

This study represented the first attempt to use CAT with military recruits. It was the first proof-of-concept experiment with adaptive tests in that setting. The principal objectives were (1) to test the feasibility of CAT-ASVAB in the recruit population, and (2) to corroborate empirically the theoretical advantages claimed for adaptive tests.

Study 1 Method

This study, which was reported previously by McBride & Martin (1983), used the method of equivalent tests administered to independent examinee groups. All tests measured a single ability—verbal ability—and all tests were computer administered. Each examinee took two forms of an ex-

perimental test, and a criterion test of the same ability. Data were collected in two phases. In the first phase, the tests were administered on a remote terminal controlled by a time-shared minicomputer system. That system proved incapable of administering adaptive tests on more than one terminal at a time, so in the interest of data collection efficiency, arrangements were made to administer tests simultaneously on four terminals controlled by a different minicomputer using a real-time executive system. The experimental aspects of the second phase of the study were identical to those of the first phase, except that up to four examinees could take tests simultaneously.

Examinees. All examinees were Marine Corps recruits tested in their first few days of recruit training. In the first phase, 196 examinees were tested; in the second phase, 270.

Tests. The experiment used five tests of verbal ability. One was a 50-item test constructed from obsolete forms of an operational ASVAB test. The other four were experimental tests, all constructed from a pool of 150 items specially developed and calibrated for the project; IRT calibration used the 3-parameter logistic (3PL) model. Two 30-item alternate forms of a conventional test were constructed. Two 30-item alternate adaptive tests were also constructed, but this happened dynamically under computer control. The adaptive tests used Owen's (1969) Bayesian sequential adaptive testing procedure for selecting items and estimating ability (scoring).

Procedure. Each examinee was assigned at random to take either the conventional or the adaptive experimental tests, followed by the criterion test. All tests were administered by computer. Both forms of the experimental tests were interleaved, so that each pair of items presented to the examinee contained one item from each form. This unusual arrangement was designed to balance fatigue and practice effects across the two forms, and to equalize the opportunities of both adaptive forms to select the best test items. Experimental test scores were computed after each pair of items were administered; thus, there were alternate form test scores for every test length from 1 through 30.

Analyses. The primary purpose was to compare the reliability and validity of the adaptive and conventional tests as a function of test length. For every test length, the correlations of scores on the two experimental forms with each other and with the criterion test score were computed. The alternate experimental test score correlations were reliability coefficients; the experimental test scores' correlations with the criterion test were concurrent validity coefficients.

Study 1 Results

Table 6-1 summarizes the reliability and concurrent validity data for the adaptive and the conventional test forms at six test lengths: 5, 10, 15, 20, 25, and 30 items. As the data show, the adaptive tests had considerably higher alternate forms reliability than the conventional tests at short test lengths—5 to 20 items. At longer test lengths, there was little difference between the adaptive and conventional test reliabilities, although the adaptive tests' coefficients were still slightly higher. These reliability data are mirrored in the validity data. For each unit of test length, the adaptive tests' average validity was higher than the conventional tests' validity. All of these data are perhaps best summarized graphically. Plots of the adaptive and conventional test reliability as a function of test length, are displayed in Figure 6-1. Figure 6-2 is a similar plot showing average validity for the two test designs.

Study 1 Discussion

The mere fact that Study 1 could be conducted demonstrated the practical feasibility of using computers to administer tests to military recruits. Anecdotal reports from experimenters and observers indicated that the recruits were generally favorably disposed toward taking the computer-administered tests, and encountered little difficulty in doing so.

The experience using the time-shared remote

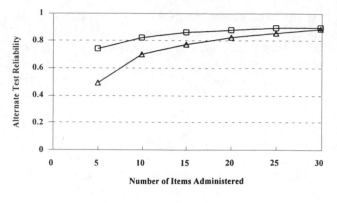

Figure 6-1
Reliability vs. Test Length for Adaptive and Conventional Tests.

computer system was another matter. The host computer was equipped with eight terminals, and capable of serving all eight simultaneously. While the adaptive testing was in progress, however, system performance was unacceptably slow if more than one terminal was used. This was apparently due to a combination of the computation-intensive nature of Owen's adaptive testing procedure, and the inefficiency of the host time-sharing computer system. The real-time system that replaced it demonstrated far superior performance, even with all four computer terminals on-line.

The data from this study corroborated a principal theoretical advantage of adaptive over conventional tests: Superior efficiency, defined in terms of the test length needed to achieve a given level of reliability or measurement precision. Figure 6-1 clearly shows that the adaptive tests' reliability was superior to the conventional tests, particularly at short to moderate test lengths. Figure 6-2 supports this, in terms of concurrent validity

Table 6-1 Reliability and Concurrent Validity Data for Adaptive and Conventional Test Forms at Six Test Lengths

	Number of Items Administered						Sample Size
	5	10	15	20	25	30	
Alternate Test Reliability							
Adaptive tests	.75	.83	.87	.89	.90	.90	355
Conventional tests	.50	.70	.78	.83	.86	.89	371
Relative efficiency	3.00	2.10	1.90	1.70	1.50	1.20	
Correlation With 50-item Criterion Test							
Adaptive tests	.73	.80	.83	.83	.84	.84	355
Conventional tests	.64	.74	.77	.79	.80	.82	371

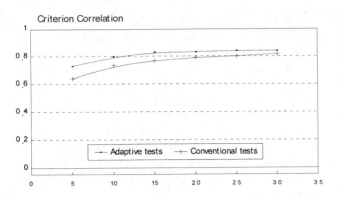

Figure 6-2
Validity vs. Test Length for Adaptive and
Conventional Tests.

against an external criterion. The relative efficiency of the adaptive tests can be evaluated by comparing the two designs in terms of the test length needed to achieve a specific degree of reliability. For example, suppose a target reliability of .80 is desired; the adaptive tests achieved it in an average of just 6 items, compared to 15 items for the conventional tests. The relative efficiency is thus 15/6, or 2.5.

Study 2: The First Battery of Adaptive Tests

The technical success of Study 1 confirmed that the theoretical promise of CAT-ASVAB could be realized in practice. It was then time to replicate the success of that study, and to extend it to include adaptive tests of other abilities. Ideally, adaptive versions of each of the ASVAB cognitive power tests would have been developed and tried out. That was not practically feasible, however, because of the expense and lead time needed to write, tryout, and calibrate hundreds of new test items using IRT models. Another obstacle was that the computer system available for adaptive testing research at the time was not equipped to display any items that involved graphics.

As an interim measure, two item banks developed and calibrated previously were made available for the research. This made it possible to administer three adaptive tests of ASVAB abilities: Word Knowledge (WK), Arithmetic Reasoning (AR), and Paragraph Comprehension (PC). In the ASVAB, those three tests made up three-fourths of the Armed Forces Qualification Test (AFQT) composite. (The fourth AFQT component at that time

was Numerical Operations [NO], a speeded test.) Trying out an adaptive battery largely parallel to the content of the AFQT was an attractive challenge, because of the important role the AFQT plays in enlistment qualification in all of the Services.

Accordingly, the decision was made that the next effort in the Marine Corps exploratory development of CAT-ASVAB would involve a battery of those three adaptive tests, and an effort to validate that battery as an alternative to AFQT. Moreno, Wetzel, McBride, & Weiss (1983) reported the details and results of that study (also see Chapter 8). It is summarized below.

Study 2 Method

Study 1 had corroborated theoretical analyses which forecast that well-constructed adaptive tests were about twice as efficient as similar conventional tests. Study 2 took that relative efficiency advantage as a given, and designed three adaptive ASVAB tests that were about half as long as their printed counterparts. As part of the study, the adaptive tests were administered to a sample of Marine recruits as part of the verification testing in addition to the paper-and-pencil. As part of Study 2, pre-enlistment and verification test scores for the recruits in the sample were obtained from personnel files. Study 2 used pre- and post-enlistment ASVAB scores, including AFQT scores, as criterion measures against which to evaluate CAT. The objective of study 2 was to determine the magnitude of the relationships between the three experimental CAT tests and their paper-and-pencil operational ASVAB counterparts.

Examinees. All examinees (N = 356) were male Marine Corps recruits in their first few days in service.

Tests. The focus of this study was on three ASVAB tests: AR, WK, and PC. Both experimental CAT and operational ASVAB tests provided the test scores used in the analyses. The experimental CAT battery consisted of CAT versions of the three tests. The CAT-AR test consisted of 15 items chosen adaptively from a bank of 225 items developed for adaptive testing use. The CAT-WK test, also a 15-item adaptive test, used an item bank containing 78 items. The CAT-PC test was an 8-item adaptive test, with an item bank containing just 25 items.

CAT-AR and CAT-WK items had been calibrated on large samples of examinees tested via paper-and-pencil, using the 3PL model. CAT-PC items, which were calibrated on item response data collected from smaller samples of examinees tested via computer, used the 1-parameter logistic (Rasch) model. Details of the item bank construction for all three tests are reported by Moreno et al. (1983). All of the adaptive tests used Owen's (1969) Bayesian sequential adaptive testing procedure for item selection and ability estimation (scoring). The paper-and-pencil ASVAB data were obtained from personnel records of the examinees' pre- and post-enlistment ASVAB scores.

Procedure. The three CAT-ASVAB tests were administered over a three-month period to 356 available Marine recruits who had just reported for basic training. The recruits routinely took the post-enlistment ASVAB battery approximately two weeks later, during their training. Pre-enlistment ASVAB testing took place from two days to six months prior to service entry. Although all ASVAB score data in the personnel records were collected, for purposes of this study the operational ASVAB scores of interest were the pre- and post-enlistment scores on AR, WK, PC, and AFQT. Thus, there were three measures of each of the three ASVAB abilities: One from the CAT test, one from pre-enlistment, and one from the post-enlistment retest. Examinees missing scores on any of the tests, and a few who had taken an obsolete pre-enlistment ASVAB form, were dropped from the analysis; 270 cases with complete data remained.

Analyses. This study assessed whether CAT tests of ASVAB abilities were as reliable as the operational versions, and whether a composite of the three CAT tests could effectively estimate AFQT scores. To address the reliability issue, product-moment correlations of the ASVAB scores on each of the three versions were computed. To address the validity issue, two multiple correlations were computed. The dependent variable in both cases was pre-enlistment AFQT score. The predictor variables in the first case were the CAT-AR, -WK and -PC scores; the post-enlistment ASVAB AR, WK, PC, and NO scores were the predictor variables in the second case.

Study 2 Results

Table 6-2 summarizes the data from Study 2—means, standard deviations, and intercorrelations among all the test scores. All correlations between same-named tests are underlined. As the data show, each CAT-ASVAB correlated slightly higher with its pre-enlistment counterpart than the ASVAB retest scores did. The CAT-AR, CAT-WK, and CAT-PC scores correlated .80, .81, and .51, respectively, with their pre-enlistment counterparts. The comparable post-enlistment tests' correlations with pre-enlistment scores were .77, .77, and .46. The correlations between CAT and post-enlistment test scores were .80 (AR), .80 (WK), and .51 (PC).

The multiple correlation of pre-enlistment AFQT with the three CAT-ASVAB scores was .87. The cor-

Table 6-2 Descriptive Statistics and Intercorrelations of Experimental CAT-ASVAB Tests, and Operational ASVAB Pre-Enlistment and Post-Enlistment Tests

Tests	# Items	Mean	s.d.	1	2	3	4	5	6	7	8	9
		Statistics						Intercorrelations				
					Pre-enlistment ASVAB								
1. AR	30	21.8	5.4	—								
2. WK	35	28.2	4.9	.48	—							
3. PC	15	11.8	2.2	.46	.57	—						
					Post-enlistment ASVAB								
4. AR	30	21.4	5.7	.77	.49	.50	—					
5. WK	35	28.1	4.9	.42	.77	.52	.48	—				
6. PC	15	11.5	2.5	.49	.52	.46	.55	.58	—			
					Computerized Adaptive Tests								
7. AR	15	.40	.82	.80	.50	.51	.80	.49	.50	—		
8. WK	15	.59	.79	.53	.81	.55	.56	.80	.60	.58	—	
9. PC	8	.08	.85	.43	.49	.51	.50	.53	.51	.52	.56	—

responding multiple correlation with post-enlistment ASVAB scores (including NO) was .85. By way of comparison, the correlation between pre-enlistment and post-enlistment AFQT scores was also .85.

Study 2 Discussion

This study was the first known comparison of a battery of computerized adaptive tests with an operational test battery. The availability of repeated measures on the operational ASVAB tests made it possible to compare CAT and paper-and-pencil tests in terms of test-retest correlation, with a comparable interval between the first and second administrations. Although the differences were not significant, each of the CAT tests had a slightly higher retest reliability than the comparable post-enlistment ASVAB test. The multiple correlation results were similar: A composite of three CAT-ASVAB tests estimated AFQT scores about as precisely (.87 vs. .85) as a composite of the same four post-enlistment tests that define the AFQT composite. Furthermore, the CAT-AFQT multiple correlation (.87) was at least as high as the AFQT test-retest correlation (.85).

These results supported the interpretation that each of the three CAT-ASVAB tests measured its respective ability variable with superior precision over P&P-ASVAB. What made these results remarkable was that the CAT tests were much shorter than their P&P counterparts. The entire battery of CAT tests consisted of 38 items (15 AR, 15 WK, and 8 PC). The combined length of the operational ASVAB tests was 80 items (30 AR, 35 WK, and 15 PC). Claims of an efficiency advantage of adaptive testing over conventional tests, predicted by theory and corroborated in Study 1, were further buttressed by extending these findings to three additional tests.

Study 3: The First Structural Analysis of Adaptive Tests

The results of Studies 1 and 2 made a strong empirical case for the proposition that adaptive testing could achieve in practice, the efficiency and measurement precision advantages that were claimed for it on the basis of theoretical analyses and simulation studies. The analyses reported so far did not, however, address the question of whether computerized adaptive tests had the same structural relationships to a broader range of cognitive abilities as their conventional printed counterparts.

Study 3 addressed this issue by means of factor analysis. No new data were collected, but additional analyses were conducted on the data collected in Study 2. Recall that ASVAB scores were transcribed from the examinees' personnel files. While Study 2 focused only on the AR, WK, and PC score data, pre- and post-enlistment scores for all 10 ASVAB tests were collected. For the purposes of Study 3, these scores were augmented with the three CAT-ASVAB test scores, and the entire matrix of intercorrelations was analyzed. The objective was to explore the congruence of the three CAT tests with the underlying structure of the ASVAB. Full details of the design and the analysis were reported by Moreno et al. (1983, pp. 7–9).

Study 3 Method

All 10 ASVAB pre-enlistment scores and their counterpart post-enlistment retest scores were collected from the personnel files of the Marine recruits who participated. Those data were combined with their ability estimates on the three CAT tests, AR, WK, and PC. Factor analysis of the intercorrelations of the test scores was conducted.

Examinees. The same 356 examinees described in Study 2 were the subjects in this study.

Variables. Between the operational ASVAB and the experimental CAT-ASVAB tests, there were a total of 23 test scores—10 pre-enlistment ASVAB scores, 10 post-enlistment ASVAB retest scores, and scores on the CAT tests of AR, WK, and PC.

Procedure. The 270 cases with complete data on current ASVAB forms were retained for data analysis.

Analysis. Product-moment correlations among the 20 ASVAB and 3 CAT-ASVAB test scores were calculated. The resulting correlation matrix was subjected to principal axes factor analysis. Four common factors were extracted, consistent with previously published ASVAB factor analysis findings, and rotated to simple structure using the varimax criterion.

Study 3 Results

Table 6-3 contains factor loadings of all 23 test scores on the four rotated principal factors. The sa-

Table 6-3 Factor Loadings of the 23 ASVAB and CAT-ASVAB Test Scores on the Four Varimax-Rotated Principal Factors

		Factor			
		I	II	III	IV
	Test	Verbal	Quant	Technical	Speed
		Pre-enlistment ASVAB			
GS	General Science	<u>62</u>	27	45	07
AR	Arithmetic Reasoning	31	<u>75</u>	21	15
WK	Word Knowledge	<u>82</u>	22	16	07
PC	Paragraph Comprehension	<u>56</u>	34	08	08
NO	Numerical Operations	04	24	12	<u>68</u>
CS	Coding Speed	13	06	00	<u>72</u>
AS	Auto & Shop Information	12	05	<u>81</u>	−02
MK	Mathematics Knowledge	31	<u>73</u>	19	26
MC	Mechanical Comprehension	35	41	<u>49</u>	11
EI	Electronic Information	34	23	<u>56</u>	02
		Post-enlistment ASVAB			
GS	General Science	<u>58</u>	33	49	07
AR	Arithmetic Reasoning	34	<u>72</u>	27	23
WK	Word Knowledge	<u>82</u>	17	23	08
PC	Paragraph Comprehension	<u>54</u>	30	17	26
NO	Numerical Operations	10	21	−08	<u>56</u>
CS	Coding Speed	06	07	04	<u>73</u>
AS	Auto & Shop Information	08	05	<u>84</u>	02
MK	Mathematics Knowledge	37	<u>72</u>	18	26
MC	Mechanical Comprehension	25	41	<u>63</u>	13
EI	Electronic Information	31	30	<u>63</u>	−01
		Computerized Adaptive Tests			
AR	Arithmetic Reasoning	35	<u>76</u>	20	21
WK	Word Knowledge	<u>83</u>	25	26	13
PC	Paragraph Comprehension	<u>54</u>	33	12	10

lient factor loadings of specific ASVAB tests were consistent with previous factor analyses of the ASVAB (cf., Waters et al., 1988).

Specifically: (1) Word Knowledge and Paragraph Comprehension tests loaded highest on one factor, the Verbal ability factor usually identified in factor analyses of the ASVAB; (2) Arithmetic Reasoning, and Mathematics Knowledge loaded highest on a second previously known factor, Quantitative ability; (3) Mechanical Comprehension (MC), Auto & Shop Information, and Electronics Information loaded highest on a third factor, Technical ability; (4) Numerical Operations and Coding Speed loaded highest on a fourth factor, Speed. The factor loadings of the pre-enlistment test scores were very similar to those of the post-enlistment scores, both in pattern and in magnitude.

The three CAT tests' factor loadings were very similar in pattern to the loadings of the same-named ASVAB tests. CAT-AR loaded highest on the Quantitative ability factor, but also had a substantial loading on Verbal ability. CAT-WK and CAT-PC loaded highest on the Verbal ability factor. Notably, all three CAT-ASVAB tests had slightly higher factor loadings than their ASVAB counterparts, on their respective two salient factors.

Study 3 Discussion

The factor analysis results provided an important complement to the data from Studies 1 and 2 on the reliability and validity of CAT-ASVAB. Those studies demonstrated that CAT's theoretical efficiency could be realized in practice, but they did not provide evidence addressing the question of whether adaptive tests, administered by computer, measured the same ability constructs as their paper-and-pencil counterparts. The factor analysis results dispelled any doubt about that question: All three of the tests in the CAT battery behaved almost identically to their counterparts in the operational P&P-ASVAB battery. Their loadings on the salient ASVAB factors were almost identical in magnitude to those of their P&P-ASVAB namesakes, and their loadings on the other factors shared the same pattern seen among the ASVAB tests.

Summary

The three studies summarized in this chapter provided convincing evidence that it was possible to develop computerized adaptive tests having all the advertised efficiency advantages. They demonstrably measured ASVAB abilities despite the substantial differences between adaptive and conventional testing in terms of the test administration medium and test design procedures. In the aggregate, the results of these studies — as well as others not reported here — provided the technical impetus that propelled the CAT-ASVAB program from an exploratory development effort to full-scale system development.

7

The Computerized Adaptive Screening Test

W. A. Sands, Paul A. Gade, and Deirdre J. Knapp

The pool of youth in the age bracket between 17 and 21 constitutes the major source of new enlistees for the Armed Services of the United States. To understand the historical context in which the Computerized Adaptive Screening Test (CAST) was developed in the early 1980s, it is important to know that the size of this pool had been declining since 1978, and forecasts indicated that it would continue to drop substantially through the late 1990s (Congressional Budget Office, 1980). This trend, viewed in conjunction with the increasing sophistication of modern weapons systems, meant that the recruiting commands of the Armed Services faced a very serious and costly challenge in attracting and enlisting a sufficient quantity and quality of young people to meet U.S. military goals for enlisted personnel (Joint Chiefs of Staff, 1982). This difficult recruiting market was made even more problematic by the intensifying of the natural competition between the Military Services. Added to the inter-Service rivalry was the competition from colleges, universities, and private employers trying to attract the same high-ability, high school graduates from this age group (Sands & Rafacz, 1983).

If the Armed Services were to meet this challenge successfully, they would have to become remarkably efficient and effective in their recruiting strategies. The best candidates would have to be located, sold on the idea of enlisting, processed for enlistment, and optimally assigned to initial training. Precious fiscal and recruiting personnel resources could not be wasted. Indeed, any tasks that reduced the time and effort spent by military recruiters on their primary mission of enlisting qualified applicants would have to be minimized

(Baker, Rafacz, & Sands, 1984). This situation provided an impetus for the introduction of groundbreaking improvements into pre-screening for the ASVAB as part of the military personnel recruiting and accessioning process.

Benefits of ASVAB Prescreening

A military applicant must achieve a minimum qualifying score on the Armed Forces Qualification Test (AFQT) composite of the ASVAB to be considered eligible for enlistment. ASVAB testing in a MEPS or METS is an expensive part of recruiting. Direct financial costs include transportation, food, and sometimes lodging, and there are indirect costs such as recruiter time to cultivate and process applicants. These substantial investments are wasted if the prospect does not achieve a qualifying AFQT score. Therefore, before making substantial investments for ASVAB testing, recruiters need a way to assess the prospect's chances of qualifying for enlistment. Beyond immediate costs, persons who are sent for ASVAB testing but fail to qualify often feel that they have wasted their time, and they return to their community with a negative attitude that can have a detrimental impact on subsequent recruiting activities (Sands, Gade, & Bryan, 1982). On the other hand, if prospective applicants who are likely to have achieved quali-

Many individuals, in addition to the authors, made significant contributions to the research, development, and evaluation of the CAST. Listed alphabetically, these people include H. G. Baker, J. D. Bryan, F. Grafton, J. R. McBride, J. McHenry, R. K. Park, R. M. Pliske, B. A. Rafacz, and L. L. Wise.

fying scores are not sent for ASVAB testing, the Services lose valuable potential recruits (Pliske, Gade, & Johnson, 1984). Obviously, the accuracy of a recruiter's decisions about sending prospects for testing is an important component of an efficient recruiting process.

The Enlistment Screening Test

The Enlistment Screening Test (EST) was first developed in 1976 by the Air Force Human Resources Laboratory (AFHRL) to provide an applicant screening tool for recruiters (Jensen & Valentine, 1976). New forms of the EST, a paper-and-pencil predictor of AFQT score, were developed in 1981 (Mathews & Ree, 1982) and 1990 (Divgi, 1990). EST-81, the version of EST that was operational when CAST was created, included 48 multiple-choice items. EST-81 items were similar to ASVAB items on the Word Knowledge (WK), Arithmetic Reasoning (AR), and Paragraph Comprehension (PC) tests (the three ASVAB tests accounting for most of the AFQT score). At the time the EST-81 was constructed, the AFQT also included Numerical Operations (NO), a speeded test, but NO items were not included on the EST because of the administration problems NO precise timing would pose on recruiters. EST-90 is larger than earlier versions (65 items) and includes WK, AR, and Math Knowledge (MK) items. MK items were added because this test replaced the speeded NO test in 1989 in computing AFQT; PC items were dropped because they were so time-consuming to administer. The EST is available for use by recruiters in all of the U.S. Military Services.

Although the EST provides relatively accurate predictions of AFQT scores for applicants (Divgi, 1990; Mathews & Ree, 1982), it suffers from many drawbacks common to paper-and-pencil tests: (1) lengthy administration time, (2) relatively poor measurement precision at the extremes of the ability distribution, (3) susceptibility to test compromise, (4) cumbersome scoring and interpretation procedures, and (5) expensive and time-consuming replacement with new editions (Sands et al., 1982).

The recruiter administers and scores the EST, and interprets the resultant scores using printed conversion tables. The test takes about 45 minutes to administer. Hand scoring by the recruiter takes additional time and introduces the chance for human error. Furthermore, because there are only two forms of the EST, an applicant might be able to compromise the test by taking it at different recruiting stations and memorizing a sufficient number of items to achieve a qualifying score (Pliske et al., 1984). Additional recruiter duties include inventorying the test booklets, removing stray marks in the booklets from previous administrations, and ordering and storing supplies. Thus, the EST is a labor-intensive instrument that consumes the time of a senior noncommissioned officer in quasi-clerical tasks (Baker et al., 1984).

At the same time in the early 1980s that the military recruiting environment was becoming ever more competitive, advances in psychometric theory and microcomputer technology made possible the operational introduction of CAT technology into the military personnel accessioning process. CAT held the promise of eliminating, or substantially reducing, the problems in the recruiting process associated with the use of EST.

The Navy's *CAST*away Joins the Army

In fiscal year (FY) 1979, the Navy Personnel Research and Development Center (NPRDC) initiated a research program called the Navy Personnel Accessioning System (NPAS). This microcomputer-based system was designed to support Navy recruiters at the level of individual recruiting stations within the Navy Recruiting Command. The system involved four integrated functions: Aptitude screening, vocational guidance, assignment prediction, and management support (Sands, 1981). The extensive NPAS R&D is documented in a series of three NPRDC reports (Baker, 1983a, 1983b; Baker, Rafacz, & Sands, 1983) and in papers presented at the annual conference of the Military Testing Association (Sands, 1980, 1981).

The Navy Recruiting Command suffered a substantial budget reduction in FY 1981 and the NPAS program was one of the R&D programs cut. A program decision-briefing and accompanying computer-based demonstration were developed and presented to Rear Admiral Miller, the Commander, Navy Recruiting Command. He was quite enthusiastic, asking many questions and actively participating in the hands-on demonstration. While his positive attitude was encouraging, his staff indicated after the session that additional budget cuts had occurred and that the Navy Recruiting Command was "going to have trouble finding the funds to put gasoline in recruiters' cars." This new information, needless to say, dampened NPRDC optimism about the fate of NPAS.

The next day, a room was set up to "show-and-tell" the NPAS to a wider audience. Navy managers and personnel representing the other Services were invited to attend the briefing and hands-on demonstration, and many of the visitors expressed interest in the project. Dr. Paul Gade, from the Army Research Institute for the Behavioral and Social Sciences (ARI), turned out to be a key player in subsequent developments.

General Maxwell Thurman, then the Commanding General of the Army Recruiting Command (USAREC) had recently directed ARI to develop computer-based tools for supporting Army recruiters in the field. The Army system was called the Joint Optical Information Network (JOIN), and employed then state-of-the-art microprocessor and videodisc technology. The JOIN system was planned to support six major functions at the Army recruiting station level: Sales presentation, aptitude screening, vocational guidance, classification and assignment, personnel training, and management support. Dr. Gade indicated that he would be interested in exploring the possibility of Army funding for the NPAS team if the Navy Recruiting Command canceled Navy support of the NPAS which subsequently occurred. Mr. Sands and Dr. Gade, in concert with the directors of their respective R&D laboratories, Dr. Martin Wiskoff (NPRDC) and Dr. Joyce Shields (ARI), crafted a three-year agreement for FY1982 through FY1984. Army funds were transferred to NPRDC to support completion of the NPAS research for the JOIN system (Sands, 1983).

The Die Is *CAST*: Developing the Test

CAST was designed to operate on a microcomputer in a military recruiting station where it would at least supplement, and perhaps replace, the conventionally administered EST. Specifically, the objective of CAST was to predict a prospect's AFQT score as well as, or better than, the EST, while reducing recruiter time and clerical burden (Sands, 1983).

Initial Item Bank Calibration and Pilot Testing

In a separate contract effort (Prestwood & Vale, 1984), University of Minnesota researchers built item banks for use in developing a CAT version of the ASVAB. Like EST-81, items were developed for three tests: WK, AR, and PC. The test items were calibrated using the three-parameter logistic (3PL) ogive item response theory (IRT)

model (Birnbaum, 1968). Thus, each item had a discrimination, difficulty, and guessing parameter estimate.

Moreno, Wetzel, McBride, and Weiss (1984) assessed the relationship between P&P and CAT versions of the ASVAB WK, AR, and PC tests (see Study 2, Chapter 6). Their research provided a *de facto* pilot test for CAST. During a three-month period in 1981, they administered the three tests to 356 recruits at the Marine Corps Recruit Depot, San Diego. Each examinee had already taken the P&P version of ASVAB to qualify for enlistment into the Marine Corps. Examinees were retested with a parallel form of the P&P-ASVAB during recruit processing. The sample size was reduced to 270 by the elimination of those with missing scores on any test and those who had taken a form of P&P-ASVAB no longer in use.

Each of the CAT tests had a fixed number of items (15 WK, 15 AR, and 8 PC). All examinees began each CAT test with the same item, which was of intermediate difficulty. The Bayesian sequential scoring method discussed by Jensema (1974b) was used. The Stratified Maximum Information (STMI) method was used to select items for administration. This strategy incorporated a randomization procedure designed to reduce item exposure.

This initial research demonstrated that military recruits and, by implication, military applicants could be administered aptitude tests on a computer with minimal intervention required by test administrators (TAs) (Baker et al., 1984). Factor analyses indicated that the CAT-ASVAB tests measured the same abilities as the P&P-ASVAB tests, while using only about half the number of items (Moreno et al., 1984). When the P&P AFQT score was regressed on the three CAT AFQT-related tests, only WK and AR, were significant predictors. The multiple correlation was .87. Because the PC test did not contribute significantly to the prediction of AFQT (after using WK and AR), and PC items are very time-consuming to administer, PC was excluded from the first operational version of CAST. The original CAST item bank included 78 WK items and 225 AR items, each with a maximum of five response alternatives.

Field Test

Field testing and initial validation of the CAST was conducted at the Los Angeles MEPS between November 1982 and January 1983 (Sands & Gade, 1983). The purpose of the study was to collect data on CAST to determine (1) the acceptability of the interactive computer dialogues, (2) the effectiveness of the WK and AR tests for predicting AFQT scores, and (3) the length for the two operational tests.

In the field test, CAST was administered to 364 Army applicants who had already completed the P&P-ASVAB. The CAST software dialogues appeared to work well with this group of examinees. Each examinee received 20 WK items and 15 AR items. Removal of persons with missing data (e.g., AFQT score) produced a usable sample of 312 persons (251 males and 61 females). Means, standard deviations, and zero-order validity estimates were computed at each possible test length for each of the two tests against the AFQT criterion. Then, to determine the best prediction model for forecasting AFQT scores from WK and AR scores, 300 separate multiple correlation analyses were performed, one for each possible combination of test lengths (20 WK x 15 AR). The multiple correlation between P&P AFQT and CAST's WK and AR tests, with one item each, was .62. At full length for each test (WK = 20 and AR = 15), the multiple correlation was .89.

Two criteria were considered in evaluating alternative combinations of test lengths: (1) accuracy—the effectiveness of the composite for predicting AFQT score, and (2) efficiency—the time required to administer the two tests. A review of the multiple correlation coefficients for the various test length combinations revealed that no single combination had a clear predictive accuracy advantage.

No timing data were available for varying test lengths. However, experience with the two types of items suggested that AR items take two to three times as long to administer as WK items. Therefore, for a constant level of predictive accuracy, it would be better to administer more WK items and fewer AR items. With this administrative efficiency in mind, the combination recommended for operational use was ten WK and five AR items. The validity estimate for the recommended combination was .85. Despite the fact that this validity estimate may have somewhat capitalized on chance factors, the validity of the composite was expected to remain high for two reasons: (1) the sample size of 312 was reasonably large, considering that only two predictor variables were involved, and (2) there was no predictor variable selection from a larger candidate set (Sands & Gade, 1983). Sands & Rafacz (1983) estimated that CAST would require about 15 minutes for administration. Based on a national sample of prospects from whom actual timing data were subsequently col-

lected, the estimate was revised by Knapp and Pliske (1986a) to a 12-minute average administration time for the ten WK and five AR items.

*CAST*ing Doubt Aside: Implementing and Cross-Validating the Test

The results of the initial validation study, conducted in the Los Angeles MEPS, indicated that CAST predicted AFQT score at least as accurately as the EST, while requiring considerably less administration time (Sands & Gade, 1983). Thus, the decision was made by the Army to implement CAST on a regional basis. By the end of 1983, CAST was fully operational in the midwestern region of the U.S.

Regional CAST Cross-Validation

The purpose of the next study was to cross-validate CAST and to provide information that could be used by Army recruiters to predict AFQT scores for enlisted applicants (Pliske et al., 1984). CAST was administered to enlistment prospects in Army recruiting stations in the midwest before they were sent to a MEPS for further entrance processing. Data were collected during January and February 1984. CAST scores were matched against ASVAB scores and demographic information available from military entrance processing data files. Matched data were available for 1,962 persons. Eighty-five percent of the sample was male; 79 percent was white (Pliske et al., 1984).

A correlation of .80 between CAST and AFQT scores was found in this cross-validation sample. While this is lower than the validity estimate of .85 obtained in the initial validation study, some shrinkage was expected due to capitalization on chance factors.

The original CAST software portrayed an examinee's performance as shown in Figure 7-1. The WK and AR scores were theta scores transformed into a common metric. The predicted AFQT (P-AFQT) score was based on regression weights reported by Sands and Gade (1983). To further facilitate the recruiters' interpretation of CAST scores, an equal percentile equating between CAST scores and AFQT scores was performed.

A second strategy for facilitating interpretation of CAST performance was based on the fact that recruiters are more interested in the AFQT category (see Chapter 1) than in exact AFQT scores. That is, the important thing to know about a prospect is his

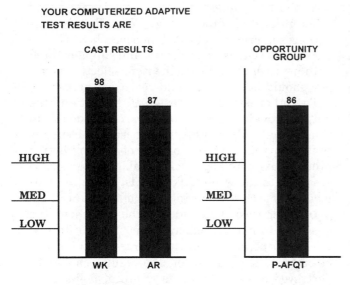

YOUR COMPUTERIZED ADAPTIVE
TEST RESULTS ARE

Figure 7-1
Sample Output from the Original CAST.

or her predicted AFQT category, since category designation determines eligibility for enlistment and, subsequently, for various enlistment programs, bonuses, and types of jobs. To assist recruiters in predicting AFQT category for a prospect, discriminant analyses were used to determine the best function for relating CAST scores to the AFQT categories of interest (I/II, IIIA, IIIB, and IV/V). Using this discriminant function, posterior probabilities of prospects being classified into the various categories were computed, based upon their CAST score. Look-up tables based on the equal percentile equating and the AFQT category probability estimates were created and provided to recruiters to assist them in deciding how to proceed with prospects having particular CAST scores. Discriminant analysis results showed that CAST did a reasonably good job of classifying prospects into AFQT categories.

National Cross-Validation

Once CAST was fully operational at the end of 1984, its performance was further evaluated in a nationwide study. The study had several objectives: (1) evaluate the prediction equation originally developed for CAST; (2) develop and evaluate a new prediction equation; and (3) describe CAST item bank usage and administration time (Knapp, 1987b).

In this study, CAST performance data were collected on 14,410 Army prospects for enlistment in 60 Army recruiting stations across the nation (Knapp, 1987b; Knapp & Pliske, 1986b). The recruiting stations were chosen to be representative of all Army recruiting stations in terms of both geographical location and population density. AFQT scores (derived from full ASVAB testing) were matched to CAST scores for only 5,929 of the 14,410 examinees, primarily because many prospects were not sent for ASVAB testing. This sample was 82 percent male and 58 percent white. The demographic characteritics of the sample are fully described in Knapp (1987b).

The operational version of the JOIN system software that administered the original CAST recorded the name and CAST score for examinees onto a "Prospect Data" diskette. This software was modified to collect additional information on special diskettes that were forwarded each month to ARI for analysis. The information collected for the study included the examinee's social security number, the item identification number for each item administered to that examinee, the response to each item, and the item response time. In addition, the operational software was modified to administer five more items beyond those used to compute the CAST score. This allowed a re-examination of the test's stopping rule.

In 1986, a change was made in the algorithm used to convert raw AFQT scores to percentiles. The AFQT scores for this test of CAST were converted to the new scale. Furthermore, in addition to cross-validating the original CAST prediction equation, the large sample of data collected permitted developing and evaluating a new prediction equation designed for the new AFQT. For developing and cross-validating a new equation for forecasting AFQT score from the WK and AR scores of CAST, the total sample (N = 5,929) was divided into a developmental sample (N = 4,166) and an evaluation sample (N = 1,763).

The first study objective concerned the evaluation of the original CAST prediction equation. The cross-validity of CAST scores, computed using the original prediction equation for predicting the revised AFQT scores (based upon 1980 norms), was .79. This value increased to .83 after correction for range restriction.

The second objective concerned development and evaluation of a new prediction equation. The AFQT scores were regressed on WK and AR scores in the development sample, yielding a multiple correlation of .79. The optimal weights determined in this development sample were employed to forecast AFQT scores in the evaluation sample, yielding a cross-validity estimate of .80. The lack of shrinkage was attributed to the large sample used in developing the equation and the fact that there were only two predictor variables (Knapp, 1987b).

The third study objective concerned adminstrative issues of item usage and testing time. Sixty-three of the 78 WK items were administered 15 or more times to the 14,410 examinees. Only 54 of the 225 AR items were administered 15 or more times. After reporting item usage figures, Knapp (1987b) pointed out that the "operational" item banks were smaller than the "actual" item banks. She noted that item characteristics of the WK item pool were more desirable than those of the AR pool; however, both item banks met minimum psychometric standards (Urry, 1974a).

To evaluate the issue of test length, multiple correlations were computed for combinations of test lengths for WK (5 to 15) and AR (5 to 10). The multiple validity coefficients ranged from .76 for both tests at a length of five, to .83 when 15 WK items were combined with ten AR items. Mean testing times for the various test lengths ranged from 14 minutes (WK = 5 items, AR = 5 items) to 25 minutes (WK = 15 items, AR = 10 items). The assessment of test lengths indicated that no changes to the stopping rule (WK = 10, AR = 5) were warranted.

As indicated by Knapp (1987b), the evidence clearly demonstrated that CAST was an effective predictive tool for the recruiter in assessing a prospect's chances of qualifying for enlistment. The revised regression equation was incorporated into the operational version of CAST in 1986.

CASTing Improvements

Although the original CAST was a major success both as a computerized adaptive test and as a pragmatic recruiting tool, it was not without some shortcomings. During the course of initial implementation and cross-validation efforts described above, ARI researchers noted several areas of potential improvement in the test. The item-level data collected in the national cross-validation (Knapp, 1987b) showed that many of the items in the WK and AR item pools were being under-utilized, while others were being severely over-exposed. There was also concern that, because the items were originally intended for experimental usage, they may not have been sufficiently

screened for gender and cultural sensitivity and differential item functioning (DIF). These observations suggested that the item pools should be reviewed, revised as appropriate, and supplemented with new items, and that the item selection strategy should be reviewed and revised if necessary.

Two other issues, the design of the test and the output provided to recruiters, were raised several times. The unifying theme of these two issues is that both relate to the nature of the prediction problem. As noted by Pliske et al. (1984), recruiters need to know how likely it is that an enlistment prospect will fall into one of several critical AFQT categories. Thus, ideally the test should be designed to make predictions most accurately at critical cutpoints rather than across the full range of performance. Moreover, the results should be portrayed to recruiters in a way that helps them interpret a prospect's performance for this purpose *and* that conveys the notion of measurement error (Knapp, 1987a).

These issues and others were addressed in a major revision of the test undertaken between 1987 and 1989. In addition, the revision also sought to refine the CAST by re-examining its psychometric foundations in light of developments in IRT and adaptive testing principles subsequent to the design of the original test. The revision and refinement of CAST are summarized below.

Item Pool

The original CAST item pools contained 78 WK items and 225 AR items. One of the problems which led to item over- and under-exposure was that items were not equally distributed across difficulty levels. For example, there were too few easy AR items, which meant that often there were not enough appropriate AR items to administer to relatively low-scoring applicants.

To address the item pool size problem, 197 new WK items and 50 new AR items were added to the item bank, thereby expanding it to 275 WK and 275 AR items. All items, including those in the original item pools, were subjected to editorial and sensitivity review and revision. All items in the enhanced item pool, including items from the original CAST, were recalibrated (Wise, McHenry, Chia, Szenas, & McBride, 1990).

The primary calibration sample included 20,037 new recruits who were given P&P tests of both new and old items. Each soldier took a test containing 50 WK and 50 AR items, yielding 700–800 responses per item for four subgroups (i.e., black and white examinees, and male and female examinees). On average, each item was administered to 3,855 examinees, including 881 blacks and 704 women.

The primary sample of soldiers, who had already met the AFQT qualification requirements, was restricted in the lower portion of the score range where only 6 percent of the sample had scored at or below the 31st percentile on the AFQT. To provide accurate parameter estimates for the easy items in the CAST item pool, a supplemental sample of 3,968 prospects was administered additional items when they took the CAST in recruiting stations. The experimental test items were presented by a program embedded in the CAST software that permitted the administering of up to six additional WK and six additional AR items per examinee. The extra items were transparent to recruiters and examinees. About 20 percent of the supplemental sample (n = 796) subsequently took the AFQT. Twenty-eight percent of those who did take the AFQT scored at or below the 31st percentile, so the goal of providing more respondents to calibrate easier items was achieved.

The primary purpose of this recalibration process was to provide information for selecting a sufficient number of items at low as well as high difficulty levels and for eliminating items that failed to discriminate between low- and high-ability individuals. In addition, items shown to be biased against blacks and females were eliminated. The final revised CAST item bank consisted of 257 WK and 254 AR items.

Testing Strategy

CAST item selection method, test length, and stopping rules were carefully examined for ways to improve the CAST testing strategy. After advantages and disadvantages of various methods were reviewed, the Stratified Maximum Information (STMI) method for selecting items, used by the original CAST, was retained, as it maximized the information value of the item for a particular individual test administration without the unacceptable computation delays or predictable sequences of items produced by other methods (Wise et al., 1990). Although the basic item selection strategy remained unchanged, its application was slightly modified to further limit item overexposure. Software programmers were also able to increase the speed at which new items were presented to examinees.

CAST used prior normal distributions of ability with a mean of 0 and a standard deviation of 1 for WK and AR tests to determine the starting point for test administration. A strategy of using the performance on the WK test to set the prior ability estimate for the AR test was examined. The decision was to retain the original starting point strategy, based on one overriding consideration—test fairness. Because the Bayesian scoring strategy of CAST tends to regress toward the starting point, and different individuals and groups of individuals would be likely to have different starting points, the potential for differential bias (or the appearance of bias) was too great a cost for possible minor benefits in reduced testing time.

A fixed test length of 10 WK and 5 AR items was used for the original CAST administration. Two alternatives were considered in revising CAST: Adopting a variable-length stopping rule, or changing the fixed-length of either or both CAST tests. After reviewing several simulation studies comparing variable- and fixed-length adaptive testing procedures, Wise et al. (1990) concluded that variable-length stopping rules based on the reliability of the ability estimate offered no advantage in precision over fixed-length tests, and that fixed-length tests were probably more fair to lower ability examinees.

A variation of the variable-length stopping rule was also considered. After reviewing recruiter feedback during experimental CAST administrations, Wise et al. concluded that recruiters were willing to trade off increased test administration time for increased precision of prediction at the lowest AFQT boundary of interest (between AFQT categories IIIB and IV). They also found that the original CAST fixed-lengths of 10 WK and 5 AR items worked well, except for examinees of lower ability who were near that critical test cut point. To increase test precision for these candidates, the length of both tests was increased by three items for examinees whose estimated ability placed them at or below the 65th percentile. Thus, the current version of CAST uses a conditional, fixed-length stopping rule. The shorter version is used for persons scoring above the 65th percentile, while three additional items are administered to persons scoring at or below the 65th percentile.

CAST uses a Bayesian sequential estimation (BSE) procedure to estimate intermediate as well as final ability estimates for both WK and AR tests. Alternative methods that might improve CAST's precision for calculating both estimates were explored (Wise et al., 1990). The three methods—

The computerized adaptive screening test (CAST) predicts your probable performance on the Armed Forces qualification test (AFQT). The figure presented below shows your predicted range of performance on AFQT. Chances are 68 out of 100 that you would perform within the shaded range of performance. Chances are 90 out of 100 that you would perform within the highlighted range of performance. You are most likely to perform near the center of the shaded area. These probabilities are based on data that was provided by about 6,000 examinees who have taken both the CAST and the AFQT.

CAST RESULTS

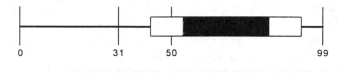

PREDICTED AFQT PERFORMANCE

Figure 7-2
"Sliding Bar" CAST Display Alternative.

BSE, expected a posteriori, and maximum likelihood estimation—were evaluated for correlations with ability, variance of the estimators, and computational difficulty. The results showed that the BSE procedure was nearly as accurate as the alternatives, was far less complex, and required less computation time. The decision was to retain the BSE scoring procedure.

The recruiters interpreted the predicted AFQT quite literally and were frustrated when the CAST-predicted AFQT score did not exactly match the AFQT score obtained at a MEPS or METS. The obvious answer was to change the display provided, to make it easier to interpret CAST performance properly.

Knapp (1987a) suggested two basic alternatives to USAREC. In the "sliding bar" option, the CAST "score" is represented by a bar illustrating the 68 percent and 90 percent confidence intervals around the predicted AFQT score. The bar is displayed on a predicted AFQT scale that shows the critical AFQT category cut points between AFQT categories IIIA and IIIB at the 50th percentile, and between categories IIIB and IV at the 31st scale point. No point prediction is provided. This score reporting format is illustrated in Figure 7-2.

The second option gives the probability that the prospect will be categorized in one of two or more AFQT categories and illustrates the probabilities with bar charts. This option is illustrated in Figure 7-3. Note that both display alternatives force the recruiter to view the CAST predictions as im-

perfect estimates of AFQT, and focus on the prediction of AFQT categories rather than AFQT scores. CAST software currently is capable of providing either or both score display options (Park & Dunn, 1991). USAREC has programmed the software for recruiters to display only the sliding bar output.

Your CAST score estimates how well you will do on the Armed Forces Qualification Test (AFQT). Your score means:

¥ There is a 75% chance you will get an AFQT score of 1, 2, or 3A. A score of 1—3A may qualify you for enlistment bonuses.

¥ There is a 25% chance you will get an AFQT score of 3B. A score of 3B probably will qualify you to enlist.

¥ There is a 0% chance you will get an AFQT score of 4 or 5.

¥ A score of 4 —5 probably will not qualify you to enlist.

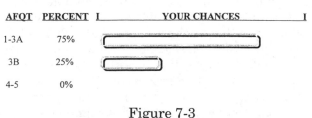

Figure 7-3
"Bar Chart" CAST Display Alternative.

Evaluation

The validity coefficient of the revised CAST for predicting AFQT was estimated by Wise et al. (1990) to be .82, based on the P&P items administered to soldiers in the primary recalibration sample, and not on a cross-validation of the revised CAST. In 1989 the AFQT was revised, with NO replaced by MK and the weighting of the tests changed. The .82 validity estimate is based on this latest version of the AFQT as the criterion.

Test fairness was examined in two ways. First, each test item was checked for differential item functioning (DIF) across black/white and male/female examinee subgroups. A small number of items was dropped from the item pools based on these analyses. Second, differential prediction analyses were conducted. The results were consistent with similar analyses from the original CAST data (Knapp, 1987a) and with results commonly reported in the literature. That is, there were intercept differences indicating performance level differences between subgroups. There were minor slope differences as well, but they indicated that the performance of black examinees, and to a smaller extent females, is overpredicted with the use of a common regression line. Such overprediction is not ordinarily considered to be a problem, though in times of military mobilization that perspective might change.

The final step in analyzing the CAST revision was to conduct simulated administrations of the revised CAST with a hypothetical sample of examinees to evaluate usage frequency of each item and to assess the accuracy of score estimates. The hypothetical sample simulated the 1980 *Profile of American Youth* (DoD, 1982) AFQT estimates and was systematically selected to provide simulated examinees at all ability levels.

The simulation results showed that overuse of certain items in the pool was dramatically reduced. No item was used more than 23 percent of the time, and most were used 14 percent or less. The simulation also allowed the correlation of true and estimated WK and AR scores. These estimates were quite high, .97 for WK and .99 for AR.

CAST or EST?

In the early years of CAST, Army recruiters were given the option of administering a prescreening test (either CAST or EST) to determine whether an applicant should be sent forward to a MEPS or METS for ASVAB testing. Today, Army recruiters must administer either the CAST or the EST to all applicants and use the test results to determine who will take the ASVAB.

Although there are no official statistics on how often CAST is administered to potential applicants in Army recruiting stations, USAREC personnel estimate that recruiters use the CAST instrument about 40 percent of the time. Although recruiters we contacted liked the CAST and the JOIN system, there are several reasons why most preferred the P&P EST.

First, a recruiter can make essentially the same sales and pre-qualification presentation either on the system that later incorporated JOIN (Electronic Information Delivery System [EIDS]) or deskside using a paper-based presentation package. With the P&P system, still pictures and recruiter dialogue replace the JOIN professional video disk presentations of the features and benefits of Army service designed to match the prospect's dominant buying motives. Although a JOIN system can be moved, it is not conveniently portable.

Second, EST can be administered to multiple applicants at the same time. This is not an unusual requirement, as recruiters often meet with groups of young people at schools and other central locations. The EIDS system limits the administration of CAST to one person at a time. Moreover, it is often located in a busy part of the recruiting station to allow all recruiters easy access. As a result, some Army recruiters chose the EST simply to prevent applicants from being distracted by traffic through the computer area.

Third, EIDS software requires recruiters to move through a relatively large number of sales presentation screens before the CAST can be accessed. This significantly compromises the administration time advantage of CAST over EST. Add to this a requirement to administer tests to several prospects at once, and the CAST time advantage disappears. Examinees may get frustrated with the length of EST, but for recruiters, EST has the time advantage under certain conditions.

Finally, recruiters say they often use EST rather than CAST because it allows them to determine whether applicants are having difficulty with the verbal or arithmetic items. Recruiters indicated that if applicants are having difficulty qualifying on the verbal items, but would qualify on the arithmetic items, they could be coached sufficiently to pass the EST, or the CAST for that matter, and the subsequent ASVAB. Since the current version of CAST, unlike earlier versions, gives only an overall estimate of AFQT score, recruiters are unable to use CAST to determine where coaching might help.

They feel this is a particular disadvantage for applicants who are not native English speakers. Using CAST or EST, or even ASVAB scores, to help devise coaching strategies for passing the ASVAB is, of course, a dubious practice. Recent research has shown that military recruiters commonly practice coaching for the ASVAB, most often with low-aptitude prospects (Palmer & Busciglio, 1996). Their results show that the impact of most coaching on ASVAB is probably negligible. However, it is clear that from the recruiter's perspective, CAST is a somewhat less useful tool than the EST for coaching the ASVAB and, as a result, is somewhat less likely to be used.

It would be a mistake to assume from the preceding discussion that recruiters do not like CAST very much; they do. All recruiters we contacted said they would use CAST rather than EST if they had CAST on a notebook computer. They felt that this would allow them to make their presentations and pre-qualify applicants "over the kitchen table." Furthermore, recruiters like giving applicants a printout of the CAST results from the EIDS system. This together with the printouts of Army pay and benefits tailored to the applicant's desired enlistment options are considered powerful recruiting tools. Laptop computers capable of administering CAST are currently being issued to all Army recruiters.

CASTing a Backward Glance

The pilot test of CAT-ASVAB WK, AR, and PC items conducted on Marine Corps recruits in 1981 (Moreno et al., 1983, 1984) and the initial validation of the CAST conducted in 1982–83 (Sands & Gade, 1983) were important CAT-ASVAB milestones for two reasons. First, from the perspective of CAT theory, those studies were among the first to clearly demonstrate that computerized adaptive tests could be equated with conventional P&P tests presumed to be measuring the same construct (Wainer et al., 1990). Second, from an applied perspective, the studies showed that CAT-ASVAB test scores could predict P&P-ASVAB test scores with an accuracy approaching the test-retest reliability of the P&P-ASVAB tests, and in substantially less time than the P&P AFQT estimator, EST.

Accomplishments

Implementation of R&D. The successful completion of the R&D for CAST was a major accomplishment in many dimensions. From an absolute frame of reference, the CAST is an accurate, predictive, psychometrically sound instrument. From a relative frame of reference, this computer-based measurement tool is as accurate as the P&P-EST that it was designed to replace, while requiring considerably less time to administer. CAST was implemented nationwide on the JOIN system in 1984 for use by Army recruiters in screening prospects for enlistment. This represented the first large-scale, nationwide implementation of CAT (Sands & Gade, 1983). As such, it was the forerunner of decentralized CAT, such as the DoD CAT-ASVAB program.

Inter-Service cooperation. CAST was not a part of CAT-ASVAB, but provided an operational demonstration of much of the technology of the CAT-ASVAB program. Competition and rivalry between the Services are legendary. However, there are examples of inter-Service cooperation that are extremely productive, conserving scarce research dollars, and shortening the time between the conception of an idea and the successful implementation of an R&D product. Recruiting operations are very similar for all the U.S. Military Services; thus the CAST instrument had a high potential for technology transfer. The joint cooperation of the Army and Navy in this research is an exemplar of a trend in military psychology: Decreasing research parochialism and increasing cooperative research efforts by individual Service laboratories (Wiskoff, 1985). As discussed in more detail elsewhere (Baker et al., 1984), the development, evaluation, and implementation of CAST under this inter-laboratory agreement constituted an excellent example of leveraging the Government research dollar.

Lessons Learned

Although CAST has been a significant R&D success story, some lessons can be learned from the experience of implementing CAT.

Delivery system. The CAST software was programmed in several languages, starting with CBASIC, and the software has been installed on several different hardware systems. The computer hardware originally used for the development of the CAST system included an Applied Computer Systems microcomputer and a Perkin-Elmer Data Systems 1200 video display terminal. Later, the CAST system was transferred to an Apple II-Plus microcomputer system, with 48K random access memory, a Z-80 softcard, two 5-1/4 inch floppy disk drives, a numeric keypad, and a video display terminal.

The Army recruiting environment needed a more sophisticated system, including videodisk capabilities. The original JOIN microcomputer system was developed under contract for the Army. It had several innovative features, including a detachable keypad with color-coded keys which facilitated administration of CAST to examinees who were not computer-literate. Though it was state-of-the-art when designed, the JOIN hardware system was outdated by the time it was implemented. It had the appearance of a dinosaur, despite its ground-breaking features. USAREC and its R&D researchers had come face-to-face with the realities of outfitting hundreds of recruiting offices with up-to-date computer systems with unique requirements not satisfied by off-the-shelf equipment.

In the early 1990s, USAREC replaced the original JOIN microcomputer system with a general use system, known as EIDS, which had been developed for a variety of Army applications. This reduced the R&D costs for USAREC, but also reduced the tailored nature of the equipment for recruiting purposes (e.g., there is no longer a detachable keypad for examinee use). And again, the equipment is rather archaic looking.

Obviously, it is difficult to keep up with technology. Although rapid advances in computer technology are likely to continue to be the norm, the magnitude of progressive improvements may not be as great as they were in the earlier years—at least for this type of testing. This might minimize the problem of delivering a flashy new computerized test via a decidedly dowdy piece of equipment.

Understanding the user. Two types of users are usually associated with CAST, the individual recruiter and the R&D sponsor (in this case, USAREC). Rather than poll recruiters, CAST researchers and USAREC tended to infer recruiter needs based on experience. Recruiters are not trained to interpret test scores, so the way in which test results are presented needs to be changed. Considerable effort has been expended on figuring out display alternatives that would be most meaningful. Who knew that recruiters would be interested in test (WK and AR) performance? They are not supposed to need this information, but the fact is that they want it. We should have asked. Moreover, no matter how valid or short the test is, recruiters will favor a P&P alternative until the test is truly transportable. They will also continue to use paper-based tests whenever they are dealing with more than a couple of prospects simultaneously.

Researchers provided USAREC with a test that was ahead of its time, or at least on the forefront of testing technology. However, ten years later several of the advantages of CAT have not been realized. In particular, the option of on-line calibration of new test items has not been attempted—this despite discussion of how this might best be accomplished from a psychometric perspective (Wise et al., 1990) as well as a delineation of the functional requirements for an automated calibration data system (Park & Rosse, 1991). A major task for researchers is to encourage military sponsors to support continued efforts to ensure that CAST remains a high-quality, innovative testing system.

*CAST*ing the Future

What of the future of CAST? Historically, the CAST instrument has served two major functions: (1) a tool for more applied CAT research, and (2) a useful functional application of CAT to the operational military recruiting environment. Perhaps the vision for the future of CAST is seen best in extrapolations of, and comparisons to, this historical perspective.

Applied Research

The future of CAST as an applied research tool may differ somewhat from the form it has taken in the past—that of demonstrating the utility of CAT as a cost-effective replacement for equivalent P&P tests. The potential of CAST may be largely realized through its use as a cost-effective, time-sensitive research tool for providing estimates of cognitive ability in a variety of human resources research efforts.

As psycho-social research moves more toward computerized data collection, the use of CAST to provide ability estimates for other purposes becomes more feasible. For example, CAST nearly became part of the National Survey of Families and Households (NSFH) and would have provided a cognitive ability estimate, AFQT, for every member of the sample. This became possible because the NSFH is administered by in-person interviewers using a computer-assisted personal interview (CAPI) protocol on a notebook computer. It would have been a technically simple matter to place CAST on the interviewers' notebooks and train them to use it. Unfortunately, there was not enough time to pretest the effects of administering CAST on increasing the time required for interviews and on its potential effects on the answers and cooperativeness of respondents. Although CAST was not used in this NSFH research, this example illustrates the potential use of the instrument to support applied research.

More recently, the CAST WK item bank was administered to a small sample (n = 149) of youth who had enlisted in the Army, but had not yet entered active duty. The goal was to see if a CAST-type test could be administered over the telephone and produce a quick, reasonable estimate of AFQT. Such a tool would be very useful in identifying potential high quality youth for marketing research purposes. Initial results were very promising, yielding a correlation of .78 between the telephone-administered WK and actual AFQT (Laurence, McCloy, & Legree, 1996; Legree, Fischl, & Gade, in press).

Operational Applications

The Joint Recruiting Information Support System (JRISS) is a Joint-Service program that was initiated in 1994 to incorporate state-of-the-art computer technology and data management systems into the business of military recruiting. When fully implemented, JRISS will result in all military recruiters having a laptop computer that can interface with USMEPCOM data bases. This will allow for one-time data entry for military applicant information *and* permit wider use of CAST within the Army and across all of the Services. The Navy has already been using the CAST in over 100 of its recruiting stations since June 1993.

In anticipation of the fielding of laptop computers to all Service recruiters, JRISS has funded a project to make modifications to the CAST. These modifications are intended to adjust the item selection and scoring systems to target critical AFQT cutpoints better, assure the security of test items, and generally upgrade the software. The revised CAST is likely to emerge with a different name—a simple step to encourage recruiters to evaluate it on its own merits, rather than by reputation (e.g., as an "old" Army test).

Some additional research efforts should also be completed before wider implementation of the CAST. For example, CAST should be cross-validated with the CAT-ASVAB. This may seem a trivial point, given the demonstrated validity of original CAST to predict P&P-ASVAB scores. However, this step is prudent to assure that CAST continues to serve its vital prescreening function in a CAT-ASVAB environment. This precaution becomes more critical because the new CAST was never cross-validated with the P&P-ASVAB after being revised. Further item pool development, updating, and testing are also essential for CAST to continue as a valid AFQT predictor. Fortunately, the JRISS program will provide the technology to conduct these activities more efficiently in the future.

First Generation—
The Experimental
CAT-ASVAB System

The successful demonstrations of CAT's validity and efficiency, summarized in the chapters of the previous part, stimulated the DoD decision to pursue full-scale research and development of CAT-ASVAB. Ultimately, that development resulted in the operational implementation of CAT-ASVAB in all Military Entrance Processing Stations in the U.S. Enroute to CAT-ASVAB's operational implementation, three generations of CAT-ASVAB systems were developed. The first generation system is the subject of the three chapters of this part; later parts will deal with the following generations.

The first generation of full-scale CAT-ASVAB research began with the development of an experimental CAT-ASVAB battery and a computer system to deliver it. The battery consisted of a set of psychometric procedures—that is, an adaptive testing strategy—and nine banks of calibrated test items for adaptive testing use. The chapters in this part describe the development of the adaptive testing strategy, the items banks and delivery system, and the research conducted to validate CAT as an alternative to the conventional ASVAB.

In **Chapter 8**, McBride, Wetzel, and Hetter summarize the research they conducted that led to decisions about the psychometric procedures used in CAT-ASVAB for adaptive item selection, ability estimation, and test scoring. Their chapter discusses the pros and cons of alternative strategies for adaptive testing that had been proposed prior to 1979. It also summarizes a program of computer simulation research that selected the strategy that best satisfied a number of sometimes conflicting criteria, and describes the hybrid strategy that was ultimately chosen.

In **Chapter 9**, Wolfe, McBride, and Sympson provide an overview of the development of two key

components of the experimental CAT-ASVAB system: A delivery system and a full-battery item bank. The delivery system was a network of Apple III computers that could administer the tests on seven computers simultaneously, while a test administrator controlled test administration and monitored testing progress from an eighth computer. Although not extraordinary by today's standards, the experimental CAT-ASVAB delivery system was a breakthrough in the early 1980s. The item bank was likewise a breakthrough development. It included banks of 30 to 200 calibrated adaptive test items in all nine subject matter areas of the ASVAB, as well as computer-administered versions of ASVAB's two speeded tests.

In **Chapter 10**, Segall, Moreno, Kieckhaefer, Vicino, and McBride summarize research that used the experimental CAT-ASVAB system to collect the data for the initial validation of CAT-ASVAB's equivalence to the paper-and-pencil version of the battery. In that research, over 7,500 military recruits of all Services, scheduled for training in 23 job specialties, took the experimental CAT-ASVAB tests. The CAT-ASVAB tests were about half the length of the printed ones, in terms of number of items; test-administration times were commensurately shorter. Factor analyses established that the CAT and printed versions of ASVAB were measuring the same ability constructs. Multiple correlation analyses established that the predictive validity of CAT-ASVAB was highly similar to that of printed ASVAB, despite CAT-ASVAB's shorter test lengths and test times. This chapter describes in some detail the design, analyses, and results of the experimental CAT-ASVAB validation studies, and draws conclusions about its implications for future research and for operational implementation of CAT-ASVAB.

8

Preliminary Psychometric Research for CAT-ASVAB: Selecting an Adaptive Testing Strategy

James R. McBride, C. Douglas Wetzel, and Rebecca D. Hetter

This chapter describes the research Navy Personnel Research and Development Center (NPRDC) conducted to choose the adaptive testing strategy employed in the initial version of CAT-ASVAB. That research consisted of a series of computer simulation studies comparing the psychometric merits of alternative strategies for adaptive testing. These computer simulation studies were conducted in two phases. The first phase provided comparative data on several adaptive testing strategies. Based on the data, the most promising strategies were chosen for further study. In the second phase, the strategies chosen from phase one were evaluated in more depth, and derivative strategies designed to enhance test security were evaluated. Following the second phase, one strategy was chosen to be implemented in the experimental CAT system. The remainder of this section will summarize the background for this research, and describe its purpose and rationale. Both theoretical and empirical research had demonstrated the technical merits of adaptive testing, but little was known about the relative merits of alternative "strategies" for adaptive testing.

Adaptive Testing Strategies

In adaptive testing, test questions are selected for each examinee individually, with the objective of matching the difficulty of the test to the ability of the individual, and maximizing the efficiency of the test. A "strategy" for adaptive testing is defined by the specific procedures used to select items. One fundamental component in any adaptive testing strategy is the method used for matching the test questions to examinee ability. Another fundamental component is the criterion for stopping the test. In some adaptive testing strategies, a third component is integral to one or both of the first two: The method used to score the test. Each of these components is discussed in more detail below, followed by a summary of several adaptive testing strategies. Test scoring alternatives will be discussed first, followed by criteria for stopping an adaptive test, and methods for selecting items.

Alternatives for Adaptive Test Scoring

Before the explication of item response theory (IRT), (Lord, 1980a) scoring adaptive tests was problematical because different examinees responded to sets of test questions that could differ in number, difficulty, and other psychometric characteristics. The problem was how to assign scores on a common scale to examinees who had taken such different tests. IRT solved this problem by providing both a common scale for expressing both item difficulty and examinee ability, and a means for estimating an examinee's location on that scale from his or her performance on a specific set of test questions with known scale values, or parameters.

In principle, IRT resolved the adaptive test scoring problem because it provided a means of locating all examinees on the same scale of ability (θ)—that is, scoring tests—based on the patterns of their right and wrong answers to appropriately calibrated test questions, regardless of which questions—or how many—were administered. All of the adaptive testing strategies studied in this research employed IRT methods for test scoring. Nonetheless, test scoring procedures differentiated some of the strategies. One source of such differences was the role of test scoring in selecting individually tailored sets of test questions. A second difference was the specific method used to compute test scores using IRT. Each of these is discussed below.

Alternative roles of test scoring in adaptive test item selection. In the simplest adaptive testing strategies, the tailoring of the test to individuals is independent of test scoring. Test questions are arranged in advance into a logical structure, largely based on their difficulty parameters. The selection of questions for an individual examinee is governed by "branching rules"—specifications for moving from one part of the structure to another, contingent on test performance. Weiss' stratified adaptive ("stradaptive") strategy is an example of this kind of strategy. In a stradaptive test, questions are arranged into several mutually exclusive sets, graduated in terms of item difficulty, called "strata." After each question, the next one is chosen from a more difficult stratum if the answer were right, or an easier stratum if the answer were wrong. Test scoring takes place only after the test has been completed.

In other adaptive testing strategies, item selection is based on intermediate test scores—that is, test scores computed at one or more points during the test itself. Two-stage testing is one example of such a strategy. In the first stage of the test, each examinee answers a small set of test questions, and a test score is computed. In the second stage, the examinee is given an easier or a harder set of test questions, contingent on the score from the first stage.

In the case of two-stage adaptive testing, the intermediate test score might be a traditional number-correct score; alternatively, it could be an IRT ability estimate based on the pattern of right and wrong answers. Some of the more sophisticated adaptive testing strategies rely heavily on intermediate scoring based on IRT. For example, an IRT score—ability estimate—may be computed after every question, and the next question administered may be one that maximizes some function of the difference between the apparent location of the examinee ("ability") and the known location of each test question ("difficulty") on the IRT scale. Adaptive testing strategies of this kind are computation-intensive; that is, they require IRT computations be made after every test question, both to update the examinee's intermediate test score, and to select the optimal question to administer next.

Alternative methods for IRT-based adaptive test scoring. At the time the research reported here was conducted, there were two predominant approaches to IRT ability estimation, or test scoring. One was a Bayesian sequential ability estimation technique proposed by Owen (1969; 1975), and more fully explicated by Urry (1971). The other was a maximum likelihood estimation (MLE) technique proposed by Birnbaum (1968) and explicated by Lord (e.g., Lord & Novick, 1968; Lord, 1980a; Wingersky & Lord, 1973). (Owen's methods are all predicated on normal ogive item response models.)

The most widely used MLE techniques are predicated on logistic ogive response models. The logistic ogive can be made closely similar to the normal ogive with a simple rescaling of the underlying metric; they are treated here as practically interchangeable. The Owen and MLE approaches are summarized in the following paragraphs.

Owen (1969) proposed an adaptive testing strategy with three key elements: (a) a normal ogive IRT model with unique parameters is fitted in advance to each test question, (b) test scoring by means of Bayesian sequential ability estimation follows each test question, and (c) the next question selected minimizes the expected value of the Bayesian posterior variance. Owen's Bayesian sequential ability estimation procedure has proven useful in adaptive testing strategies using other item selection criteria, as well. That procedure begins with a prior distribution of ability—in effect, an assumption that the examinee is a member of a population with a normal distribution of ability, with known mean and variance. After each test question, the mean and variance are updated using a statistical procedure that combines the information in the prior distribution with the observed score (right or wrong) on the most recent test question, and the parameters of that question's IRT model. The updated values of the ability distribution parameters specify a normal "posterior" distribution, which is used as the prior distribution for the next question. This process continues until the end of the test. At that point, the posterior mean is used as the estimate of the examinee's ability scale location. Owen's formulas for updating the prior mean is as follows:

$$\mu(\theta_i | u_i) = \frac{\int \theta \, P(u_i | \theta) h(\theta) d\theta}{\int P(u_i | \theta) h(\theta) d\theta} \qquad (8\text{-}1)$$

Adaptive test scoring using Owen's procedure takes into account just one item response at a time. All previous information is absorbed into the parameters of the prior distribution, which changes after each question. In contrast, scoring based on Birnbaum's maximum likelihood estimation technique makes no distributional assumptions, and takes into account all of the item response data at once—the parameters of each item's logistic IRT model, and the examinee's scores (right or wrong) on each item. From these data, it is possible to calculate the likelihood of the specific pattern of item scores at any point on the ability scale. The point at which that likelihood is highest is the ability estimate. The formula for maximum likelihood ability estimation is as follows:

$$L(u_1, u_2, \ldots u_n) = \prod_{i=1}^{n} P_i^{u_i} Q_i^{1-u_i} \qquad (8\text{-}2)$$

Alternative Criteria for Stopping an Adaptive Test

Adaptive tests can be either fixed-length or variable-length. A fixed-length adaptive test is stopped after a specified number of questions. A variable-length test is stopped after some other criterion has been satisfied, such as error of estimation of the examinee's ability. The "stopping rule" is an important element of an adaptive testing strategy.

For a fixed-length adaptive test, the stopping rule might be to administer the same number of items as a counterpart conventional test. Alternatively, the length might be set significantly shorter than that of the conventional test, to take advantage of the measurement efficiency that is typical of adaptive tests.

A criterion for a variable-length adaptive test might be to stop the test as soon as a satisfactory level of measurement precision has been reached. Such a stopping rule might be predicated on the value of (a) the posterior variance in a test using

Owen's sequential procedure or another Bayesian-motivated approach to ability estimation, or (b) the test information function in a test using maximum likelihood ability estimation. Birnbaum showed that the test information function is inversely proportional to the square of the standard error of the ability estimate. In developing an adaptive test, a key design issue is whether to use fixed-length or variable-length, and what specific value of test length or measurement precision to employ.

Alternative Criteria for Adaptive Test Item Selection

In his review of different strategies for adaptive testing, Weiss (1974a) described a variety of criteria for item selection in an adaptive test. McBride (1979) divided adaptive item selection criteria into (a) mathematically-based strategies, and (b) those which involved simple mechanical branching rules. The "mechanical" strategies were appealing because they made few computational demands, and thus presented few obstacles to satisfactory implementation on the microcomputers available at the time. The mathematically-based strategies, on the other hand, were theoretically much more efficient than the mechanical strategies, but required enough computation during the test that they could be challenging to implement on microcomputers, particularly those with the 8-bit processors available in the 1970s. A brief discussion of "mechanical" and mathematical item selection criteria follows.

Mechanical branching criteria. Some strategies involve adaptive item selection by means of predetermined branching rules, selecting items from a predetermined logical structure. Examples include the pyramidal strategy, Weiss' stratified adaptive ("stradaptive") strategy, and Lord's "flexilevel" strategy. In each of these strategies, test items are placed in advance in a logical structure such as a binary tree; the adaptive test proceeds by moving from one position to another in the structure according to a simple branching rule that is contingent on the result (right or wrong) to the previous item. None of these strategies requires ability estimates (test scores) to be computed until the test is completed.

Mathematical item selection criteria. Other strategies involve selecting test items so as to maximize or minimize some mathematical objective function. Usually, this also requires computing an updated score, or ability estimate, after each item response. The two dominant criteria for adaptive item selection were maximum information (Lord, 1977) and minimum pre-posterior risk (Owen, 1975). Adaptive testing strategies that used the maximum information item selection criterion usually also employed maximum likelihood estimation to update examinee ability between items (e.g., Lord, 1977). The Owen item selection strategy was typically employed in conjunction with Bayesian sequential updating between items (e.g., Urry and associates).

In short, the two predominant mathematically-based adaptive testing strategies being seriously evaluated in the mid-1970s were a maximum likelihood/maximum information (MLMI) strategy, and a Bayesian-motivated sequential strategy proposed by Owen and advanced by Urry. Each had advantages and disadvantages. The advantage of the MLMI strategy was that item selection could be done by reference to lookup tables computed in advance. This strategy required almost no computation at item selection time. The disadvantage of the MLMI strategy was that the maximum likelihood ability estimation step that had to be performed after every item response used an iterative numerical approximation technique that was occasionally computation-intensive, and was prone to convergence failure. It was not uncommon for the MLMI procedure to yield an indeterminate ability estimate during the test itself and even at test completion.

The Owen/Urry adaptive testing strategy did not suffer from the disadvantage of the MLMI iterative ability updating procedure. Its ability estimates were rapidly computed, and not subject to convergence failure. This advantage was more than offset by the computation-intensive item selection procedure, however. After each item response, the objective function had to be computed for every unused item. For large item banks, the computational load was demanding, and extremely time-consuming on small computers.

An obvious solution to the disadvantages of the MLMI and Owen/Urry strategies was to create a hybrid strategy that retained the advantages and avoided their disadvantages. Several researchers, including McBride, developed such hybrids. For the Marine Corps project, Wetzel and McBride (1983) evaluated a hybrid that used Owen's Bayesian sequential procedure to update ability after each item response, and selected items sequentially by referring to precomputed item information lookup tables.

Alternative Adaptive Testing Strategies

In the above, we have alluded to three areas in which choices must be made in designing an adaptive test—choices as to alternative roles and methods of test scoring, choices among alternative criteria for adaptive test item selection, and a choice between fixed- and variable-length adaptive tests. In principle, an option within one of these areas could be combined with any options within the other two. Each possible combination of such options constitutes a unique adaptive testing strategy.

Weiss' (1974a) review of adaptive testing strategies discussed virtually every strategy that had been proposed at the time. For each of the strategies he reviewed, there was a proponent who either developed it or advocated it to some degree. However, many more strategies could be defined, simply by selecting another unique combination of methods for scoring, item selection, and stopping the test. In concept, the number of alternative adaptive strategies is limitless. This makes it impossible to compare all possible strategies for the purpose of choosing the "best" one.

Every strategy—and every variant of scoring, item selection, and stopping rule—can be expected to have some advantages and disadvantages compared to others. Our objective was ultimately to select an adaptive testing strategy that would be practically feasible, psychometrically efficient, and useful in a large-scale testing program.

To be practically feasible, it had to be capable of satisfactory implementation on microcomputers of the kind that were commercially available at the time (the early 1980s). That meant its computational and data storage and retrieval requirements had to be well within the capabilities of computers with 8-bit microprocessors and very limited memory and mass storage resources.

Psychometric efficiency is a relative concept, gauged by comparing two or more strategies in terms of their test information functions (TIFs). We sought an adaptive strategy that would be approximately twice as efficient as a well-designed conventional test, and practically as efficient as the most efficient strategies.

For an adaptive test strategy to be useful in a large-scale testing program, it also had to be, among other things, stable and secure. A strategy would be considered unstable if it were prone to failure to select an item or estimate an ability. It would not be considered secure if some features of it made the test readily susceptible to compromise.

By the late 1970s, there was a growing body of research evaluating adaptive testing strategies. Little of this research was based on data from human subjects. For the most part, the evaluations were based either on theoretical analyses or on computer simulations. Prior to 1975, virtually all of the research literature reported comparisons of single adaptive strategies with conventional test designs.

In the mid-1970s—following Weiss' (1975) review of strategies for adaptive testing, the first comparisons among two or more adaptive strategies began to appear. Computer simulation studies by Vale (1975) and McBride (1976b) provided data comparing several adaptive strategies against one another and against conventional test designs. These IRT-based studies were useful, but the interpretation of their results was limited. Because they did not take into account the inevitable presence of error in the estimation of IRT item parameters, one could not be confident that the results would apply to the more realistic situation in which item parameters were fallibly estimated rather than known. Crichton (1981) addressed this shortcoming in a series of simulation studies that included item parameter estimation errors. Her results could not be used with complete confidence because the estimation errors she employed followed statistical distributions that were somewhat gratuitously assumed, without a sound theoretical or empirical basis. If actual distributions of item parameter estimation errors differed from the ones used in her simulation studies, her results might not be replicated. NPRDC's program of research to choose an adaptive testing strategy for use in the CAT-ASVAB program was designed to circumvent the shortcomings of previous research in the field.

Method

Described below is a series of computer simulation studies that evaluated and compared alternative adaptive testing strategies. These studies differed in their particulars, but all used a common approach. That approach is summarized here. The sections that follow describe the specifics of three separate studies.

The authors developed a system of computer programs designed to simulate adaptive testing strategies with as much verisimilitude as possible. To that end, the simulation process began by specifying a bank of "tryout" items intended for use in a CAT item bank. This specification took the form of a large set of item parameter values, a, b, c. Each a_i, b_i, c_i triplet specified the parameters of one item's 3-parameter logistic item (3PL) response model. Simulated item responses of large numbers of examinees to the tryout items were generated, using established procedures for model sampling. The simulated item response data were analyzed using available computer programs for item parameter estimation, resulting in a triplet of *estimated* parameters for each item:

$$\hat{a}_i, \ \hat{b}_i, \ \hat{c}_i$$

Based on the estimated item parameters, a subset of items was selected for use in the CAT item bank. The criteria for this selection followed the suggestion of Urry (1974b): Items with a wide range of estimated b-parameters were selected. No items with estimated a-parameters lower than .80 or estimated c-parameters above .33 were included in an adaptive item bank. Simulated conventional tests were specified by selecting some of the same items used in the adaptive banks. "Peaked" conventional tests were designed by selecting items with a narrow range of estimated b-parameters; "rectangular" conventional tests were designed by selecting items with a wide range and flat distribution of estimated b-parameters. Once the conventional tests and adaptive test item banks were specified, each adaptive and conventional test design being studied was "administered" to large examinee samples via computer simulation. In the computer simulations, the actual item parameters were used as the basis for generating item responses, but item selection and ability estimation were based on the *estimated* item parameters. This ensured that the effects of item parameter estimation errors were reflected in the psychometric characteristics of the resulting tests.

Using this common paradigm, a series of computer simulation studies was carried out to address technical questions leading to the choice of an integrated adaptive testing strategy to be implemented in the research and development of CAT-ASVAB. Alternative approaches to item branching, test scoring, compromise reduction, and test termination were evaluated in terms of several criteria.

The sample data in the simulation studies differed along two dimensions: (a) the size and characteristics of the adaptive test item banks, and (b) the distribution of ability in the simulated examinee samples. The earliest simulation studies used item banks that were ideally designed, in terms of the distributions of their simulated item parameters. In an ideal item bank, the distribution of b-parameters is approximately uniform, and there is no correlation between the estimated difficulty (b-) and discrimination (a-) parameters. In actual practice, it is rare to be able to construct an ideal item bank. To increase the verisimilitude of this line of research, the later simulation studies in the series used item banks with parameter distributions similar to those seen in practice.

Two different kinds of ability distributions were employed in various parts of all the studies. In some studies, the objective was to evaluate the psychometric properties of tests, conditional on specific levels of ability. For those studies, uniform distributions of examinee ability were simulated. Typically, a large sample of examinees at each of several equally spaced points on the ability continuum were simulated, and separate analyses were made of the data at each ability point. In other studies, the objective was to evaluate the marginal properties of the test in a typical population of examinees. This approach was used, for example, to evaluate test reliability. For those studies, examinee samples were drawn randomly from a normal distribution of ability.

Three of the simulation studies are summarized below.

Simulation Study 1: Comparing Leading Types of Strategies

The computer simulation study described here was conducted to compare a leading mechanical adaptive testing strategy against two mathematical strategies, in the presence of realistic errors in the estimates of item parameters, and to compare each of the adaptive strategies with conventional test designs. An earlier study in this series, described by Wetzel and McBride (1983), showed that the two mathematical strategies were superior in precision and efficiency to the mechanical strategy. The earlier study, however, used only the actual item parameters to estimate ability and select test items. The purpose of Study 1 was to evaluate whether the mathematical strategies maintained their superiority in conditions characterized by realistic errors in item parameter estimation.

Study 1 Method

Study 1 began with the specification of a pool of 400 "items," each a candidate for inclusion in the CAT item bank. Items ranged in difficulty from $b = -3.00$ to 3.00; in discrimination (a) from 0.2 to 2.0; and in lower asymptote (c) from 0 to $.3$. Wetzel & McBride (1983) describe how (a) artificial item responses to these 400 items were generated for a sample of 2,000 simulated examinees; (b) IRT parameters were estimated from the item response data; and (c) an "ideal" adaptive test item bank consisting of 223 simulated items meeting Urry's criteria was selected from the 400 original items.

Independent variable: alternative test designs. Study 1 included four test designs, three adaptive and a conventional peaked design. The adaptive designs included a mechanical strategy (Weiss' stradaptive procedure) and two mathematical strategies: Owen's Bayesian sequential procedure, and a hybrid Bayesian procedure. The hybrid procedure used Bayesian sequential updating to estimate examinee ability after each item, but used pre-computed item information tables to reduce the computation required for item selection. There were 36 tables, each representing an interval of .125 units on an IRT ability/difficulty scale, covering the range from -2.25 to $+2.125$. Each table contained a list of test items arranged in descending order of item information value, computed from estimated item parameters, at the center of the interval. To select an adaptive test item, the table with an interval containing the current ability estimate was located, and the unused item with the highest estimated information value at the center of the interval was chosen. This table look-up item selection procedure is very similar to the procedure described by Lord (1977) for his Broad Range Tailored Test. Each simulated test was 15 items long.

Dependent variables. The dependent variable was the value of the test information function, which was computed for each simulated examinee by summing the information values of the items selected for that examinee. Those values are computed from the item parameters and the examinee's simulated ability level. Test information is an index of measurement precision. Its reciprocal square root is an index of measurement error. Two values of test information were computed for each examinee. An estimated test information value was computed using the item parameter estimates. The actual information value was computed from the true values of the item parameters.

Simulated examinee samples. Nineteen examinee samples were simulated. Each sample consisted of 100 examinees with identical ability parameters. The 19 ability parameters ranged from -2.25 to $+2.25$, at .25 intervals.

Study 1 Results

The results of this comparison of four test design strategies are presented graphically. Figure 8-1 displays the mean actual test information for the four strategies at each of the 19 sampled ability levels. The figure shows that the peaked conventional test design achieved its maximum test information value at the center of the ability range, as it was designed to do, and that test information declined rapidly as ability levels departed from the center. The three adaptive test information plots show a different picture: Test information was fairly high (over 10) over the ability range from −2.0 to +2.0. Both Owen's Bayesian procedure and the hybrid Bayesian procedure had noticeably higher information values than the stradaptive procedure over the same range. Differences between Owen's procedure and the hybrid procedure were small. In some cases, Owen's procedure was somewhat superior, and in other cases the hybrid was superior.

Study 1 Discussion

The two Bayesian-derivative strategies clearly had larger test information functions (TIF) values than the stradaptive procedure, over the entire range of simulated examinees. The study described here was just part of a more complex and comprehensive study described by Wetzel & McBride (1983). The part of it presented here was arguably the most important, because it formed the basis for choosing to use a mathematical optimization strategy rather than a mechanical branching strategy in the CAT-ASVAB.

The results were presented in terms of TIF values, which index measurement precision. The relative efficiency of two different test designs can be computed easily, by calculating the ratio of their TIFs at each ability level. That ratio can be interpreted as relative test length. For example, a test with an information function value of 20 at a given ability level is twice as efficient as one with an information function value of 10. The inferior test would have to be lengthened by a factor of two to achieve the larger information function value, at least at that one ability level. The ratios of the Bayesian test strategies to the stradaptive one at each of the 19 simulated ability levels would indicate that the stradaptive test would have to be lengthened substantially to attain the same levels of measurement precision the Bayesian tests achieved in just 15 items. Hence, both Bayesian strategies were markedly more efficient than the stradaptive strategy in this study.

Since there were only small differences between the two Bayesian strategies in precision and efficiency, the hybrid Bayesian strategy was chosen

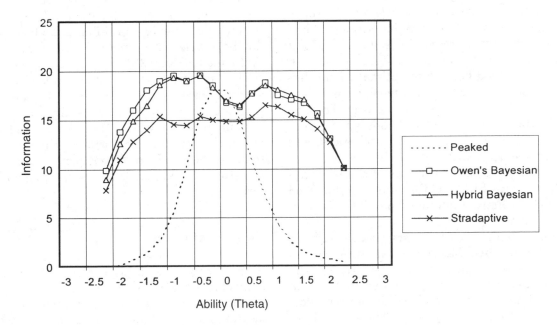

Figure 8-1
Average Test Information of Four Test Design Strategies.

for further study. The hybrid strategy was preferable because it required far less computation to select the next item than Owen's procedure, and was therefore advantageous for use on small computers.

Simulation Study 2: Comparing Refinements to Enhance Test Security

One factor that motivated the initiation of the CAT-ASVAB program was concern about test security. Adaptive testing was considered more secure in some ways than paper-and-pencil testing: There were no test booklets to pilfer, and each examinee received an individually tailored test. However, the very feature that makes the mathematical optimization strategies so efficient also makes them prone to a new kind of security breach. If each test begins with the same initial estimate of examinee ability, there is only one possible sequence of test items for any given sequence of right and wrong answers. This makes mathematical strategies like the ones in Study 1 tantamount to optimal mechanical branching strategies. Adaptive test security could easily be breached by means of an organized effort to identify the first, second, third, and subsequent items in a sequence of right answers. Examinees who answered the first five to ten items right would almost certainly achieve high scores, even if they did poorly on later items.

This shortcoming could just as easily be remedied if the adaptive item selection strategy could be modified to avoid predictable sequences of test items, especially in the early stages of the test. However, any modification to optimal item selection could be expected to reduce measurement precision as well as test efficiency somewhat. The purpose of Study 2 was to evaluate one approach to the problem of predictable item sequences, and to determine the magnitude of the adaptive efficiency/precision loss for variants of the basic approach. As with Study 1, this was accomplished by means of computer simulation of adaptive test administration.

A single adaptive strategy was used throughout Study 2—the hybrid Bayesian strategy. A key feature of item selection using that strategy is the choice of the best unused item listed in a lookup table of items chosen for high values of item information at a single ability point. The general approach used to eliminate predictable sequences of

test items was to modify that item selection somewhat, by selecting the set of k best items, and choosing one of them at random. The larger the value of k, the more random the sequence of items. If every item in the set had identical item information values, there would be no loss of precision. In fact, however, the items in the table vary considerably in their local information values. Consequently, the larger the value of k, the greater the loss of precision. One purpose of Study 2 was to determine how quickly precision decreased as k increased. Values of k ranging from 1 to 40 were evaluated in the study.

Another variant of the same approach was also tried out in Study 2. In this variant, the set size k was reduced after each item; the rate of this reduction could also be varied. For example, if k were initially set at 10, the first item chosen would be a random draw from among the 10 best items at the initial ability level. K could be reduced to a smaller number, say 8, and the second item presented would be drawn randomly from among the 8 best items at the new ability level (ability is updated after each item). If k were further reduced by 2 after each item, the sixth and subsequent items selected would be the best ones available at their respective ability levels. Thus, in this particular example, this security procedure would entail no further precision loss after the fifth item in the test.

These two versions of the item selection security procedure can be distinguished by calling the first one a "fixed set size" procedure and the second one a "shrinking set size" procedure. Numerous variants of them can be created by specifying different initial values for k, and different reduction rates for the set size. A number of such variants were evaluated in Study 2.

The full study evaluated various fixed and shrinking set size specifications in conjunction with four different adaptive testing strategies. It is summarized by Wetzel & McBride (1986). In the end, the hybrid Bayesian strategy was determined to be the most advantageous. Only the portion of the study dealing with that strategy will be described here.

Study 2 Method

Study 2 began by specifying an adaptive testing bank of 200 "items," with their true IRT difficulty, discrimination, and lower asymptote parameters distributed consistent with our experience with actual adaptive test item banks. Details are described by Wetzel & McBride (1986). The estimated item parameters were obtained, as before, by generating simulated item responses from a large number of examinees, then fitting 3PL ogives to the simulated response data. The LOGIST program (Wood, Wingersky, & Lord, 1976) was used to estimate the item parameters; true parameters were known, of course.

Independent variable: alternative secure item selection procedures. A total of seven alternative procedures were simulated in Study 2. Five different "fixed set sizes" were used. Sets of size 1 (optimal item selection), 5, 10, 20, and 40. Two different sequences of "shrinking set size" were used for the portions of the study dealing with that alternative. In the first, the set size was reduced systematically from 5 items to 1 item, in increments of 1. We refer to this as the "5-4-3-2-1" procedure. In the second, set size was reduced from 10 items to 2 items, in increments of 2. We refer to this as the "10-8-6-4-2" procedure. Data for a 15-item adaptive test using each of the seven alternative procedures was generated by computer simulation, using the same design described above for Study 1, with 100 simulated examinees at each of 19 equally spaced intervals of ability.

Dependent variables. As in Study 1, the value of the TIF was computed for each simulated examinee by summing the information values of the items selected for that examinee. Two values of test information were computed for each examinee. An estimated test information value was computed using the item parameter estimates. The actual information value was computed from the item parameters themselves.

An additional dependent variable was used in Study 2: The "fidelity coefficient" (Urry, 1983)—the correlation of the ability estimates (scores) from each variant adaptive test strategy with the actual ability parameters of the simulated examinees. Urry argued that this was a better term than validity coefficient for simulation studies. We follow Urry's suggestion.

Simulated examinee samples. As in Study 1, to evaluate adaptive test information 19 examinee samples were simulated, each consisting of 100 examinees with identical ability parameters, at equally spaced intervals from -2.25 to $+2.25$. To evaluate the correlation of adaptive test scores with the actual ability parameters, samples of 1,900 examinees with ability normally distributed (0,1) were also simulated.

Table 8-1 Fidelity Coefficients of Scores From Simulated Adaptive Tests Using the Hybrid Bayesian Strategy With Five Different Set Sizes for Random Item Selection of Nearly Optimal Items[a]

	Set Size				
	1	5	10	20	40
Fixed set size	.953	.955	.952	.951	.936
Shrinking set size	na	.957	.957	na	na

[a] All test lengths = 15 items.
  N = 1,900 simulated examinees from N (0,1).
  na = not applicable.

Study 2 Results

The fidelity coefficients of the simulated adaptive tests using each of the five fixed set size specifications are listed in Table 8-1. As the data indicate, the correlations of observed scores with true scores were .95 or higher for every set size except 40. Figure 8-1 displays the average test information value at 19 ability levels, for simulated adaptive tests using six of the seven set size specifications (fixed set size 5 is omitted for clarity). For the fixed set sizes, the figure shows that average test information declined as set size increased. For the two shrinking set size specifications, average information was approximately equivalent to the information levels observed for set size 1—i.e., optimal item selection.

Discussion

Fidelity coefficients were high—approximately .95 —for every set size, shrinking as well as fixed, except 40. This would suggest that drawing items at random from nearly optimal sets of up to 20 items results in little degradation in measurement precision. Figure 8-2, which shows estimates of measurement precision as a function of ability level for each of the set size specifications, tells another story. While there was little decrease in test information at any level for set sizes up to 10 items, the information achieved by tests using set sizes of 20 and 40 was noticeably lower. Wetzel & McBride concluded as follows: (a) as long as the set size is small (10 or less), little of the efficiency of adaptive tests will be lost if items are selected randomly from a small set of nearly optimal items; (b) if set size is small to begin with and gets progressively smaller (by means of shrinking set size) the adaptive test strategy may be virtually as effi-

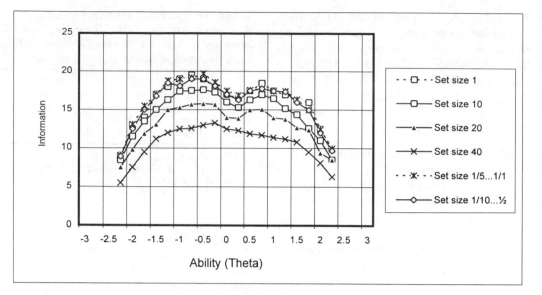

Figure 8-2
Test Information for Various Randomization Strategies.

cient as the strategy that chooses the optimal item every time.

Simulation Study 3: Comparing Fixed- and Variable-Length Tests

The two previous studies used the same adaptive test stopping rule: Terminate the test after a fixed number of items have been administered. A conceptually appealing alternative is to vary the test length, stopping as soon as a pre-specified level of precision has been attained. This has the objective of producing test scores with the same degree of measurement error, a highly desirable property from a statistical point of view. To attain this, however, test length would be expected to vary from one examinee to another, perhaps widely. If all else were equal, we would expect test length to increase as ability levels departed from the initial adaptive test ability level. Additionally, we would expect test length to vary with ability level, reflecting ability-specific differences in the aggregate information levels of the items in the item bank.

Theoretical considerations aside, there are practical rationales for preferring fixed test length. For one, if test length varies widely, test administration time may be extremely variable. This might be undesirable. For another, examinees taking relatively short tests might object if they received lower scores than other examinees who took some-

what longer tests. This could pose problems of public acceptance, not to mention legal defensibility. One purpose of Study 3 was to evaluate the tradeoff between fixed- and variable-length adaptive testing. How long are variable-length tests, compared to those with fixed length? How precise are fixed-length adaptive tests, compared to variable-length tests with their precision specified in advance?

Study 3 Method

In Study 3, an adaptive testing item bank of 194 "items" was simulated. As in Study 2, the distributions of actual IRT item parameters were similar to those of a real item bank—in this case a CAT-ASVAB Word Knowledge test item bank. Estimated item parameters used in the simulations were obtained in a manner similar to Study 2.

Independent variable: Fixed- versus variable-length stopping rules. Three adaptive test designs were simulated in Study 3. One strategy used a fixed-length stopping rule; those simulated tests terminated after 15 items. The other two strategies used variable-length stopping rules, both based on the value of the Bayes posterior variance computed after each item. For one, a posterior variance of .0638 was the termination criterion. This value would be expected to result in a fidelity coefficient of .94 or greater, in a normal (0,1) examinee ability population (Urry, 1983). In the second strategy, a critical posterior variance of .0526 (fidelity ≥ .95) was specified. The two critical posterior variance values were selected to produce fidelity coefficients similar to those of a fixed-length adaptive test, as observed for the 15-item tests simulated in Study 2. Both variable-length tests were limited to a maximum of 30 items.

Dependent variables. The dependent variables included average test information values (as in Studies 1 and 2), average adaptive test length, and the average values of the Bayes posterior variance. All of these variables were measured at each of 19 levels of ability. Additionally, fidelity coefficients were computed for a separate, normally distributed sample.

Simulated examinee samples. As in Study 2, to evaluate adaptive test information 19 examinee samples of size 100 were simulated, at equally spaced intervals from −2.25 to +2.25. To evaluate the correlation of adaptive test scores with the actual ability parameters, samples of 1,900 examinees with ability normally distributed (0,1) were also simulated.

Study 3 Results

In the tests administered to normally distributed examinee ability samples, the fidelity coefficient for the 15-item fixed-length test was .961. Coefficients for the two variable-length tests were .955 and .957.

Figure 8-3 displays mean test length at each ability level for all three adaptive tests. The fixed-length tests, of course, all had the same length, 15 items. The variable-length test with the less rigorous stopping criterion varied in mean length from 10 to 30 items, and was shorter than 15 items at ability levels from −2.25 to +1.50. Above +1.50 mean test length increased toward the 30-item limit. The test with the more rigorous (.05) stopping criterion varied in length from 12 to 30 items. Over the ability range from −2.25 to −.25 its mean test length equalled or exceeded 15. From +.25 to +1.50, it was less than 15, and from +1.75 to +2.25 it increased toward the limit.

Figure 8-4 shows average test information for two of the simulated tests—the fixed length test and the variable length test with the more rigorous .0526 stopping rule criterion—at each of the 19 ability levels. As expected, the information function of the test with the more rigorous variable-length stopping criterion was higher than that of the less rigorous test. The information function level of the fixed-length test was between the two variable-length tests from −2.25 to 0. From 0 to +1.50, the fixed-length test had higher levels of information than either variable-length test. From +1.75 to +2.25, the fixed-length test's information value decreased.

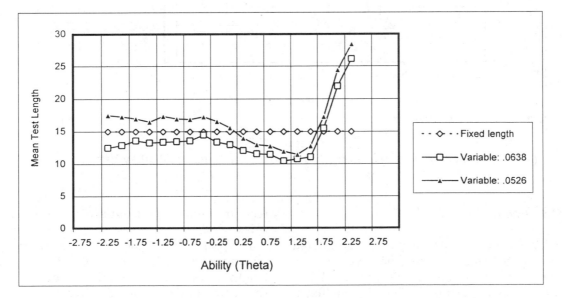

Figure 8-3
Fixed vs. Variable Length: Mean Test Length vs. Ability Level.

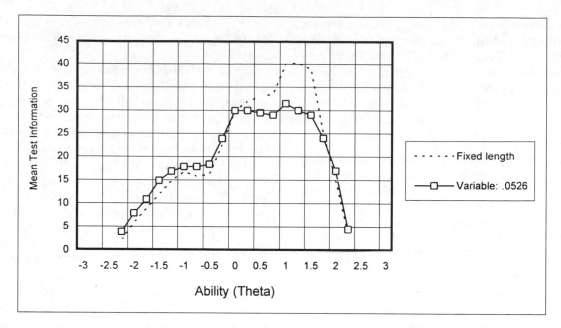

Figure 8-4
Fixed vs. Variable Length: Test Information vs. Ability Level.

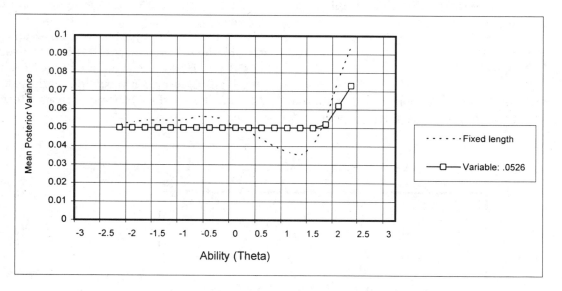

Figure 8-5
Fixed vs. Variable Length: Posterior Variance vs. Ability Level.

Study 3 Discussion

The fidelity coefficients obtained by the simulated variable-length tests exceeded .95, and were so close to each other in magnitude that the difference was of no importance. The 15-item fixed-length test fidelity coefficient reached .96. Differences in fidelity coefficients of all three tests were too small to be important. Neither the fixed-length test nor the variable-length tests were superior in this regard.

The posterior variance stopping criterion was a maximum value. It was possible for the variable length tests to attain posterior variance lower than the criterion. Figure 8-5 displays the average posterior variance as a function of ability for the same two tests as Figure 8-4. The posterior variance of the two variable-length tests was slightly below (and thus better than) the criterion from -2.25 to $+1.75$; above $+1.75$, posterior variance increased for all three tests. The mean posterior variance of the fixed-length test lay between the two variable-length means from -2.25 to 0, and was lower than both from $+.25$ to $+1.50$.

The test length of the variable-length tests varied systematically with ability level. In some cases, these tests averaged somewhat less than 15 items. At the highest ability levels (where there was little test information to begin with), the variable-length tests were much longer than 15 items, yet were not proportionally superior to the fixed-length test in terms of test information or posterior variance. The average levels of test information were also similar in magnitude, with the variable-length tests superior to fixed-length when they were longer, and with fixed-length superior when the average length of the other tests was less than 15.

Perhaps most noteworthy is what appears to be an inconsistency between the posterior variance and the test information plots. The former showed approximately constant mean levels of measurement precision throughout most of the range of ability represented in the simulations. On the other hand, average test information was not constant at all. It ranged from less than 10 to more than 20 and more for both of the variable-length tests. The lesson in this is that terminating adaptive testing when a specified level of posterior variance has been attained does not guarantee equal measurement precision when a different gauge—TIF values—is applied.

Conclusions

The three simulation studies summarized in this chapter were illustrative of the direction and the results of a much larger program of adaptive test simulations conducted by the authors from 1979 through 1985 and beyond. These simulation studies provided data evaluating a wide variety of adaptive testing strategies on a set of common criteria. The criteria included test reliability, measurement precision, and computational demands. In the end, the following general conclusions were reached:

• Mathematically complex strategies were found to be superior to simpler, mechanical strategies in terms of reliability and measurement efficiency.

• Among the mathematically complex strategies, a Bayesian sequential procedure and a maximum

likelihood procedure were found to be equally efficient, but both showed evidence of technical problems. Maximum likelihood ability estimates frequently failed to converge, causing difficulties in both item selection and test scoring. The Bayesian sequential strategy included an extremely computation-intensive item selection procedure that caused unacceptably long system response times on the 8-bit microcomputers of the late 1970s and early 1980s, and even on some fairly powerful minicomputers.

• A hybrid strategy was designed that combined the best properties of both approaches, and this eliminated the technical problems. However, this hybrid strategy had features that made test compromise likely.

• A variant of the hybrid strategy was designed to reduce the likelihood of test compromise, and was found to be virtually as efficient as the original hybrid.

• The use of variable-length adaptive testing, intended to yield equal measurement precision at all levels of examinee ability, was not found to be advantageous over fixed-length adaptive test administration.

These five broad conclusions, based on simulation studies like the ones reported in this chapter, led to the choice of adaptive testing strategy used in the experimental CAT-ASVAB system described below. Much of the early empirical data on the reliability, efficiency, and predictive and construct validity of adaptive testing were obtained using that experimental system. Almost all of the features of the adaptive strategy used in the experimental CAT system have been maintained in the CAT-ASVAB system now in operational use. A noteworthy exception is the random item selection procedure; it was displaced by an item exposure control method developed by Sympson and Hetter, described in Chapter 13.

The experimental system's hybrid adaptive strategy is summarized here: Owen's Bayesian sequential ability updating procedure was used to estimate ability after each item during the adaptive tests. Each adaptive test was fixed-length. The length differed across the nine ASVAB adaptive tests, but the 15-item length used in the above simulations is representative. A maximum information table lookup procedure was used to minimize computation during item selection. A shrinking set size procedure for randomly selecting one item from a set of nearly optimal items was used to improve security and discourage test compromise.

Development of the Experimental CAT-ASVAB System

John H. Wolfe, James R. McBride, and J. Bradford Sympson

The Navy Personnel Research and Development Center's (NPRDC's) experimental work on computerized adaptive testing (CAT) began in 1979 with an adaptively administered verbal test, using a Burroughs 1717 minicomputer (McBride & Martin, 1983). Unfortunately, that system was too slow to test more than one examinee at a time. (See also Chapter 5.)

CAT versions of three tests from the Armed Services Vocational Aptitude Battery (ASVAB) were developed: Arithmetic Reasoning (AR), Paragraph Comprehension (PC), and Word Knowledge (WK) (Moreno, Wetzel, McBride, & Weiss, 1984). The tests were administered to recruits at the Marine Corps Recruit Depot in San Diego, using four alphanumeric terminals connected to a time-shared computer at the University of Minnesota over leased lines. Items containing graphics could not be administered with that system.

By 1981, it became evident that further research progress required the development of a better platform for administering CAT. The ideal platform would be portable, self-contained, easy to program, able to present items with graphical content, and capable of rapid interaction when processing examinee responses. Fortunately, microcomputers that could meet these requirements began to become commercially available. NPRDC undertook the development of what became the first CAT microcomputer network with a shared pool of items and a graphics capability (Quan, Park, Sandahl, & Wolfe, 1984).

The battery that was developed in this study was an experimental version of CAT-ASVAB consisting of nine power tests and two speeded tests. The tests corresponded to those in the paper-and-pencil battery (P&P-ASVAB) except that the P&P-ASVAB Auto and Shop Information Test had been divided into two tests, to address concerns about dimensionality. Table 9-1 shows the content areas, test lengths, and item pool size for the battery used in the research program. Aspects of the developmental test work are described below.

Item Pool Development for Power Tests

For each content domain of the ASVAB power tests, a large pool of items of varying difficulty was constructed. Items were administered to several thousand examinees in paper-and-pencil mode. Because of the large number of items, each examinee received a subset of the full pool of items but the sets overlapped, permitting calibration of all items on a common scale (Sympson & Hartmann, 1985). The LOGIST program was used to estimate each item's parameters using a 3-parameter logistic (3PL) model.

The item pool development for the experimental CAT-ASVAB was carried out in two phases. In the first phase, about 450 items were written for each of five content areas: General Science (GS), Arithmetic Reasoning (AR), Word Knowledge (WK), Paragraph Comprehension (PC), and Mathemat-

Table 9-1 Tests in P&P-ASVAB and CAT-ASVAB

Test	Number of Items	Test Length	Test Time (minutes)	Source of Items
P&P-ASVAB				
General Science (GS)	25	25	11	
Arithmetic Reasoning (AR)	30	30	36	
Word Knowledge (WK)	35	35	11	
Paragraph Comprehension (PC)	15	15	13	
Numerical Operations (NO)	50	50	3	
Coding Speed (CS)	84	84	7	
Auto and Shop Information (AS)	25	25	11	
Mathematics Knowledge (MK)	25	25	24	
Mechanical Comprehension (MC)	25	25	19	
Electronics Information (EI)	20	20	9	
CAT-ASVAB				
General Science (GS)	197	15	Untimed	Phase 1
Arithmetic Reasoning (AR)	166	15	Untimed	Phase 1
Word Knowledge (WK)	194	15	Untimed	Phase 1
Paragraph Comprehension (PC)	95[a]	10	Untimed	Phase 1; Forms 8/9/10
Numerical Operations (NO)	50	50	2.5	ASVAB Form 8B
Coding Speed (CS)	84	84	5.5	ASVAB Form 8B
Auto Information (AI)	168	15	Untimed	Phase 2
Mathematics Knowledge (MK)	190	15	Untimed	Phase 2
Mechanical Comprehension (MC)	70	15	Untimed	ASVAB Forms 8/9/10
Electronics Information (EI)	192[b]	15	Untimed	Phase 2
Shop Information (SI)	135	15	Untimed	Phase 1

Note: Tests in this table are listed in the order of administration for the validity study.

[a] 48 PC items were in the pool during Navy and Marine Corps testing. This pool was subsequently supplemented with P&P-ASVAB items and increased to 95.

[b] 59 EI items were in the pool during Navy testing. These items were from P&P-ASVAB Forms 8/9/10. These items were then replaced with EI items from Phase 2 of the experimental CAT-ASVAB item pool development.

ics Knowledge (MK). As a first step in item calibration, items were pretested and responses obtained on approximately 300 military recruits per item. Items were calibrated using a procedure described by Urry (1976). Those items with low discrimination were removed from the pools. In the next step, items remaining in the pools were tested and item responses obtained on approximately 1,500 military applicants per item. Items were calibrated using LOGIST (Sympson & Hartmann, 1985).

In the second phase of the study, about 450 items were written and pretested for each of four content areas: Automotive Information (AI), Shop Information (SI), Mechanical Comprehension (MC), and Electronics Information (EI). The items were pretested and then calibrated using ANCILLES (Urry, 1976). Items low in discrimination were removed from the pools and item responses were collected on the remaining items. Items were then calibrated using LOGIST (N = 1,500).

A review of the nine ASVAB content areas for the power tests was conducted by Patricia Mitchell. This review showed that one of the computer content areas, MC, was very different from the P&P-ASVAB version in content. The MC items obtained in the second phase were not used; an item pool made up of MC items from P&P-ASVAB Forms 8, 9, and 10 and calibrated using LOGIST (N = 1,500) was used instead. Another problem was that many PC items were not independent (there were several questions from one paragraph) or would not fit on the screen. These items were discarded and the pool was supplemented with items from P&P-ASVAB Forms 8, 9, and 10.

At first data collection in the validation phase (see Chapter 10), item pool development for some of the tests had not been completed. The Navy data collection was started with five power tests: GS, AR, WK, PC, and MK.

At the start, the PC test consisted of those items from phase 1 that were suitable for computer administration. The MC test was added during the latter part of the Navy data collection. Since final item parameter estimates on EI, AI, and SI were not yet available, an interim pool of P&P-ASVAB EI items was included, and AI and SI were included with ANCILLES parameters (based on small sample sizes). Prior to the start of data collection for the Marine Corps, EI was replaced with the pool developed for the experimental CAT-ASVAB. Prior to the start of data collection for the Air Force, PC was supplemented with P&P-ASVAB items. ANCILLES parameters were used for administration of AI and SI throughout the data collection. At the end of data collection, these two tests were rescored using LOGIST parameters.

Item Pool Development for Speeded Tests

The items in the speeded tests were taken from P&P-ASVAB Form 8B. The speeded tests were administered in a conventional fashion, with examinees answering the same items in the same sequence. In NO, items were displayed three at a time on the screen. The test terminated when a time limit of 2.5 minutes was reached or when the examinee answered all 50 items. In CS, seven items were displayed on a screen, the format used in P&P-ASVAB. The test was terminated when a time limit of 5.5 minutes was reached or when the examinee had answered all 84 items. An examinee's score on a speeded test was the number of items answered correctly within the time limit.

Adaptive Algorithms

For each item, an information function was computed that determined the amount of information provided for a person at each level of ability. Then, an "infotable" of 36 ability level rows by 20 item ID columns was constructed. For each ability level, the IDs of the 20 most informative items were listed in order of decreasing information. The 36 ability levels cover the range -2.250 to $+2.125$ in steps of .125 standard deviation. During adaptive testing, a running estimate is kept of the examinee's ability. On the basis of each current estimate, the next item presented is selected from the unused items in the appropriate row of the infotable.

The infotable method is much faster than the Bayesian evaluation of the posterior error for each item after each examinee response, because the infotable is constructed prior to test administration and remains the same for all examinees. The examinee's ability estimate was updated each time a test item was answered.

Owen's approximation to the posterior mean (Owen, 1975) was used to update the ability esti-

mate during test administration. For each test, the prior distribution had a mean of 0.0 and a standard deviation of 1.0. The estimate after the last item was used as the score for a power test. Each test was terminated after a fixed number of items. Table 9-1 above shows the test length for each of the tests.

Because every examinee's initial ability estimate was 0.0 at the beginning of the text, strict application of the infotable method of selecting the most informative item would cause every examinee to receive the same first item. As such a test progresses, the examinees' ability estimates start to diverge from one another, so that the infotable selects different items for different examinees. However, early in the test, examinees tend to receive the same items. Such items are more likely to be remembered or discussed among examinees after the test, and their security possibly compromised through overexposure.

The experimental CAT-ASVAB item selection incorporated a procedure to reduce overexposure of certain highly informative items (Wetzel & McBride, 1986). To control the exposure of the items early in the test, a simple randomization method was used. For example, in the B-5-4-3-2-1 strategy, the first item that an examinee received was randomly chosen from among the best five items in the infotable row for ability 0.0. The second item was selected from among the best four items in the next appropriate row of the infotable, and so on. The fifth and succeeding items were the best unused items in the infotable row for the examinee's ability level.

The B-10-2-2-2-2 strategy to control item overexposure randomly selected the first item from among the best 10 questions; thereafter randomly from the best two items in the appropriate infotable row. The B-10-8-6-4-2 strategy randomly selected from the best 10 questions for question 1, from the best eight items for question 2, and so on. For the fifth and later items, one item was chosen randomly from among the best two in the appropriate row.

Hardware

Apple III Computers

The Apple III computer, which had just become available at the beginning of the project, was selected for the CAT delivery system. Unlike the Apple II computer models available at the time, the Apple III displayed lower as well as upper case letters on its screen, displayed 80 characters instead of 40, had higher resolution graphics, and contained up to four times as much random access memory (RAM). The Apple III computer provided adequate graphics resolution at about the same price as a graphics terminal. By providing a computer, rather than just a terminal to each examinee, it became feasible to test several examinees at the same time, with no degradation in interactive response time.

A modified keyboard was used for test administration. On the main keyboard, all but six keys were covered up. The remaining keys were labeled A, B, C, D, E, and Help. On the numeric keypad, the digits 0–9 remained the same, but three additional keys were relabeled "Yes," "No," and "Erase." The Yes key served to confirm and enter responses, while the No and Erase keys permitted the administration of free-response items on an experimental basis.

Corvus Multiplex Disk

It was obvious that a single floppy disk drive could not contain all of the CAT-ASVAB items and software, and that a hard (Winchester) disk would be needed. In 1982, a 20-megabyte hard drive cost about $5,500. Fortunately, the Corvus Corporation marketed a hard drive with a multiplexor that allowed up to eight Apple computers to share the same disk. Hardwicke, Eastman, and Cooper (1984) describe the physical layout and operation of the CAT equipment. The software and items were write-protected, so several Apples could read the same files "simultaneously." Examinee records were kept separately for each Apple III node in the network. Each examinee record could be accessed only by the Apple computer administering his/her test.

Software: Apple Pascal/SOS

The development of the complex CAT software was greatly facilitated by the use of a high-level structured programming language, Apple *Pascal*, which was based on the University of California-San Diego (UCSD) p-system. The compiler translated *Pascal* source code into a machine-independent p-code, which was then interpreted into executable machine instructions. Although the code ran more slowly than that produced by today's compilers, which compile directly into machine instructions, it was very efficient in the amount of RAM it used, so it became possible to fit

some very complex programs into the Apple III's 256K bytes of memory. Programming was also facilitated by Apple's Sophisticated Operating System, which was one of the first microcomputer systems to have a hierarchical file structure with subdirectories within directories.

Testing System Features

At the beginning of a testing session, the system presented computer familiarization instruction and practice to the examinee. The examinee then entered a unique identification number, using the numeric keypad. The TA entered additional personal data about the examinee after the testing session, using an Apple III computer with a full keyboard.

The test administration module had a look-ahead procedure. While the examinee was inspecting an item on the screen, the system would identify the best items to present next if the examinee answered the current item correctly or incorrectly. These two items were read from the hard disk into main memory. As soon as the examinee answered the current item, the next item could then be presented immediately. The test administration module provided several options for feedback: none, right-wrong feedback, or remedial question feedback. The last was used in the practice items given during test instructions. Scoring results could be provided to the examinee after a test or at the end of the entire test session.

If the TA observed an examinee having difficulty, or if the examinee raised a hand, the proctor first would try to handle any difficulty that did not involve the content of a specific item. Then the proctor had options to continue with the session, exit and resume testing later, skip certain procedures, or terminate the current test and begin the next test in sequence.

When an examinee finished a test, it was scored and the sequence of item responses, response latencies, and the intermediate estimates of ability were written onto a record in a file containing all examinee data. At least once a week, these files had to be transferred to floppy disks, consolidated with other files, and sent to a mainframe computer for statistical analyses.

The system had many more functions than simple test administration. Since it was a research system, it had to be highly flexible. Modules were created for entering and editing item text and graphics. Whenever a new item was entered or deleted, the module automatically entered or deleted its item parameters and recreated infotables. It was also necessary to manipulate tests at the test level, including interactive instruction and familiarization screens.

Another module managed alternative strategies for item selection, exposure control, and stopping rules. A test could be stopped after a fixed time limit, after a fixed number of items had been administered, or when the measurement error in the examinee's ability estimate had dropped to a specified value.

The system was used not only for administering CAT-ASVAB tests but also for developing new speeded tests of cognition where reaction time, inspection time, and working memory tests were administered. Several studies comparing the reliability and validity of P&P-ASVAB and CAT-ASVAB were carried out. These studies are described in Chapters 8 and 10.

Summary and Conclusions

The Apple III CAT system was a microcomputer network that was capable of delivering both textual and graphical items and contained all features necessary for a CAT-ASVAB delivery system. Important research data were collected, and experience with the system enabled detailed specifications to be developed for the operational CAT-ASVAB system that succeeded it.

10

Validation of the Experimental CAT-ASVAB System

Daniel O. Segall, Kathleen E. Moreno, William F. Kieckhaefer, Frank L. Vicino, and James R. McBride

The experimental CAT-ASVAB system, described in the previous chapter, was the first system that included tests that covered all ASVAB content areas. This made the system a very important research tool for conducting preliminary evaluations of the feasibility of replacing P&P-ASVAB with CAT-ASVAB. In 1982 through 1985, the experimental system was used to conduct a Joint-Service validity study. The primary objective of this study was to examine how well CAT-ASVAB predicted military training school performance, as compared to P&P-ASVAB. Secondary objectives were: (1) to assess the construct validity of CAT-ASVAB, and (2) to determine the amount of time needed to administer the CAT-ASVAB.

Background

The P&P-ASVAB has been validated against a variety of criteria, including job performance, paper-and-pencil written aptitude test scores, and attrition (Vineberg & Joyner, 1982; Armor, Fernandez, Bers, & Schwarzbach, 1982). The P&P-ASVAB is most commonly used as a predictor of performance in the Services' technical training courses.

P&P-ASVAB Predictive Validity Research

Composites on P&P-ASVAB Forms 5/6/7 (operational between July 1976 and September 1980)

predicted final grade and test scores in a variety of Air Force, Navy, and Army schools, but were generally poorer predictors of completion time criteria. AFQT is a composite score of ASVAB tests that is used to qualify applicants for enlistment. Until January 1989, AFQT was a composite of four tests: Arithmetic Reasoning (AR), Word Knowledge (WK), Paragraph Comprehension (PC), and Numerical Operations (NO). The AFQT was found to be a predictor of passing the Army Skills Qualification Test (SQT) (Greenberg, 1980; Armor et al., 1982). Greenberg reported that AFQT scores and selector composites had modest positive relationships with SQT scores in Army schools. Similar modest correlations were reported between P&P-ASVAB Forms 6/7 selector composites and final school grade or days-to-completion in 31 Navy "A" schools in a concurrent validity study (Swanson, 1978). Swanson also conducted several predictive validity studies, and found "good" prediction of final school grade in 19 Navy "A" schools (1978), and later in 79 Navy "A" schools and 22 Basic Electricity and Electronics (BE/E) schools (1979). Further, Swanson et al. (1978) examined the predictive validity of ASVAB Forms 5/6/7 selector composites for predicting training performance in corresponding schools. These composites were found to be predictive of final school grade in 9 Army schools, 26 Air Force Schools, and 25 Navy schools. In Swanson's predictive studies, the validity of the selector composites for predicting completion time was lower than that for final school grade.

P&P-ASVAB Forms 8/9/10 (operational between October 1980 and September 1984) predicted school performance criteria as well as Forms 5/6/7. When Forms 8/9/10 were introduced, Sims and Hiatt (1981) estimated validities for them by simulating composites using Forms 6/7 data. They concluded that except for the Clerical composite, Forms 8/9/10 yielded equal or better validity coefficients. Booth-Kewley (1983) reported comparable validity coefficients for P&P-ASVAB 5/6/7 and 8/9/10 for predicting final school grade in the Navy strategic weapon systems electronic "A" school. Forms 8/9/10 correlations with final school grade in Navy BE/E courses were significant, but the test validities were poor for predicting completion time (Baker, 1983b). Maier and Truss (1983) reported that all P&P-ASVAB tests and composites (except the Clerical) had satisfactory validity for predicting final school grades in Marine Corps training, but had little relationship to completion time. Similarly, Forms 8/9/10 AFQT predicted trainability in a variety of clusters of Marine Corps training specialties, and corresponding selector composite validities exceeded those of the AFQT, except for the Clerical composite (Maier, 1983).

Low validities of the Clerical or Administrative composites have also been documented in the Air Force (Mullins, Earles, & Ree, 1981; Wilbourn, Valentine, & Ree, 1984) and in the Army (Weltin & Popelka, 1983). Further, Weltin and Popelka noted that including the AR test in the composite would increase the validity, but it would also increase intercorrelations among the selector composites.

Wilbourn et al. (1984) studied 70 Air Force schools which used final school grade as the training performance criterion. AFQT was a good predictor of completion of Air Force basic training performance. Relatively high validity coefficients were reported for schools which used the General composite (WK, AR, PC) and the Electronics composite (GS, AR, MK, EI), moderate coefficients for the Mechanical composite (GS, AS, MC), and low validity for the Administrative composite (WK, PC, NO, CS).

Computerized Adaptive Testing Research

The validities of adaptive and conventional tests have been examined in academic settings. Bejar and Weiss (1978) examined the construct validity of two computerized adaptive and two paper-and-pencil conventional biology tests. These researchers reported that "Out of four comparisons, the adaptive procedure was somewhat more valid in one, and somewhat less valid in another. However, in all instances, the adaptive procedure was at least 25 percent shorter on the average than the conventional paper-and-pencil testing procedure. Thus, in a practical sense, the adaptive testing procedure was considerably more valid in all instances" (p. 17). Thompson and Weiss (1980) administered computerized conventional and adaptive tests to college students. Both stratified and Bayesian adaptive tests were more predictive of grade point average and ACT achievement test scores than the conventional test. The stratified tests were shorter than the conventional tests, while the Bayesian tests were slightly longer. However, there were no differences between the adaptive tests in predicting the external criteria.

Some research in military settings has compared computerized versions of conventional and adaptive tests. McBride (1980) studied computerized conventional and adaptive tests of verbal ability in a Marine Corps sample. Short adaptive tests had higher reliabilities than conventional tests of the same length, but differences in reliability decreased with increasing test length. None of the validity differences were statistically significant. In a replication of McBride's (1980) study, Martin, McBride, and Weiss (1983) reported concurrent validity coefficients for adaptive tests that were consistently higher than those for conventional tests. For example, an adaptive test of 11 items had a concurrent validity equivalent to a 27-item conventional test. In both of these studies, the criterion measure was the score on a long conventional test given at the same time as the predictor tests.

Sympson, Weiss, and Ree (1984) conducted a predictive validity study using two ASVAB tests. Three AR and three WK tests were administered on a computer in conventional, Owen's Bayesian adaptive, or stratified maximum information adaptive mode to subjects scheduled for later attendance at an Air Force training school. While validity coefficients did not differ significantly for adaptive and conventional tests of equal length, the stratified maximum information adaptive strategy achieved approximately equal validities to the conventional ASVAB while using one-third to one-half the items.

The Computerized Adaptive Screening Test (CAST) and the Enlistment Screening Test (EST) (the paper-and-pencil predecessor of the CAST) were compared as predictors of AFQT. In a field test of the CAST, Sands and Gade (1983) reported that a 15-item composite (10 WK and 5 AR items) was as valid a predictor of the AFQT as the 48-item EST. Pliske, Gade, and Johnson (1984) reported that CAST was at least as good a predictor of AFQT as EST, even though it was a much shorter test (discussed more fully in Chapter 7).

Moreno, Wetzel, McBride, and Weiss (1984) reported that correlations between CAT-ASVAB and P&P-ASVAB were of equal magnitude to P&P-ASVAB test-retest correlations for AR, WK, and PC tests in a Marine Corps sample. This was true even though the CAT-ASVAB tests included about half as many items as the P&P-ASVAB. Further, the three CAT-ASVAB tests explained 75 percent of the variance in pre-enlistment AFQT, while the four post-enlistment AFQT tests explained 73 percent of pre-enlistment AFQT variance. Thus, the evidence suggests that the CAT-ASVAB should be as valid a predictor of training performance as the P&P-ASVAB.

Factor Analytic Studies

Factor analytic studies contribute further evidence of the similarity of P&P-ASVAB and CAT-ASVAB tests. P&P-ASVAB Forms 6/7 were analyzed to yield four factors: Verbal, Mathematics, Shop, and Attitude (Sims & Hiatt, 1981). The tests comprising the P&P-ASVAB were altered between ASVAB Forms 6/7 and Forms 8/9/10, and factor analyses of the latter commonly yield a four-factor solution consisting of Verbal Ability, Quantitative or Mathematical Ability, Speeded Performance, and Technical Knowledge or Technical Information (Ree, Mullins, Mathews, & Massey, 1982; Kass, Mitchell, Grafton, & Wing, 1983; Moreno et al., 1984). When CAT-ASVAB tests were included in the analyses, they had very similar factor loadings to their corresponding P&P-ASVAB tests (Moreno et al., 1984).

Summary

The literature indicates CAT has validities as high as or higher than conventionally administered counterparts even though they are generally shorter and, thus, take less time to administer. Further, at the time of this study, CAT-ASVAB tests measuring verbal and math abilities had yielded equal validities and similar factor structures when compared to the corresponding P&P-ASVAB tests. To this end, it was important to examine CAT-ASVAB and P&P-ASVAB validities across all ASVAB content areas and for a broad spectrum of Service jobs.

Approach

The approach used to collect the data for this research was very similar across all four Services. Since the data collection effort extended from June 1982 to March 1984, there were some variations. This section first describes the general approach and research design. Then, the sample, test instruments, criterion variables, and test administration procedures are described in more detail. Differences in approach between Services are noted.

Research Design

To compare the predictive validity of CAT-ASVAB and P&P-ASVAB, 23 training courses, across the four Services, were selected. They were chosen to ensure that (1) a broad spectrum of Service training programs was represented, (2) all P&P-ASVAB tests were included as predictor composites of the schools, and (3) enough examinees would be available for testing to allow meaningful comparisons between the CAT-ASVAB and the P&P-ASVAB.

To make comparisons between CAT-ASVAB and P&P-ASVAB, scores on both batteries were needed. The general approach used was a repeated measures design in which recruits took CAT-ASVAB and a partial P&P-ASVAB. The partial P&P-ASVAB was made up of those tests used to compute the selection composite score for an individual examinee's Service specialty. For example, the Navy radioman specialty uses four P&P-ASVAB tests in computing the selection composite score: WK, PC, NO, and CS. Therefore, any recruits scheduled to attend training as a Navy radioman were given only these four P&P-ASVAB tests. Order of administration of the CAT-ASVAB and P&P-ASVAB was counterbalanced so that approximately one-half of the examinees in a given session took CAT-ASVAB followed by P&P-ASVAB, and the other half reversed the order.

The CAT-ASVAB and the partial P&P-ASVAB were administered after recruits had arrived for basic training and were conducted under nonoperational conditions. For some of the analyses, scores on a full P&P-ASVAB battery were needed, so the "scores of record," or the scores used for accessioning into the military, were also collected. Therefore, for each examinee, there were two types of P&P-ASVAB scores: The P&P-ASVAB pre-enlistment scores used for accessioning and the P&P-ASVAB scores obtained from post-enlistment testing. For purposes of this chapter, the battery from which the scores of record were obtained will be called the pre-enlistment P&P-ASVAB and the partial battery will be referred to as the post-enlistment P&P-ASVAB. In addition to the aptitude test scores, school performance data were collected on each examinee, along with demographic data, such as race and educational level.

Sample

Examinees were military recruits scheduled for training in one of the 23 military Service specialties selected for this study. Over all Services, 7,518 examinees were tested: (1) 1,411 Navy recruits at the Navy Recruit Training Center, San Diego, from June 9, 1982 through January 28, 1983; (2) 2,054 Marine Corps recruits at the Marine Corps Recruit Depot, San Diego, from February 24, 1983 through December 9, 1983; (3) 1,487 Air Force recruits at Lackland Air Force Base, San Antonio, from May 23, 1983 through September 8, 1983; and (4) 2,566 Army recruits at Fort Jackson, South Carolina, from September 20, 1983 through March 30, 1984 and at Fort Dix, New Jersey, from October 7, 1983 through March 5, 1984. Table 10-1 shows the number of recruits tested for each military specialty, and the selection composites and performance criteria used.

Test Instruments

P&P-ASVAB. P&P-ASVAB Forms 8A and 9A were used for post-enlistment test administration. The score for a test was the number of items answered correctly for that test.

CAT-ASVAB. The CAT-ASVAB used in this study was the experimental version of this battery, described in Chapter 9. At the start of data collection, item pool development for some of the tests had not been completed. The Navy data collection was started with five power tests: GS, AR, WK, PC, and MK. The PC test consisted of those items from phase 1 of the item calibration that were suitable for computer administration. During the latter part of the Navy data collection, MC was added. Since final item parameter estimates on EI, AI, and SI were not yet available, an interim pool of P&P-ASVAB EI items was included, and AI and SI were included with ANCILLES (Urry, 1976) parameters (based on small sample sizes). Before data collection started for the Marine Corps, EI was replaced with the pool developed for the experimental CAT-ASVAB system. Prior to the data

collection for the Air Force, PC was supplemented with P&P-ASVAB items. ANCILLES parameters were used for administration of AI and SI throughout the data collection. At the end of data collection, these two tests were rescored using LOGIST (Wood, Wingersky, & Lord, 1976) parameters.

The speeded tests were administered in a conventional fashion, with all examinees answering the same items in the same sequence. The score on a speeded test was the number of items answered correctly within the time limit. Chapter 9 provides a more detailed description of the experimental CAT-ASVAB system, including psychometric procedures.

Test Administration

CAT-ASVAB power test items were selected using maximum information. To save computation time, an information "look-up" table was used. Item selection incorporated a procedure to reduce overexposure of certain highly informative items (Wetzel & McBride, 1986). Owen's approximation to the posterior mean (Owen, 1975) was used to update the ability estimate during power test administration. For each test, the prior distribution had a mean of 0.0 and a standard deviation of 1.0. The estimate after the last item was used as the score for a power test. Each test was terminated after a fixed number of items.

Training Performance Criteria

When available, an official course grade was used as the training performance criterion for a particular specialty. For courses where a final course grade was not available, other criteria were developed from available data, as shown in Table 10-1.

Navy. As indicated in Table 10-1, the official final school grade was the criterion of training performance for four of the six schools in the Navy specialties. Completion time was the criterion for the Radioman and Electronics Technician schools. Since these two schools are self-paced, completion time is often used as a performance measure.

Marine Corps. Where an official final course grade was available—in six of the eight Marine Corps schools in the study—that score was used as a training performance criterion. Other criteria were also used. Aviation Fundamentals is a self-paced course in the Navy's Basic Electricity and Electronics school. Completion time is often used

Table 10-1 Training Courses, Asvab Selection Composites, and Performance Criterion Measures Used in Validating the Experimental Cat-asvab

Training Course	Number Tested	Final Number	Selection Composite[a]	Performance Criterion
Navy				
1. Radioman (RM)	252	186	VE+NO+CS	Completion Time
2. Mess Management Specialist (MS)	222	170	VE+AR	Final School Grade
3. Hospital Corpsman (HM)	228	192	VE+MK+GS	Final School Grade
4. Electronics Technician (ET)	230	143	MK+EI+GS+AR	Completion Time
5. Hull Maintenance Technician (HT)	229	170	VE+MC+AS	Final School Grade
6. Sonar Technician-Surface (STG)	250	205	MK+EI+GS+AR	Final School Grade
Marine Corps				
1. Aviation Basic Electricity and Electronics Aviation (6300)	317	228	AR+GS+MK+EI	Final Course Grade & Completion Time
2. Machinist Mate (6011)	358[b]	181	AR+AS+MC+EI	Final Course Grade
3. Aviation Structures Mechanic (6091)	358[b]	69	AR+AS+MC+EI	Final Course Grade
4. Administration Clerk (0151) Pendleton/Lejeune	373[c]	39/72	VE+NO+CS	Final Course Grade
5. Motor Transport Specialist (3500)	202	151	AR+AS+MC+EI	Final Course Grade
6. Basic Combat Engineer (1371)	240	123	AR+AS+MC+EI	Sum of All Module Scores
7. Field Radio Operator (2531)	206	128	AR+GS+MK+EI	Sum of Tests (two)
Air Force				
1. Electronic Principles (AVNC)	164	147	AR+GS+MK+EI	Mean of Common Module Scores
2. Aircraft Maintenance Specialist (MECH)	270	245	GS+2AS+MC	Final School Grade
3. Administration Specialist (ADMIN)	290	208	VE+NO+CS	Final School Grade
4. Security Specialist (SP)	617	456	AR+VE	Final School Grade
5. Medical Specialist (MED)	146	95	AR+VE	Final School Grade
Army				
1. Infantry (11X)	376	329	AR+CS+AS+MC	Sum of Task NO-GO Scores[c]
2. Motor and Generator Mechanic (63B)			NO+AS+MC+EI	
Fort Dix/	330	198		Average of Module Scores
Fort Jackson	306	186		Percent Correct[d]
3. Motor Transport Operator (64C)	392	277	VE+NO+AS+MC	Sum of Test Scores[c]
4. Administrative Specialist (71L)	490	145	VE+NO+CS	Sum of Module minus Weighted Typing Score[c]
5. Medical Specialist (91B)	429	225	VE+GS+MK+MC	Final School Grade
6. Telecommunications Center Operator (72E)	243	169	VE+NO+CS+AS	Sum of Module Scores

[a] AR: Arithmetic Reasoning; WK: Word Knowledge; PC: Paragraph Comprehension; NO: Numerical Operations; GS: General Science; MK: Mathematics Knowledge; EI: Electronics Information; CS: Coding Speed; AS: Auto and Shop Information; VE: Verbal Composite [WK + PC].

[b] A total of 358 examinees were tested from the pre-enlistment field. Some eventually were assigned to 6011 training, others to 6091.

[c] These performance criteria required combining NO-GO scores. Therefore, higher scores on these criteria indicate poor performers.

[d] This was a percent correct on the end-of-course performance test.

as a performance criterion, so completion time was included as a criterion for the Marine Corps Aviation Fundamentals course. For the remaining two courses, Basic Combat Engineer and Field Radio Operator, the final course grade was on a pass or fail basis with fewer than 5 percent failing. Analyses of module scores for the engineering course showed that the sum of module scores best accounted for performance in that course. Analyses of the test scores for the radio course revealed that the first and second halves of the course should remain separate. Here, the sum of the first four test scores served as one criterion, and the sum of the last four served as the second criterion.

Air Force. The official final school grade was the criterion of training performance for four of the five Air Force schools. The Air Training Command at Lackland Air Force Base provided the data. For examinees attending the Electronic Principles course, the Faculty Development Division at Keesler Air Force Base provided the module scores used to compute the Mean of Common Module Scores.

Army. Where an official final course grade was available and showed score variation, that score was included as a training performance criterion. The final course grade served as the criterion of training performance in one of the seven courses in the Army study. For the remaining courses, the final course grade was either a "GO" or a "NO GO," with over 90 percent receiving a "GO."

Two Army schools used other internal performance measures which served as performance criteria. The Motor and Generator Mechanic school at Fort Dix maintained an average of module scores, and the Motor and Generator Mechanic school at Fort Jackson recorded the percent correct on the end-of-course performance test. For the remaining schools, criterion development procedures determined which combination of available data best represented training performance. These procedures suggested the sum of module scores as the criterion for the Telecommunications Center Operator. For the Infantry, Motor Transport Operator, and Administrative Specialist schools, the performance criteria required combining NO-GO scores; in these cases, high scores reflect poor performance.

A problem which this study shares with previous ASVAB validity studies concerns the lack of adequate criteria measuring trainee skills. In addition to academic tests, all the schools included in this study had skills tests. Unfortunately, the results of those tests were recorded only as "pass" or "fail," and few failures (less than 5 percent) ever occurred. Nevertheless, interviews with instructors in each of the courses indicated that they believed skills tests were better indicators of training performance than academic tests.

Procedures

As mentioned, examinees were given the pre-enlistment P&P-ASVAB prior to entrance into the military, and the post-enlistment P&P-ASVAB and CAT-ASVAB during their time at basic training. Following basic training, examinees went to training for their Service specialty. At the conclusion of training for the specialty, criterion performance data were collected for each examinee.

Test session. At each test site, two testing areas were used: One for P&P-ASVAB testing and one for CAT-ASVAB testing. The session started in the P&P testing area after the test administrators (TAs) gave an introduction on the purpose of the testing. Then they randomly divided the examinees into two groups: Those who would take the CAT-ASVAB first and those who would take the P&P-ASVAB first. Examinees assigned to the CAT-ASVAB group were taken to that testing area, and the rest remained in the P&P-ASVAB testing area. At the end of the first test session, after a short break examinees given the CAT-ASVAB during the first session then took the P&P-ASVAB, and those given the P&P-ASVAB were then given the CAT-ASVAB.

Administration of the experimental CAT-ASVAB. Examinees were seated at a computer and received general verbal instructions from the TA. Then they began a programmed familiarization sequence on using the keyboard to answer test items, and completed sample questions that gave them practice answering test items. Examinees could review both of these sequences prior to the actual test administration.

CAT-ASVAB tests appeared in the following order: GS, AR, WK, PC, MK, NO, CS, EI, MC, and AI. As mentioned earlier, when testing began in the Navy, all items pools had not been put into the system. As a pool was available, and to keep some consistency of order across Services, SI was added to the end of the current battery. This is the reason that the order of the CAT-ASVAB tests was not the same as the order typical of the P&P-ASVAB tests.

Examinees answered items in the order presented and could not skip an item. When the test was completed, examinees received feedback on the computer screen. This took the form of ability estimates (theta), posterior variances, item scores, and percentiles. For the speeded tests, feedback was presented in the form of number of items attempted and number answered correctly.

Administration of a post-enlistment P&P-ASVAB. Before a P&P-ASVAB test session started, an examinee's record was checked to determine what form of the pre-enlistment P&P-ASVAB had been given. If an examinee had taken Form 8A, Form 9A was assigned and vice versa.

As mentioned earlier, the post-enlistment P&P-

ASVAB contained only those tests required for an examinee's selection composite (see Table 10-1). The same directions, instructions, and test items used in operational settings were used with one exception. Overall directions and test instructions, normally read aloud by the TA, were read by the examinees in this study.

As required in a P&P-ASVAB test session, examinees recorded their responses to items on a scannable answer sheet. Navy and Marine Corps examinees used answer sheets from the operational testing. However, examinees in the Air Force and Army recorded their answers on a research answer sheet, and then test scores were converted so that they would be equivalent to scores obtained using operational answer sheets.

Procedural problems. Prior to the testing for this study, and on the same day, examinees in the Marine Corps had been given P&P-ASVAB Form 7 as a retest. This was not discovered until after data collection for the CAT-ASVAB study had started. Three tests of Form 7 were administered, but only AR test data were part of this study. Thus, Marine Corps examinees received three versions of the AR test on the same day: P&P-ASVAB Form 7, post-enlistment P&P-ASVAB Form 8A or 9A as part of this study, and CAT-ASVAB as part of this study.

Missing data. The number of recruits tested in each Service specialty and the number of recruits in the final sample used for predictive validity analyses (final N) were shown in Table 10-1. In some cases, there is a large discrepancy between number of examinees tested and number in the final sample. A wide variety of factors contributed to this missing data problem.

In the Marine Corps a primary reason for loss of cases was that at the time of post-enlistment testing for this study, Marine Corps examinees had not been assigned to one military occupational specialty (MOS). At that time the Marine Corps recruited individuals into general occupational fields and later assigned the individual to one of the several MOS in that occupational field. Since this study was concerned with specific training schools, it was necessary to test far more Marine Corps recruits in the relevant general occupational field than were needed in the final sample of a specific MOS, since recruits might be assigned to any of several MOSs in that occupational field. Another reason for loss of cases in the final sample for predictive validity analyses was that the sample sizes for some specific MOSs were so small that they could not be included in the analyses.

A number of examinees in each training category did not have criterion scores. Since the examinees were just beginning recruit basic training at the time of testing, there were several reasons why training criteria might not have been available. These reasons included:

- Failure to complete basic training

- Change of rating, MOS, or AFSC

- Incorrect recording of the social security number or AFSC

- Holds for medical reasons

- Discharges prior to completing the assigned training

- Recycles through training

- School drops

- Failure to complete assigned training

All examinees tested who had valid predictor data, were included in those analyses that did not require criterion data.

Results and Discussion

As noted in the opening of this chapter, the purposes of this study were to (1) compare the predictive validity of CAT-ASVAB and P&P-ASVAB, (2) assess the construct validity of CAT-ASVAB, and (3) determine the amount of time needed to administer CAT-ASVAB. To evaluate these issues, the following research questions were addressed:

- Determine what method is appropriate for combining relevant CAT-ASVAB tests so that they could be compared with the corresponding P&P-ASVAB scores for Auto and Shop Information (AS) and Verbal Ability (VE = [WK and PC]).

- Compare the validity of CAT-ASVAB and P&P-ASVAB selector composites.

- Determine whether CAT-ASVAB and P&P-ASVAB tests measure the same aptitudes.

- Compare testing times for CAT-ASVAB and P&P-ASVAB.

Where appropriate, CAT-ASVAB was compared to both the pre-enlistment and post-enlistment ASVABs, so that all available information could be summarized and reported. The reader should keep in mind that the most appropriate comparisons are between post-enlistment P&P-ASVAB and CAT-ASVAB, since these two tests were administered close in time and under nonoperational conditions.

Specification of CAT-ASVAB AS and VE

CAT-ASVAB AS (the Auto and Shop composite for the CAT-ASVAB) and CAT-ASVAB VE (the Verbal Ability composite of the Word Knowledge and Paragraph Comprehension tests for the CAT-ASVAB) both consisted of two separately administered adaptive tests. The scores from the separate tests had to be combined in each instance before comparisons with the corresponding P&P composite or test scores could be made. At the time of this study, an equating between CAT-ASVAB and P&P-ASVAB tests did not exist. Therefore, the current methods for computing these scores, described in Chapter 19, could not be used. The approach taken to combine the tests was to determine a linear combination using integer-valued weights.

This procedure resulted in a correlation between CAT-ASVAB AS and P&P-ASVAB AS that (1) did not significantly differ from optimal weighting, (2) did not require AI and SI scores to be scaled prior to weighting, and (3) determined weights that were easily replicated from sample to sample. A method for testing linear hypotheses of regression weights, described in Draper and Smith (1981, pp. 102–107), was used to determine the best linear combination using the integer-valued weights. The following regression model was specified:

$$E(Y_{P\&P}) = \beta_0 + \beta_1 X_{CAT1} + \beta_2 X_{CAT2} \quad (10\text{-}1)$$

where $Y_{P\&P}$ is the raw score on the P&P-ASVAB test, and X_{CAT1} and X_{CAT2} are scores on the two separately tailored CAT-ASVAB tests. The equations for the null hypotheses of interest were as follows:

$$H_0: \beta_1 - \beta_2 = 0 \quad (10\text{-}2)$$

$$H_0: \beta_1 - 2\beta_2 = 0 \quad (10\text{-}3)$$

$$H_0: \beta_1 - 3\beta_2 = 0 \quad (10\text{-}4)$$

$$H_0: \beta_1 - 4\beta_2 = 0 \quad (10\text{-}5)$$

The first hypothesis is equivalent to the hypothesis of equal regression weights. The second states that β_1 is equal to twice β_2, etc. This framework allows testing hypotheses about the relative size of the parameters. These conditions were substituted into the original model to obtain four reduced models.

Results showed that for the CAT-ASVAB AS composite, the constraint ($\beta_1 = 2\beta_2$) resulted in a multiple correlation that nearly equaled the optimal multiple correlation. For the CAT-ASVAB VE composite, the constraint ($\beta_1 = 3\beta_2$) was equivalent to the optimal correlation to within .001. Based on these results, CAT-ASVAB composite scores were calculated as

$$\text{CAT-ASVAB AS} = (2\theta_{AI} + \theta_{SI}) \quad (10\text{-}6)$$

$$\text{CAT-ASVAB VE} = (3\theta_{WK} + \theta_{PC}) \quad (10\text{-}7)$$

where θ_{AI}, θ_{SI}, θ_{WK}, and θ_{PC} are the Owen's (1975) Bayesian ability estimates for the CAT-ASVAB AI, SI, WK, and PC tests.

Selector Composite Validity

This section examines the prediction of school criteria from CAT-ASVAB and P&P-ASVAB selector composites. Of specific interest is the relative amount of variance in the criteria accounted for by linear combinations of CAT-ASVAB and P&P-ASVAB tests. Did CAT-ASVAB and P&P-ASVAB tests predict school performance equally well?

Three separate equations were specified using school selector composite tests. The first equation predicted the criterion from the appropriate CAT-ASVAB selector composite tests. The second predicted the criterion from the appropriate pre-enlistment P&P-ASVAB selector composite tests, and the third used post-enlistment P&P-ASVAB composite tests as predictors. Regression weights for each equation were estimated using the method of least-squares. Multiple correlations for each of the three prediction equations were also calculated.

Hypotheses for the difference between CAT-ASVAB and each P&P-ASVAB multiple correlation were tested for each school. An automated hypothesis testing procedure similar to one recommended by Lord (1975) tested the difference between two dependent multiple correlations using the following procedure:

Let $\xi = R_{CAT\text{-}ASVAB} - R_{P\&P\text{-}ASVAB}$ the difference between the two multiple correlations of interest. To test the hypothesis $H_0: \xi = 0$, the values of $\hat{\xi}/\hat{\sigma}_{\hat{\xi}}$ were computed, where $\hat{\sigma}_{\hat{\xi}}^2$ is the asymptotic sampling variance of $\hat{\xi}$. (This variance is computed numerically.) The rejection region for H_0 consists of both tails of the asymptotic distribution of $\hat{\xi}/\hat{\sigma}_{\hat{\xi}}$. In the current problem, this distribution is normal with zero mean and unit variance.

Table 10-2 displays the multiple correlations for prediction equations using CAT-ASVAB, pre-enlistment P&P-ASVAB, and post-enlistment P&P-ASVAB composite tests. Values of the standardized difference statistic $\hat{\xi}/\hat{\sigma}_{\hat{\xi}}$, for testing the two hypotheses $H_0: R_{CAT\text{-}ASVAB} - R_{PRE\text{-}ASVAB} = 0$ and $H_0: R_{CAT\text{-}ASVAB} - R_{POST\text{-}ASVAB} = 0$, are listed in the last two columns of Table 10-2 labeled "CAT-PRE" and "CAT-POST," respectively. Among the 56 comparisons shown in Table 10-2, only one significant difference occurred between the CAT-ASVAB and

Table 10-2 Comparison of Multiple Correlations for Prediction Equations Based on CAT-ASVAB and P&P-ASVAB

| School | N | Multiple Correlations | | | Standardized Differences | |
		CAT-ASVAB	PRE-ASVAB	POST-ASVAB	CAT-PRE	CAT-POST
			Navy			
RM	186	.41	.38	.41	.53	.13
MS	170	.47	.48	.41	−.24	1.08
HM	192	.57	.55	.60	.52	−1.11
ET	143	.41	.43	.48	−.30	−1.31
HT	170	.40	.44	.38	−.90	.46
STG	205	.46	.43	.49	.84	−.51
			Marine Corps			
6300	228	.52	.47	.49	1.37	.74
6300	228	.61	.59	.58	.66	.98
6011	181	.39	.28	.31	1.95	1.49
6091	69	.57	.54	.53	.41	.64
0151						
Camp Pendleton	39	.43	.36	.35	.37	.46
Camp Lejeune	72	.24	.25	.14	−.08	.58
3500	151	.39	.30	.39	1.64	.01
1371	123	.69	.65	.67	1.10	.61
2531	128	.24	.27	.10	−.27	1.62
2531	128	.34	.26	.26	.94	.98
			Air Force			
AVNC	147	.57	.47	.59	2.09*	−.53
MECH	245	.57	.59	.51	−.89	1.95
ADMIN	208	.26	.28	.24	−.20	.40
SP	456	.53	.48	.49	1.67	1.42
MED	95	.65	.61	.62	.76	.64
			Army			
11X	329	.24	.24	.30	−.00	−1.39
63B						
Ft. Dix	198	.64	.66	.62	−.46	.69
Ft. Jackson	186	.44	.44	.47	.13	−.69
64C	277	.49	.46	.45	.71	1.27
71L	145	.41	.49	.48	−1.60	−1.18
91B	225	.66	.61	.62	1.78	1.29
72E	149	.21	.18	.28	.35	−.99

*p ≤ .05

P&P-ASVAB; for the Air Force Electronics Principles (AVNC) school, the CAT-ASVAB multiple R was larger than the corresponding multiple R for the P&P-ASVAB.

Construct Validity

This section addresses the question of whether P&P-ASVAB and CAT-ASVAB tests measure the same aptitudes. Previous research had yielded four factors (Verbal, Quantitative, Technical, and Speed) from analyses of various forms of the P&P-ASVAB

and the CAT-ASVAB (Ree et al., 1982; Moreno et al., 1984). Presented here are the results of a factor analysis of CAT-ASVAB and pre-enlistment P&P-ASVAB test scores. Pre-enlistment P&P-ASVAB test scores were used in this analysis instead of post-enlistment scores because examinees took only selected post-enlistment P&P-ASVAB tests.

Pearson correlation coefficients were computed between all pre-enlistment P&P-ASVAB and CAT-ASVAB test scores. A modified principal factoring procedure was performed, such that the main diagonal elements of the correlation matrix were replaced with initial communality estimates given by squared multiple correlations. The four factors with eigenvalues greater than 1.0 were extracted. Successive estimates of communalities were obtained by determining the variance accounted for by the factors extracted from the reduced matrix and substituting them into the diagonal of the new reduced matrix. This iterative process was repeated until the difference between successive communality estimates was negligible. Recruits with data on all CAT-ASVAB and pre-enlistment P&P-ASVAB tests were included in these analyses. Consequently, the total number of examinees with complete data was $N = 6,710$.

The analyses were followed by varimax rotation yielding the four final factors. The factor loadings were examined and the factors were labeled as follows: Verbal, Technical-Mechanical, Mathematical-Quantitative, and Speed. The varimax rotated factor solution is presented in Table 10-3.

The pattern of factor loadings for CAT-ASVAB tests was very similar to that of their corresponding P&P-ASVAB tests. The WK, GS, and PC tests loaded highest on the Verbal factor. The AS, MC, and EI tests had the highest factor loadings on the Technical factor, while MK and AR factor loadings were the greatest on the Mathematical factor. Finally, the two speeded tests, CS and NO, loaded highest on the Speed factor.

It appears that the CAT-ASVAB tests measure the same aptitude components as their corresponding P&P-ASVAB tests. Further, this pattern of results is similar to those found in previous studies factoring CAT-ASVAB and P&P-ASVAB tests (Ree et al., 1982; Kass et al., 1983; Moreno et al., 1984).

Test Completion Times

One of the potential advantages of CAT-ASVAB over P&P-ASVAB is the reduction in the number of items administered and, therefore, in total test time. In this study, examinees taking the CAT-ASVAB were permitted an unlimited time period, except on the speeded tests, whereas the P&P-ASVAB was administered with set time limits for each test. Still, the smaller number of items administered by the CAT-

Table 10-3 Varimax Rotated Factor Matrix for Pre-enlistment P&P-ASVAB and CAT-ASVAB Across Services ($N = 6,710$)

Test	Factor				Final Community Estimate
	Technical	Verbal	Math	Speed	
PRE-ASVAB					
AR	.30	.25	.66	.25	.66
WK	.21	.83	.14	.05	.75
PC	.19	.57	.18	.15	.41
NO	−0.11	−0.06	.19	.66	.49
GS	.43	.63	.25	−0.01	.65
CS	−0.03	.04	.03	.69	.48
AS	.82	.16	.02	−0.07	.70
MK	.20	.28	.76	.25	.76
MC	.66	.23	.34	−0.03	.61
EI	.64	.31	.17	−0.05	.53
CAT-ASVAB					
AR	.33	.32	.70	.20	.75
WK	.20	.86	.18	.05	.81
PC	.17	.67	.24	.16	.57
NO	−0.03	.13	.29	.64	.50
GS	.38	.72	.31	−0.01	.75
CS	−0.05	.13	.10	.73	.56
AS	.90	.15	.04	−0.09	.84
MK	.11	.32	.71	.28	.69
MC	.66	.24	.31	−0.03	.59
EI	.66	.42	.24	−0.05	.67
Eigenvalue	3.95	3.91	2.75	2.16	
Common Variance	30.9%	30.6%	21.5%	16.9%	

Table 10-4 Distribution of Test Completion Times Across Services[a] ($N = 7,513$)

Test	P&P-ASVAB Time (minutes)	CAT-ASVAB Percentiles						
		50	75	80	85	90	95	99
AR	36	13.2	16.5	17.4	18.7	20.3	23.4	29.7
WK	11	3.5	4.2	4.4	4.7	5.1	5.8	7.5
PC	13	9.9	12.5	12.6	13.4	14.4	16.5	20.1
GS	11	4.5	5.3	5.6	5.7	6.3	7.0	8.9
AI	—	5.0	5.9	6.2	6.5	6.9	7.5	9.2
SI	—	4.5	5.1	5.3	5.6	5.9	6.5	7.7
AS	11	9.3	10.5	10.9	11.2	11.8	12.7	15.1
MK	24	7.6	9.5	10.0	10.7	11.7	13.6	17.9
MC	19	9.9	11.8	12.3	12.9	13.7	15.1	18.1
EI	9	4.7	5.5	5.8	6.1	6.4	7.1	8.8
TOTAL	144	74.4	84.0	86.4	89.5	94.1	100.0	116.6
Instruction Time (minutes)[b]		30.8	34.5	35.5	36.8	38.4	41.6	47.6

[a] Numbers in the table represent completion times in minutes. Times for the speeded tests, NO and CS, are included in total test time.
[b] The instruction time is the total amount of time spent in test instructional sequences.

ASVAB and its self-paced nature were expected to lower test times. Test times were compared for the CAT-ASVAB and P&P-ASVAB tests, with the entire sample for each Service included these analyses.

Since instruction time is not included in P&P-ASVAB test administration times, for each CAT-ASVAB test completion times were calculated by subtracting the test instruction time from the total time expended on that test. The completion time for CAT-ASVAB AS was the sum of the completion times for the CAT-ASVAB AI and SI tests. Because the speeded tests, NO and CS had set time limits, completion times for these tests are not presented. Total completion time for the battery, which includes the times for the two speeded tests, was computed by summing over test completion times for each examinee. Familiarization/instruction times were computed by summing over test instruction times for each examinee. The times required by different percentages of examinees to finish the CAT-ASVAB were examined. Elapsed time was computed for various completion-time percentiles.

P&P-ASVAB time limits and CAT-ASVAB test times for scores at specified percentiles across all Services are presented in Table 10-4. The total completion times at specified percentiles are shown, at the bottom of the table, fifty percent of the examinees completed CAT-ASVAB within 74 minutes. Ninety-nine percent completed CAT-ASVAB within 117 minutes.

Table 10-4 also shows the amount of time spent in test familiarization/instructional sequences for CAT-ASVAB at specified percentiles. CAT-ASVAB and P&P-ASVAB could not be compared for this variable as P&P-ASVAB instruction time does not have a time limit and no data were available.

The CAT-ASVAB achieved a substantial reduction in administration time over the P&P-ASVAB. This reduction in time can be examined for two different administration formats: Self-Paced and Group-Paced. In Self-Paced administration, the examinees proceeded through the CAT-ASVAB independent of the progress of other examinees. Upon completing the CAT-ASVAB, each examinee was free to begin the next stage of entrance processing. Thus time saved on ASVAB testing translated to a direct savings for an applicant in terms of total processing time. Table 10-4 shows that the typical (50th percentile) CAT-ASVAB testing time was about half the P&P-ASVAB testing time.

In the Group-Paced administration format, examinees began the CAT-ASVAB simultaneously with other examinees. In this format, all examinees in the group must complete the CAT-ASVAB before they proceed on to the next stage of their entrance processing. Thus in the Group-Paced format, the administration time required for the group was contingent primarily upon the time required by its slowest members. Table 10-4 shows the CAT-ASVAB time by which 99 percent of the recruits had completed the test was about 80 percent of that required by the P&P-ASVAB. Thus, even in the Group-Paced administration format, the CAT-ASVAB can reduce total testing time by about one-fifth.

The CAT-ASVAB testing times reported here may be different than what would be observed for an operational CAT-ASVAB, for several reasons. First, the distribution of ability might be different in this sample than in the military applicant population. Second, the operational software and hardware would be different. Third, motivational differences between operational and nonoperational testing might affect testing times.

Conclusions

Results of this study supported operational implementation of CAT-ASVAB. Results showed that CAT-ASVAB measures the same abilities as the P&P-ASVAB, and is as valid, even though the CAT test lengths are substantially shorter. As demonstrated by the test time analyses, the shorter CAT-ASVAB test lengths translate into a significant time savings.

Results of this study do not necessarily mean that there are no differences between CAT-ASVAB and P&P-ASVAB validities, only that the differences are most likely small. Sample sizes used in this study were not large enough to detect small differences in validities. In addition, before generalizations can be made from the current research to the operational CAT-ASVAB system, several concerns should be noted. The operational computer hardware, software, and psychometric procedures differ substantially from the experimental system used in the present research. These differences between the experimental and operational systems are expected to have varying degrees of impact on test performance, test time, and attitudes toward CAT.

PART

IV

Second Generation—Full-Scale CAT-ASVAB Systems

The chapters in the preceding parts described research and development that was undertaken primarily for two reasons: Initially, to demonstrate that the theoretical advantages of CAT over conventional testing could be achieved in practice; and, that done, to extend the proof-of-concept research from a few adaptive tests to the entire ASVAB battery. That work showed convincingly that a computerized adaptive version of the ASVAB had all of the reliability, construct validity, and criterion-related validity of the conventional version, and about double its efficiency.

With the evidence from the 1st generation CAT-ASVAB system in hand, it was time to prepare a system for full-scale operational use in the military entrance processing system. The experimental CAT-ASVAB system was not suitable for operational use: Its computer system had been developed as an interim system for research purposes only. It was never intended for nationwide deployment, which would require portable computer equipment. The experimental test item banks, which had served their research purposes well, were likewise inadequate for an operational system. Their item parameter distributions were not ideal, and their numbers were not large enough to support alternate forms of CAT-ASVAB.

Consequently, a 2nd-generation CAT-ASVAB system was developed, beginning about 1985. That system had two parallel item banks, so that alternate forms of CAT-ASVAB would be available for retest purposes, as well as to enhance test security. It would be delivered by a more capable computer system: A portable one with a more powerful processor, larger amount of volatile memory, greater mass storage capacity, and superior graphics display resolution. It would feature a number of psychometric enhancements, including a refined pro-

cedure for test scoring, and a more sophisticated approach to item exposure control. Previous reliability, construct validity, and predictive utility research would be corroborated using the new system. Finally, before introducing it into operational use, scores from the full-scale CAT-ASVAB system would need to be equated to those of the conventional ASVAB, so that the new version of the test could be used interchangeably with the old.

The 10 chapters of this part describe the research and development of the 2nd generation CAT-ASVAB system. Their sequence is organized into three sections: Chapters 11 through 14 deal with the preparation of the system. Chapters 15 through 19 cover research related to its evaluation, including equating. Chapter 20 describes an operational test and evaluation of the system in entrance processing stations, a final prerequisite to full-scale operational implementation.

System preparation. The development and evaluation of the 2nd generation item pools is described in **Chapter 11** by Segall, Moreno, and Hetter. They describe research spanning the gamut from item specification through psychometric characteristics of the resulting item pools. In **Chapter 12** Segall, Moreno, Bloxom, and Hetter describe research conducted to refine earlier CAT-ASVAB psychometric procedures involved in test administration; this research addressed topics such as adaptive test item selection and ability estimation, as well as test scoring procedures for both the adaptive and the speeded tests. Chapter 12 includes guidelines addressing such issues as stopping rules for adaptive tests, as well as considerations pertaining to omitted responses and changing answers in adaptive tests. **Chapter 13,** by Hetter and Sympson, describes the method used to control item exposure in CAT-ASVAB. Their method was developed specifically to ensure that CAT-ASVAB items were exposed no more often than the items in the printed ASVAB's alternate forms, ensuring that CAT-ASVAB is no more vulnerable than printed ASVAB forms to compromise from item exposure. In **Chapter 14**, Rafacz and Hetter describe their work in developing the 2nd generation CAT-ASVAB delivery system; topics addressed in this chapter range from the concept of operations through system development to software and system acceptance testing.

System evaluation. Chapters 15 through 17 describe research that addressed three issues that often come up in discussions of converting tests from paper-and-pencil to computerized administration. **Chapter 15**, by Vicino and Moreno, describes a pilot study of human factors in CAT-ASVAB; the study addressed topics ranging from examinees' attitudes toward computerized testing to human factors engineering concerns such as fatigue and display legibility. **Chapter 16** describes research that addresses the defensibility of using paper-and-pencil test data to calibrate test items for use in computerized testing; Hetter, Segall, and Bloxom summarize previous research on this issue, and present their own findings. In **Chapter 17**, Moreno and Segall describe their research to address the questions of whether the CAT version of ASVAB measures the same ability variables as the printed version, and whether there are differences in measurement precision between them. In **Chapter 18**, Wolfe, Moreno, and Segall recount new research into the predictive validity of CAT-ASVAB; this research, which used the 2nd generation CAT-ASVAB system as well as a number of innovative, computer-administered tests, extended the predictive validity results of the 1st generation system to a number of additional military job specialties.

The major implication of all of the research recounted through Chapter 18 is that CAT-ASVAB had been demonstrated to be equivalent or superior to printed ASVAB in terms of ability constructs measured and relationships to military job training performance. One crucial piece of evidence remained to be demonstrated before CAT-ASVAB could be introduced into use alongside the paper-and-pencil versions, with its scores interpreted using paper-and-pencil norms: That was whether the two versions could be equated satisfactorily. The difficult technical issues in equating an adaptive test to a conventional one were laid out in detail in a report by Green, Bock, Humphreys, Linn, and Reckase (1984a). In **Chapter 19**, Segall places the capstone on the psychometric research that was prerequisite to operational implementation by describing the technical procedures he developed and applied to equate CAT-ASVAB test and composite scores to those of the printed version.

Preparing for operational implementation. With equating complete, the 2nd generation CAT-ASVAB system was technically ready for operational use. An operational test and evaluation (OT&E) was conducted to ensure it could be integrated well into the applicant processing procedures in use in the Military Entrance Processing Stations. In **Chapter 20**, Moreno describes the OT&E in some detail, covering a variety of topics ranging from the concept of operations to user acceptance and system performance. The OT&E was successful, and less than a year after it began, the decision was made to implement CAT-ASVAB in all U.S. Military Entrance Processing Stations.

CHAPTER
11

Item Pool Development and Evaluation

Daniel O. Segall, Kathleen E. Moreno, and Rebecca D. Hetter

By the mid-1980s, an item pool had been constructed for use in the experimental CAT-ASVAB system (Chapter 9), and had been administered to a large number of subjects participating in research studies. However, this pool was ill-suited for operational use. First, many items had been taken from retired P&P-ASVAB forms (8, 9, and 10). Using these items in an operational CAT-ASVAB would degrade test security, since these items had broad exposure through the P&P testing program. In addition, the experimental CAT-ASVAB system contained only one form. For retesting purposes, it is desirable to have two parallel forms (consisting of non-overlapping item pools) to accommodate applicants who take the battery twice within a short time interval. To avoid practice and compromise effects, it is desirable for the second administered form to contain no common items with the initial form.

This chapter summarizes the procedures used to construct and evaluate the operational CAT-ASVAB item pools. Although specific reference is made to Forms 1 and 2, many of the same procedures were applied more recently to the development of other CAT-ASVAB forms. The first section describes the development of the primary and supplemental item banks. Additional sections discuss dimensionality, alternate form construction, and precision analyses. The final section summarizes important findings with general implications for CAT item pool development.

Development and Calibration
Primary Item Banks

The primary item banks for CAT-ASVAB Forms 1 and 2 were developed and calibrated by Prestwood, Vale, Massey, and Welsh (1985). The P&P-ASVAB Form 8A was used to outline the content of items written in each area. However, important differences between the development of adaptive and conventional (paper-and-pencil) item pools were noted, which led to several modifications in P&P-ASVAB test specifications:

- *Increased range of item difficulties*
Domain specifications were expanded to provide additional easy and difficult items.

- *Functionally independent items*
The Paragraph Comprehension test (as measured in P&P-ASVAB) typically contains reading passages followed by several questions referring to the same passage. Items of these types are likely to violate the assumption of local independence made by the standard unidimensional IRT model. Consequently, CAT-ASVAB items were written to have a single question per passage.

- *Unidimensionality*
In the P&P-ASVAB, auto and shop items are combined into a single test. However, to help satisfy the assumption of unidimensionality, Auto and

Shop Information were treated as separate content areas: Large non-overlapping pools were written for each, and separate item calibrations were conducted.

About 3,600 items (400 for each of the nine content areas) were written and pretested on a sample of recruits. The pretest was intended to screen about half of the items for inclusion in a large-sample item calibration study. Items administered in the pretest were assembled into 71 booklets, with each booklet containing items from a single content area. Examinees were given 50 minutes to complete all items in a booklet. Data from about 21,000 recruits were gathered, resulting in about 300 responses per itcm. IRT item parameters were estimated for each item using the ASCAL (Vale & Gialluca, 1985) computer program.[1]

For each content area, a subset of items with an approximately rectangular distribution of item difficulties was selected for a more extensive calibration study. This was accomplished from an examination of the IRT difficulty and discrimination parameters. Within each content area, items were divided into 20 equally spaced difficulty levels. Approximately equal numbers of items were drawn from each level, with preference given to the most highly discriminating items.

The surviving 2,118 items (about 235 items per content area) were assembled into 43 P&P test booklets, similar in construction to the pretest (each booklet containing items from a single content area; 50 minutes of testing per examinee). Data from 137,000 applicants were collected from 63 Military Entrance Processing Stations (MEPSs) and their associated Mobile Examining Team Sites (METSs) during late spring and early summer of 1983. Each examinee was given one experimental form and an operational P&P-ASVAB. After matching booklet and operational ASVAB data, about 116,000 cases remained for IRT calibration analysis (providing about 2,700 responses per item). Within each content area, all experimental and operational P&P-ASVAB items were calibrated jointly using the ASCAL computer program. This helped ensure that the item parameters were properly linked across booklets, and provided IRT estimates for several operational P&P-ASVAB forms on a common metric.

Table 11-1 Linking Design

Calibration	P&P-ASVAB Form							
	8A	8B	9A	9B	10A	10B	10X	10Y
			Common Forms					
Primary			X	X	X	X	X	X
Supplemental	X	X	X	X	X	X		

Supplemental Item Bank

An analysis of the primary item banks (described below) indicated that two of the content areas, Arithmetic Reasoning (AR) and Word Knowledge (WK), had lower than desired precision over the middle ability range. Therefore, the item pools for these two content areas were supplemented with additional items taken from the experimental CAT-ASVAB system (166 AR items; and 195 WK items). The supplemental items were calibrated by Sympson and Hartmann (1985) using a modified version of LOGIST 2.b. Data for these calibrations were obtained from a MEPS administration of P&P booklets. Supplemental item parameters were transformed to the "primary item-metric" using the Stocking and Lord (1983) procedure. The linking design is shown in Table 11-1.

The primary calibration included six P&P-ASVAB forms; the supplemental calibration included a different but overlapping set of six P&P-ASVAB forms. The two sets of parameters were linked through the four forms common to both calibrations: 9A, 9B, 10A, and 10B. The specific procedure involved the computation of two test characteristic curves (TCCs), one based on the primary item calibration, and another based on the supplemental item calibration. The linear transformation of the supplemental scale that minimized the weighted sum of squared differences between the two TCCs was computed. The squared differences at selected ability levels were weighted by a $N(0,1)$ density function. This procedure was repeated for both AR and WK. All AR and WK supplemental IRT discrimination and difficulty parameters were transformed to the primary metric, using the appropriate transformation of scale.

Item Reviews

Primary and supplemental items were screened using several criteria. First, an Educational Testing Service (ETS) panel performed sensitivity and

---

[1] ASCAL is a joint maximum-likelihood/modal-Bayesian item calibration program for the three-parameter logistic item response model.

quality reviews. The panel recommendations were then submitted to the Service laboratories for their comments. An Item Review Committee made up of NPRDC researchers reviewed the Service laboratories' and ETS reports and comments. When needed, the committee was augmented with additional NPRDC personnel having expertise in areas related to the item content under review. The committee reviewed the items and coded them as unacceptable, marginally unacceptable, less than optimal, and acceptable, in each of the two review categories (sensitivity and quality).

Item keys were verified by an examination of point-biserial correlations, computed for each distractor. Items with positive point-biserial correlations for incorrect options were identified and reviewed.

The display suitability of the item screens was evaluated for: (a) clutter (particularly applicable to PC), (b) legibility, (c) graphics quality, (d) congruence of text and graphics (do words and pictures match?), and (e) congruence of screen and booklet versions. In addition, items on the Hewlett Packard Integral Personal Computer (HP-IPC) screen were compared to those in the printed booklets. Displayed items were also examined for: (a) words split at the end of lines (no hyphenation allowed), (b) missing characters at the end of lines, (c) missing lines or words, (d) misspelled words, and (e) spelling discrepancies within the booklets. After the items were examined on the HP-IPC, reviewers presented their recommendations to a review group, which made final recommendations.

Options Format Study

The primary item pools for AR and WK consisted of multiple-choice items with five response alternatives, while the supplemental items had only four alternatives. If primary and supplemental items were combined in a single pool, examinees would probably receive a mixture of four- and five-choice items during the adaptive test. There was concern that mixing items with different numbers of response options within a test would cause confusion or careless errors by the examinee, and perhaps affect item difficulties.

The authors conducted a study to examine the effect of mixing four- and five-option items on computerized test performance. Examinees in this study were 1,200 male Navy recruits at the Recruit Training Center, San Diego, California. The task for each examinee was to answer a mixture of 4-

and 5-option items. These included 32 WK items followed by 24 PC items administered by computer using a conventional nonadaptive strategy.

Subjects were randomly assigned to one of six conditions. Specific items administered in each condition for WK are displayed in Table 11-2. Examinees assigned to Conditions A or B received items of one type exclusively: Examinees assigned to Condition A received items 1–32 (all 5-option items), examinees assigned to Condition B received items 33–64 (all 4-option items). Items in Conditions A and B were selected to span the range of difficulty. Note that 4- and 5-option items were paired {1,33}, {2,34}, {3,35}, . . . so that items in the same position in the linear sequence would have similar item response functions (and consequently similar difficulty and discrimination levels). Examinees assigned to Condition C received alternating sequences of 5- and 4-choice items (5, 4, 5, 4, . . .). Examinees assigned to Condition D received a test in which every fourth item was a 4-option item (5, 5, 5, 4, 5, 5, 5, 4, ...). In Condition E, every 8th item administered was a 4-option item. Finally, in Condition F, an equal number of randomly selected 4- and 5-option items were administered to each examinee. The first item administered was randomly selected from {1 or 33}, the second item was selected from {2 or 34}, etc. An example assignment for this condition is given in the last column of Table 11-2. Note for this condition, assignments were generated independently for each examinee. An identical design was used for PC, except that only 24 items were administered to each examinee. Three different outcome measures were examined to assess the effects of mixing item formats: item difficulty, test difficulty, and response latency.

Item difficulty. For Conditions C, D, E, and F, item difficulties (proportion of correct responses) were compared with those of the corresponding items in the Control Conditions (A or B). For example, comparison of difficulty values in Condition C included pairs: {Condition C, Item 1} with {Condition A, Item 1}; {Condition C, Item 34} with {Condition B, Item 34}; etc. The significance of the difference between pairs of item difficulty values were tested using a 2×2 chi-square analysis. For WK, only seven of the 160 comparisons (about 4.4%) produced significant differences (at the .05 alpha level). For PC, only one of the 120 comparisons of item difficulty was significant.

Test difficulty. For examinees in Conditions C, D, and E, two number-right scores were

Table 11-2 Options Format Study: WK Item Lists Presented in Control and Experimental Conditions

Control		Experimental			
Condition A (5-Option)	Condition B (4-Option)	Condition C (Mixed: 1:1)	Condition D (Mixed: 3:1)	Condition E (Mixed: 7:1)	Condition F (Random: 1:1)
1	33	1	1	1	1
2	34	34	2	2	2
3	35	3	3	3	3
4	36	36	36	4	36
5	37	5	5	5	37
6	38	38	6	6	6
7	39	7	7	7	39
8	40	40	40	40	40
9	41	9	9	9	41
10	42	42	10	10	10
11	43	11	11	11	43
12	44	44	44	12	12
13	45	13	13	13	13
14	46	46	14	14	14
15	47	15	15	15	47
16	48	48	48	48	16
17	49	17	17	17	49
18	50	50	18	18	50
19	51	19	19	19	51
20	52	52	52	20	20
21	53	21	21	21	21
22	54	54	22	22	54
23	55	23	23	23	55
24	56	56	56	56	24
25	57	25	25	25	57
26	58	58	26	26	58
27	59	27	27	27	27
28	60	60	60	28	28
29	61	29	29	29	29
30	62	62	30	30	30
31	63	31	31	31	63
32	64	64	64	64	64

computed: One based on 4-option items, and another based on 5-option items. Number-right scores from corresponding items were computed for examinees in the Control conditions A and B. The number of items entering into each score for each condition are displayed in the second and fifth columns of Table 11-3. The significance of the difference between mean number-right scores across the Experimental and Control groups was tested using an independent groups t statistic. The results are displayed in Table 11-3. None of the comparisons displayed significant results at the .05 alpha level.

Response latencies. For examinees in Conditions C, D, and E, two latency measures were computed: One based on 4-option items, and another based on 5-option items. Latency measures were also computed from corresponding items in the Control conditions A and B. Mean latencies were compared across the Experimental and Control groups (Table 11-3). None of the comparisons displayed significant results at the .05 alpha level.

Discussion. Mixing items with different numbers of response options produced no measurable effects on item or test performance. This result

Table 11-3 Options Format Study: Significance Tests for Test Difficulties and Response Latencies

| | | Word Knowledge | | | Paragraph Comprehension | |
| | | *t*-value | | | | *t*-value | |
Condition	No. Items	Difficulty	Latency	No. Items	Difficulty	Latency
		Comparison With 5-Option Control					
Condition C	16	.06	−.85	12	−.08	−1.77
Condition D	24	−1.09	.47	18	−.21	−.64
Condition E	28	−.24	−.98	21	−1.82	.67
		Comparison With 4-Option Control					
Condition C	16	−1.83	1.49	12	1.30	−.72
Condition D	8	−1.35	1.84	6	−.98	−1.92
Condition E	4	1.35	−.07	3	−1.40	−.28

differed from those reported by Brittain and Vaughan (1984), who studied the effects of mixing items with different numbers of options on a P&P version of the Army Skills Qualification Test. They predicted errors would increase when an item with *n* answer options followed an item with more than *n* answer options, where errors were defined as choosing nonexistent answer options. Consistent with their hypothesis, mixing items with different numbers of answer options caused an increase in errors.

Likely explanations for the different findings between the current study and the Brittain and Vaughan (1984) study involve differences in medium (computer versus P&P). In the Brittain and Vaughan study, examinees answered questions using a standard 5-option answer sheet for all items, making the selection of a nonexistent option possible. However, in the current study, software features were employed which helped eliminate erroneous responses. (These software features are common to both the current study and the CAT-ASVAB system.)

First, after the examinee makes a selection among response alternatives, he or she is required to confirm the selection. For example, if the examinee selects option "D," the system responds with:

> If "D" is your answer press ENTER.
> Otherwise, type another answer.

That is, the examinee is informed about the selection that was made, and given an opportunity to change the selection. This process would tend to minimize the likelihood of careless errors.

A second desirable feature incorporated into the CAT-ASVAB software (and included in the options

format study) was the sequence of events following an "invalid-key" press. Suppose, for example, that a particular item had only four response alternatives (A, B, C, and D) and the examinee selects "E" by mistake. The examinee would see the messages:

> You DID NOT type A, B, C, or D.
> Enter your answer (A, B, C, or D)

Note that if an examinee accidentally selects a nonexistent option (i.e., "E"), the item is not scored incorrect; instead, the examinee is given an opportunity to make another selection. This feature would also reduce the likelihood of careless errors. These software features, along with the empirical results of the options format study, addressed the major concerns about mixing four- and five-choice items.

Dimensionality

One major assumption of the IRT item selection and scoring procedures used by CAT-ASVAB is that performance on items within a given content area can be characterized by a unidimensional latent trait or ability. Earlier research showed that IRT estimation techniques are robust against minor violations of the unidimensionality assumption, and that unidimensional IRT parameter estimates have many practical applications in multidimensional item pools (Reckase, 1979; Drasgow & Parsons, 1983, Dorans & Kingston, 1985). However, violations of the unidimensional adaptive testing model may have serious implications for validity and test fairness. Because of the adaptive nature

Table 11-4 Treatment Approaches for Multidimensional Item Pools

Approach	Calibration	Item Selection	Scoring
1. Unidimensional Treatment	Combined calibration containing items of each content type	No constraints placed on item content for each examinee	A single IRT ability estimate computed across items of different content using the unidimensional scoring algorithm
2. Content Balancing	Combined calibration containing items of each content type	Constraints placed on the number of items drawn from each content area for each examinee	A single IRT ability estimate computed across items of different content using the unidimensional scoring algorithm
3. Pool Splitting	Separate calibrations for items of each content	Separate adaptively tailored tests for each content area	Separate IRT ability estimates for each content area

of the test, and the IRT scoring algorithms, multidimensionality may lead to observed scores which represent a different mixture of the underlying unidimensional constructs than intended. This could alter the validity of the test. Furthermore, the application of the unidimensional model to multidimensional item pools may produce differences in the representation of dimensions among examinees. Some examinees may receive items measuring primarily one dimension, while others receive items measuring another dimension. This raises issues of test fairness. If the pool is multidimensional, two examinees (with the same ability levels) may be administered items measuring two largely different constructs, and receive widely discrepant scores.

In principle, at least three approaches exist for dealing with multidimensional item pools (Table 11-4). These approaches differ in the item selection and scoring algorithms, and in the item calibration design:

1. *Unidimensional Treatment*. This option essentially ignores the dimensionality of the item pools in terms of item calibration, item selection, and scoring. A single item calibration containing items spanning all content areas is performed to estimate the IRT item parameters. No content constraints are placed on the selection of items during the adaptive sequence—items are selected on the basis of maximum information. Intermediate and final scoring are performed according to the unidimensional IRT model, and a single score is obtained based on items spanning all content areas.

2. *Content Balancing*. This approach balances the numbers of administered items from targeted content areas. A single item calibration containing items spanning all content areas is performed to estimate the IRT item parameters. During the adaptive test, items are selected from *content-specific* subpools in a fixed sequence. For example, the content balancing sequence for General Science could be LPLPLPLPLPLPLPL (L = Life Science, P = Physical Science). Accordingly, the first item administered would be selected from among the candidate Life Science items. The second item administered would be selected from the physical science items, and so forth. Within each targeted content area, items are selected on the basis of IRT item information. Intermediate and final scores are based on the unidimensional ability estimator computed from items spanning all content areas.

3. *Pool Splitting*. Item pools for different dimensions are constructed and calibrated separately. For each content area, separate adaptive tests are administered and scored. It is then usually necessary to combine final scores on the separate adaptive tests to form a single composite measure that spans the separately measured content areas.

For each item pool, a number of criteria were considered in determining the most suitable dimensionality-approach, including: (a) statistical factor significance, (b) factor interpretation, (c) item difficulties, and (d) factor intercorrelations. The relation between these criteria and the recommended approach is summarized in Table 11-5.

Table 11-5 Decision Rules for Approaches to Dimensionality

Case	Statistical Factor Sig.	Interpretable Factors	Overlapping Item Difficulties	Factor Correlations	Approach
1.	No	—	—	—	Unidimensional
2.	Yes	Yes	Yes	High	Content Bal.
3.	Yes	Yes	Yes	Low	Split Pool
4.	Yes	Yes	No	—	Unidimensional
5.	Yes	No	Yes	—	Unidimensional
6.	Yes	No	No	—	Unidimensional

Statistical Factor Significance

The first, and perhaps most important criterion for selecting the dimensionality-approach is the factor structure of the item pool. If there is empirical evidence to suggest that responses of an item pool are multidimensional, then content-balancing or pool-splitting should be considered. In the absence of such evidence, item pools should be treated as unidimensional. Such empirical evidence can be obtained from factor analytic studies of item responses using one of several available approaches, including TESTFACT (Wilson, Wood, & Gibbons, 1991) and NOHARM (Fraser, 1988). The full item-information procedure used in TESTFACT allows the statistical significance of multidimensional solutions to be tested against the unidimensional solution using a hierarchical likelihood ratio procedure.

This strong empirical emphasis recommended here is not shared by all adaptive testing programs. The adaptive item selection algorithm used in the CAT-GRE (Stocking & Swanson, 1993) incorporates both item information and test plan specifications. The test plans are based on expert judgments of content specialists. Accordingly, there is likely to be a disconnect between the test plan specifications and the empirical dimensionality of the item pools. This can lead to situations where constraints are placed on the presentation of items that are largely unidimensional. In general, overly restrictive content-based constraints on item selection will lead to the use of less informative items, and ultimately to test scores with lower precision.

Factor Interpretation

According to a strictly empirical approach, the number of factors could be determined by statistical considerations, and items could be allocated to areas based on their estimated loadings. Items could be balanced with respect to these areas defined by the empirical analysis. However, a major drawback with this approach is the likelihood of meaningless results, both in terms of the number of factors to be balanced, and in the allocation of items to content areas. Significance tests applied to large samples would almost certainly lead to high-dimensionality solutions, regardless of the strength of the factors. Furthermore, there is no guarantee that the rotated factor solution accurately describes the underlying factors.

The alternative judgmental approach noted above would divide the pool into areas on the basis of expert judgments. The major problem with this approach is that without an examination of empirical data, it is not possible to determine which content areas affect the dimensionality of the pool. Choice of content areas could be defined at several arbitrary levels. As Green et al. (1982) suggest, "There is obviously a limit to how finely the content should be subdivided. Each item is to a large extent specific."

In CAT-ASVAB development, we formed a decision rule based on a compromise between the empirical and judgmental approaches. If a pool was found to be statistically multidimensional, items loading highly on each factor were inspected for similarity of content. If agreement between factor solutions and content judgments was high, then balancing was considered, otherwise balancing was not considered.

Item Difficulties

Another important criterion for selecting among dimensionality-approaches concerns the overlap of item difficulties associated with items of each content area. The overlap of item difficulties can provide some clues about the causes of the dimensionality, and suggest an appropriate remedy. Lord (1977) makes an important observation:

> Suppose, to take an extreme example, certain items in a test are taught to one group of students and not taught to another, while other items are taught to both groups. This way of teaching increases the dimensionality of whatever is measured by the test. If items would otherwise have been factorially unidimensional, this way of teaching will introduce additional dimensions. (p. 24)

If a pool contains some items with material exposed to the entire population (say nonacademic content), and other items are taught to a subpopulation (in school—academic content), then we would expect to find statistically significant factors with easy items loading on the nonacademic factor, and moderate to difficult items loading on the academic factor. Application of the unidimensional item selection and scoring algorithms would result in low ability test-takers receiving easy (nonacademic) items, and moderate to high ability test-takers receiving academic items. Thus the unidimensional treatment would appropriately tailor the content of the items according to the standing of the test-taker along the latent dimension. Note that content balancing in this situation could substantially reduce the precision of the test scores. For example, if an equal number of items from each content area were administered to each examinee, then low ability examinees would receive a large number of uninformative difficult items; and conversely, high ability examinees would receive a large number of uninformative easy items.

We would expect to observe a different pattern of item difficulty values if substantially non-overlapping subgroups were taught different material. In this instance, we would expect to observe two or more factors defined by items with overlapping difficulty values (falling within a common range). Here, an appropriate remedy would involve content balancing or pool-splitting, since different dimensions represent knowledge of somewhat independent domains.

Factor Correlations

A final consideration for selecting among dimensionality-approaches concerns the magnitude of the correlation between latent factors. Different approaches might be desirable depending on the correlation between factors estimated in the item factor analysis. If factors are highly correlated, then content balancing may provide the most satisfactory results. In this instance, the unidimensional model used in conjunction with content balancing is likely to provide an adequate approximation for characterizing item information, and for estimating latent ability.

If the correlations among factors are found to be low or moderate, then the usefulness of the unidimensional model for characterizing item information and estimating latent abilities is questionable. When the factors have low correlations, pool-splitting is likely to provide the best remedy. Separate IRT calibrations should be performed for items of each factor; separate adaptive tests should be administered; and final adaptive test scores can be combined to form a composite measure representing the standing among examinees along the latent composite dimension.

Choosing Among Alternative Approaches

Table 11-5 summarized different possible outcomes and the recommended approach for each. If an item factor analysis provides no significant second, or higher order factors, then the pool should be treated as unidimensional (Case 1). If statistically significant higher order factors are identified, these factors relate to item content, and item difficulties of each content span a common range, then consideration should be given to content balancing (Case 2, if the factor intercorrelations are high), or to pool-splitting (Case 3, if the factor intercorrelations are low to moderate). For reasons given above, if the statistical factors are not interpretable (Case 5 and 6), or if the item difficulty values of each content area span non-overlapping ranges (Case 4 and 6), then unidimensional treatment may provide the most useful approach.

Results and Discussion

In earlier studies of the Auto-Shop content area, a decision was made to apply the pool-splitting approach: This content area was split into separate auto and shop item pools (Case 3, Table 11-5). As described in an earlier section, these pools were calibrated separately. The decision to split these pools was based on the moderately high correlation among the auto and shop dimensions. In the analysis described below, the auto and shop pools were examined separately, and subjected to the same analyses as other pools.

The first step in the dimensionality analysis involved factor analyses using item data (Prestwood et al., 1985). Empirical item responses were analyzed using the TESTFACT computer program (Muraki, 1984), which employs full information item factor analysis based on IRT (Bock & Aitkin, 1981). While the program computes item difficulty and item discrimination parameters, guessing parameters are treated as known constants and must be supplied to the program. For these analyses, the guessing parameters estimated by Prestwood et al., were used. For all analyses, a maximum of four factors were extracted, using a stepwise procedure. An item pool was considered statistically multidimensional if a change in chi-square (between the one-factor solution and the two-factor solution) was statistically significant (at the .01 alpha level). If the change in chi-square for the two-factor solution was significant, the three- and four-factor solutions were also examined for significant changes in chi-square. Since items within a pool were divided into separate booklets for data collection purposes, all items within a pool could not be factor analyzed at once. Therefore, subsets of items (generally, all items in one booklet) were analyzed. The number of statistically significant factors found across booklets was not necessarily identical. In such cases, the factor solutions examined were the number found in the majority of the booklets. The number of statistically significant factors found for each item pool is summarized in Table 11-6. For those item pools showing statistical evidence of multidimensionality, items were reviewed to determine whether the pattern of factor loadings was related to content, mean difficulty parameters were computed by content area, and factor intercorrelations were examined. These results are displayed in Table 11-6.

Based on the factor analyses, PC and MC were found to be unidimensional (Case 1, Table 11-5). All other item pools were multidimensional, with GS and MK having four factors and AR, WK, AI, SI, and EI having two factors. For those areas having two factors, the pattern of factor loadings was readily apparent. Items that loaded highly on the first factor were nonacademic items (i.e., taught to the whole group through everyday experiences). Items that loaded highly on the second factor were academic items (i.e., taught to a subgroup through classroom instruction or specialized experience). Means of IRT difficulty parameters for academic and nonacademic items are displayed in Table 11-7. As indicated, the mean difficulty values for nonacademic items were much lower than those for academic items. Accordingly, AR, WK, AI, SI, and EI were treated as unidimensional item pools (Case 4, Table 11-5).

The GS pool appeared, in part, to follow a different pattern than the five pools discussed above. An examination of the factor solutions and item content provided some evidence for a four-factor solution interpreted as (a) nonacademic, (b) life science, (c) physical science, and (d) chemistry. This interpretation is supported by the fact that many

Table 11-6 Dimensionality of CAT-ASVAB Item Pools

Item Pool	No. Significant Factors	Interpretable Factors	Overlapping Item Difficulties	Factor Correlations	Case	Approach
GS	4	Yes	Yes	High	2	Content Bal.
AR	2	Yes	No	—	4	Unidimensional
WK	2	Yes	No	—	4	Unidimensional
PC	1	—	—	—	1	Unidimensional
AI	2	Yes	No	—	4	Unidimensional
SI	2	Yes	No	—	4	Unidimensional
MK	4	No	Yes	—	5	Unidimensional
MC	1	—	—	—	1	Unidimensional
EI	2	Yes	No	—	4	Unidimensional

Table 11-7 Mean IRT Item Difficulty (b) Parameters

Item Content	AR	WK	AI	SI	EI
Nonacademic	−2.37	−2.30	−2.28	−2.15	−1.51
Academic	.30	.47	.48	.57	.61

Table 11-8 Item Pools Evaluated in Precision Analyses

Condition	Content Area	Label	Form	Supplemented	Target Exposure Rate
1	GS	GS-1	1	No	1/3
2	GS	GS-2	2	No	1/3
3	AR	AR-1	1	No	1/6
4	AR	AR-2	2	No	1/6
5	AR	AR_s-1	1	Yes	1/6
6	AR	AR_s-2	2	Yes	1/6
7	WK	WK-1	1	No	1/6
8	WK	WK-2	2	No	1/6
9	WK	WK_s-1	1	Yes	1/6
10	WK	WK_s-2	2	Yes	1/6
11	PC	PC-1	1	No	1/6
12	PC	PC-2	2	No	1/6
13	AI	AI-1	1	No	1/3
14	AI	AI-2	2	No	1/3
15	SI	SI-1	1	No	1/3
16	SI	SI-2	2	No	1/3
17	MC	MC-1	1	No	1/3
18	MC	MC-2	2	No	1/3
19	MK	MK-1	1	No	1/6
20	MK	MK-2	2	No	1/6
21	EI	EI-1	1	No	1/3
22	EI	EI-2	2	No	1/3

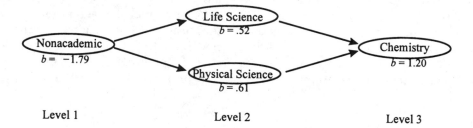

Figure 11-1
General Science Dual Track Instruction.

high schools offer a multiple-track science program (Figure 11-1). At Level 1, students have little or no formal instruction. At Level 2, some students receive training in life science, while others receive physical science training. Finally, at Level 3, some members of both groups are instructed in chemistry. Notice that each higher level contains only a subset of students contained in the levels directly below it. For example, not everyone completing a life science or a physical science course will receive instruction in chemistry. The mean IRT item difficulty values (displayed in Figure 11-1) also support this interpretation of dimensionality. The life science and physical science items are of moderate (and approximately equal) difficulty. The chemistry items appear to be the most difficult, and nonacademic items least difficult. These findings are supportive balancing content among life and physical science items (Case 2, Table 11-5). Nonacademic and chemistry items should be administered to examinees of appropriate ability levels. (See Chapter 12 for additional details on the GS content balancing algorithm.)

For MK, the pattern of factor loadings associated with the two-, three-, or four-factor solutions could not be associated with item content. Consequently, the MK item pool was treated as unidimensional (Case 5, Table 11-5).

Alternate Forms

In developing the item pools for CAT-ASVAB, it was necessary to create two alternate test forms so that applicants could be retested on another form of CAT-ASVAB. Once the item screening procedures were completed, items within each content area were assigned to alternate pools. Pairs of items with similar information functions were identified, and assigned to alternate pools. The primary goal of the alternate form assignment was to minimize the weighted sum-of-squared differences between the two pool information functions. (A pool information function was computed from the sum of the item information functions.) The squared differences between pool information functions were weighted by a $N(0,1)$ density.

The procedure used to create the GS alternate forms differed slightly from the other content areas because of the content balancing requirement. GS items were first divided into physical, life, and chemistry content areas. Domain specifications provided by Prestwood, Vale, Massey, & Welsh (1985) were used for assignment to these content areas. Once items had been assigned to a content area, alternate forms were created separately for each of the three areas.

Precision Analyses

Precision is an important criterion for judging the adequacy of the items pools, since it depends in large part on the quality of the pools. Precision analyses were conducted separately for the 22 item pools displayed in Table 11-8. The content area and form are listed in columns two and four. The target exposure rate (for the battery, i.e, across the two forms) is provided in the last column. This target was used to compute exposure control parameters according to the Sympson-Hetter algorithm (Chapter 13). The fifth column shows whether the pool included supplemental items. The third column provides a descriptive label for each condition used in the text and tables.

As would be expected, the results of any precision analysis would show various degrees of precision among the CAT-ASVAB tests. But how much precision is enough? The precision of the P&P-

ASVAB offers a useful baseline. It is desirable for CAT-ASVAB to match or exceed P&P-ASVAB precision. Accordingly, precision criteria were computed for both P&P-ASVAB and CAT-ASVAB.

It is important to evaluate the impact of using the CAT-ASVAB item selection and scoring algorithm on precision, since the precision of adaptive test scores depends on both, the quality of the item pools, and on the adaptive testing procedures. The specific item selection and scoring procedures used are described in Chapter 12. For each adaptively administered test, the precision of the Bayesian modal estimate was evaluated. For each item pool, two measures of precision were examined: (a) score information, and (b) reliability.

Score Information

Score information functions provide one criterion for comparing the relative precision of the CAT-ASVAB with the P&P-ASVAB. Birnbaum (1968, Section 17.7) defines the information function for any score y to be

$$I\{\theta, y\} \equiv \frac{\left(\frac{d}{d\theta}\mu_{y|\theta}\right)^2}{\text{Var}(y|\theta)}. \quad (11\text{-}1)$$

This function is by definition inversely proportional to the square of the length of the asymptotic confidence interval for estimating ability θ from score y. For each content area, information functions can be compared between the CAT-ASVAB and the P&P-ASVAB. The test with greater information at a given ability level will possess a smaller asymptotic confidence interval for estimating θ.

CAT-ASVAB score information functions. The score information functions (SIFs) for each CAT-ASVAB item pool were approximated from simulated test sessions. For a given pool, simulations were repeated independently for 500 examinees at each of 31 different θ levels. These θ levels were equally spaced along the $[-3, +3]$ interval. At each θ level, the mean m and variance s^2 of the 500 final scores were computed. The information function at each selected level of θ can be approximated from these results, using (Lord, 1980a, eq. 10-7)

$$I\{\theta, \hat{\theta}\} \approx \frac{[m(\hat{\theta}|\theta_{+1}) - m(\hat{\theta}|\theta_{-1})]^2}{(\theta_{+1} - \theta_{-1})^2 s^2(\hat{\theta}|\theta_0)}, \quad (11\text{-}2)$$

where θ_{-1}, θ_0, θ_{+1} represent the successive levels of θ. However, the curve produced by this approximation often appears jagged, with many local variations. To reduce this problem, information was approximated by

$$I\{\theta, \hat{\theta}\} \approx$$

$$\frac{\left[\dfrac{m(\hat{\theta}|\theta_{+1}) + m(\hat{\theta}|\theta_{+2})}{2} - \dfrac{m(\hat{\theta}|\theta_{-1}) + m(\hat{\theta}|\theta_{-2})}{2}\right]^2}{\left[\dfrac{\theta_{+1} + \theta_{+2}}{2} - \dfrac{\theta_{-1} + \theta_{-2}}{2}\right]^2 \left[\dfrac{1}{5}\sum_{k=-2}^{+2} s(\hat{\theta}|\theta)\right]^2}$$

(11-3)

$$=$$

$$\frac{25[m(\hat{\theta}|\theta_{+2}) + m(\hat{\theta}|\theta_{+1}) - m(\hat{\theta}|\theta_{-1}) - m(\hat{\theta}|\theta_{-2})]^2}{(\theta_{+2} + \theta_{+1} - \theta_{-1} - \theta_{-2})^2 \left[\sum_{k=-2}^{+2} s(\hat{\theta}|\theta_k)\right]^2}$$

(11-4)

where θ_{-2}, θ_{-1}, θ_0, θ_{+1}, θ_{+2} represent successive levels of θ. This approximation results in a moderately smoothed curve with small local differences.

P&P-ASVAB Score information functions. The P&P-SIF for a number right score x was computed by (Lord, 1980a, eq. 5-13)

$$I\{\theta, x\} = \frac{\left[\sum_{i=1}^{n} P_i'(\theta)\right]^2}{\sum_{i=1}^{n} P_i(\theta)Q_i(\theta)}$$

(11-5)

This function was computed for each content area by substituting the estimated P&P-ASVAB (9A) parameters for those assumed to be known in Equation (11-5).

A special procedure was used to compute SIF for AS since this test is represented by two tests in CAT-ASVAB. The AS-P&P (9A) test was divided into AI and SI items. SIFs (eq. 11-5) were computed separately for these AI-P&P and SI-P&P items to simplify comparisons with the corresponding CAT-ASVAB SIFs. Parameters used in the computation of these SIFs were taken from the joint calibrations of P&P-ASVAB and CAT-ASVAB items. In these calibrations, AS-P&P items were separated and calibrated among CAT-ASVAB items of corresponding content (i.e., AI-P&P items were calibrated with AI-CAT, and SI-P&P with SI-CAT items). However, two AS-P&P (9A) items appeared to overlap in AI/SI content, and appeared in both AI and SI calibrations. For computations of score information, these two items were included in both AI-P&P and SI-P&P information functions. This represents a conservative approach (favoring the P&P-ASVAB), since we are counting these two items twice in the computations of the P&P-ASVAB SIFs.

Score information results. CAT-ASVAB SIFs were computed for each of the 22 conditions listed in Table 11-8. For comparison, the P&P-ASVAB SIF (for 9A) was computed. The SIFs for the CAT-ASVAB equaled or exceeded the P&P-ASVAB SIFs for all but four conditions: 3, 4, 7, and 8. These four exceptions involved the two pools of AR and WK that consisted of only primary items. When these pools were supplemented with additional items (see conditions 5, 6, 9, and 10) the resulting SIFs equaled or exceeded the corresponding P&P-ASVAB SIFs.

Table 11-9 lists the number of items used in selected SIF analyses. The number of times (across simulees) that an item was administered was recorded for each SIF simulation. The values in Table 11-9 represent the number of items that were administered at least once during the 15,500 simulated test sessions. A separate count for pri-

Table 11-9 Number of Used Items in CAT-ASVAB Item Pools

| Content Area | Exposure Rate | Number of Used Items | | | | | |
| | | Form 1 | | | Form 2 | | |
		Primary	Supp.	Total	Primary	Supp.	Total
GS	1/3	72	—	72	67	—	67
AR	1/6	62	32	94	53	41	94
WK	1/6	61	34	95	55	44	99
PC	1/6	50	—	50	52	—	52
AI	1/3	53	—	53	53	—	53
SI	1/3	51	—	51	49	—	49
MK	1/6	84	—	84	85	—	85
MC	1/3	64	—	64	64	—	64
EI	1/3	61	—	61	61	—	61

mary and supplemental items is provided for AR and WK.

Reliability

A reliability index provides another criterion for comparing the relative precision of the CAT-ASVAB with the P&P-ASVAB. These indices were computed for each pool and for one form (9A) of the P&P-ASVAB. The reliabilities were estimated from simulated test sessions: 1,900 values were sampled from a $N(0,1)$ distribution. Each value represented the ability level of a simulated examinee (simulee). The simulated tests were administered twice to each of the 1,900 simulees. The reliability index was the correlation between the pairs of Bayesian modal estimates of ability from the two simulated administrations. The CAT-ASVAB reliabilities were computed separately for each pool. The item selection and scoring procedures match those used in CAT-ASVAB (Chapter 12).

The P&P-ASVAB reliabilities were computed from simulated administrations of Form 9A. The following procedure was used to generate number right scores for each of the 1,900 simulees:

STEP 1: The probability of a correct response to a given item was obtained for a simulee by substituting the (9A) item parameter estimates and the simulee's ability level into the three-parameter logistic model.

STEP 2: A random uniform value in the interval [0,1] was generated and compared to the probability of a correct response. If the random number was less than the probability value, the item was scored correct; otherwise it was scored incorrect.

STEP 3: Steps 1 and 2 were repeated across test items for each simulee. The number right score was the sum of the responses scored correct.

Steps 1 through 3 were repeated twice to obtain two number-right scores for each simulee. The reliability index for the P&P-ASVAB was the correlation between the two number-right scores.

A special procedure was used to compute reliability indices for AS. These items on the P&P version (9A) were divided into two components: AI and SI. This split corresponded to the assignment made in the item calibration of these content areas. A reliability index was computed separately for each component.

Reliability indices were computed for each of the 22 conditions and are listed in Table 11-10. For

Table 11-10 Simulated Reliabilities ($N = 1,900$)

Test	Form	Test Length	Exposure Rate	Reliability r
GS	CAT-1	15	1/3	.902
	CAT-2	15	1/3	.900
	ASVAB-9A	25		.835
AR	CAT$_s$-1	15	1/6	.924
	CAT$_s$-2	15	1/6	.924
	CAT-1	15	1/6	.904
	CAT-2	15	1/6	.903
	ASVAB-9A	30		.891
WK	CAT$_s$-1	15	1/6	.934
	CAT$_s$-2	15	1/6	.936
	CAT-1	15	1/6	.912
	CAT-2	15	1/6	.913
	ASVAB-9A	35		.902
PC	CAT-1	10	1/6	.847
	CAT-2	10	1/6	.855
	ASVAB-9A	15		.758
AI	CAT-1	10	1/3	.894
	CAT-2	10	1/3	.904
	ASVAB-9A	17		.821
SI	CAT-1	10	1/3	.874
	CAT-2	10	1/3	.873
	ASVAB-9A	10		.651
MK	CAT-1	15	1/6	.933
	CAT-2	15	1/6	.935
	ASVAB-9A	25		.854
MC	CAT-1	15	1/3	.886
	CAT-2	15	1/3	.897
	ASVAB-9A	25		.807
EI	CAT-1	15	1/3	.875
	CAT-2	15	1/3	.873
	ASVAB-9A	20		.768

comparison, the P&P-ASVAB reliability (for 9A) was computed and displayed in the same table. Exposure rates and test lengths are also provided. The estimated CAT-ASVAB reliability indices exceeded the corresponding P&P-ASVAB (9A) values for all 22 conditions.

Summary

The procedures described in this chapter formed the basis of the item pool construction and evaluation procedures. Large item pools were pretested and calibrated in large samples of applicants. Two item pools (WK and AR) were supplemented with additional items, and a special study was conducted to evaluate adverse consequences of mixing 4-option supplemental items with other 5-option items. Extensive analyses were conducted to evaluate each pool's dimensionality. For pools found to be multidimensional, these analyses aided in selecting the most appropriate approach for item selection and scoring. Finally, extensive precision analyses were conducted to evaluate the conditional and unconditional precision levels of the item pools, and to compare these precision levels with the P&P-ASVAB.

Based on the score information analyses, the precision for the primary AR and WK pools over the middle ranges of ability was inadequate. By supplementing these pools with experimental CAT-ASVAB items, the precision was raised to an acceptable level. Why was it necessary to supplement these pools, and what lessons can be applied to the construction of future pools?

One clue comes from the distribution of difficulty parameters obtained from surviving items (those items in the pools that have a greater than zero probability of administration). An examination of this distribution indicates a bell shaped distribution, with a larger number of difficulty values appearing over the middle ranges, and fewer values appearing in the extremes. Note that the target difficulty distribution for item writing and for inclusion in the calibration study was a uniform distribution. This suggests that there were actually an excess of items in the extremes (which had zero probabilities of administration), and for WK and AR, a deficiency of items over the middle ranges. Future development efforts should attempt to construct banks of items with bell shaped distributions of item difficulty values, similar to those constructed for P&P tests.

A bell shaped distribution of item difficulties has at least two desirable properties for CAT. First, larger numbers of items with moderate difficulty values are likely to lead to higher precision over the middle range, since the adaptive algorithm is likely to have more highly discriminating items to choose from. This may be especially desirable if it is important to match the precision of a P&P test which peaks in information over the middle ability ranges. Second, the Sympson-Hetter exposure control algorithm (Chapter 13) places demands on moderately difficult items, since the administration of these items is restricted. Because of the restrictions placed on these items, more highly informative items of moderate difficulty are necessary to maintain high levels of precision.

Although CAT-ASVAB precision analyses indicated favorable comparisons with the P&P-ASVAB, many strong assumptions were made in the simulation analyses which may limit applicability of these findings to operational administrations with real test-takers. Such assumptions (including unidimensionality, local independence, and knowledge of true item functioning) are almost certainly violated to some extent in applied testing situations. Therefore, it is important to examine the precision of these pools with live test-takers who are administered tests using the same adaptive item selection and scoring algorithms evaluated here. Such an evaluation is described in Chapter 17.

12

Psychometric Procedures for Administering CAT-ASVAB

Daniel O. Segall, Kathleen E. Moreno, Bruce M. Bloxom, and Rebecca D. Hetter

This chapter describes the psychometric procedures used in CAT-ASVAB administration and scoring, and summarizes the rationale for selecting these procedures. Key decisions were based on extensive discussions by the staff at the Navy Personnel Research and Development Center (NPRDC) and by the CAT-ASVAB Technical Committee, which occurred from about the mid- to late 1980s. For many key psychometric decisions, there was an understandable tension between two camps within the CAT-ASVAB project. One camp wanted to extensively study each decision, first by reviewing the literature, then by carefully enumerating all possible alternatives, then by studying empirically all possible alternatives from carefully designed and implemented research studies, and then, and only then, choosing from among the alternatives. The other camp was less concerned with making optimal decisions, and more concerned with the efficient allocation of resources needed to field an operational system. The tension between these two camps produced an adaptive testing battery (CAT-ASVAB) that achieved a remarkable balance between scientific empiricism and the drive to produce an operational system.

The experimental system (Chapters 8, 9, and 10) provided a useful and important starting point for the specification of psychometric procedures. By the mid-1980s, data from over 7,500 subjects had been collected and analyzed. These data, to a large extent, supported the usefulness of many experimental system procedures—validities for predicting success in training were as high or higher than the P&P-ASVAB. However, the absence of many necessary features (test time-limits, help dialogs, item seeding, stringent exposure control, and user-friendly rules for changing and confirming answers) meant that extensive psychometric changes would be required before CAT-ASVAB could be administered operationally.

From about 1985 to 1989, an extensive review of CAT-ASVAB psychometric procedures was conducted by NPRDC and the CAT-ASVAB Technical Committee. Virtually every characteristic of the system having psychometric implications was studied. Because of the necessary time and resource constraints, different decisions were based on different amounts of knowledge and understanding of each issue. Many important decisions were based on extensive empirical studies involving live or simulated data, conducted by project staff. Other decisions were based on existing work reported in the literature. And still other choices fell into the "it don't make no never mind" category. In documenting the psychometric procedures of the CAT-ASVAB, examples of each type can be found. Although not all decisions were based on a complete and thorough investigation of the issues, it is a tribute to those involved that the fundamental decisions made during this period have withstood the test of time. In this chapter, three major areas are discussed: power test administration, speeded test administration, and administrative requirements.

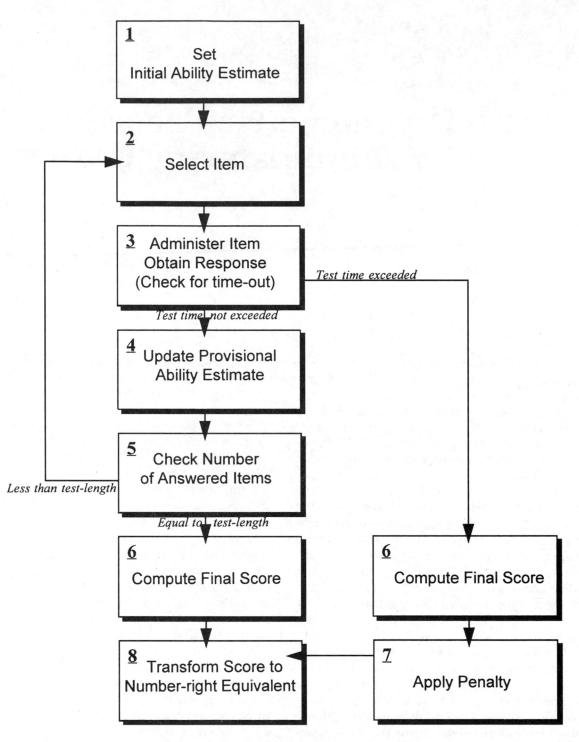

Figure 12-1
Steps in CAT-ASVAB Item Selection and Scoring.

Power Test Administration

All power tests contained in the CAT-ASVAB are administered using an adaptive testing algorithm. The eight basic steps involved in item selection and scoring are displayed in Figure 12-1. Details of each step are provided below.

1. Initial Ability Specification

The first step in item selection is to set the initial ability estimate $\hat{\theta}_0 = 0$ (i.e. equal to the mean of the prior distribution of abilities). The mean (and standard deviation) of the prior were set equal to the observed moments of IRT scores (Bayesian modal estimates) calculated from the calibration sample used to estimate IRT item parameters (Chapter 11). By specifying the initial ability estimate in this way, the first administered item will be among the most informative for average ability examinees.

2. Item Selection

Given an initial or provisional ability estimate, the second step in the adaptive algorithm is to choose the next item for presentation to the examinee. CAT-ASVAB uses item response theory (IRT) item information (Lord, 1980a, eq. 5-9) as a basis for choosing items. Selecting the most informative item for an examinee is accomplished by the use of an information table. To create the tables for each content area, items were sorted by information at each of 37 θ-levels, equally spaced along the interval $[-2.25, +2.25]$. The use of information tables avoids the necessity for computing information values for each item in the pool between the presentation of successive items; these values are essentially computed in advance. The General Science test is content-balanced among three content areas due to concerns about dimensionality. For this test, separate information tables were created for each of the three content areas: life science, physical science, and chemistry.

An item is chosen from the appropriate information table and selection is based on the provisional ability estimate (denoted by $\hat{\theta}_n$) calculated from the n previously answered items. The midpoint of θ-interval in the information table closest to the provisional estimate is located, and items with the greatest information in that θ interval are

considered in turn for administration. The selection of an item within a given θ-interval of the information table is subject to two criteria. First, the item must not have been previously administered to the examinee during the test session. Second, item selection is conditional on the application of the exposure control procedure (see Chapter 13). According to this exposure control algorithm, once an item is considered for administration, the system generates a random number between 0 and 1 and compares this random number to the exposure control parameter for the item. If the value of the exposure control parameter is greater than or equal to the random number for the item, the item is administered. If the value of the exposure control parameter is less than the random number, the item is not administered, and is marked as having been selected—the item is not considered for administration at any other point in the test for that examinee. In this case the next most informative item in the interval is considered for administration, and a new random number is generated. This process is repeated until an item passes the exposure control screen. This procedure places a ceiling on the exposure of the pool's most informative items.

The General Science test follows this same procedure, except that the allocation administers roughly the same proportion of each content area as found in the reference P&P form (8A). The following allocation vector is used to determine the information table from which to select the next item:

$$L, P, L, P, L, P, L, P, L, P, L, P, L, P, L, C,$$

where L = Life Science, P = Physical Science, C = Chemistry. Accordingly, the first item administered in the General Science test is selected from the Life Science information table, the second item administered is selected from the Physical Science information table, and so on.

3. Item Administration

Once the item has been selected, the third step is to display the item and obtain the examinee's response. The administrative requirements involved in item presentation and gathering responses are described in a following section. Each adaptive test has an associated time-limit (Table 12-1). If this time-limit is reached before the examinee has answered the last item, the test is terminated, a

Table 12-1 Time-Limits (minutes) and Test Lengths* for CAT-ASVAB Tests

	GS	AR	WK	PC	NO	CS	AI	SI	MK	MC	EI
Time-limit	8	39	8	22	3	7	6	5	18	20	8
Test-length	16	16	16	11	50	84	11	11	16	16	16

*For all power tests, the test-lengths include one experimental item. Therefore, the number of items used to score the test is the test-length minus one.

final score is computed (Step 6), and a scoring-penalty is applied (Step 7).

Ideally, pure power tests should be administered without time-limits. This is especially true of adaptive power tests which are scored using IRT methods which do not explicitly consider the effects of time-pressure on response choice. However, the imposition of time-limits on all tests was necessary for administrative purposes. When scheduling test sessions and paying test administrators, it would not be practical to allow some examinees to take as long as desired. The power test time-limits were initially based on response times of recruits in the Joint-Services validity study (see Chapter 10). Those time limits were later modified from test finishing times gathered from about 400 applicants participating in the SED study (Chapter 19). The time-limits were set so that over 95 percent of the examinees taking the test would complete all items without having to rush. In practice, each adaptive test displays completion rates of over 98 percent.

4. Provisional Scoring

After the presentation of each item, the scored response is used to update the provisional ability estimate. A sequential Bayesian procedure (Owen, 1969; 1975) is used for this purpose. This updated ability estimate is used to select the next item for administration (in Step 2). This procedure was selected for intermediate scoring because it is computationally efficient compared to other Bayesian estimators, and because it provided favorable results in empirical validity studies (Chapter 10).

5. Test Termination

Each CAT-ASVAB test is terminated after an examinee has completed a fixed number of items or reaches the test time-limit, whichever occurs first. The fifth step in the adaptive algorithm is to check to determine if the examinee has answered the prescribed number of items for the test (Table 12-1). If the test-taker has, then a final score is computed

(Step 6); otherwise, a new item is selected (Step 2) and administered (Step 3).

A number of rationales support the decision to use fixed-length testing in the CAT-ASVAB, as opposed to variable-length testing in which additional items are administered until a pre-specified level of precision has been obtained. First, simulation studies have shown that fixed-length testing is more efficient than variable-length testing. Highly informative items are typically concentrated over a restricted range of ability. In variable-length testing, examinees falling outside this range tend to receive long tests, with each additional item providing very little information. For these examinees (usually at the high and low ability levels) the incremental value of each additional item quickly reaches the point of diminishing returns, leading to a very inefficient use of the examinees' time and effort. Also, with fixed-length testing, test-taking time is less variable across examinees, making the administration of the test and the planning of post-testing activities more predictable. Administering the same number of items to all examinees avoids the public-relations problem of explaining to non-experts why different numbers of items were administered.

6. Final Scoring

A final Owen estimate can be obtained by updating the estimate with the response to the final test item. However, the Owen estimate, as a final score, has one undesirable feature: The final score depends on the order in which the items are administered. Consequently, it is possible for two examinees to receive the same items, provide the same responses, but receive different final Owen ability estimates; this could occur if the two examinees received the items in different sequences. To avoid this possibility, the mode of the posterior distribution (Bayesian mode) is used at the conclusion of each power test to provide a final ability estimate. This estimator is unaffected by the order of item administration, and provides slightly greater precision than the Owen estimator.

In selecting a procedure for computing the final

ability estimate, various alternatives were considered. The posterior mode was chosen for the following reasons:

1. Although the posterior median gives estimates that are slightly more precise in simulations, the posterior mode is more established in the research literature.

2. After transformation to the number-right metric, the score based on the posterior mode correlates .999–1.000 with the posterior mean number right obtained by numerical integration.

3. Iterative computation of the posterior mode (with Owen's approximation to the posterior mean as the initial estimate), is more rapid than computation of the posterior mean obtained by adaptive quadrature numerical integration.

4. Maximum likelihood (ML) estimation was not used because of the possible bimodality of the likelihood function and it is undefined for all correct or incorrect response patterns. Also, ML estimates had lower validity for predicting success in training. This latter result was obtained by re-computing final scores with ML estimates for subjects participating in the Joint Service Validity Study (Chapter 10), and by computing the corresponding validity coefficients. These values were lower than validity coefficients computed from final scores based on Bayesian procedures.

7. Penalty for Incomplete Tests

The Bayesian modal estimator (BME) has one property that is problematic in the context of incomplete tests. As with Bayesian estimators in general, the BME contains a bias that draws the estimate toward the mean of the prior. This bias is inversely related to test length. That is, the bias is larger for short adaptive tests, and smaller for long adaptive tests. A low-ability examinee could use this property to his or her advantage. If allowed, a low-ability examinee could obtain a score at, or slightly below, the mean by answering only one or two items. Even if the items were answered incorrectly, the strong positive bias would push the estimator up toward the mean of the prior. Consequently, below-average applicants could use this strategy to increase their score by answering the minimum number of items allowed.

To discourage the use of this strategy, a penalty procedure was developed for use in scoring incomplete tests (Segall, 1988). The fact that the tests are timed almost ensures that some examinees will not finish, whether intentionally or not. In general, it is desirable for a penalty procedure to have the following properties:

· *The size of the penalty should be related to the number of unfinished items.* That is, applicants with many unfinished items should generally receive a more severe penalty than applicants with one or two unfinished items.

· *Applicants who (a) have answered the same number of items and (b) have the same provisional ability estimate should receive the same penalty.*

· *The penalty rule should eliminate "coachable" test-taking strategies (with respect to answering or not answering test items).*

The penalty procedure used in CAT-ASVAB satisfies the above constraints by providing a final score that is equivalent (in expectation) to the score obtained by guessing at random on the unfinished items. The size of the penalty for different test lengths, tests, and ability levels was determined through a series of 240 simulations. The following example provides the basic steps used in determining penalty functions.

Example Penalty Simulation:
Electronics Information—Form 2
Penalty for 2 unanswered items

1. Sample 2,000 true abilities from the uniform interval $[-3, +3]$.

2. For each simulee, generate a 13-item adaptive test; obtain a provisional score on the 13 item test with the BME, denoted as $\hat{\theta}_{13}$.

3. For each simulee, provide random responses for the remaining two items, with the probability of a correct response equal to $p = .2$; and then re-score using all 15 responses with the BME. Denote this final estimate as $\hat{\theta}_{15}$.

4. Regress $\hat{\theta}_{15}$ on $\hat{\theta}_{13}$, and fit a least-squares line predicting $\hat{\theta}_{15}$ from $\hat{\theta}_{13}$. This regression equation becomes the penalty function for: EI (Form 2); 13 answered items.

Figure 12-2 displays the outcome of this last step. By regressing the final estimate $\hat{\theta}_{15}$ on the provisional estimate $\hat{\theta}_{13}$, we can obtain an expected penalized $\dot{\theta}$ for any provisional $\hat{\theta}_{13}$. The final results of the simulation are slope and intercept parameters for the penalty function

$$\dot{\theta} = A + B \times \hat{\theta}_{13}. \qquad (12\text{-}1)$$

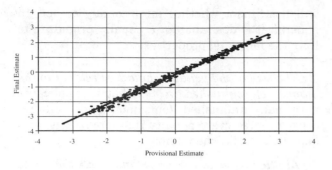

Figure 12-2
Penalty Function for EI—Form 2.

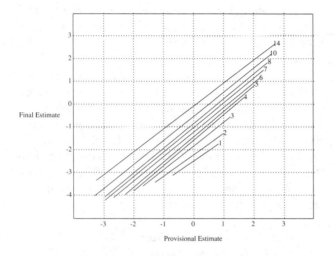

Figure 12-3
Selected Penalty Functions (by number of completed items) for EI—Form 2.

Since this simulation is conditional on (1) number of unfinished items, (2) test, and (3) test form, separate (A, B) parameters must be obtained from each of the

$$(15 \times 6 \times 2) + (10 \times 3 \times 2) = 240$$

simulations. To apply this penalty, these three pieces of information are used to identify the appropriate (A, B) parameters, which are applied to the provisional BME estimate to compute the final penalized value.

Figure 12-3 displays selected functions for different numbers of completed items for EI Form 2. Note how these functions satisfy all the requirements stated earlier:

1. The size of the penalty is positively related to the number of unfinished items.

2. Applicants who have answered the same number of items and have the same provisional ability estimate will receive the same penalty.

3. The procedure eliminates coachable test-taking strategies. There is no advantage for low ability examinees to leave items unanswered, and applicants should be indifferent about guessing at random on remaining items, or not answering them at all.

One undesirable consequence of the penalty procedure is a degradation in the precision of the final ability estimate. The penalty may not in general be correlated with the applicant's ability level. This degradation is expected to be small, however, mainly due to the infrequent application of this procedure. The time-limits for each power test allow almost all test-takers to finish. Table 12-2 provides the completion rates for those participating in the CAT-ASVAB Score Equating Verification (SEV) study (Chapter 19). As indicated by the distribution of unfinished items (Table 12-2), the penalty procedure was applied to a small number of applicants, and among those receiving a penalty, almost all received a mild value.

Table 12-2 Frequency of Incomplete Adaptive Power Tests ($N = 6,859$)

	Number of Unfinished Items										
Test	0	1	2	3	4	5	6	7	8	9	≥ 10
General Science (GS)	6,762	52	18	13	3	4	2	1		2	2
Arithmetic Reasoning (AR)	6,788	47	14	5	1	3	1				
Word Knowledge (WK)	6,820	18	6	4	4	3	2		1		1
Paragraph Comprehension (PC)	6,807	36	10	6							
Auto Information (AI)	6,820	28	9	2							
Shop Information (SI)	6,779	52	20	5	2	1					
Mathematics Knowledge (MK)	6,797	29	10	9	8	3	1	1	1		
Mechanical Comprehension (MC)	6,843	12	1	1	2						
Electronics Information (EI)	6,833	16	7		1	1			1		

8. Number-Correct Transformation

For each power test, the BME (or penalized BME if incomplete) is converted to an equated number correct score. Procedures used to obtain the equating transformations for converting scores are described in Chapter 19. Composite scores used for selection and classification are calculated from these number-right equivalents using the same formulas applied to the P&P-ASVAB reference form (8A).

Seeded Items

One advantage of computer-based testing is the ability to intersperse new, experimental test items among operational items to obtain calibration data. This is referred to as "seeding" items. Data collected on seeded items can be used to estimate IRT item parameters. This approach eliminates the need for special data collection efforts for the purpose of item-tryout and calibration.

In CAT-ASVAB, each power test includes one seeded item. An examinee's response to this item is not used to estimate the examinee's provisional or final score. The seeded item is administered as the second, third, or fourth item in a test, with the position being randomly determined by the computer software at the time of testing. This approach, using only one seeded item per power test and administering it early in the test, was taken so that it would not be apparent to the examinee that the item is experimental. As a result, the examinee should answer the item with the same level of motivation as other items in the sequence. In full-scale implementation of CAT-ASVAB, one interspersed item per test will produce calibration data on enough new items to satisfy new form development requirements.

Speeded Test Administration

The two speeded tests, Numerical Operations (NO) and Coding Speed (CS), are administered in a linear conventional format. For examinees receiving the same form, all receive the same items in the same sequence.

The speeded tests are scored using a rate score. In computerized measures of speeded abilities, rate scores have several advantages over number-right scores. First, rate-scores do not produce distributions with ceiling effects which are often observed for speeded tests scored by number-right. This is an especially important consideration when converting highly speeded tests from P&P medium to computer—the P&P time-limit imposed on the computerized version will produce higher number-right scores, possibly leading to ceiling effect. This result can often be traced to speed of answer entry: Entering an answer on a keyboard is faster than filling in a bubble on an answersheet. Number-right scoring on a computerized measure of speeded abilities would require careful consideration of time-limit specification with special attention given to the shape of the score-distribution. P&P-ASVAB time-limits applied to the computerized versions of NO and CS produced unacceptably large ceiling effects. Additionally, rate-scores have higher reliability estimates than number-correct scores (computed in an artificially imposed time interval).

For CAT-ASVAB running on the Hewlett Packard Integral Personal Computer (HP-IPC), the rate score was defined as

$$\hat{R} = \frac{P_g}{T_g} \times C, \qquad (12\text{-}2)$$

where

$$T_g = \left(\prod_{i=1}^{n} T_i\right)^{\frac{1}{n}} \qquad (12\text{-}3)$$

is the geometric mean of screen times T_i and P_g is the proportion of correct responses corrected for guessing, which is

$$P_g = 1.25P - .25 \qquad (for\ CS) \qquad (12\text{-}4)$$

$$P_g = 1.33P - .33 \qquad (for\ NO) \qquad (12\text{-}5)$$

where P is the proportion of correct responses among attempted items. If the proportion in the numerator of Equation 12-2 were not corrected for guessing, an applicant could receive a very high score by pressing any key quickly, without reading the items. Such an examinee would receive a low proportion correct, but a high rate score because of the fast responding. Correcting the score for chance guessing eliminates the advantage associated with fast random responding. The constant C in Equation 12-2 is a scaling factor which allows the rate score $\hat{R}$ to be interpreted as the number of correct responses per minute. For NO, $C = 60$, and for CS, $C = 420$.

It is important to note one problem with the geometric rate score that arises when an examinee guesses at random on a portion of the items. If an examinee answers a portion of the test correctly, and then responds at random to the remaining items very rapidly, the rate score (based on the geometric mean of response latencies) can be very large. An examinee could use this fact to game the test and artificially inflate his or her score. However, a rate score computed from the arithmetic mean of the response times does not suffer from this potential strategy. For this reason, in a later version of CAT-ASVAB (the version to be used in nationwide implementation) the geometric mean in Equation 12-3 was replaced by the arithmetic mean. The geometric mean was originally selected for CAT-ASVAB because results of an early analysis (Wolfe, 1985) showed that in comparison with the arithmetic mean, the geometric mean possessed slightly higher estimates of reliability and slightly higher correlations with the pre-enlistment ASVAB speeded tests. However, in a similar analysis conducted on larger samples with more recent data (Chapter 17), no significant differences in precision or validity was found between rate-scores based on the arithmetic and geometric means.

For the speeded tests, response-choices and latencies for screens interrupted by a "help" call are not included in the rate-score. Time spent on a question interrupted by a help-call may be atypical of the examinee's response latency to other items. Although the examinee is returned to the same item after a "help" call, he or she has unrecorded time for thinking about the interrupted item. This may make the performance on the item systematically better than other items in the test.

Rate scores (for each speeded test) are converted to an equated number correct score (see Chapter 19). As with the adaptive power tests, composite scores used for selection and classification are calculated from these number-right equivalents using the same formulas applied to the P&P-ASVAB reference form (8A).

Administrative Requirements

Changing and Confirming an Answer

When the examinee selects an answer to a power test question, the selected alternative is highlighted on the screen. If the examinee wants to change an answer, he or she can press another answer key, and that response is highlighted in place of the first answer. When the examinee's choice is final, pressing the "Enter" key initiates scoring of the response using the answer that is currently highlighted, followed by presentation of the next

item. Therefore, once "Enter" is pressed, the examinee cannot change the answer to that item. This procedure parallels, as closely as possible, the paper-and-pencil procedure of allowing the examinee to change the answer before moving on to the next question. Changing an answer once the "Enter" key is pressed and the next item selected is not allowed because of the adaptive nature of the test.

On the speeded tests, the examinee's first answer initiates scoring the response; there is no opportunity to change an answer. Allowing examinees to change answers on speeded tests would be problematic for several reasons. If examinees were allowed to change responses to speeded tests, a choice between two (undesirable) options must be made on how to measure item latency, since item latencies are used in scoring these tests. One measure of latency might be from screen presentation to response entry, ignoring time to confirmation. This, however, could lead to a strategy where examinees press the answer key as quickly as possible, then take longer to confirm the accuracy of their answer. Another measure of latency might be from screen presentation to pressing of the "Enter" or confirmation key. This approach, however, may add error to the measurement of ability, as speed in finding and pressing "Enter" could add an additional component to what the test measures.

Omitted Responses

In CAT-ASVAB, examinees are not allowed to omit items. The branching feature of adaptive testing requires a response from each examinee on each item as it is selected. Allowing examinees to omit items during the test is likely to lead to less than optimal item selection and scoring, and may lead to various compromise strategies. While it would be possible to allow omitted responses on the speeded tests, since they are administered in a conventional manner, there is no psychometric or examinee advantage for doing so.

Screen Time-Limits

In addition to test time-limits, each item screen has a time limit. The purpose is to identify an examinee who is having a problem taking the test, but is reluctant or unable to call for assistance. Two objectives were used to set the screen time-limits. First, very few test-takers should exceed the time-limit. Second, the ratio screen and test time-limits should be unacceptably large. That is, it is important to ensure that if the examinee needs help, that not too much of the test time has expired before help is called. Screen time-limits differed among the nine adaptive power tests, and are displayed in Table 12-3. These screen time-limits were first used in the CAT-ASVAB pretest (Chapter 15), resulting in very few examinees who exceeded the limit.

Help Calls

A machine-initiated "help" call is generated by the CAT-ASVAB system if an examinee times out on a screen or presses three invalid keys in a row. An examinee-initiated "help" call is generated when an examinee presses the "Help" key. "Help" calls stop all test timing and cause the system to bring up a series of "help" screens.

After a machine-initiated or examinee-initiated "help" call has been handled, all tests return to the screen containing the interrupted item, and the examinee is able to respond to the item. For speeded test scoring, the examinee's response to the item on the interrupted screen is not counted toward the score. Interrupting a speeded test distracts the examinee and adds error to the latency measure. Since speeded tests use item latency in obtaining the test score, these latencies should be as accurate as possible. On adaptive power tests, the item is scored and is used for computing the examinee's provisional and final scores. Power tests do not use latencies in scoring the test, and test time limits are liberal. Therefore, any distraction caused by an interruption should have a minimal effect on the accuracy of the examinee's score.

Display Format and Speed

The format of power test items displayed by the computer is as close as possible to the format used in the paper-and-pencil item calibration booklets. This was done to minimize any effects of format differences on item functioning. Speeded test items are presented in a format similar to paper-and-pencil ASVAB speeded test items so that the tests will be comparable across media. For NO, one item is presented per screen. For CS, seven items are presented per screen.

For the power tests, a line at the bottom, right-hand corner of the screen displays the "number of items" and "time" remaining on the test. The time shown is rounded to the nearest minute until the last minute, when the display shows the remaining time in seconds. This procedure provides standardization of test administration, ensuring that all examinees have the means of pacing themselves during the test. This procedure, however, is not used for the speeded tests. Since these tests are scored with a rate score, pacing against the test time-limit is not advantageous—the optimal strategy is to work as quickly and accurately as possible. Having a "clock" on the screen during the speeded tests would be disadvantageous to any examinee who looked at it, since time spent examining the clock would be better spent answering items.

For all tests, the delay between screens is no more than one second. In addition, the entire item is displayed at once, and does not "scroll" onto the screen. These conventions were adopted since long delays in presenting items, variability in the rate of presentation of items, and occasional partial displays of items would probably contribute to additional unwanted variability of examinee performance—that is, error variance. Also, test-taking attitude might be adversely affected.

For a newer implementation of CAT-ASVAB presented on PC-based hardware (rather than HP-IPC), it was necessary to insert a delay between screens. The PC computers that are being used in nationwide implementation of CAT-ASVAB are much faster than the HP-based systems. With these fast machines, concerns about delays in item presentation disappeared, but a new concern appeared—items being presented too quickly. For this reason, the new system has a software-controlled constant delay of .5 second between screens.

Summary

CAT-ASVAB procedures described in this chapter have, nearly without exception, proven to be efficient and reliable, and therefore have been imple-

Table 12-3 Test Screen Time-Limits (seconds)

GS	AR	WK	PC	NO	CS	AI	SI	MK	MC	EI
120	380	100	390	30	120	120	110	220	240	120

mented in the operational version of CAT-ASVAB administered in locations throughout the United States. The empirical consequences of these psychometric procedures and the relation of the resulting CAT scores to the P&P-ASVAB are documented in several other chapters, which include an evaluation of alternative forms reliability and construct validity (Chapter 17), an evaluation of predictive validity (Chapter 18), the equating of CAT-ASVAB to P&P-ASVAB (Chapter 19), and the consequence of calibration medium on CAT-ASVAB scores (Chapter 16). The favorable outcomes of these studies provide the best evidence to date of the soundness of these choices.

CHAPTER

13

Item Exposure Control in CAT-ASVAB

Rebecca D. Hetter and J. Bradford Sympson

Conventional paper-and-pencil (P&P) testing programs attempt to control the exposure of test questions by developing parallel forms. Test forms are usually administered at the same time to large groups of individuals and then discarded. Computerized adaptive tests require substantially larger item pools, and the cost of developing and discarding parallel forms becomes prohibitive. However, computer-based testing systems can control when and how often items are administered, and the development of procedures for controlling the exposure of test questions has become an important issue in adaptive testing research.

CAT achieves maximum precision when each item administered is the most informative for the current estimate of the examinee's ability level. For any ability estimate, only one item satisfies this requirement; therefore, when ability estimates are the same for different examinees, the item administered must also be the same. In the CAT-ASVAB, examinees begin the test under the assumption that they have equal abilities. Under a maximum-information selection rule, the most informative item would be the same for every examinee, the second item would be one of two choices (one after a correct answer, another after an incorrect one), and so on. As a consequence, the item sequence in this case is predictable and the initial items are used more frequently—thus becoming overexposed.

Early CAT-ASVAB research with the Apple III microcomputers used a procedure aimed at reducing sequence predictability and the exposure of initial items (McBride & Martin, 1983). In this procedure, called the 5-4-3-2-1, the first item is randomly selected from the best (most informative)

five items in the pool, the second item is selected from the best four, the third item is selected from the best 3, and the fourth item from the best 2. The fifth and subsequent items are administered as selected. The ability estimate is updated after each item. While this strategy reduces the predictability of item sequences, its net effect is substantial use and overexposure of a pool's most informative items.

To reduce the amount of item exposure and satisfy the security requirements of the operational CAT-ASVAB, a probabilistic algorithm was developed by Sympson and Hetter (1985). The algorithm was specifically designed to (1) reduce predictability of adaptive item sequences and overexposure of the most informative items, and (2) control overall item use in such a way that the probability of an item being administered (and, thereby "exposed") to any examinee can be approximated to a pre-specified maximum value. The algorithm controls item selection during adaptive testing through the use of previously computed parameters (K_i) associated with each item.

Computation of the K_i Parameters

To calculate the K_i, simulated adaptive tests are administered to a large group of simulated examinees ("simulees") whose "true" abilities are randomly sampled from an ability distribution representative of the real examinee population. Test administrations are repeated until certain values (to be defined below) converge to a pre-specified expected exposure rate.

For the CAT-ASVAB, 1,900 "true" abilities were

drawn from a normal distribution of ability, $N(0,1)$. To simulate examinee responses, a pseudo-random number was drawn from a uniform distribution in the interval $(0,1)$. If the random number was less than the three-parameter logistic model (3PL) probability of a correct response, the item was scored correct; otherwise it was scored incorrect. The CAT-ASVAB item parameters and the "true" abilities were used to compute the 3PL probabilities. The actual steps in the computations are described below.

Steps in the Sympson-Hetter Procedure

Steps 1 to 3 are performed once for each test. Steps 4 through 8 are iterated until a criterion is met.

1. Specify the maximum expected item-exposure rate r for the test. In the CAT-ASVAB battery, the rates were set to match those of the P&P-ASVAB, which comprises six forms. Four of the tests in the ASVAB battery are used to compute the Armed Forces Qualification Test (AFQT) composite score, which is used to determine enlistment eligibility. The AFQT tests in the six P&P forms are different; but each non-AFQT test is used in two forms. This results in exposure rates $r = \frac{1}{6}$ for AFQT tests, and $r = \frac{1}{3}$ for non-AFQT tests. The CAT-ASVAB has two forms and to approximate the same values, expected exposure rates were set to $r = \frac{1}{3}$ for AFQT tests ($\frac{1}{6}$ over two forms) and $r = \frac{2}{3}$ for non-AFQT tests ($\frac{1}{3}$ over two forms).

2. Construct an information table (infotable) using the available item pool. An infotable consists of lists of items by ability level. Within each list, all the items in the pool are arranged in descending order of the values of their information functions (Birnbaum, 1968, Section 17.7) computed at that ability level. In the CAT-ASVAB, infotables comprise 37 levels equally spaced along the $(-2.25, +2.25)$ ability interval.

3. Generate the first set of K_i values. If there are i items in the item pool, generate an i-long vector containing the value 1.0 in each element. Denote the ith element of this vector as the K_i associated with item I.

4. Administer adaptive tests to a random sample of simulees. For each item, identify the most informative item i available at the infotable ability level (θ) nearest the examinee's current ability estimate $(\hat{\theta})$ then generate a pseudo-random-number x from the uniform distribution $(0,1)$. Administer item i if x is less than or equal to the corresponding K_i. Whether or not item i is administered, exclude it from further administration for the remainder of this examinee's test. Note that for the first simulation, all the K_i's are equal to 1.0 and every item is administered, if selected.

5. Keep track of the number of times each item in the pool is selected (NS) and the number of times that it is administered (NA) in the total simulee sample. When the complete sample has been tested, compute $P(S)$, the probability that an item is selected, and $P(A)$, the probability that an item is administered given that it has been selected, for each item:

$$P(S) = \text{NS/NE} \qquad (13\text{-}1)$$

$$P(A) = \text{NA/NE} \qquad (13\text{-}2)$$

where NE = total number of examinees.

6. Using the value of r set in Step 1, and the $P(S)$ values computed above, compute new K_i as follows:

$$\text{If } P(S) > r, \text{ then new } K_i = r/P(S) \qquad (13\text{-}3)$$

$$\text{If } P(S) \leq r, \text{ then new } K_i = 1.0 \qquad (13\text{-}4)$$

7. For adaptive tests of length n, ensure that there are at least n items in the item pool that have new $K_i = 1.0$. Items with $K_i = 1.0$ are always administered when selected, since the random number is always less than or equal to 1. If there are fewer than n items with new $K_i = 1.0$, set the n largest K_i equal to 1.0. This guarantees that all examinees will get a complete test of length n before exhausting the item pool.

8. Given the new K_i, go back to Step 4. Using the same examinees, repeat Steps 4, 5, 6, and 7 until the maximum value of $P(A)$ that is obtained in Step 5 (maximum across all the items in the test) approaches a limit slightly above r and then oscillates in successive simulations.

The K_i obtained from the final round of computer simulations are the exposure-control parameters to be used in real testing.

Use of the K_i During Testing

The process works as follows: (1) Select the most informative item for the current ability estimate, (2) Generate a pseudo-random number x from a uniform $(0,1)$ distribution. (3) If x is less than or equal to the item's K_i, administer the item; if x is greater than the K_i, do not administer the item, identify the next most-informative item, and repeat (1), (2), and (3). Selected but not-administered items are set aside and excluded from further use for the current examinee; items are always selected from a set of items that have been neither administered nor set-aside. Note that for every examinee, the set of available items at the beginning of a test is the complete item pool.

Simulation Results

For the CAT-ASVAB tests, the maximum $P(A)$ values obtained in Step 5 approached the r values after five or six iterations. Table 13-1 shows $P(A)$ results for two AFQT tests, Paragraph Comprehension (PC) and Arithmetic Reasoning (AR). For both tests, the expected exposure rate r had been set equal to ⅓.

Precision

When the exposure-control algorithm is used, optimum precision is not achieved since the best item (most informative) is not always administered. To evaluate the precision of the CAT-ASVAB tests, score information functions were approxi-

Table 13-1 Maximum Usage Proportion $P(A)$ by Test and Simulation Number

Simulation Number	Paragraph Comprehension Test	Arithmetic Reasoning Test
1	1.000	1.000
2	0.540	0.562
3	0.412	0.397
4	0.361	0.367
5	0.364	0.357
6	0.352	0.354
7	0.359	0.345
8	0.349	0.358
9	0.357	0.352
10	0.357	0.365

mated from simulated adaptive test sessions conducted with and without exposure control. The sessions were repeated independently for 500 examinees at each of 31 different theta levels equally spaced along the $(-3, +3)$ interval. These theta levels are assumed to be true abilities for the simulations. Infotables and simulated responses were as in the K_i simulations above. Score information was approximated using Equation 11-4.

Figures 13-1 and 13-2 present score information

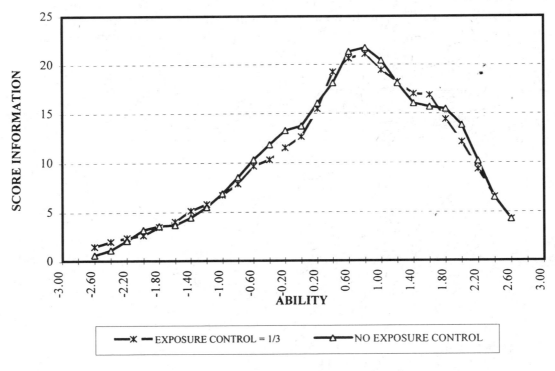

Figure 13-1
Score information by ability: Arithmetic Reasoning Test

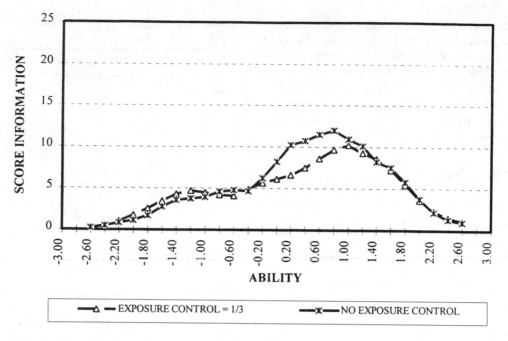

Figure 13-2
Score information by ability: Paragraph Comprehension Test

curves for Arithmetic Reasoning (AR) and Paragraph Comprehension (PC), respectively. The loss of precision due to the use of exposure control is very small and uniform across the theta range in AR, and more noticeable in the average ability region for PC. There are no losses or some gains at the extremes of the ability distribution. Results for the remaining tests were similar.

Summary

These results indicate that the use of exposure-control parameters does not significantly affect the precision of the CAT-ASVAB tests and will reduce the exposure of their best items. Future work should evaluate actual item use from the CAT-ASVAB operational administration data.

ACAP Hardware Selection, Software Development, and Acceptance Testing

Bernard Rafacz and Rebecca D. Hetter

This chapter discusses the development and acceptance testing of a computer network system to support the Computerized Adaptive Testing—Armed Services Vocational Aptitude Battery (CAT-ASVAB) program from 1984 to 1994. During that time, the program was devoted to realizing the goals of the Accelerated CAT-ASVAB Project (ACAP).

Since 1979, under the CAT-ASVAB program that has been described in the earlier chapters, the Joint Services have been developing a computer system to support the implementation of the CAT strategy at testing sites of the United States Military Entrance Processing Command (USMEPCOM). In 1984, a full-scale development (FSD) contracting effort was initiated with the expectation of using extensive contractor support to design and manufacture a unique computer system that could be used at USMEPCOM. In 1985, the FSD effort was terminated and the ACAP was initiated, primarily because the contracting effort was consuming too many resources to commence, let alone complete, the desired system. In addition, the recent advent of powerful microcomputer systems on the commercial market encouraged program managers to pursue the use of off-the-shelf microcomputers in contrast to developing a system unique to the project.

The implementation concerns for the ACAP system focused primarily on the psychometric requirements of the CAT-ASVAB system—specifically, the evaluation of CAT-generated aptitude scores and the equating of these scores to the paper-and-pencil ASVAB (P&P-ASVAB) aptitude scores. To meet this requirement, the Joint Services decided that all the computer support components should be in place so that the psychometric research could be conducted without confounding by factors other than those affecting operational use of such a system. Therefore, the ACAP was required to develop a computer system capable of supporting all of the functional specifications of CAT-ASVAB in a time frame consistent with continued support of the program.

In brief, ACAP was tasked to develop a CAT-ASVAB computer system to refine the operational requirements for the eventual system and to conduct the psychometric research efforts for evaluating CAT scores with those of the P&P-ASVAB. To this end, ACAP tried to identify and address these requirements as much as possible in an operational environment. This was accomplished by using commercially available computer hardware in a field test of CAT-ASVAB functions at selected USMEPCOM sites. At those sites, CAT-ASVAB testing was implemented in accordance with the specifications for the original contracting effort, and in accordance with specifications from new psychometric requirements that arose during the course of ACAP development. The design and development of the computer system to support CAT-ASVAB progressed along two obviously interrelated dimensions: computer hardware and software.

ACAP Hardware Selection

The hardware needed for the CAT-ASVAB system had to be selected before the operating system and programming language could be identified. Specifically, a Local CAT-ASVAB Network (LCN) of interconnected computers was to administer CAT-ASVAB to applicants for enlisted military service at any of approximately 64 Military Entrance Processing Stations (MEPSs) or approximately 900 Mobile Examining Team Sites (METSs) within US-MEPCOM. In addition, a Data Handling Computer (DHC) at each MEPS handles communication of information between the LCN units and a CAT central research facility. The DHC also stores examinee testing and equipment utilization data for six months, as required.

Original Hardware Specifications and Design

The hardware configuration envisioned by the Joint Services in the original contracting effort involved transportable computer systems at the MEPSs and METSs, based on the concept of a "generic" LCN. A generic LCN consists of six examinee testing (ET) stations monitored (via an electronic network) by a single test administrator (TA) station and peripheral support equipment (e.g., mass storage devices and printers). Under a networked configuration, a single TA station must allow the TA to monitor up to 24 ET stations (i.e., administer the CAT-ASVAB to 24 examinees simultaneously). The CAT-ASVAB portability requirements specify that each generic LCN consist of up to eight components weighing a total of no more than 120 pounds, each component weighing no more than 23 pounds. Environmental requirements for operating temperature, humidity, and altitude are also specified. The TA and ET stations must be interchangeable so that each TA and ET station can serve as the backup for any other station in the LCN.

The LCN computer hardware specifications have remained relatively unchanged as follows: Each ET station consists of a response device, a screen display, and access to sufficient random access memory (RAM) and/or data storage for administration of any CAT-ASVAB test; the amount of RAM required depends on the specific application software and networking design used. The ET stations are tied to a TA station by networking cables. Each

TA station is essentially an ET station with a mass storage device and full-size keyboard. The failure of one station must not affect the performance of any other unit in the LCN. Each TA station has a very portable printer and modem. All components operate on ordinary 110 VAC line current. Battery packs are not used because they add weight and require additional logistic support.

In the METSs, the LCN operational requirements would be as follows: Each LCN administers the CAT-ASVAB to military applicants scheduled for testing at the METS. Initially, an Office of Personnel Management (OPM) examiner would pick up the LCN equipment at a staging area (USMEPCOM, 1983), transport it to the test site (sometimes a hotel room), carry it from the vehicle to the test site, and configure it for testing. When the system is ready for testing (i.e., "booting" and loading of source code/data files are completed), the TA solicits personal data (name, Social Security number [SSN], etc.) from each examinee and enters this information into the system at the examiner's TA station. Then, the TA instructs each examinee to sit at a specified ET station and start testing, without further TA assistance. Examinee item response information is stored on a nonvolatile medium (e.g., micro floppy disk) to allow the test to continue at another ET station in the event the original ET station fails during a testing session. Finally, the TA is expected to monitor the various testing activities at the ET stations (e.g., CAT-ASVAB testing progress status and use of a "Help" function). After all examinees at a METS have completed testing, the TA sends the entire Examinee Data File (consisting of the personal data, item level responses, test scores, and composite scores) to the DHC unit at the associated MEPS, using a modem and dial-up telephone line, if available. If this is not possible (e.g., no telephone line at the test site), the examiner transfers the data after the equipment is returned to the staging area. Finally, the TA packs up and returns all equipment to the staging area.

MEPS equipment is stationary, but otherwise identical to METS equipment. In contrast to most METSs, each TA at a MEPS testing site must be capable of monitoring 24 ET stations simultaneously. In addition, on start-up, the TA obtains the latest software and testing data from the DHC unit at the MEPS via either a hard-wired connection or a transportable medium. At the end of testing, testing data are sent to the DHC using the same medium. An LCN at the MEPS would not use dial-up telephone lines.

The MEPS site implementation of CAT-ASVAB also includes a DHC unit to collect data daily from each LCN in the associated MEPS administrative segment, including any LCNs at METSs. These data are to be compiled and organized on the DHC for:

· Daily transmission of an extract of examinee data collected that day to the USMEPCOM minicomputer located at the MEPSs.

· Periodic transmission of all examinee data to the Defense Manpower Data Center (DMDC).

· Archiving of all examinee and equipment utilization data at the MEPSs for at least six months.

The MEPS DHC also must be capable of receiving new software, test item bank updates, and instructions from DMDC and telecommunicating this information to field LCN units.

ACAP Hardware Development

The three generic computer system designs being considered for use as the local computer network for the CAT-ASVAB program were discussed by Tiggle and Rafacz (1985). The three designs differed in how they stored and provided access to test items during test administration. Storing test items on removable media (e.g., 3.5-inch micro floppy disks) or a central file server (e.g., a hard disk) had disadvantages with security, media updating, ease of use, maintenance, reliability, and response time.

The design selected emphasizes the use of RAM. Each TA and ET station requires at least 1.5 megabytes (MB) of internal RAM, which can accommodate all the software and data needed to administer the CAT-ASVAB tests. In case of LCN failure, each ET station can operate independently of any other station in the network. The ET station needs one micro floppy disk drive and an electroluminescent or LCD technology display screen. In addition, the TA station can perform the functions of an "electronic" file server. The TA station could have a large amount of total RAM available, which provides great flexibility in the total number of alternate forms available during any one test session.

This design offers many advantages, including a large degree of flexibility with respect to design options. The ET stations can operate as standalone devices (i.e., without the use of the TA station). This being the case, it would be virtually impossible for an examinee's test session to fail to

be completed; each ET station would be a backup station for every other station in the LCN. This design is very reliable because it minimizes use of mechanical devices. Finally, the design provides a very high level of security because volatile RAM is erased when the power to the computer is turned off.

LCN monitoring and the system response time requirements are not functionally related. The computer hardware can be configured so that the data storage requirements (for any one CAT-ASVAB form) reside at the ET station. Therefore, the response time display of test items can be independent of the LCN. The item display process takes place at RAM speed, resulting in a maximum response time on the order of 1 second, which is well within CAT-ASVAB specifications.

The hardware procurement for ACAP was negotiated by the Navy Supply Center, San Diego, using a brand name or equivalent procurement strategy. This resulted in the selection of the Hewlett Packard Integral Personal Computer (HP-IPC) to meet the specifications. Each ET station consists of the following components in a single compact and transportable (25-pound) package:

· One 8 MHz 68000 CPU with 1.5 MB of internal RAM with an internal data transfer rate (RAM to RAM) of 175 KB/second.

· One read-only memory (ROM) chip with 256 KB of available memory containing a kernel of the UNIX operating system.

· One microfloppy disk drive (710 KB capacity) with data transfer rate (disk to RAM) of 9.42 KB/second.

· One adjustable electroluminescent display with a resolution of 512 (horizontal) by 255 (vertical) pixels (screen size 9 inches measured diagonally; 8 inches wide by 4 inches high).

· One custom-built examinee input device (essentially a modification of the standard HP-IPC keyboard).

· One Hewlett Packard Interface Loop (HP-IL) networking card.

· One integrated ink-jet printer for use when the ET station must serve as a backup to the TA station.

Each TA station is configured identically to the ET station, but includes 2.5–4.5 MB of internal RAM and a full-size ASCII keyboard.

In summary, each generic LCN (i.e., six ET stations tied to a single TA station) consists of seven transportable components weighing a total of approximately 175 pounds. Using the HP-IL networking card and special network driver software achieves a network data transfer rate of approximately 9KB per second.

The data handling computer (DHC) system, also based on the HP-IPC, consists of the following components:

· One ET station with a full-size keyboard.

· Two 55 MB hard disk drives (primary and backup data archive units).

· One cartridge tape drive unit; periodically, a cartridge tape of examinee testing data is to be sent to NPRDC.

· Telecommunications hardware to communicate with the MEPS minicomputer.

ACAP Software Development

ACAP documentation specified "C" as the programming language for software development because it was native to the UNIX operating system on the selected hardware and had the following characteristics that greatly aided software development, performance, and testing: (1) support of structured programming, (2) portability, (3) execution speed, (4) concise definitions and fast access to data structures, and (5) real-time system programming. The following paragraphs briefly describe the ACAP software development effort.

Technically, the approach to the software development efforts proceeded along traditional lines; that is, a top-down structured design approach was used, consistent with current military standards for software development (e.g., DOD-STD-2167A). The functional requirements for each of the three software packages—TA station, ET station, and DHC—were identified and developed to assist in developing a macro-level design for each package, that is, how the software is going to work from the standpoint of the user/operator.

These requirements also served as the basis for developing detailed computer programming logic to support the main functions within the macro-level design. A thorough study of this logic permitted the identification of the primitive routines and procedures that were necessary (e.g., a routine was required to confirm the correct insertion of a disk into the disk drive, and to solicit and confirm the entry of ET station identification numbers). Then, using the primitive routines, main stream (logic) drivers were developed to link the primitives into a working system that mirrors the functional requirements of the macro-level design. The software was then tested, errors were identified and corrected, and retesting continued until all portions of the software worked together as required. Occasionally, the software design had to be modified as the impact of the interaction among various routines became more complicated and/or specifications were more clearly defined.

TA Station Software

To design the software for the TA station, the functions to be supported by the TA station were compiled. The following outline describes generic TA station functions:

1. The TA must prepare and communicate all software and data necessary for CAT-ASVAB test administration to ET stations in the LCN.

2. The TA must be able to identify examinees by means of a unique identifier (e.g., SSN) and to record (in a retrievable file) other examinee personal data. In addition, it should be easy for the TA to add or modify any of the personal data.

3. The software for the TA station must randomly assign (transparent to the TA) an examinee taking CAT-ASVAB to one of the two CAT-ASVAB forms used. This assignment is subject to the condition that examinees who have previously been administered a CAT-ASVAB form must be retested on the alternate CAT-ASVAB form. In addition, the software must maintain an accounting of examinee assignments and be prepared to develop new assignments if any station in the LCN fails.

4. During examinee testing (in the networking mode of operation), the TA station must be able to receive a status report on the progress of examinees upon demand.

5. The TA station must be able to move the completed testing data recorded from an ET for additional processing and at that time produce appropriate hard copy of testing results.

6. The TA station must be able to store the testing data for all examinees who have gone through

the TA station collection process in a nonvolatile medium (i.e., a Data Disk) for later communication to the parent MEPS.

7. Finally, it must be almost impossible for an examinee's testing session not to be completed. If an examinee's assigned ET station fails, that examinee must be reassigned to another available station and continue testing at the beginning of the first uncompleted CAT-ASVAB test. Likewise, if the TA station fails, the LCN fails, or electrical power is interrupted, the TA must be able to recover and continue the testing session promptly.

In actual use, simply installing a system disk (called a TA disk) and turning on the power to the TA station begins boot-up operations to prepare the LCN for subsequent processing. At this point the TA would normally select the networking mode of operation for the current testing session. The standalone mode is a failure recovery procedure, in the event the TA station or the network supporting the LCN failed. After performing several network diagnostic tests, the TA transmits testing data to the ET stations in the LCN, then the program provides instructions for loading the data from three system disks which contain test administration software, item level data files (encoded), and supporting data (seeded test items, information tables, and item exposure control values). After these data and software are loaded into RAM of the TA station, the system disks are secured.

The TA station randomly identifies a CAT-ASVAB test form with each ET station so that approximately 50 percent of the ET stations receive each of the two CAT-ASVAB forms. The TA station then proceeds to broadcast the test administration software and data files (one at a time, alternately) to the ET stations requiring a given form, then to the remaining stations. Therefore, while one set of stations (identified with one of the two forms) is receiving one file of test items, the remaining stations are storing the test items received into RAM.

At this point the TA identifies the current testing session in terms of the date and approximate starting time for the session, and the Main Menu is displayed. The Main Menu displays the primary functions performed by the TA during a testing session, as explained below:

• PROCESS is a means for the TA to identify examinees to be tested in terms of their name, SSN, and test type information. The PROCESS func-

tion also includes creating a new list of examinees for testing, editing current examinee information, adding (or deleting) an examinee for testing, and providing a screen and/or printed list of examinees for testing.

• The ASSIGN option randomly directs (unassigned) examinees to unassigned ET stations in the network; equivalently, it randomly assigns each examinee to one of the two CAT-ASVAB test item bank forms. The examinee assignments are recorded on the TA disk at the TA station, printed at the TA station, and then broadcast to the ET stations in the LCN. Unassigned stations may serve as failure recovery stations. At this point, the TA would direct the examinees to sit at the seats corresponding to their assigned ET station, whereupon they receive computer-controlled general instructions that start CAT-ASVAB test administration.

• During the testing session the TA can use the STATUS option for a screen report on the progress of examinees during testing. This report includes the examinee's name, SSN, total time accumulated since the CAT-ASVAB began, the test being administered, the accumulated time on that test, and the expected completion time for the entire battery of CAT-ASVAB tests. The examinee's recruiter uses the expected completion time to assist in scheduling.

• The SUBMIT option in the Main Menu enables the TA to enter into a menu-driven dialogue with the TA station that records various personal information from the examinee's USMEPCOM Form 714-A. This information includes Service and component for which the examinee is being processed, gender, education level and degree code, and race/population group.

• At the end of examinee test administration, the TA uses the COLLECT option to retrieve (one at a time, or automatically upon test completion) the examinee's testing data from the assigned ET station. The TA station printer then produces a score report that includes equated number-right scores (interchangeable with the P&P-ASVAB scores) and an AFQT percentile score.

• By selecting the RECORD option, the TA can record (COLLECTed) examinee testing data on a set of microfloppy disks (identified as MASTER and BACKUP Data Disks) for subsequent transfer. The MASTER Data Disk is sent to the parent MEPS for processing, while the BACKUP Data

Disk remains secured at the testing site and is sent to the MEPS, if needed.

As briefly mentioned above, the software in the ACAP system includes the capability of supporting various failure recovery operations. The interested reader is referred to Rafacz (1995) for additional information.

ET Station Software

The design of the software for the ET station was based on the psychometric requirements for CAT supplemented by specifications associated with the computer administration of any test, improved psychometric procedures, and requirements unique for military testing. During testing, the ET stations are only required to communicate with the TA station at the end of administration of each item (and before the next item is displayed) to provide status information to the TA station.

In addition to the purely psychometric functions supporting the use of the CAT technology, the software design considers the functions supporting computer operations at the ET station. During examinee test administration, two operations are of concern: Failure recovery at the ET station and examinee implicit and explicit requests for help. The ET station software design with respect to all functions supported is discussed below:

1. Placing an ET disk in the disk drive of the ET station initiates the following boot-up operations: performing hardware verification procedures (screen, disk drive, and keyboard), soliciting the mode of operation for the computer (networking or standalone), requesting the ET station computer identification number, and verifying that the ET station computer clock has been set to the correct date and time.

Normally the TA selects the networking mode of operation. If the standalone mode is selected, broadcasting of software and data files is not required. In that case, the ET station reads the necessary testing data and software directly from the ACAP system disks. In addition, ET station assignments, dictated by the TA station and test type (initial or retest), are entered manually by the TA at each ET station. Finally, examinee testing information recorded on the ET disk is collected manually by moving the ET disk to the TA station at the conclusion of examinee testing.

2. Now, the ET station is ready to receive test item data files and software from the TA station. The first file is the actual test administration software which, once received, terminates the boot-up program, and then monitors receipt of the following data files (from the TA station) to support examinee test administration: power and speeded test item text, graphic, and item parameter files; information table files; and exposure control parameters for power test items. Each power test item file is stored in the ET station RAM, which is designed to support subsequent random retrieval (according to the information table associated with each power test).

3. After an ET station has received all of the required data files, it is ready to receive the examinee assignment list from the TA station. Once this list is received, the ET station prepares to administer the test to the assigned examinee. This requires confirming that the correct form of test items has been loaded for the assigned examinee. If not, the ET station requests the ACAP system disks and the correct testing data files are loaded into RAM; this incorrect form loading rarely happens.

4. Now that the ET station is ready to administer the CAT-ASVAB test to the assigned examinee, the TA must give the examinees verbal instructions and direct each examinee to the assigned ET station. The TA verifies the displayed SSN with the examinee and modifies it, if necessary. The examinee presses the Enter key on the keyboard of the ET station when requested to begin CAT-ASVAB test administration, in accordance with the interactive dialogues specified by Rafacz and Moreno (1987). The dialogue for the remainder of examinee test administration is between the ET station (software) and the examinee; neither the TA nor the TA station is involved.

5. Initially, the computer screen presents the examinee with information on how to use the ET station keyboard. The examinee learns how to use all of the keys labeled ENTER, A, B, C, D, E, and HELP.

6. Next, the examinee is trained on how to answer the power test items. Training on how to respond to the speeded test items is given just before these tests are administered. The examinee can ask to repeat the training on how to use the keyboard and answer test items. If a second request occurs, the ET station halts the interactive dialogue with the examinee so that the TA can be called to enter a pass code for the interactive dia-

logue to continue. The ET station software describes the current situation, and then requests that the TA monitor the examinee's progress briefly before continuing with normal duties.

7. At this point, four power tests (General Science [GS], Arithmetic Reasoning [AR], Word Knowledge [WK], and Paragraph Comprehension [PC]) are administered. For each test, the examinee is initially presented with a practice item. The examinee is given an indication that the answer is correct or incorrect, and the opportunity to ask to repeat the practice item. The second request initiates a call to the TA, who must enter a pass code to repeat the practice item. Finally, the examinee is ready to be administered the actual test items.

As the power test items are displayed, the examinee answers the test item by pressing the key corresponding to the alternative selected and then confirms the answer by pressing the Enter key. Any other answer can be selected before Enter is pressed. Selection of a valid response alternative highlights only that alternative on the screen until another alternative is selected. Pressing an invalid key results in an error message being briefly displayed. As each item is displayed on the computer screen, the lower right corner of the screen presents the number of the item being administered, relative to the total number of items, and the number of minutes remaining in the test.

While the examinee studies the test item, his or her performance is recorded by the software monitoring the keyboard. Overall, if the examinee does not confirm a valid response within the maximum item time limit, the test is halted and a TA implicit help call is initiated. In addition, if the examinee fails to complete the specified number of test items in the allotted maximum time limit for the *entire test*, the test is automatically terminated (without a TA call) and the examinee continues with the next CAT-ASVAB test. If the examinee presses an invalid key, an error message is briefly displayed. Three invalid keypresses result in an implicit help call. Pressing the Help key initiates the explicit help call sequence. For speeded tests, a valid key response (A, B, C, D, or E) at this point results in the immediate display of the next test item. For power tests, a valid key response (A, B, C, D, or E) must be followed by the confirmation key (Enter) to generate the display of the next item.

8. The test continues until the number of items administered (including one seeded item for a power test) equals the required test length or the maximum test time limit has been reached. As soon as the examinee completes the test, certain examinee test administration information is recorded in the ET station RAM and on the ET disk. For each item administered, this information includes the item identification code, the examinee-selected response alternative, the time required to select (but not confirm) the response, the new estimate of ability based on the selected response, and any implicit or explicit help call. In addition, the Bayesian modal estimate for the test is recorded, as is information on the examinee's performance on the practice screens for the test. This information is also recorded on the ET disk (a nonvolatile medium) as a backup if the ET station fails during testing.

9. The Numerical Operations (NO) and Coding Speed (CS) speeded tests are administered after the first four power tests. As with the power tests, practice test items are administered first. The examinee can repeat the practice items up to three times before a TA call is initiated. Examinee test administration of the speeded tests differs from the power tests. The speeded test items are administered in the sequence in which they appear in the item file, without using any adaptive testing strategy. In addition, the examinee does not confirm an answer by pressing the Enter key; rather, the ET station selects the first valid keypress (A, B, C, D, or E) as the examinee's answer. The display format of the CS test items is also different in that seven items are displayed on the same computer screen; NO and the power tests display only one item per screen. Rate scores are recorded as the examinee's final speeded test score (see Chapter 11). In all other respects, speeded test administration (including the availability of implicit and explicit help calls and the recording of examinee performance information) is identical to that of the power tests.

10. Once the speeded tests are completed, the examinee is administered the remaining five power tests (Auto Information [AI], Shop Information [SI], Mathematics Knowledge [MK], Mechanical Comprehension [MC], and Electronics Information [EI]). The procedure for administering these tests is identical to that for the original four power tests. Once the EI test is completed, the examinee's testing performance is stored in the ET station RAM and onto the ET disk into a single file identified by examinee SSN. The TA station collected this SSN file for subsequent compilation onto a Data Disk. The ET station instructs the ex-

aminee to return to the TA station for further instructions and the examinee then is excused. The ET station is now available for testing some other examinee whose assigned station has failed during the testing session.

During examinee test administration, normal administration activities can be interrupted to accommodate situations involving an examinee's need for assistance. These situations are either implicit help requests where the software of the ET station infers that the examinee needs assistance or explicit help requests where the examinee presses the red Help key on the keyboard. Rafacz (1995) discusses in some detail the implementation of help calls in the ET station software.

Data Handling Computer (DHC) Software

Software development was less critical for the DHC than for the ET and TA stations because the DHC serves primarily as a manager of examinee testing data *after* test administration. The DHC has two primary functions:

- **Data compilation.** The DHC compiles and organizes examinee testing data recorded on the data disks from the testing sites. Data recorded on a data disk must be removed and stored on a nonvolatile medium for subsequent communication to users of the CAT-ASVAB system. Appropriate backup mechanisms must be in place before data are purged from a data disk; once purged of its data, the data disk is returned to a testing site for reuse.

- **Data distribution.** The DHC must be able to communicate the examinee testing data to users of the system. Specifically, an extract of each examinee's testing record must be communicated to the USMEPCOM (System 80) minicomputer at the parent MEPS. In addition, all of the examinee testing data must be sent to DMDC for software quality assurance processing and communicating the data to other users of the CAT-ASVAB system.

DHC software must also ensure that the DHC collects each examinee's testing data only once and distributes each compiled data set only once to each user. An override mechanism must be available to send the information again if the original information is lost in transit. Finally, it must be possible for the DHC to recover from a hardware failure. Details concerning the functions and software development issues for the DHC may be found in Folchi (1986) and Rafacz (1995).

Item Pool Automation

In addition to the development of the TA, ET, and DHC software, a requirement of ACAP was to automate the item pools for each of the two forms of the CAT-ASVAB. The automation phase involved preparing the individual components (text, graphics, and item parameters) of candidate test items for storage and administration on the ACAP microcomputer system.

Power Test Items

The ACAP power test items consisted of two components for items with text only, and three components for items with graphics. The first two components, the item text files and the item parameter files, existed on magnetic media. The third component, the graphics, existed only as black-and-white line drawings in the experimental booklets used in calibrating the source item bank, the Omnibus Item Pool (Prestwood, Vale, Massey, & Welsh, 1985).

The graphics were captured from the experimental booklets and processed before text and parameters were merged. The ACAP Image Capturing System (Bodzin, 1986) was used. It consisted of an IBM PC-compatible computer, the Datacopy 700 Optical Scanner, the *Word Image Processing System* (WIPS) (Datacopy Corporation, 1985a), and the HP-IPC. The process also required the program, *boxit16*, which calculates the optimal size for the display of each image on the HP-IPC screen. During the process of scaling an image to the optimal size for the HP-IPC screen, information was lost, reducing the quality of the image. The image was restored to the original quality of the booklet drawing using the *WIPS Graphic Editor* (Datacopy Corporation, 1985b).

After capturing and editing, the graphic images were transferred to the HP-IPC. Additional processing was necessary before the images could be used with the ACAP test administration program. Special-purpose programs were written to display the images, verify the integrity of the file transfer, define the optimal image size for the HP-IPC screen, and rewrite the file header. Any image editing necessary was performed using *yage*, the graphics editor written for the HP-IPC.

The item text and parameter files were transferred to the HP-IPC and reformatted before being merged with the graphics portion of the items. Reformatting included reducing the size of the files and inserting specific characters recognized by the test administration software. Finally, the item text file, item parameter file, and images were merged in the Item Image Editor using a program called *edit*, written specially for this purpose. The graphic components were compressed as the items were stored to conserve storage space.

Speeded Item Files

The speeded items were prepared by the Armstrong Laboratory and delivered on IBM-formatted 5.25-inch diskettes. Speeded items, which consist of item text only, had to be modified to be compatible with the ACAP test administration software. These modifications were made using the Unix editor, *vi*.

System Documentation

Documentation requirements that apply to ACAP primarily deal with the design, development, use, and maintenance of the software supporting the ACAP network. For each of the three software systems (TA and ET stations, and DHC), user/operator manuals, programmer's reference manuals, and system test plans were developed for each of the three phases of the ACAP.

To support the use of the ACAP network at selected MEPSs in an operational mode (and provide examinee scores of record), the user of the system, USMEPCOM, has declared its requirements for system documentation, apart from the original Stage 2 RFP. These requirements use DOD-STD-7935A Automated Data Systems [ADS] Documentation as the specification source document. In summary, the following documentation is nearing completion for each phase of the ACAP in accordance with the standard:

• ACAP system—Functional Description, System/Subsystem Specification, Data Requirements, and Data Element Dictionary (four documents)

• A Programmer's Maintenance Manual and a System Test Plan for the TA station, ET station, and DHC software systems—(six documents)

• A User's Manual for all of the ACAP software systems (one document)

• An Operations Manual for the TA station, and an Operations Manual for the DHC (two documents)

System Testing Procedures

The approach used to test the software was important to the design and development of the ACAP system. Several things could be done during design and development to avoid (or at least minimize) the generation of software errors. Choice of the programming language was an important decision. The selection of "C" as the programming language for ACAP was based upon its support of structured programming, including concise definitions, fast access to data structures, and a repertoire of debugging aids. These are the characteristics of a language that minimize the chances of errors being created in the software under development.

In addition, appropriate programming standards and practices must be used as the software is designed and developed. For example, the software was designed as modular units with minimal interaction among the units. The modules were executed by a main "driver" program that controls the sequence of executions and verifies the results produced. Above all, the use of "long logic jumps" should be avoided. Appropriate software development standards were used for the specific application area; in the ACAP, as much as possible, DOD-STD-2167A was used.

Once the ACAP software was developed, it was necessary to test the software, locate errors, make necessary corrections, and retest the software until no errors were found. However, there were so many logic flow paths that it was physically impossible to test even a small proportion of such paths in a reasonable period of time. To address this concern, the Stage 2 RFP required the development of built-in test (BIT) software for use within the CAT-ASVAB system.

The BIT procedures that were used for the ET station (the most logically complex package) included adding software with the capability of reading examinee responses directly from a separate (scenario) file in contrast to the keyboard. This "scenario" file also included predetermined response latencies for test items as well as various testing times for the tests. By using the scenario files, many different logic flow paths and testing configurations were evaluated yet no (real) examinee was involved in actual test administration.

Once a scenario was completed, the system tester surveyed the output data to confirm that the information recorded matched that specified in the scenario. For the most part, any differences were attributed to software errors, which were then quickly located and corrected. By using such BIT techniques, it was possible within ACAP to minimize the time required to test a logic path within the software. Because more logic paths were tested, uncertainty as to errors that still might be "hidden" in the software was reduced.

Documents describe in detail the testing procedures for evaluating software performance, and the checklists to be completed by system testers to record the testing activities.

Software Acceptance Testing

In addition to system testing, software acceptance testing was conducted. While system testing is generally conducted by software designers and developers, software acceptance testing is conducted by an independent group knowledgeable in how the system should function.

Software acceptance testing was a critical element from the beginning of the development of the CAT-ASVAB system. The concerns for quality were twofold and equally relevant. One involved how a user would interact with the system—where a user might be a test administrator or an applicant taking the test—and the other involved the accuracy of the test scores. In a computerized-adaptive test, ensuring accuracy is a complex and difficult process. It means checking for things such as: Clear and consistent item-screen displays, precise timing (of instruction sequences, help calls, response times, time limits), the integrity of parameter files throughout test administration, the selection of the proper item in the adaptive sequence, and the calculation and recording of the final scores.

There were three different kinds of checks: Configuration management, psychometric performance, and software performance. Some of the checks are simple but tedious, some are manual and extremely detailed, some are complex and computerized. Many of the CAT-ASVAB software acceptance procedures were instituted from the start, others were developed as we learned from experience in using the system, and from feed-

back from trainers, examinees, and test administrators. All the checks were performed every time the software changed, and required substantial amounts of time from numerous members of the project staff. The rigorous execution of these checks has contributed significantly to the consistently high quality of performance of the CAT-ASVAB system.

Configuration Management

The ACAP system uses three distinct hardware and software systems: the ET station, the TA station, and the DHC. As the first step in configuration management, each system's components were identified: Computers, memory boards, interface boards, and hard disk size and type. Commercial software and versions used in each system were documented, and copies of the programs were archived. The commercial software included the operating system, compilers, various libraries, and numerous utilities.

For each system, every component or module of any software specifically developed for CAT-ASVAB was identified and listed. Included were source code and executables for all programs, subroutines, and procedures; parameter files; and compilation files (such as UNIX "make" files). Source code and executables for programs specifically developed for CAT to support software development were also included.

The next step was recompilation of all the software. A computer with a hard disk (called the ATG system, for Acceptance Testing Group) was set aside to be used solely for recompilation and was restarted with all the commercial system and utilities software used by the CAT-ASVAB. The following steps were completed for every recompilation:

1. The software development team delivered diskettes containing source and executable programs to the ATG. Next, all the source and executable CAT-ASVAB files from the prior version were erased from the hard disk.

2. The new source files were loaded from the diskettes and compiled. Executables were created and compared (bit by bit) to those delivered by the development team. If there were no differences, the programs became the "acceptance testing" version of the software. If differences were found, the documented results were provided to the software developers and the diskettes returned.

After corrections were made by the software development team, Steps 1 and 2 were repeated. This process ensured that the correct version of the software was used in subsequent checks. Software specifically developed for the CAT-ASVAB was tested after every change that required recompilation, regardless of the magnitude of the change. The complete system was tested whenever any file in any of the three components changed.

Software Performance

Once the executable programs were accepted after recompilation, members of the ATG took simulated tests, following prescribed scenarios. The tests covered a wide variety of conditions, some designed to check system specifications and others to replicate situations that occur in the field during operational testing. They included manual tests of menu screens, such as TA options during an examinee's help call, and examinee's options to repeat a practice problem. They also included checks of item and test elapsed times, performance of failure/recovery procedures, screen sequences, and others. In these checks, a test is taken and all responses are given following a prescribed scenario. For test and item times, a stop-watch is used, and the values recorded. The stop-watch value is then checked against the value in the output file. Failures are simulated by turning off the computer, performing the prescribed recovery, examining the output file, and processing it through the quality-control programs.

Speeded tests. Since these tests are not adaptive, and the item sequence is known, the displayed item screens are checked manually against printed copy. The response times are checked with a stop-watch.

Power tests. A computer program developed in-house reads the following values from the results of a CAT test (let this be Test 1): The seed used by the pseudo-random number generator, the unique identification number (UID) of all the items administered, and the examinee's responses to the items. Using the UIDs, the program reads the text of the corresponding items from the original archived text files, and prints the items (with the corresponding responses) in the form of a "booklet." The items appear in the same sequence as they were administered in the original CAT test.

The booklet is then used to take a second test (Test 2) on an HP-IPC. Test 2 is administered with the operational software, except for the random-generator seed, which is forced to be the same value as in Test 1. Using the same seed generates the same random number, which will lead to selection of the same first item. The reviewer compares the item on the screen to the one printed in the "booklet," then gives the answer printed in the booklet. When this is done for every item, all subsequent items are the same as in the original Test 1.

Psychometric Performance

Examples of psychometric performance are checks to ensure that the computer file that contains the examinee's answers matches what happened during test administration, that the proper questions are selected during adaptive testing, that the time limits are correctly enforced by the software and hardware (for both power and speeded tests and individual items), that the correct keys are used to score the items, and that the items displayed on the screen are the same as those recorded on the output file. Some of these checks were automated, others had to be performed manually. The main procedures are described below.

Quality Control Program 1. This program checks structure and format by screen type, the ranges for all the variables, test time-outs against allotted times, and the sum of elapsed item times for all the tests. It also computes the raw and standard test scores for all of the power and speeded tests, the AFQT, and the Service composite scores, and compares them against the recorded values.

Quality Control Program 2. This program checks adaptive item selection and scoring in power tests, and scoring in the speeded tests. The software reads the output of a CAT-ASVAB test and simulates a second test (a replication) using the examinee's responses and the seed for the pseudo-random number generator from the first one.[1] To ensure independence of results, the program runs on a computer system different from the operational HP-IPC; information tables, item parameters, keys, and exposure control parameters are read from the original archived files, not from the operational diskettes. The program simulates an adaptive test and compares the results, at every

---

[1] Random numbers are used in CAT-ASVAB by the exposure control algorithm, and to place an experimental not-scored item in the adaptive sequence.

step, with the original results. Discrepancies are identified and printed, including those in items selected and their order, and in all the ability estimates: The intermediate Owen's Bayesian and the final Bayesian mode. Optionally, random numbers, exposure control parameters, and information table indices for every item are also printed. All CAT-ASVAB test protocols—operational, research, and simulated—are processed through these two programs.

ACAP System Summary

To summarize the ACAP system[2] development and acceptance testing efforts: The ACAP computer network can be used as the delivery vehicle for CAT-ASVAB as specified by the Joint-Services in the Stage 2 RFP. For all critical functions, the ACAP system provides a capability meeting, if not exceeding, functional requirements specified in the Stage 2 RFP.

The Stage 2 RFP documented CAT-ASVAB system performance requirements over nine evaluation factors: (1) performance, (2) suitability, (3) reliability, (4) maintainability, (5) ease of use, (6) security, (7) affordability, (8) expandability/flexibility, and (9) psychometric acceptability. Rafacz (1995) describes in some detail the extent to which

the ACAP computer network system met the requirements of each factor to support the SED and SEV phases of the ACAP. The OT&E functions of expanded examinee score reporting and the installation of ECAT tests demonstrate the capability of the ACAP system to meet the psychometric criteria for acceptability. Installing the variable-start mechanism, as well as other OT&E enhancements that involve the operator interface, further improve the image of the system in terms of suitability and ease of use.

Finally, it should be observed that the computer software developed to support CAT-ASVAB functions on the HP-IPC has proven to be based on a very flexible and powerful design. Using a large RAM-based design for the ET station has made overall software design and structure less complicated. The net effect was to make it easier for system developers to isolate critical coding segments and minimize the ripple effects due to software errors associated with related functions. For example, the software routines needed to support recovery of the ET station in a failure situation are not dependent on the software of any other station in the testing room. Furthermore, the multitasking feature of the UNIX operating system was useful during software development because the system permitted the execution of multiple tasks; text editing, compiling, and executing tasks could proceed concurrently on the same development system. In addition, the ease with which TAs used the system in the field during OT&E implementation (Chapter 20) clearly indicates a system that can effectively serve as the delivery vehicle for CAT-ASVAB.

---

[2] The following individuals contributed significantly to the design and development of the software, database and/or acceptance testing activities of the ACAP: Dennis Cheng, Anthony Dunlap, John S. Folchi, Al Gallegos, Carolyn Huynh, Gloria James, John Rehling, Amado Santiago, Stu Sunderman, Elizabeth R. Wilbur, and Gail Winford.

15

Human Factors in the CAT System: A Pilot Study

Frank L. Vicino and Kathleen E. Moreno

Upon completion of the Accelerated CAT-ASVAB Project (ACAP) system, described in the previous four chapters, the first empirical study to be conducted was an evaluation of the human-machine interface and attitudes toward CAT-ASVAB. By 1986, at the time this study was conducted, thousands of recruits had taken CAT-ASVAB on the experimental system. Nearly all participants appeared to understand the computer-presented instructions well enough to proceed through the battery with a minimum of test administrator intervention. However, before CAT-ASVAB could be used operationally, concerns about the user interface needed be addressed. It was believed that the favorable results obtained in prior studies on CAT-ASVAB concerning the instructions may not generalize to the population of interest: *military applicants*. This concern was fueled by at least three important observations. First, the instructions for the operational ACAP system had undergone extensive revisions to accommodate necessary changes for an operational battery. Second, everyone participating in prior studies had taken the ASVAB before (on paper-and-pencil). Because of the similarity of content across CAT and P&P versions, prior exposure to the ASVAB may have led to a greater understanding of the computer presented instructions. (This may have been especially true of the instructions for the two speeded tests, NO and CS.) The third important observation noted that all subjects participating in previous studies were generally of middle or high ability levels. (They scored above the 35th-percentile of American Youth on the AFQT.) Military applicants, however, span the entire range of ability. Instructions understandable to middle and high ability test-takers (recruits) may not be understandable to low ability applicants. At the time this study was conducted, preparations were underway for the empirical, psychometric evaluation of CAT-ASVAB and the equating of CAT-ASVAB to P&P-ASVAB. It was crucial that the instructions and other aspects of the user interface be finalized prior to start of these studies. This was especially true for the equating study. If major flaws were revealed during the equating, then the entire study would need to be repeated.

Objectives

The objectives of this study were to examine:

1. Test-takers' attitudes toward, and acceptance of, CAT-ASVAB.

2. Human factors aspects of CAT-ASVAB:

   (a) Legibility of test items

   (b) Comprehension of instruction

3. Effects of fatigue.

4. Effects of ambient conditions.

5. Test administration factors (e.g., displayed clock time, test administrator support).

6. The effect of computer familiarity/experience and applicant gender on examinee attitudes and acceptance of CAT-ASVAB.

Much research has been done on the attitudes toward, and human factors aspects of, computer-based tests (Ackerman, 1985; Burke, Michael, & Normand, 1986; Hedl, O'Neill, & Hansen, 1973; Lukin, Dowd, Plake, & Kraft, 1985; Nellis et al., 1980; Skinner & Allen, 1983; Slack & Slack, 1977; Walter & O'Neill, 1974). Interest in CAT has stimulated similar research (Garrison & Baumgarten, 1986; Mitchell, Hardwicke, Segall, & Vicino, 1983; Moe & Johnson, 1986; Schmidt, Urry, & Gugel, 1978; Yoes & Hardwicke, 1984). Early studies showed that many initial users exhibited anxiety and other negative responses to the computer tasks, whereas the later studies, in general, showed the users to be highly positive toward computers. This may be due to the fact that by the mid-80s computers were becoming more commonplace. Nevertheless, reactions to computer tasks are largely dependent on the software interface.

The ACAP system was designed with state-of-the-art graphics and what we hoped were user-friendly software and response keys. Instructions had been written at the sixth to seventh grade reading level so that applicants across all ability levels could read and understand them. Even so, it was important to examine applicants' perceptions and experience with the CAT-ASVAB system and procedures before we settled on the system design.

Methodology

Three hundred and four examinees (231 military applicants, 73 high school students) representing a full range of AFQT categories (five progressively scaled AFQT categories derived from the ASVAB) were given the CAT-ASVAB test. To increase sample representation in the lower AFQT categories, many of the high school students were chosen from special education classes.

Examinees were tested in groups, with each subject taking the CAT-ASVAB, followed by a comprehensive questionnaire. The questionnaire contained 42 items and took approximately a half hour to complete. Of the 42 items, 38 required scaled responses and four items were open-ended. The questionnaire included items from earlier questionnaires used by Schmidt et al. (1978) and Mitchell et al. (1983), in addition to items recommended by the CAT Working Group Psychometric Committee. The questionnaire explored concerns about screen legibility, instruction comprehension, user fatigue, time pressures, ambient conditions, and CAT-ASVAB test administration factors.

In addition, four to eight examinees per session (total of 90) were selected for a more in-depth, systematic structured interview. The interviewee selection was stratified by test completion times, to ensure representation of those who had responded quickly, as well as those who took longer to complete the test. Finally, observers using a comprehensive observer's checklist monitored the procedures, process, and test setting, during the test session. This chapter summarizes the results of the analysis of the questionnaire responses and the on-site observations.

Summary of Results

Questionnaire Results

Questionnaire results are briefly discussed below.

Attitudes toward computerized test. Examinees felt very comfortable using the test computer, enjoyed taking the test, and would rather take a computer test than use a test booklet. The only exception to this highly positive attitude was at a high school, where students neither agreed nor disagreed about feeling uneasy during the test.

Legibility. Examinees found that reading from the screen was easier than from a written page. Most examinees also found that the test questions were easy to read, the lines of the test questions were not too close together, reading the lettering was easy, there was enough contrast between the screen and the letters, the letters were not too small, and the question format was not confusing.

Comprehension of instructions. Examinees strongly agreed that the test instructions were easy to understand. In addition, they had no problem with the instruction format. They neither agreed nor disagreed, however, to having enough practice time, or to needing computerized instructions to the test.

Fatigue. Examinees neither agreed nor disagreed that they felt extremely tired at the end of the test. They were also noncommittal concerning eye strain during the test. Approximately 50 percent of the examinees, however, indicated that they experienced eye fatigue by the end of the test.

Ambient test conditions. Overall lighting appeared adequate, and no glare conditions were experienced by the military examinees, whereas the high school students expressed some problems with lighting/glare. The two types of examinees, however, were tested at different locations, with different lighting conditions. Neither ambient noise, nor movement by people who were finishing and leaving the room at different times, distracted the examinees.

Test administration factors. Examinees had no difficulty in finding or pressing the desired keys. Further, they felt that using the keyboard was easier than using separate answer sheets. A clock showing the time remaining on the test was projected on the screen to assist examinees in pacing their responses; this form of assistance was viewed positively by the military applicants and as neutral by the high school students. The examinees agreed that the test administrator (TA) was helpful. More than half of the examinees, however, were bothered by not being able to go back to a previous question to change an answer. Examinees found the speeded tests easy to understand, and were not disturbed by finding that one of the tests included four answer options instead of five. The applicants neither agreed nor disagreed to having enough time to answer the speeded items. For the power tests, examinees felt that they were given enough time to respond. In addition, they disagreed that "the test questions appeared on the screen too fast."

Computer experience and attitude toward CAT-ASVAB. Generally, both computer-naive and experienced examinees exhibited positive attitudes toward CAT-ASVAB. Both the computer-naive and experienced examinees enjoyed taking the test on the computer and would rather take a computer test than use a test booklet. The computer-naive examinees disagreed with the statement that they felt uneasy during the test; the computer-experienced examinees *strongly* disagreed with that statement. The computer naive examinees agreed that they felt comfortable using the test computer; the computer-experienced examinees *strongly* agreed with that statement.

Examinee gender and attitude toward CAT-ASVAB. Both males and females exhibited a positive attitude to the computerized adaptive test. Both genders enjoyed taking the computerized test and would rather take a computerized test than use test booklets. In addition, both genders felt comfortable using the computer test and did not feel uneasy.

The four open-ended items in the questionnaire and the responses to them were as follows:

Please list anything about the test and/or instructions which you think should be changed.

Sixty-one percent of the examinees responded with written statements. Of those responses, 67 percent indicated that no changes were needed. The only other major category of response was a desire to have an opportunity to review and change responses to past items (12%).

What do you think are the benefits or advantages of this computer testing system?

Eighty-five percent of the examinees responded to the above statement. Of those who responded, the following represent the major response categories, along with associated percentages:

Response Category	Percent
Faster	39
Easier	18
Self-paced	10
Less writing	6

What do you think are the drawbacks or disadvantages of this computer testing system?

Eighty percent of the examinees responded to the above question. Of those responses, the following lists the major response categories along with associated percentages:

Response Category	Percent
No disadvantages	39
Can't go back	23
Eyes become tired	12

Please make other comments on this test which you feel have not been covered by any of the items in this questionnaire.

Twenty percent responded to the above question. Of those responses, the following are the major response categories, along with associated percentages:

Fifty-three percent were highly favorable (i.e., great idea, save time, prevent cheating).

Thirty percent suggested some changes or improvements (i.e., darker room, larger screen, administration in morning).

Thirteen percent expressed some negative opinions (i.e., hard on eyes, uncomfortable during test).

On-Site Observations

On-site observations supported questionnaire results. Overall, the examinees seemed to have positive attitudes toward taking the test on the computer. Examinees who appeared nervous at the start of the battery seemed to relax by the time they had completed the keyboard familiarization sequence. While the software seemed user-friendly, and "help" calls were infrequent, observers did become aware of some problems summarized below.

Instructions on the CS test seemed to be the most difficult for examinees to understand. In addition, some examinees pressed invalid keys on both of the speeded tests, due to differences between the speeded tests and power tests in entering answers to items. On a power test, an examinee enters the answer to an item and then confirms the answer by pressing the Enter key. On the speeded tests, an examinee enters the answer to an item, then the system immediately goes to the next item. Changing an answer is not allowed and confirmation of an answer is not required. In fact, pressing the Enter key during administration of a speeded test is considered invalid and generates an error message. Those examinees who did not read the instructions carefully, or did not understand the instructions, continued to press the Enter key after a response on the speeded tests.

During the CAT-ASVAB keyboard familiarization sequence and CAT-ASVAB test instruction screens, highlighting is used to emphasize certain words. Observers noted that some examinees were reading only highlighted portions of certain screens.

Some examinees did not understand the purpose of the Help key. They thought that by pressing the Help key they could receive help from the TA in answering the questions.

Some examinees did not understand some of the words used in the instructions. For example, some did not understand the word "proctor."

Summary

Based on the results of the pilot study, some changes were made to the CAT-ASVAB software. Instructions were rewritten in certain places to make them clearer. For example, speeded test instructions were rewritten to emphasize that examinees were *not* to press the Enter key after responding to an item. The word "proctor" was changed to "test administrator." Highlighting of words on keyboard familiarization and test instruction screens was also re-examined and modified in some cases. Overall, however, the changes that needed to be made to the system in response to this trial administration were minimal.

16

Evaluating Item Calibration Medium in Computerized Adaptive Testing

Rebecca D. Hetter, Daniel O. Segall, and Bruce M. Bloxom

CAT provides efficient assessment of psychological constructs (see Weiss, 1983). When combined with item response theory (IRT), CAT uses item parameter estimates to select the most informative item for administration at each step in assessing an examinee's abilities. In addition, these item parameters are used to update both point and interval estimates of each examinee's score.

A practical concern in the initial development of a CAT is whether items must be calibrated from data collected in a computerized administration or whether equally accurate results could be obtained by calibrating the items from data collected in a paper-and-pencil (P&P) administration. For example, in the development of the CAT version of the Armed Services Vocational Aptitude Battery (CAT-ASVAB), item parameter estimates were available only from a P&P administration of the items (Prestwood, Vale, Massey, & Welsh, 1985), because computers were not available at the testing sites. This made it important to assess whether scores obtained on the CAT-ASVAB using the P&P-based item calibration had the same precision and interpretation as scores obtained from a computer-based calibration of the items.

Previous Research

Generally, research comparing the effects of computer-based and P&P-based administration of cognitive tests has dealt primarily with the medium of administration (MOA) of the actual test rather than the MOA used for calibrating items. Although the investigators did not always explicitly address CAT, the work provided results that were suggestive of the potential importance of three MOA effects.

Two studies by Moreno and her colleagues examined the effect of MOA on the construct assessed by the tests. Observed-score factor analytic and correlational studies (Moreno, Wetzel, McBride, & Weiss, 1984; Moreno, Segall, & Kieckhaefer, 1985) suggested that the factor pattern of a cognitive battery has the same hyperplane pattern whether the tests are administered by conventional P&P or adaptively by computer. A meta-analytic study by Mead and Drasgow obtained correlations close to 1.00 between computerized and P&P versions of the same power tests when the correlations were corrected for attenuation, whether the computerized tests were adaptive or nonadaptive. The findings of Mead and Drasgow imply that the disattenuated correlations among tests of different traits are essentially the same whether the traits are measured using the same

Excerpted from an article published in *Applied Psychological Measurement,* Vol. 18, (3), September 1994, pages 197–204, by Hetter, Segall, and Bloxom. Reprinted by permission.

MOA or a different MOA. However, this implication had yet to be tested empirically.

Researchers also have examined MOA effect on test precision. Green, Bock, Linn, Lord, and Reckase (1984) suggested that nonsystematic MOA effects could degrade CAT precision if the tests were administered and scored using P&P-based item calibrations. They noted that such effects could arise when some items were affected (e.g., in difficulty) by MOA and other items were not. Divgi (1986a) and Divgi and Stoloff (1986) found that item response functions (IRFs) estimated from items administered adaptively by computer differed from IRFs obtained from a conventional P&P administration of the same items. However, these differences were not systematically related to the content of the items and, when applied to the scoring of adaptively administered items, produced only slight effects on final test scores. Moreno and Segall (Chapter 17) showed that even if nonsystematic effects of calibration error resulted from using a P&P-based calibration in an adaptive test, the adaptive test still could have greater reliability than a longer, conventional P&P test.

Although these results were reassuring about the relative precision of CAT and P&P tests, what remained to be demonstrated was whether the medium used to obtain item parameters affects CAT precision. Specifically, the issue was whether or not nonadaptive computer-administered items produce a calibration that results in CAT scores with greater reliability than scores produced from a P&P-based calibration.

Previous work investigated MOA effect on the score scale of the tests. Green et al. (1984) suggested that MOA could also have a systematic effect on the score scale—for example, by making the items more difficult or easier to a similar extent. Empirical results reported by Spray, Ackerman, Reckase, and Carlson (1989) and Mead and Drasgow (1993) indicated that computer-administered items can result in slightly lower mean test scores than P&P-administered items. Spray et al. (1989) investigated whether effects were general to all items or specific to certain items. They found no MOA effect for most of their items, which made their results inconclusive. An important issue that remained to be investigated was whether MOA effects on the score scale of a test are systematic—that is, removable by a transformation (e.g., linear) of the score scale—or nonsystematic—that is, altering the reliability of scores of some items, but not others.

Study Purpose

This study compared effects on CAT-ASVAB scores of using a P&P calibration versus a computer-based calibration. The two primary effects investigated were (1) the construct being assessed, and (2) the reliability of the test scores. The specific question was the extent to which adaptive scores obtained with computer-administered items and a P&P calibration corresponded to adaptive scores obtained with the same computer-administered items (and responses) and a computer calibration. A secondary inquiry concerned the influence of calibration medium on the score scale: The extent to which IRT difficulty parameters obtained with a P&P calibration corresponded to those obtained with a calibration of the same items from a nonadaptive computer administration.

Method

At each testing session, examinees were randomly assigned to one of three groups. Fixed blocks of power test items were administered by computer to one group of examinees (Group 1) and by P&P to a second group (Group 2). Those data were used to obtain computer-based and P&P-based three-parameter logistic (3PL) model calibrations of the items. Then each calibration was used to estimate IRT adaptive scores (θs) for a third group of examinees who were administered the items by computer (Group 3). The effects of the calibration MOA (CMOA) on the construct being assessed and on the reliability of the test scores were assessed by comparative analyses of the θs using the alternative calibrations. CMOA effects on the score scale were assessed by comparing IRT difficulty parameters from computer-based and P&P-based calibrations.

Examinees

Examinees were 2,955 Navy recruits stationed at the Recruit Training Center in San Diego: 989 in Group 1, 978 in Group 2, and 988 in Group 3. A simulation study by Hulin, Drasgow, and Parsons (1983, pp. 101–110) indicated that larger samples produce little improvement in the precision of IRFs and test scores, given the 40 items used in these calibrations. ASVAB scores were obtained from file data for nearly all examinees and were used to assess whether the groups were comparable in ability level.

Calibration Tests

Items were taken from item pools developed for the CAT-ASVAB by Prestwood et al. (1985). Forty items from each of four content areas—General Science (GS), Arithmetic Reasoning (AR), Word Knowledge (WK), and Shop Information (SI)—were used (160 items total). Although only 4 of the 11 CAT-ASVAB tests were included in this study, MOA tests were administered in the same order as in the CAT-ASVAB. The three groups received exactly the same instructions, the same practice problems, and the same items, in the same order and with the same time limits. The items were conventionally administered in order of ascending difficulty, using the 3PL model difficulties obtained by Prestwood et al.

The P&P test employed a booklet and an optically-scannable answer sheet; the booklet format was the same as that used in the original P&P calibration by Prestwood et al. The computer-administered format was the same as that used in CAT-ASVAB (one item per screen, no return to previous items, no omits allowed). Practice problems and instructions were printed on the booklet and read aloud by the proctor for the P&P group (Group 2), and presented on the screen, with the option-to-repeat, for the computer groups (Groups 1 and 3). Tests were timed; however, time limits were liberal. Test order and time limits were: GS—19 minutes, AR—36 minutes, WK—16 minutes, and SI—17 minutes.

Item Calibrations

IRT parameter estimates based on the 3PL model (Birnbaum, 1968) were obtained in separate calibrations for computer Group 1 (calibration C1) and for P&P Group 2 (calibration C2). The response data sets on which the calibrations were based were labeled U1 and U2, respectively. The calibrations were performed with LOGIST 6 (Wingersky, Barton, & Lord, 1982), a computer program that uses a joint maximum-likelihood approach. Response data set U3 from Group 3 (the second computer group) was not used in the calibrations. The design with the corresponding notations is shown in Table 16-1.

Scores

For each examinee in Group 3, two $\hat{\theta}$s were computed for each test (see Table 16-2). All $\hat{\theta}$s were based on the U3 responses. $\hat{\theta}$s for variables X_{GSC}, X_{ARC}, X_{WKC}, and X_{SIC} (where C is computer CMOA) were calculated using the computer-based item parameters (C1). Scores for variables X_{GSP}, X_{ARP}, X_{WKP}, and X_{SIP} (here P is P&P CMOA) were calculated using the P&P-based item parameters (C2). All $\hat{\theta}$s were based on simulated CATs, computed as described below, using only 10 of the 40 responses from a given examinee.

Adaptive scores. To compute the adaptive $\hat{\theta}$s, 10-item adaptive tests were simulated using actual examinee responses. As in CAT-ASVAB, a normal (0, 1) prior distribution of θ was assumed. Owen's (1975) Bayesian scoring was used to update $\hat{\theta}$, and a Bayesian modal estimate was computed at the end of the test to obtain the final $\hat{\theta}$. Items were adaptively selected from information tables on the basis of maximum information. An information table consists of lists of items by θ level; within each list, all items in the pool (40) are arranged in descending order of the values of their information functions computed at that θ level. The information tables used in this study were computed for 37 θ levels equally spaced along the (−2.25 to 2.25) interval.

ASVAB scores. The Armed Forces Qualification Test (AFQT) scores were obtained from the enlistment records of most examinees. These scores, which all the Military Services use to determine eligibility for enlistment, were used to assess the equivalency of the three groups.

Table 16-1 Calibration Design

Group	Medium	Data Set/ Item Responses	Item Parameters/ Calibrations
1	Computer	U1	C1
2	P&P	U2	C2
3	Computer	U3	—

Covariance Structure Analysis

The equality of $\hat{\theta}$s calculated from P&P and computer-estimated item parameters was investigated using covariance structure analysis based on the eight variables defined in Table 16-2.

The formal model was defined as follows. Let a random observation i from Group 3 be denoted as Y_{ti}, where t denotes one of four adaptive tests (GS, AR, WK, or SI). In the adaptive test, item selection and scoring are assumed to be based on item parameters representative of a population of item parameters, where the population consists of parameters obtained from each of a large number of CMOAs. A large number of hypothetical media of administration can be defined from various combinations of item display format (defined, in turn, by the choice of font, color, and display medium) and response format (defined, in turn, by the choice of format of the answer sheet or automated input device). The random observation is assumed to be on a standardized score scale with a mean of 0 and a variance of 1. The 1×4 vector of observations, $Y_i = \{Y_{ti}\}$, is assumed to be from a multivariate normal random variable with a 4×4 correlation matrix, Φ. A standardized random observation based on the use of item parameters from a specific CMOA is denoted W_{tmi} and is assumed to have a linear regression on Y_{ti},

$$W_{tmi} = P_{tm}Y_{ti} + e_{tmi}. \qquad (16\text{-}1)$$

The ρ_{tmi} are errors assumed to have a multivariate normal distribution and to be independent of each other and of the Y_{ti}. They are interpreted as errors in test scores due to nonsystematic departure of item parameters from the population-representative item parameters used to obtain Y_{ti}. These errors are a combination of various CMOA effects not definable by a linear transformation of the score scale, such as sampling variation of the parameter

estimates and variation due to the interaction of specific item contents and the CMOA. Note that, because the W_{tmi} and Y_{ti} are both standardized variables, the regression coefficient, ρ_{tm}, is the correlation between these variables, and the error variance is $1 - \rho^2_{tm}$. Also, note that the equivalence of ρ_{tm} across CMOA for each test can be taken as an indicator of similar amounts of nonsystematic calibration error across CMOA.

From these definitions of W_{tmi} and Y_{ti}, it follows that the observed score on test t in medium m can be written as

$$X_{tmi} = \sigma_{tm}W_{tmi} + \mu_{tm}, \qquad (16\text{-}2)$$

where σ_{tmi} and μ_{tmi} are the observed scale standard deviation and location (mean) parameters, respectively. If the CMOA has no linear effect on the score scale for test t, then σ_{tmi} and μ_{tmi} are the same for all m (i.e., for all CMOA).

The covariance matrix Σ among the eight variables can be modeled in terms of several parameter matrices:

$$\Sigma = \Lambda(\mathbf{R}^{1/2}\,\mathbf{J}\Phi\mathbf{J}'\,\mathbf{R}^{1/2} - \mathbf{R} + \mathbf{I})\Lambda, \quad (16\text{-}3)$$

where Λ and $\mathbf{R}$ are 8×8 diagonal matrices with elements

$$\Lambda = $$
$$diag\{\sigma_{GSC}, \sigma_{ARC}, \sigma_{WKC}, \sigma_{SIC}, \sigma_{GSP}, \sigma_{ARP}, \sigma_{WKP}, \sigma_{SIP}\}$$

and

$$R = $$
$$diag\{\rho_{GSC}, \rho_{ARC}, \rho_{WKC}, \rho_{SIC}, \rho_{GSP}, \rho_{ARP}, \rho_{WKP}, \rho_{SIP}\}.$$

The Λ matrix contains the standard deviations of the observed variables and the R matrix contains the reliability parameters. These reliability parameters measure only one source of error variance: The random error variance in test scores arising from sampling errors in item parameters. These reliability parameters do not measure error in the traditional sense, which measures the error in test scores associated with the sampling of items from an infinite pool of items.

The matrix J is 8×4 with

$$\mathbf{J} = \begin{bmatrix} \mathbf{I}_4 \\ \mathbf{I}_4 \end{bmatrix} \qquad (16\text{-}4)$$

where $\mathbf{I}_4$ is a 4×4 identity matrix. Additionally, let $\mathbf{I}_8$ denote an 8×8 identity matrix.

In Equation 16-3, Φ is a 4×4 symmetric matrix with diagonal elements equal to 1. The Φ matrix contains the disattenuated correlations among the four tests. Note that in this context,

Table 16-2 Variable Definitions

Variable	Content Area	Responses	Item Parameter Calibration Medium
X_{gsc}	GS	U3/Group 3	Computer
X_{arc}	AR	U3/Group 3	Computer
X_{wkc}	WK	U3/Group 3	Computer
X_{sic}	SI	U3/Group 3	Computer
X_{gsp}	GS	U3/Group 3	P&P
X_{arp}	AR	U3/Group 3	P&P
X_{wkp}	WK	U3/Group 3	P&P
X_{sip}	SI	U3/Group 3	P&P

Table 16-3 Model Constraints

Constraint	Parameters			
A	$\Phi_{cc} = \Phi_{pc} = \Phi_{pp}$			
B	$\rho_{GSC} = \rho_{GSP},$	$\rho_{ARC} = \rho_{ARP},$	$\rho_{WKC} = \rho_{WKP},$	$\rho_{SIC} = \rho_{SIP}$

the correlations are corrected for calibration error only. These correlations are not corrected for attenuation due to measurement errors.

From Equation 16-3, the disattenuated correlation matrix among the eight variables is given by:

$$\mathbf{J \Phi J'} = \begin{bmatrix} \Phi_{cc} & \Phi_{pc} \\ \Phi_{cp} & \Phi_{pp} \end{bmatrix} \quad (16\text{-}5)$$

where the three non-redundant submatrices are constrained by the model to be equivalent: $\Phi_{cc} = \Phi_{pc} = \Phi_{pp} (= \Phi)$. From classical test theory, the product $\mathbf{R}^{1/2} \, \mathbf{J \Phi J' R}^{1/2}$ represents the correlation matrix among observed variables, with the eight reliability parameters along the diagonal. Consequently, the sum $\mathbf{R}^{1/2} \, \mathbf{J \Phi J'} \, \mathbf{R}^{1/2} - \mathbf{R} + \mathbf{I}_8$ represents the correlation matrix among observed variables, with 1s in the diagonal. Finally, by pre- and post-multiplying the observed correlation matrix by Λ (the 8×8 diagonal matrix of standard deviations), the observed covariance matrix Σ is obtained.

In addition to estimating the model given by Equation 16-3, an additional model was examined to test the equivalency of the reliability parameters across the CMOA. The constraints imposed by the two models are summarized in Table 16-3. Model 1 imposed constraint A, which equated the disattenuated correlations across the CMOA. Model 2 imposed both constraints A and B, where B constrained the reliability parameters. Consequently, in Model 2, the reliability values for each test were constrained to be equivalent across the two calibration media. Model parameters were estimated by normal-theory maximum-likelihood using the SAS procedure CALIS (SAS Institute, 1990).

Models 1 and 2 represent a hierarchy of nested models. Consequently, the χ^2 difference test can be used to examine the statistical significance of each set of constraints. Significance tests were performed on each set of constraints listed in Table 16-3. For both models, the likelihood ratio χ^2 statistic of overall fit was calculated. To test the equivalency of disattenuated correlations across the CMOA ($\Phi_{cc} = \Phi_{pc} = \Phi_{pp}$), the likelihood χ^2 value for Model 1 was used. To test the equivalency of the reliability parameters, the difference between

the χ^2 values of Models 1 and 2 was evaluated. Under the null hypothesis, this difference was distributed as χ^2 with 4 degrees of freedom (df).

Results

Group Equivalence

Two examinees in Group 3 had fewer than 10 valid responses for WK and SI and were eliminated from all subsequent analyses of these two tests. Thus, the Group 3 sample sizes were 988 for GS and AR and 986 for WK and SI. An analysis of variance indicated a nonsignificant difference among the three group means on AFQT. This result provided some assurance that the three groups were equivalent with respect to ASVAB aptitude.

Difficulty Parameter Comparison

A comparison of the IRT difficulty parameters across the two media for Groups 1 and 2 provided one assessment of the effects of using alternative CMOA on the score scale. Ideally, the parameters from the two media should fall along a diagonal (45°) line. Systematic effects on the score scale would cause the points to fall along a different line (if linearly related), or curve (if non-linearly related). Non-systematic effects would influence the degree of scatter around the line.

Figure 16-1 (a–d) displays the plots of difficulty parameters estimated from the two CMOAs, for each of the four tests. As each plot indicates, the parameters fell along the diagonal with a small degree of scatter. This result is consistent with small or negligible effects of the calibration media on the score scale.

Covariance Structure Analysis Results

The sample correlation matrix among the eight $\hat{\theta}$s for Group 3 is displayed in Table 16-4. Also displayed in the table are the means and standard deviations of these variables.

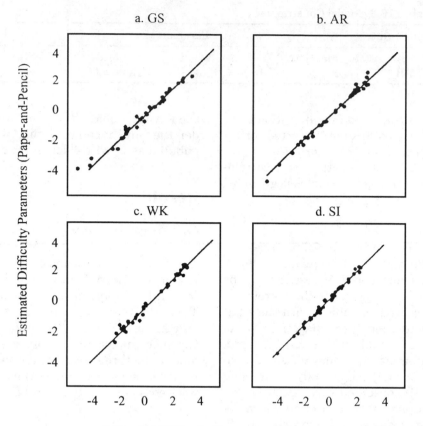

a. GS b. AR c. WK d. SI

Estimated Difficulty Parameters (Paper-and-Pencil)

Estimated Difficulty Parameters (Computer)

Figure 16-1
Paper-and-Pencil Versus Computer Estimated Difficulty Parameters.

Table 16-4 Means, Standard Deviations, and Correlations Among Group 3 Scores

Variable	X_{GSC}	X_{ARC}	X_{WKC}	X_{SIC}	X_{GSP}	X_{ARP}	X_{WKP}	X_{SIP}
X_{GSC}								
X_{ARC}	.504							
X_{WKC}	.734	.446						
X_{SIC}	.601	.354	.496					
X_{GSP}	.970	.506	.728	.587				
X_{ARP}	.507	.981	.449	.351	.506			
X_{WKP}	.737	.450	.980	.500	.730	.451		
X_{SIP}	.605	.351	.490	.956	.587	.349	.494	
Mean	.025	−.027	.012	.042	.069	−.068	.034	.012
SD	.857	.927	.877	.866	.863	.947	.853	.896

The estimated parameters of Model 1 are displayed in Tables 16-5 and 16-6. As indicated by the $\hat{\rho}$ columns of Table 16-6, the reliability values for both CMOAs were quite high, approaching 1.0. These results indicate that a very small amount of random error among test scores was attributable to estimation errors among item parameters. The estimated σ values for each CMOA are provided in the last two columns of Table 16-6.

The results of overall fit for Models 1 and 2 are displayed in Table 16-7. As indicated in this table, the likelihood ratio χ^2 value for Model 1 was nonsignificant, which provides support for the equivalency of the disattenuated correlation matrices: $\Phi_{cc} = \Phi_{pc} = \Phi_{pp}$. This result indicates that CMOA did not alter the constructs measured by the four tests.

The χ^2 test based on differences between Models

Table 16-5 Model 1: Estimated Disattenuated Correlation Matrix $\hat{\Phi}$

Test	GS	AR	WK	SI
GS	1.00			
AR	.52	1.00		
WK	.75	.46	1.00	
SI	.62	.36	.51	1.00

Table 16-6 Model 1: Estimated Reliabilities $\hat{\rho}$ and Standard Deviations $\hat{\sigma}$

| Test | $\hat{\rho}$ | | $\hat{\sigma}$ | |
	Computer	P&P	Computer	P&P
GS	.983	.958	.857	.863
AR	.978	.985	.927	.947
WK	.976	.984	.877	.853
SI	.956	.957	.866	.896

Table 16-7 Model Evaluation: Tests of Overall Fit

Model	Constraints	df	χ^2	p-value
1	A	14	14.066	.44
2	A, B	18	19.267	.38

1 and 2 indicated no difference between reliability parameters across the two calibration media ($\chi^2 = 19.267 - 14.066 = 5.201$, $df = 18 - 14 = 4$, $p = .27$). This result supports the contention that the reliability of CATs is independent of the medium used to calibrate the item parameters.

Summary

The good fit of Model 1 to the data indicated that, for the four tests, the disattenuated correlations among the scores based on the computer-based calibration, Φ_{cc} did not differ significantly from the disattenuated correlations among the scores based on the P&P-based calibration, Φ_{pp}; and neither of these sets of correlations differed significantly from the disattenuated cross-correlations of scores based on the two types of calibration, Φ_{PC}. This is consistent with the lack of within-trait medium-of-administration correlational effects found by Mead and Drasgow (1993). It also extends the conclusions drawn by Mead and Drasgow to the consistency of disattenuated correlations between traits.

The results from the comparison of Models 1 and 2 indicated that, for the four tests, equal amounts of non-systematic error variance ($1 - \rho^2_{tm}$) were obtained with the use of the computer-based and P&P-based item calibrations. This is generally consistent with—and extends—the findings of Divgi (1986b) and Divgi and Stoloff (1986), in which the computer-based calibration was based primarily on data from adaptively administered items.

The secondary effect under investigation was the influence of calibration medium on the score scale. A comparison of the difficulty parameters across the two media indicated very little or no distortion in the scale. For all four tests, the difficulty parameters tended to fall along a diagonal (45°) line.

An important practical implication of the results of this study is that item parameters calibrated from a P&P administration of items can be used in power CATs of cognitive constructs—such as those found on the CAT-ASVAB—without changing the construct being assessed and without reducing reliability. The descriptive analyses of difficulty parameters suggest little or no effect of calibration medium on the score scale. However, Green et al. (1984) noted that if scale effects do exist, they can be corrected by equating to a reference form that defines the score scale to be used for selection and classification decisions. When this is done, distortions in the mean, variance, and higher moments of the observed scores have no effect on selection and classification decisions.

17

Reliability and Construct Validity of CAT-ASVAB

Kathleen E. Moreno and Daniel O. Segall

One of the most important steps in evaluating the first operational CAT-ASVAB forms was to empirically demonstrate that the CAT-ASVAB tests were as reliable as their P&P counterparts, and that they measured the same constructs. While this step is important for any new test form, this was especially true for the first two forms of CAT-ASVAB. First, CAT was a new method of testing, never having been used before in a large-scale testing program. Second, the P&P-ASVAB had a long history of use, demonstrating its predictive validity, and therefore, the importance of measuring a particular set of constructs. Third, CAT-ASVAB and P&P-ASVAB would be in use at the same time, and scores from the two versions must be interchangeable.

Data collection for this study was conducted in 1988–89, after development of the CAT-ASVAB item pools, initial evaluation of these pools, and development of the HP-based CAT-ASVAB system. Data analyses were completed early in 1990 and results of the study played a significant role in the decision to use CAT-ASVAB operationally.

Earlier Research

Earlier studies showed that computerized adaptive testing (CAT) results in more reliable scores than conventional paper-and-pencil testing methods. Kingsbury and Weiss (1981) found that the alternate form reliability for a computerized adaptive word knowledge test was higher than that of a corresponding conventional test administered by computer. McBride and Martin (1983) found that adaptive verbal and arithmetic reasoning tests were more reliable than corresponding conventional tests administered by computer.

Previous studies have also shown that the adaptive testing methodology can be used to measure constructs traditionally assessed by conventional, paper-and-pencil tests. A comparison of the relationship between three CAT-ASVAB and corresponding P&P-ASVAB tests showed that the patterns of factor loadings for the two versions were very similar (Moreno, Wetzel, McBride, & Weiss, 1984). A validity study comparing an experimental version of CAT-ASVAB to the P&P-ASVAB found the same result (Moreno, Segall, & Kieckhaefer, 1985). In a meta-analysis of such studies, Mead and Drasgow (1993) found that medium of administration—computer versus paper-and-pencil—has little effect on power tests. Results for speeded tests were mixed.

These studies, as a whole, provided valuable information on the reliability and validity of CAT instruments. However, until the study described in this chapter was conducted, only a limited number of content areas had been examined in other research studies. In addition, the reliability and construct validity of a test is dependent on the quality of the item pools and the item selection and scoring procedures. The study described in this chapter provided information on the reliability and validity of tests in the first two operational forms of CAT-ASVAB—01C and 02C.

Method

Design

This study used an equivalent groups design, with examinees randomly assigned to one of two groups. Group 1 was administered Form 01C of the CAT-ASVAB in the first testing session, followed by Form 02C of the CAT-ASVAB in the second session. Group 2 was administered Form 9b of the P&P-ASVAB, followed by Form 10b of the P&P-ASVAB. There was an interval of five weeks between the first test and the second test. This interval was constant for all examinees. A five week interval was chosen because applicants taking the ASVAB must wait 30 days before retesting.

Examinees

Two thousand ninety male Navy recruits stationed at the Recruit Training Center in San Diego served as examinees in this study—1,057 in the CAT-ASVAB group and 1,033 in the P&P-ASVAB group. A substantial percentage of the subjects did not have complete data because they did not return for the second of the two tests. After examinees with incomplete data were eliminated, the sample sizes were 744 for CAT-ASVAB and 726 for P&P-ASVAB.

Test Instruments

P&P-ASVAB. The P&P-ASVAB consists of ten tests—eight power tests and two speeded. The content areas, test lengths, and test time limits are described in Chapter 1, Table 1-1. Each test consists of items with difficulty levels that span the range of abilities found in the military applicant population. Most tests, however, are peaked at the middle of the ability distribution. There are six forms of the P&P-ASVAB in operational use at any given time. All operational forms have been equated to a common paper-and-pencil reference form (8A).

CAT-ASVAB. CAT-ASVAB forms 01C and 02C were used in this study. These are the two forms that were developed for initial operational implementation of CAT-ASVAB. Item pool development is described in Chapter 11. The psychometric procedures used to administer the tests were identical to those used operationally, and are described in Chapter 12. The computer system used to administer the tests was the HP-IPC, described in Chapter 14.

Procedures

All examinees had taken an operational P&P-ASVAB to qualify for entrance into the Navy. As part of the present study, they took either a non-operational CAT-ASVAB or a non-operational P&P-ASVAB, with the scores used for experimental purposes only. Upon arrival at the test site, examinees were given general instructions explaining the experimental testing and signed a privacy act statement allowing use of the data for research purposes. Then they were seated in the appropriate room (CAT-ASVAB or P&P-ASVAB), based on a random assignment list. CAT-ASVAB was administered following procedures developed for operational implementation; P&P-ASVAB was administered following procedures outlined in the ASVAB Test Administrator Manual. At the conclusion of testing, TAs collected additional data from the examinees' personnel records, including population group, ethnic group, date of birth, education, operational ASVAB test form, operational ASVAB test scores, and date of enlistment.

Scores

All analyses for both the CAT-ASVAB and the P&P-ASVAB tests were based on standard scores. ASVAB standard scores are scaled to have a mean of 50 and a standard deviation of 10 in the 1980 youth population (DoD, 1982). Since CAT-ASVAB is equated to P&P-ASVAB Form 8A, standard scores for the CAT-ASVAB tests were obtained by converting the final theta estimate to the equated raw score, and then using P&P-ASVAB Form 8A conversion tables to obtain standard scores.

Data Editing

A data editing procedure which compared non-operational scores to operational scores was used to eliminate "unmotivated" examinees (Segall, 1996). After editing, the sample size was 701 for the CAT-ASVAB group and 687 for the P&P-ASVAB group. One limitation of the structural modeling procedure (CALIS) is that samples used in multi-group analyses must be of equal size; to satisfy this requirement, 14 examinees were selected at random and deleted from the CAT group. The final sample size in both groups was 687.

Data Analyses

Evaluation of equivalent groups. To assure the equivalency of the two samples, demographic variables were checked by (1) comparing the two groups on race and years of education, and (2) comparing the distribution of operational test scores by the two groups.

No significant differences between the CAT and P&P groups were found on race or years of education. For both variables, a χ^2 test for the differences between distributions indicated no significant difference. For each test of the operational ASVAB, a Kolmogorov-Smirnov [K-S] test was conducted to evaluate the difference between the score distributions for the two groups. There were no significant differences among the ten tests examined.

Correlational analyses. To compare alternate form reliabilities, Pearson product-moment correlations were computed between alternate forms of both batteries: CAT-ASVAB and P&P-ASVAB. Fisher's z transformation was used to evaluate the difference between CAT-ASVAB and P&P-ASVAB reliabilities, for each content area. Cross-medium Pearson product-moment correlations were computed between examinee performance on CAT-ASVAB tests and operational P&P-ASVAB tests, and compared to correlations between non-operational and operational P&P-ASVAB tests.

Structural analysis. If CAT-ASVAB and P&P-ASVAB are to be used interchangeably, it is essential for the two versions of the battery to measure the same traits. This issue was investigated using structural modeling. The analysis described below was performed separately for each of the ten content areas contained within the ASVAB. To begin, we defined six variables that represent standardized test scores on different versions of the ASVAB. The notational convention is provided in Table 17-1. All six variables were assumed to represent a single content area (e.g., General Science).

Further, let Σ_c represent the 3×3 covariance matrix of C_1, C_2, X_o^c (for the CAT group) and Σ_p represent the 3×3 covariance matrix of X_1, X_2, X_o^p, (for the P&P group). Each covariance matrix can be expressed in terms of several parameter matrices:

$$\Sigma_c = \Lambda_c(\mathbf{R}_c\Phi_c\mathbf{R}_c - \mathbf{R}_c^2 + \mathbf{I})\Lambda_c \quad (17\text{-}1)$$

Table 17-1 Variable Definitions for the Structural Analysis

Variable	Medium	Form	Group
C_1	CAT	1	CAT
C_2	CAT	2	CAT
X_o^c	P&P	Operational	CAT
X_1	P&P	9B	P&P
X_2	P&P	10B	P&P
X_o^p	P&P	Operational	P&P

and

$$\Sigma_p = \Lambda_p(\mathbf{R}_p\Phi_p\mathbf{R}_p - \mathbf{R}_p^2 + \mathbf{I})\Lambda_p \quad (17\text{-}2)$$

The model given by Equation 17-1 refers to the covariance matrix among three tests measuring a common content area (two CAT forms and one P&P form) for the CAT group. The model given by Equation 17-2 refers to the covariance matrix among three tests measuring the same content area (three P&P forms) for the P&P group. In Equation 17-1 the parameter matrices for the CAT group take the following form:

$$\Lambda_c = \begin{pmatrix} \sigma(C_1) & 0 & 0 \\ 0 & \sigma(C_2) & 0 \\ 0 & 0 & \sigma(X_o^c) \end{pmatrix},$$

$$\mathbf{R}_c = \begin{pmatrix} \sqrt{\rho(C_1)} & 0 & 0 \\ 0 & \sqrt{\rho(C_2)} & 0 \\ 0 & 0 & \sqrt{\rho(X_o)} \end{pmatrix},$$

and

$$\Phi_c = \begin{pmatrix} 1 & 1 & \rho(C, X_o) \\ 1 & 1 & \rho(C, X_o) \\ \rho(C, X_o) & \rho(C, X_o) & 1 \end{pmatrix}, \quad (17\text{-}3)$$

where $\sigma(C_1)$, $\sigma(C_2)$, and $\sigma(X_o^c)$ denote the standard deviations of C_1, C_2, and X_o^c, respectively, and $\rho(C_1)$, $\rho(C_2)$, and $\rho(X_o)$ denote the reliabilities of C_1, C_2, and X_o^c. In Equation 17-3, we assume that $\rho(C_1, X_o) = \rho(C_2, X_o)$ [= $\rho(C, X_o)$], where $\rho(Y, Z)$ denotes the correlation between Y and Z, corrected for attenuation.

In the model given in Equation 17-1, the Φ_c matrix represents the disattenuated correlation matrix among C_1, C_2, and X_o^c. From classical test theory, we see that the product $\mathbf{R}_c\Phi_c\mathbf{R}_c$ provides the correlation matrix of observed variables, with the diagonal elements equal to the test reliabilities. Consequently, the sum $\mathbf{R}_c\Phi_c\mathbf{R}_c - \mathbf{R}_c^2 + \mathbf{I}$ provides the correlation matrix among the observed C_1, C_2, and X_o^c, with one's in the diagonal. Finally, by pre- and post-multiplying this correlation matrix by Λ_c (which contains the standard deviations), we obtain Σ_c the covariance matrix among the observed C_1, C_2, and X_o^c.

The parameter matrices for the P&P group model, given by Equation (17-2), take on a similar form:

$$\Lambda_p = \begin{pmatrix} \sigma(X_1) & 0 & 0 \\ 0 & \sigma(X_2) & 0 \\ 0 & 0 & \sigma(X_o^p) \end{pmatrix}, \quad (17\text{-}4)$$

$$\mathbf{R}_p = \begin{pmatrix} \sqrt{\rho(X_1)} & 0 & 0 \\ 0 & \sqrt{\rho(X_2)} & 0 \\ 0 & 0 & \sqrt{\rho(X_o)} \end{pmatrix}, \quad (17\text{-}5)$$

and

$$\Phi_p = \begin{pmatrix} 1 & 1 & 1 \\ 1 & 1 & 1 \\ 1 & 1 & 1 \end{pmatrix}, \quad (17\text{-}6)$$

where $\sigma(X_1)$, $\sigma(X_2)$, and $\sigma(X_o^p)$ denote the standard deviations of X_1, X_2, and X_o^p, and $\rho(X_1)$ and $\rho(X_2)$ denote the reliabilities of X_1 and X_2.

Several constraints imposed by the model should be noted. First, the reliability of X_o^p is assumed to be equivalent to the reliability of X_o^c. That is, the reliability of the operational form is assumed to be equivalent for the CAT and P&P groups. This assumption is imposed by constraining the lower diagonal elements of the $\mathbf{R}_c$ and $\mathbf{R}_p$ matrices to be equal.

Second, the disattenuated correlation between the two CAT forms is assumed to be 1. This constraint is imposed by fixing the (2, 1) element (and its transpose) of the Φ_c matrix equal to 1. We make an additional assumption, which is consistent with this constraint, that $\rho(C_1, X_o) = \rho(C_2, X_o)$. That is, we assume that the disattenuated correlation between CAT and P&P is the same for both forms of CAT. This assumption is imposed by constraining the appropriate elements of the Φ_c matrix to be equivalent.

Third, the disattenuated correlations among the P&P-ASVAB forms (for the P&P group) are assumed to be equal to 1. This constraint is imposed by fixing all elements of the Φ_p matrix equal to 1.

The multigroup model given by Equations 17-1 and 17-2 is exactly identified since there are 12 unknown parameters and 12 nonredundant covariance elements among the two 3×3 covariance matrices. These 12 parameters were estimated by normal-theory maximum-likelihood using the SAS procedure CALIS (SAS Institute, 1990).

Results and Discussion

Table 17-2 displays the correlations between alternate forms for CAT-ASVAB and P&P-ASVAB. Seven of the ten CAT-ASVAB tests displayed significantly higher alternate form reliabilities than the corresponding P&P-ASVAB tests. The other three tests displayed nonsignificant differences. Also displayed in Table 17-2 are the correlations between the operational and non-operational forms for the CAT and P&P groups. It is important to note that CAT-ASVAB tests correlated as highly with the operational P&P-ASVAB as did alternate forms of the P&P-ASVAB.

A separate covariance analysis was performed for each of the ten content areas contained within the ASVAB. Table 17-3 lists the estimated re-

Table 17-2 Alternate Form and Cross-Medium Correlations

| | Alternate Form Reliability | | Correlations With Operational P&P-ASVAB | | | |
| | CAT | P&P | CAT Form 01C | CAT Form 02C | P&P Form 9B | P&P Form 10B |
Test						
General Science	.843**	.735	.83	.82	.79	.73
Arithmetic Reasoning	.826**	.773	.81	.75	.76	.72
Word Knowledge	.832	.811	.83	.81	.81	.78
Paragraph Comprehension	.535	.475	.54	.43	.48	.38
Numerical Operations	.817**	.708	.60	.60	.65	.56
Coding Speed	.770	.747	.57	.54	.65	.62
Auto and Shop Information	.891**	.776	.83	.83	.76	.74
Mathematics Knowledge	.883**	.819	.86	.83	.83	.80
Mechanical Comprehension	.749*	.703	.69	.64	.66	.65
Electronics Information	.727**	.648	.73	.72	.66	.65

*Statistically significant ($p < .05$)
**Statistically significant ($p < .01$)

Table 17-3 Test Reliabilities

| | CAT-ASVAB | | P&P-ASVAB | | |
Test	$\hat{\rho}(C_1)$	$\hat{\rho}(C_2)$	$\hat{\rho}(X_1)$	$\hat{\rho}(X_2)$	$\hat{\rho}(X_o)$
General Science	.86	.82	.80	.67	.78
Arithmetic Reasoning	.89	.77	.82	.73	.72
Word Knowledge	.86	.81	.84	.79	.78
Paragraph Comprehension	.67	.43	.59	.38	.37
Numerical Operations	.79	.84	.82	.61	.52
Coding Speed	.81	.73	.79	.70	.54
Auto and Shop Information	.89	.89	.80	.76	.74
Mathematics Knowledge	.92	.85	.85	.79	.80
Mechanical Comprehension	.80	.70	.73	.68	.61
Electronics Information	.74	.71	.66	.64	.66

Table 17-4 Disattenuated Correlations Between CAT- and P&P-ASVAB

Test	$\hat{\rho}(C, X_o)$	$SE(\hat{\rho})$	$\chi^2(df = 1)$	p
General Science	1.01	.018	.55	.456
Arithmetic Reasoning	1.02	.021	1.13	.287
Word Knowledge	1.02	.017	.80	.370
Paragraph Comprehension	1.11	.082	2.12	.145
Numerical Operations	.94	.044	1.73	.189
Coding Speed	.86	.043	9.12	.002
Auto and Shop Information	1.02	.020	.83	.363
Mathematics Knowledge	1.00	.015	.001	.975
Mechanical Comprehension	.99	.035	.13	.715
Electronics Information	1.05	.031	3.20	.074

liabilities for CAT-ASVAB and P&P-ASVAB forms. Table 17-4 provides $\hat{\rho}(C, X_o)$, the maximum likelihood estimate of the disattenuated correlation between CAT and P&P. Table 17-4 also provides SE $(\hat{\rho})$, the asymptotic standard error of $\hat{\rho}(C, X_o)$.

The hypothesis that $\rho(C, X_o) = 1$ was tested for each content area by fixing all elements of Φ_c equal to 1 and re-estimating the remaining model parameters. The χ^2 goodness-of-fit measure provides a test of the null hypothesis that $\rho(C, X_o) = 1$. Under the null hypothesis, this measure is χ^2-distributed with $df = 1$. The χ^2 and p-values for each content area are listed in the last two columns of Table 17-4.

The test reliabilities shown in Table 17-3 display the same pattern of differences across media as those shown in Table 17-2. The multigroup model provides a separate reliability estimate for each form, whereas the analysis provided in Table 17-2 provides a single estimate. However, for each content area, the alternate form correlations (Table 17-2) fall at about the midpoint of the two separate reliability estimates given in Table 17-3. For example, the GS (CAT-ASVAB) alternate form correlation of .84 (Table 17-2) falls at the midpoint of

the separate Form 01C and 02C reliabilities of .82 and .86 (Table 17-3). A similar pattern is evident for other tests.

From Table 17-4, we observe that the first form administered (C_1 and X_1) tended to have higher reliabilities than the second form administered (either C_2 or X_2). That is, for most tests we observe that $\hat{\rho}(C_1) > \hat{\rho}(C_2)$, and $\hat{\rho}(X_1) > \hat{\rho}(X_2)$. This pattern is evident for both CAT-ASVAB and P&P-ASVAB. One possible cause is a difference in precision between the forms. Another possible cause is motivation—examinees tend to be less motivated for the second administration of the battery than for the first. Since the order of form administration was not counterbalanced (CAT Form 01C and P&P Form 9B were always administered first, followed by CAT Form 02C or P&P Form 10B), it is impossible to isolate the cause of the difference. However, since the construction procedures for both CAT-ASVAB and P&P-ASVAB attempted to assure equal precision among forms, and the simulation results reported in Chapter 11 indicate that this goal was achieved, we speculate that the within-medium differences in reliabilities are due to motivational effects.

Table 17-4 displays $\hat{\rho}(C, X_o)$, the disattenuated correlations between CAT-ASVAB and the operational P&P-ASVAB. Although the theoretical upper limit of a correlation coefficient is 1.00, no upper bound was placed on the estimates obtained in this analysis. However, those estimates exceeding 1.00 imply that the population disattenuated correlation is equal to or less than 1.

As indicated by the significance tests in Table 17-4, only one test displayed a disattenuated correlation significantly different from 1. This was the nonadaptive speeded test, Coding Speed (CS). This test had an estimated disattenuated correlation of .86 ($\chi^2 = 9.12$, $df = 1$, $p = .002$). We know from examinee feedback that some had difficulty understanding the instructions, which are administered by computer. During P&P-ASVAB administration, test administrators often work through several examples to help examinees understand the task. Although several example questions are given on the CAT-ASVAB for CS, some examinees may need more practice. Because of the difficulty in understanding the CAT-ASVAB instructions for CS, the CAT version may have had a higher general ability ("g") component than its P&P counterpart.

The findings (from Table 17-4) indicate that none of the disattenuated correlations between CAT-ASVAB and P&P-ASVAB power tests were significantly different from 1.00. Of course, one reason for this lack of significance may be due to a lack of power to detect small or moderate sized differences. However, the standard error of estimate of $\hat{\rho}$, ($SE(\hat{\rho})$), displays a narrow confidence interval around nearly all estimated correlations. Consequently, even if the population $\rho(C, X_o)$ is less than 1 for one or more adaptive tests, it is improbable that it would fall below .97. This is true for nearly all adaptive tests examined.

Summary

Taken together, the estimated test reliabilities and disattenuated cross-medium correlations provide a compelling case for the virtues of CAT. Many concerns about the validity of CAT scores have been cited in the literature. These concerns include the impact of medium of administration (i.e., use of computers to administer tests), adaptive item selection, IRT techniques used in scoring, and paper-and-pencil calibration of item parameters. The findings of this study indicate that the aggregate effect of these threats to reliability and validity appears to be minimal or nonexistent. The results demonstrate that the adaptive tests within CAT-ASVAB measure the same traits measured by the P&P-ASVAB, with equal or greater precision, and with test lengths only half as long as their P&P counterparts.

18

Evaluating the Predictive Validity of CAT-ASVAB

John H. Wolfe, Kathleen E. Moreno, and Daniel O. Segall

Although CAT can be expected to improve reliability and measurement precision, the increased reliability does not necessarily translate into substantially greater validity. In fact, there is always a danger when changing item content or format that the new test may be measuring a slightly different ability, which may not relate to, or predict outcomes as well as, the old test. Findings of the earlier validity study of the experimental item pools (Chapter 10), therefore, did not necessarily generalize to the new, operational item pools.

The purpose of the research reported here was to evaluate whether the predictive validities of CAT-ASVAB forms 01C and 02C are as high as the P&P-ASVAB. A secondary purpose was to verify that the CAT-ASVAB tests are measuring the same abilities as their P&P-ASVAB counterparts. While the construct validity of the operational CAT-ASVAB forms had already been evaluated as part of an alternate forms study (Chapter 17), data collected as part of this study provided an opportunity for a second check.

The research was designed to answer three questions:

• Whether the means and standard deviations of the pre-enlistment ASVAB scores were the same for the CAT and P&P groups. This test was done to verify that the groups were equivalent.

• Whether the correlations between pre-enlistment and post-enlistment ASVAB were the same for CAT and P&P groups. This test was done to verify

that the two media of test administration measured the same abilities.

• Whether the validities of the tests for predicting final school grades (FSGs) were the same for P&P-ASVAB and CAT-ASVAB.

Method

Participants in this study were drawn from Navy recruits at the Navy Recruit Training Center, Great Lakes. Subjects were in one of two research projects—the Navy Validity Study of New Predictors (NVSNP) or the Enhanced Computer Administered Test (ECAT) study. Recruits were chosen for participation in the present study if they had been pre-assigned to enter one of a specified list of technical schools following their basic training. They were randomly assigned to either CAT-ASVAB or P&P-ASVAB test groups. Some months later, the school records were obtained to determine the examinees' FSGs and other criteria of school performance. The examinees' pre-enlistment ASVAB scores were also obtained.

For the ASVAB (post-enlistment) testing at Great Lakes, the recruits spent a morning as subjects in the NVSNP or ECAT experiments. In the afternoon, for the present study, they were administered either the CAT-ASVAB or the P&P-ASVAB in separate rooms. Assignments between the two conditions were made by a computer program at the test site that used a random number generator.

Table 18-1 CAT and P&P Sample Sizes

Code	School	CAT	P&P
	Navy Validity Study of New Predictors		
AD	Aviation Machinist's Mate	49	43
AMS	Aviation Structural Mechanic—Structures	43	46
AO	Aviation Ordnanceman	49	45
BT/MM	Boiler Technician/Machinist Mate	408	401
GMG	Gunner's Mate—Phase I	155	169
HM	Hospitalman	230	255
HT	Hull Technician	152	170
OS	Operations Specialist	457	447
	Enhanced Computer Administered Test Study		
AC	Air Traffic Controller	29	21
AE	Aviation Electrician's Mate	80	91
AMS	Aviation Structural Mechanic—Structures	75	61
AO	Aviation Ordnanceman	78	59
AV	Avionics Technician (AT, AQ, AX)	184	179
EM	Electrician's Mate	402	375
EN	Engineman	356	378
ET	Electronics Technician	29	30
FC	Fire Controlman	370	399
GMG	Gunner's Mate—Phase I	221	195
MM	Machinist Mate	368	409
OS	Operations Specialist	367	333
RM	Radioman	18	16
Total	School Completions	4,120	4,122
Others	Others tested	1,550	1,599

Table 18-1 gives sample sizes and school lists for the recruits. The sample sizes are for "school completers" who had FSGs of record. The row labeled "Others" shows examinees who took the post-enlistment test at Great Lakes but who had no FSGs of record. They include recruits who never went to the designated schools or who dropped out before completing training.

Statistical Analyses

The equivalence of means and standard deviations was tested with a t-test for differences in means and the F-test for ratios of variances, respectively. To correct for any differences between the groups, validities and pre-post correlations were corrected for range restriction, based on their correlations with the pre-enlistment ASVAB, using the 1991 Joint-Services recruit population ($N = 650,278$) as the reference population and all ten ASVAB tests as explicitly selected variables (see Chapter 24).

Post-enlistment scores were treated as implicitly selected. Corrections were made separately in each sample.

The pre-post uncorrected correlation differences were tested with the Fisher transformation: $Z = \tanh^{-1}(r)$. Let r_1 be the pre-post correlation for the CAT group and r_2 be the pre-post correlation for the P&P group. The following Z is approximately normally $(0,1)$ distributed:

$$Z = \frac{\tanh^{-1}(r_1) - \tanh^{-1}(r_2)}{\sqrt{\dfrac{1}{N_1 - 3} + \dfrac{1}{N_2 - 3}}} \tag{18-1}$$

The pre-post corrected correlation differences were tested using a modified version of an asymptotic test developed by Hedges, Becker, and Wolfe (1992), where N-2 replaces N in the original formula to produce better performance in small samples (see Samiuddin, 1970). Let corrected correlations be designated by capital R and uncorrected correlations by lower case r. Let $c = R/r$.

The following Z is asymptotically normally (0,1) distributed:

$$Z = \frac{R_1 - R_2}{\sqrt{\dfrac{[c_1(1 - r_1^2)]^2}{N_1 - 2} + \dfrac{[c_2(1 - r_2^2)]^2}{N_2 - 2}}}. \quad (18\text{-}2)$$

Validities of each test for predicting FSG in each school sample were computed and corrected for range restriction. Differences in validities were tested using the same formulas as above. Because many of the sample sizes were small, it was necessary to combine evidence across samples. For each ASVAB test, a combined Z was computed by the formula

$$Z = \frac{\sum_{i=1}^{k} Z_i}{\sqrt{k}}, \quad (18\text{-}3)$$

where i ranges over the $k = 21$ samples. The combined Z was referred to the normal (0,1) distribution for significance.

The final results were expressed in terms of significance tests for each ASVAB test. No attempt was made to explicitly adjust the significance levels to correct for the multiple significance tests performed in the study, but isolated results that were "significant" at the p < .05 level should generally be disregarded, since one would occur 40 percent of the time in any set of 10 hypothesis tests if they were independent. In the ASVAB they are not independent, of course, but similar considerations apply.

Results

Table 18-2 compares the *pre-enlistment* ASVAB scores for the CAT and P&P groups. There are no significant differences between the CAT and P&P groups in their means on pre-enlistment ASVAB tests. In comparing standard deviations, a "significantly" larger value was found for the CAT PC test, but the result could be spurious, since 24 significance tests were performed in this table. The randomization procedure for allocating examinees between conditions should be considered successful.

Table 18-3 shows the correlations between the CAT-ASVAB tests and the pre-enlistment ASVAB, the correlations between the post-enlistment P&P-ASVAB and the pre-enlistment ASVAB, and their differences. Since examinees were selected on the basis of their pre-enlistment scores, range-corrected results were calculated. Nine of the tests differ significantly in their uncorrected pre-post correlations, but this number shrinks to three in the corrected analysis. NO and CS, the two speeded nonadaptive tests in the CAT-ASVAB, had significantly lower correlations with the corresponding pre-enlistment tests than did the P&P tests, indicating that they measure a different construct or measure the same construct differently. The

Table 18-2 Pre-Enlistment ASVAB Comparison for the CAT and P&P Groups

ASVAB Test	Mean			Standard Deviation		
	CAT	P&P	t Diff.	CAT	P&P	F Diff.
General Science (GS)	52.99	52.98	0.10	7.26	7.11	1.04
Arithmetic Reasoning (AR)	52.51	52.48	0.19	6.92	6.94	1.01
Word Knowledge (WK)	52.55	52.64	−0.96	5.22	5.25	1.01
Paragraph Comprehension (PC)	52.83	52.94	−1.01	5.78	5.62	1.06*
Numerical Operations (NO)	53.73	53.82	−0.73	6.65	6.56	1.03
Coding Speed (CS)	52.47	52.40	0.57	6.81	6.85	1.01
Auto and Shop Information (AS)	53.98	53.83	0.95	7.96	7.88	1.02
Mathematics Knowledge (MK)	54.26	54.27	−0.10	6.62	6.58	1.01
Mechanical Comprehension (MC)	54.32	54.25	0.44	7.81	7.75	1.02
Electronics Information (EI)	52.59	52.52	0.52	7.80	7.72	1.02
Verbal (VE) = [WK + PC]	52.73	52.83	−1.05	5.00	4.99	1.00
AFQT = [VE + AR + NO/2]	58.39	58.50	−0.35	17.32	17.08	1.03

*p < .05
N: CAT = 5,670; P&P = 5,721.

Table 18-3 Pre-Post Correlations for Combined Navy and Ecat Samples

| | CAT-ASVAB | | P&P-ASVAB | | Z of Difference | |
Test	Uncorrected	Corrected	Uncorrected	Corrected	Uncorrected	Corrected
GS	.718	.812	.716	.812	0.22	0.00
AR	.752	.843	.719	.821	3.84**	2.26*
WK	.558	.719	.587	.747	−2.30*	−1.73
PC	.424	.634	.383	.597	2.61**	1.54
NO	.591	.696	.643	.734	−4.49**	−2.82**
CS	.603	.692	.665	.733	−5.54**	−3.24**
AS	.808	.842	.784	.835	3.50**	0.97
MK	.743	.834	.734	.839	1.06	−0.52
MC	.651	.745	.626	.733	2.25*	0.93
EI	.623	.712	.634	.729	−0.97	−1.31
VE	.762	.866	.733	.852	3.51**	1.47
AFQT	.830	.915	.810	.907	3.26**	1.17

*$p < .05$
**$p < .01$

Table 18-4 CAT Group and P&P Group Predictive Validities for School Final Grades

| | Uncorrected | | | Range-Corrected | | |
Test	CAT Group	P&P Group	Z (diff)	CAT Group	P&P Group	Z (diff)
		Pre-Enlistment ASVAB				
GS	.232	.249	−1.34	.531	.513	0.07
AR	.330	.319	0.81	.603	.576	0.29
WK	.202	.216	−0.62	.468	.473	−0.28
PC	.204	.222	−1.04	.467	.466	−0.17
NO	.118	.135	−1.04	.351	.348	0.15
CS	.193	.150	1.19	.362	.350	0.44
AS	.192	.215	−0.69	.370	.373	−0.35
MK	.298	.261	1.19	.559	.544	0.46
MC	.263	.289	−0.84	.505	.499	−0.48
EI	.220	.250	−0.94	.457	.457	−0.49
VE	.225	.246	−1.08	.495	.487	−0.28
AFQT	.376	.373	−0.30	.626	.615	−0.04
		Post-Enlistment ASVAB				
GS	.244	.231	0.84	.528	.477	0.41
AR	.337	.328	0.25	.580	.556	0.26
WK	.227	.272	−1.98*	.476	.503	−0.87
PC	.260	.243	0.83	.510	.461	0.87
NO	.136	.133	−0.31	.377	.321	0.82
CS	.226	.182	1.32	.395	.320	1.38
AS	.174	.220	−1.38	.310	.428	−2.01*
MK	.286	.319	−1.68	.521	.530	−0.79
MC	.273	.286	−0.25	.505	.516	−0.51
EI	.231	.267	−1.90	.453	.492	−0.81
VE	.258	.284	−1.06	.528	.519	−0.05
AFQT	.387	.396	−0.68	.630	.617	−0.73

*$p < .05$
N: CAT = 4,120; P&P = 4,122

CAT-ASVAB speeded tests were scored with a rate score—the proportion correct (corrected for guessing) divided by the mean of all screen times—whereas the P&P speeded tests were scored by number of items correct within a given time limit. The latter measure has the disadvantage of having a ceiling, which many examinees attained, of all items correct within the time limit. The computerized version is able to distinguish between fast and very fast examinees, but the shape of the score distribution changed so that it did not correlate with the pre-enlistment test as well as another P&P test can.

Table 18-4 shows the predictive validity coefficients for both pre-enlistment and post-enlistment ASVAB for predicting final school performance for the CAT and P&P groups. Note that the uncorrected pre-enlistment validities were usually lower than their post-enlistment counterparts, but this was not true for the corrected validities. Among the 48 significance tests presented in this table, two, uncorrected WK and corrected AS, were barely "significant" at the .05 level, a result that could easily occur by chance. The two computerized speeded tests that had significantly lower pre-post correlations in Table 18-3 have validities that were at least as high as the P&P versions.

Summary

The results of this research show no reason to doubt that CAT-ASVAB is as valid as P&P-ASVAB. The two computerized speeded tests yield measures that are not precisely equivalent to their P&P counterparts, but they may be better in some ways and are no less valid. The results of this study support the findings reported in Chapter 17.

19

Equating the CAT-ASVAB

Daniel O. Segall

During an extended operational test and evaluation (OT&E) phase, both the CAT-ASVAB and the P&P-ASVAB were used operationally (Chapter 20) to test applicants for the Military Services. At some testing sites, applicants were accessed using scores from the CAT-ASVAB, while at most other sites applicants were enlisted using scores obtained on the P&P-ASVAB. To make comparable enlistment decisions across the adaptive and conventional versions, an equivalence relation (or equating) between CAT-ASVAB and P&P-ASVAB was obtained. The primary objective of this equating was to provide a transformation of CAT-ASVAB scores that preserves the flow rates currently associated with the P&P-ASVAB. In principle, this can be achieved by matching the P&P-ASVAB and equated CAT-ASVAB test and composite distributions. This equating allowed cut-scores associated with the existing P&P-ASVAB scale to be applied to the transformed CAT-ASVAB scores without affecting qualification rates.

The equating study was designed to address three concerns. First, the equating transformation applied to CAT-ASVAB scores should preserve flow rates associated with the existing cut scores based on the P&P-ASVAB score scale. Second, the equating transformation should be based on operationally motivated applicants, since the effect of motivation on CAT-ASVAB equating has not been thoroughly studied. Third, subgroup members taking CAT-ASVAB should not be placed at a disadvantage relative to their subgroup counterparts taking the P&P-ASVAB.

The first concern was addressed by using an equipercentile procedure for equating the CAT-ASVAB and the P&P-ASVAB. By definition, this equating procedure identifies the transformation of scale that matches the cumulative distribution functions. Although this procedure was applied at the test level, the distributions of all selector composites were also evaluated to ensure that no significant differences existed across adaptive and conventional versions.

The concern over motivation was addressed by conducting the CAT-ASVAB equating in two phases: (1) score equating development (SED) and (2) score equating verification (SEV). The purpose of SED was to provide an interim equating of the CAT-ASVAB. During that study, both CAT-ASVAB and P&P-ASVAB were given nonoperationally to randomly equivalent groups. The tests were nonoperational in the sense that the performance on the tests had no impact on examinees' eligibility for the military—all participants in the study were also administered an operational P&P-ASVAB form that was used for enlistment decisions. This interim equating was used in the second phase (SEV) to select and classify military applicants. During the SEV phase, applicants were administered either an operational CAT-ASVAB or an operational P&P-ASVAB. Both versions used in the SEV study did have an impact on applicants' eligibility for military service. This new equating obtained in SEV was based on operationally motivated examinees, and was later applied to applicants participating in the OT&E study.

The third concern, regarding subgroup performance, was addressed through a series of analyses conducted on data collected during the score equating study. Analyses examined the performance of blacks and females for randomly equivalent groups assigned to CAT-ASVAB and P&P-ASVAB conditions.

This chapter describes the essential elements of the CAT-ASVAB equating. These include the data collection design, sample characteristics, smoothing and equating procedures, composite equatings, and subgroup performance.

Data Collection Design and Procedures

Data for the SED and SEV equating studies were collected from six geographically dispersed regions within the continental United States: Boston, MA; Richmond, VA; Jackson, MS; Omaha, NE; San Diego, CA; and Seattle, WA. Within each region is a Military Entrance Processing Station (MEPS), and associated with each MEPS are a number (between 3 and 16) of Mobile Examining Team Sites (METSs). Each MEPS and associated METSs were included in the data collection for a two- to three-month period. Within each location, testing continued until a pre-set applicant quota had been satisfied. The quotas were based on the applicant flow through the sites during a two-month period prior to testing. The six regions were selected to provide a representative and diverse sample of military applicants. Taken together, they were expected to provide nationally representative samples with respect to race, gender, and AFQT distributions. Data collection for the SED study occurred from February 1988 to December 1988, and from September 1990 to April 1992 for the SEV study.[1]

In both studies (SED and SEV), each applicant was randomly assigned to one of three groups. Each group was assigned a different form of the ASVAB. Examinees in one group were given P&P-ASVAB (Form 15C), while examinees in the other two groups were given either Form 1 or Form 2 of the CAT-ASVAB (denoted as 01C and 02C, respectively). The random assignment involved a two-step process. First, the names of all examinees were entered into the random assignment and selection program. This automated program assigned, at random, two-thirds of the applicants to CAT-ASVAB, and the remaining one-third to P&P-ASVAB (15C). The second step in the process involved randomly assigning each CAT-ASVAB examinee to an examinee testing station; each CAT station was randomly assigned either 01C or 02C, thus ensuring random assignment of examinees to CAT-ASVAB forms.

In the SED data collection, after taking either a nonoperational CAT-ASVAB form or P&P-ASVAB 15C, each applicant was administered an operational P&P-ASVAB form. This operational form was used for enlistment and classification purposes. The nonoperational forms were administered in the morning, and the operational forms were administered in the afternoon of the same day, following a break for lunch.

In the SEV study, all examinees were administered only one form of the ASVAB. All forms were administered under operational conditions, where the results (for both CAT-ASVAB and P&P-ASVAB) were used to compute operational scores of record. In the SEV study, the equating transformation used to compute operational scores of record for the CAT-ASVAB was obtained from the SED equating.

Data Editing and Group Equivalence

A small number of applicants were screened from the SED and SEV data sets using a procedure suggested by Hotelling (1931). This procedure identifies cases that are unlikely, given that the observations are sampled from a multivariate normal distribution. For the SED data, a 10×1 vector of difference scores was obtained between the operational and nonoperational versions of the ASVAB taken by each examinee (each element of the vector corresponded to one of the 10 content areas). The inverse of the covariance matrix of difference scores was pre- and post-multiplied by the vector of centered difference scores to obtain an index for each examinee. Examinees with a large index value were those with an unlikely score pattern, and therefore excluded from the analysis. In a similar manner, the 10×1 vector of operational scores for the SEV data (obtained from either CAT-ASVAB or P&P-ASVAB) was used to calculate the covariance matrix, the inverse of which was pre- and post-multiplied by the vector of centered observed scores. Examinees with a large index value were those with an unlikely score pattern, and were therefore excluded from the analysis.

In both data sets (SED and SEV) less than one percent of the sample was deleted. For the SED study, the final sample sizes were: 2641 (01C), 2678 (02C), 2721 (15C). For the SEV study, the final sample sizes were: 3446 (01C), 3413 (02C), and 3520 (15C). The SED sample contained about 18 percent females, and 29 percent blacks, with corresponding percentages of 21 and 24 in the SEV sample.

---

[1] The beginning of the SEV Study in September 1990 was an especially noteworthy date, since it marked the first operational use of CAT-ASVAB.

The equating design relies heavily on the assumed equivalence among the three groups: (1) 01C, (2) 02C, and (3) P&P-ASVAB 15C. Consequently, it is useful to examine the equivalence of these groups with respect to available demographic information. The numbers of females, blacks, and whites in each group are approximately equal. Two χ^2 analyses for assessing the equivalence of proportions across the three conditions were performed. The χ^2 significance tests for gender (SED: $\chi^2 = 2.95$, $df = 2$, $p = .23$; SEV: $\chi^2 = .20$, $df = 2$, $p = .90$) and race (SED: $\chi^2 = 2.98$, $df = 4$, $p = .56$; SEV: $\chi^2 = 7.57$, $df = 4$, $p = .11$) were nonsignificant, supporting the expectation of random equivalency across groups. In addition, the data collection and editing procedures resulted in groups of approximately equal sizes. For both the SED and SEV data sets, the χ^2 test of equivalent proportions of examinees across the three groups was nonsignificant (SED: $\chi^2 = 1.20$, $df = 2$, $p = .55$; SEV: $\chi^2 = 1.74$, $df = 2$, $p = .42$). These findings are consistent with expectations based on random assignment of applicants.

Smoothing and Equating

The objective of equipercentile equating is to provide a transformation of scale that will match the score distributions of the new and existing forms (Angoff, 1971). This transformation, which is applied to the CAT-ASVAB, allows scores on the two ASVAB versions to be used interchangeably, without disrupting applicant qualification rates.

One method for estimating this transformation involves the use of the two empirical cumulative distribution functions (CDFs). Scores on CAT-ASVAB and P&P-ASVAB could be equated by matching the empirical proportion scoring at or below observed score levels. However, this transformation is subject to random sampling errors contained in the CDFs. The precision of the equating transformation can be improved by smoothing either (1) the equating transformation, or (2) the two empirical distributions that form the equating transformation. For discrete number-right distributions, a number of methods and decision rules exist for specifying the type and amount of smoothing (e.g., Fairbank, 1987; Kolen, 1991).

The precision of any estimated equating transformation can be decomposed into a *bias* component and a *variance* component. Smoothing procedures that attempt to eliminate the bias will increase the random variance of the transformation. A high-order polynomial provides one ex-

ample. The polynomial may track the data closely, but may capitalize on chance errors and replicate poorly in a new sample. On the other hand, smoothing procedures that attempt to eliminate the random variance do so at the expense of introducing systematic error, or bias, into the transformation. Linear equating methods often replicate well, but display marked departure from the empirical transformation. It should be noted that whatever equating method is used, the choice of method, either implicitly or explicitly, involves a trade-off between random and systematic error.

One primary objective of the CAT-ASVAB equating was to use smoothing procedures that provided an acceptable trade-off between random and systematic error. In this study, smoothing was performed on each distribution (CAT-ASVAB and P&P-ASVAB) separately. These smoothed distributions were used to specify the equipercentile transformation.

Two different smoothing procedures were used. One method designed for continuous distributions (Kronmal & Tarter, 1968) was used to smooth CAT-ASVAB distributions. Another method designed for discrete distributions (Segall, 1987b) was used to smooth P&P-ASVAB distributions. These procedures are described below.

One additional concern arose over the shape of the equating transformation in the lower score range, where data are sparse. Typically, most equating procedures provide a transformation that is either undefined or poorly defined over this lower range. This problem was overcome by fitting logistic tails to the lower portion of the smoothed density functions. These tails achieved two desirable results. First, the distributions were extended to encompass the lower range, thus defining the equating transformation over the entire score scale. Second, by pre-specifying the fit-point of the tail, the distribution (and consequently the equating transformation) above that point was left unaltered by the tail. Consequently, the tail-fitting procedure altered the equating only over a pre-specified lower range; the equating transformation above that range was unaltered. The details of the fitting procedures are described in conjunction with the density estimation procedures below.

Smoothing P&P-ASVAB Distributions

The procedure used to smooth the P&P-ASVAB, developed by Segall (1987b), estimates the smoothest density that deviates from the observed density by a specified amount. Roughness is measured by

$$R = \sum_{j=1}^{n-2} [\hat{h}_j - 2\hat{h}_{j+1} + \hat{h}_{j+2}]^2, \qquad (19\text{-}1)$$

where $\hat{h}_j$ is the smoothed density estimate for the bin (or score level) j, and n is the number of bins. The index R can be viewed as a discrete analog to the squared integrated second derivative—an index which has wide application as a measure of roughness for continuous distributions.

The deviation of the estimated density from the empirical density can be measured by

$$X^2 = 2N \sum_{j=1}^{n} \dot{h}_j \ \ln(\dot{h}_j/\hat{h}_j), \qquad (19\text{-}2)$$

where $\dot{h}_j$ is the empirical sample proportion at score level j, and N is the sample size. The index X^2 is the likelihood ratio statistic and is asymptotically χ^2 distributed with $df = n - 1$. Notice that if the solution is constrained to have a small X^2, the estimated $\hat{h}_j$ and empirical $\dot{h}_j$ will deviate very little from one another, and the roughness index R is likely to be large. On the other hand, if the solution is allowed to have a large value of X^2, the resulting density is likely to have a small value of roughness R, but possesses a large deviation between the estimated $\hat{h}_j$ and the empirical $\dot{h}_j$. In effect, the constraint imposed on X^2 determines the trade-off between smoothness and the degree of deviation between the empirical and estimated densities.

The procedure used here placed the following constraint on X^2:

$$X^2 = df - 2 = n - 3. \qquad (19\text{-}3)$$

The rationale for this constraint can be obtained from the following considerations. Suppose that our smoothed $\hat{h}_j$ was the true density and the observed $\dot{h}_j$ was generated from observations that were sampled from this density. What value of X^2 would we be most likely to observe? The most likely value would be equal to the mode of the χ^2 distribution, which occurs at $n - 3$.

The density estimation procedure then minimizes roughness given by Equation 19-1, subject to the constraint that $X^2 = n - 3$. Several other constraints are imposed on the $\hat{h}_j$ to ensure that the solution defines a density: $\hat{h}_j > 0$ (for $j = 1$, $2, \ldots, n$), and $\Sigma_{j=1}^{n} \hat{h}_j = 1$. As a consequence of these constraints, the smoothed $\hat{h}_j$ deviate from the observed sample values by an amount to be expected by sampling error, and the resulting solution is the smoothest possible with this degree of deviation. The solution that satisfies the above constraints is obtained using an iterative numeri-

cal procedure that solves $n + 2$ simultaneous nonlinear equations.

The logistic CDF

$$F(x) = \frac{1}{1 + \exp[-\sigma(x - \mu)]} \qquad (19\text{-}4)$$

was used to specify density values for the lower tail of the discrete distributions. The function closely approximates the normal CDF and is often used as a substitute, since it provides mathematically tractable expressions for both the density and the distribution functions. Although the function is usually used to define a continuous CDF, it is used here to define a discrete density at bin x by

$$g(x) = F\left(x + \frac{1}{2}\right) - F\left(x - \frac{1}{2}\right). \qquad (19\text{-}5)$$

The first step in the tail-fitting process involved finding the largest x-value, x_r, from the smoothed solution that contained no more than 5 percent of the distribution. Once x_r was identified, two constraints were placed on the logistic function

$$g(x_r) = F\left(x_r + \frac{1}{2}\right) - F\left(x_r - \frac{1}{2}\right) = \hat{h}_r, \qquad (19\text{-}6)$$

and

$$\sum_{j=1}^{r} g(x_j) = F\left(x_r + \frac{1}{2}\right) - F\left(-\frac{1}{2}\right) = \sum_{j=1}^{r} \hat{h}_j. \qquad (19\text{-}7)$$

The first constraint given by Equation 19-6 ensures that there is a smooth fit of the logistic tail to the estimated density defined by $\hat{h}_j$. This is accomplished by constraining the last bin of the tail $g(x_r)$ to equal the estimated value of the smoothed solution at that bin, $\hat{h}_r$. The second constraint given by Equation 19-7 ensures that the proportion contained in the logistic tail will equal the proportion contained in the tail of the smoothed solution. It follows from this constraint that together, the logistic tail and the upper portion of the smoothed solution will define a density (i.e., sum to 1). Once the above constraints are imposed, values for μ and σ can be obtained through an iterative numerical procedure.

Smoothed distributions were estimated for each of the 10 P&P-ASVAB tests. (Separate estimates were obtained for the SED and SEV data sets.) Figures 19-1 and 19-2 display the smoothed solutions and the fitted tails for two tests (General Science and Arithmetic Reasoning) of the P&P-ASVAB 15C estimated from SEV data. The empirical proportions for each bin are indicated by the height of the bar. The smoothed (or fitted) density values

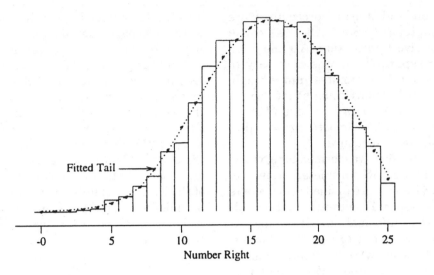

Figure 19-1
Smoothed and Empirical Density Functions P&P-ASVAB 15C (General Science)

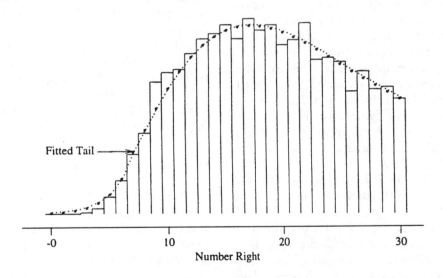

Figure 19-2
Smoothed and Empirical Density Functions P&P-ASVAB 15C (Arithmetic Reasoning)

are indicated by the small bullets joined by the dotted lines. The point at which the tail was joined to the smoothed solution $\{x_r, g(x_r)\}$ is indicated by an arrow in each figure.

Smoothing CAT-ASVAB Distributions

The procedure developed by Kronmal and Tarter (1968) was used to smooth the CAT-ASVAB distributions. This procedure, which was designed for smoothing continuous distributions, provides a Fourier estimate of the density function, using trigonometric functions. To obtain a useful density estimate, it is necessary to smooth the series by truncating it at some point. Kronmal and Tarter provide expressions that relate the mean integrated square error (MISE) of the Fourier estimator to the sample Fourier coefficients. The MISE expressions are used to specify a truncation point for the series, making it possible to specify an optimal number of terms in the series.

The distributions of penalized modal estimates (for seven adaptive power tests) and rate scores (for the two speeded tests) were smoothed using the Kronmal and Tarter method. Details about the item selection and scoring procedures are provided in Chapter 12. Since the CAT-ASVAB measures Automotive Information (AI) and Shop Information (SI) separately, it was necessary to combine the two ability estimates into a single score; this composite measure must be formed because the P&P-ASVAB measures both content areas within a single test (AS). Smoothing was performed on the composite measure.

This composite measure was formed for each examinee using estimated AS parameters from P&P-ASVAB-9A. The AS items were divided into two sets based on their content: (1) auto-information (AI) items, and (2) shop-information (SI) items. AI items were calibrated among CAT-ASVAB AI items, and similarly SI items were calibrated among CAT-ASVAB SI items (Prestwood, Vale, Massey, & Welsh, 1985). For each applicant, the expected number-right scores were obtained. In each case, the expected number-right scores were computed from the sum of item response functions evaluated at the examinee's estimated ability level. One expected number right score τ_{AI} was obtained from the AI-9A item parameters and the examinee's penalized ability estimate $\dot{\theta}_{AI}$. The other expected number-right score τ_{SI} was obtained from the SI-9A item parameters and the examinee's penalized ability estimate $\dot{\theta}_{SI}$. A composite measure was formed: $\tau_{AS} = \tau_{AI} + \tau_{SI}$. A smoothed density estimate of this composite measure was obtained in the subsequent equating analyses.

The logistic CDF given by Equation 19-4 was also used here to smooth the lower portion of the Fourier estimate where data are sparse. This tail fitting involved several steps. First, the proportion contained in the tail p_t was specified according to the proportion contained in the tail of the corresponding discrete (P&P-ASVAB) distribution given by Equation 19-6. That is, $p_t = \sum_{i=1}^{r} \hat{h}_j$. Next, the value of x_c was specified using the inverse Fourier estimate. That is, x_c is the value below which p_t proportion of the distribution falls, according to the Fourier estimator. The values x_c and p_t were used to constrain the CDF, such that $F(x_c) = p_t$. This constraint imposed in this manner ensures the equivalence of the three proportions: (1) the proportion in the continuous logistic tail below x_c, (2) the proportion in the Fourier series tail below x_c and (3) the proportion in the fitted discrete tail. A second constraint, $\partial F(x_c)/\partial x_c = d_c$ was added to ensure that the density value of the logistic tail at the join-point x_c equals the density of the Fourier estimate d_c at x_c. This constraint provided a continuous transition between the Fourier estimate

and the logistic tail. Once the above constraints were imposed, values of μ and σ were obtained using an iterative numerical procedure.

Tail fitting posed a special problem for the CAT-ASVAB AS composite. The AS scores are on the τ metric, due to the transformation used to combine the AI and SI scores. This τ metric is bounded on the upper and lower ends over the interval $(\sum_{i=1}^{25} c_i, 25)$. Consequently, scores below $\sum c_i$ are undefined. If the τ scores are smoothed directly, and a tail is fit to this smoothed distribution, much of the logistic tail falls below $\sum c_i$, over a range that is undefined. This problem was circumvented by transforming the AS τ scores using the arcsin transform

$$ w = \sin^{-1}\left[\frac{\tau - \sum_i c_i}{25 - \sum_i c_i}\right]^{\frac{1}{2}}, \qquad (19\text{-}8) $$

and performing the smoothing and fitting to the w-values. This change of metric achieved two desirable results. First, the distribution of the transformed scores w appeared more "normal-like" than did the distribution of τ scores. Second, the transformation helps contain the logistic tail within the defined interval. This becomes evident after transforming the metric of the smoothed w distribution back to the original τ-metric using the inverse of Equation 19-8

$$ \tau = \sin^2(w)\left(25 - \sum_i c_i\right) + \sum_i c_i. \quad (19\text{-}9) $$

Since 01C and 02C were smoothed separately, 20 density estimates were obtained for both the SED and SEV studies. Figures 19-3 and 19-4 display the smooth Fourier estimates and the fitted tails for 2 of the 10 tests of the CAT-ASVAB (01C), using data collected from the SEV study. In Figures 19-3 and 19-4, the empirical histograms for the CAT-ASVAB distributions are indicated by the height of the bar. The smoothed (or fitted) density functions are displayed by the dotted lines. The fitted logistic tail is displayed by the dotted curve to the left of the join-point (indicated by the solid bullet).

Equating Transformations

The smoothed distributions were used to specify the equipercentile transformation for the CAT-ASVAB. In each study (SED and SEV), there were a total of 20 equatings, one for each content area of each CAT-ASVAB form. For each P&P-ASVAB number-right score, an interval of the continuous CAT-

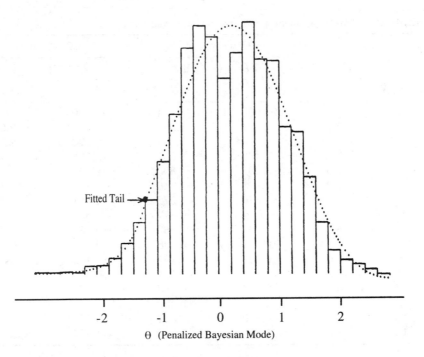

Figure 19-3
Smoothed and Empirical Density Estimates: CAT-ASVAB (Form 01), (General Science)

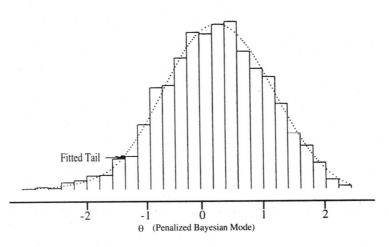

Figure 19-4
Smoothed and Empirical Density Estimates: CAT-ASVAB (Form 01), (Arithmetic Reasoning)

ASVAB scores that contained the same estimated proportion was obtained. A sample conversion table for Paragraph Comprehension (PC), based on SEV data, is provided in Table 19-1. The column labeled $\hat{h}$ displays the smoothed 15C density estimate. The next two columns provide the CAT-ASVAB lower and upper limits (LL, UL) of score intervals which contain that proportion for the smoothed estimate based on 01C, and the last two columns contain the score interval for 02C.

Figures 19-5 and 19-6 compare the equating functions based on the smoothed densities with functions based on the empirical unsmoothed distributions for two of the 20 equatings obtained in the SEV study. The smoothed function is indicated by the bullets joined by solid lines. The dog-leg portion of the function obtained from the tail fitting procedure is indicated by a large bullet. The unsmoothed transformation is indicated by the dotted function. For both the smoothed and

Table 19-1 Paragraph Comprehension Conversion Table

Raw Score X	$\hat{h}$	C1 (Form 1) $LL \le \theta < UL$		C2 (Form 2) $LL \le \theta < UL$	
		LL	UL	LL	UL
0	0.0	−999.000	−3.484	−999.000	−3.497
1	0.1	−3.484	−2.923	−3.497	−2.976
2	0.2	−2.923	−2.483	−2.976	−2.566
3	0.4	−2.483	−2.081	−2.566	−2.192
4	0.9	−2.081	−1.695	−2.192	−1.833
5	1.9	−1.695	−1.316	−1.833	−1.481
6	2.3	−1.316	−1.072	−1.481	−1.207
7	3.2	−1.072	−0.877	−1.207	−0.931
8	5.1	−0.877	−0.667	−0.931	−0.673
9	7.3	−0.667	−0.438	−0.673	−0.449
10	10.0	−0.438	−0.164	−0.449	−0.218
11	13.2	−0.164	0.154	−0.218	0.061
12	16.2	0.154	0.483	0.061	0.447
13	17.0	0.483	0.839	0.447	0.908
14	14.2	0.839	1.321	0.908	1.374
15	8.0	1.321	999.000	1.374	999.000

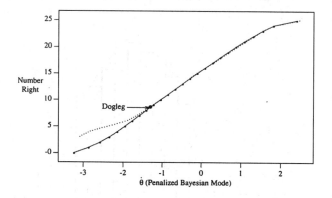

Figure 19-5
Smoothed and Empirical Equating Transformation for General Science (Form 01)

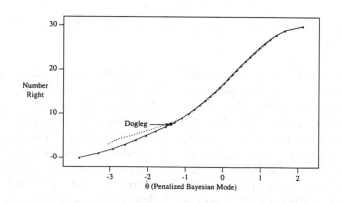

Figure 19-6
Smoothed and Empirical Equating Transformation for Arithmetic Reasoning (Form 01)

unsmoothed transformations, each number-right (on the y-axis) is plotted against the midpoint of the CAT-ASVAB score interval (on the x-axis). The agreement between the smoothed and unsmoothed functions is very high above the dogleg portion. Notice that the tail appears to provide a smooth extrapolation of the equating function over the lower range, and does not affect the agreement between the smoothed and empirical functions above the dogleg portion. Also notice that the dogleg provides a monotonic increasing function for mapping CAT-ASVAB scores into number-right scores.

Composite Equating

Equating the CAT-ASVAB to the P&P-ASVAB involves matching test distributions using an equipercentile method. This distribution matching provides a transformation of the CAT-ASVAB ability estimates to number-right equivalents. Once this transformation is specified for each test, raw-score equivalents can be computed. These raw-score equivalents provide the basis for computing Service-specific selection composites, as well as the AFQT and Verbal (VE) composites.

One concern is that the distributions of CAT-ASVAB composites might differ systematically from P&P-ASVAB composite distributions. Such a difference could be caused by differences in test reliabilities. A more reliable CAT-ASVAB would have higher covariances among tests. Since the variance of a composite is partially affected by the covariance among tests, differences in composite variances could result as a consequence of differences in reliabilities. Higher order moments of the composite distributions could be affected in a similar manner. Thus it is important to assess the need for equating CAT-ASVAB/P&P-ASVAB composites by examining the similarity of composite distributions.

Sample and Procedures

The sample consisted of 10,379 military applicants tested during the SEV data collection phase. The steps involved in computing composite score distributions differed among the three conditions (01C, 02C, and 15C), and are described below.

Each CAT-ASVAB content area was equated to the P&P-ASVAB using the procedures described in the preceding section. This equating was performed separately for each CAT-ASVAB form. First, CAT-ASVAB ability estimates were transformed to raw

score equivalents using the smoothed equating transformations. Next, raw scores (from 15C) and raw score equivalents (from 01C and 02C) were transformed to standard scores using the standardization based on the 1980 reference population. This standardization is derived from the means and variances of P&P-ASVAB 8A administered in the reference population. Then, sums of test standard scores were computed for the 29 Service composites and for the AFQT. The VE composite was also computed from the sum of WK and PC raw scores. A list of Service composites is provided in Table 19-2. After the sums were obtained, the appropriate scale conversion was applied to place each composite score on the metric used for classification decisions.

Each CAT-ASVAB composite distribution (for 01C and 02C) was compared to the corresponding 15C composite distribution. Two different methods were used to examine the significance of the differences. First, the Kolmogorov-Smirnov (K-S) two-sample test was used to detect overall differences between 01C and 15C, and between 02C and 15C. Since this test is not highly sensitive to differences of a specific nature (e.g., differences in variances), an F-ratio test was also used to test the differences between 01C and 15C variances, and between 02C and 15C variances. Both significance tests were performed on all 31 composites.

Results and Discussion

Of the 62 comparisons examined using the K-S tests, only one was significant at the .01 level. This comparison was between CAT-Form 2 and 15C for the Navy EG composite. Two of the 62 variance comparisons (Table 19-2) were significant at the .01 level. These significant variance differences existed between both CAT-ASVAB forms and 15C for the Navy EG composite.

The results of the K-S and F-ratio tests are generally indicative of no differences between CAT-ASVAB and P&P-ASVAB composite score distributions, with the possible exception of the Navy EG composite. It is possible that the significant differences were due to Type I errors that occur when a large number of comparisons are made. In this study, over 124 comparisons were made. Finding at least three significant differences (at the .01 level) is highly probable, even when no true differences exist between the composite distributions.

However, this same Navy composite exhibited significant variance differences (between CAT-ASVAB and P&P-ASVAB) in the SED analysis (Se-

Table 19-2 Significance Tests of Composite Standard Deviations

Composite	Standard Deviation			F-ratio	
	C1	C2	15C	C1 vs. 15C	C2 vs. 15C
Army					
GT = AR + VE	16.02	15.97	15.62	1.053	1.045
GM = GS + AS + MK + EI	16.07	15.72	16.38	1.039	1.086
EL = GS + AR + MK + EI	16.59	16.23	16.37	1.026	1.017
CL = AR + MK + VE	15.69	15.74	15.79	1.013	1.006
MM = NO + AS + MC + EI	15.88	15.71	15.97	1.012	1.034
SC = AR + AS + MC + VE	16.60	16.44	16.52	1.010	1.010
CO = AR + CS + AS + MC	16.29	16.02	16.32	1.003	1.037
FA = AR + CS + MK + MC	16.27	16.15	16.12	1.019	1.003
OF = NO + AS + MC + VE	14.97	14.89	15.24	1.036	1.048
ST = GS + MK + MC + VE	16.22	16.12	16.07	1.019	1.006
Navy					
EL = GS + AR + MK + EI	29.31	28.68	28.92	1.027	1.017
E = GS + AR + 2MK	30.15	30.32	30.38	1.016	1.004
CL = NO + CS + VE	17.97	17.94	17.90	1.008	1.004
GT = AR + VE	14.84	14.79	14.45	1.053	1.047
ME = AS + MC + VE	21.48	21.44	21.62	1.013	1.017
EG = AS + MK	12.75	12.89	13.89	1.187*	1.161*
CT = AR + NO + CS + VE	24.67	24.57	24.28	1.033	1.024
HM = GS + MK + VE	21.26	21.26	21.02	1.023	1.023
ST = AR + MC + VE	22.37	22.13	21.66	1.067	1.044
MR = AR + AS + MC	22.84	22.56	22.81	1.002	1.023
BC = CS + MK + VE	18.72	18.69	18.64	1.009	1.005
Air Force					
M = GS + 2AS + MC	25.61	25.22	26.08	1.037	1.069
A = NO + CS + VE	24.41	24.32	24.16	1.021	1.013
G = AR + VE	25.03	24.85	24.58	1.038	1.022
E = GS + AR + MK + EI	24.43	23.97	24.43	1.000	1.038
Marine Corps					
MM = AR + AS + MC + EI	17.30	17.02	17.06	1.028	1.005
CL = CS + MK + VE	14.64	14.62	14.59	1.007	1.005
GT = AR + MC + VE	16.91	16.72	16.37	1.067	1.043
EL = GS + AR + MK + EI	16.59	16.23	16.37	1.026	1.017
AFQT = AR + MK + 2VE	23.78	23.79	23.87	1.008	1.006
All Services					
VE = PC + WK	7.44	7.42	7.21	1.065	1.060

*$p < .01$
Note: See key of abbreviations.

gall, 1989). That is, the results found here were consistent with those found in the SED study. Therefore it is unlikely that both sets of significant differences were due to Type I errors. Consequently, it is prudent to examine the consequence of not equating this composite, under the assumption that the observed differences are not subject to sampling errors. That is, suppose the observed differences in composite distributions were treated as true differences; what consequence would this difference have on flow rates?

The Navy training schools that select on EG all employ a cut-score of 96. An analysis of the proportion of applicants scoring at or above 96 on each of the CAT-ASVAB forms and 15C shows that $P(X \geq 96|01C) = .704$, $P(X \geq 96|02C) = .709$, and $P(X \geq 96|15C) = .668$. Consequently, if the observed sample differences were treated as true

Exhibit 19.1: Key Service and DoD Composite and Test Acronyms in Table 19-2

Service Composites					
Army	Navy	Air Force	Marine Corps	DoD	ASVAB Tests
GT = General Technical	EL = Electronics	M = Mechanical	MM = Mechanical Maintenance	AFQT = Armed Forces Qualification Test	AR = Arithmetic Reasoning
GM = General Maintenance	E = Basic Electricity and Electronics	A = Administrative	CL = Clerical		AS = Auto and Shop Information
EL = Electronics	CL = Clerical	G = General	GT = General Technical		CS = Coding Speed
CL = Clerical	GT = General Technical	E = Electronics	EL = Electronics Repair		EI = Electronics Information
MM = Mechanical Maintenance	ME = Mechanical				GS = General Science
SC = Surveillance/ Communications	EG = Engineering				MC = Mechanical Comprehension
CO = Combat	CT = Cryptologic Technician				MK = Mathematics Knowledge
FA = Field Artillery	HM = Hospitalman				NO = Numerical Operations
OF = Operations/Food	ST = Sonar Technician				PC = Paragraph Comprehension
ST = Skilled Technical	MR = Machinery Repairman				WK = Word Knowledge
	BC = Business & Clerical				

differences, then about 4 percent additional CAT-ASVAB applicants would qualify for schools using the Navy EG composite. This difference is relatively small.

Subgroup Comparisons

Although equipercentile equating matches CAT-ASVAB and P&P-ASVAB distributions for the total applicant sample, it does not necessarily guarantee a match for distributions of subgroups contained in the sample. This result follows from the fact that the two versions (CAT-ASVAB and P&P-ASVAB) are not parallel. Although we might expect small differences in subgroup performance across the two versions as a result of differences in measurement precision, a multitude of other factors could also cause group differences. It is therefore instructive to examine the performance of subgroups to determine whether any are placed at a substantial disadvantage by CAT-ASVAB. Two subgroups were examined in this analysis: (1) females and (2) blacks.

Test Comparisons

The equating transformation based on the total edited sample ($N = 10,379$) was applied to members of the two subgroups who had taken CAT-ASVAB. For each subgroup, the subgroup's performance on CAT-ASVAB was compared with its performance on the P&P-ASVAB. All 10 content areas were examined, as well as the VE and AFQT composites. For each test and composite, three sta-

tistics for assessing distributional differences were computed. The K-S test was used to identify overall differences; the F-ratio statistic was used to identify differences in variances; and the t-test was used to test mean differences. In instances where overall differences are found, the t-test can be used to identify which version (CAT-ASVAB or P&P-ASVAB) provides an advantage, on the average, to members of the specified subgroup.

Tables 19-3 and 19-4 provide the results of the significance tests for females and for blacks, respectively. Among the comparisons for females, two tests (PC and AS) displayed significant differences at the .01 alpha level. For both tests, P&P-ASVAB applicants possessed an advantage. Among the comparisons for blacks, two tests (AS and MK) displayed significant differences. For both tests, CAT-ASVAB applicants displayed a slight advantage.

Only two of 24 female and black comparisons show a significant disadvantage for CAT-ASVAB test-takers. Both involved female comparisons. One difference was for PC, and represents about one standard score unit, or about 1/10 of a standard deviation. Since PC is never used in a composite without WK, comparisons involving the VE composite are more relevant than PC alone. The VE composite comparisons were nonsignificant for females. The other difference was for AS and is discussed below.

Supplemental Auto/Shop Analyses

Among the subgroup differences, those found for females on AS are especially noteworthy. Females

Table 19-3 Female Differences Between P&P-ASVAB and CAT-ASVAB Versions in the SEV Study

Test	K-S Z Value	K-S p	F Ratio F Value	F Ratio p	t test t	t test p	t test $\bar{X}_{cat}$	t test $\bar{X}_{pp}$	Advantage
GS	.426	.993	1.10	.178	.11	.912	48.02	47.98	None
AR	.660	.777	1.03	.662	−1.15	.252	48.56	49.03	None
WK	.502	.963	1.03	.634	.39	.699	51.08	50.95	None
PC	1.776	.004	1.03	.720	−2.82	.005	51.37	52.35	P&P-ASVAB
NO	1.223	.100	1.00	.993	−2.22	.026	54.61	55.34	None
CS	1.082	.192	1.03	.706	−1.98	.047	55.71	56.44	None
AS	3.075	.001*	1.27	.001*	−7.23	.001*	42.05	44.37	P&P-ASVAB
MK	.724	.671	1.00	.958	.58	.560	52.29	52.05	None
MC	.718	.680	1.11	.124	−1.48	.140	45.34	45.89	None
EI	.967	.307	1.01	.832	−1.20	.231	44.75	45.19	None
VE	.548	.925	1.04	.611	−.56	.573	51.21	51.40	None
AFQT	.777	.582	1.05	.511	−.58	.563	50.99	51.62	None

*$p < .001$ CAT-ASVAB: $N = 1,184$;   P&P-ASVAB: $N = 620$

Table 19-4 Black Differences Between P&P-ASVAB and CAT-ASVAB Versions in the SEV Study

Test	K-S Z Value	K-S p	F Ratio F Value	F Ratio p	t test t	t test p	t test $\bar{X}_{cat}$	t test $\bar{X}_{pp}$	Advantage
GS	.790	.561	1.02	.769	−.88	.381	44.78	45.07	None
AR	.364	.999	1.00	.988	−.53	.599	45.22	45.38	None
WK	.762	.607	1.10	.114	−.16	.871	46.76	46.81	None
PC	.778	.580	1.08	.176	−1.05	.292	47.20	47.56	None
NO	.595	.870	1.07	.252	1.24	.217	52.21	51.79	None
CS	.671	.759	1.02	.719	.76	.450	51.30	51.05	None
AS	1.704	.006	1.22	.001	2.43	.015	45.00	44.27	CAT-ASVAB
MK	1.504	.022	1.08	.184	3.00	.003	49.71	48.69	CAT-ASVAB
MC	1.137	.151	1.03	.578	1.23	.217	44.98	44.59	None
EI	.973	.300	1.23	.001	1.36	.174	44.76	44.31	None
VE	.732	.657	1.05	.385	−.54	.590	46.78	46.95	None
AFQT	.834	.490	1.11	.081	.25	.803	38.73	38.52	None

CAT-ASVAB: $N = 1,649$; P&P-ASVAB: $N = 830$.

Table 19-5 Analysis of Covariance of Female Differences on the Auto/Shop Test (SED Study)

Group	N	Operational $\bar{X}$	Nonoperational Unadjusted $\bar{X}$	Nonoperational Adjusted $\bar{X}$
CAT-ASVAB	873	10.75	9.64[c]	9.66[c]
P&P-ASVAB	478	10.86	11.20[p]	11.15[p]

Note. c = Nonoperational CAT-ASVAB; p = Nonoperational P&P-ASVAB

traditionally score lower than males on AS, resulting in fewer opportunities for women in jobs requiring this knowledge. Lower scores for women on CAT-ASVAB AS have the potential for reducing still further the number of women qualifying for these traditionally male jobs. Although two differences were identified for black applicants across CAT and P&P versions, these differences are potentially beneficial to black applicants taking CAT. Black applicants taking CAT-ASVAB are likely to have higher qualification rates than blacks taking P&P-ASVAB (although this increase may be small).

Similar female differences on AS were obtained in the SED study (Segall, 1989), with females scoring about 2.7 standard score points higher on AS-P&P than on AS-CAT. Because of these noteworthy female differences on AS, supplemental analyses were performed on data collected during the SED study to investigate potential causes. The plausibility of four different causal factors were examined, including: Group equivalence, precision, dimensionality, and dimensionality/precision interaction.

Group equivalence. The group equivalence hypothesis asserts that females taking CAT-ASVAB

were less able on AS than females taking P&P-ASVAB, and that this difference contributed to the observed difference between CAT-ASVAB and P&P-ASVAB scores. Although applicants were randomly assigned to CAT and P&P versions, random assignment does not ensure equivalent groups; highly significant differences can occur by chance.

To test this hypothesis, an analysis of covariance was performed using data from the SED study. The dependent variable was the nonoperational score on AS; the independent variable was version (either CAT or P&P); the covariate was the operational AS score. The results are summarized in Table 19-5.

Although females taking CAT-ASVAB scored lower (on their operational AS test) than females taking P&P-ASVAB, this difference is very small, and does not account for the relatively large difference in nonoperational means on AS. This is apparent from the adjusted means presented in Table 19-5. It is unlikely that the difference in AS means was caused by unequal groups, especially since the finding was replicated in the SEV study.

Precision. This hypothesis states that the increased precision of CAT-ASVAB will magnify the difference between high and low scoring subgroups in comparison to P&P-ASVAB. The direction of the female performance on CAT-ASVAB AS was consistent with the precision hypothesis. However, the hypothesis does not correctly predict the direction of the difference for black applicants on AS; black applicants as a group scored lower on AS than white applicants. In accordance with the precision hypothesis, we would expect blacks to score significantly lower on CAT than on P&P, but just the reverse was true. Blacks scored significantly higher on AS-CAT than on AS-P&P. Although precision most likely contributes to the female differences, some additional factor must be invoked to account for black performance.

Dimensionality. This hypothesis asserts that the difference in female Auto/Shop performance between CAT-ASVAB and P&P-ASVAB is caused by a difference in the test's Verbal loading. This hypothesis is based on the following suppositions. First, AS-CAT has a lower verbal loading than AS-P&P (15C). Second, males and females have a large difference in mean AS knowledge, with males scoring higher. Third, males and females differ less in their verbal abilities than in their AS knowledge. If test performance is a composite of verbal and AS dimensions, then the test that gives the lowest relative weight to the verbal dimension will provide the lowest mean test performance for females. (In reasoning through this argument, it is helpful to remember that the equating forces the means and variances on the combined "male + female" group to be equivalent across the CAT and P&P versions.)

To investigate this hypothesis, the relation between the test's reading grade level (RGL) and mean female performance was examined. Here we are assuming that the RGL for an AS test is an indicator of the magnitude of its verbal loading. In addition to the P&P reference form (15C), three other P&P-ASVAB forms were included in this analysis: 15, 16, and 17. After these forms were equated on the combined male+female sample, significant differences in mean female performance were identified (Monzon, Shamieh, & Segall, 1990). For each of the four P&P-ASVAB forms, the Flesch index was calculated, and mean female performance was computed from a sample of applicants tested during the IOT&E of these forms (Table 19-6).

For the CAT-ASVAB, a complication arises when computing the RGL of an applicant's test: Because of the adaptive nature of the test, different applicants receive different questions, and consequently some degree of variation in RGL is likely among

Table 19-6 Reading Grade Level Analysis of ASVAB Versions of the Auto/Shop Test

ASVAB Version	Reading Grade Level (RGL)	Auto/Shop Mean (Females)
CAT	7.1	41.54
P&P-16	7.5	42.17
P&P-17	7.6	42.81
P&P-15	7.9	42.57
P&P-8A	8.5	43.36

applicants taking CAT-ASVAB. Furthermore, the RGL of individual items may be correlated with item difficulty, causing low-ability examinees to receive a lower "RGL" test than high-ability examinees. To address this issue, a separate RGL index was computed for female CAT-ASVAB examinees in the SED study. The exact item text was reconstructed from the examinee protocol, and then the RGL was computed from this item text. These two steps were repeated for examinees in the female sample, and an average RGL was calculated across the 407 female examinees. RGL and mean CAT-ASVAB AS performance are shown in Table 19-6.

There is a nearly perfect rank ordering between mean female performance and RGL. These results are consistent with the hypothesis that the difference in female Auto/Shop performance between CAT-ASVAB and P&P-ASVAB is (at least partially) due to differences in their verbal loadings.

Dimensionality/precision interaction. Although the RGL analysis supports the role of dimensionality in explaining differences in female performance across CAT and P&P versions, several questions remain. First, does dimensionality account for the entire difference in female Auto/Shop means across CAT- and P&P-ASVAB? Second, what role does precision play in accounting for female differences? Third, does dimensionality also account for the difference in the performance of blacks across CAT- and P&P-ASVAB?

To address these issues, a confirmatory factor analysis was performed using data collected in the SED study. This analysis modeled observed means as well as observed covariances among selected tests. The objective was to describe the differences in subgroup performance on AS as a function of (1) the Verbal and AS loadings, (2) precision, and (3) the mean latent ability of each subgroup. For this analysis, eight subgroups were defined by crossing ASVAB version with gender and race (Table 19-7).

The observed means and covariances for two tests were included in the analysis: Auto/Shop (AS) and Paragraph Comprehension (PC). The

Table 19-7 Subgroup Sample Sizes for Structural Equations Model

Group	Version	Gender	Race	N
1	P&P	M	White	1,521
2	P&P	M	Black	534
3	P&P	F	White	311
4	P&P	F	Black	179
5	CAT	M	White	2,981
6	CAT	M	Black	1,128
7	CAT	F	White	546
8	CAT	F	Black	345

Table 19-8 Structural Model Parameter Definitions

Group	Means $E(\xi_{re})$	$E(\xi_{as})$	$Cov(\xi_i, \xi_j)$
White Male	κ_1	κ_2	Φ_1
Black Male	κ_3	κ_4	Φ_2
White Female	κ_5	κ_6	Φ_3
Black Female	κ_7	κ_8	Φ_4

structural relations between x (the observed number-right score) and two latent variables τ_{re} (latent reading proficiency) and τ_{as} (latent AS knowledge) are given by the equations

P&P-ASVAB:

$$x_{pc} = \nu_1 + \lambda_1\tau_{re} + \delta_1, \qquad (19\text{-}10)$$

$$x_{as} = \nu_2 + \lambda_2\tau_{re} + \lambda_3\tau_{as} + \delta_2, \quad (19\text{-}11)$$

CAT-ASVAB:

$$x_{pc} = \nu_3 + \lambda_4\tau_{re} + \delta_3, \qquad (19\text{-}12)$$

$$x_{as} = \nu_4 + \lambda_5\tau_{re} + \lambda_6\tau_{as} + \delta_4. \quad (19\text{-}13)$$

Note that the slopes λ's and intercepts ν's are allowed to vary across CAT and P&P versions for corresponding tests. The covariance matrix of measurement errors for P&P is parameterized by a 2×2 matrix $\Theta_1 = E(\delta\delta')$, where $\delta' = [\delta_1, \delta_2]$. Similarly for CAT, the variance-covariance matrix of measurement errors is denoted by $\Theta_2 = E(\delta\delta')$, where $\delta' = [\delta_3, \delta_4]$. Table 19-8 provides additional model parameters which include the latent means and covariances among the reading and AS dimensions for each of the four groups defined by race and gender.

Particular constraints were placed on model parameters across the eight groups defined by version, race, and gender. First, the slopes λ's and intercepts ν's depend only on version and are not influenced by subgroup. Second, means κ's and covariances Φ's of the latent variables vary only according to subgroup (defined by race and gender), and are not dependent on version. Finally, variances of measurement errors Θ depend only on version, and are not dependent on subgroup. These constraints can be summarized by the following equations

P&P-ASVAB:

White Males: Ω_1
$$= f(\nu_1, \nu_2, \lambda_1, \lambda_2, \lambda_3, \Theta_1; \kappa_1, \kappa_2, \Phi_1) \quad (19\text{-}14)$$

Black Males: Ω_2
$$= f(\nu_1, \nu_2, \lambda_1, \lambda_2, \lambda_3, \Theta_1; \kappa_3, \kappa_4, \Phi_2) \quad (19\text{-}15)$$

White Females: Ω_3
$$= f(\nu_1, \nu_2, \lambda_1, \lambda_2, \lambda_3, \Theta_1; \kappa_5, \kappa_6, \Phi_3) \quad (19\text{-}16)$$

Black Females: Ω_4
$$= f(\nu_1, \nu_2, \lambda_1, \lambda_2, \lambda_3, \Theta_1; \kappa_7, \kappa_8, \Phi_4) \quad (19\text{-}17)$$

CAT-ASVAB:

White Males: Ω_5
$$= f(\nu_3, \nu_4, \lambda_4, \lambda_5, \lambda_6, \Theta_2; \kappa_1, \kappa_2, \Phi_1) \quad (19\text{-}18)$$

Black Males: Ω_6
$$= f(\nu_3, \nu_4, \lambda_4, \lambda_5, \lambda_6, \Theta_2; \kappa_3, \kappa_4, \Phi_2) \quad (19\text{-}19)$$

White Females: Ω_7
$$= f(\nu_3, \nu_4, \lambda_4, \lambda_5, \lambda_6, \Theta_2; \kappa_5, \kappa_6, \Phi_3) \quad (19\text{-}20)$$

Black Females: Ω_8
$$= f(\nu_3, \nu_4, \lambda_4, \lambda_5, \lambda_6, \Theta_2; \kappa_7, \kappa_8, \Phi_4) \quad (19\text{-}21)$$

where Ω_k is the model implied moment matrix for group k. The parameters contained in the function $f(\ )$ illustrate the dependence of each of the eight moment matrices on the model parameters defined above.

Maximum likelihood estimates of the model parameters were obtained using LISREL VI (Jöreskog & Sörbom, 1984). To identify the model, several additional constraints were necessary. These constraints fixed the origin and unit for the two latent variables. First $\kappa_1 = \kappa_2 = 0$ (latent means for white males). Second, the diagonal elements of Φ_1 were set equal to 1 (i.e., the latent variances for white males were fixed at one). And third, the variances of measurement errors were fixed at values calculated from the alternate forms reliability study (Chapter 17):

$$\Theta_1 = \begin{pmatrix} 3.686 & 0 \\ 0 & 5.372 \end{pmatrix}, \qquad (19\text{-}22)$$

and

$$\Theta_2 = \begin{pmatrix} 3.904 & 0 \\ 0 & 2.396 \end{pmatrix} \qquad (19\text{-}23)$$

The overall fit of the model implied moment matrices to the observed moment matrices is provided by two fit statistics: $\chi^2 = 47.07$, ($df = 14$), and $GFI = .996$. In general, these values indicate a relatively good fit. Parameter estimates for each equation are

P&P Estimates:

$$x_{pc} = 11.673 + 1.885\xi_{re} + \delta_1 \quad (19\text{-}24)$$

$$x_{as} = 16.512 + 4.547\xi_{re} + 3.197\xi_{as} + \delta_2 \quad (19\text{-}25)$$

CAT Estimates:

$$x_{pc} = 11.658 + 1.847\xi_{re} + \delta_3 \quad (19\text{-}26)$$

$$x_{as} = 16.734 + 4.378\xi_{re} + 4.170\xi_{as} + \delta_4. \quad (19\text{-}27)$$

Notice that as predicted, the loading for x_{as} on the reading dimension is higher for P&P than for CAT (4.547 vs. 4.378). Also notice that x_{as} has a different loading on the latent Auto/Shop dimension across CAT and P&P versions, 4.170 (for CAT) vs. 3.197 (for P&P). This last result is most likely due to CAT's greater precision. The estimated latent means κ's for each subgroup on each dimension are provided in Table 19-9. The estimated means κ's, slopes λ's and intercepts ν's can be used to specify model implied means for the observed indicator variable x_{as}. For each subgroup, two means can be computed, one for CAT and another for P&P:

P&P-ASVAB

$$\mu_{as}^k = \nu_2 + \lambda_2\kappa_{re}^k + \lambda_3\kappa_{as}^k, \quad (19\text{-}28)$$

CAT-ASVAB

$$\mu_{as}^k = \nu_4 + \lambda_5\kappa_{re}^k + \lambda_6\kappa_{as}^k, \quad (19\text{-}29)$$

(for $k \in \{\text{WM, BM, WF, BF}\}$). A comparison of the model implied means with the observed means across subgroups and versions provides an indication of how well the model predicts differential subgroup performance. Substituting the estimated parameters into the above equations provides us with the results displayed in Table 19-10. The last column lists the difference between the observed and model-implied means shown in the first two columns. The observed differences in subgroup performance can be accurately described by the structural model. That is, differences in mean per-

Table 19-9 Latent Subgroup Means

Subgroup	Means (κ)	
	$\mathrm{E}(\xi_{re})$	$\mathrm{E}(\xi_{as})$
White Males	(0)	(0)
Black Males	−1.106	.104
White Females	.137	−1.558
Black Females	−.691	−1.392

Note. ( ) indicates fixed value

Table 19-10 Observed and Implied Auto/Shop Means

Subgroup	Observed	Implied	Diff.
	P&P ASVAB		
White Males	16.660	16.512	.148
Black Males	11.307	11.816	−.509
White Females	12.334	12.150	.184
Black Females	9.016	8.920	.096
	CAT-ASVAB		
White Males	16.667	16.734	−.067
Black Males	12.516	12.326	.190
White Females	10.752	10.834	−.082
Black Females	7.864	7.907	−.043

formance across CAT and P&P versions are consistent with the model predictions, which describe a subgroup's performance as a function of: (1) the Verbal and AS loadings, (2) precision, and (3) the mean subgroup latent ability.

Impact assessment. According to the Dimensionality/Precision Model, AS-CAT provides a measure of AS knowledge that is slightly less contaminated by reading proficiency than AS-P&P. From the standpoint of increased classification efficiency and possibly validity, this makes the use of CAT-ASVAB more desirable. However, one of the goals of the equating was to achieve, to the extent possible, an equating that places no subgroup at a substantial disadvantage. Since during an extended implementation phase, both CAT-ASVAB and P&P-ASVAB will be administered operationally, it is desirable for applicants of various subgroups to be indifferent about which of the two versions they receive. If women score lower on the average on AS-CAT, then they might prefer the P&P-ASVAB.

The general question of impact arose during a consideration of the SEV phase, in which a planned sample of 7,500 applicants was to take an operational version of CAT or P&P. Data for addressing the impact on Navy school-qualification rates were available. The specific question was: Among the 7,500 military applicants to be tested during SEV, how many female Navy recruits would be expected to fail their assigned rating entry requirements as a consequence of lower AS performance on CAT-ASVAB?

Data addressing this question came from three sources. The first source was data collected during the SED equating study. From this sample of about 8,000 applicants, a series of conditional probabilities were computed. The series produced the top portion of the probability tree displayed in Figure 19-7. Examinees in each box in the left column were repeatedly divided into exclusive non-

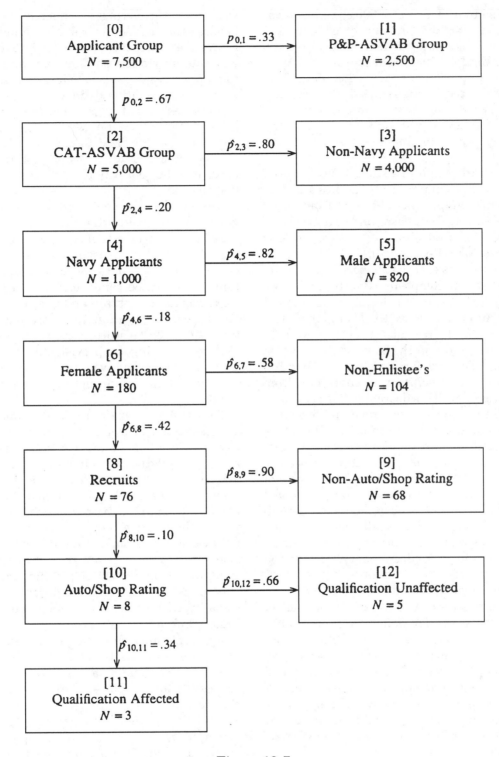

Figure 19-7
Estimated Auto/Shop Effect

overlapping subgroups. First, the applicant group [Box 0] was divided into those taking CAT [Box 2] and those taking P&P [Box 1]. The applicants taking CAT [Box 2] were divided into Navy applicants [Box 4] and non-Navy applicants [Box 3]. The Navy applicants [Box 4] were divided into female applicants [Box 6] and male applicants [Box 5]. The numbers in each successive group were tallied and used to compute the conditional probabilities reported in Figure 19-7.

A second sample of about 27,500 examinees was used to determine the probability of a female-Navy-applicant becoming a female-Navy-recruit. These data were obtained from the Defense Manpower Data Center using accession data from FY89. As indicated in Figure 19-7, female Navy applicants [Box 6] were divided into recruits [Box 8] and nonenlistees [Box 7], and the resulting frequencies were used to compute the conditional probabilities.

Finally, a third sample of about 10,500 was used to determine the remaining probabilities in Figure 19-7. This sample was obtained from PRIDE (a Navy Recruiting Database) and was based on recruits accessed from June 1989 through May 1990. Female-Navy-Recruits in [Box 8] were divided into those who entered a job that used Auto/Shop in its selector composite [Box 10] and those entering a job that used a selector composite not containing Auto/Shop [Box 9]. Using the same sample of 10,500, the recruits in [Box 10] were divided into two groups on the basis of qualification status change. For each female recruit in [Box 10], three standard score points were subtracted from her composite score. This decrement was based on the mean difference between female performance on CAT-ASVAB and P&P-ASVAB in the SED study—about 2.7 standard score points. The reduced composite score was then compared to the cut-score used for the school she had entered. The number of women having their qualification status changed from qualified (before the decrement) to unqualified (after the decrement) was tallied and included in [Box 11]. The women not having their qualification status altered by the decrement were included in [Box 12].

The conditional probabilities obtained from these frequencies were used to estimate the effect of lower AS-CAT scores for women on their qualification status: Among the 7,500 military applicants to be tested during SEV, three female Navy recruits would be expected to fail their assigned rating entry requirements as a consequence of lower AS performance on CAT-ASVAB. This analysis suggests that the impact on qualification rates is very small, both for SEV and for an extended OT&E of CAT-ASVAB.

Summary

The present study addresses three major concerns about equating CAT-ASVAB and P&P-ASVAB versions. First the use of an equipercentile procedure ensures that the transformation applied to CAT-ASVAB scores preserves flow rates into the military, and into various occupational specialties. Smoothing procedures were used to increase the precision of the transformation estimates. Although equating was performed at the test level, the equivalence of CAT-ASVAB and P&P-ASVAB composite distributions was verified to ensure that the use of CAT-ASVAB would not disrupt flow rates dependent on the equivalence of these composite distributions.

Second, the equating study was conducted in two phases to ensure that the transformation was based on operationally motivated applicants. The first phase, SED, was used to obtain a preliminary equating based on data collected under nonoperationally motivated conditions. The second phase, SEV, was used to obtain an equating transformation based on operationally motivated examinees (whose CAT-ASVAB scores were transformed to the P&P metric using the provisional SED equating). This latter equating was used in the OT&E phase to collect data on concepts of operation (Chapter 20).

The third issue examined by the equating study addressed the concern that subgroup members taking CAT-ASVAB should not be placed at a disadvantage relative to their subgroup counterparts taking the P&P-ASVAB. Results indicate that although it is desirable for exchangeability considerations to match distributions for subgroups as well as the entire group, this may not be possible for a variety of reasons. First, differences in precision between the CAT-ASVAB and P&P-ASVAB versions may magnify existing differences between subgroups. Second, small differences in dimensionality, such as the verbal loading of a test, may cause differential subgroup performance. Although some subgroup differences observed in CAT-ASVAB are statistically significant, their practical significance on qualification rates is small. Once CAT-ASVAB fully replaces the P&P-ASVAB, the exchangeability issue will become less important. The small differences in subgroup performance displayed by CAT-ASVAB may be a positive consequence of greater precision and lower verbal contamination. Ultimately, in large-scale administrations of CAT-ASVAB, we may observe higher classification efficiency and greater predictive validity than is currently displayed by its P&P counterpart.

CAT-ASVAB Operational Test and Evaluation

Kathleen E. Moreno

By Spring of 1990, the technical development and evaluation of CAT-ASVAB were nearing completion. Empirical studies had shown that CAT-ASVAB tests measured the same abilities as their P&P-ASVAB counterparts, and were as reliable, and in many cases, more reliable. The Score Equating Development study (SED) eliminated concerns about equating CAT to P&P. The one psychometric study remaining to be conducted was the Score Equating Verification (SEV), which would provide final equating tables for the Accelerated CAT-ASVAB Project (ACAP) system. By 1990, therefore, CAT-ASVAB was psychometrically ready for nationwide implementation. Psychometric readiness, however, was not the only factor influencing a decision on nationwide implementation of CAT-ASVAB. There were two other very important factors to consider: (1) the cost effectiveness of nationwide implementation, and (2) the impact on operational procedures of implementing computer-based testing.

A 1988 cost/benefit analysis had shown that the cost effectiveness of CAT-ASVAB was questionable. (See Chapter 23 for details.) This study, however, was limited in that it considered using CAT in very much the same way as the P&P-ASVAB was being used. The study neglected to take into account the flexible nature of CAT, and placed CAT-ASVAB in the 1980s' group-paced, lock-step processing environment of the MEPSs/METSs. In addition, there had never been an opportunity to collect empirical data on how CAT would perform in an operational environment. While SED had been conducted in the MEPSs/METSs environment, it was a nonoperational research study that required administration of CAT-ASVAB and P&P-ASVAB to equivalent groups, and therefore, required the typical lock-step processing. SEV, while operational, still required the group-administered, lock-step processing.

During the 1989–90 time frame, there was little Service policymaker support for nationwide implementation of CAT-ASVAB. This could be contributed in part to the negative findings of the 1988 cost–benefit analysis. In fact, most people in the Joint-Service ASVAB arena felt that the program should be stopped until results from the Enhanced Computer Administered Test (ECAT) study (Chapter 24) were available. During the 1990–91 time frame, however, several events occurred that put CAT-ASVAB back on track. First and foremost, Captain James Kinney became Director of the Recruiting and Retention Programs Department, the Navy office that managed the CAT-ASVAB program. Coming from a recruiting background, Captain Kinney immediately saw the potential benefits of CAT-ASVAB. He tasked NPRDC with developing a plan for limited implementation of CAT, and convinced those in his chain of command to support the idea. Second, several of the higher level managers in various recruiting commands visited SEV

Many people played important roles in the CAT-ASVAB Operational Test and Evaluation, including all NPRDC researchers assigned to the CAT-ASVAB program, numerous personnel at the CAT-ASVAB MEPSs, and various USMEPCOM and DMDC personnel. This was truly a joint effort, and credit for the success of this effort should be shared by all organizations and individuals involved. Special thanks go to Captain James Kinney and Dr. Clessen Martin for providing the leadership and policy support necessary to make OT&E a reality.

sites and saw CAT-ASVAB in operation. As did Captain Kinney, they also saw the potential benefits of CAT-ASVAB and became strong supporters of the program. Third, DMDC, as lead agency for ASVAB, was tasked to look at CAT-ASVAB concepts of operation and to conduct a new cost–benefit analysis. Empirical data on an operational CAT-ASVAB system would provide valuable information in conducting their analyses. DMDC, therefore, supported limited implementation of CAT-ASVAB as a means of collecting the necessary data. These combined events led to development of a plan for the CAT-ASVAB Operational Test and Evaluation (OT&E) and to approval of this plan.

Operational Test and Evaluation Issues

Since data from the OT&E would be used in helping to define CAT-ASVAB concepts of operation and in conducting a new cost–benefit analysis, careful consideration was given to the issues that needed to be addressed. The goal was to collect the most valuable information possible while minimizing the impact on the MEPSs' mission of processing applicants. Following is a list of the questions asked:

• *Flexible-start.* Since all test instructions are automated, CAT-ASVAB allows for a "flexible-start," where examinees start the test at different times. This "flexible start" procedure gives applicants and recruiters more flexibility compared to the conventional group-administered testing procedure, but how does it affect other applicant processing operations, such as applicant check-in and medical examination?

• *Processing of test scores.* Since scores are automatically computed, does CAT-ASVAB save a substantial amount of score processing time? Are procedures for electronically transmitting scores to the main processing computer easy to use and reliable?

• *Equipment needs.* How much equipment is needed at each site and how are equipment needs affected by the "flexible-start" procedure?

• *TA training and performance.* How much time should be allowed for test administrator (TA) training and how does the amount of training impact TA performance?

• *User acceptance.* What are the reactions of applicants, recruiters, and MEPS personnel to CAT-ASVAB? Do the flexibility and shorter test times provided by CAT-ASVAB make it easier to schedule applicants for testing, save recruiter and MEPS personnel time, and reduce travel costs?

• *Security issues.* Is the system secure? Extended operational data collection allows the assessment of procedures for identifying potential security problems. It also allows the evaluation of the effectiveness of item exposure control.

• *Administration of experimental tests.* Can experimental tests be easily added to the end of the battery? Since CAT-ASVAB takes less time than the P&P-ASVAB, the Services might be able to add experimental tests to the end of CAT-ASVAB, allowing for pilot testing and data collection to evaluate adverse impact.

• *System performance.* Does the system meet all operational requirements? Is the software easy to use? How does the hardware perform?

Approach

The general approach was to implement CAT-ASVAB at a small number of operational sites, provide some specific guidelines for its use, such as flexible start times, and see what happens. Prior to implementation at a site, program managers met with the MEPS personnel in the selected area to prepare them for this new way of testing. Data collection for this effort began in June 1992, and for the purposes of this study, ended in February 1993. The CAT-ASVAB OT&E system, however, remained in operational use until 1996, when it was replaced by the "next generation" CAT-ASVAB system.

Test Sites

The military uses two types of sites to administer the ASVAB: Military Entrance Processing Stations (MEPSs) and Mobile Examining Team Sites (METSs). MEPSs are stationary sites where all processing, including aptitude testing and medical examinations, is conducted. There are approximately 65 MEPSs nationwide. At the MEPSs, military personnel administer the ASVAB and conduct test sessions four or five days a week. METSs are usually temporary sites that offer only ASVAB testing. There are approximately 600 METSs nationwide. If an applicant passes the test at a METS, he or she must go to the associated MEPS for all other processing. Office of Personnel Management personnel usually administer the ASVAB at a METS and testing schedules vary widely, from four sessions a week to one session a month.

Four MEPSs were selected as CAT-ASVAB OT&E sites: San Diego; Jackson, MS; Baltimore; and Denver. These MEPSs were selected based on location and number of applicants tested. In addition, one METS was selected: Washington, DC. This METS operates under the Baltimore MEPS. It was selected based on the suitability of the facilities for computer-administration, and the number of weekly test sessions. At all the OT&E sites, CAT-ASVAB was administered to all military applicants. The CAT-ASVAB test scores served as the scores of record for these applicants.

A fifth MEPS was added as the study got underway—Los Angeles MEPS. In May 1992, the Los Angeles MEPS was partially burned during the Los Angeles riots. The MEPS was forced to move to temporary quarters, and lost the capability to score P&P-ASVAB and to provide medical processing. Applicants in the Los Angeles area were bused to San Diego for this part of the processing. USMEPCOM, concerned that San Diego would be processing over twice their normal load and implementing a new system at the same time, asked the San Diego MEPS managers if they wanted to delay implementation of CAT-ASVAB. San Diego, however, was anxious to begin the implementation, as the MEPS personnel in San Diego viewed CAT-ASVAB as a means to help with their overload. In fact, after the system had been in operational use in San Diego for a few weeks, the San Diego MEPS Testing Officer proposed setting up CAT-ASVAB testing at the temporary Los Angeles site as well. This way, applicants could be tested near home, and bused to San Diego for medical processing only if they qualified on the aptitude battery. This approach would save a substantial amount of time and money. In full support of this request, the Navy, as lead Service, sought and received approval to use CAT-ASVAB operationally in Los Angeles on a temporary basis only. CAT-ASVAB was such a benefit to the MEPS, the Commander asked to have Los Angeles included permanently in the OT&E. The Navy, agreeing to pay all costs associated with the addition of this site, sought and received approval from the Manpower Accession Policy Steering Committee (MAP) to continue the OT&E in Los Angeles.

To allow for comparisons between CAT-ASVAB and P&P-ASVAB, five control MEPSs, administering P&P-ASVAB, were selected: Philadelphia, New Orleans, Portland, San Antonio, and Fresno. Several factors were considered in selecting the control sites, including: (1) size/throughput, as indicated by the number of examinees tested; (2) demographic characteristics of the examinees, including score levels on the AFQT, percent completing high school, and gender and race distributions; and (3) geographic size of the region served, as indicated by percent tested in the central MEPS and the number and size of the METSs associated with each MEPS. Statistics from a 13 month period (Oct. 91 through Oct. 92) were used in selecting the control MEPSs.

Data Collection Procedures

Data were collected using several instruments: CAT-ASVAB; administration of questionnaires to recruiters, applicants, and MEPS personnel; on-site observation; and interviews.

CAT-ASVAB. In the natural course of administering CAT-ASVAB, data on all interactions between the applicant and the computer system are saved. This includes item response data, item response latencies, test times, instruction times, number and type of help calls, and failure/recovery information (if a computer failure occurs). Any unusual events, such as an applicant leaving during testing, are also documented by the TAs.

On-site observations. During the first month of testing at each site, NPRDC researchers were on-site to observe test administration. After this first month, periodic visits were made to each site. Based on these observations, the reactions of TAs, recruiters, and applicants to CAT-ASVAB were documented.

Interviews. Researchers who were conducting on-site observations also conducted informal, unstructured interviews with MEPS personnel and recruiters. In addition, informal interviews were conducted periodically over the phone.

Questionnaires. Two separate questionnaires were developed, one for recruiters and one for applicants. Recruiter questionnaires contained 25 questions, with the majority of the questions focusing on meeting testing goals, factors affecting amount of travel, flexibility of scheduling applicants for testing, and effects of immediate scores. Recruiter questionnaires administered at CAT-ASVAB sites contained an additional seven questions about their reactions to CAT-ASVAB. Recruiter questionnaires were administered several months after the start of the OT&E to give recruiters using the OT&E sites a chance to evaluate CAT-ASVAB.

Table 20-1 Questionnaire Sample Sizes

	Number of Persons		
	OT&E Sites	Control Sites	Total
Recruiter Questionnaires	167	175	342
Applicant Questionnaires	1,550	1,497	3,047

Applicant questionnaires contained 23 questions designed to measure examinees' general reactions to the test battery, focusing on test length, difficulty, fairness, clarity of instructions, and feelings of fatigue and anxiety. Applicant questionnaires were administered for one to two months following the start of the OT&E. Table 20-1 shows the sample sizes.

Results

Flexible-Start Assessment

At the start of the OT&E, all of the CAT-ASVAB MEPSs used a flexible-start option. Each MEPS set an arrival window during which applicants could come in and start the test. For example, at the San Diego MEPS, applicants could arrive and begin the test anytime between the hours of 4:00 p.m. and 6:00 p.m. Recruiters and applicants found that flexible start reduced scheduling problems. MEPS personnel were initially concerned about the flexible start option because it was so different from the fixed start time for group administration. They found, however, that the procedure worked well. The one disadvantage of using flexible start was that it required two MEPS personnel to be available during the arrival window, one to check applicants in and one to administer the test.

As the OT&E continued, MEPSs that tested in the afternoon or evenings continued to use flexible start. The MEPSs, however, discovered that CAT-ASVAB made the concept of one-day processing very feasible. Some of the MEPSs began conducting early morning sessions so that the applicant could complete processing the same day. In these early morning sessions, the MEPSs tended to minimize flexible start, keeping the arrival window very short so that all applicants would be finished early enough to complete other processing.

Processing of Test Scores

CAT-ASVAB does save TAs a substantial amount of time in processing test scores. When adminis-

tering the P&P-ASVAB, all answer sheets must be scanned, which is tedious and time-consuming. At the MEPSs, CAT-ASVAB scores were transferred to the main computer by carrying a disk from the testing room to another room, where the data were uploaded in a matter of minutes. Data transfer procedures were very reliable. In the "next generation" system, this process was further simplified by the use of a computer network. Scores are transferred from the testing network to the main computer at the touch of a key.

At the Washington, DC METS, scores were telecommunicated to the main computer at the Baltimore MEPS. This procedure proved to be less reliable than desired, due to the use of obsolete hardware and software. With the OT&E system, Washington METS personnel had to coordinate the exact time of the transfer with Baltimore MEPS personnel to ensure that the computer receiving the data was in the "host," or receiving, mode. To complicate the situation, host mode had a timeout feature that automatically took the computer out of this mode after a certain number of minutes. If all data transfer steps were not followed in the exact order at both ends, the transfer failed. This problem, however, will disappear once CAT-ASVAB is transitioned to a new system for METSs use, and an updated data communications program can be used.

Equipment Needs

Each of the CAT-ASVAB OT&E sites, with the exception of the Los Angeles MEPS, had enough equipment to test maximum session sizes for that MEPS. However, the use of flexible start and the shorter testing time of the CAT-ASVAB battery reduce equipment requirements. It is estimated that, on the average, a MEPS requires half as many computers as examinees in a maximum session. For example, Los Angeles, one of the largest MEPSs in the country, had 30 computers during the OT&E, with the capability of testing 60 applicants in the same amount of time as a typical P&P-ASVAB test session. In fact, Los Angeles has tested larger numbers than this in an evening session. Equipment needs are less than projected in earlier studies, reducing the cost of implementing CAT-ASVAB nationwide.

Test Administrator Training and Performance

The instruction program that was initially developed to train CAT-ASVAB TAs took about four days of classroom training. At the beginning of the OT&E, it became clear that MEPS personnel could not devote four days exclusively to CAT-ASVAB training. Therefore, for the OT&E effort, the training program was changed to include two days of classroom training and two days of on-the-job training (OJT). This revised training program for TAs has been successful, both at the MEPSs and METS.

During the classroom part of the training, TAs met all course objectives. The two days of OJT seemed adequate for training TAs to run the system under normal conditions. In addition, observation of performance on the job confirmed this conclusion.

While very few problems were encountered in training, one problem that was noted is that due to the high turnover in TAs and scheduling difficulties, "group-administered" classroom training is not ideal. Therefore, a self-administered, computer-based training program using an intelligent tutoring system is being developed.

Another problem that was encountered was TA performance under unusual conditions. Occasionally, a site experienced some type of system failure and the TA did not know how to recover. While the system was designed to recover from all failures, and procedures for all types of failure/recovery were documented in the User's Manual, certain types of failures happened so infrequently that TAs needed assistance in the recovery. In these cases, TAs called NPRDC for guidance. This demonstrates the need for some type of "help line," particularly during nationwide use of the system.

Overall, CAT-ASVAB helped streamline test administration procedures, making it easier for TAs to perform their duties. They no longer needed to read instructions, time tests, or scan answer sheets. Automating these functions also resulted in standardization across all the testing sites.

User Acceptance

Recruiters' reactions. Based on interview results, recruiters' reactions were very positive overall. Recruiters were very enthusiastic about the shortened testing time and the immediate scores provided by CAT-ASVAB. Some recruiters felt that because of the standardized testing environment, CAT-ASVAB is a fairer test than the P&P-ASVAB. Some recruiters reported traveling a substantial extra distance so that their applicants could test on CAT-ASVAB rather than P&P-ASVAB. Recruiters, however, expressed some concerns about the differences between CAT-ASVAB and P&P-ASVAB. For example, some feared that CAT-ASVAB might be more difficult than the P&P-ASVAB because it is computer-administered. Other recruiters received reports from high ability examinees that the test was really difficult and, therefore, believed that their applicants would have a better chance qualifying with the P&P-ASVAB. It was also difficult for recruiters to understand how a test with 16 items could provide a number-correct score of 35. It was found that conducting sessions where recruiters could see a demonstration of CAT-ASVAB, learn how the test worked, and have the opportunity to ask questions would address these concerns. As a result of this finding, educational materials on the CAT-ASVAB system were developed prior to nationwide implementation, and were distributed to MEPSs and recruiting personnel.

Questionnaire results showed few differences between the reactions of recruiters from the OT&E sites and the control sites. At both types of sites, recruiters felt that the availability of immediate scores and a more flexible testing schedule would greatly increase their productivity. About 65 percent of the recruiters at CAT-ASVAB sites felt that CAT-ASVAB saved them 30 to 90 minutes of time per testing session. About 33 percent felt that applicants were more willing to take the ASVAB when it was CAT-ASVAB, while 11 percent felt it decreased the applicants' willingness. About 16 percent felt that taking CAT-ASVAB instead of the P&P-ASVAB increased the applicants' willingness to enlist, compared to five percent who felt it decreased it. About 25 percent of the recruiters were willing to travel at least 30 minutes more so that applicants could take CAT-ASVAB.

Applicants' reactions. In comparing questionnaire responses from the CAT-ASVAB examinees to the responses from the P&P-ASVAB examinees, the two groups were significantly different on most questions. These differences were small, with both groups giving positive responses about the ASVAB. P&P-ASVAB examinees were slightly more positive than CAT-ASVAB examinees on the following issues: General feelings about the test, feelings of anxiety, test difficulty, and amount of eye strain. CAT-ASVAB examinees were slightly more positive than P&P-ASVAB examinees on the following: General fatigue, test fairness, test length, time pressures during the test, clarity of instructions, convenience of testing schedule, test enjoyability, and the interest level of the test. There were no significant differences between the two groups on distractions from the surrounding environment.

Some of the significant differences in reactions to the tests could be attributed to the adaptive nature of CAT-ASVAB. For example, high ability examinees are administered more difficult test items than they would typically take on a P&P-ASVAB. This may cause them to be more fatigued at the end of the test and to perceive the test as being very difficult, possibly increasing their anxiety level. On the other hand, because CAT-ASVAB is an adaptive test, and therefore, much shorter than the P&P test, examinees were more positive about test length.

Some of the differences in reactions to the test, however, could be attributed to the medium of administration: computer versus paper-and-pencil. Taking the test on the computer causes eye strain slightly more often, but is perceived as more enjoyable, more interesting, and having less time pressure. Computer administration also offers flexibility in the testing schedule; examinees are not required to start the test as a group.

Since CAT-ASVAB was administered with a flexible test start time, the finding of no significant difference in terms of environmental distractions was positive. Initially, there was some concern that examinees coming and going during a CAT-ASVAB test session would disturb examinees taking the test. Questionnaire results and on-site observations alleviated this concern. Once the examinee started the test, the focus was on the test, not the surrounding environment. Overall, examinees' reactions to CAT-ASVAB were very positive. In general, we found that most examinees preferred taking CAT-ASVAB to the P&P-ASVAB.

Reactions of MEPS personnel. Based on interviews and on-site observations, the reactions of MEPS personnel have been overwhelmingly enthusiastic. Initial skepticism on the part of the MEPS commanders at the OT&E sites soon gave way to "couldn't live without it" attitudes. TAs also had a very positive reaction to CAT-ASVAB, preferring it to administering the P&P-ASVAB. TAs felt that CAT-ASVAB allowed them to make much more efficient use of their time. These positive reactions are the reason that the CAT-ASVAB system remained in op-

erational use at the OT&E MEPSs, even after data collection for purposes of the OT&E had ended.

Test Security

CAT-ASVAB test items reside on several floppy disks that are never accessible to applicants. In addition, test item files are encrypted. During test administration, the items are loaded into volatile computer memory, disappearing when the computer is turned off. Test compromise from theft of items is much less likely with CAT-ASVAB than P&P-ASVAB. Another security issue does exist, however, and that is security of the computer equipment. MEPSs are very secure, making computer theft unlikely. During the OT&E, no computer equipment was stolen from a MEPS or METS. This may become more of a problem, however, if future use of CAT-ASVAB includes the use of portable notebook computers in the METSs.

Administration of Experimental Tests

To date one experimental test has been added to the CAT-ASVAB, Assembling Objects (AO), a spatial test. From an implementation standpoint, the addition of this test was "painless." Since it is computer administered, no booklets had to be printed or answer sheets modified. An additional software module was simply added to the CAT-ASVAB test administration software. In addition, since CAT-ASVAB takes so much less time than the P&P-ASVAB, there were few complaints about the small amount of additional testing time needed to administer the AO test.

System Performance

The OT&E has shown that the CAT-ASVAB system meets all ASVAB testing requirements, and that the software is fairly easy to use. It has also helped to identify procedures that could be automated and incorporated into the system to streamline ASVAB testing (e.g., the automatic generation of forms typically completed by hand). In addition, it has helped to identify CAT-ASVAB procedures that are unnecessary or too time-consuming. Some of the general findings are:

• Random assignment of examinees to machines is not necessary. This procedure requires entering names and social security numbers at the TA station before testing can start, therefore delaying the start of testing. The purpose of this procedure was to ensure that, when session sizes were smaller than the number of computers in the room, the same machines were not used over and over. It is much more efficient, however, to tell the TAs to space the examinees out. Elimination of this procedure will prevent accidently seating the examinee at a computer designated for another examinee.

• The stand-alone mode of operation takes too long and requires the handling of too many disks. This procedure could not be changed for the HP Integral Personal Computer-based system (HP-IPC), as the system has no hard disk drive and the floppy drive will not read high density disks. In the "next generation" system, however, stand-alone mode has been streamlined as much as possible.

• The interactive screen dialogues need to be less wordy. If the screens are too wordy, the TAs tend not to read them.

• Procedures in general need to be streamlined. There are too many cases where the TA must remember that a certain procedure must be completed before another, or at a certain point in the session. While, during the course of the OT&E, procedures have been streamlined and automated, due to limitations of the HP-IPC based system and the network for this system, certain desirable changes could not be made. These types of changes, however, have been incorporated into the design of the "next generation" system.

The hardware performed very well during the course of the OT&E. The HP-IPCs that were used in this evaluation were purchased in the 1985 to 1987 time frame. They were used at the OT&E sites until the end of 1996. By current computer standards, they were, therefore, fairly old. Yet, hardware problems were minimal. The majority of the hardware problems were with the floppy drives and the memory boards. All other computer components performed well above expectation. During the OT&E, non-functioning equipment was shipped to NPRDC for repair, and repairs were performed by NPRDC staff. Since these machines were obsolete, the most challenging part of repairing the equipment was to purchase needed parts within a reasonable time frame. Another challenge was to keep track of equipment inventory, since there was a lot of movement of equipment between MEPSs and NPRDC. For nationwide implementation, the simplest approach to equipment maintenance is to have an on-site maintenance contract. This approach, however, must be evaluated for cost-effectiveness.

Summary

The OT&E marked the turning point in the CAT-ASVAB program, and is the program's biggest achievement. This is true from both a manager's and researcher's perspective. From a manager's perspective, the OT&E demonstrated that CAT-ASVAB meets the needs of recruiters, applicants, MEPS personnel, and USMEPCOM Headquarters. It led to the enthusiastic support of CAT-ASVAB by MEPS and recruiting personnel, which in turn influenced the outcome of the 1993 cost–benefit analysis. Due to the success of the OT&E, in May 1993, the MAP approved implementation of CAT-ASVAB at all MEPSs nationwide. This marked the high point in the CAT-ASVAB program.

From a researcher's perspective, there has been no greater reward than conducting the CAT-ASVAB OT&E. After years of hard work in developing and evaluating the system, we were able to not only see the system in operational use, but to become an integral part of this limited operational implementation. We were able to go out into the operational environment and interact daily with the users of the system—MEPS personnel, applicants, and recruiters. While we expected the system to work well, we did not necessarily expect such a strongly favorable reaction from all the users of the system. For the numerous researchers who have contributed to this program, and in particular, for those researchers working on the program during this effort, the CAT-ASVAB OT&E made those years of hard work all worthwhile.

Third Generation— Building a System for Nationwide Implementation

The research summarized in the previous part culminated in a decision to institute CAT for AS-VAB administration through the Military Entrance Processing Stations. Obsolescence and commercial unavailability of the 2nd generation computer equipment made it necessary to develop a 3rd generation delivery system, using different computers. The obsolescence of the 2nd generation system had several implications, addressed by the chapters of this part. For one, a new computer platform had to be chosen and all of the CAT-ASVAB software had to be modified to be compatible with it. In **Chapter 21**, Unpingco, Rafacz, and Hom describe the considerations involved in selecting the new computers and the network to link them, as well as in converting the CAT-ASVAB software to run on the new system.

In addition, the substitution of computer equip-ment raised the psychometric question of the equivalence of tests administered on the old and new computers. In **Chapter 22**, Segall enumer-ates the issues that the new computer raised in this respect, and recounts the design and results of research conducted to investigate the compara-bility of test scores obtained using the old com-puter and a number of variants of a new one.

Another implication of the introduction of a new computer system is that it invalidated previous cost analyses. As a consequence, new concepts of operations had to be considered, and new analyses of costs and benefits had to be conducted. In **Chapter 23**, Wise, Curran, and McBride review prior cost analyses, and describe a study of several al-ternative concepts of ASVAB operations, and the results of cost comparisons among them that ac-counted for the cost of the new equipment.

21

Development of a System for Nationwide Implementation

Vincent Unpingco, Irwin Hom, and Bernard Rafacz

The 1993 approval to implement CAT-ASVAB nationwide started a new phase in the CAT-ASVAB program. One major aspect of this phase of the program was to develop a new CAT-ASVAB system. While the Hewlett Packard—Integral Personal Computer (HP-IPC), used for the Accelerated CAT-ASVAB Project (ACAP), had served its purpose well, by 1993 it was obsolete and no longer manufactured. Developing a new system involved selecting a new computer platform and networking system, designing an input device comparable to the one used in ACAP, and developing new test administration software. This chapter describes all phases of the system development for nationwide implementation of CAT-ASVAB.

Computer Hardware Selection

Computer hardware selection consisted of four steps: (1) developing hardware requirements, (2) conducting a market survey of available systems, (3) evaluating these systems, and (4) developing hardware specifications. In selecting the hardware for nationwide implementation, lessons learned from ACAP were extremely valuable. This was particularly true while conducting the initial step—developing hardware requirements.

Hardware Requirements

The hardware requirements for a new CAT-ASVAB computer system were based on the capabilities of the HP-IPC, with input from the operational CAT-ASVAB MEPS personnel. The new computer system had to meet or exceed system specifications in certain areas. Other requirements, however, were new, having been developed as a result of our experience with the HP-IPC.

Hardware requirements as defined by the ACAP system. The hardware and software system for ACAP was designed, developed, and implemented using the HP-IPC running under a UNIX (System V) operating system. The HP-IPC meets the following requirements:

Portability. The HP-IPC is a portable computer system. It is classified as a transportable suitcase-type portable. It weighs 25.3 pounds, and can be (somewhat) easily assembled and disassembled and moved from one location to the other. It is fully self-contained, with a built-in monitor, floppy disk drive, ink jet printer, and detachable keyboard. It is designed for ease of operation and flexibility.

The 1993 decision to implement CAT-ASVAB nationwide was limited to implementation at Military Entrance Processing Stations (MEPSs). Since MEPSs are permanent sites, they do not require portable systems (i.e., they can use desktop computers). The only sites requiring portable computers are the Mobile Examining Team Sites (METSs), which are typically temporary sites requiring equipment set-up and take-down for each session. However, since implementation at METSs is under consideration, it was necessary to select a computer platform that would meet the needs of both types of sites. To fulfill this requirement, we decided to evaluate desktop computers for MEPSs and portable notebooks for METSs. The advantage in using desktop computers where possible is that they are less costly, easier to maintain, easier to upgrade, and less susceptible to theft. There are some disadvantages to having two types of computers. First, there is a potential for increasing the amount of effort dedicated to software development and software acceptance testing. Second, both types must be equated to the ASVAB reference form, increasing the cost and complexity of score equating.

In evaluating systems for portability the following factors were considered: weight, size, ability to easily assemble, disassemble, and move from one location to the next; and ability to operate as a stand-alone unit. Based on experiences in the field, the new system had to have a substantial size and weight advantage over the HP-IPC system. A portable computer system should be under 10 pounds, and 7 pounds if possible.

Adaptability. The HP-IPC system provides for two additional expansion slots that can be used for additional (random access memory [RAM]) and (input/output) interface capabilities. While only one printer per test site is required, the HP-IPC system comes with a built-in ink jet printer and an IEEE-488 interface, which allows for additional peripherals. The HP-IPC system has a 3.5 inch floppy disk drive. It also has a detachable keyboard, facilitating modifications to the examinee input device.

The new computer system had to be expandable, allowing for specific system growth on the system's main-board. It had to have a minimum of four megabytes of RAM, expandable to 16. A minimum of two I/O interfaces were required, one containing a parallel and serial port for attaching a printer and/or modem, and one for network interfacing. The new system had to be equipped with a 3.5 inch floppy disk drive to allow for flexibility in software design, and had to have the ability to link to a printer or other peripherals as required for operational field use. Ease of keyboard modification or attachable add-on keypads was considered highly desirable.

Performance capabilities. The HP-IPC runs under an eight megahertz (MHz) processing speed. It is capable of multi-tasking. The new computer system processor speed requirement was based on 1993 industry standards which were faster than 8 MHz. (The minimum computer processor speed evaluated was 25 MHz.) While multi-tasking is desirable for software development purposes, it is not necessary for operational examinee test administration or associated system functions needed during test administration.

Monitor. The HP-IPC has a monochrome monitor with a 512 (horizontal) x 255 (vertical) pixels electroluminescent display. The screen size is 9 inches measured diagonally, 8 inches wide by 4 inches high. The display can be configured for up to 31 lines with up to 85 characters per line, but the ACAP system uses dot matrix dimensions of 5 x 8 dots embedded in a 7 x 11 field. At this resolution, it is possible to display 23 lines with 73 characters per line on the HP-IPC screen.

To display graphics items clearly, the monitor video resolution screen for the new computer system was required to have as a minimum the 1993 industry standard Video Graphics Adapter (VGA). The number of lines per screen and characters per line of the ACAP system was also a minimum requirement so that each item will fit on one screen. The new system did not need to meet other monitor specifications for the HP-IPC, as an equating was conducted prior to implementation. It was required as a minimum that all new computer systems have a built-in external VGA monitor adapter, SVGA being more desirable.

New requirements. The new system had to meet requirements in addition to those met by the HP-IPC system. One of the biggest problems with the HP-IPC was it did not sell well in the marketplace, and it was very specialized, making parts costly and hard to obtain. To whatever extent possible, the new system needed to be a commonly used computer system so that replacement parts could be procured near the test sites. This would substantially reduce maintenance costs, would provide for future growth of the system, and would delay system obsolescence. The HP-IPC does not have internal storage capability, limiting system flexibility and expansion capabilities dramatically. The new system had to have internal mass storage capability. This would allow for growth and flexibility in system applications. In addition, a portable system should have upgrade capability similar to that of a desktop computer. A portable system should also have a minimum FCC Class B certification.

Types of Available Systems

An evaluation of the computer systems that were on the market in 1993 took into consideration the various types of microprocessors and the types of portable computers.

Types of microprocessors. There were three predominant microprocessors on the market which fit the personal computer systems profile: Intel (80386/80486/80586) based or compatible, Motorola (68000/680xx) based, and RISC (Reduced-Instruction-Set-Computer) based microprocessors. Intel normally operates under the Disk Operating System (DOS), but does have UNIX and other operating systems capability. Motorola normally operates under a UNIX operating system. RISC runs under a UNIX operating system and is the newest microprocessor on the market.

Types of portable computers. There were two basic categories of portables: Those weighing under or over 15 pounds. Styles that fit in the first category are the handheld, the notebook, and the laptop; they usually resemble a clamshell design. These systems are typically referred to as notebooks and portables. Styles that fit in the second category are suitcase and, occasionally, those having the clamshell design. These systems are typically referred to as transportables or luggables.

Transportable computers, similar to the HP-IPC, do not meet minimum size and weight requirements for temporary sites and are too expensive for permanent sites. For these reasons, this category of computers was eliminated from consideration.

Evaluation of Available Systems

A wide variety of desktops (for MEPSs) and notebooks (for METSs) were evaluated as meeting the minimum system requirements. Portable notebook computers, in particular, have grown substantially in performance capability and peripheral expansion capability over the past several years. Previous notebook computer systems seemed to lack the ruggedness needed for operational field use, but technological advancements have established their durability for operational field use. There are certain expansion disadvantages to notebook computers, but performance and physical characteristic advantages outweigh the disadvantages.

The Motorola and RISC-based portable and desktop computers, while meeting minimum specifications, are very limited in type, quantity and production, and are expensive to purchase, maintain, and upgrade. Systems using the Intel microprocessor, on the other hand, are relatively low cost, widely available, and easy to maintain and upgrade. Based on these findings, IBM-PC/AT (Intel-based compatible) computers were selected as best suited for the new computer platform.

Computer Specifications

Table 21-1 lists the primary computer specifications for the desktop computers and the notebook/laptop computers. These are *not* minimum specifications needed to run CAT-ASVAB software, but specifications that we felt would provide the Government with a reliable, easily maintainable system that has the capability for future expansion. In developing these specifications, we tried to project what would be standard equipment when procuring the systems for implementation. These specifications apply to both the Test Administrator (TA) station and the Examinee Testing (ET) stations.

Keyboard Specifications

The one difference between an ET station and a TA station is the type of keyboard required. Where the TA station requires a full Enhanced AT 101 type keyboard, the ET station requires a modified AT 101 type keyboard. Required modifications include relocating the "A," "B," "C," "D," and "E" keys, labeling the space bar as "ENTER," labeling the F1 key as "HELP," and covering all unused keys. A lot of time and effort went into figuring out how to meet these requirements and still have a durable, easily maintainable keyboard. The ACAP system used a template to cover unused keys and labels to mark the keys needed to take the test. While this method worked reasonably well, over time the templates warped, moved slightly inhibiting key depression, or came unfastened. We experienced some problem with key labels coming off. To avoid these problems, we decided to use blank keycaps on all unused keys. The item response keys ("A," "B," "C," "D," and "E") are the original keys moved to the proper location. The "HELP" key (F1) and "ENTER" key (space bar) were labeled using the same process normally used in labeling commercial keyboards. Figure 21-1 shows a picture of the modified ET keyboard.

Network Selection

Networking of computer systems allows for more efficient administration of CAT-ASVAB, particularly at large sites. Networking helps to eliminate redundancy in procedures, saving a substantial amount of test administrator time when more than ten ET stations are being operated at any one time. For this reason, the HP-IPC CAT system

Table 21-1 CAT-ASVAB Hardware Specifications

	Desktop	Notebook
Microcomputer Platform	IBM PC/AT (Intel-Based Compatible)	
Microprocessor (CPU)	80486DX (Intel or Intel Compatible) microprocessor 8KB Internal cache memory 33 MHz or faster	25 MHz or faster
Mainboard/Motherboard	33 MHz PCI or VLB I/O BUS rated speed CMOS/ROM BIOS configuration option, during boot-up Expansion slots, 6 minimum	
RAM	30 or 72 pin SIMM type modules, with a minimum of 4 MB, expandable to 64 MB	4 MB, expandable up to 16 MB of RAM
	70ns or faster RAM	
External I/O Bus	One RS-232 Serial I/O port (9-pin) One Parallel I/O port	1 external keyboard/keypad port, built-in 1 external mouse port, built-in mouse support must be Microsoft compatible
Display/Video Interface	Super Video Graphics Array (SVGA) reflective color LCD	Dual scan color
	Extended graphics resolution modes, 640 (horizontal) X 480 (vertical) pixels 1MB VRAM	
	Screen Size, 14″ measured diagonally .28 mm dot-pitch Non-interlaced and interlaced monitor support 15-pin (DB15) cable, 6 ft.	Screen Size, 9.5″ measured diagonally Display text up to 80 characters by 25 lines Viewing angle: greater than "TBS/TBD" degrees in a horizontal plane 1 external VGA/SVGA port
Floppy Diskette Drive	3.5″ 1.44 MB High Density Floppy Disk (HD FDD)	
Internal Hard Disk Drive	80MB Internal Hard Disk Drive (80MB measured using no compression software or hardware)	
	ALL IDE drives must be capable of supporting a second IDE drive from various manufacturers.	
Notebook Size		NTE Size (d,w,h) 8.3″ x 11″ x 1.8″
Notebook Weight		NTE 6.3 lbs in weight

Note. Cells that span both desktop and notebook columns are requirements for both.

provided the capability of networking, via a local area network (LAN). This is also a requirement of the new desktop computers, but not the portable computers. At this time, notebook computers will not have the capability of networking, as they will be used at the smaller test sites. Networking requires a network interface controller (NIC), cable, and software that runs it. In selecting these components of the network, several options were considered.

Network Hardware

Network interface controller. PC networking hardware consists of using an NIC that provides the physical connection between a computer and the network medium. Several NIC protocols were evaluated.

Arcnet. In 1977, DataPoint Corporation developed Arcnet as a proposed inexpensive solution

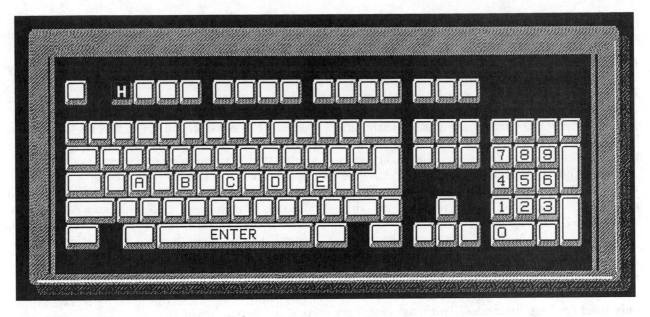

Figure 21-1
Modified ET Keyboard.

to connectivity. This protocol allowed up to 255 nodes. Arcnet gives each node a unique ID address in incremental order. It uses a token-passing scheme where a token (sequence of characters) travels to each station according to ascending node addresses. When a PC receives a token, it holds that information and queries other PCs about their ability to accept tokens. When a recipient is available, the system sends the token and continues sending the token to other recipients until the last node receives the token. Because a node may transmit only when it has the token and only after getting an okay from the recipients, Arcnet performance is slow. The data transfer rate is 2 Mbps baseband operation. This may be acceptable if the number of workstations is moderate and their volume of network messages is light. Otherwise, the system will get bogged down by constant group interaction, heavy transmission, or large files. Arcnet's specific hardware and software requirements, along with its proprietary protocol, make it an unpopular network for PCs.

Ethernet. The Xerox Corporation invented this protocol in the early 1970s. It uses a communication technique called Carrier Sense Multiple Access/Collision Detection (CSMA/CD). Workstations with information to send would "listen" for network traffic. If the workstations detect traffic, they pause and listen again until clear. Once there is no traffic, they broadcast the packet (series of bytes) in both directions. The data packets identify the destination workstation by a unique address. Each

workstation reads the header of the packet, but only the destination node reads the entire packet. Multiple workstations may transmit simultaneously. When this happens and messages collide, a message goes out to cancel the transmission; the workstation waits a random amount of time and then re-transmits. Ethernet has the advantage of packing the maximum number of messages on the network and producing high-speed performance. This popular protocol (IEEE 802.3) has a data transfer rate of 10 Mbps baseband operation. Because many different platforms support Ethernet, this makes it simple and easy to use Ethernet to link to various computer systems.

Token ring. IBM originally designed this network protocol. It works similarly to Arcnet's token passing scheme, except the tokens travel in one direction on a logical ring and pass through every node to complete the circuit. When a workstation receives the token, it can either transmit a data packet or pass the token to the next station. In this procedure, each node between the originating workstation and the data's destination regenerates the token and all of its data before passing it on. Upon reaching its destination, usually the file server, the receiver reads the data, acknowledges them, and sends the message back into the ring to return to the sender. Again, each workstation along the way reads and re-transmits the token. This scheme creates considerable overhead, but assures successful data transmission. Depending on whether twisted-pair or shielded two-pair cabling is used, the data transfer rate is 4 Mbps or 16 Mbps baseband, respectively (IEEE 802.5).

The protocol of choice is Ethernet. We base this on its popularity and the following four factors. It is a low cost network; the protocol is inherently reliable; it is fast; and it has a variety of cabling options. There are many manufacturers of Ethernet NICs that are 100 percent compatible with standards set by the IEEE 802.3 committee. Eight-bit and sixteen-bit controllers are available for the Industry Standard Adapter (ISA) bus found in desktop PCs. These controllers plug into any open ISA slot and come with connectors for thick-net, thin-net, twisted-pair, or a combination.

Cabling. There are four cabling topologies available for Ethernet: Thin-net (10Base2), thick-net (10Base5), twisted-pair (10BaseT), and fiber optics (10BaseF). Fiber optics is expensive and is only used for long distances. Thick-net is seldom used because its thick cables are hard to work with and bulky.

Twisted-pair uses concentrators (hubs) to link the workstations together. This range of ports allows designing networks with simple point-to-point twisted-pair cabling or using structured cabling systems. This gives total flexibility on monitoring and managing the network. Such a setup is easy to configure. If a station fails or the connection between a station and hub fails, all other stations continue to operate. However, if a hub fails, all the stations connected to that hub cease functioning. Twisted-pair cabling provides the capability of running at 100 Mbps.

Thin-net cables are easy to move and connect to workstations. In this type of setup, the trunk segment acts as backbone for all the workstations. Each end of the trunk is a BNC 50-ohm terminator which ends the network signal. Up to five trunks may be connected using a repeater that strengthens network signals. Each trunk supports a maximum of 30 workstations. The nodes connect to the trunk using BNC T-connectors. The biggest advantage of thin-net is that it is low in cost. The disadvantages are that network and station errors are harder to diagnose, if one station goes down there is the potential for all stations to go down, and it can run only at 10 Mbps.

Network Software

There were three options for network software: Writing our own network operating system (NOS); selecting a commercial, server-based NOS; or using a peer-to-peer NOS.

Custom developed. Writing our own NOS would be a very large scale project. First, we would need to select the NIC to use and to develop drivers for that card. Hundreds of NICs are available and programming drivers are different for each. We would have to solicit technical information from the manufacturer of each NIC we considered. Some NICs come with drivers, but these are usually used for linking with commercial NOS. In the event that a manufacturer discontinued an NIC, developing new drivers would become necessary. Similarly, we would need to provide updates to drivers whenever an NIC changed in revision. Once we completed development of drivers, we would need to write a suite of functions to conform with the IEEE 802.3 ethernet protocol.

Server-based. The major manufacturers of server-based networks are Novell NetWare and Banyan VINES. With this type of network, each workstation attaches to the server via a protocol driver and workstation shell that loads into memory. The protocol driver creates, maintains, and terminates connections between network devices. The shell intercepts application requests and figures out whether to route them locally either to DOS or to the network file server for processing by the NOS. This creates very little overhead as the workstations interact only with the server. Configuring a PC for use in a server-based network is quite simple. Drivers come with the NIC, which makes it easy to link with the NOS. Finally, manufacturers supply updates to drivers of each product.

Peer-to-peer. With peer-to-peer networks, only a subset of network commands is available. Major packages are Artisoft's LANtastic and Novell's NetWare Lite. This type of network is also configurable as server-based, although that configuration would involve more overhead. Peer-to-peer networks load seven terminate-and-stay-resident (TSR) drivers into memory. These drivers take over the operating system by assuming that each workstation will communicate with all the others. In the CAT-ASVAB configuration, this is not true. ET stations communicate with the TA station, but not with other ET stations. For peer-to-peer networks, processing appears slower whenever a workstation transmits to the server. Each workstation monitors all input and output. Another shortcoming is their compatibility with networks on other platforms. The main advantage of this type of LAN is the sharing of resources with other nodes without implementing a dedicated server. Many good features exist in peer-to-peer networks which are missing in server-based networks. However, these features are enhancements that the CAT-ASVAB environment does not require.

Other considerations. Each server-based and peer-to-peer system is unique to the manufacturer and is not easily cross-compatible. For instance LANtastic is not directly compatible with NetWare Lite. To get the NOS from two vendors to talk to each other usually requires purchasing additional software to link the two. Things to consider are compatibility, stability, connectivity options, ease of use, and technical support issues. There are many more Novell CNEs (Certified Network Engineers) than Banyan certified engineers. Most important is to standardize and not consider low-end products. If the manufacturer of a proprietary system goes out of business, support and parts supplies are no longer available (LAN: The Network Solutions Magazine, September 1993). When looking at hardware and software configurations on PCs and other platforms (VAX, Sun, Apple), Novell is used as the measure of network compatibility. Many products carry Novell's stamp of approval indicating "YES NetWare Tested and Approved."

The CAT-ASVAB TA station is required to communicate with the MEPCOM Integrated Resource System (MIRS) system. Initial specifications showed MIRS to be a UNIX workstation running ethernet and Transmission Control Protocol/Internet Protocol (TCP/IP). Novell's NetWare 3.11, the version on the market at the time of this evaluation, already included the TCP/IP Transport, which is a collection of protocols, application programming interfaces, and tools for managing those protocols. Other NOSs support TCP/IP through add-on packages which increase network traffic and can slow down response times.

Network Selected

After considering CAT-ASVAB's current and future network requirements, the following networking hardware and software were selected: An ethernet NIC, twisted-pair cabling, and Novell NetWare, a server-based NOS. To maintain compatibility across all types of computers, we decided that the file server, required by this networking option, must meet the same computer specifications as the TA and ET stations. This combination of hardware and software was found to meet all CAT-ASVAB current and projected networking requirements and to be cost-effective.

Software Development

Since the CAT-ASVAB software running on the HP-IPC was in operational use during the time that CAT-ASVAB software was being developed for the IBM-PC compatible, names were assigned to each to avoid confusion. The former is referred to as HP-CAT and the latter as PC-CAT. HP-CAT functional requirements were used as a baseline for the development of PC-CAT, with some exceptions. In particular, "lessons learned" from the CAT-ASVAB Operational Test and Evaluation (OT&E) were used in modifying the functional requirements. Differences between the functionality of HP-CAT and PC-CAT are noted in the paragraphs below.

Minimum System Requirements

Since the computer platform selected for the next generation CAT-ASVAB is an IBM PC/AT compatible, single-user computer, PC-CAT is written for this machine with a minimum configuration of an Intel 80386 CPU, 640 K of conventional memory and at least three megabytes of extended memory. The speed of the CPU must be at least 25 megahertz. A multi-syncing VGA monitor (interlaced or non-interlaced) with a minimum resolution of 640 x 480 is required. While we had the option of programming the system to run under Windows, we elected to develop an MS-DOS based system. We had learned from the ACAP system that taking the simplest and cleanest approach possible minimizes problems in the field. Windows offered no advantage and requires substantially more resources. PC-CAT requires MS-DOS 5.0 or higher. PC-CAT is fully upwards compatible, but not downwards compatible.

Programming Language

From a technical standpoint, the programming language of choice remained "C". The primary reason for this choice was that HP-CAT had been written in the C language and many of the psychometric routines for test administration were transportable to the new system (i.e., item selection, test scoring, expected test completion time). About 80 percent of the code, however, was rewritten and designed specifically for the MS-DOS environment. This is a reasonable approach since much of the original OT&E software (dating back to 1986; Folchi, 1986) was designed and written when not all the functions to be supported were known. Over time, as more and more software was added and/or revised to reflect new functional specifications, the required "re-engineering" produced a greater level of convolution in software logic and inefficiency in software that would not have been the case if all of the functions were known at the start. Now that all of the functions are known, and in fact, in the case of the TA station, simplified, the more preferred path, and the one ultimately selected, was to design and write new software relative to the new environment, but taking advantage of that software from the OT&E code that reflected common functions.

A further technical consideration was the choice of a C compiler to support software development and execution. Among those features which characterized HP-CAT was the use of RAM as an electronic storage medium for testing data, particularly the test item files (Rafacz, 1994). This reduced the need to access a mechanical device such as a floppy drive to retrieve test items, thus minimizing wear-and-tear on those devices. Most importantly, however, the storage of test items in volatile RAM provided maximum security for the items because they disappeared once power was removed. Needless to say it was desirable to use the same type of design for PC-CAT, but within an MS-DOS environment. This required using a compiler that included expanded memory capabilities, analogous to that available on the HP-CAT system via the UNIX operating system. The Borland C++ 3.1 compiler provided the necessary capability.

To support software development, a comprehensive collection of functions, referred to as the "In-house Library," was developed. Most of these functions are written in Intel assembly with some intricate C coding. The In-house Library includes graphics functions and functions to control the use of expanded memory, keyboard interrupts, and high resolution timings. The In-house graphics functions are faster than Borland C compiler routines.

Software Components

There are two major software components in PC-CAT—the Examinee Testing (ET) station software and the TA station software. Unlike HP-CAT, PC-CAT does not include Data Handling Computer (DHC) software, as these functions will be handled by the MEPS MIRS system. Like HP-CAT, PC-CAT can function in either a networking mode or a stand-alone mode of operation.

ET software. The functionality of the ET software for PC-CAT is almost identical to that of HP-CAT. There are some differences, however. First, with PC-CAT both forms of CAT-ASVAB are loaded into memory, allowing for selection of form at the ET station. In comparison, HP-CAT could store only one form in memory, not because the capability did not exist, but rather because the cost of RAM was too prohibitive. The net result is that PC-CAT enjoys a simplification of some of the software routines concerning the placement of examinees at stations and certain failure recovery situations. Second, because the specification for the random assignment of examinees to testing stations has been removed, test administrators may now seat examinees essentially in a "free-form" format. Test administrators enter the examinee's social security number at the ET station. In networking mode, the TA station will "get" the examinee identifying information from the file server. This will allow the examinee to start testing immediately, since it is no longer necessary to identify examinees at the TA station prior to examinees commencing testing. Third, all scoring will be done at the ET station. In HP-CAT, the final theta estimate was computed at the ET station, but all subsequent scoring was done by the TA station software. This change allows all psychometric routines to be part of one software component—the ET station software, making software modifications and the associated acceptance testing more straightforward.

There are four main software modules that make up the ET station software: the keyboard familiarization sequence module, the test instruction module, the test administration module, and the "Help" module. The ET station software allows some flexibility in test administration by reading certain information from files. For example, screen.dat is a file of all text dialogs and screens. Therefore, screen text can be changed without changes to the source code. Subtest.cat is a software configuration file for modifying administration of items. This file contains such information as the tests to administer, the order of test administration, the number of items in the test pool, the test length, test time, and the screen time-out limits. Et.cfg is a file that tells the ET station the type of computer (notebook or desktop) that is being used. All item information, such as item text and graphics, exposure control parameters, IRT parameters, and information tables, is external to the source code. Item text, graphics, and item parameters are stored in a database created using "Itemaker," a program developed specifically for CAT-ASVAB. Exposure control parameters and information tables are stored in ASCII text files.

As with HP-CAT, PC-CAT automatically creates backups of applicant data files. If the system is operating in networking mode, applicant data are stored both on the hard drive of the File Server and the hard drive of the ET Station. If the system is operating in stand-alone mode, applicant data are stored on the hard drive and floppy drive of the ET Station. If the network fails during testing, each ET Station automatically switches to stand-alone mode, using the hard drive as the primary data depository and the floppy drive as the backup.

TA software. Unlike the ET station, the TA station for PC-CAT has been simplified at the functional level. As previously mentioned, the removal of the requirement for the random assignment of examinees to stations simplifies maintaining information on examinees and the availability of stations, as was necessary when designing the OT&E system. In fact, there is now no requirement for the TA station software to be concerned with where examinees are located in the testing room with respect to either test form or station availability. In addition, the immediate availability of either CAT-ASVAB test form at an ET station eliminates operator need to be concerned with where to place examinees when starting tests and, more importantly, in a failure recovery situation. In essence, any available station in the testing room may now be used to start a new examinee for testing, or to continue the testing session of an examinee whose station has failed.

The TA station functional specifications for the new system involve a number of requirements. Upon bootup, the software performs file maintenance activities and requests that the operator confirm the system clock time. The operator then selects the mode of operation for the testing session—network or stand-alone. At a MEPS, the network option will normally be selected; the stand-alone mode will be a failure recovery alternative. At a METS, only the stand-alone mode can be selected as the computers will not be electronically tied together as a "networked" configuration. The operator then enters TA and test session identifying information. Subsequently, the main screen is displayed. This screen allows you to monitor examinee progress and perform all necessary test administrator functions for the session.

About two-thirds of the main screen is used to display the status of examinees in the test session. There are nine data fields:

1. The SSN data field displays applicants' social security numbers. This information is transferred from the ET stations to the TA station. The word "Available" indicates that an applicant is not assigned to the test station. This data field also displays the number of stations and peripherals in the network that are not booted up. These stations and peripherals are referred to as "off-line."

2. The NAME data field displays applicants' last names.

3. The STATION ID (Station ID) data field displays ET station identifying numbers.

4. The FORM/TYPE data field displays the test form and test type assigned to the applicant. "I" indicates an initial test type; "R" indicates a retest; "C" indicates a confirmation test.

5. The TOTAL TIME data field displays the amount of time the applicant has been taking CAT-ASVAB.

6. The SUBTEST data field displays the abbreviated name of the test on which the applicant is currently working. It also indicates when an applicant needs help by displaying the word "HELP."

7. The TEST TIME data field displays the amount of time the applicant has been taking the test.

8. The END TIME data field displays an estimate of when the applicant will complete CAT-ASVAB. The estimate is in hours and minutes with an error factor that becomes smaller with each test.

9. The STATUS/AFQT data field displays letters representing the testing status of each applicant and applicants' AFQT test scores upon completion of testing. At the start of testing, the field is dash-filled. Each dash represents a single step in the testing progress of the applicant. When an applicant's name has been submitted, the first dash becomes an "S," for already submitted. When the examinee completes testing, the second dash becomes a "C." When an applicant's results are transferred to MIRS, the third dash becomes an "R." When an applicant's unverified score report (described in Chapter 14) has been printed, the fourth dash becomes a "P." If all processing steps are complete, the last dash becomes a "D." If the network detects that the applicant's machine has failed, the last dash becomes an "F." The system automatically performs all of these functions, except SUBMIT.

The arrow keys can be used to move up and down in the list of applicants and to select an applicant for editing of the applicant's identifying information, printing a report, or other available functions.

At the very bottom of the main screen, an electronic banner displays various testing activities. If a computer fails, the banner displays a message telling the test administrator that a station failed, giving the station's identifying information. If an applicant is in "HELP" a message is also displayed. Although this information is contained in the data fields described above, the moving banner is more likely to draw the TA's attention.

Immediately above the banner is a list of all available functions. To select a function, the TA presses the key associated with the function.

1. "N" sorts applicants by name.

2. "S" sorts applicants by SSN.

3. "T" sorts applicants by ET Station ID number.

4. "M" switches between modes of display. There are two modes of display: Session mode and current mode. Session mode, which is the default mode, displays all applicants who have tested during the session. Current mode displays only those applicants currently testing. The mode that the TA software is in is displayed at the top, right-hand side of the main screen.

5. "P" provides the test administrator with options to reprint the unverified score reports or the Aptitude Testing Processing List (ATPL), or to print a test session status report. (When an individual applicant completes testing the unverified score report is automatically printed. When all applicants have completed testing, the TA station automatically prints the ATPL, a standard USMEPCOM form that includes such information as the examinee's last name, SSN, test form administered, Service processing for, sex, AFQT score, and test type. The reprint option is available in case another copy of these reports is needed.)

6. "D" allows the TA to collect applicant test data with a diskette rather than having CAT-ASVAB automatically download the data from the ET Stations to the File Server Station. The only time the TA will use this option is when the network fails during testing.

7. "E" allows the TA to electronically send applicant test data files to MIRS. (MIRS, in turn, sends the data to a central repository at USMEPCOM.) If the connection between the CAT-ASVAB system and MIRS is not functional, the data are automatically written to a floppy disk so they can be "manually" transferred to MIRS.

8. "INS" (the Insert key) allows you to add applicants to the test session at the TA station.

This option is functional only in Stand-Alone mode.

9. "ESC" ends the test session.

In summary, the functional capability of the TA station emulates that of the HP-CAT system, but at both a simpler and more encompassing level. The TA station user-interface for PC-CAT is significantly different from that of HP-CAT. HP-CAT required the user to go through a number of menus to perform functions. Until the user became very familiar with the system, he could easily "get lost," not knowing how to get to a certain menu or where to locate certain functions. With PC-CAT, once the user has "logged into" the TA station, everything is on one screen. In addition, all functions that could be automated have been, requiring less computer-user interaction.

Summary

In 1996, USMEPCOM procured the computer hardware for nationwide implementation. When the hardware specifications were written, the procurement was expected to take place in the 1994/95 time frame. While the CAT-ASVAB hardware requirements did not change between 1994 and 1996, what was available on the market did. As a result, the system that was actually procured exceeds some of the specifications. Most notable, the CPU is a pentium, running at 100 MHz, with eight megabytes of RAM and a 630 megabyte hard drive. As with the hardware, the networking software has also been upgraded. While initially programmed to run under NetWare 3.1, CAT-ASVAB now runs under NetWare 4.1.

The PC-CAT system is a streamlined, up-to-date version of HP-CAT. This new system is a cost-effective system that allows for ease in operating CAT-ASVAB and in maintaining the CAT-ASVAB software and equipment. There are several main advantages of the PC-CAT system over the HP-CAT system. First, there have been many advances in computer technology since 1985 when the HP-CAT system was selected. Notebook computers are now available that are much smaller, lighter, and more capable than computers available in 1985. Second, prices of computers in general have come down drastically, making both powerful notebooks and desktops available at relatively low cost. Third, the additional computer resources and a better understanding of the operational requirements have given designers an opportunity to make the system more efficient.

22

The Psychometric Comparability of Computer Hardware

Daniel O. Segall

An important issue in the development and maintenance of a computerized adaptive test concerns the comparability of scores obtained from different computer hardware. Previous studies (Divgi & Stoloff, 1986; Spray, Ackerman, Reckase, & Carlson, 1989) have shown that medium of administration (computer versus paper-and-pencil) can affect item functioning. It is conceivable that differences among computer hardware (monitor size and resolution, keyboard layout, physical dimensions, etc.) can also influence item functioning. For example, particular monitor characteristics may influence the clarity and accuracy of graphics items. Variations in clarity and accuracy among monitors may, in turn, affect examinee's performance on particular items. If this effect is sufficiently large, then variation in hardware components can affect three important psychometric properties of the test, including: (1) the score scale, (2) precision, and (3) construct validity.

An example of *score scale* effects is provided by small low-resolution monitors which might make intricate graphics items difficult to interpret, increasing their difficulty. This effect would lower the mean of the observed scores for this monitor type, and perhaps affect higher order moments of the observed test score distribution as well. If variation among hardware affects the observed score distribution, then separate equatings would be required to place scores obtained from different hardware on a common score scale. The data required to estimate these adjustments however may be costly, since samples of 2,500 examinees may be required for each hardware configuration to perform an adequate equipercentile equating.

A large hardware effect can, in addition, influence the *precision* of the estimated scores. For example, the use of low-resolution monitors may increase the difficulty of particular graphics items, while having no effect on the difficulty of other non-graphics items. This misspecification of the difficulty parameters of some (but not all) items is likely to introduce both systematic and nonsystematic errors in the estimated abilities. If a particular hardware configuration increased the difficulty of some items, we would expect the mean of the estimated abilities to decrease by some amount. If this increase in difficulty is not uniform across items, however, we would expect a random error component to be introduced as well, lowering the precision of the estimated abilities. Poor resolution monitors (for example) may also lower the item's discrimination level, which in turn would affect the precision of the estimated abilities. The introduction of random error is perhaps somewhat more serious than the introduction of systematic error, since no monotonic score scale transformation can equate test reliabilities.

A large hardware effect can also alter the *construct validity* of the test or battery. For example, individual differences in visual acuity may affect scores obtained from poor resolution monitors. Those examinees with poor or average eyesight may be at a disadvantage relative to those with above average acuity for answering some graphics items. In this event, the constructs measured by some graphics tests (e.g., Mechanical Comprehension [MC]) may actually be influenced by the accuracy and resolution of the monitor. For low resolution monitors these tests would measure a combination of visual acuity and mechanical knowledge—for high quality monitors these tests would measure only mechanical knowledge. Consequently, it is instructive to examine the effect of hardware characteristics on the constructs measured by the tests. These effects can be examined through an evaluation of construct validity (i.e., test intercorrelations).

There is some evidence to suggest that speeded tests contained in the ASVAB (Coding Speed [CS] and Numerical Operations [NO]) may be especially sensitive to small changes in test presentation format—more so than the adaptive power tests. In paper-and-pencil (P&P) presentation of these tests, the shape of the bubble on the answer sheet has been found to have a significant effect on the moments of number-right scores (Bloxom et al., 1993; Ree & Wegner, 1990). Since speed is a significant component of these tests, larger bubbles require more time to fill, and thus produce lower scores on average. In these studies, no answer sheet effect was found for power tests.

Although previous work on speeded tests (which focused on effects of P&P presentation forms) may not be directly transferable to the study of computer administered speeded tests, this work suggests that different hardware effects may exist for computer administered power and speed tests. Characteristics of input devices, for example, which affect the speed of input, are likely to affect speed-test scores. It is unclear however that power tests would be similarly affected, since these scores are based primarily on response-accuracy, and are only indirectly affected by response-latency.

The study reported here examines the effects of particular hardware characteristics on psychometric properties of the CAT-ASVAB. The objective of this work is to provide some insight into the exchangeability of different hardware—whether machines of different makes and models can be used interchangeably, and which hardware characteristics must remain constant among testing platforms to ensure adequate precision and score interpretation. The effects of several different hardware characteristics were examined on the score scale, precision, and construct validity of CAT-ASVAB test scores.

Method

A total of 3,062 subjects recruited from the San Diego area participated in the study. Subjects were recruited from local colleges and universities, high schools, trade schools, and employment training programs and were paid $40.00 for ap-

proximately 3.5 hours of testing. Subjects consisted of 17 through 23-year-olds responding to advertisements in local, college, and high school newspapers.

Procedures

All subjects were scheduled for a session date and time (either morning or afternoon) prior to the day of testing. For each session, examinees were processed in the order in which they arrived. Upon arrival, TAs inspected photo-identification to verify subjects' identities and ages. Each subject was asked to read and sign a consent form which provided background information on the ASVAB, and agreement by the subject to participate in the research study. The consent form also informed subjects that as part of the study, they will take a computerized test which takes approximately three and a half hours to complete; will take the test to the best of their ability; and will receive a check for $40.00 at the conclusion of the test.

After signing the Consent Form, each subject was randomly assigned[1] to one of 28 computers. As described below, each of the 28 computers belonged to one of 13 experimental conditions.

Experimental Conditions

Thirteen experimental conditions were defined by specific combinations of computer hardware and test presentation format. These are displayed in Table 22-1. Column abbreviations along the top row denote the following:

1. **STA** Computer station number (from 1–28)

2. **CT** Computer type

   A. Panasonic notebook (386 CPU); monochrome LCD

   B. Dell subnotebook (386 CPU); monochrome LCD

   C. Texas Instruments (486 CPU); monochrome LCD

   D. Toshiba (486 CPU); active color matrix display

---

[1] This assignment was performed using random assignment sheets which contained a pseudorandom permutation of integers from 1 to 28. The first examinee seated was assigned to the first station listed on the sheet; the second examinee seated was assigned to the second station on the sheet, etc. A different sheet (containing a different random permutation) was used for each test session. This assignment resulted in roughly equal proportions of subjects assigned to each of the 28 computer stations.

Table 22-1 Experimental Conditions

STA[1]	CT[2]	MNF[3]	Type[4]	Monitor[5]	COND[6]	Input[7]	Order[8]
1	A	Pans	N	Mono	1	Pad-G	C1
2							C2
3					2	Full	C1
4							C2
5							C1
6							C2
7	B	Dell	S	Mono	3	Full	C1
8							C2
9					4	Pad-D	C1
10							C2
11	C	TI	N	Mono	5	Pad-G	C1
12							C2
13					6	Tmp	C1
14							C2
15					7	Full	C1
16							C2
17	D	Tosh	N	Color-HC	8	Full	C1
18							C2
19	E	Dell	D	Mono	9	Pad-G	C1
20							C2
21	F	Datl	D	Mono	10	Pad-G	C1
22							C2
23				Color-HC	11	Full	C1
24							C2
25				Color-LC	12	Full	C1
26							C2
27				Color-HC	13	Pad-G	C1
28							C2

E. Dell desktop (486 CPU); monochrome VGA monitor

F. Datel (486 CPU)

3. **MNF** Manufacturer

Pans Panasonic

Dell Dell Microsystems

TI Texas Instruments

Tosh Toshiba

Datl Datel

4. **Type** Computer Type

D Desktop

N Notebook

S Subnotebook

5. **Monitor** Computer Monitor

Mono Monochrome (VGA)

Color-HC Color (High Contrast—White letters with blue background)

Color-LC Color (Low Contrast—Purple letters with blue background)

6. **COND** Condition (from 1–13) denoting how data from the 28 stations are combined for analyses

7. **Input** Input device

Full Full keyboard where labels "A–B–C–D–E" were placed over the "S–F–H–K– :" keys, respectively. The space bar was labeled "ENTER", and the "F1" key was relabeled "HELP". All other keys were covered with blank labels.

Pad Keypad—17 keys (either G: Genovation, or D: Dell) where labels "HELP–A–B–C–D–E" were placed over the "-–7–9–5–1–3" keys, respectively.

Tmp Template, where all keys except the "F1", "spacebar", and "S–F–H–K–:" keys were removed from the full keyboard. A flat piece of plastic with rectangular holes (for the 7 remaining keys) was placed over keyboard. The "F1" and "spacebar" keys were relabeled "HELP" and "ENTER", respectively. The "S–F–H–K–:" were relabeled "A–B–C–D–E" respectively.

8. **Order** First form administered—Each examinee received both forms of the CAT-ASVAB, with indicated form (C1 or C2) administered first.

Hardware Dimensions

The 13 experimental conditions were constructed to examine five issues related to the effects of particular hardware characteristics on the measurement properties of observed test scores. Using the design outlined above, each of these questions can be addressed by contrasting selected conditions in which all hardware characteristics remained constant—except for the characteristic of interest. A sixth set of conditions was added to address the similarity of scores obtained from different hardware configurations which employ a common input device. The six research questions and associated conditions are provided below.

Input device. Do differences in input devices used by examinees to enter responses affect scores? This can be addressed by a comparison of Conditions 5–6–7, which used the 'keypad,' 'full keyboard,' and 'template' input devices, respectively.

Color scheme. Does the use of different background and foreground colors affect scores? This can be addressed by a comparison of Conditions 11 and 12. Condition 11 presented questions using white letters (foreground) with a blue background (denoted as high-contrast). Condition 12 used purple letters presented on a blue background. In this latter condition (denoted as low-contrast), the contrast between the foreground and background was greatly reduced due to the similarity of colors.

Monitor. Do differences in monitor types (color or monochrome) affect scores? This issue can be examined by contrasting Conditions 10 and 13, which used monochrome and color monitors, respectively.

CPU. Do differences in CPU (make or model) affect scores? This question can be addressed by a comparison of Conditions 9 and 10, which used CPUs from different manufacturers.

Portability. Do differences in portability affect scores? This issue can be addressed by a comparison of Conditions 1–4–9 (Notebook–Subnotebook–Desktop); Conditions 2–3–7 (Notebook–Subnotebook–Notebook); and Conditions 8–11 (Notebook–Desktop). Note that the same input device was used within each of these three subsets.

Input device invariance. Can similar scores be obtained from different hardware configurations using the same input device? This contrast (which contrasts Conditions 1, 4, 5, 9, 10, and 13) anticipates that differences (where they exist) might be caused primarily by the input device. This may be especially true for speeded tests. By holding input-device constant across different hardware configurations, the remaining differences (if any) can be assessed.

Instruments

All subjects participating in the study were administered both forms (C1 and C2) of the CAT-ASVAB (see Chapter 11). Dependent measures consisted of the 22 (11 tests × 2 forms) scores. For the 18 adaptive power tests, these scores were based on Item Response Theory (IRT) ability estimates, and were set equal to the mode of the posterior distribution. The four speeded tests were scored using chance corrected rate scores. Scoring details are provided in Chapter 12.

The software that administers the CAT-ASVAB runs under the MS-DOS operating system, requires 4 megabytes of RAM, and requires a VGA video card and monitor. The same software was used in all conditions, with only minor modifications required to accommodate differences in input devices.

Analyses and Results

Under the null hypothesis of no hardware effects, the 22 test variables should display equivalent first, second, and cross moments among the 13 experimental conditions. Stated more formally, under the null hypothesis

$$\mu_1 = \mu_2 = \cdots = \mu_{13} \qquad (22\text{-}1)$$

and

$$\Sigma_1 = \Sigma_2 = \cdots = \Sigma_{13} \qquad (22\text{-}2)$$

where μ_k is a 22-element vector containing the test means for the k-th condition, and Σ_k is the 22×22 covariance matrix for the k-th condition. Taken jointly, the parameters $\{\mu_k, \Sigma_k\}$ (for $k = 1, 2, \ldots, 13$) contain useful information about hardware effects on the score scale, reliability, and construct validity of the battery. This becomes evident by noting that common measures of these properties are functions of these parameters. Score scale effects can be assessed from a comparison of means and variances across conditions; reliability effects can be examined from a comparison of alternate form reliabilities (across conditions); and construct validity effects can be measured from a comparison of test intercorrelations, or from a comparison of disattenuated test intercorrelations. Since all these measures are functions of elements contained in $\{\mu_k, \Sigma_k\}$, the statistical significance of the hardware effects (on the score scale, reliability, and construct validity) can be tested directly from (22-1) and (22-2). That is, if (22-1) and (22-2) hold, then so does the equivalence of score scale, reliability, and construct validity across conditions. This is noteworthy, since standard significance tests exist for testing (22-1) and (22-2). Below, the equivalence of the means and covariance matrices are tested separately. Where differences were found, additional analyses were conducted to help isolate the hardware related cause.

Homogeneity of Covariance Matrices

The likelihood ratio statistic

$$\lambda = \frac{\Pi_{k=1}^{13} \left| \hat{\Sigma}_k \right|^{n_k/2}}{\left| \hat{\Sigma} \right|^{N/2}} \qquad (22\text{-}3)$$

was used to test the significance of the difference among the 13 covariance matrices, where $\hat{\Sigma}_k$ is ML estimate of the 22×22 covariance matrix for the k-th group, $\hat{\Sigma}$ is the estimated covariance matrix for the total group, n_k is the sample size of the k-th group, and $N = \Sigma_{k=1}^{13} n_k$ is the total sample size. Under the assumption that the observations were sampled from a normal distribution, $-2 \log \lambda$ is asymptotically chi-square distributed with $df = 3,036$. However, in the current application of the test statistic, the asymptotic distribution of λ may not hold since most groups had relatively small sample sizes. For testing the significance of the difference among covariance matrices, the distribution of λ was approximated by a bootstrap method. This was accomplished using the following procedure:

1. Compute the statistic given by Equation 22-3 and denote the statistic value as λ_0.

2. Compute $\mathbf{x}_j$ ($j = 1, \ldots, N$), where $\mathbf{x}_j$ is the 22 element vector of difference scores calculated from the difference between the raw observations and the respective group mean vector.

3. Sample N observations ($\mathbf{x}_j$'s) with replacement.

4. Divide the N sampled values into 13 groups of sizes $n_1, n_2, \ldots, n_{13}$.

5. Compute the 13 covariance matrices from the set of bootstrapped values.

6. Compute the λ statistic given by Equation 22-3 from the bootstrapped covariance matrices.

7. Perform 10,000 replications of Steps 3–6, computing $\lambda_1, \lambda_2, \ldots, \lambda_{10000}$.

8. Compute prob($\lambda > \lambda_0$), the proportion of λ values greater than the sample value λ_0. If this proportion is small, we reject the null hypothesis of equivalent covariance matrices.

The bootstrap procedures outlined above resulted in an estimated prob $(\lambda > \lambda_0) = .4785$, which leads us to accept the null hypothesis of equivalent covariance matrices. Thus, there appears to be no effect of hardware on the reliability, construct validity, or on the variance of the score scale. Effects of hardware on the score-scale location parameters (means) are examined below.

Homogeneity of Means

To test the equivalence of means across the 13 hardware configurations, separate one-way ANOVAs were computed for each of the 11 tests contained in CAT-ASVAB. The dependent measure in each analysis was the average of the two scores obtained from like-named tests of forms C1 and C2. The results and summary statistics for the nine adaptive power tests are provided in Table 22-2. As indicated, none of the power tests displayed significant mean differences.

Table 22-3 displays results for the two speeded tests. For each test, three scores were examined:

Rate the proportion-correct (corrected for chance guessing) divided by the mean response time.

RT the average response latency (seconds) computed from the answered (reached) items.

P the proportion of correctly answered items calculated from reached items only.

The dependent measure was the average of these variables across the two CAT-ASVAB forms. As indicated in Table 22-3, significant mean differences

Table 22-2 ANOVA Results and Summary Statistics (Power Tests)

Condition	N	Statistic	Means (m) and SD (s)								
			GS	AR	WK	PC	AI	SI	MK	MC	EI
1	210	m	.34	.27	.41	.02	−.71	−.62	.65	−.52	−.47
		s	.88	.96	.84	.91	.71	.77	.97	.93	.91
2	433	m	.28	.12	.28	−.02	−.75	−.77	.55	−.59	−.41
		s	.92	1.00	.90	.94	.74	.81	1.04	.93	.94
3	228	m	.27	.12	.27	−.03	−.80	−.72	.55	−.52	−.41
		s	.96	1.03	.92	.97	.71	.80	1.03	.89	.91
4	210	m	.32	.26	.33	.05	−.79	−.76	.71	−.52	−.44
		s	1.03	.99	1.01	.97	.74	.78	.92	.85	.95
5	228	m	.31	.22	.32	.05	−.69	−.68	.60	−.49	−.35
		s	.91	.97	.86	.89	.69	.76	.98	.89	.86
6	222	m	.33	.22	.33	.01	−.77	−.70	.65	−.57	−.39
		s	.85	.95	.91	.96	.74	.74	.92	.86	.89
7	218	m	.24	.18	.25	.00	−.72	−.73	.59	−.61	−.45
		s	.93	1.00	.87	.91	.71	.78	.94	.84	.88
8	224	m	.28	.29	.31	−.02	−.82	−.78	.60	−.57	−.48
		s	.87	1.00	.87	.97	.67	.74	1.00	.86	.92
9	217	m	.24	.08	.26	−.05	−.73	−.78	.56	−.66	−.43
		s	.88	.89	.91	.94	.69	.78	.96	.83	.90
10	218	m	.28	.23	.32	.04	−.81	−.75	.62	−.57	−.45
		s	.96	.92	.94	.94	.71	.77	.92	.79	.92
11	225	m	.32	.24	.34	.02	−.71	−.66	.56	−.52	−.35
		s	.95	.94	.91	1.02	.73	.78	1.00	.90	.94
12	217	m	.28	.24	.27	−.01	−.68	−.70	.63	−.46	−.35
		s	.94	.91	.88	.91	.76	.78	.98	.91	.92
13	213	m	.27	.23	.24	−.05	−.80	−.75	.64	−.57	−.52
		s	.94	.94	.90	.96	.65	.76	.98	.85	.92
ANOVA		F value	.27	1.12	.53	.31	1.01	.91	.55	.85	.75
		P value	.99	.34	.89	.99	.44	.54	.88	.60	.70

for response time (RT), accuracy (P), and rate were found for NO. For CS, significant and marginally significant differences were found for response time (RT) and rate, respectively. Additional comparisons were made among speeded test rate-score means (Rate) to help relate the significant findings to specific hardware characteristics.

Table 22-4 displays ANOVA results for the six research issues. The second column displays those conditions included in each ANOVA. The results for NO (columns 3 and 4) indicate significant effects for "input-device," portability," and "input-device-invariance." Note however, most significant effects can be attributed to the Dell subnotebook used in Conditions 3 and 4 (full-keyboard and keypad conditions, respectively). An inspection of the means for Condition 3 and 4 (Table 22-3) indicates that this computer provides the lowest rate scores among all 13 conditions. This may have been due to the monitor which consisted of a liquid-quartz display. As indicated in the bottom row of Table 22-4, by excluding the Dell subnotebook Condition

non-significant mean differences were found when the same input-device (keypad) is used across remaining notebook and desktop computers (Conditions 1, 5, 9, 10, and 13).

The results for CS also display significant effects for "portability." However, unlike NO, no effect of input device is observed, and the portability effect does not appear to be directly related to the Dell subnotebook computer. Some characteristic difference between desktop and notebook computers (other than input device) appears to affect mean rate-scores on CS. Because of the inconsistency of these results, it is difficult to attribute the exact cause of the difference to a specific hardware characteristic.

Discussion

Among the five hardware dimensions examined, none were found to affect the psychometric properties of the adaptive power tests contained in the

Table 22-3 ANOVA Results and Summary Statistics (Speeded Tests)

Condition	N	Statistic	Means (m) and SD (s)					
			Numerical Operations			Coding Speed		
			Rate	RT	P	Rate	RT	P
1	210	m	21.64	2.83	.93	10.33	5.28	.89
		s	5.43	.76	.07	3.20	1.46	.15
2	433	m	21.83	2.89	.94	10.27	5.38	.89
		s	5.91	.82	.06	3.18	1.39	.16
3	228	m	21.09	2.97	.94	9.81	5.54	.88
		s	5.38	.82	.06	3.49	1.39	.17
4	210	m	19.50	3.10	.91	9.88	5.40	.89
		s	5.33	.79	.09	3.05	1.41	.17
5	228	m	21.63	2.85	.94	10.37	5.49	.92
		s	4.90	.66	.06	3.01	1.33	.13
6	222	m	23.78	2.66	.94	10.91	5.14	.90
		s	6.29	.76	.05	3.16	1.31	.13
7	218	m	22.74	2.79	.94	10.72	5.19	.90
		s	6.23	.83	.06	3.12	1.43	.14
8	224	m	21.66	2.87	.94	9.73	5.43	.87
		s	5.62	.75	.07	3.59	1.38	.18
9	217	m	21.39	2.90	.93	10.36	5.40	.90
		s	5.47	.84	.07	3.09	1.45	.14
10	218	m	21.47	2.91	.93	10.21	5.35	.89
		s	5.30	.87	.07	2.97	1.36	.16
11	225	m	22.07	2.84	.93	10.47	5.30	.90
		s	6.40	.75	.08	3.30	1.41	.15
12	217	m	21.39	2.94	.94	10.08	5.52	.90
		s	5.65	.78	.05	3.00	1.45	.14
13	213	m	21.52	2.86	.93	10.27	5.29	.89
		s	5.38	.68	.07	3.31	1.33	.16
ANOVA		F value	6.22	3.67	2.94	2.50	1.68	1.28
		P value	.00	.00	.00	.00	.06	.22

Table 22-4 ANOVA for Selected Comparisons (Speeded Tests)

Factor	Conditions	Numerical Operations		Coding Speed	
		F value	P value	F value	P value
A. Input Device	5,6,7	7.71	.001**	1.76	.173
B. Color Scheme	11,12	1.38	.240	1.75	.187
C. Monitor	10,13	.01	.928	.04	.841
D. CPU	9,10	.02	.881	.27	.602
E. Portability	1,4,9	9.91	.001**	1.59	.205
	2,3,7	4.41	.012*	4.40	.013*
	8,11	.51	.477	5.30	.022*
F. Input Device Invariance	1,4,5,9,10,13	5.25	.001**	.76	.577
	1,5,9,10,13	.08	.987	.10	.981

*p < .05; **p < .001

CAT-ASVAB. This result is noteworthy, since it suggests that some future changes in input device, color scheme, monitor, CPU, and portability may not necessarily lead to changes in reliability, construct validity, or the score scale of the adaptive power tests. Thus some variation in hardware may be permissible without the need for separate power test equating transformations.

However, some effects on rate scores were observed for the two speeded tests. For NO, these significant effects appeared to be caused by differential effects of hardware on both response latency and accuracy. Furthermore, scale-location of the rate-score was influenced by the type of input device. Some input devices appeared to allow for faster responding, which resulted in higher rate scores. When the same input device was used on desktop and notebook computers, no differences in psychometric score properties were identified. For CS, "portability" effects were identified—causing differences in scale-location between desktop and notebook computers. Although the difference appears to be related to response-speed rather than to response-accuracy, it is difficult to attribute the exact cause of the difference to a specific hardware characteristic.

Although the results suggest that computer administered power tests are insensitive to hardware changes, prudence should be exercised when altering any characteristic of an existing test with an established score scale, or when considering the exchangeability of scores obtained from different hardware configurations. This caution grows out of experiences with paper-and-pencil tests, where seemingly trivial differences, such as differences in-line-length or spacing can have a related effect on observed score distributions. When considering variation in hardware among computer administered tests, it may be useful to consider the following two factors.

1. *To what extent is the test speeded?* To the extent that speed influences test scores, hardware is likely to have an increasing effect on the score scale. Among the 11 tests studied here, there was a clear demarcation between power and speed. Although each of the nine power tests had an associated time-limit, these time-limits typically allow (in a military applicant population) over 98 percent of all examinees to complete all questions. Thus any small differences in response times caused by different hardware are unlikely to result in an increase in the frequency of unanswered items. Conversely, for the two speeded tests, scores are determined by dividing the percent correct by the item latencies. For these tests, it is very obvious how different hardware may cause different response times. However, the issue becomes more complicated when changes are being considered for power tests that have completion rates somewhere between the two extremes, say 90 percent. If the power test is sufficiently speeded, it is conceivable that latency-related hardware changes may increase the numbers of incomplete tests by a large enough amount to significantly alter the score scale.

2. *To what extent is the item appearance dependent on the hardware?* In the current study, the item appearance on different computers was almost identical. The same software was used to administer the adaptive tests on different computers. In each condition VGA monitors were used. Although both text and graphics were presented, the position and relative dimensions of all text and graphics remained relatively constant across conditions. The software presented text using a standard DOS fixed-width font, which resulted in identical line-breaks and spacing across conditions. Variations involving more extensive alterations in appearance (i.e., changes in font and line-breaks) may have larger effects than the ones identified in this study.

Although the adaptive power test results are encouraging, caution should be exercised when generalizing these results to other tests and other hardware configurations. Some meaningful (but small) effects may have been present, but were not detected because of insufficient power. In some instances, small changes in the score scale can have important consequences for selection decisions. The samples used in this study may not have been large enough to detect small but important effects caused by different hardware. A useful and important follow-on study would: (a) consist of a small number of conditions (say one desktop and one notebook condition), and (b) employ large samples (say 2,500 subjects per condition). If present, such a study could detect these small but important effects of hardware on the score scale. If this future large sample study replicates the current findings, then added confidence can be given to the hardware-invariance property attributed to adaptive power tests.

23

CAT-ASVAB Cost and Benefit Analyses

Lauress L. Wise, Linda T. Curran, and James R. McBride

The original Department of Defense (DoD) CAT-AS-VAB development tasking memo (5 January 1979) assigned responsibility to the Air Force for item development, to the Army for procurement and implementation, and to the Navy for psychometric development, provision of a test-bed system, and chairing the inter-Service committee for "determining the feasibility and cost advantages of utilizing CAT in the Department of Defense." (Note that this tasking memo was co-signed by the Under Secretary of Defense for Research and Engineering, later Secretary of Defense, William J. Perry.) The first of the original objectives for CAT-ASVAB was that it: "Be cost competitive with the paper-and-pencil (P&P) ASVAB for maintenance, administration, support, and advanced development."

By 1985, it was clear that the psychometric objectives for CAT-ASVAB were being met, and an effort to develop and evaluate alternative plans for deploying the system was launched. This chapter describes the approach, issues, and results of two major efforts to determine how CAT would be used operationally and whether the benefits associated with operational CAT testing justified the new equipment and other incremental costs.

CAT-ASVAB was originally sold with the promise that it could be cost-competitive with P&P testing and, at the same time, offer significant advantages. Some of the incremental advantages originally identified included (1) improved accuracy, particularly at the low and high ends of the ability scale; (2) improved test security as there would be no test booklets to "lose"; (3) significant reduction in testing time; and (4) improvement in the accuracy and speed of scoring. Additional benefits

were identified as CAT-ASVAB development progressed, including (1) simplified test form development through on-line calibration of new items; (2) improved test and item monitoring through the availability of item response data; and (3) expanded forms of assessment, such as psychomotor testing, made feasible by the availability of a computerized testing platform.

Given that the new system would require significant investment in computer hardware, the question of whether it could, in fact, be cost-competitive with the existing P&P system was a big one. The question assumed even larger significance as Defense procurement regulations covering the acquisition of computer hardware were expanded. It became not just a matter of soliciting fair and competitive bids. An economic analysis showing expected returns on investments was required for most computer purchases.

Issues in Operational Use

After the technical success of the new CAT system, three general issues remained to be addressed. These were:

• *Where and how will the new system be used?* Installation and use in the Military Entrance Processing Stations (MEPSs) would be reasonably straightforward, although issues involving the frequency and timing of testing sessions and individual versus group starts had to be addressed. The use of the new system in Mobile Examining Team Sites (METSs) was more problematic, as the equipment would have to be set up and taken down each time and stored somewhere between testing sessions. Some questioned whether the use of CAT-ASVAB at METSs was feasible at all. In this chapter, the complete specification of where and how CAT-ASVAB would be used is referred to as the *concept of operation* for the system. A great deal of effort was put into defining and evaluating numerous alternative operational concepts (The Concepts of Operations Planning and Evaluation [COPE] project).

• *How much will it cost to install and operate?* The evaluation of the cost of alternative operational concepts involved several factors. Estimates of the type and number of machines were required, along with analyses of potential changes in test administration, travel and storage costs, and any required site modifications.

• *What are the extent and value of benefits from the use of the new system?* CAT-ASVAB was not designed to reduce operational costs, but, rather, to provide additional selection benefits without significantly increasing operational costs. Benefits such as reduced test development costs could be given a dollar value. Other benefits such as stronger test security or improved test monitoring were more difficult to value. More important, although equally difficult to evaluate, was the impact on recruiting costs associated with shorter testing sessions, changes in the location and frequency of testing, and possibly changes in the effect of aptitude testing on the prospect's willingness to enlist. Finally, the most heroic assumptions were required in evaluating the impact of improvements to selection and classification decisions because of greater accuracy in assessing applicant aptitudes.

Summary of the 1987 and 1988 Economic Analyses

A decision by the Assistant Secretary of Defense (Manpower and Logistics) to accelerate the CAT-ASVAB program (Sellman, 1988) led to a departure from the normal approach to system life cycles for computer resources as detailed in DoD-STD-2167. It was estimated that the normal life cycle process would delay implementation until 1993 or later. Nonetheless, it was clear that CAT-ASVAB would involve significant costs for computer equipment and might also require site modification costs. Consequently, an economic analysis of costs and potential benefits associated with the new CAT-ASVAB system was launched under the direction of the Of-

fice of the Chief of Naval Personnel, as Executive Agent for CAT-ASVAB development (Automated Sciences Group & CACI, Inc. 1988).

Limitations and Assumptions

A contract to conduct the required economic analyses was awarded to Automated Sciences Corporation and CACI, Inc. In discussions with the project officer, several limiting assumptions were made that allowed the analyses to proceed within the schedule and scope of the intended effort. Based upon these limiting assumptions, the analyses:

• Excluded consideration of the DoD Student Testing Program

• Assumed implementation in existing MEPSs and METSs

• Assumed then current testing loads (FY81 through FY85)

• Used a life cycle through 2001, ten years after targeted implementation

• Did not consider alternative concepts of P&P testing

• Did not investigate issues related to technical adequacy of CAT-ASVAB

Alternatives Considered

The then operational P&P-ASVAB testing system was the baseline Option 1. Six computer-based alternatives to P&P testing (Options 2 through 7 below) were identified in the initial (1987) economic analysis. The two basic alternatives considered were CAT testing at all current sites and testing at the MEPSs only. Variations included testing at some (high-volume) but not all METSs, local versus centralized storage of METSs equipment, and introduction of a screening test that could be used by recruiters to minimize the additional burden of sending applicants to MEPSs, as required by the MEPS-only option. Specific options and related cost considerations are summarized briefly here.

• *Option 2, Full plus Local Storage,* included testing at both MEPSs and existing METSs. Semipermanent, networked systems would be used in the MEPSs and portable, stand-alone systems would be used at METSs. The METS equipment would be stored locally between testing sessions.

An estimated total of 10,500 computers would be required.

• *Option 3, Full plus Central Storage,* included both MEPS and METS testing as in Option 2. In Option 3, METS equipment would be stored centrally and shared across METSs, increasing transportation costs but decreasing the total number of machines that would be required. The estimated number of computers would be reduced to 7,000; however test administrator (TA) costs would nearly double.

• *Option 4, MEPSs Only,* specified elimination of all METS testing. Set-up and storage requirements would be eliminated and machine requirements would be significantly reduced, but travel costs and inconvenience for recruiters and applicants associated with sending everyone to a MEPS for testing would increase.

• *Option 5, MEPSs plus High-Volume METSs,* was a compromise between the cost and convenience of Options 2 and 3 and the savings and inconvenience of Option 4. Computer requirements would be reduced in comparison to Options 2 and 3, but the convenience of some alternative testing sites would be maintained.

• *Option 6, Screening plus MEPS,* included the use of the Computerized Adaptive Screening Test (CAST) (see Chapter 7) at recruiting stations to screen out applicants who were unlikely to meet aptitude qualifications. The number of applicants sent to MEPSs for testing and the associated travel and lodging costs could thus be substantially reduced.

• *Option 7, Portable Screening plus MEPSs,* was similar to Option 6, except that the screening test was designed to be administered on portable, hand-held computers. This would enable recruiters to administer the screening test in the field rather than having to bring youth into recruiting stations for testing.

Cost Analysis

Baseline costs for continuing P&P testing were estimated through analyses of actual costs over the FY81 through FY85 time period (Table 23-1).

Total baseline costs for a P&P-ASVAB 10-year life cycle were estimated by rounding the annual figures up to $14 million and multiplying by 10, giving a baseline of $140 million. In various presentations, an additional $70 million, covering current

Table 23-1 Baseline Annual Costs for P&P-ASVAB Testing in MEPSs and METSs, FYs 1981–85

Cost Categories	Cost (Thousands)
Testing Personnel	$12,180
Other Personnel	496
Travel and Transportation	593
Printing and Supplies	105
Test Development	500
Total Annual Cost	$13,674

operations for the 5-year period preceding implementation (e.g., FY87 through FY91) was added to each option.

Alternative costs for CAT-ASVAB included estimates of how the above "operations and support" costs would change and also added estimates for two other categories of costs: R&D and investment. *R&D costs* included remaining development, transition costs, and project management. They ranged from a total of $6 million to $8 million depending primarily on whether research to develop additional METS options would be required. *Investment costs* included purchase of new equipment, site modifications, shipping and installation, training, and project management.

Benefits Analysis

No attempt was made to estimate the impact of the new system on recruiting. The analysis of benefits focused, instead, on estimating the value of improved prediction of job success. The formulation developed by Cronbach and Gleser (1965) to assess the value of improved performance was used. In this approach, the value of improved performance is computed as the *product* of the following factors:

N Number of selections (310,000 annually)

T Average tenure of selectees (6.04 years)

SD_y Annual value of a one standard deviation increase in performance (estimated at $4,662, which was 20 percent of average salary)

R_i Increment in predictive validity (estimated as .005)

$\overline{X}$ The average standardized score of selectees ranging from 0 (if all applicants are selected) to large positive numbers as selection rate decreases with a corresponding increase in the value of test information for identifying the best candidates (estimated at .35 using a cut-off at the 20th percentile)

Using these figures, the value of the very modest increment in predictive validity was estimated as $15.276 million annually or roughly $153 million over the 10-year life cycle of the new system.

For each alternative, a return on investment (ROI) rate was estimated by taking the ratio of *net* benefit to initial investment. Net benefit is the difference between the value estimated above and the total operating costs necessary to produce that benefit. Initial investment costs included hardware acquisition, site preparation, and installation and training.

Results of the 1987 Economic Analysis

Table 23-2 summarizes the results from the initial (1987) economic analysis. Fifteen-year costs (5 years pre-implementation through 10 years post) for the alternatives ranged from $204 million for Option 7 to $292 million for Option 3, all generally comparable to the $210 million baseline estimate for continuing P&P testing. Based upon the benefits analysis described above, all of the CAT-ASVAB options showed a very significant ROI.

After reviewing the initial economic analysis, the Manpower Accession Policy Steering Committee (MAP) and the Assistant Secretary of Defense for Force Management and Personnel requested more information on benefits and a more detailed analysis of costs for three of the options. The initial analyses were judged sufficient to rule out the three options requiring the highest initial investment ($20 million or more)—Options 2 and 3 that required equipping all current METSs and Option 6 that required equipping all recruiting stations. Along with the three remaining alternatives (4, 5, and 7), a fourth concept, supported by MEPS personnel, was added in the subsequent analyses.

Revised Economic Analyses

To avoid confusion with the earlier analyses, the alternatives considered in the 1988 economic analysis were labeled A through D rather than 1 through 4. The four alternatives were: (A) MEPSs Only, (B) MEPSs plus High Volume METSs, (C) MEPSs plus Mobile Screening, and (D) MEPSs plus Mobile Testing Vans. The first three alternatives were Options 4, 5, and 7, respectively, from the prior analyses.

Concept D in this analysis involved administration of CAT-ASVAB in mobile vans. This approach would provide greater testing convenience to applicants and recruiters, while avoiding problems associated with maintaining fixed testing sites with a requirement to store the equipment between testing sessions. The downside of this approach was the significant costs that would be required for acquiring and maintaining the vehicles as well as the computers.

The report of the 1988 economic analysis (ASG & CACI, 1988) provided a great deal of detail on assumptions and costs for each option. Testing sites to be used in each MEPS area, average driving distances with associated travel and meal and lodging costs, and the size and frequency of testing sessions at each site were all documented as part of the cost analyses. The result was a much more focused attempt to assess the "cost competitiveness" of alternative CAT-ASVAB concepts.

On the benefits side, sensitivity analyses were conducted to determine the extent to which different assumptions influenced the results. For the most part, however, the benefits were viewed as unquantifiable. The final report stated:

The most significant benefits of CAT-ASVAB implementation remain to be quantified. This is because empirical data proving that CAT provides an econom-

Table 23-2 Life Cycle Cost Estimates for Alternative Operational Concepts: 1987 Economic Analyses[a]

Alternative Operational Concepts	Life Cycle Costs (Millions of Dollars)				Return on Investment (Percent)
	R & D	Investment	Operations and Support	Total	
1. Baseline—P&P Testing	0	0	210	210	NA
2. Full + Local Storage	8	28	233	269	261
3. Full + Central Storage	8	20	264	292	254
4. MEPSs Only	6	5	221	232	1,190
5. MEPSs + High-Volume METSs	6	16	239	261	464
6. MEPSs Screening	7	27	207	231	359
7. Portable Screening + MEPSs	8	11	185	204	842

[a] Automated Sciences Group & CACI, 1988.

ically significant improvement in selection and classification of enlistees has not yet been produced and analyzed.

Table 23-3 summarizes the cost findings from the revised economic analysis. The detailed analyses did lead to some changes in the overall estimates, mostly increases. Estimated costs for the MEPS plus Screening option (C, previously Option 7) increased significantly, in large part because the assumption was made that all applicants with predicted scores above the 10th percentile would be encouraged to go to the MEPSs for testing, greatly reducing the effectiveness of screening procedures in comparison to prior estimates.

The general conclusion drawn from the revised economic analyses was that CAT-ASVAB was necessarily more costly than P&P testing. Significant increases in predictive validity would be required to justify the extra expense and CAT-ASVAB had not been designed to seek significant improvements in prediction. Consequently, an expanded battery taking advantage of a computerized testing platform was needed.

After policy consideration of the results of the 1988 economic analysis, implementation decisions were put on hold and efforts were directed toward development and testing of an Enhanced Computer Administered Test (ECAT) Battery. The development and evaluation of this expanded battery is documented in Chapter 24.

The Concept of Operations Planning and Evaluation (COPE) Project

As described above, the completion of the original economic analysis was followed by a period of retrenchment. NPRDC continued CAT-ASVAB development with the completion of comparability and equating studies. A Joint-Service committee (Technical Advisory Selection Panel [TASP]) evaluated new tests and selected some of them for inclusion in the ECAT battery. A Joint-Service ECAT validity study was launched.

In 1989 responsibility for P&P-ASVAB R&D was transferred from the Air Force to the Defense Manpower Data Center (DMDC). A Personnel Testing Division was created in Monterey, California to handle this assignment and a staff of about 20 researchers and test developers was put in place.

Working with the Manpower Accession Policy Working Group (MAPWG) and under the guidance of the MAP, DMDC set out to conduct a new study of CAT-ASVAB implementation options. The study was designed to build on data from the ECAT validity study to evaluate alternative content for the ASVAB, as well as evaluating alternative test location and administration strategies.

Another component in the confluence of events supporting a new evaluation was the CAT-ASVAB Operational Test and Evaluation (OT&E) launched by the Navy. At the completion of the equating studies, CAT-ASVAB was ready for operational use. The equating studies had demonstrated the feasibility of operational testing, but with several significant limitations. Previously testing had always been conducted by outside contractors. No one was certain whether operational staff would be able to handle the increased complexity of CAT-ASVAB test administration. Further, no attempt had been made to gather information on recruiter attitudes and practices in response to operational use of CAT-ASVAB. Finally, more information was needed to estimate machine requirements. Details of the OT&E that resulted in response to these needs are provided in Chapter 20.

In 1991, after several rounds of discussion by the MAPWG, DMDC issued a request for proposals for contractor support in designing and conducting another evaluation of alternative concepts for ASVAB testing. The study was to be considerably broader in scope than the previous effort. A new testing concept using digital response pads was to

Table 23-3 Life Cycle Cost Estimates for Alternative Operational Concepts: 1988 Economic Analyses

Alternative Operational Concepts	Life Cycle Costs (Millions of Dollars)				Percent Increase
	R & D	Investment	Operations & Support	Total	
Baseline (P&P)—Testing	0	0	223	223	NA
A. Centralize—Testing	9	5	226	240	8
B. High Volume—METSs	9	10	280	299	34
C. CAT +—Screening	10	11	224	245	10
D. Mobile—Testing	9	31	315	355	59

be included, as was consideration of changes to the content of the ASVAB test battery based on ECAT validity results. The Human Resources Research Organization (HumRRO) was selected as the prime contractor to conduct the study.

In the summer of 1991, while alternative contractor proposals were being reviewed, DMDC formed an advisory panel consisting of operational personnel from USMEPCOM and recruiting or recruiting policy personnel from each Service. The purpose of the panel, which became known simply as the COPE panel, was to provide guidance on the need for, and feasibility of, alternative concepts for aptitude testing as seen from the perspective of the system's administrators and clients. It was hoped that the panel would help in identifying specific costs and cost savings that might be associated with different approaches. The first meeting of the panel included an overview of the nature and scope of the proposed project and discussion by panel members of their views on priorities for enhancements.

Evolution of Alternative Concepts

A considerable effort was expended in defining, refining, and redefining the alternative concepts for aptitude testing to be evaluated. Complete specification of a single alternative involved addressing questions of what was administered (current AS-VAB, augmented ASVAB, or partial ASVAB), where it was administered (in MEPSs, at METSs, at contractor facilities ranging from community colleges to dedicated testing centers), how it was administered (P&P, digital response pads, desktop computers, notebook computers). In fact, a complete plan required answering the questions of whether, what, and how testing would be conducted at each type of site, yielding a very large number of possible alternatives.

Digital response pad (DRP) testing. Just as a new evaluation of operational concepts for CAT-ASVAB was being launched as part of the comprehensive review of the contents and use of the ASVAB, an alternative approach to testing was proposed by staff at USMEPCOM. The proposal was to use digital response pads (DRPs) to record examinee responses. The response pads, which were about the size of a hand-held calculator, were relatively inexpensive to buy in quantity and easy to transport. Responses to all of the ASVAB items could be stored in a single pad and then uploaded through a "docking station" either to a PC or,

via modem, to a mainframe for nearly immediate scoring.

DRP testing would greatly reduce scoring delays at remote sites without the cost and "lugability" problems associated with the use of personal computers. It did require continued use of printed test booklets and so did not improve test security. This approach also did not support adaptive selection of items, so that test length was not reduced. Subsequent research did suggest, however, that considerable savings in testing time could be achieved for most examinees through self-paced administration, where all of the oral instructions were given at the beginning of the battery.

Separation of test content issues. As preliminary results from the ECAT validation study became available, two things were clear. First, no unambiguously large gains in validity were likely. Large gains were evident only where the criterion was limited to special measures of psychomotor performance and only for a limited number of occupations. Second, a number of issues, including practice and coaching effects and adverse impact, would have to be resolved before most of the tests could be used operationally. A special subcommittee of the MAPWG was formed to review the ECAT results and make recommendations on possible near-term changes to the content of the ASVAB. The subcommittee, dubbed the ASVAB Review Technical (ART) Committee, was chaired by Dr. Bruce Bloxom of DMDC and included Frances Grafton from the Army, Dr. Dan Segall and Dr. Clessen Martin from the Navy, Dr. Lonnie Valentine from the Air Force, and Dr. Bill Sims from the Center for Naval Analyses. Several others served in "ex officio" capacities.

As it evolved, the economic analyses were divided into two parts. The cost of enlistment processing was related primarily to the length and not the content of the battery. Evaluation of benefits relating to reduction in recruiting and enlistment processing costs proceeded independent of considerations of changes to the content of the battery, assuming only that the overall length would be held constant. At the same time, NPRDC had demonstrated the equivalence of scores from different modes of testing, so evaluation improvements to selection and classification decisions resulting from changes to the battery could proceed independent of considerations regarding the medium and location of testing. The remainder of this chapter focuses on the cost–benefit issues.

Leverage points. The COPE study began with a careful analysis of the current approach to aptitude testing as it was embedded in the overall enlistment screening process. The idea was to identify potential "leverage points," areas involving significant costs where savings through alternative concepts might be plausible. As described below, the approach taken in this study was much broader than the approach used in the prior study, encompassing the entire recruitment and enlistment process and not just aptitude testing. Some key costs that were identified were: (1) recruiter time, (2) TA costs, and (3) travel, lodging, and meal costs associated with bringing applicants to the MEPSs for testing and, in many cases, housing them overnight. The COPE panel was particularly helpful in pointing to the need for more immediate scoring at remote sites as one important leverage point. Delays in score processing cause recruiters to have to spend more time keeping in touch with applicants and, in some cases, lose applicants as other opportunities arise for them. Specific leverage points identified in the review of baseline operations (Hogan, McBride, & Curran, 1995) included:

- Improvements to the quality of the job match

- Reduced testing time

- Local testing

- Earlier job-specific information

- Overnight stays

- MEPS processing

The first ASVAB review workshop. In addition to four or five meetings each of the MAPWG and COPE panel and numerous meetings between the contractor (HumRRO) and DMDC staff, two workshops were held to identify the most feasible concepts of operations. The first workshop was held at the HumRRO offices in the Spring of 1992. The workshop was attended by planners and policy experts from each Service in addition to members of the MAPWG and COPE panel. The goals of this first workshop were to (1) review the range of alternative concepts and help set priorities for the ones to be evaluated, and (2) review and augment the debt and benefit factors to be considered in the evaluation. At the conclusion of the first workshop, a greatly reduced set of options had been identified. For example, options involving two stages of testing, AFQT administered locally at METSs, and an augmented battery requiring special testing devices later at the MEPSs were essentially eliminated.

Alternative concepts. After additional refinement, the following concepts were selected for inclusion in the economic analyses:

1. *Baseline:* Continued use of P&P testing at all current sites.

2. *DRP in MEPSs and at METSs:* Continued testing at all current sites using DRPs.

3. *CAT-ASVAB in MEPSs and DRP at METSs:* Use of networked desktop computers in the MEPSs and DRPs at current METSs.

4. *P&P in MEPSs and CAT at METSs:* An attempt to focus on changes in METS testing where gains are most needed.

5. *P&P in MEPSs and DRP at METSs:* Limited introduction of new technology at the point where quick scoring is most needed.

6. *CAT in MEPSs and CTCs and DRP at METSs:* As many METSs as possible replaced by contract testing centers (CTCs) with dedicated computer testing equipment; DRP used at remaining METSs.

7. *CAT in MEPSs and at METSs:* Networked desktop computers would be used at MEPSs and notebook computers would be used at METSs. Some METSs might have to be closed or relocated if CAT could not be accommodated.

8. *CAT in MEPSs, CTCs, and Large METSs; DRPs Elsewhere:* A hybrid approach similar to the identification of "high-volume" METSs in the previous study.

As the study progressed, it became clear that a number of feasibility issues would have to be addressed before either CAT or DRP could be used operationally at METSs, or before CTCs could be engaged. CAT-ASVAB was already being used operationally in some MEPSs. An evaluation was needed of the option of going ahead with full-scale MEPS implementation while testing continued on the feasibility of different METS approaches. Consequently, a ninth option was added:

9. *CAT in MEPSs and P&P at METSs:* Implement established CAT-ASVAB procedures now, even though the most pressing problems are at the METSs.

Development of the Cost Model

The model developed for assessing the costs of alternative operations divided costs into three general categories. *Operational costs* included test form development and printing, test administration and scoring costs, and travel, meal, and lodging costs, as well as medical screening and other enlistment processing costs. *Recruiting costs* included, primarily, the recruiter salaries and related costs. *Person-Job match costs* included costs associated with training attrition and marginal or substandard performance on the job by individuals inappropriately selected for a given job. As indicated above, this last category was used only in evaluating changes to the test battery; analysis of alternative operational concepts was limited to the first two cost categories.

Stage-of-processing model. A model of the costs associated with different stages of applicant processing was developed. Initial recruiter contact, aptitude testing, medical assessment, Service counseling and assignment, and the time in the delayed entry program (DEP) were identified as distinct stages at which applicants might opt or be screened out prior to enlistment. An applicant flow model, indicating the proportion of applicants who continue from each stage to the next, was developed. Some concepts, such as immediate scoring at METSs, might reduce losses at one stage or another, thus reducing the number of initial recruiter contacts needed to produce a fixed number of enlistments. The basic idea of the stage-of-processing model was that unit (per applicant) costs could be estimated for each stage and then multiplied by the number of applicants processed through that stage under a given concept to get total costs for the stage. Overall costs were estimated by summing the total costs from each stage. A more detailed discussion of this approach may be found in Hogan et al. (1995).

Capital costs. In analyzing different options, the cost of capital equipment was broken out separately from other processing and development costs. This amount represented the "investment" necessary to produce savings and other benefits. Some capital costs, associated primarily with scanning equipment, were identified for the current, baseline testing concept. Alternatives involving CAT or DRP testing would reduce or eliminate the need for scanners, reducing one area of capital costs in exchange for investments in other areas. After deliberation, a 5-year life-cycle was estimated for computer and DRP equipment. Capital costs were thus amortized over a 5-year period.

One-day processing. As the study progressed, USMEPCOM was going forward with plans for a significant upgrade of the computers used in each of the MEPSs. Part of the justification for new hardware and software was that it could speed processing through the MEPSs. Because of the length of processing in the MEPSs, many applicants, including virtually all of those who undergo aptitude testing in the MEPSs, are brought in and tested the night before processing and then housed overnight. The shorter time requirements of CAT-ASVAB and the immediate availability of scores would enable more applicants to be brought in the morning of processing, complete their aptitude testing, and be ready by mid-morning for medical screening and counseling, eliminating the need for an overnight stay. The variable completion time of CAT-ASVAB was actually an advantage in comparison to "lock-step" testing, as it allowed applicants to flow more smoothly into medical processing.

Results of the Cost Evaluation

A spreadsheet model was developed that computed estimates of each type of costs as a function of assumptions associated with each alternative concept. Examples of these assumptions included the proportion of applicants tested at MEPSs versus METSs and the proportion of MEPS examinees requiring an overnight stay. Table 23-4 summarizes the resulting annualized cost estimates for baseline operations and each of the alternative testing concepts.

The second ASVAB review workshop. Results from the cost analyses were reviewed by DMDC, the MAPWG, and the Defense Advisory Committee on Military Personnel Testing (DAC). In addition, a second ASVAB Review Workshop was held at HumRRO in Spring 1993 to develop specific recommendations based upon these findings and also to review proposals for changes to the content of the ASVAB.

All of the alternatives resulted in substantial estimated savings relative to current P&P testing. As mentioned above, the feasibility of some of the options for METS testing had yet to be demonstrated. Implementing CAT in the MEPSs required only a very modest capital investment. The savings in the first year would more than pay for the estimated (unamortized) five-year capital investment costs. Proceeding at once with implementation in the MEPSs was the first recommendation derived from these results.

The need for improvements to METS testing had been clearly laid out and the cost analysis results indicated that very substantial savings could plau-

Table 23-4 Estimated Costs for Alternative Concepts: 1993 Study

	Annual Costs (Millions of Dollars)			
Operational Concept	Capital Cost (Amortized)	Processing & Development	Recruiting Costs	Annualized Total
1. Baseline: All P&P—(Total Annual Costs)	.287	76.761	472.990	550.039
	Savings/(Costs) Relative to Baseline (Millions)			
2. DRP in MEPSs and METSs	(.306)[a]	1.233	.844	1.772
3. CAT in MEPSs—DRP at METSs	(.609)	3.675	1.970	5.035
4. P&P in MEPSs—CAT at METSs	(2.690)	1.250	2.524	1.083
5. P&P in MEPSs—DRP at METSs	(.200)	.916	.898	1.614
6. CAT in MEPSs & at CTCs—DRP at METSs	(.579)	3.539	2.023	4.984
7. CAT in MEPSs—CAT at METSs	(2.808)	3.661	3.582	4.435
8. CAT in MEPSs, CTCs, Large—METS; DRP elsewhere	(1.537)	3.570	2.758	4.791
9. CAT in MEPSs—P&P at METSs	(.378)	2.751	1.082	3.454

[a] ( ) indicates negative costs [savings].

sibly be achieved through such improvements. The second recommendation drawn from these results was that DoD should proceed with all due haste to an operational tryout of METS testing concepts.

Comparison of First and Second Cost–Benefit Studies

The two major CAT-ASVAB cost–benefit studies (ASG/CACI and HumRRO) took somewhat different approaches and reached dramatically different conclusions. The first study showed large net cost increases and focused on improved selection and classification decisions to find benefits from CAT. The second study held the quality of selection and classification decisions constant and found very significant operational savings. How did such very different results come about?

Military Entrance Processing Command (USMEPCOM) Enthusiasm

A key change in the attitude of USMEPCOM personnel occurred between the two studies and was a major factor in the different outcomes. At the time of the first study, USMEPCOM had a natural and healthy "it ain't broke, so why fix it?" perspective. Enlistment testing was working satisfactorily under the current system and they wanted to make sure that any proposed changes were thoroughly researched and adequately resourced. They did not want to be left implementing changes that might lead to unforeseen problems which they did not have the resources to deal with.

By the time of the second study, the CAT OT&E was underway and the staff at several MEPSs felt comfortable with the feasibility of CAT. In addition, while the current system did not break, it became "seriously bent" in two significant respects. The Los Angeles MEPS was burned to the ground during the riots that followed the initial acquittal of police in the Rodney King beating. Most of the enlistment processing that had been handled by the Los Angeles MEPS was diverted to San Diego, one of the CAT-ASVAB OT&E sites. ASVAB testing did take place at a temporary site in the Los Angeles area. The MEPS commander, through HQ USMEPCOM, requested that Los Angeles be added as a fifth OT&E site to speed up testing and scoring at this temporary site. The request was approved and the CAT computers were installed. A total of 30 computers could be accommodated at the temporary site, but by staggering starting times, as many as 80 applicants were tested on some evenings. Scores were transmitted via modem to the San Diego MEPS so that applicants who qualified could be sent for further processing as soon as the next day. The use of CAT-ASVAB at Los Angeles allowed enlistment testing to continue despite the loss of the MEPS.

The other serious concern with the current system related to the USMEPCOM System 80 computers used in each MEPS. They were old and would soon be impossible to maintain. The need for improved hardware and information processing software was evident and CAT-ASVAB was seen as a potentially important component of the justification for the new system that was becoming increasingly critical.

At the beginning of the CAT OT&E, the word

passed down to the MEPS commanders was that this was likely to be just a temporary test; they should support it, but not become too attached to it. Within a year, a very different attitude prevailed and all five of the MEPS commanders at the OT&E sites were extremely reluctant to revert back to P&P testing. The concept of "one-day" testing that became a major component of CAT-ASVAB savings was developed and promoted by USMEPCOM staff. Without their enthusiastic support, a very different outcome might have been reached.

Recruiter Involvement

A second factor that led to the different results in the second study was the involvement of recruiters in the planning and review of the evaluation and the inclusion of recruiting costs in the overall cost model. With the military downsizing following the end of the Cold War, recruiting resources were being cut faster than requirements. At the same time, interest in military careers was declining, making the recruiters' jobs more difficult than ever. Involving recruiters in the specification of issues to be addressed and in the design of alternative concepts was a significant factor and led to a much greater acceptance of the final results.

Other Factors

A number of significant environmental changes between 1988 and 1992 also contributed to the different results. The costs of desktop computers were greatly reduced at the same time that their capacity increased. Notebook computers became much more common and affordable. The development of DRP testing was another factor that led to differences in the concepts considered. One additional factor was increased interest in computerized testing, even adaptive testing, as plans for computer administration of tests, such as the Educational Testing Service Graduate Record Examination, were developed and implemented.

Summary and Conclusions

A number of lessons about cost–benefit analyses can be drawn from the CAT-ASVAB experience. One example is the importance of a very tangible demonstration of the feasibility of proposed operational concepts. Until the OT&E gave USMEPCOM personnel a chance to try out the new approach, a healthy skepticism existed that limited thinking about possible alternatives and retarded acceptance of any new system.

Another consideration was the importance of documenting tangible cost savings. The use of "utility dollars" as the measure of output identified in the initial study did not create a great deal of enthusiasm on the part of policy makers being asked to pay for the new system. Only when specific cost savings were identified was approval granted.

A final lesson, although not new, is the importance of involving all stakeholder groups in defining the options to be considered and designing and reviewing the evaluation of these options. Without the participation of recruiters and operational USMEPCOM personnel, in addition to the system developers, successful results would have been unlikely.

In May 1993, the MAP approved the implementation of CAT-ASVAB at all MEPSs and urged all due haste in developing, testing, and evaluating alternatives for automating METS testing. This decision represents the successful conclusion of a very long process of CAT-ASVAB design and development.

VI

Current Status and Beyond

The final chapters deal with three disparate topics related to CAT-ASVAB, but not integral to the research and development that prepared for its introduction into operational use. **Chapter 24** describes research that focused on the possibility of adding some innovative tests to the CAT-ASVAB battery to take advantage of unique capabilities of computer-administered testing that were not exploited in the development of CAT-ASVAB itself. Wolfe, Alderton, Larson, Bloxom, and Wise describe research to evaluate ECAT, a battery of innovative tests including measures of non-verbal reasoning, spatial abilities, psychomotor skills, and perceptual speed.

Chapter 25 discusses the impact of CAT-ASVAB research and development on a number of other computerized testing programs. In it, McBride makes the point that not only did the CAT-ASVAB program culminate in operational use of CAT for DoD personnel selection testing; it also had the indirect effect of disseminating computerized adaptive testing technology to other testing applications, in both the public and private sectors.

In **Chapter 26**, Segall and Moreno underscore that CAT-ASVAB research and development did not cease with the decision to implement it nationwide. Two complete new item pools have already been developed, making a total of four alternate forms of CAT-ASVAB available. Plans are in place to develop new, nationwide ASVAB norms by administering CAT-ASVAB Form 4 in the 1997 Profile of American Youth. The new CAT-ASVAB-based norms will provide a basis for developing new score scales for ASVAB tests and composites, and thus for improving on the scales based on the paper-and-pencil versions of the tests. Research is in progress to address some test security issues, unique to adaptive testing, that make it desirable to improve on the test item exposure control procedures already incorporated in CAT-ASVAB. New approaches to item calibration and equating are being explored; if successful, these could result in substantial improvements in the cost and efficiency of developing new test forms by collecting data on-line during the operational tests. Last, but not least, work is in progress to explore the use of multidimensional adaptive testing, which has the potential to yield substantial improvements in the efficiency of the already highly efficient adaptive tests of CAT-ASVAB.

Following Chapter 26, two sections include an extensive **reference list** of nearly 300 citations from the book and a **list of acronyms** frequently used in the 26 chapters.

CHAPTER
24

Expanding the Content of CAT-ASVAB: New Tests and Their Validity

John H. Wolfe, David L. Alderton, Gerald E. Larson,
Bruce M. Bloxom, and Lauress L. Wise

The widespread availability of CAT-ASVAB computers will facilitate the use of new types of tests that could not be administered in paper-and-pencil mode, such as tests of working memory, psychomotor ability, and reaction time. New computer-based tests could, in turn, improve the ASVAB's validity, resulting in better selection and classification and hence decreased school attrition and better on-the-job performance. This prospect led to the validity study described in this chapter, the Enhanced Computer Administered Tests (ECAT) project.[1]

The ECAT project began when the Assistant Secretary of Defense (Force Management and Personnel) redirected the CAT-ASVAB program to "include a Joint-Service validation of the Services' new computerized cognitive and psychomotor tests" (Sellman, 1988). The project was planned and approved jointly by representatives from DoD, Army, Navy, Air Force, and Marine Corps, with the Navy as Executive Agent and the Navy Personnel Research and Development Center (NPRDC) as lead laboratory.

Before the project began, a meta-analysis study was performed to estimate how great an increase in the ASVAB's validity might be attainable by the addition of new tests (Schmidt, Hunter, & Dunn, 1987). That study concluded that the addition of perceptual speed tests could raise the ASVAB's

mean validity by .02. If psychomotor tests were added, the validity might be improved by an additional .01, for a combined increase of .03. Assuming the ASVAB's mean validity to be about .60, these increases represent 3 percent and 5 percent improvements, respectively. Although these increases appear small, Schmidt et al. concluded that they could result in hundreds of millions of dollars worth of personnel performance improvement annually in the Armed Services because of the large number of people selected and classified by the ASVAB.

McHenry, Hough, Toquam, Hanson, and Ashworth (1990) reported mean validity increases from Project A spatial and psychomotor tests of .02 and .04 for predicting Core Technical Proficiency and General Soldiering Proficiency, respectively. Wolfe, Alderton, and Larson (1993) validated several of the nonpsychomotor ECAT tests in nine Navy schools (see also Wolfe & Alderton, 1992). They found mean validity increases of .016 over a mean ASVAB validity of .70, corrected for range restriction and criterion unreliability. The largest increases, up to .06, were obtained for hands-on laboratory performance measures. Working Memory, Figural Reasoning, and Spatial composites each produced increases in validity as high as .055 for predicting Avionics Lab, Hull Technician Lab, and Aviation Ordnance, while Perceptual Speed had smaller validity increments. Carey (1994) validated eight of the nine ECAT tests against mechanical job performance in the Marine Corps.

---

[1] Additional information about ECAT can be found in a special issue of *Military Psychology,* Vol 9(1), 1997.

The validity increases were .012 for predicting hands-on performance tests for automotive mechanics and .016 for helicopter mechanics. Job knowledge criteria showed negligible increases in validity (.003). Carey found that one spatial visualization test, Assembling Objects (AO), produced as much validity increase as the entire ECAT battery for predicting hands-on criteria.

Collectively, these findings seem to generally confirm the Schmidt et al. (1987) conclusions about probable validity gains from adding new tests to the ASVAB. The ECAT study was designed to determine (more precisely) probable validity gains and to identify the aptitude constructs that might make the greatest contribution.

ECAT Tests and Factors

The ECAT battery consists of nine tests, as shown in Table 24-1, reproduced from Alderton & Larson (1992).

Three of the tests are cognitive ability tests that require computer administration: Integrating Details, Mental Counters, and Sequential Memory. Three of the tests—Assembling Objects, Spatial Orientation, and Figural Reasoning—were computer-administered versions of the Army's Project A paper-and-pencil spatial tests (Peterson et al., 1990). Three of the tests are psychomotor tests reproduced from Project A: One-Hand Tracking, Two-Hand Tracking, and Target Identification. Since most of the ECAT tests are quite novel, a brief description of each test is given.

Nonverbal Reasoning Tests

Mental Counters (CT)—a complex 40-item working memory test. Each screen contains three horizontal lines, arrayed left to right. Each line represents a counter with an initial value of zero. During an item, boxes appear sequentially, one at a time, either above or below one of the three lines. If a box appears above a line, the value for that counter is incremented by 1. If a box appears below a line, that counter is decremented by 1. On each trial, either five or seven boxes appear. The boxes appear at one of two rates, either one every 1.33 seconds or one every .75 second. The task is to make a series of rapid calculations and to select, from a four-alternative multiple-choice menu, the set of correct final counter values. Number of correct responses is the summary score.

Sequential Memory (SM)—a complex test of working memory. Each item consists of three to five horizontally arrayed dots on the screen. Each dot is given a numerical value which must be memorized. The item is then presented in a series of 5 to 7 "calls" to the dots, in which each call is announced by briefly turning one of the dots into an "X." The person must report the digit string that corresponds to the order in which the dots were "called." In the second half of the test, after all the calls for an item have been made, the examinee is told to translate each number in the ordered number list into a different number and then type in the new ordered list. There are 10 items in the first part of the test and 25 in the second part of the test. The test score is the proportion of digits correct.

Figural Reasoning (FR)—a figural inductive reasoning (or series extrapolation) test. Items use a combination of geometric forms and arbitrary figures presented in a series of four frames. The task is to induce the transformation rule controlling the series and then select one of five alternatives that correctly completes the series. The test score is the number correct of 35 items.

Table 24-1 Tests in the Joint-Service ECAT Battery

Construct	Test	Description
Non-Verbal Reasoning	Mental Counters (CT)*	40-item working memory test using figural content
	Sequential Memory (SM)*	35-item working memory test using numerical content
	Figural Reasoning (FR)	35-item series extrapolation test using figural content
Spatial Ability	Integrating Details (ID)*	40-item spatial problem-solving test
	Assembling Objects (AO)	32-item spatial and semi-mechanical test
	Spatial Orientation (SO)	24-item spatial perception/rotation test
Psychomotor Skill	One-Hand Tracking (T1)*	18-item single-limb psychomotor tracking test
	Two-Hand Tracking (T2)*	18-item multi-limb psychomotor tracking test
Perceptual Speed	Target Identification (TI)*	36-item reaction-time-based figural perceptual speed test

*Requires computer administration.

Spatial Ability Tests

Integrating Details (ID)—a complex, 40-item spatial problem-solving test. Each item consists of two separate screens. The first screen contains from two to six regular geometric puzzle pieces that must be mentally fused to form a complete object. This is much like a jigsaw puzzle. Having connected all of the puzzle pieces, the individual must remember the final object, then press a response key. The puzzle pieces are replaced by a new screen with a single completed object. The task is to indicate if the displayed object is the product of the original puzzle pieces. Accuracy is the test score.

Assembling Objects (AO)—a spatial construction test. Each item consists of a frame with several (2–6) separate elements. The task is to choose from four alternatives the answer that correctly represents how the elements should be connected. There are 32 items in the test. The first 15 items are semi-mechanical items with labels indicating how the elements should be connected. The final 17 items consist of a disheveled jigsaw and four complete ones; the task is to choose the correct alternative. The test score is number correct.

Spatial Orientation (SO)—a spatial perception test. Each of the 24 items consists of an environmental view, such as a bridge over a river or a house with an apparent horizon. These views are rotated away from the "natural" horizon. At the bottom of the frame is a circle with a dot on the perimeter. The task is to rotate the frame around the view until it corresponds with the natural horizon and determine where the dot on the circle would be located. This information is used to select which of five alternatives correctly shows the dot after rotation. The test score is the number of items correct.

Psychomotor Skill

One-Hand Tracking (T1)—a psychomotor test that uses a response pedestal. Each item begins with a "path" on the computer screen. The path is a contiguous string that goes up/down and/or right/left, parallel with the sides of the screen, making only 90-degree turns. At one end of the path is a diamond indicating the path's termination point. Starting at the other end is a box that travels forward along the path. The subject moves a joy-stick that controls the movement of a "cross-

hair." The task is to keep the cross-hair on the moving box. Items vary in terms of the length of the path which is inversely related to the speed at which the box moves (total item duration is thus constant). For each item, the "score" is the average absolute Cartesian pixel distance between the cross-hair and the moving box (a distance reading is taken every 50 ms during the item). The test score is the average distance-off-target across 18 items.

Two-Hand Tracking (T2)—a psychomotor test that has exactly the same structure and task constraints as the One-Hand Tracking test. The difference is that cross-hair movement is controlled by two slide potentiometers: One slide controls horizontal (left/right) movement while the other controls vertical (up/down) motion. One hand must be used for each slide control. Number of items, scoring, and final score are the same as for One-Hand Tracking.

Perceptual Speed

Target Identification (TI)—a hybrid test combining aspects of choice reaction time and spatial mental rotation tests. Each item consists of a target figure in the top half of the screen and three alternative figures in the bottom half. The figures are schematic line drawings of simple objects, such as trucks, helicopters, and tanks. The target may be rotated, distorted (e.g., shrunken), or both, but the alternative answers will be in a "natural" upright position. The task is to select the correct alternative as rapidly as possible. Before each item, examinees must simultaneously press four "Home" buttons, two on the left and two on the right side of the response pedestal, essentially pinning their hands. As soon as the examinee decides upon an answer, either hand may be used to press the button corresponding to the selected alternative. The test score is the average correct decision time across the 36 items, with decision time defined as the time between item presentation and button release.

The Schmid-Leiman (1957) factoring given in Table 24-2 (orthogonalized hierarchical solution) shows that these nine tests measure three underlying factors: Working Memory, Spatial Ability, and Psychomotor Ability. Additional factor analysis of the combined ASVAB and ECAT battery (Alderton & Larson, 1992) shows seven factors which are the union of the ECAT factors and the usual four factors found in the ASVAB (Verbal, Mathe-

Table 24-2 Factor Analyses of ECAT

Test	"g"	Spatial Ability	Psychomotor Ability	Working Memory
Mental Counters (CT)	.690	.130	−.046	**.313**
Sequential Memory (SM)	.643	.019	.000	**.583**
Figural Reasoning (FR)	.703	**.210**	−.002	.149
Integrating Details (ID)	.751	**.279**	−.018	.009
Assembling Objects (AO)	.757	**.281**	−.036	−.003
Spatial Orientation (SO)	.677	**.231**	−.057	.033
One-Hand Tracking (T1)	−.484	.004	**.696**	−.017
Two-Hand Tracking (T2)	−.524	−.017	**.716**	.009
Target Identification (TI)	−.402	−.082	.241	−.021

Note: Entries in bold correspond to Promax loadings greater than .40. ECAT = Enhanced Computer Administered Test.

Table 24-3 Range-Corrected Correlations Among ASVAB and ECAT Factor Scores

Factor	Verbal	Math	Technical	Clerical Speed	Working Memory	Spatial Ability	Psychomotor Ability
Verbal	1.000						
Math	0.722	1.000					
Technical	0.672	0.558	1.000				
Clerical Speed	0.489	0.647	0.166	1.000			
Working Memory	0.491	0.641	0.387	0.472	1.000		
Spatial Ability	0.587	0.711	0.603	0.420	0.789	1.000	
Psychomotor Ability	−0.365	−0.405	−0.430	−0.271	−0.480	−0.605	1.000

matical, Technical, and Speed). It was encouraging to verify that the ECAT battery was indeed measuring ability factors not measured by the ASVAB.

Unfortunately, the factors turned out to be highly correlated, both within and between the ASVAB and ECAT batteries. Table 24-3 shows the intercorrelations of the (regression-weighted estimates of) factor scores derived from separate factor analyses of ASVAB and ECAT. The correlation of .722 between ASVAB Verbal and Math factors is less than the .789 correlation of Working Memory and Spatial Ability, and only slightly larger than the .711 correlation between Math and Spatial Ability. The high intercorrelations between the ASVAB and ECAT factors limit the potential improvement in validity that the ECAT battery can achieve.

Adverse Impact

From inspection of the content of the sample items, one can conclude that the ECAT tests are relatively knowledge-free as compared to the ASVAB (that is, they do not require knowledge acquired through formal education). They may be described as tests of fluid intelligence, rather than the crystallized intelligence measured by the ASVAB. This aspect should mean that the ECAT tests would have less adverse impact on educationally disadvantaged subgroups. Table 24-4 confirms this hypothesis. It shows the differences in mean test scores between Caucasians and blacks, Asians, and Hispanics. The four tests with the largest adverse impact all were ASVAB tests—General Science, Word Knowledge, Auto-Shop Information, and Mechnical Comprehension. The subgroups differ on which tests had the least adverse impact, but the ECAT tests compared favorably with the ASVAB tests. Since the sample was explicitly selected by ASVAB scores, correction for range restriction would increase the estimates of adverse impact for ASVAB tests more than for ECAT tests.

Sample and Procedures

Subjects were military recruits scheduled for technical training in a military occupational specialty in the Navy, Army, and Air Force. In the Navy, subjects were tested at the Great Lakes Recruit Training Center early in basic training, usually four weeks before beginning their specialized training. In the Army and Air Force, recruits were tested at

Table 24-4 Subgroup Differences in ASVAB and ECAT Test Means

Variable	White-Black Z	White-Asian Z	White-Hispanic Z
Years of Education	−.058*	−.288**	.133**
AFQT	.736**	.302**	.370**
General Science (GS)	.818**	.609**	.475**
Arithmetic Reasoning (AR)	.753**	.187**	.293**
Word Knowledge (WK)	.736**	.755**	.532**
Paragraph Comprehension (PC)	.515**	.375**	.219**
Numerical Operations (NO)	.023	−.189**	.022
Coding Speed (CS)	.142**	−.073	.051
Auto-Shop Information (AS)	1.106**	.829**	.638**
Math Knowledge (MK)	164**	−.396**	−.017
Mechanical Comprehension (MC)	.901**	.430**	.440**
Electronics Information (EI)	.719**	.358**	.344**
Mental Counters (CT)	.656**	−.100	.089*
Sequential Memory (SM)	.445**	.139*	.248**
Integrating Details (ID)	.729**	−.023	.116**
Assembling Objects (AO)	.713**	.010	.097*
Spatial Orientation (SO)	.694**	.165*	.169**
Figural Reasoning (FR)	.546**	.103	.196**
One-Hand Tracking (T1)	−.565**	−.292**	−.026
Two-Hand Tracking (T2)	−.701**	−.314**	−.113**
Target Identification (TI)	−.485**	−.400**	−.179**

Note. $*p < .05$, and $**p < .01$. ASVAB = Armed Services Vocational Aptitude Battery. ECAT = Enhanced Computer Administered Test. Z values = Differences in ECAT sample means divided by the Caucasian group standard deviations.

the beginning of their specialized training. In all cases, there was a lag of two to six months between testing and criterion performance, so the validation was predictive rather than concurrent. There were 10,963 examinees with complete test scores after minor data editing. Demographically, the sample was 95.5 percent male, 72.0 percent white, 15.8 percent black, 6.2 percent Hispanic, and 2.1 percent Asian.

The samples described in this chapter all came from students at military technical training schools. Instead of relying on final school grades (FSG), as has been traditional for most validation studies conducted in Service schools, every effort was made to collect information on practical skills taught in shop, laboratory, simulator, or other exercises.

School performance criteria were obtained for 13 Navy schools, two Air Force courses, and three Army schools. Kieckhaefer et al. (1992) describe the development of the ECAT criteria. They collected data on every quiz, homework assignment, and laboratory/shop/exercise for samples of several hundred students at each school. Based on factor analysis, they constructed composites of scores designed to measure different dimensions of achievement in each school. Altogether, 77 criteria were used for predictor validation among 18 schools.

For purposes of summarizing the data, it is convenient to select one criterion per school. A set of *a priori* rules was constructed to select the best criterion for each school. The first rule was to select a performance measure in preference to a written test, if possible. Such measures include shop work, live-firing of weapons, and tracking performance in combat simulations. Traditionally, the ASVAB has been validated against FSG scores as a measure of school achievement. However, it was not expected that psychomotor ability, for example, would improve performance on the written tests that usually form the basis for FSG scores. Also, an earlier study by Wolfe et al. (1993) found the largest incremental validities with laboratory criteria. Thus, whenever possible, the analysis stressed hands-on performance measures. Only where such measures were unavailable was a grade or written test score used for a school.

Other *a priori* standards for selecting the best criterion included reliability, face validity, and lateness in the curriculum. The final primary set of criteria, one for each school, was termed "internal criteria," since laboratory or simulator performance scores are generally not reported outside the school. Table 24-5 lists these criteria and their abbreviations, used in reporting the results. One school (Army 19K) was dropped from the study because none of its criteria proved to be reliable. Two schools (11H and ATC) were each split into two samples because of curriculum differences.

The composite scores were means of tests or laboratory scores, so if a student missed one or two tests, a criterion score could still be computed. In most cases, some criterion performance data were incomplete or missing for students who dropped out of the classes before finishing the course. For this reason, non-academic dropouts were excluded from the validity analyses. Academic failures were included in the analyses unless they dropped out so early that there were not enough data to construct composite criteria from more than two scores.

Hypotheses

Although the criterion development produced a great deal of psychometric information about the criteria, including internal reliabilities, the psychological aspects of the criteria were not well documented. In most cases, we were unable to generate specific hypotheses about which test should predict which criterion. Two exceptions were:

· Mental Counters was expected to predict air traffic control operations. This test not only measures working memory, but is also a test of information processing speed. The examinee is presented with a series of screens for each item at a computer-controlled rate. He or she not only has to keep track of three counters in working memory, but has to do it quickly enough to be ready for the

Table 24-5 Internal Criteria for ECAT Validation

Code	Course Title	Criterion	Description
		Army Schools	
11H(A)	Heavy Antiarmor Weapons Crewman (HMMWV Curriculum)	TO_1	M966 TOW simulator tracking event 1 Total
11H(B)	Heavy Antiarmor Weapons Crewman (ITV Curriculum)	ITVTOW	ITV TOW simulator tracking total events 1–3
13F	Field Artillery Fire Support Specialist	FIRING	Firing composite of 1 written test + 3 live firing tests
		Air Force Schools	
APS	Apprentice Personnel Specialist (73230)	AFPT70	Air Force performance test (words per minute typing)
ATC	Apprentice Air Traffic Control Operator (27230)	BLK5A	Basic approach control operation (perf test—standardized hours)
		Navy Schools	
AC	Air Traffic Controller	PERF	Mean of 4 performance tests
AE	Aviation Electrician's Mate	SUM2	Average of performance tests loading on factor 2
AMS	Aviation Structural Mechanic—Structures	PERF	Average of performance tests and practical work
AO	Aviation Ordnanceman	PRACTL	Average of all practical work
AV	Avionics Technician	PERFORM	Average of all Performance Tests
EM	Electrician's Mate	PHASE 1	Average of all Phase I tests
EN	Engineman	FSG	Final school grade*
ET(AEF)	Electronics Technician— Advanced Electronics Field	PERF	Average of Phase II Performance tests
FC	Fire Controlman	RADAR	Average of all radar tests
GMG	Gunner's Mate—Gun	HALF2	Average of tests 14–27/30
MM	Machinist's Mate	FSG	Final school grade*
OS	Operations Specialist	PERF	Average of all performance tests
RM	Radioman	PHASE3	Average of all knowledge and performance tests in last phase

Note. ECAT = Enhanced Computer Administered Test, HMMWV = High Mobility Multipurpose Wheeled Vehicle, TOW = Tube-launched Optically-tracked Wire-guided missile, ITV = Improved TOW Vehicle, TO = Training Objective. *FSG (Final School Grade) was used as a criterion in those schools where no practical performance criteria were available.

next screen when it appears. It was conjectured that Air Traffic Controllers have analogous information-processing demands.

• The tracking and spatial tests were expected to predict performance on the Army's 11H School Tube Launched Optically Tracked Wire Guided (TOW) missile tracking simulator. Smith and Walker (1988) confirmed a study by Grafton, Czarnolewski, and Smith (1989) showing the validity of tracking and spatial tests for predicting 11H TOW simulator performance. The ECAT study of 11H TOW performance is a cross-validation of the previous findings.

A large number of statistical hypotheses were generated and tested in the study, using a hierarchical approach to reduce the Type I error which often results from multiple significance tests. First, the global hypothesis was tested that no validity improvement occurred in any school when all ECAT predictors were used. Then each school was individually hypothesized not to have incremental validity from the whole ECAT battery. After rejecting that hypothesis, each ECAT test was hypothesized not to improve validity in any school. Finally, for those schools and those predictors that had significant incremental validity, the hypothesis was tested that the predictor had no incremental validity in that school—that is, the school by predictor interaction was tested.

To increase statistical power, the number of new predictors in the regression was reduced by forming three two-test composites that replaced six of the original tests. The tracking composite was the sum of the z-scores for the two tracking tests, the memory composite was the sum of the z-scores for Mental Counters and Sequential Memory, and the spatial composite was the sum of the z-scores for Integrating Details and Assembling Objects. For each school, the multiple correlation from the 10 ASVAB tests was compared with the multiple correlation from the 10 ASVAB tests plus three ECAT composites plus three other ECAT tests. If a composite was significant, its constituent tests were later examined for significance.

Results

Table 24-6 compares the range-corrected zero-order validities of the ECAT tests with the ASVAB tests for each criterion. The largest test validity for a criterion is shown in boldface. Bearing in mind that the tracking and Target Identification test scores are lower for better performers, we see

that Two-Hand Tracking was the best single test for the 11H criteria, and that Mental Counters and Sequential Memory were the only other ECAT tests that had higher validities than any other tests for some schools. The other validities had quite respectable magnitudes, however, better than many of the ASVAB tests. In view of the fact that their adverse impacts are low compared with the ASVAB, they seem attractive for inclusion in a military selection battery.

Table 24-7 shows the multiple correlations of ten ASVAB tests with each criterion, the multiple correlation of 10 ASVAB tests plus six ECAT predictors, and the significance of the difference. The probability value shown on the bottom summary line is that associated with the global null hypothesis mentioned above. The corrected validities shown on the three right-most columns were corrected for multivariate range-restriction (Lawley, 1943), adjusted by their population values (Ezekiel, 1930), and corrected for criterion reliability. Large improvements in validity were obtained for the 11H ITVTOW criterion, typing speed in Personnel Specialist, and Air Traffic Control operations in both the Air Force and Navy. Significant results were obtained in four of the 13 Navy schools. Averaged across all schools, the improvement in validity was 5.0 percent.

Table 24-8 shows the validity increase from adding just one ECAT factor to the four ASVAB factors for each school where ECAT was significant. The working memory factor is primarily important in typing speed, Air Traffic Control, and Aviation Electrician written test average. The spatial ability factor shows up in 11H weapons simulator tracking, typing speed, Air Traffic Control, and Aviation Electrician. The Psychomotor Factor has a huge influence in the 11H school and produces a large validity increase in Air Traffic Control.

Table 24-9 gives individual test results for each significant school. Although the results are generally in-line with what one would expect from the factor validities, some additional information shows up. For example, a comparison of Mental Counters with Sequential Memory shows that the former is very effective in enhancing prediction of Air Traffic Control, while Sequential Memory is better for predicting typing speed.

Summary and Conclusions

At the beginning of the study, we expected that the ECAT battery would improve ASVAB mean validity by about 5 percent, or about a .03 increase in multiple correlation (Schmidt, Hunter, & Dunn, 1987).

Table 24-6 Zero-Order Validities of ASVAB and ECAT Tests

School	Criterion	N	GS	AR	WK	PC	NO	CS	AS	MK	MC	EI	CT	SM	ID	AO	T1	T2	FR	SO	TI	Memory	Spatial	Tracking
						ASVAB Tests												ECAT Tests					Two-Test Composites		
11H(A)6	TO_1	542	18	14	17	13	17	15	13	18	18	10	11	13	15	12	−21	**−23**	18	18	−12	13	15	−24
11H(B)9	ITVTOW	318	04	−06	−02	−05	−09	−08	06	−00	08	03	−06	−07	06	11	−21	**−22**	02	10	01	−07	10	−23
13F3	FIRING	821	44	**52**	45	48	33	38	33	47	42	36	37	40	42	41	−34	−32	43	41	−25	43	46	−36
APS3	AFPT70	432	14	31	26	23	28	29	03	28	14	06	30	**34**	27	22	−02	03	28	21	−05	35	27	01
ATC(A)4	BLK5A	205	22	42	19	26	20	20	19	22	35	20	**46**	30	35	32	−28	−27	40	28	−20	42	37	−30
ATC(B)4	BLK5A	295	27	39	20	19	30	21	10	38	25	17	**43**	37	33	36	−32	−29	39	37	−25	44	38	−33
AC2	PERF	76	17	28	06	19	24	33	−05	31	09	05	35	**43**	29	36	−27	−14	34	26	−02	43	36	−22
AE2	SUM2	273	**50**	**50**	36	35	24	23	36	40	46	39	39	40	43	40	−22	−20	41	38	−30	44	46	−22
AMS2	PERF	244	42	44	36	26	34	34	39	36	**46**	43	33	35	43	44	−27	−29	35	34	−30	38	48	−30
AO2	PRACTL	229	26	31	31	29	35	35	14	**38**	24	25	30	29	31	29	−25	−18	34	27	−21	33	33	−23
AV4	PERFORM	352	32	42	26	28	14	13	39	39	**47**	44	35	29	38	40	−32	−30	36	37	−14	36	43	−33
EM2	PHASE1	797	51	**62**	46	45	33	32	33	60	50	47	43	37	46	42	−24	−27	49	43	−19	44	48	−27
EN1	FSG	750	59	**60**	55	51	31	29	53	53	**60**	57	41	34	49	45	−29	−34	47	47	−28	42	52	−34
ET3	PERF	86	40	**67**	44	36	44	44	28	57	34	39	47	44	47	39	−46	−43	48	52	−37	50	48	−48
FC2	RADAR	780	54	**53**	52	50	30	29	46	43	**53**	52	31	24	40	41	−29	−35	45	41	−21	30	45	−34
GM3	HALF2	397	57	**60**	56	50	31	31	52	50	52	50	41	33	43	45	−27	−30	47	46	−24	41	48	−30
MM1	FSG	801	44	42	36	38	24	25	38	39	**43**	41	30	27	38	39	−25	−23	40	31	−20	31	42	−26
OS3	PERF	815	48	**61**	44	49	43	45	34	60	52	41	54	49	51	51	−32	−37	52	51	−26	57	56	−37
RM2	PHASE3	277	46	**53**	45	46	26	32	26	44	47	41	39	35	42	39	−18	−24	35	42	−11	41	44	−22

Note. In each row, the largest validity is printed in boldface. Decimals are omitted.

ECAT Test Measures Used as Predictors

CT = Mental Counters Proportion Correct
SM = Sequential Memory Proportion Correct
AO = Assembling Objects Proportion Correct

T1 = 1-Hand Tracking Mean 1000*log(1 + RMS (Attempted))
T2 = 2-Hand Tracking Mean 1000*log(1 + RMS (Attempted))
ID = Integrating Details Proportion Correct

TI = Target Identification Mean Clipped Decision RTs
FR = Figural Reasoning Proportion Correct
SO = Spatial Orientation Proportion Correct

Table 24-7 ECAT Incremental Validities for Internal School Criteria

School	Criterion	Sample Size	Uncorrected Multiple R				Corrected Multiple R		
			ASVAB	ASVAB +ECAT	Percent Variance	Probability of $F_{6,N-17}$	ASVAB	Increase	Percent Increase
11H(A)6	TO__1	542	.210	.269	3.031	1.52×10^{-2}	.240	.046	19.1*
11H(B)9	ITVTOW	318	.154	.350	11.203	1.51×10^{-5}	.075	.237	316.3**
13F3	FIRING	821	.444	.466	2.507	2.82×10^{-3}	.730	.007	1.0**
APS3	AFPT70	432	.294	.404	9.129	2.28×10^{-6}	.388	.079	20.4**
ATC(A)4	BLK5A	205	.322	.404	7.127	4.18×10^{-2}	.614	.079	12.9*
ATC(B)4	BLK5A	295	.312	.408	8.316	1.04×10^{-3}	.450	.100	22.2**
AC2	PERF	76	.330	.460	13.033	2.80×10^{-1}	.381	.149	39.2
AE2	SUM2	273	.440	.487	5.808	2.39×10^{-2}	.608	.022	3.7*
AMS2	PERF	244	.393	.431	3.892	1.89×10^{-1}	.650	.016	2.4
AO2	PRACTL	229	.343	.374	2.652	4.69×10^{-1}	.490	.010	2.1
AV4	PERFORM	352	.379	.409	2.853	1.48×10^{-1}	.673	.016	2.4
EM2	PHASE1	797	.474	.482	.950	2.86×10^{-1}	.729	.001	0.1
EN1	FSG	750	.584	.588	.721	5.09×10^{-1}	.763	.000	0.0
ET3	PERF	86	.482	.574	14.533	1.41×10^{-1}	.735	.075	10.2
FC2	RADAR	780	.345	.381	3.053	7.93×10^{-4}	.733	.016	2.1**
GM3	HALF2	397	.458	.467	1.033	6.87×10^{-1}	.734	.000	0.0
MM1	FSG	801	.402	.425	2.362	5.41×10^{-3}	.557	.012	2.2**
OS3	PERF	815	.523	.564	6.510	3.81×10^{-9}	.791	.025	3.1**
RM2	PHASE3	277	.420	.464	4.907	5.08×10^{-2}	.702	.017	2.4
Summary	Internal	8,490	.373[a]	.440	3.966[b]	$< 1.4 \times 10^{-17c}$	.619	.031	5.0[d]**

Note. *p < .05 for uncorrected R increase. **p < .01 for uncorrected R increase.
  1. ECAT = Enhanced Computer Administered Test, ASVAB = Armed Services Vocational Aptitude Battery, FSG = Final school grade.
  2. For definitions of schools and criteria, see Table 24-5.
[a] Mean multiple Rs are means of Wherry-shrunken Rs.
[b] Percent Variance $= 100 \times \dfrac{\Delta R^2}{1 - R^2_{ASVAB+ECAT}}$
[c] Summary probability $= P(\chi^2_{38})$.
[d] The summary percent increase is defined as 100 × the ratio of the mean increase to the mean corrected ASVAB validity.

Table 24-8 Incremental Validities From Adding One ECAT Factor to Four ASVAB Factors for Significant Internal School Criteria From Full Model

School	Criterion	Memory	Psychomotor	Spatial
11H(A)6	TO__1	.000	.055**	.003
11H(B)9	ITVTOW	.000	.178**	.039**
13F3	FIRING	.011**	.005**	.009**
APS3	AFPT70	.051**	.015*	.034**
ATC(A)4	BLK5A	.089*	.047*	.120**
ATC(B)4	BLK5A	.060**	.053**	.078**
AC2	PERF	.150*	.019	.142
AE2	SUM2	.024**	.000	.013**
AV4	PERFORM	.009	.014*	.011*
FC2	RADAR	.002*	.004	.000
MM1	FSG	.000	.000	.006**
OS3	PERF	.020**	.008**	.025**

Note. *p < .05 for uncorrected R increase. **p < .01 for uncorrected R increase.
1. ECAT = Enhanced Computer Administered Test, ASVAB = Armed Services Vocational Aptitude Battery, FSG = Final school grade.
2. For definitions of schools and criteria, see Table 24-5.

Table 24-9 Incremental Validities From Adding One ECAT Test to the ASVAB for Significant Internal School Criteria

School	Criterion	Mental Counters	Sequential Memory	Integrating Detail	Assembling Objects
11H(A)6	TO__1	.000	.000	.000	.000
11H(B)9	ITVTOW	.000	.000	.006	.056*
13F3	FIRING	.002*	.007**	.002*	.002*
APS3	AFPT70	.018**	.034**	.025**	.010*
ATC(A)4	BLK5A	.111**	.006	.026*	.015
ATC(B)4	BLK5A	.060*	.032	.014	.040*
AC2	PERF	.048	.135*	.045	.126*
AE2	SUM2	.008*	.018**	.005	.004
FC2	RADAR	.000	.005**	.000	.001
MM1	FSG	.000	.000	.003	.009**
OS3	PERF	.017**	.011**	.006**	.010**
RM2	PHASE3	.004	.000	.002	.000

School	Criterion	One-Hand Tracking	Two-Hand Tracking	Target Identification	Spatial Orientation
11H(A)6	TO__1	.036**	.044**	.000	.008
11H(B)9	ITVTOW	.159**	.172**	.000	.047*
13F3	FIRING	.006**	.002*	.002	.002*
APS3	AFPT70	.006	.028**	.000	.004
ATC(A)4	BLK5A	.030	.015	.005	.000
ATC(B)4	BLK5A	.049**	.034**	.023*	.044**
AC2	PERF	.063	.000	.000	.033
AE2	SUM2	.000	.000	.009*	.000
FC2	RADAR	.002	.004*	.000	.000
MM1	FSG	.003*	.000	.000	.000
OS3	PERF	.003*	.006**	.000	.011**
RM2	PHASE3	.000	.000	.006	.006

School	Criterion	Memory Composite	Spatial Composite	Tracking Composite	Figural Reasoning
11H(A)6	TO__1	.000	.000	.047**	.007
11H(B)9	ITVTOW	.004	.047**	.185**	.000
13F3	FIRING	.006**	.003**	.005**	.003**
APS3	AFPT70	.036**	.024**	.018**	.014**
ATC(A)4	BLK5A	.066**	.031**	.027	.060**
ATC(B)4	BLK5A	.063*	.038*	.049**	.036
AC2	PERF	.128	.123	.025	.070
AE2	SUM2	.019**	.007	.000	.003
FC2	RADAR	.003*	.000	.004*	.003
MM1	FSG	.000	.008**	.000	.009**
OS3	PERF	.019**	.012**	.005**	.007**
RM2	PHASE3	.003	.002	.000	.000

Note. $*p < .05$ for uncorrected R increase. $**p < .01$ for uncorrected R increase.
1. ECAT = Enhanced Computer Administered Test, ASVAB = Armed Services Vocational Aptitude Battery, FSG = Final school grade.
2. For definitions of schools and criteria, see Table 24-5.

In fact, the mean incremental validity turned out to be .031 using performance-oriented criteria, and much larger for some criteria. Thus, the ECAT project succeeded in accomplishing its objectives.

The validity gains were greatest in schools where the ASVAB was a poor predictor. The largest gain was .24 for the 11H school ITVTOW criterion, where the ASVAB's validity was only .08. On the other hand, ECAT was a weak predictor for most Navy schools, where the ASVAB's corrected validity often exceeded .70. Even here, however, ECAT raised the validity for predicting OS school performance by .02, starting from ASVAB's .79 validity.

The tests producing the largest gains were Mental Counters for Air Traffic Control, both Tracking tests for 11H, and Assembling Objects for 11H. The most broadly useful tests are Mental Counters, Sequential Memory, Two-Hand Tracking, and Assembling Objects. Each produced validity gains exceeding .01 in four of the 19 samples. The tracking tests appear to have specialized usefulness for the Army's 11H school and the Air Traffic Control schools.

Potentially, these validity increases could mean better hands-on job performance if recruits were classified on the basis of the relevant ECAT tests. Unfortunately, hands-on performance is seldom measured or publicly available, which is why we labeled these "internal" criteria. Because hands-on performance is nearly invisible to external decision makers without special studies, validity improvements are likely to go unnoticed. Worse, these criteria are ephemeral; they change or completely disappear when the curriculum changes, as it frequently does. It may be impossible to cross-validate a regression equation on the same school a year later because the criterion no longer exists! Mitigating this fact somewhat, the same ability that was needed to perform one laboratory exercise may show up on a different one, or on subsequent job performance.

Are any of the results reproducible? Yes, the ECAT results for the Army's 11H Heavy Antiarmor Weapons school are actually cross-validations of earlier studies at the same school by Smith and Walker (1988) who confirmed a study by Grafton et al. (1989) showing the validity of tracking and spatial tests for predicting 11H TOW simulator performance. In addition, the ECAT study found that psychomotor and spatial tests improved prediction of criteria in two different samples from the 11H school.

Another result that was replicated within the ECAT study itself was a large validity improvement from Working Memory and Spatial Ability tests for predicting Air Traffic Control operations, thus confirming one of the hypotheses of the study. The same result was found for two different samples from the Air Force ATC school and from the Navy's AC school. Because Air Traffic Control is so critical to human lives and to the safety of equipment, anything that could improve the selection of Air Traffic Controllers would be very valuable to both military and civilian aviation.

The ultimate use of these findings depends on practical and economic considerations beyond the scope of this scientific study. It is not clear, for example, that testing every incoming military enlisted applicant with the ECAT tests is an efficient way to proceed. It may be possible to give ECAT tests to only those applicants who are likely to be assigned to 11H, Air Traffic Control, or certain other specialties. Although computerized testing will become nearly universal with the full-scale implementation of CAT-ASVAB, the response pedestals needed for the psychomotor tests will not be part of that system. Each response pedestal costs more than a computer. On the other hand, further research might develop a track-ball or mouse-based tracking test that is equally effective in measuring psychomotor ability. In that case, routine psychomotor testing of all applicants might become feasible.

The overall mean incremental validity for internal criteria was remarkably close to that estimated by Schmidt et al. (1987). However, the components of the 5 percent validity increase differed from those expected by the authors. Schmidt et al. expected a 3 percent improvement from perceptual speed tests, but the only ECAT test in that category, Target Identification, showed the least gain of any of the predictors. Psychomotor and spatial ability turned out to be more important than expected. The major new result of this study was the finding that Working Memory, which Schmidt et al. might have considered to be useful mainly as providing a better estimate of general ability, was demonstrated to have specific predictive value for some occupational specialities, particularly Air Traffic Controllers.

CHAPTER

25

Dissemination of CAT-ASVAB Technology

James R. McBride

Since its beginnings in 1979, the CAT-ASVAB program was the locus of a number of technical developments, and many of those have been disseminated and used to advantage in other adaptive testing programs in both the public and private sectors. Examples include specific commercial applications of adaptive testing, other military testing programs, and an educational testing program. In addition, key technical developments from CAT-ASVAB are at the core of two other major government applications of CAT. This chapter will summarize some of the applications of CAT technology that have been the direct beneficiaries of technology developed in the course of the CAT-ASVAB program.

The principal value of technology transfer is perhaps that it makes possible widespread development of practical applications of technology in far less time and expense than the technology took to develop. Without the dissemination of CAT-ASVAB technology, a number of CAT applications that have been in use for up to 10 years might not have been economically feasible. There are at least four aspects of CAT-ASVAB technology that have been either appropriated by other CAT applications, or transferred directly to them. (1) adaptive testing strategy; (2) computer software; (3) equating technology; and (4) computerized test technical standards. Examples of the influence of the CAT-ASVAB program in each of these four areas are presented in this chapter.

Adaptive Testing Strategy

In Chapter 4, I presented a definition of a "strategy" for adaptive testing: An integrated set of methods and criteria for adaptively selecting items one by one, and for placing scores from the resulting tests on the same scale. That chapter reviewed some of the features of a variety of adaptive testing strategies that have been proposed over the years, and described the strategy eventually adopted for use in CAT-ASVAB: A hybrid strategy that administers fixed-length adaptive tests employing Bayesian procedures for ability estimation, a local maximum information criterion for item selection, and a procedure for limiting test item exposure.

CAT-ASVAB's adaptive testing strategy was adopted after extensive study of the psychometric characteristics of alternative strategies for adaptive testing, and has been demonstrated to result in efficient adaptive tests that are reliable and valid. Any test user choosing to explore or implement adaptive testing must select a strategy. In doing so, they can either conduct a research program similar to CAT-ASVAB's research into alternative strategies, or they can adopt an already-developed strategy and tailor it to their special requirements. The latter course is less time-consuming, as well as far less expensive. CAT-ASVAB developers have been generous in transferring their accumulated knowledge about various aspects of adaptive testing strategies to other prospective users of the technology; in addition, some CAT-ASVAB researchers have applied CAT-ASVAB procedures to other adaptive test programs after leaving government service.

Examples of the transfer of CAT-ASVAB's adaptive testing strategy to other programs will be given below. First, it may be useful to present a summary of some of the features of that strategy, and to differentiate it from other strategies now in use in major adaptive testing programs (e.g., the computerized adaptive versions of the Graduate Record Examination and the certification testing program of the American Board of Clinical Pathologists). Some key features that differentiate CAT-ASVAB and these programs are (1) their psychometric foundations; (2) their procedures for ability estimation; (3) their criteria for adaptive item selection; and (4) their criteria for test termination.

All of these programs use item response theory (IRT) as a general psychometric foundation. CAT-ASVAB uses the 3-parameter logistic IRT model, as does the GRE programs; the Clinical Pathologists program, in contrast, uses the 1-parameter logistic, also known as the Rasch model. These programs use a wider variety of ability estimation procedures: CAT-ASVAB is unique in this aspect of its overall strategy. It uses Owen's Bayesian sequential procedure for updating the ability estimate after each test item. Then, after the last item in each test, CAT-ASVAB computes a final ability estimate, using Bayesian modal estimation. The GRE uses maximum likelihood estimation to update the ability estimate after each item, and at the end of the test. The Clinical Pathologists program uses Rasch estimation, which in effect is a special case of maximum likelihood estimation.

In their adaptive item selection procedures, CAT-ASVAB and the GRE are similar. Both select items by referring to a pre-computed lookup table in which items are sorted in descending order of their information values at spaced intervals over the ability scale. This is referred to as a "maximum information" item selection criterion. Both programs have modified the maximum procedure somewhat to balance item usage, and thus avoid overexposure of the most informative test items. Because the Clinical Pathologists testing program uses the Rasch model, it can select items on the basis of the proximity of the item difficulty parameter to the most recent estimate of examinee ability; this is tantamount to the maximum information criterion, but is implemented in a totally different way.

The technology embodied in CAT-ASVAB's hybrid Bayesian sequential adaptive testing strategy has been transferred to a number of other adaptive tests, both within and outside of the federal government.

The first widespread practical use of adaptive testing was the Army's Computerized Adaptive Screening Test (CAST), which is available to recruiters to evaluate the likelihood that a prospective recruit will attain a qualifying score on the Armed Forces Qualification Test embedded in the ASVAB. CAST was introduced into operational use in 1985. Its development is described in some detail in Chapter 7. Suffice it to say here that CAST represented the first instance of CAT-ASVAB technology transfer. CAST, which was developed for the Army by the Navy Personnel Research and Development Center (NPRDC), is based entirely on procedures and materials pioneered in the course of CAT-ASVAB research and development. CAST's adaptive testing strategy is identical to the hybrid Bayesian sequential strategy developed for CAT-ASVAB (and reported in Wetzel and McBride, 1986). CAST's item banks were developed in early CAT-ASVAB research reported by Moreno, Wetzel, McBride, and Weiss (1983). Decisions about the composition and length of the CAST tests were also based on data reported by Moreno et al. (1983).

One of the first examples of a commercial application of CAT is the Computerized Adaptive Edition of the Differential Aptitude Tests—the Adaptive DAT—published by The Psychological Corporation (1986a). The printed versions of the DAT have been used to test millions of people since 1947, for educational placement and vocational guidance of secondary school students, and for personnel selection and career counseling of adults. The Adaptive DAT, like the CAT-ASVAB, is a system for computerized adaptive administration of a traditional multiple abilities battery. Also like the CAT-ASVAB, the Adaptive DAT takes less than half the time it takes to administer the printed version.

The linkage of the Adaptive DAT to military CAT research is very direct: From 1977 to 1983 this writer was principal investigator in the Navy's development of CAT-ASVAB. From 1985 to 1986, I directed the development of the Adaptive DAT, which uses many of the same psychometric procedures pioneered within the Department of Defense, including the hybrid adaptive strategy based on Bayesian sequential ability estimation. (Another CAT system developed by The Psychological Corporation [1986b] is the Stanford Adaptive Mathematics Screening Test, a brief test of achievement in mathematics that is suitable for use over an extremely wide range of ability—from fourth through twelfth grade. Like the Adaptive DAT, it uses the hybrid Bayesian strategy. Unlike any other adaptive test I am aware of, it also employs "differential entry levels." Initial ability estimates and difficulty levels vary depending on school grade; thus, the Stanford Adaptive Mathematics Screening Test was the first operational adaptive test to use collateral information—in this case, school grade—to guide ability estimation and item selection.

Adaptive Testing Software

Just as the evolution of strategies for adaptive testing was slow and expensive, so was the development of software systems for CAT. The earliest CAT software, developed under the direction of Abraham Bayroff of the Army Research Institute, was very limited in its application. His first system administered adaptive tests via a teletype machine. It was inherently limited to tests that could be presented in printed form, using only numbers, common typographic symbols, and upper-case alphabetic characters. His second system was far more advanced in display capability—test items were presented by projecting 35mm color transparencies on a small screen, and thus could contain anything that could be photographed. Both of Bayroff's systems were developed for use on mainframe computers, and for research purposes only; they were not easily extended to other applications, and their inherent limitations did not make them attractive candidates for adoption elsewhere.

Starting in the 1970s with the burgeoning availability of minicomputers that could support multiple users simultaneously, and then of microcomputer networks that made it feasible to test each examinee at a dedicated computer, the development of systems for adaptive testing became feasible. Feasibility is one thing; practicality is another. The first general-purpose software systems capable of administering batteries of adaptive tests, and of displaying graphical as well as text-only test items typically took two years or more to design and develop. The cost of software development was commensurate with the time involved. With few exceptions, each early CAT researcher developed a new software system for CAT administration. At first, this was essential, because of the evolution of CAT strategies themselves, and because of the rapid changes that were occurring

in computer technology. In time, however, it became feasible to develop flexible, general-purpose systems for administering CAT and other computer-based tests. Once that point was reached, the transfer of DoD-developed CAT software technology to more general use began.

One of the first vehicles of this transfer was MicroCAT (Assessment Systems Corporation, 1984). MicroCAT is an integrated system for both development and administration of tests, including but not limited to, computer administered adaptive tests. It was the first commercially available system for designing, authoring, analyzing, and administering adaptive tests. It's the kind of thing that an adaptive test developer would have to invent if it were not itself commercially available. MicroCAT was developed by David Vale of Assessment Systems Corporation under a Navy Small Business Innovations Research contract. Vale had learned his craft under David Weiss at the University of Minnesota. In fact, Weiss was a principal in Assessment Systems Corporation. Hence the link of MicroCAT to military research is a direct one involving both technology and people, and its commercial availability represents the first tangible transfer of adaptive testing software technology from DoD to public use.

Other instances of the transfer of adaptive testing software outside DoD have occurred subsequently. One such transfer took the form of publishing CAT software in the public domain. The entirety of the Navy's experimental adaptive testing software system—including source code and system documentation—was published in an NPRDC technical report by Quan, Park, Sandahl, and Wolfe (1984). This publication made it possible for the public to obtain, and use without charge, software implementations of all or part of a computer adaptive testing system, including provisions for test item bank storage and retrieval, text and graphic item design and display, examinee response processing, and features specific to adaptive testing, such as dynamic selection of test items, ability estimation, test scoring, and storage of detailed data for each test administered.

More recently, DoD and the Navy have made portions of the CAT-ASVAB software system available to other users, both within and outside the federal government. For example, some CAT-ASVAB software was incorporated into a system developed by the U.S. Department of Labor (DoL) to administer a computerized version of the General Aptitude Test Battery (GATB). Additionally, the Navy has made its software available for administration of other agencies' computerized adaptive tests, and has provided technical support in adapting the software for those agencies' use. An adaptive testing system under development for administering personnel tests for the U.S. Immigration and Naturalization Service is based entirely on the CAT-ASVAB software platform. Additionally, the NPRDC performed a similar adaptation of the CAT-ASVAB software system for use in an experimental educational test administration system developed for the North Carolina State Department of Education.

Adaptive Test Equating Methods

Among the thorniest technical challenges to the developers of CAT-ASVAB was the problem of test equating. The problem itself is straightforward: For some period of time after implementation of CAT-ASVAB, adaptive and conventional versions of the battery will be in use at the same time. Consequently, scores from both versions of the battery must be interchangeable. Adaptive tests, however, use a different score metric than conventional tests (IRT continuous ability metric rather than number correct scores), and typically have different degrees of measurement precision. Methods used to equate alternate forms of conventional tests were not applicable to the problem of equating adaptive and conventional test scores. Segall discusses this problem—and CAT-ASVAB's solution to it—in detail in Chapter 19. Solving the equating problem was essential, not only in the case of CAT-ASVAB but also for any other adaptive test developed to be used interchangeably with a conventional test. DoD and the Navy have published their equating technology, and have made it, and the expertise of its developers, available to other organizations faced with analogous situations.

The first example of this is the DoL's computerized GATB program, mentioned above. The computerized version of GATB contains both adaptive and conventional versions of many of the printed GATB tests. The computerized paper-and-pencil GATB tests are speeded by design, and measurement differences between printed and computerized implementations of speeded tests are well-documented (e.g., Greaud & Green, 1986). The adaptive versions of some of the GATB tests represent a particular challenge, as they are designed as power tests yet are to be used interchangeably with counterpart printed tests which are speeded. Through a cooperative arrangement between the U.S. DoD and DoL, NPRDC staff involved in equating CAT-ASVAB with its printed counterpart took respon-

sibility for equating the new and old versions of GATB as well. That effort is incomplete at this writing, pending collection of printed and computer-administered GATB data by DoL.

Adaptive Testing Standards

Another difficult issue arose early in the development of CAT-ASVAB as an alternative to, and replacement for, the P&P-ASVAB: The absence of precedents. The CAT-ASVAB program began in 1979; by 1982, enough research data had been accumulated to indicate that adaptive versions of some of the ASVAB tests were highly correlated with their conventional counterparts, and were much more efficient. While the early data were promising for the new technology, there were no professional standards or guidelines available to evaluate the suitability of computerized tests in general, and adaptive tests in particular, as replacements for conventional tests in ongoing testing programs.

Even though the early results were promising from a research standpoint, it was not clear what kind and amount of evidence would be required to support the use of CAT-ASVAB as a replacement for the traditional version used for DoD enlisted personnel selection. There were many unanswered questions: Would the computerized adaptive tests measure the same ability constructs as the conventional tests? What about the speeded tests? Would computerized tests be as reliable and valid as the printed ones for personnel selection? What evidence would be needed to answer the preceding questions in the affirmative? Would computerized test administration give examinees with computer experience an advantage over others? Would computerized tests put some population subgroups—such as males, females, majority or minority group members—at an advantage or disadvantage? Existing professional standards, particularly the then current *Standards for Educational and Psychological Tests* (American Psychological Association, American Educational Research Association, & National Council on Measurement in Education, 1974) neither addressed, nor anticipated, the use of computers or adaptive testing in test administration.

The absence of applicable standards was a matter of some concern; among other things, it left open the possibility that computerized adaptive testing might be technically attractive yet unacceptable on legal or other grounds. To address the absence of standards, Dr. Charles Davis of the Office of Naval Research arranged for a panel of experts, independent of the DoD, to study the matter and develop a set of technical recommendations on the kinds of research needed to evaluate the suitability and technical acceptability of a computerized adaptive version of the ASVAB. The evaluation plan proposed by that panel (Green, Bock, Humphreys, Linn, & Reckase, 1982) constituted what may be the most rigorous standards ever imposed on a psychometric test development project. Its contents were transferred to the public domain by the subsequent publication of an article in the *Journal of Educational Measurement* (Green et al., 1984) that applied similar evaluation standards to CAT in general. The contents of the evaluation plan also influenced the 1985 revision of the 1974 test standards, as well as the later *Guidelines for Computer-Based Tests and Interpretations* (American Psychological Association, 1986).

Summary

As the examples given above indicate, long before its recent introduction into large-scale operational use, CAT-ASVAB had a profound impact on other practical applications of CAT programs. The psychometric testing strategy developed in the early 1980s for the CAT-ASVAB system has been incorporated in a number of other adaptive tests, beginning as early as 1985. Software developed for CAT-ASVAB has been incorporated, in whole or in part,

into a number of other public sector adaptive testing systems; some CAT-ASVAB software has also been published in the public domain, and is potentially available for all to use. Technology initially developed for equating CAT-ASVAB test scores to scores of counterpart conventional ASVAB tests has been extended for use in other programs, notably the DoL's development of a computerized version of the GATB. Finally, and perhaps most important of all, technical standards developed specifically to guide the evaluation of CAT-ASVAB as a potential replacement for its conventional version have become de facto professional standards for evaluating any CAT system.

There is little doubt that computerized testing, in general, and CAT, in particular, is poised for a broad technology transfer to the entire spectrum of testing—cognitive testing, surveys and polling, personality measurement, clinical diagnosis, and myriad other applications. Government, industry, and academia all are carefully venturing into the unfamiliar waters. The 20-year research and development sponsored and conducted by the Military Services will provide the foundation upon which that technology is built.

Psychological testing has finally reached the point predicted over a quarter of a century ago by Dr. Bert Green: *"most of these changes lie in the future. . . . in the inevitable computer conquest of testing"* (Green, 1970).

26

Current and Future Challenges

Daniel O. Segall and Kathleen E. Moreno

The preceding chapters provide a detailed account of the research and development of CAT-ASVAB. Prior to its operational use in September of 1990, the CAT-ASVAB was one of the most thoroughly researched tests of human aptitudes and abilities in modern history. Data from over 40,000 test-takers participating in numerous empirical studies were gathered to address issues crucial to the development of a large-scale adaptive test battery. The CAT-ASVAB program has broken new ground in the field of adaptive testing, and by doing so, has set new standards for the development of other adaptive tests.

The wide-scale implementation and use of CAT-ASVAB will provide continuing technical and managerial challenges. In this chapter, we provide an update on the current (1997) status of the program, and take a look forward at some of the issues facing the program, including the development of a new score scale, the development of new forms, test security issues, and ongoing psychometric development.

Nationwide Implementation

DoD began making plans for nationwide implementation of CAT-ASVAB soon after the decision to proceed was made in 1993. The first step was the formation of a working group to develop the implementation plan. The working group was made up of representatives from four DoD agencies: OASD/FMP, USMEPCOM, DMDC, and Navy. While USMEPCOM and DMDC were responsible for the implementation, Navy, at that time, had the necessary CAT-

ASVAB expertise. Plans included procurement of the hardware, development of the software, installation of the system, training of personnel, and conducting the research necessary to use the new system operationally.

Specifications for procurement of the hardware and development of the CAT-ASVAB software are described in Chapter 21. It is important to note, however, that not only did the computer hardware have to meet specifications, but all hardware components had to be identical across all units. In addition, the keyboard had to be identical and the monitor had to be equivalent in size and clarity to that used in the initial (non-operational) equating of CAT-ASVAB forms to the P&P-ASVAB reference form. This eliminated psychometric concerns about effects of hardware differences on test performance and makes maintenance and troubleshooting of system problems easier. While meeting these requirements was a challenge for USMEPCOM (the procuring agency), these goals were met.

As the agency responsible for administering the ASVAB, USMEPCOM developed schedules for both system installation and test administrator (TA) training. The nationwide implementation of CAT-ASVAB coincided with the equating of Forms 1 and 2 to the ASVAB-P&P reference form (8A). Although these forms had been previously equated (Chapter 19), it was believed necessary to re-estimate the transformation using the new PC hardware. (These forms had been previously equated on the Hewlett-Packard hardware.) A total of 25 MEPSs participated in the IOT&E equating study. For a period of several months, applicants processed through these MEPSs were randomly assigned to either CAT-ASVAB or P&P-ASVAB. Their data was used to estimate the final transformation for Forms 01C and 02C, which will be applied to applicants taking CAT-ASVAB after the equating study is completed.

Implementation began in October 1996 at the Denver MEPS. Denver was selected as the first site to use the new system operationally because its personnel had extensive experience using the first operational, HP-based, CAT-ASVAB system. Denver personnel were so enthusiastic about CAT-ASVAB that they moved the old system to another room so that they could continue testing with it until the new system was installed, and training had been completed. They were somewhat less enthusiastic about having to test some applicants on P&P-ASVAB during the first several months of implementation to fulfill the requirements of the equating study.

The Chicago MEPS was the second site to receive the new system. Chicago, with no previous exposure to CAT-ASVAB, is a large MEPS—processing substantial numbers of applicants. Site setup at Chicago gave USMEPCOM and DMDC the opportunity to realistically evaluate training materials and procedures, and the need for CAT-ASVAB informational materials. This site was started two weeks after Denver so that problems that occurred in Denver could be resolved before the start of a second site. After Chicago, 2–3 sites were installed, trained, and started weekly. The IOT&E ended in April 1997, when sample size requirements were reached. At that point, P&P-ASVAB testing at MEPSs was no longer required. Installation at all sites was completed in June 1997.

The training program used for nationwide operational implementation followed very closely the one used in the OT&E. Training was scheduled for three to four days, and occured the week following installation. TAs received about 16 hours of classroom training, consisting of lectures, exercises, and labs. Part of the training included conducting one or two "live" test sessions, where applicants were tested using the CAT-ASVAB system. While all parts of the training have proven necessary for teaching TAs how to run the system, the most valuable part was the "hands on" experience received during the labs and live sessions.

Although an intelligent tutoring system (ITS) for training CAT-ASVAB TAs was developed during the CAT-ASVAB OT&E, the system was not used during the nationwide implementation phase. During this phase, group-administered, classroom training was more efficient and effective. The ITS, however, will be used later to train new TAs as normal turnover of TAs occurs.

As in all new systems, TAs occasionally need assistance. This is particularly true when the system is turned on at a particular site. During the initial phase of the implementation, DMDC, as the software developer, provided technical assistance to the sites. We provided sites with both office phone numbers and pager numbers, for around the clock help access. One of the most frustrating experiences for a new system user is to be unable to contact someone for help, something we want to avoid. After the initial implementation, USMEPCOM will take over this responsibility, providing a more formal "HELP" desk.

New Form Development

New forms were required for nationwide implementation of CAT-ASVAB, and for the norming study. Test items had been written in 1988 by Educational Testing Service (ETS) under contract to NPRDC (Massad, Schratz, & Anderson, 1988). Because of the lessons learned in developing the first two CAT-ASVAB forms (Chapter 11), NPRDC tasked ETS with writing 800 items for each of the AFQT content areas and 400 items for each of the remaining content areas. This was expected to provide enough high quality items to develop two new forms. These items were written to match the ASVAB 8A and CAT-ASVAB Forms 01C and 02C taxonomy. ETS reviewed the pools for content, quality, and sensitivity. However, work on these item pools was put on hold until 1993, pending the results of work on expanding the content of the ASVAB battery (Chapter 24) and other work examining the economic utility of CAT-ASVAB (Chapter 23).

In 1993, NPRDC turned over the item pools to DMDC for screening and calibration. The intention was to build two or three forms from these items, one to be used as the new reference form, and one or two other forms to be used operationally. As was done with the first two CAT-ASVAB forms (Chapter 11), about half the items were selected for a large-scale IRT calibration. (Time and examinee constraints prevented the collection of item calibration data on all items.) Rather than relying on empirical measures of difficulty and quality (i.e., pre-testing all the items in small samples of test-takers) as was done with Forms 01C and 02C (Chapter 11), the items for the new forms were screened using expert judgments. Items were selected from the ETS pools on the basis of content taxonomy coverage and estimated difficulty (Harris, 1996). Prior to producing calibration booklets, DMDC personnel reviewed all items for accuracy,

Table 26-1 CAT-ASVAB Forms 3 and 4

Content Area	Number of Tryout Items	Final Item Pools		Number Supplemented From P&P
		Form 3	Form 4	
GS	275	135	133	199
AR	360	137	136	97
WK	360	137	137	129
PC	275	68	70	0
AI	180	77	73	70
SI	180	73	73	80
MK	360	126	132	118
MC	300	106	104	112
EI	300	92	92	70
AO	180	89	89	0

sensitivity, and format. In addition to the ETS items, 180 new items for the Assembling Objects (AO) test were developed. As a result of the ECAT validity study, described in Chapter 24, AO has been approved for addition to the ASVAB battery.

Data for calibrating the items were collected in the MEPSs. Table 26-1 shows the number of items that were calibrated in each content area. Harris (1996) provides a complete description of the calibration design. Once data were collected, items were calibrated using BILOG. Procedures similar to those used for CAT-ASVAB Forms 01C and 02C (see Chapter 11) were used to evaluate the resulting forms. Dividing the item bank into three forms resulted in score information functions that were lower in some areas of the ability range than the P&P-ASVAB. Similar results were obtained when the item bank was divided into two forms. Consequently, some content areas had to be supplemented with additional highly informative items to meet the precision criterion. Most of the content areas were supplemented with new items originally intended for new forms of the P&P-ASVAB. The number of items in the final pools is shown in Table 26-1.

ASVAB Content Revisions

As mentioned above, a new test will be added to the ASVAB battery. AO was selected for inclusion in the battery because (1) it can be administered in either computer or paper-and-pencil format, and (2) it showed a decrease in adverse impact over current ASVAB tests having a spatial component (Chapter 24). Two other tests currently in the battery are candidates for removal: Numerical Opera-

tions (NO) and Coding Speed (CS). For most Services, these tests provide very little incremental validity over other tests in the battery. However, prior to operational use of AO, and prior to eliminating any tests, data must be collected to evaluate how AO might be used by each Service. To accommodate these possible changes, the order of test presentation in new ASVAB forms will be GS, AR, WK, PC, MK, EI, AI, SI, MC, AO, CS, NO. This ordering places the AFQT tests together in a block towards the beginning of the battery, places most of the technical tests together in a block, and the two speeded tests at the end. This test ordering will allow data on all tests to be collected in the upcoming norming study, allow the addition of AO, and allow the deletion of the two speeded tests without the need for special equating studies since these are presented at the end of the battery.

Instructions

Prior to the norming data collection, other changes that were considered and, in some cases, implemented were changes to CAT-ASVAB instructions. As the result of the SEV and OT&E studies (Chapters 19 and 20), we were aware that CS instructions were difficult to understand. The instructions used in Forms 01C and 02C were very similar to those used in the P&P-ASVAB. Computerized presentation of the instructions, however, provided an opportunity for making them more interactive and easier to understand. These instructions have been updated so that the computer now demonstrates how to answer the items, as opposed to the older instructions, which verbally described the procedure.

Instructions for other content areas were reviewed and slightly modified. While suggestions had been made to update the "look and feel" of CAT-ASVAB (i.e., use proportional rather than fixed-width font), we chose not to make extensive modifications with the exception of CS. There were several reasons for this. First, the CAT-ASVAB Forms 01C and 02C instructions had been used to give the test to over 80,000 test-takers. These instructions had proven to be easy to understand by applicants across the whole ability range. Second, human factors experts reviewing the instructions advised us to keep our instructions and the "look and feel" of the system the same—it was simple and worked well. Third, our experience with other software development projects had reinforced that keeping the software as simple as possible was prudent, as complexity often adds problems with no real gain.

Empirical Evaluation of New CAT-ASVAB Forms

Prior to the equating of the new forms and the use of Form 4C in the norming study, the forms were evaluated empirically (Holmes, 1996). The purpose of the empirical evaluation was to assess the reliability and construct validity of the new forms. Pairs of new and old CAT-ASVAB forms were administered to randomly equivalent groups (of about 1,000 test-takers per group) to compare the alternate forms reliability. In addition, a third randomly equivalent group was administered one new and one old form to aid in the assessment of the similarity of constructs measured by the new and old forms. Preliminary results indicate that the new forms (3C and 4C) compare favorably to the old forms (01C and 02C) in terms of precision and construct similarity. Additional data were collected to assess the effects of test reordering.

Development of New Score Scale

Data collected in the 1997 PAY (Profile of American Youth) study will serve two important purposes. First, it will provide important information about the availability of high quality youth. This information can be used by force planners to determine the levels of advertising and enlistment incentives to attract the necessary numbers of high quality applicants to fill jobs of increasing technical complexity in the military.

Data collected in the 1997 PAY study will also provide an opportunity to develop a new score-scale based on CAT-ASVAB tests administered to a current nationally representative sample of youths. The existing ASVAB score scale was constructed from P&P-ASVAB data collected in the 1980 PAY study. Table 26-2 summarizes several possible score scales based on the 1980 and 1997 PAY studies.

Option 1 presents the existing number-right (NR) score scale defined by administration of the P&P-ASVAB (Form 8A) to a nationally representative sample of youth in 1980. As indicated in Table 26-2, a linear transformation is applied to the number-right scores, denoted by X, to produce test standard scores S. The slope and intercept parameters of the transformation were specified in such a way that the mean and SD of S are equal to 50 and 10, respectively, in the 1980 youth population. As indicated in Table 26-2, CAT-ASVAB IRT ability estimates ($\hat{\theta}_c$) are placed on the number-right scale through an equipercentile equating with the P&P-8A reference form. Once on the NR scale, the same linear transformation (as used for the P&P-ASVAB) is applied to the number-right equivalents X^* to produce standard scores. This transformation is repeated for each of the 10 content areas contained in the ASVAB (see Chapter 19).

One problem with the existing score scale (given by Option 1) is that it is tied to the distribution of

Table 26-2 Score Scale Options

Option	Pop.	Scale	Scoring CAT	Scoring P&P	Non-Linear Transformation CAT	Non-Linear Transformation P&P	Linear Transformation
1	'80	NR	$\hat{\theta}_c$	X	$X^* = e(\hat{\theta}_c)$	—	$S = A + BX$
2	'80	IRT	$\hat{\theta}_c$	$\hat{\theta}_p$	—	—	$S = A + B\hat{\theta}_p$
3	'97	IRT	$\hat{\theta}_c$	$\hat{\theta}_p$	—	—	$S = A + B\hat{\theta}_c$
4	'97	IRT	$\hat{\theta}_c$	$\hat{\theta}_p$	—	$\hat{\theta}_p^* = e(\hat{\theta}_p)$	$S = A + B\hat{\theta}_c$
5	'97	IRT	$\hat{\theta}_c$	$\hat{\theta}_p$	$Y = f(\hat{\theta}_c)$	$Y^* = f(e(\hat{\theta}_p))$	$S = A + BY$

*The A and B parameters are specified so that S has a mean of 50 and an SD of 10 in the reference population.

number-right scores produced by a specific P&P-ASVAB reference form (8A). In recent administrations of the 8A test form to military applicants, ceiling effects have been observed for at least two tests (WK and PC). Consequently, the equipercentile equating for CAT-ASVAB takes the upper ability ranges and combines them into a small number of discrete intervals. Information for CAT-ASVAB scores over the upper ability ranges is lost through the course grouping required to convert ability estimates $\hat{\theta}_c$ into number-right equivalents X^*.

Option 2 avoids the ceiling-effect problem by using the natural ability metric associated with item response theory (IRT). Here, both CAT-ASVAB and P&P-ASVAB are scored by IRT (e.g., maximum of the posterior mode). Provided that the item difficulty and discrimination parameters of the CAT-ASVAB and P&P-ASVAB are properly linked, the resulting ability estimates $\hat{\theta}_c$ and $\hat{\theta}_p$ should automatically be placed on the same metric. A linear transformation can be applied to the P&P IRT ability estimates $\hat{\theta}_p$ to produce test standard scores S. The slope and intercept parameters of the transformation can be specified in such a way that the mean and SD of S are equal to 50 and 10, respectively, in the 1980 youth population. This same transformation can be applied to both CAT-ASVAB and P&P-ASVAB ability estimates.

The primary advantage of Option 2 is that it uses the IRT metric which is largely independent of the characteristics of a particular test form. By basing the scale on IRT ability estimates, the ceiling effects associated with the NR metric can be avoided. The obvious disadvantage of Option 2 is that the final scale is based on the 1980 reference group. If the distributions of proficiencies related to dimensions measured by the ASVAB have changed since 1980, then the interpretation applied to the standard-score scale may be misleading or incorrect. For example, a standard score of $S = 50$ may not be at the mean, but may be well below the mean in the current youth population. These interpretations are used to help specify qualification standards for military occupational specialties.

This problem is remedied by Option 3, where like Option 2, both CAT-ASVAB and P&P-ASVAB are scored by IRT, resulting in ability estimates which are automatically placed on the same metric. However, in this option the standard score scale is constructed using the CAT-ASVAB IRT ability estimates obtained in the 1997 PAY study. The slope and intercept parameters of the linear transformation can be specified in such a way that the mean and SD of S are equal to 50 and 10, respec-

tively, in the 1997 youth population. This same transformation can be applied to both CAT-ASVAB and P&P-ASVAB ability estimates. In this way, the various interpretations associated with standard-scores S can be made relative to a current population. However, one drawback with this approach may be that interpretations gained through experience with the old score scale may not be readily transferred to the new score scale. For example, a cut score of $S = 60$ on the 1980 and 1997 metrics may provide recruits with substantially different levels of trainability in particular occupational specialties. Thus, cut scores associated with the 1980 metric must be translated onto the 1997 metric.[1] Although the mechanics of this translation are straightforward, test users with a long history of use with the 1980 metric may have some difficulty changing over to the new score scale.

Another problem associated with both Options 2 and 3 is that distributions of observed IRT scores $\hat{\theta}_c$ and $\hat{\theta}_p$ produced by CAT-ASVAB and P&P-ASVAB may have different shapes. Consequently, the same cut-score may produce different qualification rates across the two versions. Option 4 would fix this problem through an equipercentile equating transformation $e(\ )$ applied to the P&P scores $\hat{\theta}_p$. By applying the equipercentile transformation, cut-scores applied to the transformed P&P scores $\hat{\theta}_p^*$ will display the same qualification rates as those applied to the CAT scores $\hat{\theta}_c$.

Another problem shared by Options 2, 3, and 4, deals with the large standard errors of measurement associated with extreme scores on the "theta" and standard-score scales. Test-users may be tempted to overinterpret differences in scores among those scoring along the lower and upper extremes. Variation among scores along these ranges may be due primarily to measurement errors. One remedy would involve a nonlinear S-shaped transformation of scale applied to the ability estimates ($\hat{\theta}_c$ and $\hat{\theta}_p^*$) which confined the scale to a finite interval. This transformation would compress the scale at the upper and lower extremes, while applying a nearly linear transformation to the scale over the middle ranges. The most useful transformation would balance the reduction in standard errors of measurement (SEM) at the extremes against the desire to discriminate among examinees at adjacent ability levels. The most appropri-

---

[1] A study is planned to equate scores on the P&P and CAT reference forms used in the 1980 and 1997 PAY studies. The linkage will be constructed from an equipercentile equating estimated from a sample of military applicants.

ate transformation might be one which provides high levels of score information (Birnbaum, 1968, Section 17.7) along the ability continuum.

Several criteria will provide useful information for choosing among the alternative score scale options. These include measures of test precision, including conditional SEM, the slope of the regression of the test-score on ability, and score-information (the squared ratio of the latter to the former). Other important psychometric measures for assessing the performance of composites include: (a) the generalized variance of true proficiency given observed composite score, and (b) expected ability (for each test dimension) given observed composite score. Each of the criteria can be evaluated separately for each option for CAT-ASVAB and P&P-ASVAB. Note that it is important to include the P&P-ASVAB in this evaluation, since it will continue to be administered to large numbers of applicants in the near term—until a suitable concept of operations can be identified which fully replaces the P&P-ASVAB in all remote testing locations. The most desirable score scale will provide high and comparable levels of precision across the CAT-ASVAB and P&P-ASVAB versions.

Test Security Issues

Two often cited advantages of CAT are those of flexible scheduling and immediate score reporting. CAT can provide a means of administering a self-paced exam, where different test-takers start and end the tests at different times—the automated nature of the test and the power of the computer provide a means for scoring the exam within a few seconds after completion, and provide the test-taker with immediate feedback. Compared to large group administrations often associated with P&P tests, these advantages appear compelling. In large-group administrations, the exam is administered on two or three occasions annually, and several weeks may pass before score-reports are made available.

The continuous (on-demand) testing schedule associated with CAT has a potential downside: Test items may be more susceptible to compromise than in large-group administrations. In continuous testing, examinees taking the test one day might share the item-content with friends taking the test in the future. In large-group testing, opportunities for this type of compromise are minimal, since substantially different items are administered on different occasions.

These test security issues associated with continuous testing are not unique to CAT. Although some P&P tests follow the large-group/annual (or biannual) schedule, many other P&P tests are administered on-demand, and provide immediate feedback. The P&P-ASVAB is one such battery. At many locations throughout the country, military applicants can schedule an exam on short notice, and often receive a score report within a few minutes of completion. Consequently, many of the test-compromise concerns associated with CAT apply to the P&P-ASVAB as well. However, the P&P-ASVAB has a long history of on-demand continuous testing. Trends in scores are monitored on a continuing basis to help ensure that significant compromise is not occurring among ASVAB test-takers. P&P-ASVAB provides a useful baseline for comparison with CAT-ASVAB. One way to judge the level of test security associated with CAT-ASVAB is to compare expected score gains associated with different compromise strategies across the CAT-ASVAB and P&P-ASVAB versions. From a historical perspective, an acceptable level of gain (associated with the application of a particular strategy to CAT-ASVAB) would fall at or below that gain achieved by the application of the same strategy to the P&P-ASVAB.

As indicated in Chapter 13, CAT-ASVAB uses the Sympson-Hetter algorithm to control item exposure. The algorithm uses exposure rates associated with the P&P-ASVAB as a target. This algorithm uses the target exposure rate as a ceiling on the usage of the pool's most informative items. For example, the most used items of the AR test are administered to about 1/3 of the examinee population. Considering that examinees are randomly assigned to two CAT-ASVAB forms (which have unique non-overlapping item pools), this results in maximum expected item usage rates of 1/6, which matches the usage rates of items contained within the six forms of the P&P-ASVAB. That is, for the P&P-ASVAB, examinees are randomly assigned to one of six forms, resulting in item usage rates of 1/6. Thus, with the Sympson-Hetter algorithm, observed item usage rates for CAT-ASVAB can be constrained to be less than or equal to those of a corresponding P&P-ASVAB test.

However, there are several concerns about the Sympson-Hetter algorithm that have led to a re-evaluation of the effects of possible compromise within the context of CAT-ASVAB. First, the expected item usage rates resulting from the algorithm are based on an assumed ability distribution. If the actual ability distribution differs from the assumed distribution, the observed item usage rates may differ from the expected values. This may be especially problematic at test-sites which have homogeneous test-takers. For example, examinee groups having a smaller than expected variation in proficiencies will tend to receive sets of items which have a higher than expected overlap. Thus, within homogeneous examinee groups, the Sympson-Hetter algorithm may lead to higher than expected usage rates for some items, providing an increased opportunity for exchange of item content, and an increased opportunity for item compromise.

A second concern about compromise centers on the fact that many CAT tests tend to be shorter than the P&P tests which they have replaced. For example, CAT-ASVAB test-lengths tend to be 40-percent shorter than their P&P-ASVAB counterparts. Consequently, each adaptively administered item of the short CAT test may possess a larger influence in the final score than each linearly administered item of the somewhat longer P&P test. Since CAT tests generally administer fewer items than their P&P counterparts, knowledge of a single CAT item may result in a larger score gain than knowledge of a single item administered in a conventional P&P format.

These concerns about the susceptibility of CAT to compromise motivated a simulation study (Segall, 1995) examining the expected score gains resulting from six different compromise strategies. In addition, the effects of altering several characteristics of the adaptive test on potential score gains were also investigated. Six compromise strategies examined in the study are summarized in Table 26-3. As indicated these strategies differ across three dimensions: (1) transmittal mechanism, (2) the correlation between the cheater and informant ability levels $Cor(\theta_c, \theta_I)$, and (3) the method used by the informant to select items for disclosure.

One way in which these strategies differ is in the *transmittal mechanism* of item content between informants and cheaters. One type of transmittal involves *sharing* between two friends, where the informant discloses l-items to his or her friend, the cheater. Another type of transmittal involves *item-banking,* where a number of informants contribute to a bank of items by disclosure of their test contents. The cheater then learns the contents of the l most frequently administered items from a review of the banked items.

A second way in which compromise strategies differ is in the correspondence of ability levels between informants and cheaters. Since CAT tailors the difficulty of the items to the ability level of the examinee, two friends of equal or nearly equal ability are likely to receive a greater number of common items than two friends of unequal ability. Thus the benefit to cheaters may be enhanced when their informant-friends are of similar ability levels, and lessened when their informant partners differ substantially in ability. Similarly, the benefits to cheaters of item-banking are likely to depend on the correspondence in ability levels between themselves and the group of informants. If the variation in ability is small, then all items contained in the bank would have a high probability of administration to a cheater. Under this condition, any learned item is likely to be beneficial. Conversely, if the informant/cheater group were heterogeneous in ability, then it would be unclear to the cheater which CAT items to learn, since some may have a low probability of presentation.

A third way in which compromise strategies differ is in the disclosure method used by the informant to select which test items to provide to the cheater. In one type of item disclosure, the informant provides the contents of the first l items of the test (i.e., items 1, 2, 3). In another type of item disclosure, the informant reveals the contents of items selected at random (i.e., items 2, 7, 9). In CAT-ASVAB, the first several items have a high probability of administration to examinees of all ability levels. Consequently, random informing may not be as beneficial as disclosure of the first l items administered.

For each condition, score gains associated with each of five levels of cheater ability $\theta_c \in \{-2, -1, 0, 1, 2\}$ were estimated for the AR test of the CAT- and P&P-ASVAB. For each of these ability levels, 16 levels of compromise ($l = 0, 1, \ldots, 15$) were

Table 26-3 Compromise Strategies

| Condition | Transmittal Mechanism | $Cor(\theta_c,\theta_I)$ | Disclosure Method | |
			CAT	P&P
1	Sharing	0	First l	Last l
2	Sharing	0	Random	Random
3	Sharing	.8	First l	Last l
4	Sharing	.8	Random	Random
5	Item Banking	.8	Most used	Random
6	Item Banking	0	Most used	Random

simulated, where l denotes the number of items exposed by the informant (or item bank) to the cheater. Thus within each condition, a total of $80(= 5 \times 16)$ simulations were conducted for CAT-ASVAB and P&P-ASVAB (conventional) tests. If the cheater receives an item disclosed by the informant during the adaptive item selection process, a correct response is obtained—otherwise the response is determined by the cheater's true ability level. Key features associated with each condition (Table 26-3) are summarized below.

Condition 1. This condition simulates the situation where the ability levels of the cheater and informant are uncorrelated. For the CAT test, an informant discloses the first l items to the cheater. (Since the first few items of the CAT test are those with the highest usage frequency, the disclosure of these items is likely to lead to larger score gains than the disclosure of items later in the adaptive testing sequence.) For the P&P test, the cheater disclosed the last l items of the linear test. (Since items in the P&P AR test are ordered in terms of approximate difficulty levels, these latter items will tend to be those which the cheater finds most difficult. Thus, the cheater is likely to benefit more from the disclosure of difficult questions positioned toward the end of the test than from the disclosure of easy questions positioned at the beginning of the test.) Thus in this condition, the informants in both the CAT and P&P conditions use potentially optimal disclosure strategies.

Condition 2. This condition also simulates the situation where the ability levels of the cheater and informant are uncorrelated. For the CAT test however, the informant discloses l items selected at random from among the 15 adaptively administered items. For the P&P test, the informant also discloses l randomly selected items from among the 30 linearly administered items.

Condition 3. This condition simulated the situation where the ability levels of the cheater and informant are highly correlated ($\rho = .8$). For the CAT

test, an informant discloses the first l items to the cheater. For the P&P test, the informant discloses the last l items of the linear test.

Condition 4. This condition also simulates the situation where the ability levels of the cheater and informant are highly correlated ($\rho = .8$). For the CAT test however, the informant discloses l items selected at random from among the 15 adaptively administered items. For the P&P test, the cheater also discloses l randomly selected items from among the 30 linearly administered items.

Condition 5. This strategy simulated the banking of items by a large number of informants of homogeneous ability, where the ability levels between informants and cheaters is correlated ($\rho = .8$). The l items with the highest usage rates are disclosed to the cheater.

Condition 6. This strategy simulates the banking of items by a large number of heterogeneous informants, where the ability levels between informants and cheaters are uncorrelated. The l items with the highest usage rates are disclosed to the cheater.

In each condition, 75 gain values were computed for CAT, and another 75 gain values were computed for P&P. These values represented the mean gain for a group of cheaters over a group of non-cheaters for the same fixed ability level $\hat{\theta}_c$. Each gain value was expressed in standard deviation units by dividing the differences in means by the standard deviation of observed test scores for a simulated non-cheater group with a normal (0,1) distribution of true ability.

One consistent result across all six conditions (Segall, 1995) is that the score gains for CAT are larger than those for the corresponding P&P conditions, with the largest CAT-P&P gain differences occurring for the cheaters at the lowest ability ($\hat{\theta}_c = -2$). The largest CAT score gains, and largest differences between CAT and P&P gains occur for Condition 5, where items are disclosed from a bank of compromised items created from a homogeneous group of informants. Taken as a whole, these results indicate that the Sympson-Hetter method (used in conjunction with two item-pools and a target exposure rate of 1/3) may not provide the same level of protection that is achieved by six forms of the P&P tests. These results suggest that more stringent item exposure controls should be imposed on the adaptive item selection process. Lowering levels of item exposure can be achieved by altering several characteristics of the adaptive test. The effects on score gains were examined in a second simulation study. The results are summarized below.

Approach 1. One approach for reducing CAT score gains is to increase test-length (say from 15 to 20 items) so that each adaptively administered item has less influence on the final ability estimate. Results of the simulation study indicated that longer CAT tests are less susceptible to compromise than shorter CAT tests. However, only modest reductions in compromise-gains can be achieved by lengthening the CAT test.

Approach 2. Another approach involves increasing the number of CAT forms or item pools (say from two pools to three pools). This should lower the expected score gains for CAT since each item would be administered to a smaller proportion of the examinee population. Results of the simulation study indicated that increasing the number of CAT forms (from two to three forms) had a substantial reduction in score-gain. Using three forms of CAT provided score gains equivalent or less than those observed for six forms of the P&P-ASVAB under all compromise strategies.

Approach 3. Another approach involves a reduction in the target exposure rate used in the Sympson-Hetter algorithm. Reducing the target exposure rate (from 1/3 to 2/9) provided a substantial reduction in the magnitude of CAT scores gains, with only a small degradation in the precision of the resulting scores.

Approach 4. A final strategy for lowering item exposure rates is to increase the number of items contained in the item-pool. Item pools with a larger number of items may have lower average usage rates. However, simulation results indicated that increasing pool size had little or no effect on

reducing score gains. This is probably because the extra items added to the pool did not automatically ensure a more even distribution of item usage.

Approaches 2 and 3 appeared most promising (increasing the number of CAT forms, and reducing the target exposure rate). Based in part on these results, a decision was made to develop a third CAT-ASVAB form to be administered along with CAT-ASVAB Forms 01C and 02C. Approach 3 was less desirable because CAT-ASVAB Forms 01C and 02C had already been equated using an exposure control target of 1/3. Lowering the target for these forms would have required a new equating study.

The results of the simulation study indicate that the rule of thumb which equates the target exposure rate for CAT with the number of P&P forms may not provide comparable levels of compromise-gains across CAT and P&P versions. In the development of CAT-ASVAB, the target exposure rate of 1/3 (when combined with two CAT forms) was thought to provide the same level of protection as six forms of the P&P test. The simulation results indicated that CAT compromise gains may be substantially higher for a number of different compromise strategies. These results stress the importance of examining compromise gains for specific item pools in the development of new forms, and in examining the utility of using lower target-exposure rates than might otherwise be suggested by the rule-of-thumb based on the number of P&P forms used in continuous testing programs.

Ongoing Psychometric Development

After nearly 20 years of R&D, the psychometric development of CAT-ASVAB has reached an advanced level. As with any operational testing program, however, we expect significant additional development will occur in the coming years. These include refinements in new form construction procedures and further advancements in CAT-ASVAB item selection and scoring methodology. Two areas under active investigation by DoD are outlined below.

Streamlining New Form Development

There are at least two approaches to large-scale testing that have been used with traditional P&P exams: Large-group and continuous testing. These approaches have different advantages, and are

Table 26-4 Comparison of Testing Programs

Characteristic	Testing Program Type		
	Large-Group	Continuous	Ideal CAT
Item Tryout	• Operational Motivation No Special Collection	• Non-operational Motivation Special Tryout Study	• Operational Motivation No Special Collection
Equating	• No Special Collection	• Special Equating Study	• No Special Collection
Test Security	• High	• ?	• High
Instant Scores	• No	• Yes	• Yes
On Demand Testing	• No	• Yes	• Yes

summarized in Table 26-4. Large-group testing programs traditionally offer the exam on two or three days out of the year, and require test-takers to schedule for the exam weeks in advance. A given operational form is typically administered on only one or two occasions, which results in very little opportunity for test compromise. Each test booklet usually contains some items that will contribute to the examinee's score, and some experimental items that are candidates for inclusion in new forms. In addition, an existing form may be administered to randomly equivalent groups to provide a link back to the reference score scale. After the day of testing, these large-scale programs collect all the data (usually from thousands of examinees) and perform an equating back to the reference score scale. This usually occurs in the days following the administration of the exam. Then this equating is used to transform scores back to the reference scale, and score reports are sent to the interested parties, usually several weeks after the exam. Data from the experimental items are used to construct new forms for future exams.

Continuous testing programs offer a flexible schedule with frequent testing opportunities. Scores are computed instantly at the completion of the test session. Because the same forms may be used for an extended period, test compromise is a larger concern than in large-group testing programs. For new form development, special and separate data collection efforts are required for both item-tryout studies and for equating studies. In ASVAB form development for example, large numbers of items are pre-tested on military recruits, and based on the resulting item statistics, these items are assembled into new test forms. Then, in a second data collection effort, data are collected non-operationally from other recruits for the purpose of constructing a provisional equating. In a third step, a final equating is developed from an operational administration of the new test forms, using the provisional equating to provide transformed scores. Once enough data have been

collected, a final equating based on operational administrations of the test forms is constructed, and is used to provide transformed scores until the forms are retired, and the cycle begins again.

As suggested above, continuous testing programs have at least two important advantages over large-group programs: They offer flexible test scheduling and instant scores. However, new form construction for continuous testing programs is significantly more burdensome—special tryout and equating data collection studies are required.

Adaptive testing can, in principle, combine the advantages of both types of testing programs (Table 26-4). Tests can be given on demand with instant scores; large item pools can help guard against compromise; experimental items can be seeded amongst the operational items providing item-tryout data; and provisional equating transformations can be estimated from the underlying psychometric model. Using CAT, the possibility exists for the evaluation and operational implementation of new forms without the need for special burdensome data collection studies. However, before such an idealized version of CAT can be implemented, technical details concerning the IRT calibration of items administered on-line, and the possibilities of on-line equatings must be further investigated. Some specific issues are presented below.

On-line calibration. CAT-ASVAB administers one experimental item (in each test) to each examinee. For each test-taker and test, the seed item is randomly selected from among a pool of 100 experimental items. Assuming that about 300,000 exams will be administered annually, enough data to perform an IRT calibration will be collected in about 4–6 months, providing between 1,000 and 1,500 responses per item. Since these experimental items are randomly interspersed among the operational items during presentation (Chapter 12), the respondents to the experimental items should be operationally motivated, providing high quality data for use in estimating the necessary b (difficulty), a (discrimination), and c (guessing) parameters. However, the estimation of the item parameters places special demands on traditional IRT estimation methods. When estimating the item parameters using adaptive test data, at least two problems can occur with the score scale: Systematic and random score-scale drift.

Errors in item parameter estimates can accumulate over time to systematically distort the score scale. The items administered in CAT-ASVAB will tend to have a positive bias associated with their discrimination parameters—items with a parameters that are overestimated are more likely to be administered than items whose a parameter was underestimated. When estimating the parameters of new items, the item response functions of the adaptively administered items are taken as fixed, and are used to estimate the parameter values for the new items. The bias in these adaptively administered items can result in biased estimates of the new parameters. Over several generations of adaptive pools, this can lead to a distortion of the score scale. Nonsystematic score scale drift can also occur from random errors in item parameter estimates. The errors can accumulate over time to produce distortions in the underlying IRT score scale.

DoD is investigating data collection and analysis procedures that will minimize these effects to provide a stable score scale over time (Krass, 1996). This work will build on Office of Naval Research (ONR) funded research occurring during the mid- to late 1980s. The intent of the ONR work was to evaluate four estimation procedures for use in on-line calibration:

1. Joint Maximum Likelihood: F. Lord and M. Stocking

2. Marginal Maximum Likelihood: D. Bock

3. Nonparametric Estimation: F. Samejima

4. Formula Scoring: M. Levine.

Additional evaluations will be conducted by DoD for at least two of the most promising procedures (Formula-scoring, Levine; marginal maximum likelihood, Bock).

On-line equating. In traditional P&P testing, there is a very strong and direct relation between the difficulty (and discrimination) levels of the test items and the observed distribution of number-right scores. Two P&P forms with items of slightly different difficulty or discrimination levels can have markedly different distributions of number-right scores. In adaptive testing (scored by IRT methods), there is a much weaker relation between the composition of the item pools and the distribution of estimated ability parameters. In theory, the IRT ability parameter is defined independently of the difficulty and discrimination of the test-items (Lord, 1980a). Thus for long tests and ideal item pools (many highly discriminating items), two forms of CAT constructed from independent sets of items should provide identical (or nearly identical) distributions of observed test scores. In practice, however, short adaptive tests from separate item pools may display some differences among observed score distributions.

Small but meaningful differences in observed score distributions (of Bayesian modal estimates) among different CAT-ASVAB forms have prompted the use of form-specific equating transformations. For example, Forms 01C and 02C of CAT-ASVAB have separately estimated equating transformations (back to the reference P&P-ASVAB scale; Chapter 19). Because of the large numbers of applicants tested annually, even small differences in the observed score distributions can have a meaningful impact on the numbers of qualifying applicants.

Past equating studies with both CAT- and P&P-ASVAB have included a costly and burdensome operational-calibration (OPCAL) phase. In the OPCAL phase, a provisional equating transformation is estimated from the non-operational administration of the new and reference forms. Then, a final equating is estimated in a second data collection effort (the initial operational test and evaluation), where the new and reference forms are administered operationally, using the provisional equating to provide scores of record for those taking the new forms. The empirical-OPCAL study is especially burdensome and time-consuming because all tests are administered non-operationally to large samples (about 2,500 examinees per form).

By relying more heavily on the underlying psychometric model, the empirical-OPCAL study can be replaced with a theoretical-OPCAL. This can be done for example, by simulating the distributions of adaptive test scores resulting from the new item pools by using the exact item selection and scoring algorithms used in CAT-ASVAB, and replacing the item parameters assumed to be known for the new pools with those estimated in the on-line calibration study. The provisional equating estimated from the theoretical-OPCAL could be used for an interim period during the IOT&E to collect empirical data for the final equating among new and old CAT forms. Note that if the new CAT-ASVAB forms are equated to an older CAT-ASVAB form, then the

IOT&E study would be transparent to the test-takers, and result in no additional burden. Each test-taker would take one operational form, and would be provided with a score of record on the reference score scale. Examinees taking the new form would have their scores transformed to the reference scale using the provisional transformation estimated in the theoretical-OPCAL. After sufficient data had been collected, the provisional equating (from the theoretical-OPCAL) would be replaced with the final equating estimated from test-takers in the IOT&E study.

It remains to be seen whether the theoretical-OPCAL can provide a sufficiently precise estimate of the equating transformation. On the one hand, the theoretical-OPCAL may actually provide equating transformations of higher precision than those provided by the traditional empirical-OPCAL studies. The empirical-OPCAL studies rely on data from non-operationally motivated examinees—the theoretical-OPCAL approach would use data from operationally motivated examinees to estimate item functioning, and then rely on an IRT model to predict the resulting distributions of observed test scores. On the other hand, the additional model assumptions required to predict the distributions of observed scores (unidimensionality and local independence) may be violated and result in imprecise equating transformations.

A study is underway by DoD to compare the results of theoretical- and empirical-OPCALs using historical data collected for previous CAT-ASVAB equating studies. If the theoretical approach provides an estimated equating as precise as the empirical-OPCAL (as compared to the IOT&E equating), then this approach may be used in the development of future CAT-ASVAB forms.

Although the discussion here has focused on the notion of total pool replacement (each form consisting of mutually exclusive sets of items), it may be desirable for the item-pools of new forms to overlap with previous forms. One candidate pool replacement schedule is provided in Table 26-5. Here, each form is composed of four subpools. In the example given in Table 26-5, 12 mutually exclusive non-overlapping subpools are listed across the top. Nine different forms consisting of various combinations of 12 subpools are provided along the left hand column. Form 1.0 consists of subpools (A, B, C, D); Form 1.1 consists of subpools (B, C, D, E); etc. Assuming that each subpool contains the same number of items, Forms 1.0 and 1.1 contain 75 percent of their items in common; Forms 1.0, 2.0, and 3.0 contain no common items. Thus using a form replacement strategy such as the one above, each new form would contain about 25 percent new items.

Then for each new form, two steps would be involved in the computation and evaluation of the equating transformation: (a) a provisional (theoretical) equating would be estimated, and (b) the final equating would be estimated using operational scores from randomly equivalent groups. Steps (a) and (b) could be repeated for each new form (i.e., 1.1, 1.2, 1.3, 2.0, ...). This partial pool replacement strategy might provide equating transformations which are less dependent on model assumptions made by the theoretical equating procedures.

For every item currently in the CAT-ASVAB item pool, one or two additional items were written, calibrated, and later rejected because of insufficient levels of information. Thus it is extremely important to start with sufficiently large numbers of items in the candidate item bank—in order to end up with enough high quality items in the final forms. To ensure enough items are contained in the candidate forms, it would be desirable to evaluate the relative precision of mutually exclusive successor forms (i.e., 2.0 with 1.0; and 3.0 with 2.0) before partial pool replacement is begun. For ex-

Table 26-5 Form Composition for Partial Pool Replacement

Form	Subpool											
	A	B	C	D	E	F	G	H	I	J	K	L
1.0	X	X	X	X								
1.1		X	X	X	X							
1.2			X	X	X	X						
1.3				X	X	X	X					
2.0					X	X	X	X				
2.1						X	X	X	X			
2.2							X	X	X	X		
2.3								X	X	X	X	
3.0									X	X	X	X

ample, items for Form 2.0 can be written and calibrated. The precision of the resulting 2.0 form can be evaluated and compared to Form 1.0 (Chapter 11). If the level of precision of new Form 2.0 is inadequate, it can be supplemented with additional highly informative items, until its level of precision matches that of Form 1.0. Once comparable levels of precision have been obtained, the items in the successor form (2.0) can be divided into four mutually exclusive subpools (E, F, G, H), and partial pool replacement can proceed in four steps (1.1, 1.2, 1.3, 2.0) as indicated in Table 26-5. By evaluating Form 2.0 before partial pool replacement is begun, comparable levels of precision among successor forms can be maintained across new generations.

Multidimensional Adaptive Testing

Another active area of investigation by DoD is multidimensional adaptive testing (MAT) (Segall, 1996). Under certain conditions, substantial gains in measurement efficiency can be obtained by the application of MAT item selection and scoring algorithms. When the dimensions are correlated, the responses to items of one test can provide information about the level of proficiency measured by the other tests in the battery. Rather than obtaining separate ability estimates as in unidimensional adaptive testing, MAT provides a single multidimensional vector of ability estimates for each examinee, which are updated after each response. The item selection algorithm chooses items which provide the largest decrement in the volume of the multidimensional credibility ellipsoid. One primary benefit of MAT is that this added information provided by items of correlated dimensions can lead to greater measurement efficiency—manifested by either greater precision or by reduced test-lengths. In a simulation study comparing the existing CAT-ASVAB item selection and scoring algorithms with the proposed MAT algorithms, MAT achieved greater or comparable precision with about 1/3 fewer items.

Before MAT can be applied operationally, several issues require further investigation. These areas include multidimensional item parameter estimation, exposure control, developing a common metric and orientation, and the effect of item-order on item functioning. Additional discussion of these issues is provided by Segall (1996).

Summary

Nationwide implementation of CAT-ASVAB will provide additional technical challenges and opportunities for refinements. Among the most immediate challenges are on-line calibration and on-line-equating. Improvements in these calibration and equating methodologies are expected to result in significantly less burdensome form development and evaluation procedures. Recent work also indicates that the examinee's burden can be significantly reduced by the application of multidimensional item selection and scoring algorithms. By taking advantage of the added information provided by items of correlated dimensions, test lengths can be reduced by 1/3 with no loss in precision.

With nationwide implementation of CAT-ASVAB also comes concerns over item and test compromise. Expected score gains resulting from different compromise strategies suggest that CAT may be more susceptible than originally believed. Results of simulation studies indicate that the rule-of-thumb which equates the target exposure rate for CAT with the number of P&P forms may not provide comparable levels of compromise gains across CAT and P&P versions. Decreases in score gains due to compromise can be obtained by at least two approaches. Marked improvements in test security can be obtained by the introduction of additional CAT forms, or by decreasing the target exposure rate.

Information for choosing among several score scales will be obtained from the administration of CAT-ASVAB to a nationally representative sample of youth. Justification for the revised ASVAB score scale will arise primarily from considerations of precision and interpretability. Knowledge and familiarity with the existing score scale will help define important cut-points along the new scale through an equating of the old (P&P) and new (CAT) reference forms.

CAT has reached an important threshold in military testing. Uncertainties about its utility and usefulness have been methodically and convincingly laid to rest. Finally, as the next millennium approaches, we look forward to the many challenges and opportunities for further advancements that are inherent to adaptive testing in the U.S. Armed Forces.

References

Ackerman, T. A. (1985, April). *An investigation of the effect of administering test items via computer.* Paper presented at the annual meeting of the Midwest Educational Research Association, Chicago, IL.

Alderton, D. L., & Larson, G. E. (1992, August). *ECAT battery: Descriptions, constructs, and factor structure.* Paper presented at the annual meeting of the American Psychological Association, Washington, DC.

American Educational Research Association, American Psychological Association, & National Council on Measurement in Education. (1985, August). *Standards for educational and psychological testing.* Washington, DC: American Psychological Association.

American Psychological Association. (1980). *Principles for the validation and use of personnel selection procedures.* Division of Industrial-Organizational Psychology. Washington, DC: Author.

American Psychological Association. (1986). *Guidelines for computer-based tests and interpretations.* Washington, DC: Author.

American Psychological Association, American Educational Research Association, & National Council on Measurement in Education. (1974). *Standards for educational and psychological tests.* Washington, DC: American Psychological Association.

Angoff, W. H. (1971). Norms, scales, and equivalent scores. In R. L. Thorndike (Ed.), *Educational measurement (2nd ed.)* (pp. 508–600). Washington, DC: American Council on Education.

Armor, D. J., Fernandez, R. L., Bers, K., & Schwarzbach, D. (1982). *Recruit aptitudes and Army job performance: Setting enlistment standards for infantrymen* (R-2874-MRAL). Santa Monica, CA: The RAND Corporation. (NTIS No. AD-A140 961)

Assessment Systems Corporation. (1984). *User's manual for the MicroCAT testing system* (RR 85-1). St. Paul, MN: Author.

ASVAB Working Group. (1980). *History of the Armed Services Vocational Aptitude Battery (ASVAB) 1974–1980* (A report to the Principal Deputy Assistant Secretary of Defense [Manpower, Reserve Affairs and Logistics]). Washington, DC: Author.

Automated Sciences Group & CACI, Inc.-Federal. (1988). *CAT-ASVAB program: Concept of operation and cost/benefit analysis.* Fairfax, VA: Author.

Baker, H. G. (1983a). *Navy Personnel Accessioning System (NPAS): Background and overview of the person-job matching (PJM) and recruiting management support (RMS) subsystems* (SR 83-34). San Diego, CA: Navy Personnel Research and Development Center. (NTIS No. AD-A129 325)

Baker, H. G. (1983b). *Navy Personnel Accessioning System (NPAS): II. Summary of research and development efforts and products* (SR 83-35). San Diego, CA: Navy Personnel Research and Development Center. (NTIS No. AD-A129 326)

Baker, H. G., Rafacz, B. A., & Sands, W. A. (1983). *Navy Personnel Accessioning System: III. Development of a microcomputer demonstration system* (SR 83-36). San Diego, CA: Navy Personnel Research and Development Center. (NTIS No. AD-A129 319)

Baker, H. G., Rafacz, B. A., & Sands, W. A. (1984). *Computerized Adaptive Screening Test (CAST): Development for use in military recruiting stations* (NPRDC TR 84-17). San Diego, CA: Navy Personnel Research and Development Center. (NTIS No. AD-A138 554)

Bejar, I. I., & Weiss, D. J. (1978). *A construct validation of adaptive achievement testing* (RR 78-4). Minneapolis: Psychometric Methods Program, Department of Psychology, University of Minnesota.

Betz, N. E., & Weiss, D. J. (1973). *An empirical study of computer-administered two-stage ability testing* (RR 73-4). Minneapolis, MN: Psychometric Methods Program, Department of Psychology, University of Minnesota.

Betz, N. E., & Weiss, D. J. (1974). *Simulation studies of two-stage ability testing* (RR 74-4). Minneapolis, MN: Psychometric Methods Program, Department of Psychology, University of Minnesota.

Betz, N. E., & Weiss, D. J. (1975). *Empirical and simulation studies of flexilevel ability testing* (RR 75-3). Minneapolis, MN: Psychometric Methods Program, Department of Psychology, University of Minnesota.

Birnbaum, A. (1968). Some latent trait models and their use in inferring an examinee's ability. In F. M. Lord & M. R. Novick, *Statistical theories of mental test scores.* Reading, MA: Addison-Wesley.

Bloxom, B. M., McCully, R., Branch, R., Waters, B. K., Barnes, J. D., & Gribben, M. R. (1993). *Operational calibration of the circular-response optical-mark-reader answer sheets for the ASVAB* (Report 93-009). Monterey, CA: Defense Manpower Data Center.

Bock, R. D. (1972). Estimating item parameters and latent ability when responses are scored in two or more nominal categories. *Psychometrika, 37,* 29–52.

Bock, R. D., & Aitkin, M. (1981). Marginal maximum

likelihood estimation of item parameters: An application of the EM algorithm. *Psychometrika, 46,* 443–459.

Bock, R. D., & Mislevy, R. J. (1981). Adaptive EAP estimation of ability in a microcomputer environment. *Applied Psychological Measurement, 6,* 431–444.

Bodzin, L. J. (1986). *An image capturing and editing system for the HP-Integral computer.* Unpublished paper. Naval Ocean Systems Command, San Diego, CA.

Booth-Kewley, S. (1983). *Validation of the Armed Services Vocational Aptitude Battery Forms 5/6/7 and 8/9/10 selection criteria for strategic weapons system electronic "A" school.* San Diego, CA: Navy Personnel Research and Development Center. (NTIS No. AD-A139 029)

Branch, R. (March 7, 1995). Personal communication. North Chicago, IL: U.S. Military Entrance Processing Command.

Brittain, C. V., & Vaughan, P. R. (1984). Effects of mixing two-option and multi-option items in a test. *Proceedings of the 26th Annual Conference of the Military Testing Association Volume I* (369–374). Munich, Federal Republic of Germany: Psychological Service of the German Federal Armed Forces.

Burke, M. J., Michael, & Normand, J. (1986). *Examinee attitudes toward computer-administered psychological testing.* Paper presented at the annual meeting of the American Educational Research Association, San Francisco, CA.

Carey, N. B. (1994). Computer predictors of mechanical job performance: Marine Corps findings. *Military Psychology, 6,* 1–30.

Clark, C. L. (1975). *Proceedings of the First Conference on Computerized Adaptive Testing* (PS 75-6). Washington, DC: Personnel Research and Development Center, U.S. Civil Service Commission.

Congressional Budget Office. (1980). *Costs of manning the active duty military* (Staff working paper). Washington, DC: Author.

Crichton, L. I. (1981). *Effects of error in item parameter estimates on adaptive testing.* Unpublished doctoral dissertation, University of Minnesota, Minneapolis, MN.

Croll, P. R. (1982). *Computerized adaptive testing system design: Preliminary design considerations* (NPRDC TR 82-52). San Diego, CA: Navy Personnel Research and Development Center. (NTIS No. A118 495)

Cronbach, L. J., & Gleser, G. C. (1965). *Psychological tests and personnel decisions* (2nd ed.). Urbana, IL: University of Illinois Press.

Cudeck, R. (1985). A structural comparison of conventional and adaptive versions of the ASVAB. *Multivariate Behavioral Research, 20,* 305–322.

Datacopy Corporation. (1985a). *Datacopy Model 700 User's Guide (Version 1.4).*

Datacopy Corporation. (1985b). *Datacopy WIPS Editor User's Guide (Version 1.0).*

Department of the Army. (1965). *Marginal man and military service.* Washington, DC: Author.

Department of Defense. (1982). *Profile of American Youth: 1980 nationwide administration of the Armed Services Vocational Aptitude Battery.* Washington, DC: Office of the Assistant Secretary of Defense (Manpower, Installations and Logistics).

Department of Defense. (1985). *Defense manpower qual-*

ity: Volume I. Washington, DC: Office of the Assistant Secretary of Defense (Manpower, Installations and Logistics).

Department of Defense. (1992). ASVAB *18/19 counselor manual.* North Chicago, IL: U.S. Military Entrance Processing Command.

Divgi, D. R. (1986a). *Determining the sensitivity of CAT-ASVAB scores to changes in item response curves with the medium of administration* (Report No. 86–189). Alexandria, VA: Center for Naval Analyses.

Divgi, D. R. (1986b). *On some issues in the Accelerated CAT-ASVAB Project* (CRM 86-231). Alexandria, VA: Center for Naval Analyses. (NTIS No. AD-A178 558)

Divgi, D. R. (1990). *Calculating the performance gain due to improved validity* (CRM 89-254). Alexandria, VA: Center for Naval Analyses. (NTIS No. AD-A230 732)

Divgi, D. R., & Stoloff, P. H. (1986). *Effect of the medium of administration on ASVAB item response curves* (Report 86-24). Alexandria, VA: Center for Naval Analyses. (NTIS No. AD-B103 889)

Dorans, N. J., & Kingston, N. M. (1985). The effects of violations of unidimensionality on the estimation of item and ability parameters and on item response theory equating of the GRE verbal scale. *Journal of Educational Measurement, 22,* 249–262.

Draper, N. R., & Smith, H. (1981). *Applied regression analysis* (2nd ed.). New York: John Wiley and Sons.

Drasgow, F., & Parsons, C. K. (1983). Application of unidimensional item response theory models to multidimensional data. *Applied Psychological Measurement, 7,* 189–199.

Eitelberg, M. J. (1988). *Manpower for military occupations.* Washington, DC: Office of the Assistant Secretary of Defense (Force Management and Personnel).

Eitelberg, M. J., Laurence, J. H., Waters, B. K., with Perelman, L. S. (1984). *Screening for service: Aptitude and education criteria for military entry.* Washington, DC: Office of the Assistant Secretary of Defense (Manpower, Installations and Logistics). (NTIS No. AD-A142 167)

Ezekiel, M. (1930). *Methods of correlational analysis.* New York, NY: John Wiley and Sons.

Fairbank, B. A. (1987). The use of presmoothing and postsmoothing to increase the precision of equipercentile equating. *Applied Psychological Measurement, 11,* 245–262.

Folchi, J. S. (1986). Communication of computerized adaptive testing results in support of ACAP. *Proceedings of the Annual Conference of the Military Testing Association, 28,* 618–623. New London, CT: U.S. Coast Guard Academy. (NTIS No. AD-A226 551)

Frankel, S. (1986). *Computer adaptive tests: The engines that will drive the revolution in education.* Paper presented at the annual meeting of the American Educational Research Association, San Francisco, CA.

Fraser, C. (1988). NOHARM II. *A Fortran program for fitting unidimensional and multidimensional normal ogive models of latent trait theory.* Armidale, Australia: The University of New England, Center for Behavioral Studies.

Garrison, W. M., & Baumgarten, B. S. (1986). An application of computer adaptive testing with communication handicapped examinees. *Educational and Psychological Measurement, 46,* 23–35.

Grafton, F., Czarnolewski, M. Y., & Smith, E. P. (1989).

Relationship between Project A psychomotor and spatial tests and TOW2 gunnery performance: A preliminary investigation (ARI-WP-RS-89-1). Alexandria, VA: U.S. Army Research Institute for the Behavioral and Social Sciences.

Greaud, V. A., & Green, B. F., Jr. (1986). Equivalence of conventional and computer presentation of speed tests. *Applied Psychological Measurement, 10,* 23–24.

Green, B. F., Jr. (1970). Comments on tailored testing. In W. H. Holtzman (Ed.), *Computer-assisted instruction, testing, and guidance* (p. 194). New York: Harper & Row.

Green, B. F., Jr., Bock, R. D., Humphreys, L. G., Linn, R. L, & Reckase, M. D. (1982). *Evaluation plan for the Computerized Adaptive Armed Services Vocational Aptitude Battery* (NTIS No. AD-A115 334). Baltimore, MD: The Johns Hopkins University, Department of Psychology.

Green, B. F., Bock, R. D., Humphreys, L. G., Linn, R. L., & Reckase, M. D. (1984a). *Evaluation plan for the Computerized Adaptive Vocational Aptitude Battery* (MPL TN 85-1). San Diego, CA: Manpower and Personnel Laboratory, Navy Personnel Research and Development Center.

Green, B. F., Jr., Bock, R. D., Humphreys, L. G., Linn, R. L, & Reckase, M. D. (1984b). Technical guidelines for assessing computerized adaptive tests. *Journal of Educational Measurement,* 347–360.

Green, B. F., Bock, R. D., Linn, R. L., Lord, F. M., & Reckase, M. D. (1984). A plan for scaling the computerized adaptive Armed Services Vocational Aptitude Battery. *Journal of Educational Measurement, 21,* 347–360.

Greenberg, I. M. (1980). *Mental standards for enlistment performance of Army personnel related to AFQT/ASVAB scores* (Final report MGA-0180-WRO-02). Monterey, CA: McFann, Gray and Associates.

Hardwick, S. B., Eastman, L., & Cooper, R. (1984). *Computerized adaptive testing: A user's manual* (NPRDC TR 8432). San Diego, CA: Navy Research and Development Center.

Harris, J. (November, 1996). *Item development and sampling results for the CAT-ASVAB forms 3 and 4 item tryout.* Unpublished manuscript.

Hedges, L. V., Becker, B. J., & Wolfe, J. H. (1992). *Detecting and measuring improvements in validity* (TR-93-2). San Diego, CA: Navy Personnel Research and Development Center. (NTIS No. AD-A257 446)

Hedl, J. J., O'Neill, H. L., & Hansen, D. N. (1973). Affective reactions toward computer-based intelligence testing. *Journal of Counseling and Clinical Psychology, 40,* 217–222.

Hetter, R. D., Segall, D. O., & Bloxom, B. M. (1994). A comparison of item calibration media in computerized adaptive testing. *Applied Psychological Measurement, 18* (3), 197–204.

Hogan, P. F., McBride, J. R., & Curran, L. T. (1995). *An evaluation of alternate concepts for administering the Armed Services Vocational Aptitude Battery to applicants for enlistment* (DMDC TR 95-013). Monterey, CA: Personnel Testing Division, Defense Manpower Data Center.

Holland, J. L. (1973). *Making vocational choices: A theory of careers.* Englewood Cliffs, NJ: Prentice Hall.

Holmes, R. (1996). Reliability and construct validity of

CAT-ASVAB Forms 1, 2, 3, and 4: Preliminary results. Unpublished manuscript. DMDC.

Hom, I. (1994). *PC-CAT Examinee Testing Station Software.* San Diego, CA: RGI.

Hornke, L. F., & Sauter, M. F. (1980). A validity study of an adaptive test of reading comprehension. In D. J. Weiss (Ed.), *Proceedings of the 1979 Computerized Adaptive Testing Conference.* Minneapolis, MN: Psychometric Methods Program, Department of Psychology, University of Minnesota, 57–67. (NTIS No. AD-A095 301)

Hotelling, H. (1931). A generalization of Student's ratio. *Annual of Mathematical Statistics, 2,* 360–378.

Hulin, C. L., Drasgow, F., & Parsons, C. K. (1983). *Item response theory.* Homewood, IL: Dow Jones-Irwin.

Jensema, C. J. (1972). *An application of latent trait mental test theory to the Washington Pre-college Testing Battery.* Doctoral thesis, University of Washington. (University Microfilms 72-20, 871, Ann Arbor, MI)

Jensema, C. J. (1974a). An application of latent trait mental test theory. *British Journal of Mathematical Statistical Psychology, 27,* 29–48.

Jensema, C. J. (1974b). The validity of Bayesian tailored testing. *Educational and Psychological Measurement, 34,* 757–766.

Jensen, H. E., & Valentine, L. D. (1976). *Development of the Enlistment Screening Test (EST) Forms 5 and 6* (TR 76-42). Brooks AFB, TX: Air Force Human Resources Laboratory. (NTIS No. AD-A033 303)

Johnson, M. F., & Weiss, D. J. (1980). Parallel forms reliability and measurement accuracy of adaptive and conventional testing strategies. In D. J. Weiss (Ed.), *Proceedings of the 1979 Computerized Adaptive Testing Conference* (pp. 16–34). Minneapolis, MN: Psychometric Methods Program, Department of Psychology, University of Minnesota. (NTIS No. AD-A095 301)

Joint Chiefs of Staff. (1982). *United States military posture for FY 83.* Washington, DC: Author.

Jöreskog, K. G., & Sörbom, D. (1984). *LISREL VI, Analysis of linear structural relationships by maximum likelihood, instrumental variables, and least squares methods.* Mooresville, IN: Scientific Software.

Kass, R. A., Mitchell, K. J., Grafton, F. C., & Wing, H. (1983). Factorial validity of the Armed Services Vocational Aptitude Battery (ASVAB) Forms 8, 9, and 10: 1981 Army applicant sample. *Educational and Psychological Measurement, 43,* 1077–1087.

Kieckhaefer, W. F., Ward, D. G., Kusulas, J. W., Cole, D. R., Rupp, L. M., & May, M. H. (1992). *Criterion development for 18 technical training schools in the Navy, Army, and Air Force* (Contract N66001-90-D-9502, DO 7J08). San Diego, CA: Navy Personnel Research and Development Center.

Kingsbury, G. G., & Weiss, D. J. (1981). *A validity comparison of adaptive and conventional strategies for mastery testing* (Report 81-3). Minneapolis, MN: Department of Psychology, University of Minnesota.

Knapp, D. J. (1987a). *Display of results: Alternatives for the Computerized Adaptive Screening Test (CAST)* (Working paper 87-05). Alexandria, VA: U.S. Army Research Institute for the Behavioral and Social Sciences.

Knapp, D. J. (1987b). *Final report on a national cross-validation of the Computerized Adaptive Screening Test (CAST)* (ARI TR 768). Alexandria, VA: U.S. Army

Research Institute for the Behavioral and Social Sciences.

Knapp, D. J., & Pliske, R. M. (1986a). *An update on the Computerized Adaptive Screening Test (CAST).* Paper presented at the annual meeting of the Military Testing Association. Mystic, CT: Military Testing Association. (NTIS No. AD-A226 551)

Knapp, D. J., & Pliske, R. M. (1986b). *Preliminary report on a national cross-validation of the Computerized Adaptive Screening Test (CAST)* (ARI RR 1430). Alexandria, VA: U.S. Army Research Institute for the Behavioral and Social Sciences. (NTIS No. AD-A175 767)

Kolen, M. J. (1991). Smoothing methods for estimating test score distributions. *Journal of Educational Measurement, 28,* 257–282.

Krass, I. (1996). *Evaluation design for online calibration procedures.* Unpublished manuscript. Defense Manpower Data Center.

Kronmal, R., & Tarter, M. (1968). The estimation of probability density and cumulatives by Fourier series methods. *Journal of the American Statistical Association, 69,* 925–952.

Larkin, K. C., & Weiss, D. J. (1974). *An empirical investigation of computer-administered pyramidal ability testing* (RR 74-3). Minneapolis, MN: Psychometric Methods Program, Department of Psychology, University of Minnesota. (AD 783 553)

Larkin, K. C., & Weiss, D. J. (1975). *An empirical comparison of two-stage and pyramidal adaptive ability testing* (RR 75-1). Minneapolis, MN: Psychometric Methods Program, Department of Psychology, University of Minnesota. (NTIS No. AD-A006 733)

Laurence, J. H., McCloy, R. A., & Legree, P. J. (1996, August). *The enlistment decision and personnel quality.* Paper presented at the 104th Annual Convention of the American Psychological Association, Toronto.

Lawley, D. N. (1943). A note on Karl Pearson's selection formulae. *Royal Society of Edinburgh Proceedings, Section A, 62,* 28–30.

Legree, P. J., Fischl, M., & Gade, P. A. (in press). Testing cognitive abilities by telephone using computer adaptive test. *Intelligence.*

Lord, F. M. (1952). *A theory of test scores.* Psychometric Monograph No. 7. Princeton, NJ: Educational Testing Service.

Lord, F. M. (1970). Some test theory for tailored testing. In W. Holtzman (Ed.), *Computer-assisted instruction, testing, and guidance* (pp. 139–183). New York, NY: Harper & Row.

Lord, F. M. (1971a). The self-scoring flexilevel test. *Journal of Educational Measurement, 8,* 147–151.

Lord, F. M. (1971b). A theoretical study of two-stage testing. *Psychometrika, 36,* 227–241.

Lord, F. M. (1971c). Robbins-Munro procedures for tailored testing. *Educational and Psychological Measurement, 31,* 3–31.

Lord, F. M. (1974). Individualized testing and item characteristic curve theory. In Krantz, Atkinson, Luce, & Suppes, *Contemporary developments in mathematical psychology, 2* (pp. 106–126). San Francisco, CA: W. H. Freeman.

Lord, F. M. (1975). Automated hypothesis tests and standard errors for nonstandard problems. *The American Statistician, 29,* 56–59.

Lord, F. M. (1977). A broad range tailored test of verbal ability. *Applied Psychological Measurement,* 95–100.

Lord, F. M. (1980a). *Application of item response theory to practical testing problems.* Hillsdale, NJ: Erlbaum.

Lord, F. M. (1980b). Discussant remarks. In D. J. Weiss (Ed.), *Proceedings of the 1979 Computerized Adaptive Testing Conference* (pp. 439–441). Minneapolis, MN: Computer Adaptive Testing Laboratory, Psychometric Methods Program, Department of Psychology, University of Minnesota.

Lord, F. M., & Novick, M. R. (1968). *Statistical theories of mental test scores.* Reading, MA: Addison-Wesley.

Lukin, M. E., Dowd, T., Plake, B., & Kraft, R. G. (1985). Comparing computerized versus traditional psychological assessment. *Computer in Human Behaviors, 1,* 49–58.

Maier, M. H. (1983). *The predictive validity of the AFQT for forms 8, 9, and 10 of the ASVAB* (83-3163/27). Alexandria, VA: Center for Naval Analyses.

Maier, M. H., & Truss, A. R. (1983). *Validity of the ASVAB Forms 8, 9, and 10 for Marine Corps training courses: Subtests and current composites* (83-3107/1). Alexandria, VA: Center for Naval Analyses.

Martin, J. T., McBride, J. R., & Weiss, D. J. (1983). *Reliability and validity of adaptive tests in a military recruit population* (ONR TR 83-1). Arlington, VA: Personnel and Training Programs, Office of Naval Research. (NTIS No. AD-A129 324)

Massad, E. E., Schratz, M. K., & Anderson, G. (August, 1998). *Second generation CAT-ASVAB tests: Phase I, item authoring and review* (Contract Deliverable). San Diego, CA: Navy Personnel Research and Development Center.

Mathews, J. J., & Ree, M. J. (1982). *Enlistment Screening Test Forms 81a and 81b: Development and calibration* (AFHRL TR 81-54). Brooks AFB, TX: Air Force Human Resources Laboratory. (NTIS No. AD-A113 464)

McBride, J. R. (1975). Scoring adaptive tests. In D. J. Weiss (Ed.), *Computerized adaptive trait measurement—problems and prospects* (pp. 17–25). Minneapolis, MN: Psychometric Methods Program, Department of Psychology, University of Minnesota.

McBride, J. R. (1976a). *Research on adaptive testing 1973–1976: A review of the literature.* Unpublished manuscript. Department of Psychology, University of Minnesota, Minneapolis, MN.

McBride, J. R. (1976b). *Simulation studies of adaptive testing: A comparative evaluation.* Unpublished doctoral dissertation, University of Minnesota, Minneapolis.

McBride, J. R. (1979). *Adaptive mental testing: The state of the art* (ARI Report 423). Alexandria, VA: U.S. Army Research Institute for the Behavioral and Social Sciences. (NTIS No. 088 000)

McBride, J. R. (1980). Adaptive verbal ability testing in a military setting. In D. J. Weiss (Ed.), *Proceedings of the 1979 Computerized Adaptive Testing Conference* (pp. 4–15). Minneapolis, MN: Department of Psychology, University of Minnesota. (NTIS No. AD-A095 301)

McBride, J. R. (1982). *Computerized adaptive testing project: Objectives and requirements* (NPRDC TN 82-122). San Diego, CA: Navy Personnel Research and Development Center. (NTIS No. AD-A118 447)

McBride, J. R., & Martin, J. T. (1983). Reliability and validity of adaptive verbal ability tests in a military setting. In D. J. Weiss (Ed.), *New horizons in testing* (pp. 223–235). New York, NY: Academic Press.

McBride, J. R., & Weiss, D. J. (1976). *Some properties of a Bayesian adaptive ability testing strategy* (RR 76-4). Minneapolis, MN: Psychometric Methods Program, Department of Psychology, University of Minnesota. (NTIS No. AD-A022 964)

McHenry, J. J., Hough, L. M., Toquam, J. L., Hanson, M. A., & Ashworth, S. (1990). Project A validity results: The relationship between predictor and criterion domains. *Personnel Psychology, 43,* 335–354.

Mead, A. D., & Drasgow, F. (1993). Effects of administration medium: A meta-analysis. *Psychological Bulletin, 114, 3,* 449–458.

Mislevy, R. J., & Bock, R. D. (1981). BILOG—*Maximum likelihood item analysis and test scoring: LOGISTIC model.* Chicago, IL: International Educational Services.

Mitchell, P., Hardwicke, S. B., Segall, D. O., & Vicino, F. L. (1983). Computerized adaptive testing: A preliminary study of user acceptability. *Proceedings of the Annual Conference of the Military Testing Association, 25,* 106–111. Gulf Shores, AL: Military Testing Association.

Moe, K. C., & Johnson, M. F. (1986, August). *Participants reaction to computerized testing.* Paper presented at the annual meeting of the American Psychological Association, Washington, DC.

Monzon, R. I., Shamieh, E. W., & Segall, D. O. (1990). *Subgroup differences in equipercentile equating of the Armed Services Vocational Aptitude Battery.* Unpublished manuscript. San Diego, CA: Navy Personnel Research and Development Center.

Moreno, K. E., & Segall, D. O. (1992). CAT-ASVAB precision. *Proceedings of the 34th Annual Conference of the Military Testing Association, 1,* 22–26.

Moreno, K. E., Segall, D. O., & Kieckhaefer, W. F. (1985). A validity study of the Computerized Adaptive Testing version of the Armed Services Vocational Aptitude Battery. *Proceedings of the Annual Conference of the Military Testing Association, 27, 1,* 29–33. San Diego, CA: Military Testing Association. (NTIS No. AD-A172 850)

Moreno, K. E., Wetzel, C. D., McBride, J. R., & Weiss, D. J. (1983). *Relationship between corresponding Armed Services Vocational Aptitude Battery (ASVAB) and computerized adaptive testing (CAT) subtests* (NPRDC TR 83-27). San Diego, CA: Navy Personnel Research and Development Center. (NTIS AD-A131 683)

Moreno, K. E., Wetzel, C. D., McBride, J. R., & Weiss, D. J. (1984). Relationship between corresponding Armed Services Vocational Aptitude Battery (ASVAB) and Computerized Adaptive Testing (CAT) subtests. *Applied Psychological Measurement, 8, 2,* 155–163.

Mullins, C. J., Earles, J. A., & Ree, M. (1981). *Weighting of aptitude components based on differences in technical school difficulty* (AFHRL TR-81-19). Brooks Air Force Base, TX: Air Force Human Resources Laboratory. (NTIS No. AD-A102 045)

Muraki, E. (1984). *Implementing full-information factor analysis: TESTFACT program.* A paper presented at the annual meeting of the Psychometric Society, University of California, Santa Barbara, CA.

Nellis, J., Carlson, F. R., Gray, P., Hayes, J., Holman, M., & White, M. J. (1980). *Technology assessment of personnel computers.* Los Angeles: Center for Future Research, University of Southern California.

Olivier, P. A. (1974). *An evaluation of the self-scoring flexilevel tailored testing model.* Unpublished doctoral dissertation, Florida State University, Tallahassee, FL.

Owen, R. J. (1969). *A Bayesian approach to tailored testing* (RB-69-92). Princeton, NJ: Educational Testing Service.

Owen, R. J. (1975). A Bayesian sequential procedure for quantal response in the context of adaptive mental testing. *Journal of the American Statistical Association, 70,* 351–356.

Palmer, D. R., & Busciglio, H. H. (1996). Coaching on the ASVAB: Analysis of post-test questionnaire responses. *Military Psychology, 8, 4,* 267–278.

Park, R. K., & Dunn, M. L. (1991). *Compatibility evaluation and research on the Computerized Adaptive Screening Test (CAST). Final Report: User and programming guide.* Washington, DC: American Institutes for Research. (NTIS No. AD-A293 112)

Park, R. K., & Rosse, R. L. (1991). *Functional requirements of an automated data collection system for the Computerized Adaptive Screening Test (CAST).* Washington, DC: American Institutes for Research.

Parker, S. B., & McBride, J. R. (1990). *A comparison of Rasch and three-parameter logistic models in computerized adaptive testing.* Unpublished manuscript.

Peterson, N. G., Hough, L. M., Dunnette, M. D., Rosse, R. L., Houston, J. S., & Toquam, J. L. (1990). Project A: Specification of the predictor domain and development of new selection/classification tests. *Personnel Psychology, 43,* 247–276.

Pliske, R. M., Gade, P. A., & Johnson, R. M. (1984). *Cross-validation of the Computerized Adaptive Screening Test (CAST).* (ARI RR 1372). Alexandria, VA: U.S. Army Research Institute for the Behavioral and Social Sciences.

Prestwood, J. S., Vale, C. D., Massey, R. H., & Welsh, J. R. (1985). *Armed Services Vocational Aptitude Battery. Development of an adaptive item pool* (TR 85-19). Brooks AFB, TX: Air Force Human Resources Laboratory. (AD-A160 608)

The Psychological Corporation. (1986a). *The Computerized Adaptive Edition of the Differential Aptitude Tests.* San Antonio, TX: Author.

The Psychological Corporation. (1986b). *The Stanford Adaptive Mathematics Screening Test.* San Antonio, TX: Author.

Quan, B., Park, T. A., Sandahl, G., & Wolfe, J. H. (1984). *Microcomputer network for computerized adaptive testing* (CAT) (NPRDC TR 84-33). San Diego, CA: Navy Personnel Research and Development Center.

Rafacz, B. A. (1994). *The design and development of a computer network system to support the CAT-ASVAB program.* San Diego, CA: Navy Personnel Research and Development Center.

Rafacz, B. A. (1995). *Computerized Adaptive Testing version of the Armed Services Vocational Aptitude Battery (CAT-ASVAB): Computer system development* (NPRDC-TN-95-8). San Diego, CA: Navy Personnel Research and Development Center. (NTIS No. AD-299 806)

Rafacz, B. A., & Moreno, K. E. (1987). *Interactive screen dialogues for the examinee testing (ET) station.* San Diego, CA: Navy Personnel Research and Development Center.

Rasch, G. (1960). *Probabilistic model for some intelligence and attainment tests.* Copenhagen, Denmark: Danish Institute for Educational Research.

Reckase, M. D. (1974). *Ability estimation and item calibration using the one and three parameter logistic models: A comparative study* (RR 77-1). Columbia, MO: Tailored Testing Research Laboratory, Educational Psychology Department, University of Missouri.

Reckase, M. D. (1979). Unifactor latent trait models applied to multifactor tests: Results and implications. *Journal of Educational Statistics, 4,* 207–230.

Ree, M. J. (1977). Implementation of a model adaptive testing system at an Armed Forces Entrance and Examining Station. In D. J. Weiss (Ed.), *Proceedings of the 1977 Computerized Adaptive Testing Conference* (pp. 216–220). Minneapolis, MN: Psychometric Methods Program, Department of Psychology, University of Minnesota. (NTIS No. AD-A060 049)

Ree, M. J., Mullins, C. J., Mathews, J. J., & Massey, R. H. (1982). *Armed Services Vocational Aptitude Battery: Item and factor analysis of Forms 8, 9, and 10* (AFHRL TR-81-55). Brooks AFB, TX: Air Force Human Resources Laboratory. (NTIS No. AD-A113 465)

Ree, M. J., & Wegner, T. G. (1990). Correcting differences in answer sheets for the 1980 Armed Services Vocational Aptitude Battery reference population. *Military Psychology, 2,* 157–169.

Samejima, F. (1976). Graded response model of the latent trait theory and tailored testing. In C. L. Clark (Ed.), *Proceedings of the First Conference on Computerized Adaptive Testing* (pp. 5–15) (PS 75-6). Washington, DC: Personnel Research and Development Center, U.S. Civil Service Commission. (U.S. Government Printing Office Stock No. 006-000-00940-9)

Sands, W. A. (1980). The automated guidance for enlisted Navy applicants (AGENA) system. *Proceedings of the Annual Conference of the Military Testing Association, 22, 2,* SAN0–8. Toronto, Canada: Military Testing Association. (NTIS No. AD-A098 678)

Sands, W. A. (1981). The Navy personnel accessioning system. *Proceedings of the Annual Conference of the Military Testing Association, 23, 2* (pp. 1025–1029). Arlington, VA: Military Testing Association. (NTIS No. AD-A130 703)

Sands, W. A. (1983, August). *Computerized adaptive testing for the U.S. Army JOIN system.* Paper presented at the annual convention of the American Psychological Association, Anaheim, CA.

Sands, W. A., & Gade, P. A. (1983). An application of computerized adaptive testing in U.S. Army recruiting. *Journal of Computer-Based Instruction, 10, 3 & 4,* 87–89.

Sands, W. A., Gade, P. A., & Bryan, J. D. (1982). Research and development for the JOIN system. *Proceedings of the Annual Conference of the Military Testing Association, 24.* Brooks Air Force Base, TX: Air Force Human Resources Laboratory. (NTIS No. AD-A126 554)

Sands, W. A., & Rafacz, B. A. (1983). Field test of the Computerized Adaptive Screening Test System (CAST). *Proceedings of the Annual Conference of the Military Testing Association, 25* (pp. 112–117). San Antonio, TX: Military Testing Association.

SAS Institute. (1990). *SAS/STAT User's Guide* (4th ed.). Raleigh-Durham, NC: Author.

Schmid, J., & Leiman, J. M. (1957). The development of hierarchical factor solutions. *Psychometrika, 22,* 53–61.

Schmidt, F. L., & Gugel, J. F. (1975, August). *The Urry item parameter estimation technique: How effective?* Paper presented at the annual convention of the American Psychological Association, Chicago, IL.

Schmidt, F. L, Hunter, J., & Dunn, W. (1987). *Potential utility increases from adding new tests to the Armed Services Vocational Aptitude Battery* (TN-95-5). San Diego, CA: Navy Personnel Research and Development Center. (NTIS AD-A279 580)

Schmidt, F. L, Urry, V. W., & Gugel, J. F. (1978). *Item parameterization procedures for the future.* Washington, DC: Personnel Research and Development Center, U.S. Civil Service Commission.

Segall, D. O. (1987a). ACAP item pools: Analysis and recommendations. Unpublished manuscript. San Diego, CA: Navy Personnel Research and Development Center.

Segall, D. O. (1987b). *A procedure for smoothing discrete distributions.* Unpublished manuscript. San Diego, CA: Navy Personnel Research and Development Center.

Segall, D. O. (1988). *A procedure for scoring incomplete adaptive tests in high stakes testing.* Unpublished manuscript. San Diego, CA: Navy Personnel Research and Development Center.

Segall, D. O. (1989). *Score equating development analyses of the CAT-ASVAB.* Unpublished manuscript, Navy Personnel Research and Development Center.

Segall, D. O. (1996). Multidimensional adaptive testing. *Psychometrika, 61,* 331–354.

Segall, D. O. (1995, April). *The effects of item compromise on computerized adaptive test scores.* Paper presented at the meeting of the Society for Industrial and Organizational Psychology, Orlando, FL.

Sellman, W. S. (1988, December 14). *Memorandum for Manpower Accession Policy Steering Committee: Appointment of technical representative to a Joint-Service computerized test selection committee.* Washington, DC: Office of the Assistant Secretary of Defense.

Siegel, S. (1956). *Nonparametric statistics for the behavioral sciences.* New York, NY: McGraw-Hill.

Sims, W. H., & Hiatt, C. M. (1981). *Validation of the Armed Services Vocational Aptitude Battery (ASVAB) Forms 6, 7, 6E, and 7E* (CNA Study 1152). Alexandria, VA: Center for Naval Analyses. (NTIS No. AD-A110 025)

Skinner, H. A., & Allen, B. A. (1983). Does the computer make a difference? Computerized versus face-to-face versus self report assessment of alcohol, drug and tobacco use. *Journal of Consulting and Clinical Psychology, 51,* 267–275.

Slack, W. W., & Slack, C. W. (1977). Talking to a computer about emotional problems: A comparative study. *Psychotherapy: Theory, Research and Practice, 14,* 156–164.

Smith, E. P., & Walker, M. R. (1988). Testing psychomotor and spatial abilities to improve selection of TOW gunners. *Proceedings of the Annual Conference of the Military Testing Association, 30,* 647–652. Arlington, VA: Military Testing Association. (NTIS No. AD-A215 179)

Spray, J. A., Ackerman, T. A., Reckase, M. D., & Carlson, J. E. (1989). Effect of medium of item presentation on examinee performance and item characteristics. *Journal of Educational Measurement, 26,* 261–271.

Stocking, M. L., & Lord, F. M. (1983). Developing a common metric in item response theory. *Applied Psychological Measurement, 1*, 201–210.

Stocking, M. L., & Swanson, L. (1993). A method for severely constrained item selection in adaptive testing. *Applied Psychological Measurement, 17*.

Swanson, L. (1978). *Armed Services Vocational Aptitude Battery Forms, 6 and 7: Validation against school performance—interim report* (NPRDC TR 78-24). San Diego, CA: Navy Personnel Research and Development Center. (NTIS No. AD-A056 700)

Swanson, L. (1979). *Armed Services Vocational Aptitude Battery, Forms 6 and 7: Validation against school performance in Navy enlisted schools (July 1976–February 1978)* (NPRDC TR 80-1). San Diego, CA: Navy Personnel Research and Development Center. (NTIS No. AD-A077 158)

Swanson, L., Fischl, M. A., Ross, R. M., McBride, J. R., Wiskoff, M. F., Valentine, L. D. Jr., Mathews, J. J., & Wilfong, H. D. (1978). *Validity of the Armed Services Vocational Aptitude Battery (ASVAB) for predicting performance in Service technical training schools* (TR 77-4). Chicago, IL: Directorate of Testing, U.S. Military Entrance Processing Command.

Sympson, J. B., & Hartmann, L. (1985). Item calibrations for computerized adaptive testing (CAT) item pools. In D. J. Weiss (Ed.), *Proceedings of the 1982 Item Response Theory and Computerized Adaptive Testing Conference.* Minneapolis, MN: Computerized Adaptive Testing Laboratory, Department of Psychology, University of Minnesota. (NTIS No. AD-A163 040)

Sympson, J. B., & Hetter, R. D. (1985). *Controlling item exposure rates in computerized adaptive tests.* Paper presented at the Annual Conference of the Military Testing Association. San Diego, CA: Military Testing Association.

Sympson, J. B., Weiss, D. J., & Ree, M. J. (1984, April). *Predictive validity of computerized adaptive testing in a military training environment.* Paper presented at the annual meeting of the American Educational Research Association, New Orleans, LA.

Thompson, J. G., & Weiss, D. J. (1980). *Criterion-related validity of adaptive testing strategies* (RR 80-3). Minneapolis: Department of Psychology, University of Minnesota.

Tiggle, R. B., & Rafacz, B. A. (1985). Evaluation of three local CAT-ASVAB network designs. *Proceedings of the Annual Conference of the Military Testing Association, 23–28.* San Diego, CA: Navy Personnel Research and Development Center. (NTIS No. AD-A172 850)

Tsutakawa, R. K. (1984). *Final report on project NR 150-464 improved estimation procedures for item response functions* (RR 84-2). Columbia, MO: Department of Statistics, University of Missouri.

Urry, V. W. (1970). *A Monte-Carlo investigation of logistic mental test models.* Unpublished doctoral dissertation, Purdue University, IN.

Urry, V. W. (1971). Individualized testing by Bayesian estimation. *Research Bulletin* 171–177, Bureau of Testing, University of Washington, Seattle, WA.

Urry, V. W. (1974a). *Computer-assisted testing: The calibration and evaluation of the verbal ability bank* (Technical study 74-3). Washington, DC: Research Section, Personnel Research and Development Center, U.S. Civil Service Commission. (NTIS No. PB-258 210)

Urry, V. W. (1974b). Approximations to item parameters of mental test models and their uses. *Educational and Psychological Measurement, 34*, 253–269.

Urry, V. W. (1976). Ancillary estimators for the item parameters of mental test models. In W. A. Gorham (Chair), *Computers and testing: Steps toward the inevitable conquest* (PS-76-1). Washington, DC: U.S. Civil Service Commission.

Urry, V. W. (1977). Tailored testing: A successful application of latent trait theory. *Journal of Educational Measurement, 14*, 181–196.

Urry, V. W. (1983). *Tailored testing and practice: A basic model, normal ogive models, and tailored testing algorithms.* Washington, DC: Office of Personnel Management. (Also NPRDC TR 83-32; NTIS No. AD-A133 385)

USMEPCOM. (1983). *U.S. MEPCOM Mobile Examining Team Site requirements for computerized adaptive testing.* Director of Testing, USMEPCOM Letter Report dated December 22, 1983. Vol. I, II, and III.

Vale, C. D. (1975). Problem: Strategies of branching through an item pool. In D. J. Weiss (Ed.), *Computerized adaptive trait measurement: Problems and prospects* (RR 75-5). Minneapolis, MN: Psychometric Methods Program, Department of Psychology, University of Minnesota. (AD-A018 675)

Vale, C. D., & Gialluca, K. A. (1985). *ASCAL: A microcomputer program for estimating logistic IRT item parameters* (RR ONR 85-4). St. Paul, MN: Assessment Systems Corp. (NTIS No. AD-A169 737)

Vale, C. D., & Weiss, D. J. (1975). *A simulation study of stradaptive ability testing* (RR 75-6). Minneapolis, MN: Psychometric Methods Program, Department of Psychology, University of Minnesota. (AD-A020 961)

Vineberg, R., & Joyner, J. N. (1982). *Prediction of job performance: Review of military studies* (NPRDC TR 82-37). San Diego, CA: Navy Personnel Research and Development Center. (NTIS No. AD-A113 208)

Wainer, H., Dorans, N. J., Flaugher, R., Green, B. F., Mislevy, R. J., Steinberg, L., & Thissen, D. (1990). *Computerized adaptive testing: A primer.* Hillsdale, NJ: Erlbaum.

Wall, J. E. (1995). Briefing presented to the Defense Advisory Committee on Military Personnel Testing. Apache Junction, AZ, February 16, 1995.

Walter, G. H., & O'Neill, H. F., Jr. (1974). On-line user-computer interface: The effects of interface flexibility, terminal type, and experience on performance. *AFIPS Conference Proceedings, 43*, 379–384.

Waters, B. K. (1975). An empirical investigation of Weiss' Stradaptive Testing Model. In *Proceedings of the First Conference on Computerized Adaptive Testing* (pp. 54–63). (PS-75-6). Washington, DC: Personnel Research and Development Center, U.S. Civil Service Commission. (U.S. Government Printing Office Stock No. 006-000-00940-9)

Waters, B. K. (1974). *An empirical investigation of the stradaptive testing model for the measurement of human ability.* Unpublished doctoral dissertation, Florida State University, Tallahassee, FL.

Waters, B. K., Barnes, J. D., Foley, P., Steinhaus, S. D., & Brown, D. C. (1988). *Estimating the reading skills of military applicants: Development of an ASVAB to RGL conversion table* (HumRRO Final Report, FR-PRD-88-22). Alexandria, VA: Human Resources Research Organization.

Waters, B. K., Laurence, J. H., & Camara, W. J. (1987). *Personnel enlistment and classification procedures in the U.S. military.* Washington, DC: National Academy Press.

Weiss, D. J. (1974a). *Strategies of adaptive ability measurement* (RR 74-5). Minneapolis, MN: Psychometric Methods Program, Department of Psychology, University of Minnesota. (NTIS No. AD-A004 270)

Weiss, D. J. (1974b). *The stratified adaptive computerized ability test* (RR 73-3). Minneapolis, MN: Psychometric Methods Program, Department of Psychology, University of Minnesota. (AD 768 376)

Weiss, D. J. (1975). Computerized adaptive ability measurement. *Naval Research Reviews,* pp. 1–18.

Weiss, D. J. (1983a). *Computer-based measurement of intellectual capabilities.* Minneapolis, MN: Psychometric Methods Program, Department of Psychology, University of Minnesota. (NTIS No. AD-A144 065)

Weiss, D. J. (Ed.). (1983b). *New horizons in testing: Latent trait test theory and computerized adaptive testing.* New York: Academic Press.

Weiss, D. J., & Betz, N. E. (1973). *Ability measurement: Conventional or adaptive?* (RR 73-1). Minneapolis, MN: Psychometric Methods Program, Department of Psychology, University of Minnesota. (NTIS No. AD-A757 788)

Weltin, M. M., & Popelka, B. A. (1983). *Evaluation of the ASVAB 8/9/10 clerical composite for predicting training school performance* (ARI-TR-594). Alexandria, VA: U.S. Army Research Institute for the Behavioral and Social Sciences. (NTIS No. AD-A143 235)

Wetzel, C. D., & McBride, J. R. (1983). *The influence of fallible item parameters on test information during adaptive testing* (TR 83-15). San Diego, CA: Navy Personnel Research and Development Center. (NTIS No. AD-A128 336)

Wetzel, C. D., & McBride, J. R. (1986, October). *Reducing the predictability of adaptive item sequences.* Paper presented at the annual conference of the Military Testing Association, San Diego, CA.

Wilbourn, J. M., Valentine, L. M., & Ree, M. J. (1984). *Relationships of the Armed Services Vocational Aptitude Battery (ASVAB) Forms 8, 9, and 10 to Air Force technical school final grades* (AFHRL-TP-84-8). Brooks Air Force Base, TX: Air Force Human Resources Laboratory. (NTIS No. AD-A144 213)

Wilson, D. T., Wood, R., & Gibbons, R. D. (1991). *TEST-FACT: Test Scoring, Item Statistics, and Item Factor Analysis.* Scientific Software International, Inc. Chicago, IL.

Wingersky, S., Barton, M. A., & Lord, F. M. (1982). *LOGIST user's guide.* Princeton, NJ: Educational Testing Service.

Wingersky, S., & Lord, F. M. (1973). *A computer program for estimating examinee ability and item characteristic curve parameters when there are omitted responses* (RM 73-2). Princeton, NJ: Educational Testing Service.

Wise, L. L., McHenry, J. J., Chia, W. J., Szenas, P. L., & McBride, J. R. (1990). *Refinement of the computerized adaptive screening test.* Alexandria, VA: U.S. Army Research Institute for the Behavioral and Social Sciences. (NTIS No. AD-A231 437)

Wiskoff, M. F. (1981). Computerized adaptive testing. *Proceedings of the National Security Industrial Association First Annual Conference on Personnel and Training Factors in Systems Effectiveness.* San Diego, CA: National Security Industrial Association.

Wiskoff, M. F. (1985, August). *Military psychology and national defense: Making a difference.* Division 19 Presidential Address at the annual convention of the American Psychological Association, Los Angeles, CA.

Wolfe, J. H. (1985). Speeded tests: Can computers improve measurement? *Proceedings of the Annual Conference of the Military Testing Association, 27, 1,* 49–54. San Diego, CA: Military Testing Association. (NTIS No. AD-A172 850)

Wolfe, J. H., & Alderton, D. L. (1992). Navy incremental validity study of new predictors. *Proceedings of the Annual Conference of the Military Testing Association, 34, 1,* 39–44. San Diego, CA: Military Testing Association. (NTIS No. AD-A268 815)

Wolfe, J. H., Alderton, D. L., & Larson, G. E. (1993). *Incremental validity of new computerized aptitude tests for predicting training performance in nine Navy technical schools.* Navy Personnel Research and Development Center, Unpublished manuscript.

Wood, R. L., Wingersky, M. S., & Lord, F. M. (1976). *LOGIST: A computer program for estimating examinee ability and item characteristic curve parameters* (RM-76-6). Princeton, NJ: Educational Testing Service.

Wright, B. D. (1977). Solving measurement problems with the Rasch model. *Journal of Educational Measurement, 14,* 97–166.

Wright, B. D., & Douglas, G. A. (1977). Conditional versus unconditional procedures for sample-free item analysis. *Educational and Psychological Measurement, 37,* 47–60.

Wright, B. D., & Mead, R. J. (1977). *BICAL: Calibrating items and scales with the Rasch model* (RM No. 23). Chicago, IL: Statistical Laboratory, Department of Education, University of Chicago.

Yoes, M. E., & Hardwicke, S. B. (1984). *The effect of mode of presentation on test performance.* San Diego, CA: RGI.

List of Acronyms

ACRONYM	DEFINITION
1PL	One-Parameter Logistic IRT Model
3PL	Three-Parameter Logistic IRT Model
ACAP	Accelerated CAT-ASVAB Project
AFHRL	U.S. Air Force Human Resources Laboratory
AFQT	Armed Forces Qualification Test
AFQT CATEGORY	AFQT Score Group
AFSC	Air Force Specialty Code
AGCT	Army General Classification Test
AI	Automotive Information Test of the CAT-ASVAB
AO	Assembling Objects Test in ECAT Battery
AR	Arithmetic Reasoning Test of the ASVAB
ARI	U. S. Army Research Institute for the Behavioral and Social Sciences
ART	ASVAB Review Technical Committee
AS	Auto and Shop Information Test of the ASVAB
ASD/FM&P	Assistant Secretary of Defense for Force Management and Personnel
ASD/M&L	Assistant Secretary of Defense for Manpower and Logistics
ASVAB	Armed Services Vocational Aptitude Battery
ASVAB CEP	Armed Services Vocational Aptitude Battery—Career Exploration Program
ATG	Acceptance Testing Group
BBN	Bolt, Beranek, and Newman
BDM	BDM Federal Inc.
BME	Bayesian Modal Estimator
BRTT	Broad Range Tailored Test
BSE	Bayesian Sequential Estimation
BUPERS	Bureau of Naval Personnel

ACRONYM	DEFINITION
CAST	Computerized Adaptive Screening Test
CAT	Computerized Adaptive Testing
CAT-ASVAB	Computerized Adaptive Testing Version of the ASVAB
CATICC	CAT Inter-Service Coordinating Committee
CATWG	CAT Working Group
CBO	Congressional Budget Office
CDF	Cumulative Distribution Function
CMOA	Calibration Mode of Administration
CNP	Chief of Naval Personnel
COPE	Concepts of Operations Planning and Evaluation
CPU	Central Processing Unit
CS	Coding Speed Test of the ASVAB
CT	Mental Counters Test in ECAT Battery
CTC	Contract Testing Center
DA	U. S. Department of the Army
DAC	Defense Advisory Committee on Military Personnel Testing
DAT	Differential Aptitude Tests
DEP	Delayed Entry Program
DHC	Data Handling Computer
DIF	Differential Item Functioning
DMDC	Defense Manpower Data Center
DoD	U. S. Department of Defense
DOD-STP	Department of Defense Student Testing Program
DoL	U. S. Department of Labor
DoN	U. S. Department of the Navy
DOS	Disk Operating System
DRP	Digital Response Pad
ECAT	Enhanced Computer Administered Tests
EI	Electronics Information Test of the ASVAB

ACRONYM	DEFINITION	ACRONYM	DEFINITION
EIDS	Electronic Information Delivery System	MOA	Medium of Administration
EST	Enlistment Screening Test	MOS	Military Occupational Specialty
ET	Examinee Testing Station	NLSY79	1979 National Longitudinal Survey of Youth Labor Force Behavior
FEDSIM	Federal Computer Performance Measurement and Simulation Center	NO	Numerical Operations Test of the ASVAB
FR	Figural Reasoning Test in ECAT Battery	NOS	Network Operating System
FSG	Final School Grade	NPAS	Navy Personnel Accessioning System
FY	Fiscal Year (1 October – 30 September)	NPRDC	Navy Personnel Research and Development Center
GRE	Graduate Record Examination	NSFH	National Survey of Families and Households
GS	General Science Test of the ASVAB	NVSNP	Navy Validity Study of New Predictors
HP-IPC	Hewlett Packard Integral Personal Computer	O&M	Operations and Maintenance
HumRRO	Human Resources Research Organization	O&S	Operations and Support
		OIC	Officer-in-Charge
ID	Integrating Details Test in ECAT Battery	OASD	Office of the Assistant Secretary of Defense
IF	Interest Finder—DoD Interest Inventory	OPM	U. S. Office of Personnel Management
IOT&E	Initial Operational Test and Evaluation	OSD	Office of the Secretary of Defense
IRT	Item Response Theory	OT&E	Operational Test and Evaluation
ISA	Industry Standard Adapter	P&P	Paper-and-Pencil
JOIN	Joint Optical Information Network	P&P-ASVAB	Paper-and-Pencil Version of the ASVAB
K-S	Kolmogorov-Smirnov Statistical Test	PACE	Professional and Administrative Career Examination
LAN	Local Area Network	PAY80	1980 *Profile of American Youth Study*
LCN	Local CAT-ASVAB Network	PC	Paragraph Comprehension Test of the ASVAB
MAP	Manpower Accession Policy Steering Committee	R&D	Research and Development
MAPWG	Manpower Accession Policy Working Group	RAM	Random Access Memory
		RFP	Request for Proposal
MAT	Multidimensional Adaptive Testing	RGL	Reading Grade Level
MC	Mechanical Comprehension Test of the ASVAB	ROI	Return on Investment
		ROM	Read Only Memory
MCRD	Marine Corps Recruit Depot	SDS	Self-Directed Search
MDAC	McDonnell-Douglas Aeronautics Corporation	SED	Score Equating Development
		SEV	Score Equating Verification
MEPS	Military Entrance Processing Station	SI	Shop Information Test of the CAT-ASVAB
METS	Mobile Examining Team Site	SIF	Score Information Function
MHz	Megahertz	SM	Sequential Memory Test in ECAT Battery
MIRS	USMEPCOM Integrated Resource System	SO	Spatial Orientation Test in ECAT Battery
MISE	Mean Integrated Square Error	SSN	Social Security Account Number
MK	Mathematics Knowledge Test of the ASVAB	STMI	Stratified Maximum Information
		STRADAPTIVE	Stratified Adaptive Testing Strategy
MLE	Maximum Likelihood Estimation		
MLMI	Maximum Likelihood/Maximum Information	SVGA	Super Video Graphics Array

ACRONYM	DEFINITION	ACRONYM	DEFINITION
T1	One-Handed Tracking Test in ECAT Battery	USAREC	U.S. Army Recruiting Command
T2	Two-Handed Tracking Test in ECAT Battery	USMEPCOM	U.S. Military Entrance Processing Command
TA	Test Administrator	UID	Unique Identification Number
TASP	Technical Advisory Selection Panel	VE	Verbal Composite from the ASVAB (WK + PC)
TCC	Test Characteristic Curve		
TI	Target Identification Test in ECAT Battery	VGA	Video Graphics Adaptor
TIF	Test Information Function	WK	Word Knowledge Test of the ASVAB
TSR	Terminate-and-Stay-Resident Driver		

Index